Lecture Notes in Computer Science 14011

The series Lecture Notes in Computer Science (LNCS), including its subseries Lecture Notes in Artificial Intelligence (LNAI) and Lecture Notes in Bioinformatics (LNBI), has established itself as a medium for the publication of new developments in computer science and information technology research, teaching, and education.

LNCS enjoys close cooperation with the computer science R & D community, the series counts many renowned academics among its volume editors and paper authors, and collaborates with prestigious societies. Its mission is to serve this international community by providing an invaluable service, mainly focused on the publication of conference and workshop proceedings and postproceedings. LNCS commenced publication in 1973.

Masaaki Kurosu · Ayako Hashizume
Editors

Human-Computer Interaction

Thematic Area, HCI 2023
Held as Part of the 25th HCI International Conference, HCII 2023
Copenhagen, Denmark, July 23–28, 2023
Proceedings, Part I

Editors
Masaaki Kurosu
The Open University of Japan
Chiba, Japan

Ayako Hashizume
Hosei University
Tokyo, Japan

ISSN 0302-9743 ISSN 1611-3349 (electronic)
Lecture Notes in Computer Science
ISBN 978-3-031-35595-0 ISBN 978-3-031-35596-7 (eBook)
https://doi.org/10.1007/978-3-031-35596-7

This Springer imprint is published by the registered company Springer Nature Switzerland AG
The registered company address is: Gewerbestrasse 11, 6330 Cham, Switzerland

Foreword

Human-computer interaction (HCI) is acquiring an ever-increasing scientific and industrial importance, as well as having more impact on people's everyday lives, as an ever-growing number of human activities are progressively moving from the physical to the digital world. This process, which has been ongoing for some time now, was further accelerated during the acute period of the COVID-19 pandemic. The HCI International (HCII) conference series, held annually, aims to respond to the compelling need to advance the exchange of knowledge and research and development efforts on the human aspects of design and use of computing systems.

The 25th International Conference on Human-Computer Interaction, HCI International 2023 (HCII 2023), was held in the emerging post-pandemic era as a 'hybrid' event at the AC Bella Sky Hotel and Bella Center, Copenhagen, Denmark, during July 23–28, 2023. It incorporated the 21 thematic areas and affiliated conferences listed below.

A total of 7472 individuals from academia, research institutes, industry, and government agencies from 85 countries submitted contributions, and 1578 papers and 396 posters were included in the volumes of the proceedings that were published just before the start of the conference, these are listed below. The contributions thoroughly cover the entire field of human-computer interaction, addressing major advances in knowledge and effective use of computers in a variety of application areas. These papers provide academics, researchers, engineers, scientists, practitioners and students with state-of-the-art information on the most recent advances in HCI.

The HCI International (HCII) conference also offers the option of presenting 'Late Breaking Work', and this applies both for papers and posters, with corresponding volumes of proceedings that will be published after the conference. Full papers will be included in the 'HCII 2023 - Late Breaking Work - Papers' volumes of the proceedings to be published in the Springer LNCS series, while 'Poster Extended Abstracts' will be included as short research papers in the 'HCII 2023 - Late Breaking Work - Posters' volumes to be published in the Springer CCIS series.

I would like to thank the Program Board Chairs and the members of the Program Boards of all thematic areas and affiliated conferences for their contribution towards the high scientific quality and overall success of the HCI International 2023 conference. Their manifold support in terms of paper reviewing (single-blind review process, with a minimum of two reviews per submission), session organization and their willingness to act as goodwill ambassadors for the conference is most highly appreciated.

This conference would not have been possible without the continuous and unwavering support and advice of Gavriel Salvendy, founder, General Chair Emeritus, and Scientific Advisor. For his outstanding efforts, I would like to express my sincere appreciation to Abbas Moallem, Communications Chair and Editor of HCI International News.

July 2023 Constantine Stephanidis

HCI International 2023 Thematic Areas and Affiliated Conferences

Thematic Areas

- HCI: Human-Computer Interaction
- HIMI: Human Interface and the Management of Information

Affiliated Conferences

- EPCE: 20th International Conference on Engineering Psychology and Cognitive Ergonomics
- AC: 17th International Conference on Augmented Cognition
- UAHCI: 17th International Conference on Universal Access in Human-Computer Interaction
- CCD: 15th International Conference on Cross-Cultural Design
- SCSM: 15th International Conference on Social Computing and Social Media
- VAMR: 15th International Conference on Virtual, Augmented and Mixed Reality
- DHM: 14th International Conference on Digital Human Modeling and Applications in Health, Safety, Ergonomics and Risk Management
- DUXU: 12th International Conference on Design, User Experience and Usability
- C&C: 11th International Conference on Culture and Computing
- DAPI: 11th International Conference on Distributed, Ambient and Pervasive Interactions
- HCIBGO: 10th International Conference on HCI in Business, Government and Organizations
- LCT: 10th International Conference on Learning and Collaboration Technologies
- ITAP: 9th International Conference on Human Aspects of IT for the Aged Population
- AIS: 5th International Conference on Adaptive Instructional Systems
- HCI-CPT: 5th International Conference on HCI for Cybersecurity, Privacy and Trust
- HCI-Games: 5th International Conference on HCI in Games
- MobiTAS: 5th International Conference on HCI in Mobility, Transport and Automotive Systems
- AI-HCI: 4th International Conference on Artificial Intelligence in HCI
- MOBILE: 4th International Conference on Design, Operation and Evaluation of Mobile Communications

List of Conference Proceedings Volumes Appearing Before the Conference

1. LNCS 14011, Human-Computer Interaction: Part I, edited by Masaaki Kurosu and Ayako Hashizume
2. LNCS 14012, Human-Computer Interaction: Part II, edited by Masaaki Kurosu and Ayako Hashizume
3. LNCS 14013, Human-Computer Interaction: Part III, edited by Masaaki Kurosu and Ayako Hashizume
4. LNCS 14014, Human-Computer Interaction: Part IV, edited by Masaaki Kurosu and Ayako Hashizume
5. LNCS 14015, Human Interface and the Management of Information: Part I, edited by Hirohiko Mori and Yumi Asahi
6. LNCS 14016, Human Interface and the Management of Information: Part II, edited by Hirohiko Mori and Yumi Asahi
7. LNAI 14017, Engineering Psychology and Cognitive Ergonomics: Part I, edited by Don Harris and Wen-Chin Li
8. LNAI 14018, Engineering Psychology and Cognitive Ergonomics: Part II, edited by Don Harris and Wen-Chin Li
9. LNAI 14019, Augmented Cognition, edited by Dylan D. Schmorrow and Cali M. Fidopiastis
10. LNCS 14020, Universal Access in Human-Computer Interaction: Part I, edited by Margherita Antona and Constantine Stephanidis
11. LNCS 14021, Universal Access in Human-Computer Interaction: Part II, edited by Margherita Antona and Constantine Stephanidis
12. LNCS 14022, Cross-Cultural Design: Part I, edited by Pei-Luen Patrick Rau
13. LNCS 14023, Cross-Cultural Design: Part II, edited by Pei-Luen Patrick Rau
14. LNCS 14024, Cross-Cultural Design: Part III, edited by Pei-Luen Patrick Rau
15. LNCS 14025, Social Computing and Social Media: Part I, edited by Adela Coman and Simona Vasilache
16. LNCS 14026, Social Computing and Social Media: Part II, edited by Adela Coman and Simona Vasilache
17. LNCS 14027, Virtual, Augmented and Mixed Reality, edited by Jessie Y. C. Chen and Gino Fragomeni
18. LNCS 14028, Digital Human Modeling and Applications in Health, Safety, Ergonomics and Risk Management: Part I, edited by Vincent G. Duffy
19. LNCS 14029, Digital Human Modeling and Applications in Health, Safety, Ergonomics and Risk Management: Part II, edited by Vincent G. Duffy
20. LNCS 14030, Design, User Experience, and Usability: Part I, edited by Aaron Marcus, Elizabeth Rosenzweig and Marcelo Soares
21. LNCS 14031, Design, User Experience, and Usability: Part II, edited by Aaron Marcus, Elizabeth Rosenzweig and Marcelo Soares

22. LNCS 14032, Design, User Experience, and Usability: Part III, edited by Aaron Marcus, Elizabeth Rosenzweig and Marcelo Soares
23. LNCS 14033, Design, User Experience, and Usability: Part IV, edited by Aaron Marcus, Elizabeth Rosenzweig and Marcelo Soares
24. LNCS 14034, Design, User Experience, and Usability: Part V, edited by Aaron Marcus, Elizabeth Rosenzweig and Marcelo Soares
25. LNCS 14035, Culture and Computing, edited by Matthias Rauterberg
26. LNCS 14036, Distributed, Ambient and Pervasive Interactions: Part I, edited by Norbert Streitz and Shin'ichi Konomi
27. LNCS 14037, Distributed, Ambient and Pervasive Interactions: Part II, edited by Norbert Streitz and Shin'ichi Konomi
28. LNCS 14038, HCI in Business, Government and Organizations: Part I, edited by Fiona Fui-Hoon Nah and Keng Siau
29. LNCS 14039, HCI in Business, Government and Organizations: Part II, edited by Fiona Fui-Hoon Nah and Keng Siau
30. LNCS 14040, Learning and Collaboration Technologies: Part I, edited by Panayiotis Zaphiris and Andri Ioannou
31. LNCS 14041, Learning and Collaboration Technologies: Part II, edited by Panayiotis Zaphiris and Andri Ioannou
32. LNCS 14042, Human Aspects of IT for the Aged Population: Part I, edited by Qin Gao and Jia Zhou
33. LNCS 14043, Human Aspects of IT for the Aged Population: Part II, edited by Qin Gao and Jia Zhou
34. LNCS 14044, Adaptive Instructional Systems, edited by Robert A. Sottilare and Jessica Schwarz
35. LNCS 14045, HCI for Cybersecurity, Privacy and Trust, edited by Abbas Moallem
36. LNCS 14046, HCI in Games: Part I, edited by Xiaowen Fang
37. LNCS 14047, HCI in Games: Part II, edited by Xiaowen Fang
38. LNCS 14048, HCI in Mobility, Transport and Automotive Systems: Part I, edited by Heidi Krömker
39. LNCS 14049, HCI in Mobility, Transport and Automotive Systems: Part II, edited by Heidi Krömker
40. LNAI 14050, Artificial Intelligence in HCI: Part I, edited by Helmut Degen and Stavroula Ntoa
41. LNAI 14051, Artificial Intelligence in HCI: Part II, edited by Helmut Degen and Stavroula Ntoa
42. LNCS 14052, Design, Operation and Evaluation of Mobile Communications, edited by Gavriel Salvendy and June Wei
43. CCIS 1832, HCI International 2023 Posters - Part I, edited by Constantine Stephanidis, Margherita Antona, Stavroula Ntoa and Gavriel Salvendy
44. CCIS 1833, HCI International 2023 Posters - Part II, edited by Constantine Stephanidis, Margherita Antona, Stavroula Ntoa and Gavriel Salvendy
45. CCIS 1834, HCI International 2023 Posters - Part III, edited by Constantine Stephanidis, Margherita Antona, Stavroula Ntoa and Gavriel Salvendy
46. CCIS 1835, HCI International 2023 Posters - Part IV, edited by Constantine Stephanidis, Margherita Antona, Stavroula Ntoa and Gavriel Salvendy

47. CCIS 1836, HCI International 2023 Posters - Part V, edited by Constantine Stephanidis, Margherita Antona, Stavroula Ntoa and Gavriel Salvendy

https://2023.hci.international/proceedings

Preface

Human-Computer Interaction is a Thematic Area of the International Conference on Human-Computer Interaction (HCII). The HCI field is today undergoing a wave of significant innovation and breakthroughs towards radically new future forms of interaction. The HCI Thematic Area constitutes a forum for scientific research and innovation in human-computer interaction, addressing challenging and innovative topics in human-computer interaction theory, methodology, and practice, including, for example, novel theoretical approaches to interaction, novel user interface concepts and technologies, novel interaction devices, UI development methods, environments and tools, multimodal user interfaces, human-robot interaction, emotions in HCI, aesthetic issues, HCI and children, evaluation methods and tools, and many others.

The HCI Thematic Area covers four major dimensions, namely theory and methodology, technology, human beings, and societal impact. The following four volumes of the HCII 2023 proceedings reflect these dimensions:

- Human-Computer Interaction (Part I), addressing topics related to design and evaluation methods, techniques and tools, and interaction methods and techniques
- Human-Computer Interaction (Part II), addressing topics related to children-computer interaction, emotions in HCI, and understanding the user experience
- Human-Computer Interaction (Part III), addressing topics related to human-robot interaction, chatbots and voice-based interaction, and interacting in the metaverse
- Human-Computer Interaction (Part IV), addressing topics related to supporting health, quality of life and everyday activities, as well as topics related to HCI for learning, culture, creativity, and societal impact.

Papers of these volumes are included for publication after a minimum of two single-blind reviews from the members of the HCI Program Board or, in some cases, from members of the Program Boards of other affiliated conferences. We would like to thank all of them for their invaluable contribution, support, and efforts.

July 2023

Masaaki Kurosu
Ayako Hashizume

Human-Computer Interaction Thematic Area (HCI 2023)

Program Board Chairs: **Masaaki Kurosu**, *The Open University of Japan, Japan* and **Ayako Hashizume**, *Hosei University, Japan*

Program Board:

- Salah Ahmed, *University of South-Eastern Norway, Norway*
- Valdecir Becker, *Federal University of Paraiba, Brazil*
- Nimish Biloria, *University of Technology Sydney, Australia*
- Zhigang Chen, *Shanghai University, P.R. China*
- C. M. Nadeem Faisal, *National Textile University, Pakistan*
- Yu-Hsiu Hung, *National Cheng Kung University, Taiwan*
- Jun Iio, *Chuo University, Japan*
- Yi Ji, *Guangdong University of Technology, P.R. China*
- Hiroshi Noborio, *Osaka Electro-Communication University, Japan*
- Katsuhiko Onishi, *Osaka Electro-Communication University, Japan*
- Mohammad Shidujaman, *Independent University, Bangladesh, Bangladesh*

The full list with the Program Board Chairs and the members of the Program Boards of all thematic areas and affiliated conferences of HCII2023 is available online at:

http://www.hci.international/board-members-2023.php

HCI International 2024 Conference

The 26th International Conference on Human-Computer Interaction, HCI International 2024, will be held jointly with the affiliated conferences at the Washington Hilton Hotel, Washington, DC, USA, June 29 – July 4, 2024. It will cover a broad spectrum of themes related to Human-Computer Interaction, including theoretical issues, methods, tools, processes, and case studies in HCI design, as well as novel interaction techniques, interfaces, and applications. The proceedings will be published by Springer. More information will be made available on the conference website: http://2024.hci.international/.

General Chair
Prof. Constantine Stephanidis
University of Crete and ICS-FORTH
Heraklion, Crete, Greece
Email: general_chair@hcii2024.org

https://2024.hci.international/

Contents – Part I

Design and Evaluation Methods, Techniques and Tools

Co-creating User Journey Map – A Systematic Approach to Exploring Users' Day-to-Day Experience in Participatory Design Workshops

Wan-Ling Chang(✉) and Ying-Cih Shao

Industrial Design, National Cheng Kung University, Tainan, Taiwan, R.O.C.
WanLingChang@gs.ncku.edu.tw

Abstract. Mutual learning scaffolds co-realization and knowledge exchange between the users and designers to facilitate effective collaborative creation and decision processes in participatory design. Two common challenges recognized in mutual learning processes are how to efficiently uncover users' experience and immerse designers or engineers in users' know-how of their everyday experience. In this study, we intend to introduce a collaborative user journey map creation process among users, designers, and system engineers. Unlike other user journey maps created by the researchers and served as a reference for workshop discussion, in this study, we had the older participants, the engineers, and the designers to co-create the user journey map during the workshop to enhance mutual learning. The new user journey map building process included using LEGO® to build the participants' life space representations, interviewing the participants about their typical day experience with the living space representation and event sheets, building up the user journey map with event sheets' information and advanced interviews, and identifying the life challenges within groups. The post-interview analysis showed that the chronological and visual features of the user journey map effectively revealed older participants' life experiences and challenges with other workshop members. The new way of making user journey maps engaged all the workshop participants in the journey map co-creation activity and enhanced designers' or engineers' commitment to the mutual learning process.

Keywords: Participatory Design · User Journey Map · Mutual Learning

1 Introduction

Participatory design (PD) is a democratic approach that emphasizes empowering disadvantaged users and providing a relatively equal design decision-making setting for both users and designers or designers (Kensing & Greenbaum, 2012). To facilitate effective collaborative creation and decision processes, mutual learning scaffolds co-realization and knowledge exchange between the users and designers (Lee et al., 2017) and build common ground among the participants (Luck, 2018). While users learn the technological expertise from the system designers to understand the competence and limitation of the technology, the designers learn the "tacit knowledge" of users' everyday practices

M. Kurosu and A. Hashizume (Eds.): HCII 2023, LNCS 14011, pp. 3–17, 2023.
https://doi.org/10.1007/978-3-031-35596-7_1

through various tools and techniques revealing experiences (Robertson & Simonsen, 2012). Two common challenges recognized in mutual learning processes are how to uncover users' experience efficiently and how to immerse designers or engineers in users' know-how of their everyday experience. In this study, we attempted to address those issues by introducing a collaborative user journey map creation process among users, designers, and system engineers. While the new design of the journey map creation process enhances the effectiveness and operation of mapping users' experience, the co-creation process contributes to designers' and engineers' immersion in users' knowledge.

The user journey map, also called the customer journey map, is a data visualization method appropriated to discover users' experience incidents (Bellos & Kavadias, 2021). This approach is widely adopted in human-computer interaction research and practices, as well as in Participatory design studies. We found that, in Participatory design, user journey maps were usually created by the researchers with interviews, observations, and various ethnographic research methods before the workshops and served as reference material for workshop participants to understand the users' experience (e.g., Shin et al., 2022). Creating a user journey map involves intensive engagement of users' activity data and contextual information of the interaction instances. The off-site data collection and analysis of the user journey map may fail to encourage users' and system designers' commitment to the mutual learning process. In this participatory design project, we designed a series of techniques to engage all workshop participants in collecting contextual information and users' daily routines, arranging activity data, and laying out the experience journey.

This participatory design project targeted developing ideas for Natural Language Processing (NLP) applications with healthy older people. The participants in this project included older adults from the local communities, the NLP system engineers, and product designers. The participatory design process expended one technical knowledge workshop, two user journey map co-creation workshops, and one idea-developing workshop. We conducted this participatory design project with two local communities, and the two series of workshops were held before and after the COVID-19 pandemic in 2019 and 2022. This study primarily focuses on discussing the results of user journey map co-creation workshops. The first user journey map creation activity started with using LEGO® bricks and paper drawings to build up the physical arrangements of users' home environments and the facilities and arenas they usually attended. Then, like doll playing, the users carried the LEGO® figures around the miniatures to tell their life stories. Meanwhile, the designers interviewed the users about their typical daily routines, and the engineers took notes on the event sheets. After finishing reviews of older participants" daily activities, all the participants worked together to create the journey map based on the event sheet data and further discussion within the group. The workshop participants densified the challenges or potential opportunities to introduce NLG applications at the end of the journey map creation process.

In this study, we illustrate the details of the co-creation workshop process and operation in the Study Design and PD Workshop sections. To demonstrate the efficacy of the co-creation process of the user journey map, we present the analysis of post-interview findings and discuss how the user journey map benefited the mutual learning among all participants in the Findings and Discussion sections.

2 Study Design

The PD procedure of this co-design project with older community members contained four individual PD workshops for different purposes. The design and process of four PD workshops will be delineated in the next section. These four workshops were held on four separate days. Each of them lasted for around three hours. Prior to the PD workshops, the researchers interviewed the workshop participants about their expectations of the workshops. Furthermore, after the workshops, the post-interviews collected participants' feedback on whether their expectation was addressed and what they learned and got in the workshops. The procedures of this study were reviewed and approved by National Cheng Kung University Governance Framework for Human Research Ethics. Before each pre-interview with the participants, we obtained written informed consent from the participants. The workshop process was video and audio-recorded, and photos also documented the workshop outcomes.

The research team performed the PD procedure in this study with two local communities. Most members in both communities were people aged 65 years or over. The selected communities were close to the local university. Many community members were active and willing to take part in university research projects working with younger people. The first PD workshop with the first community was conducted in December 2019. However, from 2020 to 2022, the COVID-19 pandemic caused human interaction prohibition. There were a few times of nationwide lockdowns for that period. The governments and citizens are concerned most about the activities related to the older population. The senior community centers shut down for around two years. Even though the community centers re-opened in early 2022, the community managers set rigorous restrictions on community entrance and outsiders' interactions with older community members. To follow the governmental policy and consider the communities' concerns, we held down the research progress until the community centers were completely open to everyone in the Summer of 2022. The PD study with the second community was held from late August to early September 2022.

2.1 Workshop Participants and Locations

There are three roles of participants in the co-design workshops. In addition to the older people in the senior communities, we also included computer science engineers who were experts in NLP implementation and product designers who had experience in applying user journey maps and other design tools in the design process. Each course of the workshops had two teams. And each team had two to three older people, one to two computer science engineers, and two product designers. The participant combinations and their genders are shown in Table 1. All the older adult participants were over 65 years old and physically and cognitively healthy.

The first course of the PD workshops with the first local community was held in the laboratory room at one of the university buildings. Since the older participants lived close

Table 1. The composition of workshop participants

PD workshop course	Team #1	Team #2
Community 1	2 older people (1M, 1F) 2 NLP engineers (2M) 2 designers (2F)	3 older people (2M, 1F) 2 NLP engineers (2M) 2 product designers (1M, 1F)
Community 2	2 older people (2F) 1 NLP engineer (1M) 2 product designers (2F)	2 older people (1M, 1F) 1 NLP engineer (1M) 2 product designers (2F)

* M-Male; F-Female

to the university campus, it was easy for them to access the workshop location. Since the laboratory room was a close setting that could avoid interruption and distraction from the environment, the workshop participants were more likely to focus on the workshop process. Nevertheless, when working with the second community, only some of their members lived in the neighborhood areas, and the community managers still had some concerns about COVID. For this reason, the second course of the PD workshops was held in community building. Two workshops were held in the café space, and two workshops were held in a classroom. Since the café was a public area and open to all the community members, the researchers devoted more effort to engaging the participants in the workshop activities. But it may be because the participants were in an environment they were familiar with. The participants in the second workshop seemed more relaxed than the older participants in the first-course workshops.

3 PD Workshop

This PD project intended to explore the potential technology applications that implement NLP technology and fit into active older people's daily lives. The PD project consisted of one technical knowledge workshop, two user journey map co-creation workshops, and one idea-developing workshop. The primary goal of this PD workshop was to encourage knowledge sharing and mutual learning among various types of participants. And then, with what they learned in the workshops, the participants better understood each other, reached a higher quality of collaboration and inspired each other to generate NLP application ideas. Besides having the engineers teach other participants the NLP concepts and mechanisms, the workshop design concentrated on applying pre-designed tools and techniques to help older people reveal and organize their life problems. The researchers developed a new process of creating users journey maps, which meant documenting detailed routines of older people's everyday lives in order to discover opportunities for technological intervention. The designed user journey map process engaged all participant roles in the exploratory progress to enhance the collaboration in the group and have engineers and designers emphasize the older people. The design of the four workshops and workshop records were as follows.

3.1 Workshop 1: Learning NLP Technology

The first workshop activity aimed at having all the participants learn the targeted technology of this PD project, the NLP technology. The computer science engineers prepared a talk introducing the fundamental concepts and mechanisms of speech recognition, natural-language understanding, and natural-language generation (See Fig. 1A). Besides lectures on technical knowledge, the engineers also prepare some exemplary website services and mobile apps for other participants to interact with (See Fig. 1B). Since the recruited senior participants were active learners, they were interested in learning the technology and consistently consulted the engineers about what they felt they needed clarification about the NLP technology. Initially, older people were reticent when listening to lectures. After the designers asked questions about what the engineers introduced, they became talkative and curious about some digital applications. Especially in the workshop with the second community, one female participant explained what she learned about the NLP in her words and then confirmed whether her understandings of the NLP were correct with the engineers. The engineers told the researchers they were so surprised that the older participants could understand abstract computer processing quickly. They usually expected that older people might have difficulties understanding the new technologies and the mechanisms of how those technologies work.

Fig. 1. (A) The engineers introduced NLP technology in the first-course workshops, and (B) the older participants consulted engineer about how to operate the apps in the second-course workshops

In working with both communities, trying on those technology applications engaged the older participants in the activities in the demonstration process. They started asking questions about operating the systems and sometimes asked how those technologies worked. Interacting with the technologies also encouraged the participants to discuss their ideas of how the technology could be used and implemented in their everyday lives. When a female participant in the second-course workshops tried the speech-to-text transcription service, she was excited about it and mentioned that she would use it in her church work. She thought the software would hugely reduce her work loading of managing church meeting minutes. Many participants in the first-course workshops talked about what kind of conversational robots they would like to have in their everyday lives. The participants in the first-course workshops quickly envisioned the future of technology applications since the first workshop activity.

3.2 Workshop 2: Contextual Interview

The design of the second workshop activity was planned to involve the older participants in reviewing their daily lives and revealing the information to the engineers and designers. The workshop session started with introducing a business origami design method (Fox, 2014), which applied physical elements to help people investigate and explain complex interactions within various stakeholders, locations, and systems. The researchers implemented this method since the physical elements helped visualize the physical locations and people in the interaction circumstances and enabled workshop participants to discuss the interaction directly with those visual cues. The older participants were asked to use LEGO® bricks and paper drawings to build up the living spaces of their houses and other places they usually spent time in, such as community building. In the LEGO® building process, the designers played the roles of both facilitators and interviewers. They asked older participants questions to add details of the arrangement of the living spaces. Meanwhile, the designers and engineers helped with sketching the floor plan of the houses or using bricks to build the furniture, as the older participants described. This process intended to engage all the participants in understanding the older adults' life spaces (See Fig. 2 for an example of built life space representation).

Fig. 2. The older participants appropriated the LEGO® living space representation and told their stories to other workshop participants.

After building the physical representation of older participants' living spaces, the older participants were given LEGO® figures and role-played how they and their families interacted in their living spaces. The designers and engineers were the interviewers who asked older participants about one day of their lives and documented the detailed interactions of their life routines. The designers consulted the older participants on a typical day, from waking up in the morning to bedtime. The engineers documented all the interaction or activity events with the event sheets. The event sheets included information on the timestamp of the event, the title of the event, the location, the objects and people the older participant interacted with in the event, and the details of it (See Fig. 3). The engineers wrote one sheet for one event individually. Then they sequenced those event sheets after completing the interviews. Even though the interviews were conducted in time sequence, the older participants usually had difficulty chronicling their life routines. They often came out with some events that happened later but related to current discussions. The engineers would write another sheet for the later event and put it aside for later use. In the interviews, the designers appropriated the preset LEGO® life space representation and LEGO® figures and concentrated the senior interviewees on using them to tell stories about how they moved around the space and interacted with their family and objects (See Fig. 2). At the end of this workshop activity, the team collected a pile of event sheets for the next workshop 3.

However, some of the older participants in both courses of workshops felt uncomfortable when building the LEGO® representations. They seemed altered and questioned whether building the representations might expose their privacy to others. But after the researchers explained the abstraction of the LEGO® representation and its purposes, the older participants felt relieved and re-joined the activities. Even though the interview conversations were carried out among the older participants and the designers, the documentation work still involved the engineers in the process of understanding older people's lives. Occasionally, they asked older participants about the interviews to clarify some event details for their documentation.

Fig. 3. The engineers wrote the event sheets to documents activities the older participant mentioned in the interview.

3.3 Workshop 3: Creating the Journey Map

In the third workshop activity, the teams transferred the data in the interview event sheets to a visualized user journey map. The researchers introduced the design tool, the user journey map, to the workshop participants and gave them user journey map canvases to rearrange the event sheets' information. The user journey map contains eight types of information about each event or interaction moment, including 1) event name, 2) locations, 3) people they interact with, 4) object they interact with, 5) what they do in the event, 6) what they think in the event, 7) how they feel when the event happens, and 8) the positive or negative emotional status during the event. The event sheets contained information of types 1) to 5). So at the beginning of the activity, the designers and engineers reviewed the sequenced event sheets with the older participants, filled up post-its with the information on the sheets, and pasted the post-its in the corresponding places on the journey map canvases (See Fig. 4A). Then, the designers went through the process again and asked the older participants what they thought (type 6 information) and how they felt (type 6 information) about individual events. The engineers or other team members noted their answers on post-its and pasted them on the journey map canvases (See Fig. 4B). At the end of the journey-map-building activity, the designers consulted the participants about their emotional status of the events and drew the emotional line of changed emotions during the day.

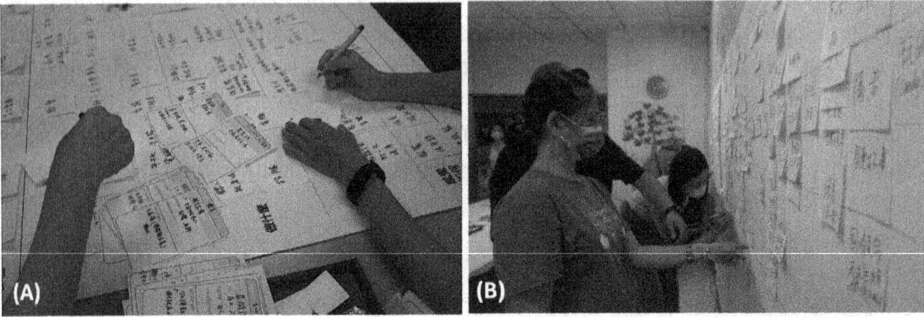

Fig. 4. (A) The teams deployed the information on post-its and pasted the notes on the journey map canvases. (B) After asking older participants their thoughts and feelings about the event, the team members pasted post-its with answers on the canvas.

While building the user journey maps, the designers, who were usually the interviewers of information needed for the journey maps, frequently asked whether the older participants wanted to add complementary information to the existing journey map. The visualization process of the older participants' everyday lives with the journey map reminded them of many additional details of the events. For example, in Fig. 5, the larger post-its on the journey map were the data collected from the event sheets and the first consultation with the older participants. The smaller post-its were the additional information the older participants added in later discussions. Moreover, the visualization of their daily events and activities gave the team a shared view of what the older participants encountered and the related information for a better understanding of their life situations. Sometimes, seeing other older participants' journey maps recalled the older participants' life experiences and some problems they also met. The user journey map seemed helpful in enhancing the discussions among the older participants and other team members.

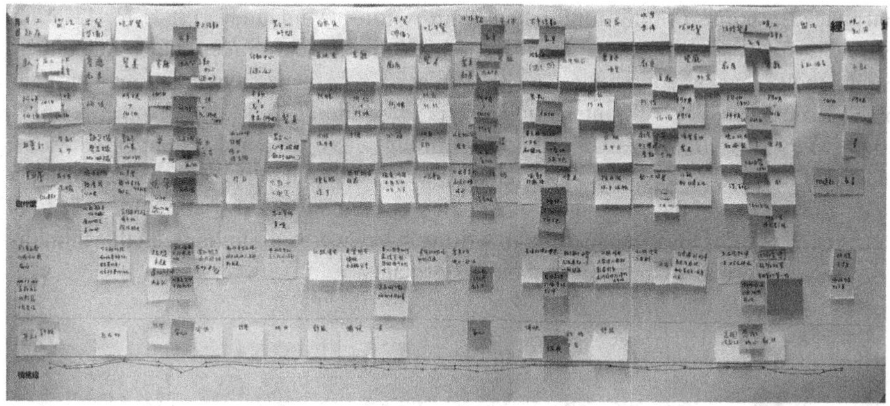

Fig. 5. A user journey map built at the end of the third workshop activity.

3.4 Workshop 4: Identifying Problems & Ideation

The final workshop activity focused on identifying the older participants' life challenges and finding preliminary ideas for implementing the NLP technologies. At first, while reviewing the user journey map in the team, the older participants were requested to identify the challenges they faced in their everyday activities. The team members wrote down those challenges on post-its with unique colors and pasted them along with the events linking to the challenges (See Fig. 6). The team walked through those challenges and then voted for those challenges they thought interesting, important, or appropriate for applying NLP technologies. However, we found that many older participants were satisfied with their current lives, and it was difficult for them to find the problems they wanted to solve. The designers might have to recall some discussions in the prior workshops and ask the older participants whether some issues they mentioned unintentionally before bothered them. Sometimes, the designers asked the older participants which issue or situation they thought could be improved to urge the older participants to think about the potential needs in their lives.

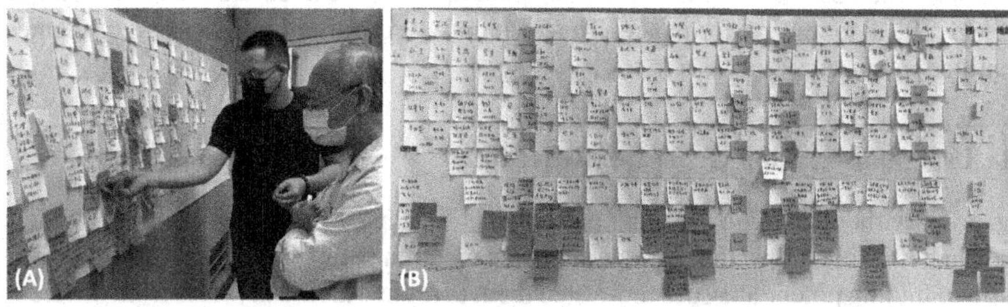

Fig. 6. (A) The engineers added the challenge notes on the journey map with the older participants. (B) The Pink post-its were the challenges of the older participants' daily life.

In the later session, the team picked up two challenges that most of the team members voted to and applied them as the topic of the idea generation activity. The researchers introduced a brainstorming tool called brain writing (VanGundy, 1984) for ideation. Brainwriting was a well-known brainstorming technique that forced the participants to extend their ideas based on others'. The designers and engineers brainstormed with the older participants. They got interesting results when adding their ideas to other people's concepts (See Fig. 7). However, the brainstorming activity seemed challenging to some older participants. They usually took a long time to come out with their ideas. Especially in the first course of the workshop, some older participants worried about the quality of their concepts after finishing their brain writing. They were unfamiliar with this thinking process and were less confident in their performance.

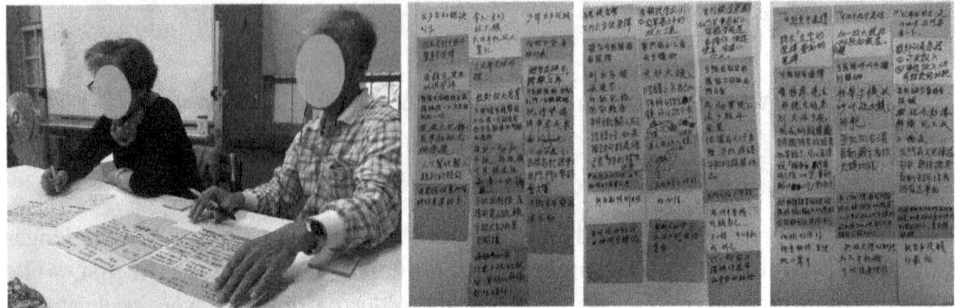

Fig. 7. The brainwriting activity and some examples of the brain writing results.

4 Findings

We conducted pre- and post-interviews with workshop participants, including the older participants, the engineers, and the designers, and collected feedback on their expectations and gains from participating in the workshops. The researchers applied qualitative analysis to code the interview contents and identified instances regarding the workshop tools and process. The abductive analysis extended those preliminary instances to include themes that revealed how the participants perceived and reflected on the workshop design and performance. This section will discuss the four primary themes identified in our analysis.

4.1 User Journey Map Generates Reflections

The primary theme among the older participants' feedback was their reflection on their lives. In both workshops, the older participants mentioned that building the user journey map and finding potential issues motivated them to review their daily lives from different perspectives. They found that they were used to life routines and did not recognize hidden problems or challenges embedded in their lifestyles. Going through the workshop process and discussing the journey maps with other participants provoked their thoughts of exploring their unseen problems and needs and discovering the potential to live a better life. They also mentioned the collaborative efforts in doing the journey map, which helped them recognize that something they thought was not a problem needed to be addressed. In addition to finding the invisible issues, the older participants talked about the journey map, guided them to examine how they live, which they did not usually do, and to identify the delightful moments they enjoyed.

All the engineers who participated in both courses' PD workshops mentioned that working on the user journey map with older people strongly changed their presumptions of the users who might use their product. The engineers who participated in the workshops were experts in NLP and had experience developing NLP products designed for senior users. They had some assumptions about how older people. For example, they thought most older people were not good at using digital technology, such as mobile phones. They had confidence that they understood the older adults' needs, but the experience in the workshops ultimately rejected their assumption. The changes triggered them to reflect on their ways of developing NLP applications and services. They said they usually sat in the laboratory and imagined how their users thought and behaved. The developing team discussed most of the functions and technical concerns. They rarely talked about the users and their needs. After the workshop, they recognized gaps between what they thought about the users and what the users thought. They said that engineers needed to reach the end users and better understand them before developing the products. Both the older and engineer participants' responses illustrated the new way of collaboratively building user journey maps to enrich their understanding of older people's life experiences and appeal to them to reflect on their current work and lives.

4.2 What They Also Learned from User Journey Map

In addition to discussing user journey map contents, the participants reflected on something they learned from the tool user journey map. The older participants in the second community reacted to how the user journey map might change how they looked at their life routines. They usually considered their life events independently, and the fragment information was attached to a specific event. After they learned the user journey map, they said that they found the benefits of rethinking their life events sequentially and could find extended viewpoints from the chronological data and their relationships. They also found that the visualized map would bring them a holistic view of the events, transforming their mindset and perspective of things.

The engineers had aspects similar to the older participants. They appreciated the process of collecting all data and implementing them in time sequence. The process of documenting the events when interviewing and then filling out the data on the user journey map collected the needed information entirely and had little information left. Some mentioned that they thought the visualization way of presenting users' experiences was structured and well-organized. This form of data presentation enabled them to find older people's problems and concerns quickly. Users' experiences represented on the journey maps also provided the evidence and analytical contexts of users' needs and function design reasoning.

The designers also mentioned in the interviews that visualizing user journey maps generated more discussion between the older participants and others. While looking at the user journey map on the wall, the older participants would report more detailed information than they provided in the interviews. We learned from those responses that the participants acknowledged the chronological and visualizing features of the user journey map and valued the benefits the tool brought. However, since the engineers were responsible for writing down the interview information on the event sheets, they also recognized the importance of well-documented interviews before the chronologic visualization of the collected data. The user journey map-building process in these PD workshops not only benefited participants' understanding of the older participants' life experiences but enhanced personal reflection and group discussions.

4.3 Learning from Other Participants

All older participants in both workshop courses believed it was never too late to learn. They actively participated in the learning activity. In the post-interviews, they mentioned learning a lot from the workshop processes and other participants. They enjoyed learning something new, especially those relating to new technology, which they did not have a chance to learn about. It was also mentioned that what they learned in the workshop regarding those NLP technologies broadened their imagination of technological capacity and applications. Besides learning about the technology, they also learned some techniques of how the designers facilitated the group work and discussion. One participant in the second-course PD workshop mentioned that she appreciated how designers guided people to review life details and identify potential problems. She learned some tips from the designers. The engineers said working with users and participating in a user-centered process was a unique experience. One engineer expected that he would just play the role of contributor at the beginning but learned much from the other participants and the workshop process at the end. The engineer mentioned that exploring the problem space before defining the problem was something new to them and turned valuable to them after the workshop. The mutual learning of technology and life experience knowledge happened among different participants in the workshop. However, the workshop design and operation also brought additional benefits to the older participants and engineers to extend their knowledge.

4.4 Inspiration Brought by Brainwriting

The brainwriting activity was reported as the most exciting activity for both the older participants and engineers. Some older participants and engineers mentioned that building their ideas based on other people's concepts extended their imagination of potential solutions to the targeted problems. Coming out with some ideas for the problems made them feel productive. The older adults especially enjoyed the brain-storming session with the engineers and designers. They thought the younger people had new and novel ideas, and they got inspiration from those ideas. The designers' and engineers' ideas acknowledged that the problems they usually considered unsolvable had solutions from other perspectives. Those ideas from the younger generation gave them some ideas of how those problems might be solved. Meanwhile, they felt embarrassed about their ideas' conservativeness and self-restriction. The engineers also thought brainwriting was inspiring. One engineer was impressed by the process and outcomes of brainwriting and planned to bring the tools back to his workplace. The designers noticed that even though all the participants engaged in the user journey map-building process, there were not many discussions among the older participants and engineers. The brainwriting session was fun and generated many active discussions when the team shared their ideas. The interactions between the older participants and the engineers seemed most impassioned throughout the whole workshop process.

5 Discussion

5.1 User Journey Map Enhanced Mutual Learning

One of the critical principles of PD is enhancing mutual learning among various stakeholders for better collaboration in the design process (Robertson & Simonsen, 2012a). In this study, the co-creation process enhanced the mutual learning process from two perspectives. At first, the same as prior research findings (such as McCarthya et al., 2018; Segelström, 2012), the visualization and chronology of the user experience contributed to the understanding and communication in the PD teams. The workshop process and the post-interview analysis showed that the built user journey map in the workshop brought the engineers and designers insights into the users' experiences and challenges. Especially for the engineers, learning the users' experiences revised the concepts they took for granted in their jobs and recognized the need to reach out to the end users and understand them before developing technological applications. Besides the engineers and designers learning of users' "tacit knowledge" (Robertson & Simonsen, 2012a) from user journey maps, the visualization of the life experience also increased older participants' recall of their tacit knowledge. As shown in Fig. 5, the older participants added more details after they put the interview data in the journey map canvas. The older participants mentioned that the user journey map provided alternative perspectives to investigate lives. Seeing other people's journeys might remind them of similar experiences. The designers also noticed that the older participants took a more active role in discussing their experience after building the user journey map. The journey map expanded the interaction among the group.

The second benefit of the co-creation process to the mutual learning process was engaging all the participants in learning about users' experiences. The typical way of creating user journey maps relied on researchers or designers collecting field-site data and analyzing them in chronological map format. The process of analyzing users' data and representing the data in sequential form was decided by the designers and researchers (e.g., Brata & Liang, 2019). Other people transcribed the data, and the users were usually less attached to the knowledge-sharing process. In some PD projects, the researchers facilitated the users to build their journey map (e.g., Broadley & Smith, 2018). In this case, the users were usually confident about the journey data they presented. However, most of the time, they had to take additional time to explain the detailed information on the map to other participants in the PD group. In this study, the research team developed a process that not only engaged the users (the older participants in this study) to uncover their experience to share among the team but also had the product creation team (the designers and engineers) participate in the process of generating the knowledge. In our research findings, the older participants were devoted to digging into their experiences and completing the journey map information. They added details to the journey map in the workshop discourses of their and other people's maps. The engineers reported that documenting users' life routines with the event sheets was beneficial and helped them engage with users' data and inspired new ideas for their future designs.

From those perspectives, the new approach of engaging all participants in creating the user journey map not only leveraged the advantages of visualizing user experience with the user journey map but also had all participants immersed with the users' data to increase the group mutual understanding and discussions. The research results validated how the co-creation of the user journey map contributed to mutual learning in PD.

5.2 Contradictory Reactions to the use of LEGO®

In this study, the research team adopted business origami techniques and applied LEGO® bricks to build the physical arrangement of people's living spaces. The visibility and tangibility of the physical representations in the business origami method enabled simulations and group discussions about the interactions in the setting (Martin et al., 2012). Since the researchers had no idea of the living spaces of the older participants, the flexible LEGO® bricks seemed an excellent tool for quickly constructing the physical arrangement of an indoor space. The research team expected that the physical arrangement of the physical space and role-play with the LEGO® figures could help the older percipients tell their life routines and illustrate how the interactions happened in various locations. In the process of the PD workshop, the researchers recognized that the LEGO® representation did help the designers imagine older participants' activities and interactions in the interview process. However, in the post-interviews, most engineers thought this process was useless and did not advance their understanding of users' experience. They did not recognize the benefits as the designers. Also, the older participants did not like the LEGO® tools and thought LEGO® were toys for the kids. Even though the prior research did not identify adult users' rejection when applying LEGO® in research activities (Schulz & Geithner, 2011), we award that the general impressions of LEGO® might critically impact participants' dealings and attitudes in operating the workshop tools. The research team should not solely focus on the efficiency of the PD workshop tools but also consider the tools' appropriation for the participants in the group.

6 Conclusion

This study developed a new PD method of having all the participants co-create the user journey maps intended to reinforce mutual learning in the PD process. This new process included four activities: 1) using LEGO® to build the participants' life space representations, 2) interviewing the participants about their typical day experience with the living space representation and event sheets, 3) building up the user journey map with event sheets' information and advanced interviews, and 4) identifying the life challenges within groups. The research team performed two courses of PD workshops with older people in two local communities. The PD workshop involved the potential users of the project (the older participants) and the product developing team (the engineers and the designers). The post-interviews demonstrated that the co-creation process benefited mutual learning from two perspectives. The visualization and chronology of the user experience contributed to understanding users' experiences and communication in the

PD teams. Also, the co-creation activity design immersed all the participants in the users' data in increasing mutual understanding and discussions. This method of co-creating the user journey maps may be an appropriate tool to support PD practices with older people, especially when the research team plan for active collaboration in the mutual learning process.

References

Bellos, I., Kavadias, S.: Service design for a holistic customer experience: a process framework. Manage. Sci. **67**, 1718–1736 (2021)

Brata, K.C., Liang, D.: An effective approach to develop location-based augmented reality information support. Int. J. Electr. Comput. Eng. **9**, 3060 (2019)

Broadley, C., Smith, P.: Co-design at a distance: context, participation, and ownership in geographically distributed design processes. Des. J. **21**, 395–415 (2018)

Fox, D.: Using the business origmai technique to understand complex ecosystems. In: Studying and Designing Technology for Domestic Life: Lessons from Home, p. 93 (2014)

Kensing, F., Greenbaum, J.: Heritage: having a say. In: Routledge International Handbook of Participatory Design, pp. 41–56. Routledge (2012)

Lee, H.R., et al.: Steps toward participatory design of social robots: mutual learning with older adults with depression. In: Proceedings of the 2017 ACM/IEEE International Conference on Human-Robot Interaction, pp. 244–253 (2017)

Luck, R.: What is it that makes participation in design participatory design? Des. Stud. **59**, 1–8 (2018)

Martin, B., Hanington, B., Hanington, B.M.: Universal methods of design: 100 ways to research complex problems, develop innovative ideas, and design effective solutions. Rockport Pub (2012)

McCarthya, S., O'Raghallaigha, P., Fitzgeralda, C., Adamab, F.: Participatory design: a key tool in the arsenal of IT management. In: Irish Academy of Management Conference (2018)

Robertson, T., Simonsen, J.: Challenges and opportunities in contemporary participatory design. Des. Issues **28**, 3–9 (2012a)

Robertson, T., Simonsen, J.: Participatory design: an introduction. In: Routledge International Handbook of Participatory Design, pp. 1–17. Routledge (2012b)

Schulz, K.-P., Geithner, S.: "Making Waves" The development of shared understandings and innovation through metaphorical methods such as LEGO Serious PlayTM. Citeseer, Hull University Business School, Hull, UK (2011)

Segelström, F.: Communicating through visualizations: service designers on visualizing user research. In: Conference Proceedings ServDes. 2009; DeThinking Service; ReThinking Design; Oslo Norway 24–26 November 2009, pp. 175–185. Linköping University Electronic Press (2012)

Shin, J.Y., Okammor, N., Hendee, K., Pawlikowski, A., Jenq, G., Bozaan, D.: Development of the socioeconomic screening, active engagement, follow-up, education, discharge readiness, and consistency (SAFEDC) model for improving transitions of care: participatory design. JMIR Formative Res. **6**, e31277 (2022)

VanGundy, A.B.: Brain writing for new product ideas: an alternative to brainstorming. J. Consum. Mark. (1984)

Integrate Gamification into Questionnaire Design

Yu-Chen Chen, Chin-Ying Chen, and Hsi-Jen Chen(✉)

National Cheng Kung University, Tainan, Taiwan
p38091070@gs.ncku.edu.tw, hsijen_chen@mail.ncku.edu.tw

Abstract. Self-report questionnaire is usually used to explore people's feelings, attitudes, or perspectives. However, some potential problems of self-report questionnaire are indicated, such as participants' careless responding, insufficient effort responding, and a lack of motivation to participate. In order to improve the motivation of responding the questionnaire, previous studies integrated gamification into the questionnaire design by creating a novel questionnaire items or scales. But, less of them discussed the situation without changing the questionnaire items or scales. Under the situation, we investigated the influence of gamification on the survey results and intrinsic motivation for responding the questionnaire. The study took the Big Five Personality Test IPIP 50 as an example to gamify and investigated 38 participants to understand the difference between the results from original and gamification versions. The results of the five personality traits from the two versions reveal highly positive correlations; moreover, compare with original version, gamification version enhances the interest/enjoyment, perceived competence, and perceived choice in intrinsic motivation, but decreases the pressure/tension. In summary, the gamification version does not obviously change the survey results and improves the intrinsic motivation. As a result, integrating gamification into questionnaire design without changing the questionnaire items or scales may be a potential approach to improve the application of gamification in questionnaire design.

Keywords: Gamification · Questionnaire Design · Intrinsic Motivation · the Big Five

1 Introduction

1.1 Background and Motivation

A questionnaire is a common research method in quantitative research. Many studies explore people's feelings, attitudes, or perspectives through self-report questionnaire. However, a lot of scholars claim potential problems of self-report questionnaire. For example, participants' careless or insufficient effort responding would interfere in the results of questionnaires [1, 2]. Careless responding is that people do not correspondingly reply to the questionnaire. About 10 to 12% students carelessly respond to the online questionnaire [1]. Insufficient effort responding means people reply to the questionnaire

M. Kurosu and A. Hashizume (Eds.): HCII 2023, LNCS 14011, pp. 18–29, 2023.
https://doi.org/10.1007/978-3-031-35596-7_2

before reading the content carefully [2]. Inattentive participants provide worse self-report data [3]. Moreover, when a questionnaire length is too long [4, 5], or participants are not interested in the research, they are less willing to respond the questionnaire and respond casually. These situations may cause participants to provide random answers or to choose the first option to reply [6] because of a lack of motivation [1, 2, 7]. Therefore, in order to improve the motivation, gamification is integrated into the questionnaire [8, 9].

Gamification is a strategy to influence or motivate people's behavior by applying game-design elements to non-game situations. Chou outlined the gamification strategies and elements and addressed eight Core Drivers in Octalysis [10]; besides, the Core Drivers were sorted into White Hat and Black Hat Motivation in gamification. Drivers causing people's positive feelings were sorted in White Hat Motivation while some drivers causing people's negative feelings were sorted in Black Hat Motivation, and the others involved in White Hat and Black Hat Motivation. Both White Hat and Black Hat Motivation were used together so as to increase the influence of gamification. Furthermore, many studies utilized Intrinsic Motivation Inventory (IMI) [11] to investigate the influence of gamification [12, 13].

Gamification were applied in many fields, including psychometric assessments and related questionnaire design. Landers, and Sanchez refer to some terms relating to gamification applications in psychometric assessments. Game-based assessment, a method combines game elements with psychometric tests and is usually utilized in job recruitment to find the appropriate candidates. The other terms are Assessment Gameful Design and Assessment Gamification which belong to design strategies. The former applies game mechanics and elements to create a novel assessment, whereas the latter makes use of mechanics and elements in an existing assessment [14]. In addition to the method and strategies, gamification elements are applied for questionnaire design to improve the experience of responding the questionnaire (e.g., fun, pleasure, and satisfaction) and to engage participants in the process [15, 16]. McCord et al. developed a text-based fantasy game through modifying the questionnaire items and adding a dialog box like in game to create the situation just like playing a text adventure game [8]. Landers & Collmus utilized narrative to transform the original items into situational judgment tests [17] and Harman & Brown integrated both narrative and illustrations into the questionnaire [9].

Generally speaking, most previous studies redesigned questionnaire items or scales when integrating gamification into the questionnaire. But less of them discussed the situation without changing the questionnaire items or scales. Consequently, we investigated the influence of gamification on the survey results and motivation of responding the questionnaire when combining the original items and scales with the gamification approach.

1.2 Purpose

The study explored the influence of gamification on the survey results and motivation of responding the questionnaire. The Big Five Personality Test IPIP 50 (retrieved from International Personality Item Pool, IPIP) [18] was taken as an example and the gamification version of IPIP 50 was created to discover appropriate and effective gamification strategies and to improve the application of gamification in questionnaire design. Our purposes are:

- To understand the influence of gamification on the survey results
- To understand the influence of gamification on intrinsic motivation of responding the questionnaire

2 Methods

Three phases were involved in our study: preparation, investigation, and analysis. First of all, we selected the questionnaire, IPIP 50 to gamify and demonstrated our gamification approach. In the next phase, the influence of gamification on the survey results and intrinsic motivation of responding the questionnaire were investigated. The results from original and gamification versions and the relationship between gamification and participants' intrinsic motivation were discussed in the final phase.

2.1 Preparation Phase

Big Five Personality Test IPIP 50. To understand the influence of gamification, we gamified the Big Five Personality Test IPIP 50 (IPIP 50). Before explaining why we chose IPIP 50, we simply introduced personality trait theory. Personality was composed of traits [19, 20] and models of personality trait classification were developed [20, 21]. The Big Five model was one of the classification generally used and the model involved five personality traits: "extroversion," "agreeableness," "conscientiousness," "emotional stability," and "openness to experience" [22, 23]. Many versions of the questionnaire measuring the Big Five personality traits were built and IPIP 50 retrieved from International Personality Item Pool (IPIP) [18] is one of the versions containing 50 items. The reliability and validity of IPIP 50 are high in Chinese context [24] and additionally, the Big Five personality traits are stable for adults [25]; as a result, we gamified IPIP 50 to compare the difference between the survey results from original and gamification versions.

Eight Core Drivers and White Hat & Black Hat Motivation. After organizing the gamification strategies and elements, Chou pointed out Octalysis composed of eight Core Drivers and classified the drivers by two kinds of motivation [10], as shown in Fig. 1.

The Core Drivers are "epic meaning & calling," "development & accomplishment," "empowerment of creativity & feedback," "ownership & possession," "social influence & relatedness," "scarcity & impatience," "unpredictability & curiosity," and "loss & avoidance." Then, the Core Drivers were briefly introduced. Epic meaning & calling was reflected when people believe they were doing something beyond themselves or were selected to do that thing. Development & accomplishment drove people's behavior by the feeling that people wanted to boost abilities or achieve goals; besides, that is also the easiest driver to design. When people kept trying novel things and combinations, that expressed empowerment of creativity & feedback. Ownership & possession referred

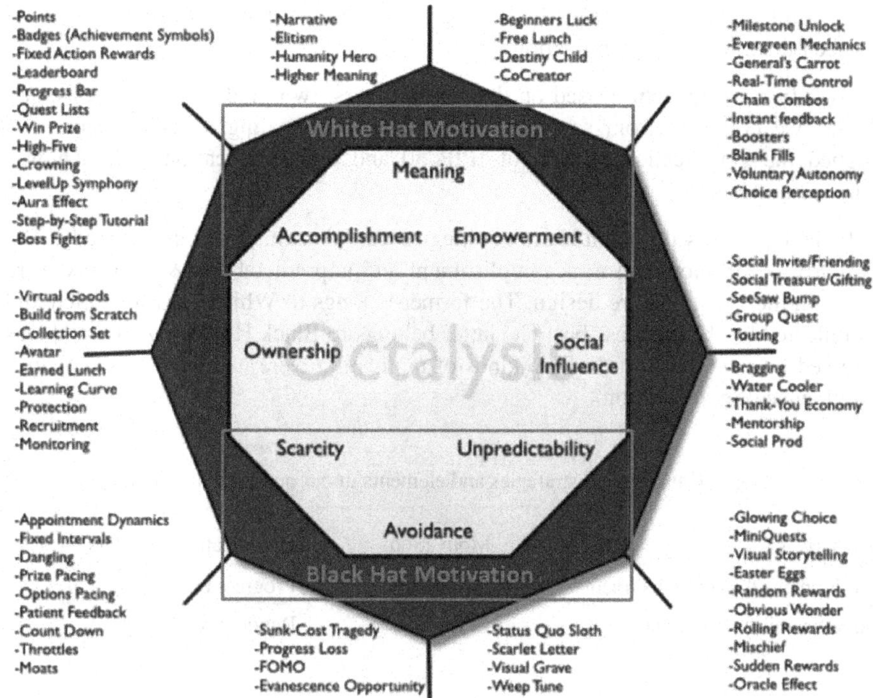

Fig. 1. Eight Core Drivers and White Hat & Black Hat Motivation [10] p.23

that when people possessed something, they would like to increase or improve it genuinely. Social influence & relatedness involved all elements relating to society, such as mentorship, social feedback, and competition with others. Scarcity & impatience was carried out when people desire to earn things that were rare, unique, or even not available right now. Unpredictability & curiosity was attractive because people were attracted inevitably by unexpected things or results. Loss & avoidance inspired people to avoid losing what they possessed or avoid admitting that their endeavor was in vain.

Moreover, Chou grouped these drivers into White Hat and Black Hat Motivation. White Hat Motivation stimulated positive emotions, like making people feel competent, fulfilled, or satisfied and involved the first three drivers (epic meaning & calling, development & accomplishment, empowerment of creativity & feedback). Black Hat Motivation triggered negative emotions, like making people feel fascinating, anxious, or addicted and included the last three drivers (scarcity & impatience, unpredictability & curiosity, and loss & avoidance). The other drivers (ownership & possession, social influence & relatedness) involved in both White Hat and Black Hat Motivation. Only carrying out White Hat Motivation would not urge people to do something immediately while only manipulating Black Hat Motivation may cause them to feel unpleasant or out of control.

Consequently, equally and properly making use of the two kinds of motivation could enhance the influence of gamification.

Gamification Approach. Based on the Core Drivers, two kinds of motivations, and troubles we collected from several students about responding a questionnaire, we designed the gamification version of IPIP 50 and our gamification approach was explained in this part.

Table 1 presents the gamification strategies and elements used in our study. The Core Drivers, development & accomplishment and unpredictability & curiosity were applied in the questionnaire design. The former belongs to White Hat Motivation and was reflected by the progress bar. The latter belongs to Black Hat Motivation and was expressed by random rewards. Two kinds of motivation were manipulated to enhance the influence of gamification.

Table 1. Gamification strategies and elements in our questionnaire design

Core Drivers	Motivation	Gamification elements
Development & accomplishment	White Hat	Progress bar
Unpredictability & curiosity	Black Hat	Random rewards

Furthermore, both pictures and text were made use of in the gamification questionnaire and the sample of gamification questionnaire is illustrated in Fig. 2 to Fig. 5. At the beginning of the gamification version, the way to earn reward was provided: each participant has a chance to win the lottery after finishing the questionnaire (see Fig. 2). Figure 3 shows the screen which they started to answer the questionnaire. As participants responded the certain numbers of items they got rewards (see Fig. 4). Figure 5, the final screen presents the winning numbers for the lottery.

Fig. 2. The way to earn reward was provided at the beginning of the gamification version

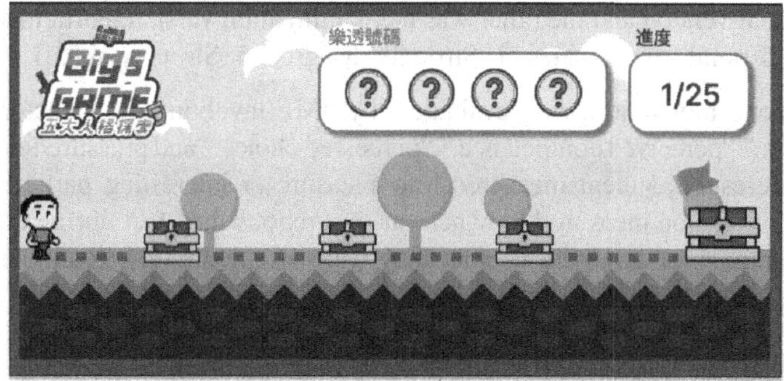

Fig. 3. The screen which participants started to answer the questionnaire

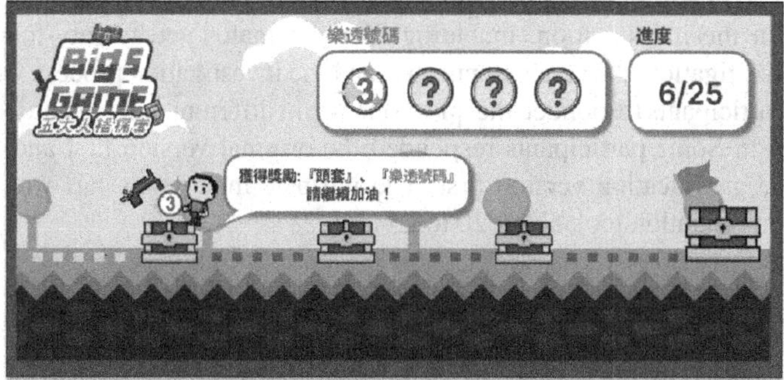

Fig. 4. Participants got rewards when they responded the certain numbers of items

Fig. 5. The winning numbers for the lottery on the final screen

2.2 Investigation Phase

Measures. The study measured the Big Five personality traits by IPIP 50 and intrinsic motivation by Intrinsic Motivation Inventory (IMI) [11]; besides, both questionnaires are self-report. IPIP 50 were divided into two parts and each part had 25 items. One part was the original version and the other was the gamification version. Participants scored each item in 5-point Likert scales (1: Strongly disagree; 5: Strongly agree).

In addition, motivation was evaluated by IMI involving four factors: "interest/enjoyment," "perceived competence," "perceived choice," and pressure/tension," and 22 items. Interest/enjoyment measured how pleasure or interesting participants' feel while pressure/tension measured how nervous or anxious they feel during the process. Perceived competence assessed whether they were satisfied with or confident of their performance. Their willingness to respond the questionnaire was evaluated in perceived choice. Moreover, participants filled out IMI in semantic differential scale (-2: Agree well with the original version; 0: Neither agree with the original nor the gamification version; 2: Agree well with the gamification version) according to the experience of responding the original and gamification version of IPIP 50.

Subject and Procedure. We invited our participants online and thirty-eight people participated in the investigation, including fourteen males and twenty-four females. Before the investigation, the research purpose and the investigation process were briefly introduced. Participants responded the questionnaire in different orders in order to reduce the order effect. Some participants responded the original version first and the others responded the gamification version first. The intrinsic motivation part was answered finally. The investigation took about 20 to 25 min.

2.3 Analysis Phase

In the phase, we analyzed the results of original and gamification versions and the relationship between gamification and participants' intrinsic motivation. First, split-half-reliability was used to inspect the results of two versions were high correlation and good internal consistency. We explored the correlation between the results of the two versions through Pearson Correlation next. Additionally, the scores of IMI in semantic differential scale were transformed, as seen in Table 2. For instance, "−2" were transformed into two numbers. One was "2" in original version and the other was "0" in gamification version. After that, Independent Sample t test was manipulated to research the motivation difference between responding the two versions.

Table 2. Scores transformation in semantic differential scale

Before transformation	After transformation	
	score in original version	score in gamification version
−2	2	0
−1	1	0
0	0	0
1	0	1
2	0	2

3 Results

The study discussed the influence of gamification on the survey results and intrinsic motivation. Thirty-eight people participated in the investigation, including fourteen males and twenty-four females from 16 to 32 years old. The results were analyzed in two parts: one is gamification questionnaire and the results of IPIP 50, and the other is gamification questionnaire and intrinsic motivation.

Table 3. Split-half-reliability in 50 items

Cronbach's α	Original version	Value	.771
		N of Items	25
	Gamification version	Value	.744
		N of Items	25
	Total N of Items		50
Correlation Between Forms			.830
Spearman-Brown Coefficient			.907
Guttman Split-Half Coefficient			.906

3.1 Gamification Questionnaire and the Results of IPIP 50

First of all, we confirmed the high correlations between the 25 original items and 25 gamification items (Spearman-Brown Coefficient = .907, Guttman Split-Half Coefficient = .906) through split-half-reliability [26], as seen in Table 3. Then, the study organized the five personality traits (extroversion, agreeableness, conscientiousness, emotional stability, and openness to experience) from original and gamification versions and examined the relationship between the two versions of each personality trait.

Pearson correlation analysis revealed the relationship between original version and gamification version in extroversion and a significantly positive correlation ($p < .05$) was found. The previous steps were iterated and the relationship between two versions in other personality traits were presented in Table 4. Similar to the result of extroversion, positive correlations between two versions in the other personality traits were significant. The correlation coefficient between the two versions of extroversion, agreeableness, and openness to experience were greater than 0.8, and the other coefficients of conscientiousness, emotional stability were greater than 0.7. Hence, a strong correlation between the results of two versions was indicated.

Table 4. Correlation of each personality trait in original and gamification versions

		the results from Gamification version				
		E (G)	A (G)	C (G)	ES (G)	O (G)
the results from Original version	E (O)	**.810****				
	A (O)		**.845****			
	C (O)			**.742****		
	ES (O)				**.740****	
	O (O)					**.802****

Note: E: extroversion, A: agreeableness, C: conscientiousness, ES: emotional stability, O: openness to experience. (O): the results from the original version; (G): the results from the gamification version

**. Correlation is significant at the 0.01 level (2-tailed)

Table 5. Difference of intrinsic motivation between original and gamification versions

	Original version		Gamification version		*t*	*p*
	M	*SD*	*M*	*SD*		
Interest/Enjoyment	.250	.3882	.639	.5345	−3.634**	.001
Perceived competence	.305	.4230	.574	.5119	−2.492*	.015
Perceived choice	.353	.4144	.611	.5071	−2.427*	.018
Pressure/Tension	.816	.5430	.158	.3260	6.403**	.000

**. The mean difference is significant at the 0.01 level. * $p < .05$. ** $p < .01$.

3.2 Gamification Questionnaire and Intrinsic Motivation

We arranged the four factors of intrinsic motivation and investigated the difference in intrinsic motivation when responding the questionnaire. Independent Sample t test demonstrated a significant difference ($p < .05$) in original and gamification versions, as can be presented in Table 5. Compare to the original version, the gamification versions inspired higher intrinsic motivation in interest/enjoyment, perceived competence, and perceived choice while the original version caused higher motivation in pressure/tension.

4 Discussion

The results demonstrate that the survey results of original and gamification versions are highly correlated, and moreover, the gamification version boosts the intrinsic motivation.

First, the high relation between the results of the two versions implies that the gamification questionnaire may not change the participants' responses. Some previous studies created new questionnaire items or scales to enhance the feeling like playing a game; instead, we integrated gamification strategies and elements with the original assessments to gamified the questionnaire. Without changing the original questionnaire items or scales may not only maintain the reliability and validity of the original assessment, but also lead to the satisfactory high correlation results of the two versions. Additionally, compared to create a novel questionnaire items or scales, our approach could save much time and cost, and could increase the opportunities promptly using in other questionnaire design. To confirm the influence of gamification, the difference of intrinsic motivation between original and gamification versions were analyzed in the next paragraph.

The results presented that the gamification version increases the interest/enjoyment, perceived competence, and perceived choice in intrinsic motivation, but decreases the pressure/tension, and the effectiveness of gamification was proved as well. In addition to retaining the original items and scales, we applied both White Hat and Black Hat Motivation to gamify the questionnaire in order to enhance the influence of gamification by inspiring the positive feeling (such as a sense of achievement) and negative feeling (such as nervousness) [10]. Furthermore, pictures and text were used to show the gamification questionnaire completely and vividly, and to create the feeling like playing a game. In sum, the gamification version improves the intrinsic motivation when responding the questionnaire and do not obviously change the results of the survey. As a result, integrating gamification into questionnaire design may be potential.

5 Conclusion

The study explored the influence of gamification on the results and intrinsic motivation of responding the questionnaire. We integrated gamification into questionnaire design and took IPIP 50 as an example. The survey results from original and gamification versions were discussed and the influence of gamification on intrinsic motivation was analyzed. The following are our main findings:

- The results of the five personality traits from original and gamification versions reveal highly positive correlations.
- Compare with original version, gamification version enhances the interest/enjoyment, perceived competence, and perceived choice in intrinsic motivation, but decreases the pressure/tension.

Limitation and Future Work. We investigated the difference between original and one gamification versions. In the gamification version, we retained the original items and scales of the questionnaire and integrated gamification elements. Because our results seem potential, more gamification versions with diverse gamification strategies and elements would be created and inspected in the future. In addition to IPIP 50, we would also apply the approach to other kinds of to understand the possibility of integrating gamification into questionnaire design.

References

1. Meade, A.W., Craig, S.B.: Identifying careless responses in survey data. Psychol. Methods **17**(3), 437 (2012)
2. Bowling, N.A., et al.: Who cares and who is careless? Insufficient effort responding as a reflection of respondent personality. J. Pers. Soc. Psychol. **111**(2), 218 (2016)

3. Maniaci, M.R., Rogge, R.D.: Caring about carelessness: participant inattention and its effects on research. J. Res. Pers. **48**, 61–83 (2014)
4. Herzog, A.R., Bachman, J.G.: Effects of questionnaire length on response quality. Public Opin. Q. **45**(4), 549–559 (1981)
5. Saucier, G.: Mini-markers: a brief version of goldberg's unipolar big-five markers. J. Pers. Assess. **63**(3), 506–516 (1994)
6. Krosnick, J.A.: Response strategies for coping with the cognitive demands of attitude measures in surveys. Appl. Cogn. Psychol. **5**(3), 213–236 (1991)
7. Huang, J.L., et al.: Detecting and deterring insufficient effort responding to surveys. J. Bus. Psychol. **27**(1), 99–114 (2012)
8. McCord, J.-L., Harman, J.L., Purl, J.: Game-like personality testing: an emerging mode of personality assessment. Personality Individ. Differ. **143**, 95–102 (2019)
9. Harman, J.L., Brown, K.D.: Illustrating a narrative: a test of game elements in game-like personality assessment. Int. J. Sel. Assess. **30**(1), 157–166 (2022)
10. Chou, Y.-K.: Actionable gamification: Beyond points, badges, and leaderboards. Packt Publishing Ltd. (2019)
11. Ryan, R.M.: Control and information in the intrapersonal sphere: an extension of cognitive evaluation theory. J. Pers. Soc. Psychol. **43**(3), 450 (1982)
12. Höchsmann, C., et al.: Effectiveness of a behavior change technique–based smartphone game to improve intrinsic motivation and physical activity adherence in patients with type 2 diabetes: randomized controlled trial. JMIR Serious Games **7**(1), e11444 (2019)
13. López-Martínez, A., et al.: Using gamified strategies in higher education: relationship between intrinsic motivation and contextual variables. Sustainability **14**(17), 11014 (2022)
14. Landers, R.N., Sanchez, D.R.: Game-based, gamified, and gamefully designed assessments for employee selection: definitions, distinctions, design, and validation. Int. J. Sel. Assess. **30**(1), 1–13 (2022)
15. Guin, T.D.-L., et al.: Myths and realities of respondent engagement in online surveys. Int. J. Mark. Res. **54**(5), 613–633 (2012)
16. Keusch, F., Zhang, C.: A review of issues in gamified surveys. Soc. Sci. Comput. Rev. **35**(2), 147–166 (2017)
17. Landers, R.N., Collmus, A.B.: Gamifying a personality measure by converting it into a story: convergence, incremental prediction, faking, and reactions. Int. J. Sel. Assess. **30**(1), 145–156 (2022)
18. Goldberg, L.R.: The development of markers for the Big-Five factor structure. Psychol. Assess. **4**(1), 26 (1992)
19. Cattell, R.B.: Description and measurement of personality (1946)
20. Allport, G.W.: Pattern and growth in personality (1961)
21. Eysenck, H.J., Strelau, J.: The biosocial approach to personality. In: Explorations in Temperament: International Perspectives on Theory and Measurement, p. 87 (1991)
22. Barrick, M.R., Mount, M.K.: The big five personality dimensions and job performance: a meta-analysis. Pers. Psychol. **44**(1), 1–26 (1991)
23. Costa, P.T., McCrae, R.R.: Personality in adulthood: a six-year longitudinal study of self-reports and spouse ratings on the NEO Personality Inventory. J. Pers. Soc. Psychol. **54**(5), 853 (1988)
24. Zheng, L., et al.: Reliability and concurrent validation of the IPIP Big-Five factor markers in China: Consistencies in factor structure between Internet-obtained heterosexual and homosexual samples. Personality Individ. Differ. **45**(7), 649–654 (2008)

25. Cobb-Clark, D.A., Schurer, S.: The stability of big-five personality traits. Econ. Lett. **115**(1), 11–15 (2012)
26. Streiner, D.L.: Starting at the beginning: an introduction to coefficient alpha and internal consistency. J. Pers. Assess. **80**(1), 99–103 (2003)

Exploring the Tensions of Self-tracking Wearable Technologies Through Design

Chiara Di Lodovico(✉)

Design Department, Politecnico di Milano, Milan, Italy
chiara.dilodovico@polimi.it

Abstract. In the last decade, the research interest in self-tracking practices mediated by wearable technologies has risen exponentially. A variety of contributions is focused on examining interaction modalities and user experiences to increase the usability and utility of such systems. However, several scholars are also committed to unveiling the inherent ethical, social and political implications of the self-tracking phenomenon, proposing an alternative perspective. Based on the review of contributions investigating polarities and issues in the landscape of self-tracking technologies, the current work proposes five interrelated tensions at play in the self-tracking domain. The tensions presented are allusion to objectivity and non-neutrality of numbers; trust in data and reliance on subjective experience; reductionism and complexity of lived phenomena; performance and wellbeing; and surveillance and self-surveillance. Rather than researching ways to avoid these tensions, the present contribution discusses the role that design may play in further exploring them. In particular, the paper illustrates studies leveraging speculative and critical design approaches to explore the ethical, political, and social issues of technologically-mediated self-tracking practices, as well as individuals' relations with data, beyond conscious interaction.

Keywords: Wearable technologies · self-tracking · data representations · tensions · speculative design

1 Introduction

Wearable technologies for self-tracking are attracting increasing research interest due to their widespread adoption, from e-health and workplace to fitness and lifestyle. Wearables will likely become a mega-trend within the next few years [28], dominated by smartwatches and activity trackers. According to Statista [31], smartwatches are expected to grow from 37 million devices in 2016 to over 253 million units by 2025. In this scenario, understanding the effects of wearable technologies for self-tracking on individuals' everyday life, identities, and behaviours has become critical, requiring attention from Human-Computer Interaction (HCI) and digital fashion researchers [45,46].

Prior studies addressing self-tracking practices acknowledge the potential of wearable technologies to offer individuals previously inaccessible information

M. Kurosu and A. Hashizume (Eds.): HCII 2023, LNCS 14011, pp. 30–46, 2023.
https://doi.org/10.1007/978-3-031-35596-7_3

about their bodies, performance and lifestyle, enabling them to leverage the acquired knowledge for self-improvement and self-reflection. However, quantified-based representations produced by self-tracking wearable technologies may yield tensions between the subjective experience of the self/body and their objectified representation in the data. Rather than seeking ways to avoid these tensions, the current study argues that they could represent interesting research paths to be explored through design.

This paper is divided into five sections. Section 4 briefly overviews wearable technologies for self-tracking, illustrating typologies, functioning processes, and data representation modalities. The third section examines research concerning the analysis and implementation of self-tracking devices to serve human empowerment from a utilitarian standpoint. Subsequently, we illustrate contributions investigating the implications at the interplay of individuals, devices, and socio-cultural forces beyond utility and usability. In this section, a selection of five tensions emerging from the analysis of the literature is presented. In the fifth section, the principles and features of speculative and critical design are presented and contextualized within the broader discourse of non-solutionist design. Here, we propose a designerly way of exploring the tensions leveraging speculative, critical design and design fiction. Our conclusions and reflections are drawn in the final section.

2 Self-tracking Practices Mediated by Wearable Technologies

The practice of self-tracking is not new. Personal diaries, bullet journaling, and weighing scales have been used for a long time as instruments to keep track of personal life aspects [57] for self-care, self-improvement and self-management, as Foucault's "technologies of the self" [18].

In the last decades, sensor-equipped wearable technologies brought self-tracking to a new level. By seamlessly detecting body signals and movements, these technologies enable automatic detection, triangulation, and interpretation of data streams offering a detailed picture of individuals' physiological and behavioural status [36,40,64]. Thanks to dedicated sensors, algorithms, and artificial intelligence techniques, these close-to-the-body systems are able to collect sensor records, pre-process and transfer filtered information for analysis through computing paradigms, process data through aggregation, clustering and classification, and compare a large set of users' information to provide a variety of visualizations, insights, and recommendations for the wearers to act upon [47]. Privileged channels and data representation modalities to convey the resulting knowledge are screen-based quantified data-driven visualizations (numbers, charts and tables, scores, icons, and text) displayed on dedicated apps, web dashboards or directly on the wearable device itself [5].

Among the most popular devices enabling the collection of personal data are smartwatches and activity trackers. Products like AppleWatch, FitBit, and Garmin, allow consumers to measure biometrics (like heart rate and blood oxygen) and monitor movements, activities performance, and location (such as steps, stairs climbed, distance travelled, sports and fitness). Moreover, like many other wearables, they claim to detect stress levels, sleep quality, and daily readiness. According to Statista [31] wearable technology will become a megatrend within the following years, as smartwatches are expected to grow from 37 million devices in 2016 to over 253 million units by 2025. The market interest in wearables is also attested by the number of devices populating Vandrico's database [3]. The platform hosts more than 400 wearables (including headbands, wristbands, smart rings, and foot-worn devices) dedicated to lifestyle, fitness, entertainment, gaming, and medical domains.

The buzz around wearables and their exponential growth are not only driven by the consumers' interest and curiosity in novel technologies. The premises and drivers contributing to the establishment of technologically-mediated self-tracking practices can be retraced to:

> the context of the current cultural moment of the belief that data are superior forms of knowledge, combined with the affordances of contemporary digital technologies that allow individuals to produce large masses of data about themselves. [35]

These discourses are directly linked with other contextual factors: the pervasiveness of the digital data economy and datafication of human phenomena; the neoliberalist culture of healthism and self-responsibility; individualisation, reinvention and self-entrepreneurship; and the importance of gaining self-knowledge as a way to work upon and improve the self [11,35,39,63–66]. The combination of the above reasons is further supported by the establishment of bottom-up worldwide movements and communities like the Quantified Self, a label for a well-established community made of

> life hackers, data analysts, computer scientists, early adopters, health enthusiasts, productivity gurus, and patients [...] believing in the notion of 'self-knowledge through numbers' [12]

Finally, the miniaturization of sensor-equipped wearable technologies, the greater accessibility and monitoring capacities of these devices, and their affordable prices are exponentially increasing the democratization and the diffusion of wearable technologies for self-tracking practices to a mainstream audience [52, 53]. In this scenario, understanding the effects of wearable technologies for self-tracking on individuals' everyday life, identities, and behaviours has become critical, requiring attention from HCI and digital fashion researchers [45,46].

3 Self-tracking Research: Towards Data Analysis, Usability, and Utility

Paralleling the diffusion of self-tracking technologies among the broader population, scholarly research has increased, generating a plethora of labels framing different shades of this emerging field of inquiry. Some examples include *Quantified Self* [68], *Personal Informatics* [33], *Personal Analytics* [69], *Lived Informatics* [58], *Self as Database* [60], *Data Double* [59], and *Data-Human Assemblage* [38]. By cross-reading these expressions it is thus possible to grasp the intertwined and dialogic interaction of two worlds. On one hand, terms like quantified, informatics, analytics, data, and database recall the data-driven and rationalistic ground upon which the tracking practice is based. On the other hand, concepts like self, personal, lived, double and assemblage capture the intimate, embodied, and ever-evolving nature of these practices. This twofold dimension is greatly illustrated by Ruckenstein's definition of "data double" adapted from Haggerty and Ericson [23]:

> the conversion of human bodies and minds into data flows that can be figuratively reassembled for the purposes of personal reflection and interaction. [59]

The desire to understand the engagement and interaction modalities individuals establish with self-tracking technologies - such as wearables - led to several empirical research in the HCI domain. According to the literature review by Epstein et al. [15], which mapped 253 publications since 2010 in the personal informatics field, the main research effort focused on investigating and designing for health and wellness, behaviour change and self-improvement, primarily relying on examination of users' interaction with commercial trackers, in lieu of the development of novel artifacts. Other research streams include exploring the motivations and reasons for individuals to adopt such technologies [10,12,22,40], identifying users' profiles and engagement modes [24,36,50,54,58], illustrating interaction models and stages [12,29,33,44], and listing abandonment reasons [6,13,47].

The majority of the above contributions, especially the ones examining abandonment motivations, provide a vast range of suggestions and design guidelines for HCI researchers and practitioners to improve current devices. Some examples include discovering and aligning the device features with the target users' expectations, supporting self-reflection and data sense-making, and building trustworthy systems for long-term use.

While the knowledge disseminated by all the above studies may dramatically contribute to implementing devices' usability and utility, supporting users' decision-making processes, and increasing the technologies' adoption rate, the utilitarian perspective may overlook ethical implications and issues [15,32,56], emerging beyond conscious interaction.

4 Widening the View: Scholarly Debate and Tensions of the Phenomenon

A growing number of scholars from HCI, science and technology studies, philosophy of technology, and critical studies are starting to elaborate on the polarities, paradoxes and implications of the self-tracking phenomenon, beyond a utilitarian view [11,39,56,61,64,65]. These works acknowledge the intrinsic complexity of forces and interplay among the self, wearables and quantified data representations, the stakeholders involved in the technology design, and societal norms and values.

Based on the review of these contributions, the current work proposes five interrelated tensions for HCI and digital fashion designers to reflect upon. The term 'tension' stands for a state of stress between different or opposing forces, arguments, or influences, possibly generating conflicts [2]. In prior contributions, similar conditions were defined as paradoxes and polarities [8,61].

In this paper, we use the term *tension* to refer to more subtle coexisting, at time opposing, conditions taking place at different levels of the interaction. The tensions illustrated below are:

- allusion to objectivity and non-neutrality of data;
- data reductionism and complexity of lived phenomena;
- trust in data and reliance on subjective experience;
- performance and well-being;
- surveillance and self-surveillance.

4.1 Allusion to Objectivity and Non-neutrality of Data

As previously stated, the mainstream paradigm for displaying personal tracking data in commercial devices is through quantified-based representations (e.g. numbers, tables, graphs, and scores) and data-driven recommendations [5].

Many scholars note that this way of framing data representations is firmly grounded in the semantic domain of science and healthcare, implicitly pointing to a straightforward and accurate relation between data and an individual's behavioural and biological states [8,25,43,65]. In addition, as Hepworth remarks referring to FitBit's user interface and experience:

> [t]heir persuasive, apparent objectivity is furthered by the modernist-influenced functionalist aesthetic commonly found in visualizations [...] to give an aesthetic appearance of objectivity and efficiency. [25]

This is even truer if we consider the widespread mainstream perception of objectivity and fairness surrounding sensors and algorithms. However, the lure of precision, authority, and trustworthiness is often far from the actual self-tracking system's capabilities [65]. Wearables-based data streams are nothing but neutral and impartial for multiple reasons.

Firstly, besides the significant improvements in micro-electronics and computing processes, accuracy issues may prevent the system from providing a reliable reading of the wearers' activities and biological data. Many researchers demonstrated that commercially viable devices might suffer from precision problems because of the technical limitations of the sensors and/or the algorithms in detecting activities and biosignals, or the misuse of the device from the user's side [9,16,17,21,42].

Secondly, as Baker [8] notes, the kind of data and interaction modalities available to the user are mediated by a plethora of stakeholders from the industry. This mediation results from the interplay of interests and biases from business managers, computer scientists, engineers, psychologists, designers, and other professionals which impact on, for instance, the ways in which data and recommendations are delivered to the users.

The tension here is traceable where virtually inaccurate and biased information are represented using a scientific authoritative semantic, alluding to an implicit inherent reliability and authority of the system.

4.2 Data Reductionism and Complexity of Lived Phenomena

The quantification and digitization of human phenomena operated by self-tracking devices are critiqued by many scholars because of their reductionist nature [61,65]. The trade-off here is between the reductive but accessible, comprehensible and actionable data-driven knowledge and the complex nature of lived experiences, that is to say qualitative, messy, and challenging to measure. The reduction may be played at different levels. Wearable technology companies frequently claim to enable the detection and assessment of wellness, stress, and sleep quality, leveraging bodily data streams and Artificial Intelligence algorithms. In turn, these are rendered through scores, numbers, and recommendations; again, conveyed as quantifiable and monitorable entities.

This reductive intervention has the potential to displace "other meaningful and possibly intangible ways of talking about a phenomenon" [43] by amplifying the visibility of specific trackable signals of the body and concealing others, not measurable by sensors and algorithms [11,64]. Baker alerts us on the risks of considering the device's readout more inclusive than it actually is, leading to what she calls *"erosion of choice"* [8], that is, the limitation of users' actions and choices, and change of behaviours and habits as adaptation to the technology constraints [39,65].

By conceptualizing ideals of healthiness, fitness, wellness, and good sleep, technology developers and the wearables industry leaders push individuals towards sociocultural stereotypes and normative bodies in line with dominant expectations and paradigms [64,65]. Van Den Eede articulates the concept *"fixed entity fallacy"* [64] to express the notion that certain phenomena can be set as unchangeable, unambiguous entities (for example, "sugar" is "bad"; "exercise" is "healthy"). Lupton [37], in the contribution "Quantified sex: a critical analysis of sexual and reproductive self-tracking using apps", captures another implication of the reduction that may be operated by self-tracking devices:

> [t]hese technologies [...] act to support and reinforce highly reductive and normative ideas of what is 'good sex' and 'good performance' by encouraging users to quantify their sexual experiences and feelings in ever finer detail and to represent these data visually in graphs and tables. The discourses of performance, quantification and normality suggest specific limited types of sexualities. Gender stereotypes are reinforced. [37]

4.3 Trust in Data and Reliance on Subjective Experience

Many scholars documented the multiple shades of the tension between the trust in the objectified data-driven version of the self, and the subjective experience of the phenomenon tracked. The following examples deepen the relations individuals may establish with this "reductive summary" [8] either by trusting it, disregarding its validity, or negotiating reliance on both data and subjective experience.

The over-trust in data and measurements can lead individuals to consider the "objective" representation provided by the device as more reliable than their subjective experience [59]. Consequently, this could lead to obsessive tracking, data dependency, and self-fulfilling prophecies [65]. Rapp and Tirabeni [54,55] observed that the tendency to rely on and trust numbers is stronger in amateur sportspeople than in professional athletes. While the former may blindly follow the data representations prompted by the wearables, the latter seem to operate a calibration between the device's readout and their own bodily feelings, considering both sources of information as important.

Other research depicted situations in which the device counterfeits the user's self-perceptions, unveiling a "false" or "alter" self [30,42]. The misalignment between the two sources may lead to reflection and negotiation strategies to deal with data uncertainty [4]. On the same line, more committed individuals may establish a dialogic relationship with sensor-based data, recontextualizing quantitative data into "qualitative narratives" in order to make sense of and learn something new about their "selves", despite commercial devices are not designed for this aim [51]. The increased self-awareness achieved through engagement with personal data in form of visualizations may lead to a change in self-perception and in the way trackers experience their bodies [30]. Van den Eede defines this phenomenon as perceiving "in an embodied manner an objectified version of the self" [64].

The spectrum of experiences illustrated above serves to highlight the continuum trade-off and tension between the system's representation of data and the subjective experience of the wearer in time and space. Pink et al. [49] acknowledge these time-related, context-dependent and situated dimensions using the expression "broken data", pointing to the iterative maintenance and repair processes integral to individuals' everyday interactions with data to complement their meaning.

4.4 Performance and Wellbeing

By seamlessly measuring and monitoring one's aspects of life and body, wearables make the otherwise extremely time-consuming activity of tracking easier to manage. One of the main reasons why people engage in self-tracking practices is to improve their fitness, health, and overall lifestyle [12]. In this scenario, individuals may experience tensions between the pleasure of performing an activity with the stress deriving from the pressure to perform. The risks of this attitude are synthesized by Baker [8] in the irony of *"well-being versus never being well enough"*.

While the performance discourse may be familiar within sports and fitness domains, de Boer [11] notes how by tracking daily life activities like eating, meditating, making steps and sleeping, these technologies are turning previously transparent actions into performative acts to be measured and optimized. Peculiar examples of this are the meditation and focus-training brain-sensing headband Muse [1] and sexual activity trackers [37] providing feedback loops, challenges, and rewards to improve the wearer's performance.

As Whitson [66] notes, the framework within which self-tracking practices and data representation designs operate is the one of gamification.

> Gamification practices, operating under the umbrella of play, foster a quantification of the self; collecting, collating and analyzing minute data and providing feedback on how to better care for one's self. This quantification of the self feeds into neoliberal governance projects that promise to make daily practices more fulfilling and fun. Enabled by increased levels of surveillance (self-monitoring and otherwise), these projects use incentivization and pleasure rather than risk and fear to shape desired behaviours. [66]

In the marathon to achieve ideals of wellness within a quantified reductionist framework, individuals may find themselves optimizing the recorded data (for example "steps") in lieu of more fundamental concepts, like "health" [11].

The other side of the coin is the diffused practice of cheating to obtain rewards [65]. The device accuracy issue, in this case, could be exploited by users to represent a fictional but performative self, gaining achievements and reaching goals without actually performing the necessary activities. The Wall Street Journal article and video "Want to Cheat Your Fitbit? Try a Puppy or a Power Drill" [7] offers an interesting outlook on this practice.

4.5 Surveillance and Self-surveillance

In the western culture of healthism and self-entrepreneurship, communities of individuals are called to be responsible for their own health and wellbeing, and invited to voluntarily measure and track aspects of their life, turning their gaze inward [39]. Whitson [66] characterize these digital quantification practices as a "surveillance apparatus" since it directly involves data collection in view of a behaviour change and gaining control over one's body and life. In disciplining and improving the self, individuals may contribute to what Lupton calls a "participatory surveillance" [35]. In this scenario, by nudging users to engage in self-surveillance, sharing personal data on social media and other digital platforms, and involving peers in monitoring activities, self-tracking leads to increasingly more intricate kinds of surveillance that converge the lines between private and public monitoring [39,61].

This is particularly relevant considering the increasing diffusion of corporate wellness programs and health insurance packages where employees and clients are invited to wear tracking devices and stimulated through competitions and rewards to perform in the workplace and beyond. As Sharon [61] argues:

> Self-tracking [...], in such accounts, is portrayed as a paradigmatic practice of contemporary surveillance society, as one of the many ubiquitous technologies used to monitor, measure, and record individuals' activities for purposes of disciplining and managing populations via an extension of the medical or "panoptic" gaze.

Here a delicate trade-off is at play between the individuals' interest in engaging in self-tracking practices to improve health and fitness, and the interests of third parties, like employers, wearable technology companies, and other stakeholders interested in exploiting personal data for multiple reasons.

In less subtle and visible power dynamics than "pushed" and "imposed" self-tracking modes [39], the signs of "neoliberal health regimes and culture of self-surveillance" [71] are disguised in the design elements and interaction flow of self-tracking devices and apps for private use. The gamification-driven user experience, the promise of empowerment through digital quantification of human phenomena, normativity towards sociocultural stereotypes, and widespread sharing of intimate personal data contribute to making wearable technologies for self-tracking extremely complex and multifaceted technologies to investigate. This raises several concerns regarding privacy issues, data ownership, and the use of intimate information by the wearable ecosystem stakeholders (and beyond), that may be overlooked in favour of the perceived comfort and convenience these technologies provide to individuals.

The tensions presented in the previous subsections enable us to grasp at a glance the complexity pervading the self-tracking practices mediated by wearable technologies, which are far from mere tools at the service of human empowerment. The first temptation for design and HCI practitioners may be to address the tensions by adopting a problem-solving and solution-oriented approach, at least trying to mitigate their negative effects on users.

Conversely, this paper argues that these tensions, far from being solvable, could be the starting point for reflecting on where design may play a crucial role. To do so, we turn to alternative design approaches [48] found in design and HCI research and practice to delineate current and future research opportunities.

In the next section, we introduce speculative design, critical design and design fiction as alternative approaches to the affirmative, problem-solving, and consumer-oriented nature of traditional design.

5 Addressing the Tensions Through Design: Alternative Design Approaches to Solutionism

Speculative design, critical design and design fiction are approaches where the act of designing artifacts, scenarios, and imaginaries is not directed towards the market, in a production-driven optic. Rather, these future-oriented and critical-oriented design approaches [70] aim to raise questions and prompt reflections on the political, ethical, and societal implications of emerging technologies by materializing issues for consideration [14,41]. Key levers for alternative designs are inherent ambiguity, ambivalence, and even contradiction of the propositions with respect to contemporary conventions and expectations [48]. The encounter with these kinds of speculative artifacts and systems

> produce a variety of 'soft' kinds of knowledge which are: subject to change; highly contextual; asks questions; doesn't provide answers; intends to be rhetorical; aspires towards messy accounts of social situations. The processes by which this knowledge is produced [...] when applied in a Research context, provide a unique (and otherwise hard to attain) way to better understand the world we live in. [34]

The words used by Lindley and Green [34] to summarize what speculative design is, contribute to strengthening the value of generating new knowledge and better understanding messiness and complexity we live in, through design.

In this paper, we argue that these alternative design approaches may serve Research through Design (RtD) inquiries, by materializing the inherent tensions of self-tracking into future-oriented plausible but fictional design artifacts. By building on existing Research through Design (RTD) investigations, we propose different ways through which HCI and digital fashion design researchers can explore the tensions emerging from the self-tracking phenomenon.

The speculative project "Quantuition" [67] aims to explore the relationship between personal biometric data and the multiple interpretations we ascribe to it. The designer imagined a future where sensors would be able to seamlessly track every aspect of one's life, and designed a fictional self-tracking system made of nanosensors collecting data from the body, and data physicalizations as edible 3D sculptures. To support the speculation, the researcher visualized the relationship between the wearer and the data via Instagram posts. The picture captions tell the hypothetical tracker's feelings and thoughts on the resulting data sculptures. Some of the data sculptures realised by the designer, made with play-doh, simulate physicalisations of the users' daily laughs and smiles, sun exposure, food supplements in response to dietary data, and activity nudges. Through the project deployment, the author engaged in reflections on how personal data should be represented and interpreted, the benefits and downsides of feedback loops produced by biometric monitoring, and the relationship between individuals and data concerning free will, agency, and control.

Another design-driven speculation is proposed by Fox et al. in the pictorial "Vivewell: Speculating Near-Future Menstrual Tracking through Current Data Practices" [19]. "Vivewell" is conceived as a fictional company presenting a product catalogue of menstrual self-tracking technologies. The products are: *Lithe*, a sensorized underwear set detecting and communicating the woman's emotional data with the partner; *Privvy*, a smart office toilet, analysing employers' urine and fecal matters to assess their health status and improve workplace efficiency and productivity; and *Vivid*, a smart menstrual disc equipped with sensors sharing newly menstruating child's data with parents. The project aims to explore the advantages, and social, economic and legal implications of the widespread collection and sharing of personal intimate data with a variety of stakeholders. Specifically, it aims to spark reflections on ways in which near-future technologies may serve novel forms of intimate surveillance, establish and reinforce power systems, and generate new threats due to pervasive self-tracking data-sharing practices.

Other projects show instead the power of exposing speculative designs to the wider audience as (fictional) commercial products.

In "Problematising Upstream Technology through Speculative Design: The Case of Quantified Cats and Dogs", [32] Lawson et al. investigate the public's reaction to near-future monitoring technologies for animals, in line with existing market trends. The team designed and presented three products from the fictional start-up "The Quantified Pet" in various focus groups, involving pet owners and animal behaviour experts. These included the smart collar *Emoti-Dog* revealing the pet's emotional state, the microchip *Cat-a-log* detecting the animal's movements and spotting its exact location in the garden, and *Litter-bug*, a non-invasive system to track the cat's dietary health and comportments. A focus group revealed, on the one side, a diffuse unconcerned enthusiasm of the pet owners, on the other side, doubts and concerts coming from professionals and experts. The latters, specifically, expressed worries about the risk that technologies could exacerbate existing issues in human-animal relations and generate new tensions in the ecosystem of pet owners, pet clinicians, and residents.

Following the same startup-like rhetoric, Søndergaard and Hansen [62] proposed the speculative fictional project *PeriodShare*: a sensor-equipped menstruation cup that seamlessly measures and posts menstrual data on social media. The team's intention was to explore the social and cultural facets of menstruation by conjecturing a situation in which data from its tracking would acquire social and economic value. *PeriodShare* was presented by a fictional start-up team at an entrepreneurial fair. The materials supporting the speculation were a mid-fidelity prototype characterized by a Do It Yourself aesthetic, a dedicated app, a Kickstarter crowd-funding campaign, and a commercial video. The researchers state that *PeriodShare* created space for discussions on a taboo topic, stimulating critical questions on the monetization of intimacy through technology and the self-tracking positivist promise of empowering individuals.

In all the above cases, the designs request the viewers to imagine their potential relation with the technology and data representations. The artifact plays the role of a trigger inviting the person to consider social, political and ethical aspects, rather than introspective ones based on actual data [67]. Conversely, developing working research prototypes and letting participants interact with their own data may elicit more introspective accounts, eliciting personal vulnerabilities and intimate meanings projected in individuals' data.

Howell et al. [27] in "Tensions of Data-Driven Reflection: A Case Study of Real-Time Emotional Biosensing" report a user study in which 17 participants were asked to wear for two days *Ripple*, a sensorized shirt responding to the wearer's skin conductance arousal parameters via colour-changing threads sewn on the garment. The researchers documented their intention to design the system according to ambiguity [20] and design for contestability principles [26]. The aim was to downplay the system's authority, making participants question the device's accuracy and reflect upon the reliability of such devices. The study results raised the author's awareness of unexpected tensions at play in data-driven reflections. Ethical concerns were related to participants not questioning the system's reliability, and users projecting their vulnerabilities onto the displayed data, to fill the gap left by the ambiguity of information.

The cases presented in this section, far from being exhaustive, offer interesting points for reflection highlighting how design can be a powerful means to make the technologically-mediated self-tracking issues visible and open to debate. By leveraging the designers' skillset and tools, researchers may convey the criticalities of the phenomenon through fictional and working prototypes, also involving people in a variety of ways. New knowledge could be generated from the recipients' interaction with the speculation artifacts, in terms of concerned and unconcerned feedback. The researchers' (self)reflection on the design practice and study deployment may offer additional insights. The reflection may not be limited to the possibility of stimulating debate but may also address the novel issues that the designs raise with respect to the existing tensions initially guiding the design process.

6 Conclusions

Self-tracking wearables are attracting increasing interest, making technologically-mediated self-tracking practices a fruitful area to be investigated. With this contribution, we call for HCI and digital fashion researchers to advance our understanding of the self-tracking implications through design.

After briefly presenting some of the current research trends in the HCI field, this contribution gathers and clusters the opinions of scholars from philosophy, science and technology, and critical studies into five intertwined and pervasive tensions crossing the self-tracking phenomenon. The tensions presented are allusion to objectivity and non-neutrality of numbers; trust in data and reliance on subjective experience; reductionism and complexity of lived phenomena; performance and wellbeing; surveillance and self-surveillance. This overview aims to offer at a glance the complexity at the interplay of individuals, wearable technologies, stakeholders involved in the technology design and sociocultural norms and values, emerging beyond deliberate and conscious interaction.

Rather than pursuing problem-solving endeavours, digital fashion and HCI practitioners and researchers may develop speculative design interventions intentionally deepening the tensions. In this vein, we suggest looking at alternative approaches to traditional design, like speculative design, critical design, and design fiction within a Research through Design inquiry framework. Designing according to emerging trends and existing tensions may help researchers gain a deeper understanding of the present and future risks of the self-tracking domain, making subtle instances more visible for consideration.

References

1. Muse^{TM} EEG-Powered Meditation & Sleep Headband. https://choosemuse.com/
2. Tension. Definition and meaning. https://www.collinsdictionary.com/dictionary/english/tension
3. Vandrico. Wearable Technology Database. https://vandrico.com/wearables.html
4. Alqahtani, D., Jay, C., Vigo, M.: The role of uncertainty as a facilitator to reflection in self-tracking. In: DIS 2020: Designing Interactive Systems Conference, Eindhoven, Netherlands, pp. 1807–1818. ACM (2020). https://doi.org/10.1145/3357236.3395448
5. Alrehiely, M., Eslambolchilar, P., Borgo, R.: A taxonomy for visualisations of personal physical activity data on self-tracking devices and their applications. In: Proceedings of the 32nd International BCS Human Computer Interaction Conference, HCI 2018, pp. 1–15. BCS Learning and Development Ltd. (2018). https://doi.org/10.14236/ewic/HCI2018.17
6. Attig, C., Franke, T.: Abandonment of personal quantification: a review and empirical study investigating reasons for wearable activity tracking attrition. Comput. Hum. Behav. **102**, 223–237 (2020). https://doi.org/10.1016/j.chb.2019.08.025
7. Bachman, R.: Want to Cheat Your Fitbit? Try a Puppy or a Power Drill - WSJ (2016). https://www.wsj.com/articles/want-to-cheat-your-fitbit-try-using-a-puppy-or-a-power-drill-1465487106
8. Baker, D.A.: Four ironies of self-quantification: wearable technologies and the quantified self. Sci. Eng. Ethics **26**(3), 1477–1498 (2020). https://doi.org/10.1007/S11948-020-00181-W
9. Baron, K.G., Abbott, S., Jao, N., Manalo, N., Mullen, R.: Orthosomnia: are Some Patients Taking the Quantified Self Too Far? JCSM J. Clin. Sleep Med. **13**(2), 351–354 (2017). https://jcsm.aasm.org/doi/pdf/10.5664/jcsm.6472
10. Baumgart, R., Wiewiorra, L.: The role of self-control in self-tracking. In: Thirty Seventh International Conference on Information Systems, Dublin, pp. 1–16 (2016)
11. de Boer, B.: Experiencing objectified health: turning the body into an object of attention. Med. Health Care Philos. **23**(3), 401–411 (2020). https://doi.org/10.1007/s11019-020-09949-0
12. Choe, E.K., Lee, N.B., Lee, B., Pratt, W., Kientz, J.A.: Understanding quantified-selfers' practices in collecting and exploring personal data. In: CHI 2014: Proceedings of the SIGCHI Conference on Human Factors in Computing Systems, Toronto, Canada, pp. 1143–1152. Association for Computing Machinery (2014). https://doi.org/10.1145/2556288.2557372
13. Clawson, J., Pater, J.A., Miller, A.D., Mynatt, E.D., Mamykina, L.: No longer wearing: investigating the abandonment of personal health-tracking technologies on craigslist. In: UbiComp 2015 - Proceedings of the 2015 ACM International Joint Conference on Pervasive and Ubiquitous Computing, pp. 647–658. Association for Computing Machinery, Inc. (2015). https://doi.org/10.1145/2750858.2807554
14. Dunne, A., Raby, F.: Speculative Everything: Design, Fiction, and Social Dreaming. MIT Press, Cambridge (2013)
15. Epstein, D.A., et al.: Mapping and taking stock of the personal informatics literature. Proc. ACM Interact. Mob. Wearable Ubiquitous Technol. **4**(4), 1–38 (2020). https://doi.org/10.1145/3432231

16. Evenson, K.R., Goto, M.M., Furberg, R.D.: Systematic review of the validity and reliability of consumer-wearable activity trackers. Int. J. Behav. Nutr. Phys. Act. **12**(159), 1–22 (2015). https://doi.org/10.1186/s12966-015-0314-1
17. Feehan, L.M., et al.: Accuracy of fitbit devices: systematic review and narrative syntheses of quantitative data. JMIR Mhealth Uhealth **6**(8), 1–19 (2018). https://doi.org/10.2196/10527
18. Foucault, M.: Technologies of the Self: A Seminar with Michel Foucault. Tavistock Publications, London (1988)
19. Fox, S., Howell, N., Wong, R., Spektor, F.: Vivewell: speculating near-future menstrual tracking through current data practices. In: DIS 2019: ACM SIGCHI Conference on Designing Interactive Systems, San Diego, CA, USA, pp. 541–552. ACM (2019). https://doi.org/10.1145/3322276.3323695
20. Gaver, W.W., Beaver, J., Benford, S.: Ambiguity as a resource for design. In: CHI 2003: Proceedings of the SIGCHI Conference on Human Factors in Computing Systems, pp. 233–240. Association for Computing Machinery (2003). https://doi.org/10.1145/642611.642653
21. Germini, F., et al.: Accuracy and acceptability of wrist-wearable activity-tracking devices: systematic review of the literature. J. Med. Internet Res. **24**(1), 1–18 (2022). https://doi.org/10.2196/30791
22. Gimpel, H., Nißen, M., Görlitz, R.A.: Quantifying the quantified self: a study on the motivations of patients to track their own health. In: Thirty Fourth International Conference on Information Systems, Milan, pp. 1–16 (2013)
23. Haggerty, K.D., Ericson, R.V.: The surveillant assemblage. In: Surveillance, Crime and Social Control (2000). https://doi.org/10.1080/00071310020015280
24. Hancı, E., Ruijten, P.A., Lacroix, J., IJsselsteijn, W.A.: The impact of mindset on self-tracking experience. Front. Digit. Health **3** (2021). https://doi.org/10.3389/fdgth.2021.676742
25. Hepworth, K.: A panopticon on my wrist: the biopower of big data visualization for wearables. Des. Cult. **11**(3), 323–344 (2019). https://doi.org/10.1080/17547075.2019.1661723
26. Hirsch, T., Merced, K., Narayanan, S., Imel, Z.E., Atkins, D.C.: Designing contestability: interaction design, machine learning, and mental health HHS public access. In: DIS 2017: Designing Interactive Systems Conference (2017). https://doi.org/10.1145/3064663.3064703
27. Howell, N., Devendorf, L., Gálvez, T.A.V., Tian, R., Ryokai, K.: Tensions of data-driven reflection: a case study of real-time emotional biosensing. In: CHI 2018: Proceedings of the SIGCHI Conference on Human Factors in Computing Systems, Montreal, QC, Canada, vol. 2018-April. ACM (2018). https://doi.org/10.1145/3173574.3174005
28. Kalantari, M.: Consumers adoption of wearable technologies: literature review, synthesis, and future research agenda. Int. J. Technol. Mark. **12**(1), 1 (2017). https://doi.org/10.1504/ijtmkt.2017.10008634
29. Kim, D.J., Lee, Y., Rho, S., Lim, Y.K.: Design opportunities in three stages of relationship development between users and self-tracking devices. In: CHI 2016: Proceedings of the SIGCHI Conference on Human Factors in Computing Systems, pp. 699–703. Association for Computing Machinery (2016). https://doi.org/10.1145/2858036.2858148
30. Kristensen, D.B., Prigge, C.: Human/technology associations in self-tracking practices. In: Self-Tracking: Empirical and Philisophical Investigations, Palgrave Macmillan, pp. 43–59 (2018). https://doi.org/10.1007/978-3-319-65379-2

31. Laricchia, F.: Global smartwatch shipment forecast 2025 (2022). https://www.statista.com/statistics/878144/worldwide-smart-wristwear-shipments-forecast/
32. Lawson, S., Kirman, B., Linehan, C., Feltwell, T., Hopkins, L.: Problematising upstream technology through speculative design: the case of quantified cats and dogs. In: CHI 2015: SIGCHI Conference on Human Factors in Computing Systems, vol. 2015-April, pp. 2663–2672. Association for Computing Machinery (2015). https://doi.org/10.1145/2702123.2702260
33. Li, I., Dey, A.K., Forlizzi, J.: Understanding my data, myself: supporting self-reflection with ubicomp technologies. In: UbiComp 2011: Proceedings of the ACM International Joint Conference on Pervasive and Ubiquitous Computing, Beijing, China, pp. 405–414. Association for Computing Machinery (2011). https://doi.org/10.1145/2030112.2030166
34. Lindley, J., Green, D.P.: The ultimate measure of success for speculative design is to disappear completely. Interact. Des. Architect. J. IxD&A **51**, 32–51 (2022). https://doi.org/10.55612/s-5002-051-002
35. Lupton, D.: Self-tracking cultures: towards a sociology of personal informatics. In: OzCHI 2014: Proceedings of the 26th Australian Computer-Human Interaction Conference, pp. 77–86. Association for Computing Machinery (2014). https://doi.org/10.1145/2686612.2686623
36. Lupton, D.: Self-tracking modes: reflexive self-monitoring and data practices. SSRN Electron. J. (2014). https://doi.org/10.2139/ssrn.2483549
37. Lupton, D.: Quantified sex: a critical analysis of sexual and reproductive self-tracking using apps. Cult. Health Sex. **17**, 440–453 (2015). https://doi.org/10.1080/13691058.2014.920528
38. Lupton, D.: Digital companion species and eating data: implications for theorising digital data-human assemblages. Big Data Soc. **3**(1), 1–5 (2016). https://doi.org/10.1177/2053951715619947
39. Lupton, D.: The diverse domains of quantified selves: self-tracking modes and dataveillance. Econ. Soc. **45**(1), 101–122 (2016). https://doi.org/10.1080/03085147.2016.1143726
40. Lupton, D.: The Quantified Self. A Sociology of Self-Tracking. Polity, Cambridge (2016)
41. Malpass, M.: Critical Design in Context. History, Theory and Practice. Bloomsbury Publishing, London (2017)
42. Marcengo, A., Rapp, A., Cena, F., Geymonat, M.: The falsified self: complexities in personal data collection. In: Antona, M., Stephanidis, C. (eds.) UAHCI 2016. LNCS, vol. 9737, pp. 351–358. Springer, Cham (2016). https://doi.org/10.1007/978-3-319-40250-5_34
43. Morozov, E.: To Save Everything, Click Here: The Folly of Technological Solutionism. Public Affairs, New York (2013)
44. Niess, J., Woźniak, P.W.: Supporting meaningful personal fitness: the tracker goal evolution model. In: CHI 2018: SIGCHI Conference on Human Factors in Computing Systems - Proceedings, vol. 2018-April. Association for Computing Machinery (2018). https://doi.org/10.1145/3173574.3173745
45. Nobile, T.H., Noris, A., Kalbaska, N., Cantoni, L.: A review of digital fashion research: before and beyond communication and marketing. Int. J. Fashion Des. Technol. Educ. **14**(3), 293–301 (2021). https://doi.org/10.1080/17543266.2021.1931476
46. Noris, A., Nobile, T.H., Kalbaska, N., Cantoni, L.: Digital fashion: a systematic literature review. A perspective on marketing and communication. J. Glob. Fashion Mark. **12**(1), 32–46 (2021). https://doi.org/10.1080/20932685.2020.1835522

47. Ometov, A., et al.: A survey on wearable technology: history, state-of-the-art and current challenges. Comput. Netw. **193**, 108074 (2021). https://doi.org/10.1016/j.comnet.2021.108074
48. Pierce, J.: In tension with progression: grasping the frictional tendencies of speculative, critical, and other alternative designs. In: CHI 2022: CHI Conference on Human Factors in Computing Systems, p. 19. ACM, New York (2021). https://dl.acm.org/doi/pdf/10.1145/3411764.3445406
49. Pink, S., Ruckenstein, M., Willim, R., Duque, M.: Broken data: conceptualising data in an emerging world. Big Data Soc. **5**(1) (2018). https://doi.org/10.1177/2053951717753228
50. Pols, J., Willems, D., Aanestad, M.: Making sense with numbers. Unravelling ethico-psychological subjects in practices of self-quantification. Sociol. Health Illness **41**(S1), 98–115 (2019). https://doi.org/10.1111/1467-9566.12894
51. Rapp, A.: Wearable technologies as extensions: a postphenomenological framework and its design implications. Hum.-Comput. Interact. **38**(2), 79–117 (2023). https://doi.org/10.1080/07370024.2021.1927039
52. Rapp, A., Cena, F.: Personal informatics for everyday life: how users without prior self-tracking experience engage with personal data. Int. J. Hum. Comput. Stud. **94**, 1–17 (2016). https://doi.org/10.1016/j.ijhcs.2016.05.006
53. Rapp, A., Marcengo, A., Buriano, L., Ruffo, G., Lai, M., Cena, F.: Designing a personal informatics system for users without experience in self-tracking: a case study. Behav. Inf. Technolo. **37**(4), 335–366 (2018). https://doi.org/10.1080/0144929X.2018.1436592
54. Rapp, A., Tirabeni, L.: Personal informatics for sport: meaning, body, and social relations in amateur and elite athletes. ACM Trans. Comput.-Hum. Interact **25**(3), 1–30 (2018). https://doi.org/10.1145/3196829
55. Rapp, A., Tirabeni, L.: Self-tracking while doing sport: comfort, motivation, attention and lifestyle of athletes using personal informatics tools. Int. J. Hum.-Comput. Stud. **140** (2020). https://doi.org/10.1016/j.ijhcs.2020.102434
56. Rapp, A., Tirassa, M.: Know thyself: a theory of the self for personal informatics know thyself: a theory of the self for personal informatics running head: a theory of the self for personal informatics. Hum.-Comput. Interact. **32**(5/6), 335–380 (2017). https://doi.org/10.1080/07370024.2017.1285704
57. Rettberg Jill, W.: Seeing Ourselves Through Technology How We Use Selfies, Blogs and Wearable Devices to See and Shape Ourselves. Palgrave Macmillan, Basingstoke (2014). https://doi.org/10.1057/9781137476661. https://library.oapen.org/bitstream/handle/20.500.12657/27826/1/1002179.pdf
58. Rooksby, J., Rost, M., Morrison, A., Chalmers, M.: Personal tracking as lived informatics. In: CHI 2014: Proceedings of the SIGCHI Conference on Human Factors in Computing Systems, pp. 1163–1172 (2014). https://doi.org/10.1145/2556288.2557039
59. Ruckenstein, M.: Visualized and interacted life: personal analytics and engagements with data doubles. Societies **4**(1), 68–84 (2014). https://doi.org/10.3390/soc4010068
60. Schüll, N.D.: Data for life: wearable technology and the design of self-care. BioSocieties **11**(3), 317–333 (2016). https://doi.org/10.1057/biosoc.2015.47
61. Sharon, T.: Self-tracking for health and the quantified self: re-articulating autonomy, solidarity, and authenticity in an age of personalized healthcare. Philos. Technol. **30**(1), 93–121 (2017). https://doi.org/10.1007/s13347-016-0215-5

62. Søndergaard, M.L.J., Hansen, L.K.: PeriodShare: a bloody design fiction. In: NordiCHI 2016: Nordic Conference on Human-Computer Interaction, Gothenburg, Sweden. ACM (2016). https://doi.org/10.1145/2971485.2996748
63. Swan, M.: The quantified self: fundamental disruption in big data science and biological discovery (2013). https://doi.org/10.1089/big.2012.0002
64. Van Den Eede, Y.: Tracking the tracker. A postphenomenological inquiry into self-tracking technologies. In: Rosenberger, R., Verbeek, P.P. (eds.) Postphenomenological Investigations Essays on Human Technology Relations, pp. 143–158 (2015)
65. Van Dijk, E., Beute, F., Westerink, J.H., IJsselsteijn, W.A.: Unintended effects of self-tracking. In: CHI 2015. Workshop on Beyond Personal Informatics: Designing for Experiences of Data, Seoul, South Korea (2015). https://www.researchgate.net/publication/274008273
66. Whitson, J.R.: Gaming the quantified self. Surveill. Soc. **11**(1/2), 163–176 (2013). https://doi.org/10.24908/ss.v11i1/2.4454
67. Wirfs-Brock, J.: Quantuition: exploring the future of representing biometric data. In: TEI 2019: ACM International Conference on Tangible, Embedded and Embodied Interaction, Tempe, AZ, USA. ACM (2019). https://www.instagram.com/jordansspeculativedesign/
68. Wolf, G.: Know Thyself: Tracking Every Facet of Life, from Sleep to Mood to Pain (2009). https://www.wired.com/2009/06/lbnp-knowthyself/
69. Wolfram, S.: The Personal Analytics of My Life (2012). https://writings.stephenwolfram.com/2012/03/the-personal-analytics-of-my-life/
70. Wong, R.Y., Khovanskaya, V.: Speculative design in HCI: from corporate imaginations to critical orientations. In: Filimowicz, M., Tzankova, V. (eds.) New Directions in Third Wave Human-Computer Interaction: Volume 2 - Methodologies. HIS, pp. 175–202. Springer, Cham (2018). https://doi.org/10.1007/978-3-319-73374-6_10
71. Zheng, E.L.: Interpreting fitness: self-tracking with fitness apps through a postphenomenology lens. AI Soc. **1** (2021). https://doi.org/10.1007/s00146-021-01146-8

User Clustering Visualization and Its Impact on Motion-Based Interaction Design

Antonio Escamilla[1,2(✉)], Javier Melenchón[1], Carlos Monzo[1], and Jose A. Moran[1]

[1] Universitat Oberta de Catalunya, Barcelona, Spain
{aescamillap,jmelenchonm,cmonzo,jmoranm}@uoc.edu
[2] Universidad Pontificia Bolivariana, Medellín, Colombia
antonio.escamilla@upb.edu.co

Abstract. Movement-based interaction design relies on sensor data analysis and higher-level feature extraction to represent human movement. However, challenges to effectively using movement data include building computational tools that allow exploring feature extraction technology as design material, and the need for visual representations that help designers better understand the contents of movement. This paper presents an approach for visualizing user clustering descriptors to enhance the practitioners' ability to use human motion in interaction design. Following a user-centered strategy, we first identified perceptions of, and barriers to, using motion-based features in a group of interaction designers. Then, a multiple-view multiple-people tracking system was implemented as a detection strategy that leverages current models for 3d pose estimation. Finally, we developed a computational prototype that performs instantaneous and short-term clustering of users in space and presents simple descriptors of the algorithm's output visually. Our approach was validated through a qualitative study with interaction designers. Semi-structured interviews were used to evaluate design strategies with and without the assistance of the computational prototype and to investigate the impact of user clustering visualization on the design of interactive experiences. From practitioners' opinions, we conclude that feature visualization allowed designers to identify detection capabilities that enriched the ideation process and relate multiple dimensions of group behavior that lead to novel interaction ideas.

Keywords: Interaction design · Machine learning · Feature visualization · Motion-based feature · User clustering

1 Introduction

Interaction design plays a crucial role in creating engaging and effective movement-based interactions. One of the key challenges in this field is finding systematic and predictable relationships between human movement and technology, which requires human movement analysis and feature interpretation. In recent

M. Kurosu and A. Hashizume (Eds.): HCII 2023, LNCS 14011, pp. 47–63, 2023.
https://doi.org/10.1007/978-3-031-35596-7_4

years, there has been a growing interest among the human-computer interaction community in exploring the possibilities of motion-based interaction design. This has led to the development of various computational frameworks for analyzing human movement, such as those proposed by [1,2,7,13]. These frameworks focus on the extraction of relevant features from human motion data, such as spatial, temporal, and qualitative characteristics, to better understand and represent the contents of human movement. However, despite the progress in this field and as concluded from the previous works, there is still a lack of understanding about how these movement characteristics are perceived by interaction designers and experienced by end users.

In our previous work [15], we gathered a group of interaction designers in a focus group study and identified perspectives and attitudes toward using motion-based features. The study explored how practitioners relate motion-based feature extraction technology and sensor-based interaction design methodologies, highlighting their perceptions of the conditions descriptors must meet to become a constructive exploration tool during concept ideation. In essence, we found that interaction designers demand features that provide valuable information for non-technical practitioners and help identify a path to design.

Beyond the type of detection system, movement features can be derived by using algorithmic methods [1,9,13,18] or by using machine learning techniques [7,19,20,23,29]. Unsupervised learning is used for detecting features of motion instead of explicitly defining rules or algorithms, offering the ability to characterize group behavior without reliance on a priori knowledge. Due to the manifested interest of interaction designers to use easy-to-understand motion-based multiple-people features [15], we decided to provide the ability to perform clustering to positional data over configurable time windows. Additionally, we followed their recommendations regarding feature interpretability and created meaningful visualizations with the extracted data. We foresee that user clustering visualization could be helpful to interaction designers when designing movement-based interactions because it allows them to identify common patterns and behaviors across different users, which can then inform the design of the interaction.

We implemented a multiple-view multiple-people tracking system and developed a computational prototype that visually describes the users' clustering to improve the practitioners' capability to use human motion in interaction design. The aim is to understand the impact of user clustering visualization on the design of interactive experiences and how the visualization of multiple user clustering descriptors encourages its use in the design of spatial-interactive experiences. We conducted an interview-based study and observed that movement information visualization provided further insights into the characteristics of movement and helped participants understand the interaction opportunities that come with it. Interaction designers harnessed such visualizations to identify detection capabilities and enrich the ideation process.

2 Background

In this section, we briefly present the related work on which we build our prototype. First, we examine algorithms and computational models to interpret human activity through feature extraction. Then, we discuss different techniques used to visualize movement and its characteristics.

2.1 Movement Feature Extraction

Significant prior work has been done in expressive gesture recognition [28], and performative art studies [1] to extract information from human movement. The *EyesWeb* processing library [8,10] proposes a set of expressive cues in a layered approach to model expressive gestures from low-level physical measures up to overall motion features. Following research [1,7,18,21] advanced in the study of human movement by using similar approaches for the analysis of expressive gestures in music and dance performances. More recent work has evolved the analysis strategy to a user-centered approach based on Interactive Machine Learning (IML) and Design by Doing [22]. Presented as a promising resource to design intricate and performative movement interactions, such as embodied movement [29], IML makes it possible to design by providing examples of correct behaviors framed in terms of supervised learning. Gillies [22] points to IML as a successful method for designing movement interaction with applications in a wide range of domains: from movement-based musical interface design [19,20] to rapid prototyping of movement in a participatory design context [11].

The *movement and computing* community has shown interest in developing computational frameworks for the analysis of human movement data in recent years. *Mova* [2] is a movement analytics framework for motion capture data integrated with a library of feature extraction methods. The framework allows examining several of the features proposed in the literature in terms of their operative or expressive qualities. *OpenMoves* [3] is a system for interpreting person-tracking data that emphasizes movement pattern recognition. The system was presented as a complement to *OpenPTrack* [27] and provides real-time centroid analysis, low-level short-time features, and higher-level abstractions based on unsupervised and supervised machine learning techniques. *Modosc* [13] is a library in the form of Max abstractions that extract movement descriptors from a marker-based motion capture system in real-time. The initial release of the library presented point descriptors like velocity, acceleration, jerk, and fluidity index along with descriptors to process groups of points such as center of mass, quantity of motion, contraction index, and bounding box. Finally, *InteractML* [23] is a node-based tool for designing movement interactions in Unity, based on the IML paradigm and tailored to non-experts with little programming experience. Nevertheless, among movement features to be used as inputs to the model, the user can only choose between position, rotation, velocity, and distance to another input.

2.2 Movement and Feature Visualization

A growing body of literature has investigated different ways of visualizing motion capture data [2,4,6,25]. Frequently applied strategies derive representations from raw data usually considering the extraction of features focused on exposing and extracting as much of the semantics as possible [6]. The analytics platform by Alemi et al. [2] uses parallel visual processing capabilities of human perception to visualize multiple features at the same time and in different forms which can be used to better understand the relationships between a particular type of movement and their corresponding measurable features. Extending Bernard et al.'s work [6] to the dance and performing arts domain, Arpatzoglou et al. [4] presented a prototype of their framework *DanceMoves* addressing these challenges. The framework's functionality offers the interactive visual analysis of dance moves, as well as comparison, quality assessment, and visual search of dance poses. The proposed similarity measures were evaluated using agglomerative clustering over a public domain dataset and the visualization features through domain experts' feedback. However, they neglect to discuss the methodology for the qualitative study that supports their conclusions. From a different perspective, *MoViz* [25] is presented as a visualization tool that enables comparative evaluation of algorithms for clustering motion capture datasets. Regarding the design of behaviors and user interface, *MoViz's* authors tried to include several information visualization design principles to make the tool intuitive, informative, and accurate in data representation. Using *LuminAI* [26] -an interactive art installation that uses machine learning to improvise movement with human dancers- as a use case, Liu et al. [25] employed *MoViz* to evaluate different gesture clustering pipelines used by the installation's AI system. As a result of this evaluation, the authors argue that the tool allowed them to identify which pipelines worked well for certain clustering datasets, which speaks to the tool's potential to better understand 'black-box' algorithms.

3 Prototype Implementation

To study the impact of user clustering visualization on motion-based interaction design, we developed a prototype to analyze human motion for interaction design purposes. Although the implementation was comprehensive by allowing a group of people to move freely with intentions of interaction within a large space, the specific contribution of this article assumes the use of the prototype as a research instrument, so the description of the system is complete yet brief.

3.1 Pose Estimation and Tracking in 3D Space

The 3d pose estimation and tracking component considers a multi-camera approach to account for large volume spaces and resolve occlusions and limited field-of-view problems. The procedure for this component consists of a sequence of steps. First, a calibration step based on using a *ChArUco* board pattern to capture properly synchronized images, and then obtain camera poses by bundle adjustment optimization. Second, a people detection and pose estimation step. To this end, we adopted the body-only *AlphaPose* estimator [17] which follows a top-down strategy. *Alphapose* is a two-step framework that first detects human bounding boxes and then independently estimates the pose within each box. In the current implementation, an off-the-shelf *YOLOV3* pre-trained detector [30] and an efficient high-accuracy pose estimator [17] are adopted. Third, a multi-view correspondence and 3d pose reconstruction step. To match the estimated 2d poses across views, we adopted the approach of Dong et al. [14] in which appearance similarity and geometric compatibility cues are combined to calculate the affinity score between bounding boxes. The bounding boxes with no matches in other views are regarded as false detections and discarded. The multi-way matching algorithm groups 2d poses of the same person in different views from which 3d poses can be reconstructed [5]. And fourth, a tracking-by-detection and filtering step to finally obtain smoothed human poses of all the people in the scene. To improve the identification ability, we compute the appearance feature similarity between non-redundant candidates and existing tracks to address the spatial distance limitation. Temporal averaging is used to fill in missing joints, while a Gaussian kernel with standard deviation σ is used to smooth each joint trajectory [31].

3.2 Feature Extraction System

The feature extraction system is based on identifying the joints in the human body and tracking all users in space. Moreover, the user's trajectory is characterized by considering a fixed number of the most recent position points updated into a circular buffer of three-dimensional data at every time step. To prevent the user from diverting his attention to technical details about algorithm tunning, we decided to reduce the prototype user intervention to its minimum. Therefore, neither algorithm parameterization nor numerical feedback is an option for the user. Below we present the features that were implemented for the present study.

Instantaneous Clustering. The instantaneous clustering feature takes the current time step's set of user centroid positions and finds clusters using the mean shift algorithm [12]. The mean shift algorithm is widely used in data analysis because it's non-parametric and doesn't require any predefined number of clusters. As Amin & Burke [3] pointed out, the mean shift algorithm fits well with the frequently changing nature of social interaction scenes and live performances.

Hotspots. The hotspots feature provides the capability to identify frequently visited areas or routes in the space. Based on the work of Amin & Burke [3], hotspots are addressed as a long-term, macroscopic form of clustering. Nevertheless, we decided to perform clustering to positional data over a fixed time window using a different algorithm. We have chosen the DBSCAN algorithm as it performs density-based clustering robust to outliers. DBSCAN works on the assumption that clusters are dense regions in space separated by regions of lower density [16], providing better hotspot visualization results compared to other clustering algorithms.

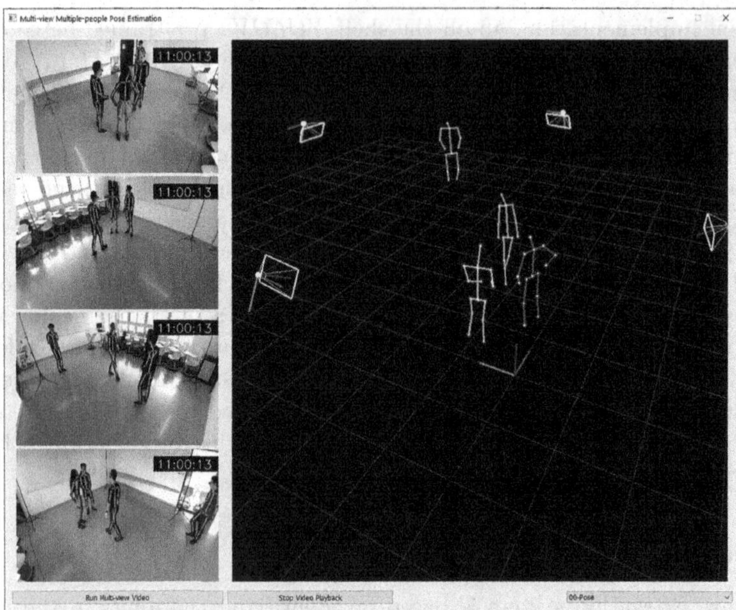

Fig. 1. Multi-view multiple-people tracking system.

3.3 Visualization Engine

The visualization engine provides visual representations of the human poses and the extracted features in a 3d view of the scene. The graphical user interface is divided into three sections (see Fig. 1): A selection section with controls for opening scenes and selecting the feature, a multi-view video playback section with the 2d pose detection results overlaid on each view, and a three-dimensional representation of the scene over which the feature visualization is rendered. The camera position in the 3d scene is controlled by the prototype user using six degrees of motion input using the keyboard keys and the mouse; allowing the user to observe the relationship between feature and space from different perspectives, navigate the 3d scene, and decide whether to focus on a smaller region or zoom outwards to get a broad overview. In addition, the prototype adheres to Tufte's conception of graphical integrity in which visual representations of data should neither overrepresent nor underrepresent its effects and phenomena [32]. Following we present the visualization strategies corresponding to each feature.

Instantaneous Clustering Visualization. To produce a meaningful feature visualization, we decided to maintain the color representation assigned to each user by the tracking module and not to change it depending on the cluster to which they belong each time step. Preliminary tests evidenced that coloring each user's pose according to the cluster produced confusing results that overrepresented the phenomenon with continuous color flips. Instead, we observed that using a fixed neutral color and a circular shape for displaying all clusters was more organic and intuitive. However, to offer a complete visual experience of the clustering attributes, we decided to represent the distance of users to the cluster's centroid to which they belong with lines on the ground plane, and the number of users in each cluster as the radius of the circle representing the cluster. As a final result, we present an instantaneous clustering visualization that prioritizes cluster position and size over cluster shape and eliminates information in the height axis (Fig. 2).

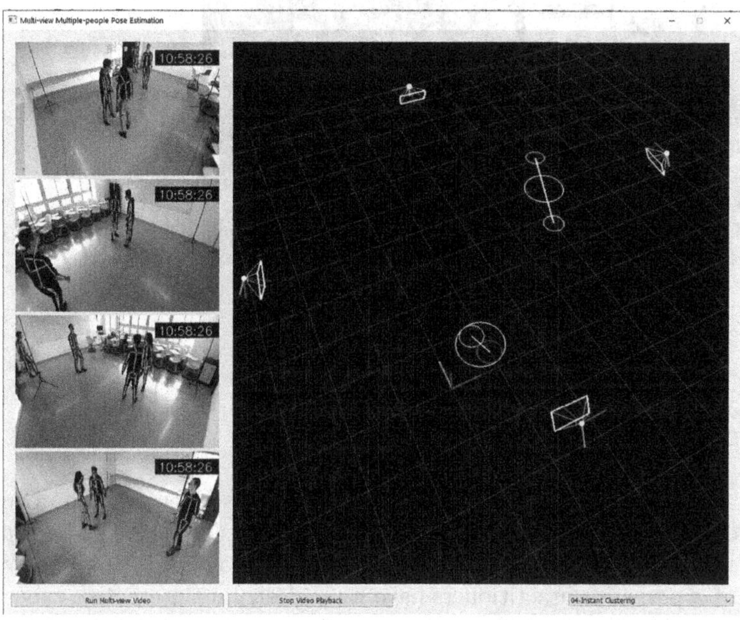

Fig. 2. Visualization of clustering over instantaneous positional data.

Hotspots Visualization. Regarding long-term clustering visualization, the prototype shows simple descriptors of the algorithm's output such as position, spread, and boundaries of clusters in a heatmap representation to enrich the user's perception of group behavior. The prototype maintains a 3d view of the scene to represent the user's trajectories and displays the hotspot representation on an emergent GUI widget (see Fig. 3). We noticed during development that the hotspot information by itself was not perceived as reliable if the trajectory information was unavailable. We believe that, in this case, as the length of the trajectories is the result of the time window considered by the clustering algorithm, its visualization allows a quick interpretation of the heatmap representation and validates the graphic outcome.

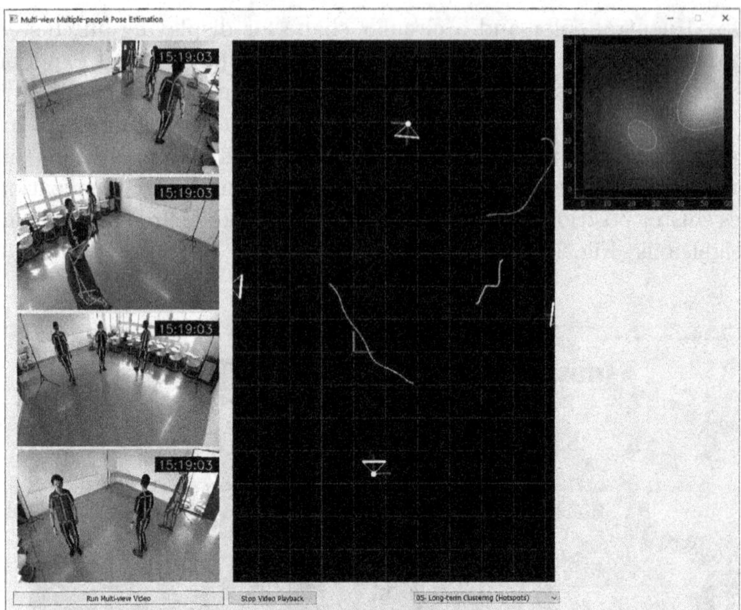

Fig. 3. Hotspot visualization

4 Proposal Assessment

A qualitative research method was used to follow a user-centered approach and to develop an understanding of interaction designers' needs and perceptions. We chose a semi-structured interview-based methodology to ensure we cover the breadth of experiences practitioners have when designing interactive experiences and observe the impact of user clustering features and their visualization in design practice.

4.1 Participants

Six interaction designers took part in the qualitative study. Three of these had participated in our previous study [15] and the other three participants were recruited specifically for this study. Nevertheless, the recruitment protocol was the same as for the previous study [15] ensuring that new participants had prior proficiency in creating full-body interactive experiences based on movement or gestures. This mix of practitioners allowed us to consider new interaction designers' perspectives and give continuity to previous participants' ideas in the prototype evaluation process. There were participants between the ages of 23 and 45 (M = 30.3, SD = 9.6), with professional experience varying from 3 to 15 years (M = 7, SD = 4.6).

4.2 Interview Method

Prior to the interview, three multi-view scenes with actors were recorded using a calibrated multi-camera system. Each scene recreated a particular situation where the grouping of people was considered suitable for the design of interactions in space. The interviews were conducted by the corresponding author using a web conferencing tool with activated webcams on both sides. The interviewer presented the research aims and briefly explained the contributions of our previous study. Two study conditions corresponding to the extracted features explained in Sect. 3.2 were considered. For each condition, we first presented a scene and discussed design strategies in the absence of any visual feedback other than the video itself. Then, we told participants that they would be presented with a user clustering visualization prototype. Finally, we asked them to interpret the user movement from the corresponding extracted feature and to express what other interactions they could think of with the information available. The discussion was repeated for the other two scenes, following up on topics of interest that arose naturally. After reviewing both conditions, participants were asked about aspects that influenced their overall experience, their thoughts on the hardship of assessing user grouping without proper visualization, and the limitations faced.

4.3 Analysis

The interview video recordings were initially reviewed as a method of immersion and preparation stage before the analysis. We used timestamps to identify interesting quotes and relevant sections, and reviewed insights retrospectively within the research team. To analyze the interview data, we first transcribed the audio recordings, then extracted discrete statements, and finally labeled them by condition. Moreover, we clustered the statements using grounded theory methods and affinity analysis [24] and then, performed open coding for major thematic groups. In a second clustering round, statements within these groups were then further analyzed and clustered into sub-categories. After multiple rounds of discussion and analysis with the research group, we observed a set of themes that emerged from the interview findings.

5 Results

The results section of this paper presents the findings from the qualitative research study. Through this method, we were able to identify several key themes and sub-categories that emerged from our analysis. As can be seen in Fig. 4, there were three main groupings that participants (P) discussed in different ways. First, participants considered user clustering visualization a valuable tool to better understand user behavior, which includes pattern identification and even anomalies in user behavior. Second, user clustering visualization helped practitioners refine their design practice and make more informed design decisions. Finally, practitioners acknowledged that this approach would be most ideally suitable during the analysis and evaluation stage or during the definition of motion-based detection strategies.

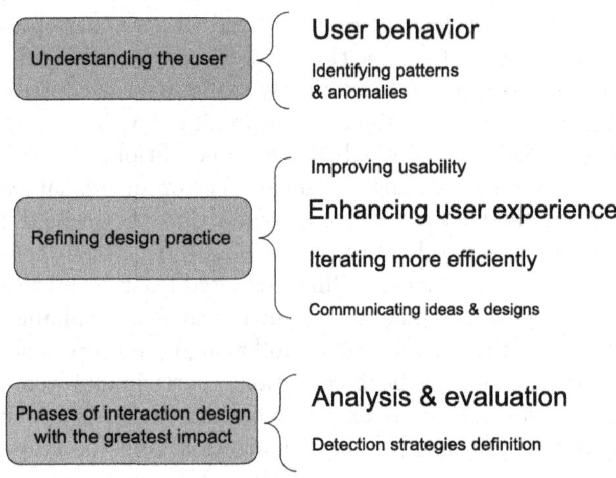

Fig. 4. Affinity analysis results with main themes and sub-categories. A bigger font size indicates that the topic was discussed by more participants.

5.1 Understanding User Behavior

One of the main themes that emerged from the data was the importance of understanding user behavior and identifying patterns and anomalies. Practitioners noted that user clustering visualization allowed them to better understand the diverse ways in which users interact with the system and identify areas where the design may be falling short.

Understanding User Behavior. Feature visualization allowed designers to understand how users move and interact with a product, providing insights into user behavior and preferences.

- "User clustering visualization helps me to see where users are having difficulty, and to identify patterns of behavior that I might not have noticed otherwise." (P4)
- "I think what matters most in that scene is where they stand and the interactions they are making in mid-air." (P2)
- "There is something interesting, and it is to understand that the feature is a specific information of the movement that opens the additional possibility of predicting the user's behavior." (P5)

Identifying Patterns and Anomalies. By visualizing movement descriptors, designers could identify patterns, such as common gestures or movements, as well as anomalies or unexpected behaviors.

- "The information provided by the prototype can be used to develop an active play installation using gross motor skills. You could analyze group patterns and make a game out of them." (P2)
- "It occurs to me that you can know two people from the same team, in what position they are one with respect to the other. And define whether they are fulfilling a condition, for example, you are 'offside' or you are not. You're ahead or you're not, those kinds of interactions. I think they are interesting." (P2)

5.2 Refining Design Practice

Another key theme that emerged from the data was the role of user clustering visualization in supporting some of the designer's work. Participants stated that user clustering visualization helped them in design practice by improving usability, enhancing user experience, iterating more efficiently, and communicating ideas and designs to other stakeholders. They noted that this approach allows them to make more informed design decisions, and to communicate their ideas more effectively to, for example, developers and engineers.

Improving Usability. With a better understanding of how users interact with a product, designers can make informed decisions about the design of movement-based interactions, resulting in improved usability.

- "Interesting! The group movement in this visualization looks natural and fluid. I would use it not only to implement an interactive experience but to measure its effectiveness." (P3)
- "User clustering visualization has been really helpful in identifying areas where the design is not working well, and in coming up with solutions to improve usability." (P5)

Enhancing User Experience. By incorporating user behavior insights into the design of movement-based interactions, designers could think of a more personalized and engaging user experience.

- "I would use the user's distance to all other clusters in a game to influence what the other groups of people produce even if to a lesser extent." (P4)
- "The interior design of commercial spaces has some rules, right? Then, depending on the user's trajectory, the intent of those rules can be reinforced with lighting, for example. Now I can detect where the user stops and based on this event, understand which are the objects, or at least the category of objects, that attract the most attention." (P6)
- "By observing a trajectory, I can be very sure of where the user has passed, and I can make redesign decisions with certainty based on an analysis over time." (P5)

Iterating More Efficiently. Feature visualization provided designers with a quick way to iterate on their design ideas, allowing them to adjust and test different options more efficiently.

- "It's just that the features make it much easier. For example, clustering and trajectories are very good for understanding how groups are formed. One now compares the features and the videos, and it is not easy to realize all the information in the movement that can be useful." (P3)
- "It helped me to see where users are having trouble and to iterate more quickly to improve the overall user experience." (P1)

Communicating Ideas and Designs. Additionally, practitioners expressed that feature visualization could be used as a tool for designers to communicate their ideas and designs to other stakeholders, such as developers, engineers, and other designers, allowing for a more collaborative design process.

- "The prototype is very useful for me to ground the idea and take it to other fields of ideation." (P1)

5.3 Impact on the Full Design-Production Cycle

Finally, practitioners commented on the stage/phase of the design-development cycle in which this approach would be most suitable. All of them were unanimous in their assessment of the prototype as an effective tool for the analysis and evaluation of group experiences; however, some other opinions also pointed toward using the prototype during the definition of motion-based detection strategies. They emphasized that clustering visualization is particularly useful in helping designers to define the specific movements or gestures that will be used to interact with the system and in validating the effectiveness of different detection strategies.

During the Analysis and Evaluation. User clustering visualization can be particularly useful in motion-based interaction design, as it can help designers understand how different groups of users interact with the system and identify potential issues or challenges. This process is typically used during the analysis and evaluation phase of the interaction design process.

- "In this scene, it was 'cool' to see a heat map with a lot of the information that I had previously with lower-level features. It's all there, and now I can analyze where they were moving! It is certainly easier for me to see it because of the type of visualization." (P3)
- "For me, it is useful not only to control the experience as such but also to measure its long-term success. This is one of the most difficult things in the design of interactive experiences since in most cases the only feedback we have is through satisfaction interviews." (P1)

During the Definition of Motion-Based Detection Strategies. To a lesser extent, the discussion of the participants focused on how user clustering visualization can be useful throughout the interaction design process, not just in the analysis and evaluation phase. One key phase where user clustering visualization was particularly valuable was in the definition and design of motion-based detection strategies.

- "When you're designing experiences, it's important that there are certain things that are kind of magical and abstract, right? But also, that they allow some understanding of how user interaction works in order to control the experience. Otherwise, people come in, and if they don't understand, they leave. So, it also seems to me that it is, in a certain way, a matter of easy understanding for the user." (P1)
- "In clustering, I see that there are several data available that are, in a certain way, parameterizable. Not only for the user, as an interaction parameter, but as a robust control event in the implementation stage." (P5)
- "I'm thinking about how long the user must take to make the gesture and how to detect it. It is these types of parameters that at the end of the day would define the rhythm of the experience." (P3)

6 Discussion

User clustering visualization is a technique used to group users based on their movement patterns and behaviors. This can be useful for interaction designers when designing movement-based interactions because it allows them to identify common patterns and behaviors across different users, which can then inform the design of the interaction. One specific benefit of user clustering visualization is that it allows designers to identify edge cases and outliers in user behavior. By understanding how these users interact with a product, designers can make informed decisions about how to handle these cases in their designs, resulting in a more inclusive and user-friendly interaction. Additionally, user clustering visualization can be used to personalize the user experience. By grouping users based on their behavior, designers can create tailored interactions for different user segments. This can lead to a more engaging and satisfying experience for users. Finally, user clustering visualization can also be used to improve the overall usability of a product. By identifying common patterns in user behavior, designers can optimize the interaction design to make it more intuitive and user-friendly for most users.

During the analysis and evaluation phase of the interaction design process, designers use various methods to gather data about users, such as interviews, surveys, and usability testing. This data is then analyzed to identify patterns and commonalities among users, which can inform the design of the final product. User clustering visualization can provide valuable insights for interaction design and can help designers create more effective and user-centered designs. For example, if a cluster of users is found to have difficulty with certain gestures or movements, the designer can take this into consideration and adjust the design to improve usability for that group. During the early stages of the design process, designers often need to define the specific movements or gestures that will be used to interact with the system. User clustering visualization can be used to identify common patterns and variations in user movement, which can inform the design of detection strategies that are robust and able to accommodate a wide range of user input. For example, imagine that you are designing a motion-based control system for a home automation system. Through user research and clustering visualization, you identify that users exhibit a wide range of hand gestures when controlling the system. Some users prefer to use simple, open-handed gestures, while others use more complex, closed-handed gestures. By understanding these variations in user movement, you can design a detection strategy that is able to accurately recognize both types of gestures. Additionally, clustering visualization can be used to validate the effectiveness of different detection strategies. By comparing the behavior of users in different clusters, designers can identify areas where the detection system may be struggling and adjust accordingly.

We argue that the visualization of user movement descriptors helps creators define better detection strategies that can lead to a more fluid interactive experience and reduced user frustration. When a motion-based detection system is able to accurately recognize a wide range of user input, it can respond to user actions more quickly and accurately. This can result in a more responsive and intuitive interface, which can make it easier for users to accomplish their tasks and reduce the likelihood of frustration. In addition, better detection strategies can also contribute to the creation of a natural user interface. When a motion-based detection system is able to recognize and respond to a wide range of user input, it can more closely mimic the way that people naturally interact with the environment. This can make the interface feel more natural and intuitive, which can reduce the cognitive load on the user and make it easier to use.

Practitioners should be aware that clustering is a complex process that requires a deep understanding of the domain, the user, and the technology. It should be approached with a critical perspective, considering the context, the goals, and the limitations of the project. Also, it's important to note that clustering visualization should be used in conjunction with other evaluation methods, such as usability testing, to provide a more comprehensive understanding of the system's performance. Moreover, the concept of a natural user interface goes beyond motion recognition. It encompasses various aspects such as the user interface, the interaction, the feedback, the aesthetics, the context, and the goals. Therefore, it's important to approach it with a holistic mindset, considering all these elements and testing the design with users.

7 Conclusion and Future Work

In summary, the feature visualization process was highly valued by the interaction designers participating in the study as it provided them with a valuable tool to structure and refine their design ideas. It helped them to understand the movement patterns of users, identify common behaviors and tailor their interactions accordingly. The visualization also allowed them to overcome the complexity of the extraction algorithms and explore the creative possibilities of using clustering and other features. The exposure to visual cues rather than numerical data was deemed crucial in their design practice as it helped them to understand user behavior in a more intuitive and graphical way. The practitioners reported that it was very difficult to abstract the meaning of the data without the prototype, and by observing a trajectory, they were able to make redesign decisions with certainty based on an analysis over time. Overall, feature visualization was seen as a powerful tool to enhance the design of movement-based interactions.

In future work, we plan to further investigate the impact of user clustering visualization on the design of interactive experiences. We will conduct user studies to evaluate the effectiveness of the system in different scenarios and domains. Additionally, we will explore the integration of other machine-learning techniques to improve the accuracy and robustness of the user clustering algorithm. Furthermore, as a new line of research, one can investigate the potential of using our approach in other fields such as crowd analysis, sports analysis, and surveillance.

References

1. Alaoui, S.F., Bevilacqua, F., Jacquemin, C.: Interactive visuals as metaphors for dance movement qualities. ACM Trans. Interact. Intell. Syst. **5**(3), 13:1–13:24 (2015)
2. Alemi, O., Pasquier, P., Shaw, C.: Mova: interactive movement analytics platform. In: Proceedings of the 2014 International Workshop on Movement and Computing - MOCO 2014, Paris, France, pp. 37–42. ACM Press (2014)
3. Amin, S., Burke, J.: OpenMoves: a system for interpreting person-tracking data. In: Proceedings of the 5th International Conference on Movement and Computing, p. 13. ACM (2018)
4. Arpatzoglou, V., Kardara, A., Diehl, A., Flueckiger, B., Helmer, S., Pajarola, R.: DanceMoves: a visual analytics tool for dance movement analysis. In: EuroVis 2021 - Short Papers, p. 5 (2021)
5. Belagiannis, V., Amin, S., Andriluka, M., Schiele, B., Navab, N., Ilic, S.: 3D pictorial structures revisited: multiple human pose estimation. IEEE Trans. Pattern Anal. Mach. Intell. **38**(10), 1929–1942 (2016)
6. Bernard, J., Vögele, A., Klein, R., Fellner, D.: Approaches and challenges in the visual-interactive comparison of human motion data. In: Proceedings of the 12th International Joint Conference on Computer Vision, Imaging and Computer Graphics Theory and Applications, Porto, Portugal, pp. 217–224. SCITEPRESS - Science and Technology Publications (2017)
7. Bevilacqua, F., Guédy, F., Schnell, N., Fléty, E., Leroy, N.: Wireless sensor interface and gesture-follower for music pedagogy. In: Proceedings of the 7th International Conference on New Interfaces for Musical Expression, pp. 124–129 (2007)

8. Camurri, A., Volpe, G., De Poli, G., Leman, M.: Communicating expressiveness and affect in multimodal interactive systems. IEEE MultiMedia **12**(1), 43–53 (2005)
9. Camurri, A., et al.: EyesWeb: toward gesture and affect recognition in interactive dance and music systems. Comput. Music J. **24**(1), 57–69 (2000)
10. Camurri, A., Mazzarino, B., Volpe, G.: Analysis of expressive gesture: the EyesWeb expressive gesture processing library. In: Camurri, A., Volpe, G. (eds.) GW 2003. LNCS (LNAI), vol. 2915, pp. 460–467. Springer, Heidelberg (2004). https://doi.org/10.1007/978-3-540-24598-8_42
11. Caramiaux, B., Altavilla, A., Pobiner, S.G., Tanaka, A.: Form follows sound: designing interactions from sonic memories. In: Proceedings of the 33rd Annual ACM Conference on Human Factors in Computing Systems, Seoul Republic of Korea, pp. 3943–3952. ACM (2015)
12. Comaniciu, D., Meer, P.: Mean shift: a robust approach toward feature space analysis. IEEE Trans. Pattern Anal. Mach. Intell. **24**(5), 603–619 (2002)
13. Dahl, L., Visi, F.: Modosc: a library of real-time movement descriptors for marker-based motion capture. In: Proceedings of the 5th International Conference on Movement and Computing, MOCO 2018, pp. 1–4. Association for Computing Machinery, New York (2018)
14. Dong, J., Jiang, W., Huang, Q., Bao, H., Zhou, X.: Fast and robust multi-person 3D pose estimation from multiple views. In: 2019 IEEE/CVF Conference on Computer Vision and Pattern Recognition (CVPR), Long Beach, CA, USA, pp. 7784–7793. IEEE (2019)
15. Escamilla, A., Melenchón, J., Monzo, C., Morán, J.A.: Interaction designers' perceptions of using motion-based full-body features. Int. J. Hum. Comput. Stud. **155**, 102697 (2021)
16. Ester, M., Kriegel, H.P., Xu, X.: A density-based algorithm for discovering clusters in large spatial databases with noise. In: KDD, vol. 96, pp. 226–231 (1996)
17. Fang, H.S., et al.: AlphaPose: whole-body regional multi-person pose estimation and tracking in real-time. IEEE Trans. Pattern Anal. Mach. Intell. (2022)
18. Feldmeier, M., Paradiso, J.A.: An interactive music environment for large groups with giveaway wireless motion sensors. Comput. Music. J. **31**(1), 50–67 (2007)
19. Fiebrink, R., Cook, P.R., Trueman, D.: Human model evaluation in interactive supervised learning. In: Proceedings of the SIGCHI Conference on Human Factors in Computing Systems, Vancouver, BC, Canada, pp. 147–156. ACM (2011)
20. Françoise, J., Candau, Y., Fdili Alaoui, S., Schiphorst, T.: Designing for kinesthetic awareness: revealing user experiences through second-person inquiry. In: Proceedings of the 2017 CHI Conference on Human Factors in Computing Systems, Denver, Colorado, USA, pp. 5171–5183. ACM (2017)
21. Friberg, A.: A fuzzy analyzer of emotional expression in music performance and body motion. In: Proceedings of Music and Music Science, vol. 10, pp. 28–30 (2004)
22. Gillies, M.: Understanding the role of interactive machine learning in movement interaction design. ACM Trans. Comput.-Hum. Interact. **26**(1), 5:1–5:34 (2019)
23. Hilton, C., et al.: InteractML: making machine learning accessible for creative practitioners working with movement interaction in immersive media. In: Proceedings of the 27th ACM Symposium on Virtual Reality Software and Technology, Osaka, Japan, pp. 1–10. ACM (2021)
24. Lazar, J., Feng, J.H., Hochheiser, H.: Research Methods in Human-Computer Interaction. Morgan Kaufmann, Burlington (2017)
25. Liu, L., Long, D., Magerko, B.: MoViz: a visualization tool for comparing motion capture data clustering algorithms. In: Proceedings of the 7th International Con-

ference on Movement and Computing, Jersey City/Virtual, NJ, USA, pp. 1–8. ACM (2020)
26. Long, D., Liu, L., Gujrania, S., Naomi, C., Magerko, B.: Visualizing improvisation in LuminAI, an AI partner for co-creative dance. In: Proceedings of the 7th International Conference on Movement and Computing, Jersey City/Virtual, NJ, USA, pp. 1–2. ACM (2020)
27. Munaro, M., Basso, F., Menegatti, E.: OpenPTrack: open source multi-camera calibration and people tracking for RGB-D camera networks. Robot. Auton. Syst. **75**, 525–538 (2016)
28. Noroozi, F., Corneanu, C.A., Kamińska, D., Sapiński, T., Escalera, S., Anbarjafari, G.: Survey on emotional body gesture recognition. IEEE Trans. Affect. Comput. **12**(2), 505–523 (2021)
29. Plant, N., et al.: Movement interaction design for immersive media using interactive machine learning. In: Proceedings of the 7th International Conference on Movement and Computing, MOCO 2020, pp. 1–2. Association for Computing Machinery, New York (2020)
30. Redmon, J., Farhadi, A.: YOLOv3: An Incremental Improvement (2018)
31. Tanke, J., Gall, J.: Iterative greedy matching for 3D human pose tracking from multiple views. In: Fink, G.A., Frintrop, S., Jiang, X. (eds.) DAGM GCPR 2019. LNCS, vol. 11824, pp. 537–550. Springer, Cham (2019). https://doi.org/10.1007/978-3-030-33676-9_38
32. Tufte, E.R.: The visual display of quantitative information. J. Healthc. Qual. (JHQ) **7**(3), 15 (1985)

eGLU-Box Mobile: A Smartphone App for Usability Testing by Italian Public Administration Webmasters

Stefano Federici[1,4(✉)], Giovanni Bifolchi[1], Marco Bracalenti[1], Alessandro Ansani[1,2], Agnese Napoletti[1], Rosa Lanzillotti[3], Giuseppe Desolda[3], Maria Laura Mele[4], Simone Borsci[5], Maria Laura de Filippis[1], Giancarlo Gaudino[6], Massimo Amendola[6], Antonello Cocco[6], Aldo Doria[6], and Emilio Simonetti[7]

[1] Department of Philosophy, Social and Human Sciences and Education, University of Perugia, Perugia, Italy
stefano.federici@unipg.it, alessandro.ansani@uniroma3.it

[2] Department of Philosophy, Communication, and Performing Arts, Roma Tre University, Rome, Italy

[3] Department of Computer Science, University of Bari Aldo Moro, Bari, Italy
{rosa.lanzillotti,giuseppe.desolda}@uniba.it

[4] Myèsis, Research and Development Company, Rome, Italy

[5] Department of Learning, Data Analysis, and Technology – Cognition, Data and Education – CODE group, Faculty of BMS, University of Twente, Enschede, The Netherlands

[6] DGTCSI-ISCTI – Directorate General for Management and Information and Communications Technology, Superior Institute of Communication and Information Technologies, Ministry of Enterprises and Made in Italy, Rome, Italy
{giancarlo.gaudino,massimo.amendola,antonello.cocco, aldo.doria}@mise.gov.it

[7] Rome, Italy

Abstract. Smartphones and tablets now offer consumers unique advantages such as portability and accessibility. Developers are also working with a mobile-first approach, and are prioritizing mobile applications over desktop versions. This study introduces eGLU-box Mobile, an application for performing a drive usability test directly from a smartphone. An experimental study was conducted in which the participants were divided into two groups: an experimental group, which used the new mobile application from a smartphone, and a control group, which used the desktop application from a computer. The participants' behavior was assessed using explicit (self-report questionnaires) and implicit measures (eye movement data). The results were encouraging, and showed that both the mobile and desktop versions of eGLU-box enabled participants to test the usability with a similar level of UX, despite some minimal (although significant) differences in terms of satisfaction of use.

Keywords: Mobile · Application · App · Computer · Desktop · eGLU-box · Eye-Tracking · Eye-Tracker · Usability

---

E. Simonetti—Independent Researcher.

M. Kurosu and A. Hashizume (Eds.): HCII 2023, LNCS 14011, pp. 64–79, 2023.
https://doi.org/10.1007/978-3-031-35596-7_5

1 Introduction

Mobile devices such as smartphones and tablets are now commonly used. Oulasvirta and colleagues [1] have reported that smartphones are more widely available and are used more often throughout the day than laptops. In addition, smartphones provide faster access to content than laptops, due to their portability. In view of this, the present study compares a mobile version of eGLU-box developed for the Italian public administration (PA), a national government, with the original version for desktop use. eGLU-box PA (in the following eGLU-box) is a web platform that allows PA webmasters in Italy to evaluate the usability of their websites and digital services [2]. It was developed based on the eGLU LG 2018.1 protocol, and is designed to run on a personal computer or Mac [3]. The eGLU-box Mobile application, which is available for both Android and iOS systems, was developed to guide these webmasters to carry out semiautomatic evaluations directly from their smartphones. In this study, we aim to evaluate the user experience of eGLU-box Mobile compared to the desktop version (eGLU-box) by observing the users' implicit (eye movement) and explicit (satisfaction, cognitive workload, and promotability) behaviors. This study forms part of the eGLU-box Mobile project supported by the former Ministry of Economic Development, now known as the Ministry of Enterprises and Made in Italy (MIMIT), together with the universities of Perugia and Bari. The aim of the project was to create a new mobile application that would allow users to use eGLU-box on devices such as smartphones and tablets. Before its launch, the application needs to be tested under laboratory conditions with participants randomly selected from the population.

1.1 eGLU-box: From Its Inception to Today

Introduction to eGLU-box. eGLU-box is software developed by the PA in collaboration with the universities of Perugia and Bari (Italy), which allows for the evaluation of the usability of websites. It is an online tool that allows PA webmasters to create usability tests for a particular website and to invite participants to carry them out. eGLU-box is a re-engineered version of a previous platform called UTAssistant [4–6], a web-based usability assessment tool that was developed to provide the PA with an online tool to conduct remote user studies. Both UTAssistant and its newer version, eGLU-box, were designed according to usability guidelines provided by GLU, a group working on usability that was founded by the Department of Public Function, Ministry for Simplification and Public Administration in 2010. Currently, eGLU-box is based on eGLU LG version 2018.1, the latest version of the protocol [3].

The eGLU-box LG Protocol: Usability Guidelines for Everyone. Version 2018.1 of the eGLU LG protocol specifies the procedure that a tool should implement to investigate the usability of a product. This is a generic tool, as the protocol is defined independently of the technology. This means that it can be applied with minimal adjustment to a variety of products and services on different distribution channels and with different technologies, such as information websites, online services, paper documents, desktop applications (for computers), and mobile applications (for smartphones and tablets). This protocol was created with the aims of: (i) describing a procedure to promote the direct involvement and observation of users in the evaluation of online sites and services; and (ii) encouraging public operators to pay greater attention to the issue of usability. The user observation procedure consists of five steps: (i) definition of the tasks (e.g., searching for specific information, filling in online forms, downloading documents) to be carried out by participants, which is done by the observer; (ii) selection of users; (iii) performance of the assigned tasks by users (during the observation, direct questions from the observer are not admitted); (iv) administration of user experience questionnaires when the tasks have been executed; (v) data analysis based on the quantitative or qualitative data collected. If carried out correctly, the entire procedure can be considered a minimum usability test, albeit simplified, and can be performed by non-experts. The protocol also provides the PA webmaster with an idea of the possible problems with interaction with the PA website and online services.

eGLU-box: From Theory to Practice. When the detailed instructions provided by the eGLU LG protocol version 2018.1 are followed, the eGLU-box platform allows even a non-expert in usability testing to conduct a usability test. eGLU-box reports the time taken for each task, its outcome, the results of the questionnaire, any registration or tracing performed by the participant as part of the task, etc. Via a single web platform, eGLU-box allows for the merging of data with different natures, which an observer would otherwise have to collect using different technologies and software, such as screen recordings, task durations, task outcomes, etc. To perform a usability test with eGLU-box, an observer (i.e., a webmaster or experimenter) accesses the platform as a "user-creator" in order to define the tasks to be performed by the users on the specific website under evaluation (Fig. 1). Furthermore, the user-creator can select one or more self-report questionnaires to be completed by the user at the end of the test, in order to measure: (i) usability, based on the System Usability Scale (SUS) [7] and UMUX-LITE [8]; and (ii) promotability, based on the Net Promoter Score (NPS) [9]. The user-creator also has the ability to add new questionnaires via the interface.

When the user-creator has set up the website that will be evaluated, the tasks and the questionnaires to be carried out, each user taking part in the usability evaluation is invited to access eGLU-box as a "user-tester". This interface provides users with a step-by-step guide to navigating the website under evaluation, and displays the tasks and questionnaires set up by the user-creator. The user's actions are recorded by eGLU-box through a webcam, screen recordings, and a microphone. eGLU-box was designed for the conduction of usability tests both remotely and in a laboratory. In this case, eGLU-box data can be combined with software that captures bio-behavioral data (such as electroencephalographic, skin conductance, heart rate, eye movement, and facial expression data) [5].

In 2022, a version of eGLU-box was developed for mobile testing (designed for both Android and iOS systems) to guide the webmasters of the PA to carry out a semiautomatic evaluation directly from smartphones and tablets.

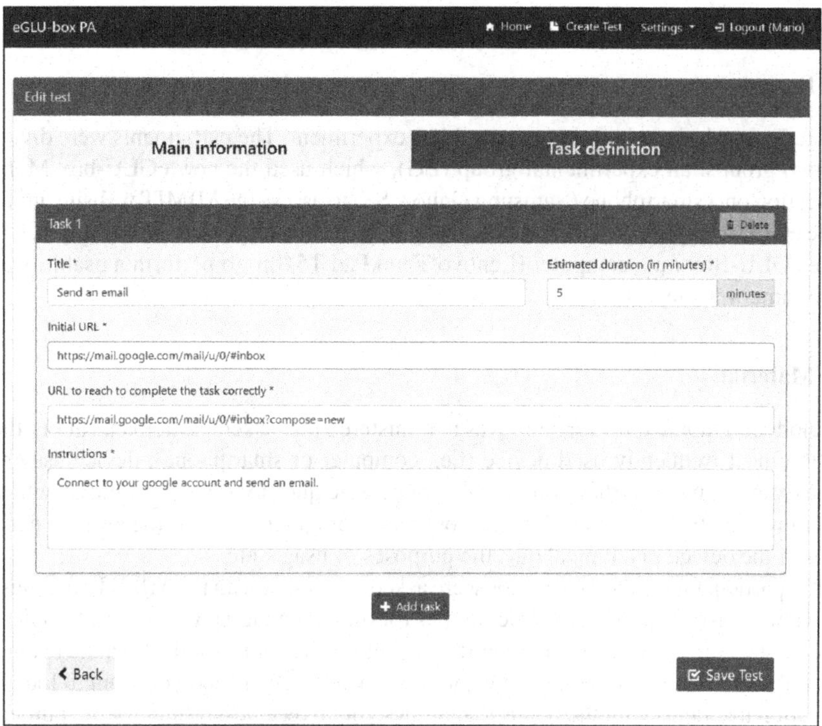

Fig. 1. A screenshot of eGLU-box (desktop version) showing the task creation screen. This figure shows an example created previously, in which the user-tester is asked to send an email via Gmail.

This study aims to evaluate the user experience with eGLU-box Mobile compared to the desktop version (eGLU-box), by observing users' implicit behaviors (eye movements) and explicit reactions (satisfaction, cognitive workload, and promotability) to the elements of this evaluation tool. The main goal was not to assess the usability of the specific interface through which participants carried out their tasks (i.e., the MIMIT website: https://www.mise.gov.it/), but to compare the experience of participants using the web and mobile versions of eGLU-box. As a semiautomatic assessment system, eGLU-Box was also designed to be used remotely by participants, with the application providing all the necessary instructions on the screen to allow participants to start and complete a usability test on their own.

2 Methods

2.1 Design

The study was designed as a between-subject experiment. The participants were divided into two groups: an experimental group (EG), which used the new eGLU-box Mobile application on a smartphone (Samsung Galaxy S8) to assess the MIMIT website, guided by the eGLU-box indications, and a control group (CG), which used the desktop version of the eGLU-Box on a computer (Lenovo ThinkPad T540p) to perform a usability test of the same website.

2.2 Material

A sociodemographic questionnaire was administered that asked participants about their age, the most frequently used device (i.e., computer or smartphone), device assigned by the experimenter. Furthermore, a series of generic questions were presented with the aim of investigating their use of smartphones and computers, such as the average period of use of the device in a typical day, the purposes of usage, etc.

The participants in the two groups were asked to interact with the MIMIT websites to achieve four tasks, which were structured as follows: (i) imagine you are the founder of a female start-up and you need to identify possible concessions for the "female business creation" category; (ii) imagine you want to buy a new vehicle and you want to look for the section that deals with the bonus that allows you to receive a refund for the purchase of low-emission vehicles; (iii) imagine you are the owner of a small farm that needs a supply of fuel, and you want to know its price; and (iv) imagine that you are the owner of a radio station that has been granted access to local broadcaster contributions, and you want to find a document containing a list of contribution amounts. All of the tasks had a maximum duration of 5 min.

After the interaction with the interface, three self-report questionnaires were administered in order to measure: (i) usability, through the SUS [7]; (ii) cognitive workload, through the Nasa Task Load Index (NASA TLX) [10]; and (iii) promotability, based on the NPS [9] for the eGLU-box application. The Partial Concurrent Thinking Aloud (PCTA) technique [11, 12] was used, in which participants were required to silently interact with the interface and ring a bell whenever they detected a problem; this bell represented a reminder signal, with the aim of aiding memorization of the moment at which the participant encountered the problem. The experimenter then needed to record what the participant was doing when the bell rang. As soon as the participant finished the test, they were invited to discuss and verbalize the problems encountered during the interaction [13]. Hence, at the end of the experimental procedure, a short interview was conducted in which the participant was asked how the interaction with the interface had gone in general, the reasons that had prompted them to ring the bell, and the observations they made regarding the application.

2.3 Participants

Forty-nine students attending the University of Perugia (eight males, 41 females) with an average age of 21.67 years (min = 18; max = 50; SD = 5.90) were recruited through social networks and academic mailing lists. A description of the sample can be seen in Table 1.

Table 1. Description of the sample, divided by sex and mean age

Group	Sex	N (%)	Mean age
Experimental	Male	4 (16.7%)	22.00
	Female	20 (83.3%)	21.60
	Total	24 (100%)	21.67
Control	Male	4 (16%)	21.50
	Female	21 (84%)	22.86
	Total	25 (100%)	23.20

In their answers to the sociodemographic questionnaire, 42 participants (85.7%) stated that they spent more time on a smartphone in a typical day, while seven (14.3%) declared that they spent more time on the computer. A total of 44 participants (89.9%) reported that they used a smartphone more often as a device for surfing the Internet, while five (10.2%) stated that they mainly used a computer for this. Twenty-two participants (44.9%) stated that they would feel more motivated to participate in an online questionnaire using a smartphone, while 27 (55.1%) said that they would prefer to use a computer. The answers to these questions can be viewed in Table 2.

Table 2. Questions about smartphone and computer use (responses from 49 participants)

Question	Answer	N (%)
In a typical day, which device do you spend more time on?	Smartphone	42 (85.7%)
	Computer	7 (14.3%)
In a typical day, which device do you use most often to search the internet?	Smartphone	44 (89.4%)
	Computer	5 (10.2%)
Which device would you be more motivated to use to participate in an experimental study (online questionnaire)?	Smartphone	22 (44.9%)
	Computer	27 (55.1%)

Participants were asked how much time they thought they spent on a smartphone and a computer in a typical day (Table 3). They reported using a smartphone between 2.5 and 3 h, while a computer was used between 1.5 and 2 h. When they were asked about their likelihood of agreeing to participate in an online study using a smartphone (Table 4), the data suggest that none of them would refuse to participate and all 44 would participate, whereas if they were asked to participate using a computer, one person would not participate and 43 would.

Table 3. Answers to the question: "How much time do you currently spend on your computer/smartphone in a typical day?" (responses from 49 participants)

Answer	Device	N (%)
None	Smartphone	0
	Computer	3 (6.1%)
Between 1 and 30 min a day	Smartphone	0
	Computer	5 (10.2%)
Between 60 (1 h) and 90 min (1 h 30 min)	Smartphone	6 (12.2%)
	Computer	8 (16.3%)
Between 90 min (1 h 30 min) and 120 min (2 h)	Smartphone	7 (14.3%)
	Computer	6 (12.2%)
Between 120 min (2 h) and 150 min (2 h 30 min)	Smartphone	6 (12.2%)
	Computer	7 (14.3%)
Between 150 min (2 h 30 min) and 180 min (3 h)	Smartphone	9 (18.4%)
	Computer	5 (10.2%)
Between 180 min (3 h) and 210 min (3 h 30 min)	Smartphone	5 (10.2%)
	Computer	5 (10.2%)
Between 210 min (3 h 30 min) and 240 min (4 h)	Smartphone	9 (18.4%)
	Computer	2 (4.1%)
More than 240 min (4 h)	Smartphone	7 (14.3%)
	Computer	5 (10.2%)

Table 4. Answers to the question: "How likely is it that you would accept an invitation to an experimental study (online questionnaire) using a computer/smartphone?" (responses from 49 participants)

Answer	Device	N (%)
Very unlikely	Smartphone	0
	Computer	0
Unlikely	Smartphone	0
	Computer	1 (2%)
Neutral	Smartphone	5 (10.2%)
	Computer	5 (10.2)
Likely	Smartphone	17 (34.7%)
	Computer	15 (30.6%)
Very likely	Smartphone	27 (55.1%)
	Computer	28 (57.1%)

2.4 Procedure

The experiment was conducted in a laboratory at the University of Perugia. The experimenter provided participants with a brief introduction to the study, randomly assigned each of them to a group (EG or CG), and assigned them an email for use in connecting to the eGLU-box. Eye-tracker calibration was performed only on participants in the CG at this time. The participants then opened the Qualtrics.xm (Provo, UT, USA) platform, via which the informed consent and the privacy policy were displayed and the sociodemographic questionnaire and the questionnaire on the frequency of smartphone and computer usage were administered. Next, the participants started to carry out the tasks through the eGLU-box platform. Before accessing the eGLU-box platform, eye-tracker calibration was performed for participants in the EG group. The tasks were the same for both groups, and eGLU-box guided participants to carry out these tasks on the MIMIT website. When these were complete, participants from both groups returned to Qualtrics to complete three self-report questionnaires (SUS, NASA TLX, and NPS) about the eGLU-box interface they had used to receive instructions, tasks and scenarios and to perform the overall assessment in a guided modality. Finally, participants were interviewed by an experimenter based on the PTCA procedure. Implicit data from eye movements were collected using a Tobii Pro Nano eye-tracker.

2.5 Data Analysis

The duration of the experiment with eGLU-box was calculated for all participants, and data from 11 participants were discarded as they were considered to be outliers. The time spent on navigation in eGLU-box was calculated by Qualtrics, using a widget that counted how much time the participant required before going to the next page. Although each participant was instructed to move to the next page only after completing the tasks in the eGLU-box, some proceeded before the task was concluded, and these data were not considered in the analysis. For this reason, the average navigation data may differ from those reported in the section on eye movement analysis. For the tasks in the eGLU-box, three possible outcomes were defined: (i) completed, i.e., the participant achieved the required goal; (ii) not completed, i.e., the participant did not reach the required goal; and (iii) missing, i.e., code problems with the eGLU-box application were encountered during the procedure (e.g., forced closure) that prevented execution, which allowed us to find possible bugs. The SUS results were transformed into grades [14, 15] ranging from F (absolutely unsatisfactory) to A + (absolutely satisfactory). Mann-Whitney U test was conducted to find a possible significant difference in the SUS results for the two groups (EG and CG), and the total score was used as the test variable. For the NPS questionnaire, the participants' scores were transformed to classify them as promoters (scores of nine or 10), passives (scores of seven or eight) and detractors (scores of between zero and six). The NPS is calculated as the percentage of promoters minus the percentage of detractors. Mann-Whitney U test was used to find a possible significant difference in the results obtained in the NPS questionnaire for the EG and CG, and the participants' responses were used as the test variable. For the NASA TLX, the Mann-Whitney U test was applied to find a possible significant difference in the final results of the scales for the two groups (EG and CG), and the total score for each scale was used as the test variable. The eye-tracking data were analyzed using Tobii Pro Lab software.

For the EG, which used a smartphone, a mobile testing accessory (MTA) was used to ensure the tracking and collection of eye movement data. The implicit measures analyzed were the area of interest (AOI), mean webpage observation time, and ocular fixation (with a threshold set to ≥ 50 ms). To perform the analyses, data from participants with a gaze sample percentage of greater than or equal to 75% were used. Eye movement data were analyzed for only 12 participants from the EG, as only these met the requirements. The mean values for the number of fixations and time of visualization of the AOIs were analyzed. AOIs were inserted by the Tobii Pro Lab software. Eye movement data were analyzed only during the interaction with the elements of eGLU-box. In the analysis phase, five AOIs were identified for the mobile application, and eight for the desktop application (see Fig. 2).

IBM SPSS version 27 software was used for analysis of the questionnaire data, and Tobii Pro Lab software version 1.207 was used for the eye movement data.

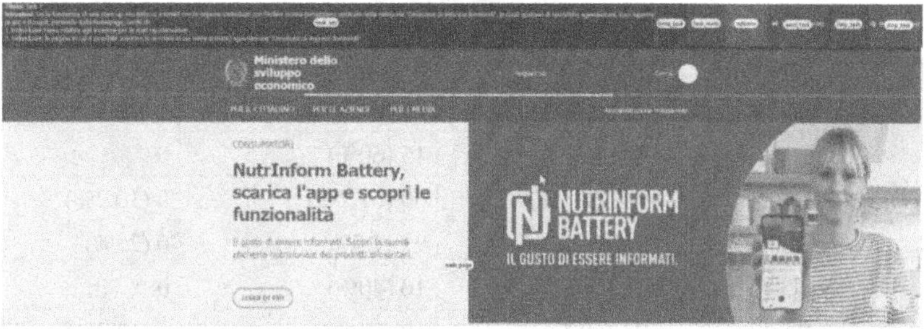

Fig. 2. Visualization of the eGLU-box platform: (a) smartphone mode; (b) computer mode. Both screens show the AOIs as colored squares or rectangles.

3 Results

3.1 Participants' Performance

On average, each participant took 6 min to complete the eGLU-box tasks, with a minimum time of 5 min and a maximum of 11 min. Of the 38 participants, 20 were allocated to the EG that used the smartphone. On average, the participants in the EG spent 6 min, with a minimum time of 5 min and a maximum of 11 min. The CG consisted of 18 participants, who used a computer to perform the tasks. On average, the participants in the CG spent 6 min, with a minimum time of 5 min and a maximum of 9 min. Mann-Whitney U test was conducted to determine whether there was a difference in the total time spent to perform tasks in eGLU-box between the two groups (EG and CG). The results indicate non-significant difference ($U = 123$, $p = .096$). A regression analysis of task achievement suggested that there were no significant differences between the EG and CG in terms of success or failure in achieving the tasks. Table 5 summarizes the performance of the participants in the two groups for each task, including missing data. On average, 40.8% of participants succeeded in carrying out the four tasks, 48.8% failed, and in about 10.7% of the cases there was a technical issue.

Table 5. Percentages of tasks completed by participants in the experimental (EG) and control (CG) groups

Task	Group	Completed	Not completed	Missing
Task 1	EG	0	18 (75%)	6 (25%)
	CG	2 (8%)	23 (92%)	0
	Total	2 (4.1%)	41 (83.7%)	6 (12.2%)
Task 2	EG	17 (70.8%)	3 (12.5%)	4 (16.7%)
	CG	23 (92%)	2 (8%)	0
	Total	40 (81.6%)	5 (10.2%)	4 (8.2%)
Task 3	EG	4 (16.7%)	15 (62.5%)	5 (20.8%)
	CG	10 (40%)	15 (60%)	0
	Total	14 (28.6%)	30 (61.2%)	5 (10.2%)
Task 4	EG	9 (37.5%)	9 (37.5%)	6 (25%)
	CG	15 (60%)	10 (40%)	0
	Total	24 (49%)	19 (38.8%)	6 (12.2%)

3.2 PCTA Interview

In the CG, 17 participants rang the bell, with a total of 22 events. However, the difficulties reported were related less to the functioning of the platform than to the difficulty of completing the tasks requested within the tested website. In fact, only two of 22 events were related to critical issues regarding the procedure, and these were particularly associated with the difficulty of understanding the requests made in one of the questionnaires (NASA-TLX). In the EG, 17 participants rang the bell, with a total of 38 events. In this case, most of the events concerned a malfunction or critical aspects of the application. Specifically, of these 38 events, three were related to the non-functioning of the hyperlinks in the tasks set by the application. In one event, the application crashed at the start of one of the tasks, requiring the user to close and reopen it. In 15 events, the participants complained that they could not read the task instructions again when they were doing it. Of these subjects, none had clicked on the button marked with the current task number, which would have displayed the instructions. Instead, the button these subjects had clicked was the one marked "?", as they expected to be able to see the instructions from there. In one event, it was reported that the participant expected to be shown the on-screen instructions again each time he performed one of the requested tasks. Another event occurred when a participant exited the application by mistake. By clicking on the icon again, the participant could restart the task they were carrying out; however, the timer did not restart from the point where it left off, and it was necessary to click on the task number to make the instructions reappear and then resume the task, with the timer restarting from 5 min. Nine of the events referred to difficulties in completing the tasks requested for the website. In one event, the instructions did not disappear from the screen even though the 5-min timer had started, making it impossible to start the task. In two events, the exact opposite occurred, i.e., the task began without the 5-min timer starting. In one event, it was not possible to move from one task to the next after communicating to the application whether or not the previous task had been completed successfully. Another participant complained that in the top bar, the application showed an excessive number of stimuli that were confusing while carrying out the tasks. In a further event, it was recommended to change the way the application works. Instead of having the participant press the button to finish the task, the application should itself show a message on the screen when the participant has reached the goal and thus finished the task. Finally, two events involved a sudden crash of the application, which required the participant to log in again and start the test from the beginning.

3.3 Usability Questionnaire

System Usability Scale (SUS). The results for the SUS questionnaire showed an average score of 63.78, with a minimum of 25.00, a maximum of 87.50 and a standard deviation of 14.43. The mean value for the EG was 58.02, with a minimum of 25.00, a maximum of 87.50 and a standard deviation of 14.28, while the mean value for the CG was 69.30, with a minimum of 40.00, a maximum of 87.50 and a standard deviation of 12.49. Mann-Whitney U test between the EG and CG showed a significant difference ($U = 160$, $p = .005$), meaning that these participants found it more satisfying to use eGLU-box from a computer than a smartphone. In the EG, eight participants (33.3%) were assigned Grade F, eight participants (33.3%) were assigned Grade D, four participants (16.7%) were assigned Grade C, one (4.2%) was assigned Grade C+, one (4.2%) was assigned Grade B, one (4.2%) was assigned Grade A−, and one (4.2%) was assigned Grade A+. In the CG, two participants (8%) were assigned Grade F, six (24%) were assigned Grade D, four (16.7%) were assigned Grade C, three (12%) were assigned grade C+, two (8%) were assigned grade B, one (4%) was assigned grade B+, two (8%) were assigned grade A−, three (12%) were assigned grade A, and two (8%) were assigned grade A+. Figure 3 shows a graph of the data divided based on the device used.

NASA TLX. The NASA TLX results showed the following weighted average values for the six scales: mental 210.20, physical 15.83, temporal 155.26, performance 124.48, effort 128.85, frustration 95.57. For the EG, the results for the weighted average values were: mental 214.37, physical 1.66, temporal 140, performance 144.37, effort 108.95 and frustration 95.41. For the CG, the results for the weighted average values were: mental 206.20, physical 2.20, temporal 101.60, performance 100.40, effort 142.80, frustration 76.60. For each scale, the Mann-Whitney U test was applied to identify a difference between the two groups. The results were not significant for any of the scales.

Net Promoter Score. At a general level, 25 detractors (51.0%), 20 passive (40.8%) and four promoters (8.2%) were identified, giving a final value for the NPS of −42.8. In the EG, 15 detractors (62.5%), eight neutrals (33.3%) and one promoter (4.2%) were identified, with an NPS value of −58.3. In the CG, 10 detractors (40%), 12 neutral (48%), and three promoters (12%) were found, giving an NPS value of −28. The data suggest that the participants would be more likely to recommend the desktop version over the smartphone version, although neither of the results were very high. Figure 4 shows the

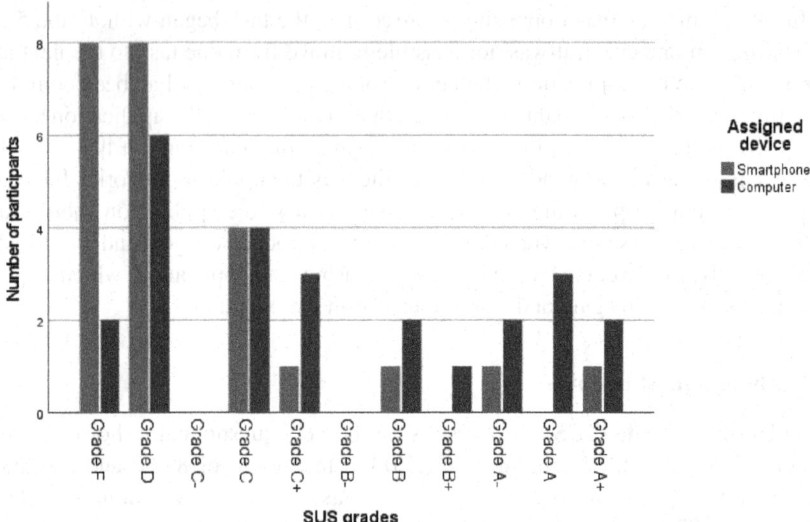

Fig. 3. Graph showing the number of participants with each grade on the SUS questionnaire. Participants were divided based on the device assigned, i.e., smartphone (EG) and computer (CG).

percentages of detractors, passives, and promoters for each device. Mann-Whitney U test was applied to the NPS scores for the CG and the EG, but no significant difference was found.

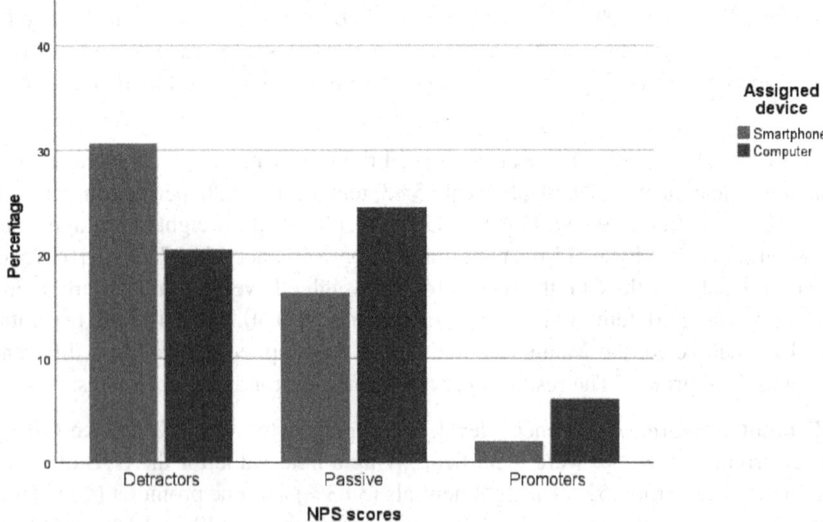

Fig. 4. Graph showing the percentages of detractors, passives, and promoters for each device, i.e., smartphone (EG) and computer (CG).

3.4 Eye Movement Analysis

Several AOIs were inserted for the smartphone device: one in the application bar, one around the help button, one around the button used to go to the next task, one around the exit button, and finally, one around the task button, which showed the time remaining and the task instructions if it was clicked. In the computer version, the following AOIs were inserted: one in the bar where the task instructions were displayed, one where the remaining time was visible, one around the task number button, one around the options button, one around the button to switch to the next task, one around the help button, one around the exit button, and finally, one around the web page. Participants looked at the webpage screen for an average of 11 min, with an average of 3,311 fixations. The eGLU-box bar was viewed for a mean total of 20 s, with a mean of 68 fixations. The exit button was viewed for only 2 s on average, with an average total of six fixations, while the help button was viewed for an average of 4 s and an average of 14 fixations. The next task button was looked at for an average of 3 s and an average number of fixations of 10, while the task number button was viewed for an average of 8 s and an average of 30 fixations.

All data from the CG met the requirement to be included in the analyses. CG participants looked at the web page for an average of 12 min with an average of 2,595 fixations. The help button was viewed for an average of 1 s with an average of three fixations. The button used to move to the next task was looked at for an average of 5 s with an average of 13 fixations, while the options button was viewed for an average of 3 s with an average of 12 fixations. The exit button was looked at for an average of 1 s and an average of two fixations, and the task instructions button was looked at for an average of 2 min and an average of 316 fixations. The task number button was looked at for an average of 4 s and an average of 14 fixations, whereas the time remaining button was viewed for an average of 4 s and an average of 14 fixations.

4 Discussion and Conclusion

In this study, we have reported pilot data from the development of eGLU-box Mobile, a version of eGLU-box for Android and iOS systems. This was designed to guide a PA webmaster to perform a semiautomatic evaluation directly from a smartphone. The aim of this study was to evaluate the user experience with eGLU-box Mobile compared to the desktop version (eGLU-box), by observing users' implicit (eye movement) and explicit (satisfaction, cognitive workload, and promotability) behaviors. From the results of the questionnaires, it can be seen that that the two applications are interchangeable.

Most participants (90%) reported spending more time interacting with a smartphone than a computer, even when browsing the Internet. In regard to which device they would be more motivated to use to answer a web questionnaire, the participants expressed a greater preference for computers (55.1%), but smartphones also achieved a significant proportion of the vote (44.9%). The same result was found when we asked how likely they would be to agree to participate in a study with a smartphone or a computer. The results were very similar and positive, indicating that a good percentage would agree to participate in both cases. It therefore seems that the participants are inclined to use smartphones as well as computers.

For the tasks performed using eGLU-box, a regression analysis did not reveal significant differences between the EG and CG participants in terms of success or failure. This indicates that both applications allow for correct use of the product. Furthermore, the results from the NPS and NASA TLX questionnaires were shown to be fairly similar, and the Mann-Whitney U test showed no significant differences between the participants in the EG and CG. This suggests that both applications gave the same results in terms of both promotability and cognitive load. Only the results of the SUS questionnaire were different, and the Mann-Whitney U test showed that the results were statistically significant. In this case, better results were found for those who had performed the tasks from the computer (CG) in terms of satisfaction with using the application.

From the PCTA interview, we discovered that one of the problems with the smartphone application may have been related to the absence of a button that clearly indicated where to find the task instructions, as these are clearly visible in the desktop application without the need to click anything. It could be deduced from the average viewing data for the AOIs that the participants in the CG looked at the area showing the instructions for the task more often, while the smartphone group almost never looked at these. This may be because it was not clear to the participants that clicking the task number button would also display the instructions. We can conclude that although the new application can be officially launched, there is still a need to make some improvements to the usability and satisfaction, such as the implementation of a clearer button that allows the user to read the task instructions again.

This study has some limitations that should be highlighted, such as the size of the sample, the homogeneity of the sample in terms of gender, and the limitations imposed by the collection of eye movements for mobile devices. For participants in the EG, recording of eye data started at the moment they logged into the eGLU-box application, while for CG participants eye data recording started immediately after device assignment. A decision was made to proceed in this way because data collection from a smartphone is much less sensitive than from a computer, which requires that the participant does not move from the position in which the calibration was performed. Therefore, in order not to require too much effort from the participants, it was decided to record the eye movements only in the part of our interest, i.e., when the eGLU-box was being used. However, this required the participant to stop the test to calibrate the eye-tracker. This procedure was not carried out for the CG, in which calibration was performed at the beginning of the experiment. This was because the sensitivity of the eye-tracker when using a computer is very high and the participant must remain motionless. It is also necessary to consider that the smartphone experiment was much more stressful than the computer one, since the capture of eye movements is much more rigid in this mode and the participant must move as little as possible.

In future studies, we intend to expand the sample size, and to include not only students but also the rest of the population.

References

1. Oulasvirta, A., Rattenbury, T., Ma, L., Raita, E.: Habits make smartphone use more pervasive. Pers. Ubiquit. Comput. **16**, 105–114 (2011). https://doi.org/10.1007/s00779-011-0412-2

2. Federici, S., et al.: Heuristic evaluation of eGLU-box: a semi-automatic usability evaluation tool for public administrations. In: Kurosu, M. (ed.) HCII 2019. LNCS, vol. 11566, pp. 75–86. Springer, Cham (2019). https://doi.org/10.1007/978-3-030-22646-6_6
3. AGID (Agenzia per l'Italia Digitale): Linee guida di design per i servizi web della pubblica amministrazione. AGID, Rome, IT (2022)
4. Desolda, G., Gaudino, G., Lanzilotti, R., Federici, S., Cocco, A.: UTAssistant: a web platform supporting usability testing in Italian public administrations. In: 12th Edition of CHItaly: CHItaly 2017, pp. 138–142 (2017)
5. Federici, S., Mele, M.L., Bracalenti, M., Buttafuoco, A., Lanzilotti, R., Desolda, G.: Bio-behavioral and self-report user experience evaluation of a usability assessment platform (UTAssistant). In: VISIGRAPP 2019: Proceedings of the 14th International Joint Conference on Computer Vision, Imaging and Computer Graphics Theory and Applications. Volume 2: HUCAPP, pp. 19–27 (2019)
6. Federici, S., et al.: UX evaluation design of UTAssistant: a new usability testing support tool for Italian public administrations. In: Kurosu, M. (ed.) HCI 2018. LNCS, vol. 10901, pp. 55–67. Springer, Cham (2018). https://doi.org/10.1007/978-3-319-91238-7_5
7. Borsci, S., Federici, S., Lauriola, M.: On the dimensionality of the System Usability Scale (SUS): a test of alternative measurement models. Cogn. Process. **10**, 193–197 (2009). https://doi.org/10.1007/s10339-009-0268-9
8. Lewis, J.R., Utesch, B.S., Maher, D.E.: UMUX-Lite: when there's no time for the SUS. In: Conference on Human Factors in Computing Systems: CHI 2013, pp. 2099–2102 (2013). https://doi.org/10.1145/2470654.2481287
9. Reichheld, F.F.: The one number you need to grow. Harv. Bus. Rev. **82**, 133 (2004)
10. Hart, S.G., Staveland, L.E.: Development of NASA-TLX (task load index): results of empirical and theoretical research. In: Hancock, P.A., Meshkati, N. (eds.) Human Mental Workload, pp. 139–184. North-Holland, Amsterdam (1988)
11. Federici, S., Borsci, S., Mele, M.L.: Usability evaluation with screen reader users: a video presentation of the PCTA'S experimental setting and rules. Cogn. Process. **11**, 285–288 (2010). https://doi.org/10.1007/s10339-010-0365-9
12. Borsci, S., Federici, S.: The partial concurrent thinking aloud: a new usability evaluation technique for blind users. In: Emiliani, P.L., Burzagli, L., Como, A., Gabbanini, F., Salminen, A.-L. (eds.) Assistive Technology from Adapted Equipment to Inclusive Environments: AAATE 2009, vol. 25, pp. 421–425. IOS Press, Amsterdam (2009). https://doi.org/10.3233/978-1-60750-042-1-421
13. Borsci, S., Kurosu, M., Federici, S., Mele, M.L.: Computer systems experiences of users with and without disabilities: an evaluation guide for professionals. CRC Press, Boca Raton (2013). https://doi.org/10.1201/b15619-1
14. Borsci, S., Federici, S., Bacci, S., Gnaldi, M., Bartolucci, F.: Assessing user satisfaction in the era of user experience: comparison of the SUS, UMUX and UMUX-Lite as a function of product experience. Int. J. Hum.-Comput. Interact. **31**, 484–495 (2015). https://doi.org/10.1080/10447318.2015.1064648
15. Sauro, J., Lewis, J.R.: Quantifying the User Experience: Practical Statistics for User Research. Morgan Kaufmann, Burlington (2012)

MobE – A New Approach to Mobile Ethnography

Jan Haentjes[(✉)], Andreas Klein, Viola Manz, Johanna Gegg, and Sarah Ehrlich

Spiegel Institut Mannheim GmbH, 80807 München, Germany
info@spiegel-institut.de
https://www.spiegel-institut.de/en

Abstract. This paper presents a novel approach in ethnographical research by using an app with gamification elements (MobE), to gain insights into users' behavior and needs. The presented app allows numerous documentation options, such as various question formats, text, voice inputs and the recording of videos. For researchers it contains an environment to give participants feedback in real-time. MobE accompanies the study-progress through gamification by using coins and level upgrades as rewards. This has the effect to reduce mobile ethnography' inherent disadvantage, that the participants' motivation can be poorly controlled. This article also contains an evaluation of the app, which was carried out by a field study with the research on truckers' activities. The evaluation included usability aspects, motivational factors, and the subjects' interest in the topic of gamification. In addition, research with the app was compared to a classical contextual interview. The evaluation showed a generally positive experience with MobE by participants. Participants perceived the gamification elements as positive and encouraging. Surveying the truckers was difficult due to their context. The comparison showed that the contextual interview generated more data than the MobE-App. The latter proving easier in deployment, while still generating sufficient information to draw statistically significant conclusions. Application of MobE-App combined with a contextual interview in a mixed methods approach are discussed to combine both advantages. Finally, through development and research with MobE, further insights could be gained that contribute to research in the ethnographic field.

Keywords: Mobile Ethnography · Gamification · User Survey · Evaluation Methods and Techniques

1 Mobile Ethnography

Ethnography is one of the most common approaches in market research (Koschel, 2018; Muskat et al., 2018). It's spectrum of research methods ranges from direct methods, such as interviews to indirect methods like participant observations (Spittler, 2001). Mobile ethnography is an emerging approach, in which data are gained with the help of mobile devices, such as smartphones and tablets (Bosio, 2017; Koschel, 2018; Muskat et al., 2018). It supersedes a central property of previous research methods - the presence of an investigator on site (Beddall-Hill et al., 2011 and Koschel, 2018). In addition,

M. Kurosu and A. Hashizume (Eds.): HCII 2023, LNCS 14011, pp. 80–92, 2023.
https://doi.org/10.1007/978-3-031-35596-7_6

it facilitates conducting a large number of surveys in parallel, which has economic advantages (Koschel, 2018). For many industries, such as tourism, health or retail, mobile ethnography significantly reduces the cost of costumer surveys (Bosio, 2017; Muskat et al., 2018; Koschel, 2018; Schlemmer et al., 2022). In addition to economic benefits, mobile ethnography enables participants to explore environments on their own thereby providing a new perspective by limiting the influence of researchers on participants (Berger, 2015; Bosio, 2017; Muskat et al., 2018).

To generate data efficiently, various mobile applications are often used to conduct studies. These apps enable participants to document their everyday experience using video, audio, or text (Bosio, 2017; Schlemmer, 2022). Specifically, apps such as 'Indeemo' (Insightplatforms, 2023), 'Field notes' (Fieldnotescommunities, 2023) or 'Over The Shoulder' (Schlesingergroup, 2023) offer photo-, video or audio-sharing functions, screen recording functions for capturing user's behavior on online websites, or geo-location triggers and tagging. Various tools for ethnographic research, combining with different qualitative research methods are also available.

A key element for the success of mobile ethnographic research is the participants' willingness to provide the necessary data. Studies show that the results and completeness of collected data in ethnographic studies are highly dependent on the motivation of the participants, which is difficult to control (Koschel, 2018). Therefore, providing this data needs to be as easy as possible for participants. In addition, entertaining elements can help to keep users engaged.

In recent years, gamification became a valid approach to convey information and increase the engagement of participants during the conduction of studies (Nacke & Deterding, 2017; Rapp et al., 2019).

Through achievable levels and coins, the MobE-App accompanies the study-progress through gamification, which should encourage the participants.

In this context, the use of gamification in mobile ethnography apps is little known and will be focused on through this approach.

2 MobE – An Application for Ethnographic Research

The MobE-App was designed by Spiegel Institut. In the field of ethnographic research, special emphasis was given to usage of context analysis, as well as generating insights into participants' behavior and needs at minimal cost. With its set of functions, it can additionally be deployed for various use cases, such as diary instrument, interactive or quantitative surveys, and short photo- or video-documentations. Compared to a classic contextual interview, Spiegel Institut expects to receive more direct impressions from various contexts, not filtered by an investigator or limited by the time or location of one interview. Special emphasis lay on gamification elements that should motivate participants to highly contribute to the survey for a certain period.

When opening the MobE-App for the first time, some short intro screens are presented, as well as a registration- or log-in-interface. Users can register themselves and can choose a username, which is used for further interaction with investigator and other participants. The app offers four main areas of interaction (Studien, Shorties, Chat and Fortschritt) in the tap bar at the bottom edge of the screen (see Fig. 1).

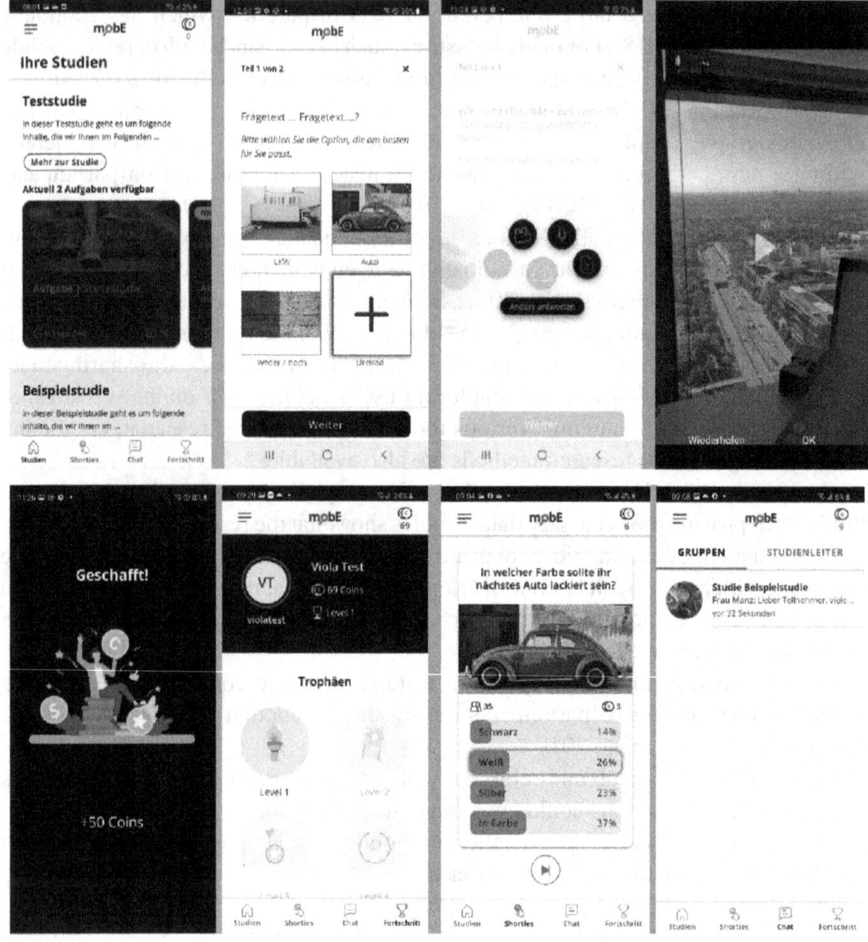

Fig. 1. Screenshots of the survey app MobE

Studien (Studies): Core element is the area "Studien" ("studies"). There, users have an overview of studies they were invited to. In every study, participants see tasks in the form of tiles. They can edit tasks, pause, and continue later. All tasks are either visible at first sight or appear a certain time after the first task has been edited. One task can consist of one or several pages. The pages can show various content elements: questions with classical quantitative answer types (single choice, multiple choice, multi-level scales, open text-fields, dial for numbers, image selection batteries) as well as central elements for uploading videos, photos, files, and voice inputs.

Fortschritt (Progress): As the app focuses on elements of gamification it puts value on an appealing look and feel. Participants shall have fun using the app. For this purpose, coins and experience points for level up can be assigned to each task by the investigator.

Participants can see their status on coins and levels in the area "Fortschritt" ("progress"). Here they have a user profile with their chosen username.

Shorties: Another central gamification element are the "Shorties", the third interaction area in the tap bar. These are short questions with maximum four answer options. The questions can be relevant for study but do not have to. After answering one shortie, participants promptly see how previous participants have answered.

Chat: Finally, the fourth and the last central area, "Chat", allows interaction among the study participants in one group channel per study. The participants can also interact with the investigator in the same channel. Here the investigator can follow up to the participant's answers or uploaded media.

Push notifications are implemented to prompt the usage of the app. Notifications can be set for new studies, new tasks, and new messages from the chat channels. Also, when the study is going to close, push notifications will be sent to inform participants about their last chance to finish their open tasks. The MobE-App is administrated via a web interface. Here the investigator can create studies and tasks, download survey data, and manage the participants. Through the second web interface, "RocketChat", the investigator has access to all chat channels.

To explore potential opportunities of the newly designed research app MobE, questions arose to what extend the app can serve as a validated survey tool. The following research questions were set:

> *Research question 1:* Are the participants motivated by the gamification elements of the app?

This question looks at motivation and satisfaction in general, as well as to what the individual gamification elements, such as the reward character, the shorties, the look, and the feel of the app made the study more enjoyable and increased engagement. Furthermore, the coins and levels were used to create a competition among the participants. The top three were rewarded an increased participation fee. Thus, gamification increased the stakes for participants. Coins and levels were one small criteria among others contributing to the "quality of participation", like length and meaningfulness of the answers.

> *Research question 2:* How easily can participants use the app in their daily lives? Are there any technical issues?

As this was the first trial for the newly designed app, the suitability of the app for research in everyday use should be investigated. Unexpected bugs could occur, possibly influencing the results.

> *Research question 3:* What are the advantages and disadvantages of the app compared to a contextual interview in terms of the quantity and quality of the results and the cost of deployment?

A comparison between the MobE-App and a classical contextual interview should also be carried out, since both approaches promise their advantages and disadvantages (Koschel, 2018). Hence, it should be evaluated if and to what extent the absence of the interviewer would lead to possibly less or poorer answers, and how clear the interpretation of these answers seemed to be.

3 Evaluation Methods and Test Procedure

For evaluation a contextual interview and a mobile ethnographic study using the MobE-App were conducted. The questions for both studies overlapped to ensure comparability of results. For evaluation, everyday tasks of truck drivers should be investigated. Data generated therein were transferred into a trucker activity summary. To compare the answers obtained from both studies, the number of entries and words per entry were counted and served as criteria. In the survey with MobE-App, participants were additionally asked about their experience of using the app in the end. Questions related to daily tasks of truckers can arise before, after or during a day. Topics included for example registration, loading, unloading and preparation.

3.1 Study 1: Mobile Ethnographic Study

Initially truckers were given smartphones with the installed MobE-App. Four participants started the survey on 26th of April, 2021 and three participants started on 27th of April, 2021. In MobE, questions and different topics for documentation were displayed in a fixed order. Before performing the tasks, each participant first went through the tutorial screens of the app to be informed about the meaning of the coins for each uploaded task. That is, one can rise in further levels after sufficient coins are collected by completing the tasks. Participants could record their observations with video, audio or text. By default, feedback was set via voice record, but participants had the choice to switch into recording with video or text. After having worked with the app for quite a while, participants were asked about their experience with MobE and the gamification elements with likert-scale items and open interview-questions. Ten participants were invited to this study. Three participants did not start the study after registration. One participant dropped out after half the study. Therefore, the final sample of the ethnographic interview consisted of $n = 7$ participants with an average age of 44.4 ($SD = 3.25$) with a range from 36 to 54 years. Six of the participants were male, one of the participants was female. The total duration of study was 14 days. After eleven days the participants got new tasks requiring 10 to maximum 30 min editing time each day. The tasks covered different fields of interest starting with the daily work routine to specific truck related questions.

3.2 Study 2: Contextual Interview

In the contextual interview, topics were observed by an interviewer on site. The interviews were conducted between 16th of June 2021 and 22nd of July 2021. The order of questions was changed dependent on the current situation of the truck drivers. The interview was conducted on a single day for a total duration of approximately eight hours. A total of $n = 10$ respondents were interviewed for the contextual interview. The sample was exclusively male. The subjects were aged between 26 and 54 with an average age of 40.4 years ($SD = 10.06$).

3.3 Results

In Study 2, three out of ten participants did not start the study after the registration process. The three participants were classic non-starters: One did not want to use the app because felt too complicated for him, one did not want to spend 30 min editing time per day, one just dropped out of the study without any further explanation.

Research question 1: Are the participants motivated by the gamification elements of the app? Conclusions of questions about gamification elements are summarized in the following bullet-points. Table 1 below shows questions in detail:

- Truckers were overall satisfied with the use of the app (1, 2, 3, 4).
- App's gamification elements such as coins, levelling up and viewing answers from other participants' shorties were rated as positive and interesting (5, 6, 7).
- Interest in gamification varied among the participants (5, 6).
- Effect on participants' motivation by the app overall was modest (8).
- Effect on participants' motivation by the gamification elements was modest (9).
- The motivation due to the competitive situation was average (10).

Table 1. Summary of rating-questions for research question 1

No.	Question	Means (1–5)	Median
1	How satisfied are you overall with the survey app mobE?	3.25 (*SD* = 1.09)	3.5
2	Using the app as a whole is fun	3.25 (*SD* = 1.09)	4
3	Answering shorties is fun	3.88 (*SD* = 1.27)	4
4	Using the app while answering tasks is fun	3.13 (*SD* = 1.05)	3.5
5	I like the fact that I get coins for completing tasks and can level up	3.63 (*SD* = 1.58)	4
6	It was interesting for me to see what other people answered to the shortie questions	3.38 (*SD* = 1.5)	4
7	The progress section with the overview of my collected coins and earned levels was interesting for me	2.88 (*SD* = 1.17)	3
8	Overall design of the app (structure, functions, look and feel) motivated me to actively participate in the survey	3.29 (*SD* = 0.7)	3
9	The reward character of the app (coins, levels) motivated me to actively participate in the survey	3.29 (*SD* = 1.03)	3
10	The announced competition (the three best study participants receive additional money) motivated me to actively participate in the survey	2.86 (*SD* = 1.25)	2

SD = Standard Derivation, *Rating*: 1 = completely disagree, 5 = completely agree.

Research question 2: How easily can participants use the app in their daily lives? Are there any technical issues? Conclusions of questions concerning the user experience are summarized in the following bullet points. Below, tables show questions in detail (see Tables 2 and 3) and experience with the technical functionality of MobE is summarized.

Table 2. Summary of rating-questions for research question 2

No.	Question	Means (1–5)	Median
1	I answered tasks in the app during my working	2.5 (*SD* = 1.22)	3
2	I used breaks to answer tasks in the app	2.5 (*SD* = 1.12)	2.5
3	I have completed tasks in the app before or after my working day	3.75 (*SD* = 0.97)	4
4	When I completed tasks during work doing so disrupted my workflow	2.25 (*SD* = 0.83)	2.5
5	When I completed tasks during work answering did not disrupt my workflow	3.8 (*SD* = 0.98)	3

SD = Standard Derivation, *Rating*: 1 = completely disagree, 5 = completely agree.

- Some truckers used the app seldom at work but rather before and after work. Thus, the app appears to be not ideally suited for documentation during a trucker's workday (1, 2, 3, 6).
- Some truckers were able to integrate the app in their workflow. When they used the app during work, it did not interrupt their workflow (4, 5).
- Half of the truckers would use the app again but would prefer a face-to-face interview in an upcoming study (7, 8).
- Some truckers were reluctant to send voice messages and preferred to use text messages (9).

Table 3. Summary of qualitative questions for research question 2

No.	Question	Answers (n)
6	Was/would it in principle be allowed/possible for you to document situations "live" at your workplace through photos, videos, voice messages?	Yes (1) No (4)
7	Would you personally participate in such a smartphone-based survey again?	Yes (3) No (3)
8	If you had the choice next time to participate in this survey via smartphone or alternatively to be accompanied and interviewed by an interviewer in your vehicle for a day: How would you choose?	Interview (4) App (1)
9	[If "answer differently" was mostly chosen] You preferred the option "text input" in "answer differently" instead of sending voice recordings. Why do you prefer text input?	Felt more comfortable (3)

Technical Functionality of MobE During Evaluation. The beta of MobE contained some technical limitations. During evaluation, MobE did not store data without an internet connection. As a result, two truckers reported some data loss. Therefore, when no constant connection was available, participants were asked to record videos and audios first with other applications and upload to the app later on. Participants were also asked to record videos no longer than one minute each, when recording via the app. Sometimes, some accidental logouts occurred while using the app. Therefore, some participants had to ask for a new password and were interrupted in their research for this time.

Research question 3: What are the advantages and disadvantages of the app compared to a contextual interview in terms of the quantity and quality of the results and the cost of deployment? To answer this research question, the number of entries and words per entries were counted and compared. In addition, the time deployed for conducting the interview and the app-survey are summarized.

Mean Number of Entries. For the participant observations of trucker activities, the number of entries per work section had a mean of 6 ($SD = 2.18$) entries. The app survey showed fewer entries per work section ($M = 4.28$, $SD = 2.64$). The following diagram depicts the individual mean values of entries per work phase. Especially for tasks during the working day, such as during the trip, loading and unloading there seem to be even more entries from face-to-face interview as from mobile ethnography. For tasks outside the trip, this difference seems to be lower (Fig. 2).

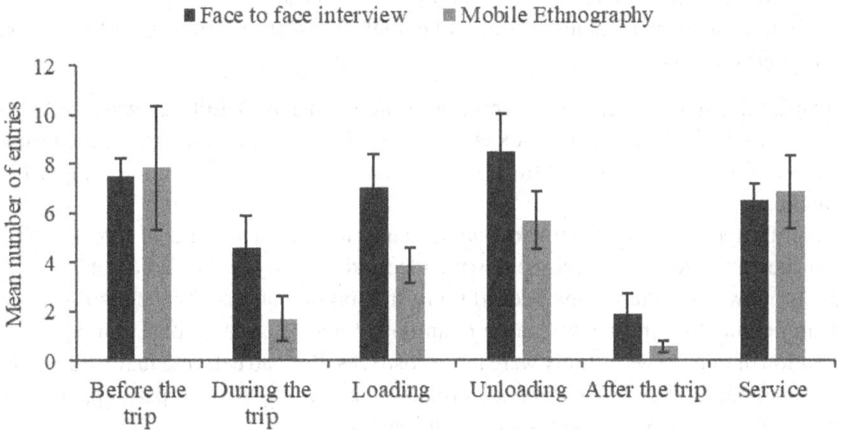

Fig. 2. Mean number of entries per work section, compared between two methods.

Mean Number of Words Per Entry. In the trucker surveys, the number of words per entry had an average of 40.31 ($SD = 20.38$) words for the contextual interview. The entries of the app surveys had fewer words on average ($M = 24.86$, $SD = 13.96$). As with the number of entries, there is a tendency for the differences to be higher especially during the working day (Fig. 3).

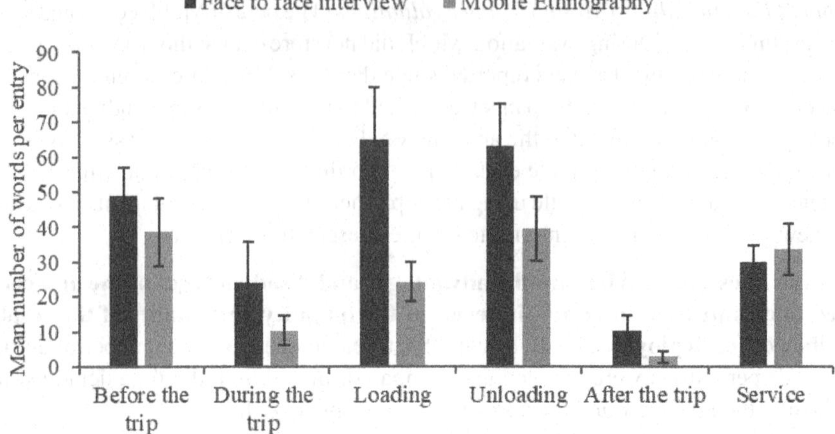

Fig. 3. Mean number of words per work section, compared between two methods.

Effort in Preparation, Conduction, and Evaluation of Mobile Ethnographic Study. As MobE was not available in app-stores or iOS yet, separate smartphones with an installed MobE-App were provided. All in all, the MobE-study needed more preparation than the interview. This includes preparation of mobile phones, as various accounts and SIM-cards had to be set up and the formulation of unambiguous instructions, that can be understood without an interviewer. In comparison, conducting the personal interview was less time-intensive because order and explanations of questions could be adapted by the interviewer on site.

During the study, interviews were more time intensive. A full day was needed per interview, as the interview itself took eight hours and additional time was needed for the researcher for travelling. In contrast, the app survey required only limited input from researchers.

Overall, the data quality of text-, audio- and video output gathered through MobE was sufficient. Questions could be downloaded individually or as a complete package. Data output was structured and needed no further modifications. As seen in the results, by using contextual interviews, more quantitative and qualitative data can be gained. Evaluation of interviews initially were more costly, as they had to be manually transcribed and formatted. However, the data gathered was less ambiguous as participants' body language and facial expressions added additional texture.

4 Discussion

Results show that through the MobE-App a database could be assembled. Further, the app was predominantly rated as positive and motivating by the truckers. Some truckers were able to integrate participation in the study into their working routine, others conducted the surveys before and after their working day. Minor technical issues might have slightly reduced the number of responses gathered through the app. Further, the significance of the small sample must be treated with caution.

4.1 Gamification

Applicated gamification elements such as the shorties, coins and levels were rated as positive. Perceived motivation, as described by participants, varied between "modest" and "good". These tendencies are in line with literature that gamification has positive effects on motivation. Therefore, it can be concluded that gamification constitutes a valid addition to surveys with mobile ethnography, as it maintains or improves motivation of participants (Nacke & Deterding, 2017; Rapp et al., 2019). As in the literature, there is a tendency for users to evaluate gamification differently (Kim, 2015; Santos et al., 2021). For some it increases their engagement, whereas for other's it has little to no impact.

Without technical issues the impact on motivation would likely have been even higher. Similarly, an easier integration in the work environment would have further increased gamification's positive effect on engagement. Thus, it is advised to repeat the study with an improved beta version and in a more suitable work environment. In addition, a direct comparison with an app version without gamification could further clarify the effect of gamification.

The competitive part was assessed as average and wasn't perceived as predominantly positive. One explanation for this could be that truckers might not think the competition fair, as participants cover different areas, such as construction or long-haul, and they thus elect not to engage. To test this conjecture the study should be replicated with participants from more similar backgrounds.

An active commentary option could have had a positive effect on the participants' motivation as it would allow experimenters to give additional motivating feedback and respond quickly to ambiguities.

4.2 Context

The truck-segment as a context for using mobile applications for ethnographic research did not prove to be entirely suitable from the truckers' point of view. Some truckers reported engaging with the app only before or after their working, as the app would have interfered with their work. This is also confirmed by the differences in entries and words per entry, as entries entered outside of work were on average longer than entries entered during working time. In addition, recording videos was not always possible due to prohibitions against video recording or too much background noise. Many truckers pointed out that they would use the app again but would prefer a personal interview for the next time.

From an organisations' perspective, nevertheless, there were some advantages to using the app. Despite the environment, it was possible to generate a decent amount of data through MobE. Thus, the app allowed the organisation to gain initial insights, some of which would not have been captured by a traditional interview, with few resources and at low cost. Hence, the study drew out the advantage of integrating different response formats, such as text, audio or video. For example, if an environment was too noisy for a video, the participants could switch to another format like text. However, not only because of the context but also because of the differing personalities of participants, did it prove to be useful to allow multiple response formats. Some drivers reported that they felt uncomfortable with voice messages and preferred to communicate with text. For further research examining the choice of response-format in relation to personality or the relation between response-format and the length of the answer could be considered.

4.3 Comparison of Contextual Interview and Mobile Ethnography

Different advantages and disadvantages of a face-to-face interview and mobile ethnography emerged, which should be considered and balanced with against each other's, when designing further research.

Through the interview better results in quantity as well in quality, could be gained. This is in line with existing literature (Koschel, 2018). An interviewer on site can better clarify answers by building up a personal relationship. This study also showed that visiting participants' work environment deepens the interviewer's understanding of the participants' response, leading to better evaluation afterwards. On the other hand, these benefits can involve the risk that results will be influenced by the interviewers' perspective and inherent biases. Additionally, the higher cost in time and financial resources have to be considered. In this study, an interview lasted about eight hours on average. The above-mentioned advantages could decrease when less time is planned for an interview.

Letting participants explore a context via an app can be even more efficient in time and costs. With an app, multiple studies can be conducted contemporaneously, making it easier to generate a larger sample size. Also, an app gives the researchers access to a more diverse group of participants, as it removes geographical limitations and other constrains. Further, environments with restrictions or danger zones can be accessed much easier. More advantages are that participants are less influenced by an interviewer and report their experiences entirely from their own perspective. However, these freedoms carry the risk that data will depend on the respondent's motivation and understanding of interview questions. Participants then could drop out of the study or the quality of gained data will be low. The upper experiment also showed a higher effort to evaluate the data output, as no interviewer had experienced the context. The MobE-App offers some solutions to counteract these disadvantages of mobile ethnography. Gamification elements are one possibility to increase participants' motivation. Through some comment options interviewers could build up a personal relationship with participants, guide them and get a better understanding of their statements. On top of that, in comparison to a face-to-face interview, the slight barrier via the app could reduce the feeling of being observed and social desirability.

Overall, both approaches give sufficient access to user-contexts, while having different merits and demerits. Hence, future studies would benefit from a mixed methods approach with an application of both methods, as demonstrated by this experiment (Schlemmer et al., 2022). On the one hand, a high level of detail could be achieved using a contextual interview. On the other hand, MobE could be used to give additional validation and further texture to participants' interview responses.

4.4 Recommendation for Further Research in Mobile Ethnography

Development of MobE has revealed many recommendations for further research in mobile ethnography.

- Design app-login as simple as possible or provide a ready-made account to reduce dropouts at the beginning.
- Make app-instructions easy and easily comprehensible to avoid any misunderstandings and thereby increase the reliability of data.
- Design an easy password-reset to avoid that participants stay logged out for longer or discontinue the study.
- Allow a permanent communication between participants and interviewers for example via chat to facilitate a quick response to any questions.
- Send push notifications to keep participants engaged.
- Create incentives, such as virtually collected coins and level advancements, linked to real incentives, to keep participants motivated.
- Adapt gamification to the target audience.
- Provide constant overview of the progress to the participant.
- Allow temporary data storing on the smartphone when offline to avoid loss of data due to no internet connection.
- Allow different response formats, such as audio, video or text, to meet individual needs and allow for response options in each context.

5 Summary

With MobE an approach was presented to let users explore their context with an app containing gamification-elements. The evaluation concluded that a sufficient amount of data could be generated by the app and gamification elements were ranked positively. Gamification and an integrated communication option could counteract previous disadvantages of mobile ethnography, making it an even more valuable alternative to a face-to-face interview. As seen in this study, context has a high impact on how an app for mobile ethnography can be applied. Future studies should keep this limitation in mind and if necessary, adapt the procedure to the given context of research.

References

Berger, R.: Now I see it, now I don't: Researcher's position and reflexivity in qualitative research. Qual. Res. **15**(2), 219–234 (2015)

Beddall-Hill, N., Jabbar, A., Al Shehri, S.: Social mobile devices as tools for qualitative research in education: iPhones and iPads in ethnography, interviewing, and design-based research. J. Res. Center Educ. Technol. **7**(1), 67–90 (2011)

Bosio, B., Rainer, K., Stickdorn, M.: Customer experience research with mobile ethnography: a case study of the Alpine destination Serfaus-Fiss-Ladis. In: Qualitative Consumer Research. Emerald Publishing Limited (2017)

Fieldnotescommunities: Field Notes (2023). https://www.fieldnotescommunities.com/de

Muskat, B., Muskat, M., Zehrer, A.: Qualitative interpretive mobile ethnography. Anatolia **29**(1), 98–107 (2018)

Insightplatforms: Indeemo (2023). https://www.insightplatforms.com/platforms/indeemo/

Kim, B.: Designing gamification in the right way. Libr. Technol. Rep. **51**(2), 29–35 (2015)

Koschel, K.-V.: Mobile Ethnographie in der qualitativen Markt- und Konsumforschung. In: Theobald, A. (ed.) Mobile Research, pp. 131–144. Springer, Wiesbaden (2018). https://doi.org/10.1007/978-3-658-18903-7_10

Nacke, L.E., Deterding, S.: The maturing of gamification research. Comput. Hum. Behav. **71**, 450–454 (2017)

Rapp, A., Hopfgartner, F., Hamari, J., Linehan, C., Cena, F.: Strengthening gamification studies: current trends and future opportunities of gamification research. Int. J. Hum. Comput. Stud. **127**, 1–6 (2019)

Santos, A.C.G., et al.: The relationship between user types and gamification designs. User Model. User-Adap. Inter. **31**(5), 907–940 (2021). https://doi.org/10.1007/s11257-021-09300-z

Schlemmer, P., Stickdorn, M., Kristiansen, E., Schnitzer, M.: A mixed methods stakeholder satisfaction study of sports events based on the case of the 2016 international children's games. In: Journal of Convention & Event Tourism, vol. 23, no. 1, pp. 41–62. Routledge (2022)

Schlesingergroup: Over the Shoulder (2023). https://www.schlesingergroup.com/de/uber-uns/qualitativ/over-the-shoulder/

Spittler, G.: Teilnehmende Beobachtung als Dichte Teilnahme. Zeitschrift für Ethnologie 1–25 (2001)

A Comparative Analysis of Institutional Ethical Codes of Conduct for the Practice of Design

Ana O. Henriques[1(✉)], Victor M. Almeida[1], Sónia Rafael[2], and José Gomes Pinto[3]

[1] CIEBA – Artistic Studies Research Center, Faculty of Fine-Arts, University of Lisbon, Largo da Academia Nacional e Belas Artes, 1249-058 Lisboa, Portugal
{ana.gfo.henriques,victoralmeida}@campus.ul.pt

[2] ITI/LARSyS, Faculty of Fine-Arts, University of Lisbon, Largo da Academia Nacional e Belas Artes, 1249-058 Lisboa, Portugal
srafael@campus.ul.pt

[3] CICANT – Centre for Research in Applied Communication, Culture, and New Technologies, Lusófona University, Campo Grande 376, 1749-024 Lisboa, Portugal

Abstract. The present article is aimed as a comparative analysis of ethical codes of conduct for the practice discipline of design. This discussion is especially relevant in the broader context of a discussion surrounding the important topic of ethics in design. Especially considering the present and increasing chasm we are witnessing in both academic design discourse and the practical implications thereof within the design profession. As such, this investigation is intended to bridge the gap between these realms, presenting a dissection of the current state of the dialogue between ethics and design in a professional context. In order to accomplish that, an analysis of the proposed ethical codes of conduct by eight high-profile institutions in the design space was conducted with the added purpose of determining whether they converge enough to be redundant or diverge too much and become ambiguous, both ultimately contributing to their dilution.

Keywords: Ethics in Design · Codes of Conduct · Comparative Analysis

1 Introduction

Design is a lot more than praxis. As argues Ezio Manzini, it is, primarily, a process through which to perceive and act upon the world [1]. As such, the act of designing implies an inherent form of "material (re)configuration" [2] based upon intent. Doing so, however, requires purpose. Indeed, as per Herbert Simon, to design is to "[devise] courses of action aimed at changing existing situations into preferred ones" [3] (p. 111). Our designs, likewise, are the product of intention, derived from the interactions between agent, outcome, and process.

In the words of Ece Canlı, "all designed things (from artifacts, spaces, sites, technologies, images to sartorial, digital, medical and cyber instruments) … act back and reconfigure the world;" and, in so doing, also our "identities, selves, … our everyday

M. Kurosu and A. Hashizume (Eds.): HCII 2023, LNCS 14011, pp. 93–107, 2023.
https://doi.org/10.1007/978-3-031-35596-7_7

lives, environments, social structures, politics, relationships, movements, habits, value judgments and so forth [2] (p. 11)—thus highlighting the inherent link between our designs and our ethics.

Designing—that is, the creation of material alternatives—requires deliberate acts based upon intent. This is, at its core, an ethical matter. Indeed, finding the best design solutions is, in essence, inherently a question of which are the best set of choices in a given situation to fulfill a given purpose. These kinds of choices regarding what one should or should not do, what is good and what is best, are the primary concern of ethics as a field of study; namely, the philosophy branch dealing with the foundations for these such decisions.

Ethics, as a discipline, is concerned with the human experience—"the good life" [4]—ranging from the individual to the collective. Here we see the importance of ethics in guiding our design choices; the difficulty, however, lies in how one can define 'best.' Views on 'good' can differ quite a bit depending on our social context and cultural values, making the summary of any concrete and broadly applicable answers an exceedingly challenging task.

This is, precisely, the motivation behind the establishment of ethical codes of conduct as documents which typically state the goals, views, values, and rules of any entity which has them—in essence, their ethos. According to The Ethics & Compliance Initiative "every organization, regardless of size, focus, or status, should have a code of conduct in place" [5] (p. 3).

Despite their significance, the usefulness of ethical codes of conduct has become somewhat taken for granted. This is the motivation behind the research presented in this paper, which looks at the most relevant ethical codes of conduct within design organizations in order to ultimately assess their impact.

2 Why Ethics Matters

As discussed, or designs carry with them ethical implications with increasing impact to our societies, which is especially true of areas of development focused on technological advancement. This was the impetus behind James Moor's formulation of his Moor's Law, where he postulates that, with the growing impact of technological development, the accompanying ethical problems upsurge as well [6]. This is posited to happen due to the growing number of stakeholders; or, in other words, real people who are suffering the consequences of such steep technological development—a speed which, as a side effect, produces goods and services which have yet to be morally or legally vetted [7].

As a result, the consequences of our designs largely remain poorly thought out. As such, an ethical agent, the HCI designer/researcher/technologist in particular, must be aware of their responsibility and exercise caution. Indeed, technology should not be seen as a default solution to pre-existing existing ethical quandaries because its possible repercussions are, as of yet, too ill-defined. Rather, technology should be considered an aspect to the development of society, which will, ineluctably, generate some amount change, and which our equally changing ethics must address [8].

It is of note, however, that ethics specifically applied to technology is a fairly recent concept. Technoethics, as a field of study, was originally developed in the 1970s by Mario

Bunge, under the view that those most intimately responsible for bringing technological artifacts into being—like the engineers and technologists—were equally accountable for the ethical consequences derived from innovation and use [9]. Bunge advocated for the development of new ethical frameworks to answer the specific challenges brought about by technological breakthroughs upon society [9]. In his own words, "the technologist must be held not only technically but also morally responsible for whatever he designs or executes: not only should his artifacts be optimally efficient but, far from being harmful, they should be beneficial, and not only in the short run but also in the long term" [9] (p. 72).

Progress in areas such as transportation, medicine or communication technologies is intimately related with ethical questions with rising complexity. Increased reliance on new technology, therefore, calls into question the fundamental underpinnings of formerly solid institutions and societal conventions, creating policy concerns about the modification and subsequent implementation of new laws, ethical guides, and professional codes of conduct [9].

Science and technology-led innovation is, in this way, becoming deeply embedded within the pillars of our shifting societies, be it through cultural, labour and educational sectors, private and public affairs, public institutions, or social practices [10]. This means that unregulated technological development is taking an active role in redefining key aspects of our lives—visible in things such as how governments make decisions, how students learn, how healthcare is provided, how ethnic groups preserve their cultures, how business is conducted, and even how scientific discoveries are handled.

All this underscores just how much technological development requires a thorough examination of its social and ethical implications, as well as the need to carry out extensive research on that front. Expansive theorization is thus necessary in order to leverage the indisputable good that such breakthroughs might facilitate while also protecting us against the harm.

3 Methodology

3.1 Methodological Approach

To fulfill this research's main objective of assessing the impact of ethical codes of conduct within design organizations, a comparative analysis of each document was conducted. This was done in order to be able to dissect their contents and determine whether and where they converge and diverge. The eight documents under this probe are as follows:

- *Design Business + Ethics*, published by the American Institute of Graphic Arts [11];
- *Code of Ethics for Professional Designers*, published by the French Designers Alliance [12];
- *Code of Ethics*, published by the Australian Graphic Design Association [13];
- *Code of Conduct*, published by the Chartered Society of Designers [14];
- *Ethics for Starving Designers*, published by the Ethics for the Starving Designer project (henceforth referred to as ESD) [15];
- *GDC Code of Ethics*, published by the Graphic Designers of Canada [16];

- *Model Code of Professional Conduct for Communication Designers*, published by the the International Council of Design[1] (ICoD), the International Council of Societies of Industrial Design, and the International Federation of Interior Architects/Interior designers [17];
- *Code of Ethics*, published by the Industrial Designers Society of America [18].

These were chosen for four principal reasons. Namely, because, first of all, they exist in a state robust enough to facilitate a substantive analysis, they were the most cited and influential proposals written specifically for the practice of design, they were published by noteworthy as well as organizations, and because these were the design organizations with the most members.

3.2 Data Collection and Analysis

This review was conducted in accordance with methods for data categorization aimed at comparative analysis. Specifically, the data was largely collected following Card Sorting methods of data categorization [19] and presented through data visualization methods for the purpose of sense-making and effective communication [20].

Upon an attentive reading of each document, each individual mentioned topic was isolated and documented. In doing so, some broad trends started to emerge, and Card Sorting was then used to group these topics in coherent clusters through a method of hybrid sorting for subsequent comparative analysis. These categories, which occasionally intersect, include "social responsibilities," "personal responsibilities," "responsibilities to designers," "professional responsibilities," and "responsibilities to the code."

After the sorting, each topic was tabulated individually and the frequency with which each category is represented was counted as well. This was done in order to facilitate the presentation of the data, which was designed to follow the criteria proposed by Stephen Few. Namely, whether it clearly illustrated the relationship between the variables, whether it accurately represents the quantities, whether it is easy to compare them, whether it facilitates the visualization of the ranked order of values, and whether it indicates how people could use the information [20].

4 Results

After a careful reading of these documents, through comparative analysis, each specific topic was isolated, and the contents were organized into the afore mentioned five separate categories through Card Sorting (see Table 1).

The results were then tabulated and summarized in Table 2 and Fig. 1.

From an immediate initial reading, one can quickly glean that all the documents under review reference all of the set categories with the exception of the "responsibilities to designers" category, which is only referenced in three [15, 16, 18] of the eight documents.

The graph in Fig. 2 represents the breakdown of each of the set categories, based on the individual topics covered in the codes of conduct. As depicted in Table 2, some topics were assigned overlapping categories when appropriate. In such cases, each referenced topic was counted once in each of the categories to which they belong. A closer

[1] Previously known as ico-D and formerly as ICOGRADA.

Table 1. Card Sorting results.

<table>
<tr><th colspan="5">CATEGORIES</th></tr>
<tr><th>Professional Responsibilities</th><th>Personal Responsibilities</th><th>Social Responsibilities</th><th>Responsibilities to the Code</th><th>Responsibilities to Designers</th></tr>
<tr><td colspan="2">Uphold the integrity of the profession</td><td>Support free speach and freedom of assembly</td><td>Follow the code/do not violate the code</td><td>Responsibilities of employers</td></tr>
<tr><td colspan="2">Be qualified and keep improving knowledge and skills</td><td>Accessibility</td><td>Encourage others to follow the code</td><td>Responsibilities of educators</td></tr>
<tr><td>Conflicts of interest</td><td colspan="2">Responsibility for the endorsement of the client and the product</td><td>Follow the local codes when practising overseas when there is no conflict</td><td></td></tr>
<tr><td>Responsibility to the client</td><td colspan="2">Responsibility for preventable consequences</td><td></td><td></td></tr>
<tr><td>Plagiarism/copyright/ licensing</td><td colspan="2">Commit time to doing good</td><td></td><td></td></tr>
<tr><td>Do not hinder other designer's work</td><td>Virtuosity</td><td>Environment</td><td></td><td></td></tr>
<tr><td>Professional minutia</td><td>Contingency</td><td>Follow the law</td><td></td><td></td></tr>
<tr><td>Honesty and transparency</td><td>If you must accept unethical work, compensate for it in some way</td><td>Improve society</td><td></td><td></td></tr>
<tr><td>Wage fairness</td><td></td><td>Protect human rights</td><td></td><td></td></tr>
<tr><td></td><td></td><td>Responsibility for public safety and well-being</td><td></td><td></td></tr>
<tr><td></td><td></td><td>Respect for the audience</td><td></td><td></td></tr>
<tr><td></td><td></td><td>Do not harm</td><td></td><td></td></tr>
</table>

reading of this data (see Fig. 2) illustrates, unequivocally, that the "professional responsibilities" category is overrepresented in detriment of all the others and especially that of "responsibilities to designers."

Additionally, we also see that the most mentioned topics are largely those pertaining to the "professional responsibilities" category, along with the "follow the code/do not violate the code" topic from the "responsibilities to the code" category (see Table 2 and Fig. 1). We also see that the least mentioned category is "responsibilities to designers" and the least mentioned individual topics are "contingency," "if you must accept unethical

Table 2. Each topic covered in the texts by category in every document [11–18].

Categories	Topics	AIGA	AFD	AGDA	CSD	ESD	GDC	ICoD	IDSA
Social Responsibilities	Environment	•	•	•	•	•	•	•	
	Follow the law				•		•		•
	Improve society		•				•	•	
	Protect human rights	•					•		•
	Responsibility for public safety and well-being	•				•			•
	Respect for the audience	•				•	•	•	
	Do not harm	•					•		
	Accessibility						•		•
Social and Personal Responsibilities	Commit time to doing good						•		
	Responsibility for the endorsement of the client and the product	•				•			
	Responsibility for preventable consequences					•			
	Support free speech and freedom of assembly	•							
Personal Responsibilities	Virtuosity		•			•			
	Contingency					•			
	If you must accept unethical work, compensate for it in some way					•			

(continued)

Table 2. (*continued*)

Personal and Professional Responsibilities	Uphold the integrity of the profession	•	•	•	•	•	•	•	•
	Be qualified and keep improving knowledge and skills	•	•				•		•
Professional Responsibilities	Conflicts of interest	•	•	•	•		•	•	•
	Responsibility to the client	•	•	•	•	•	•	•	•
	Plagiarism/ copyright/licensing	•	•	•	•		•	•	•
	Do not hinder other designer's work		•	•	•	•	•	•	•
	Professional minutia	•	•	•	•	•	•	•	•
	Honesty and transparency	•	•	•	•		•	•	•
	Wage fairness	•	•	•	•	•	•	•	•
Responsibilities to designers	Responsibilities of employers					•	•		
	Responsibilities of educators					•			•
Responsibilities to the Code	Follow the code/do not violate the code	•	•	•	•	•	•	•	•
	Encourage others to follow the code				•				•
	Follow local codes when practicing overseas where there is no conflict (stressing the importance of following a code)			•			•	•	

work, compensate for it in some way," "responsibilities of educators," "commit time to doing good," "responsibility for preventable consequences," and "support free speech and freedom of assembly"—each mentioned only once and which largely belong to the "personal responsibilities" category, with some overlap with the "social responsibilities" and "responsibilities to designers" categories. It is also worthy of note that the only topics

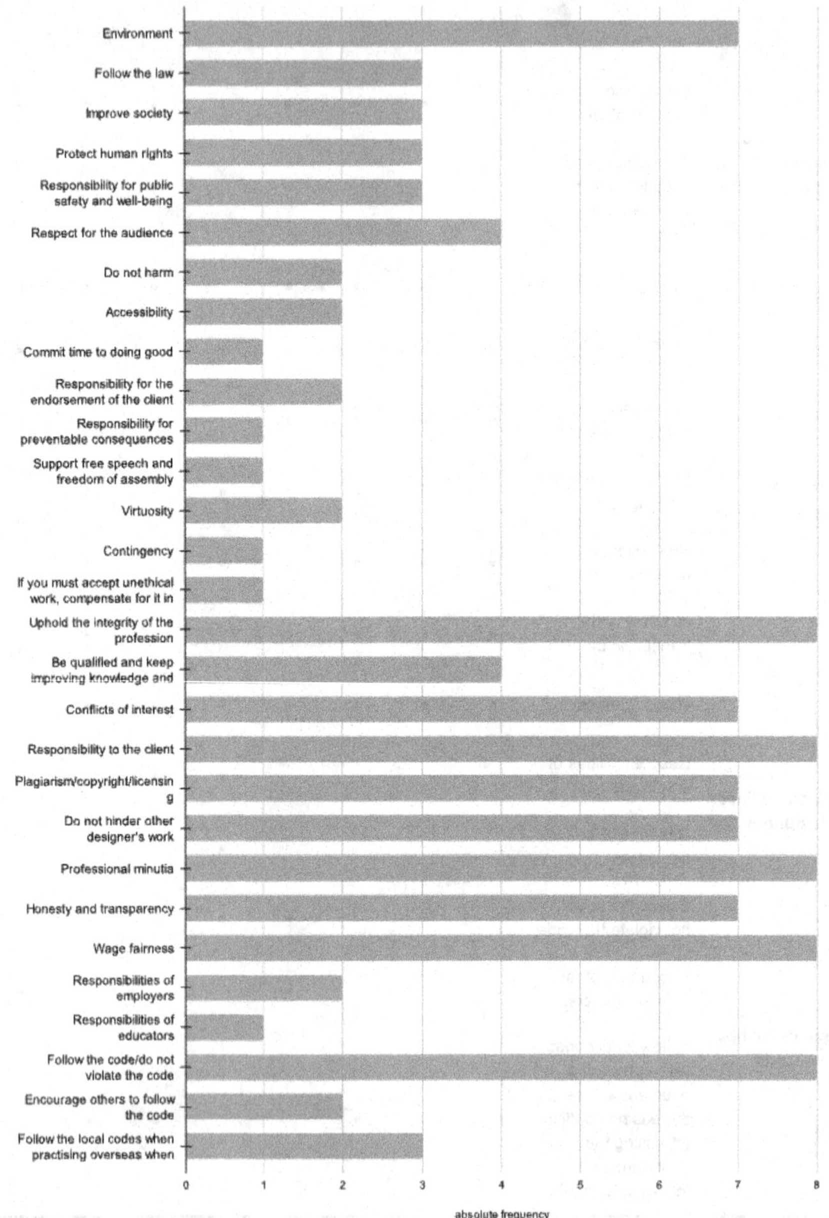

Fig. 1. Bar graph of the absolute frequency by topic for all documents [11–18].

listed by all the documents are "responsibility to the client," "professional minutia," "wage fairness," "," and "follow the code/do not violate the code"—which, except for the latter all belong to the "professional responsibilities category."

All this underscores a troubling trend, highlighted by the word cloud below (see Fig. 3) showing how the most used words are, collectively, "client," "designer," and "professional.". This will be addressed in the following Discussion section.

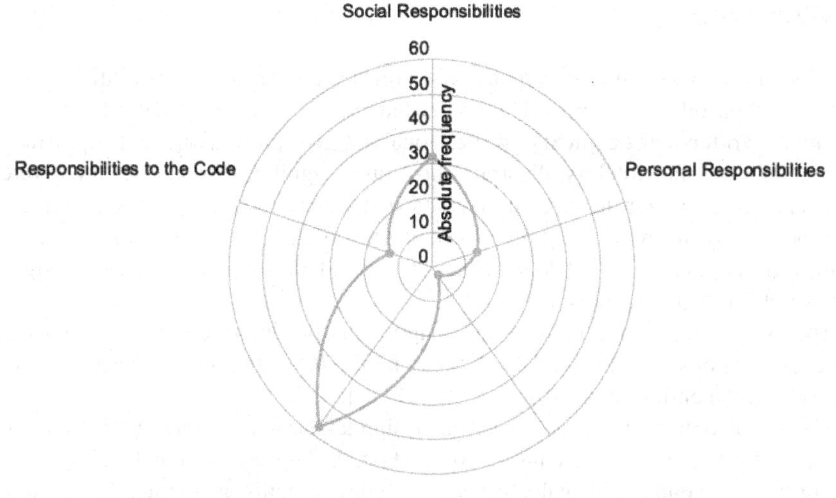

Fig. 2. Graph of absolute frequency of each category as they are covered in the probed codes of conduct [1–18].

Fig. 3. Word cloud of the corpus under analysis [11–18]. Obtained using Orange, an open-source platform for data analysis and visualization.

5 Discussion

The raw data shows, primarily, a major focus on "professional responsibilities" in contrast with all the other categories. This somewhat makes sense, given that these are codes of conduct written in the context of professional design organizations for the practice of design. This gap, nonetheless, illustrates how other significant categories are severely underrepresented within these documents. This matters, as these are the only related texts specifically meant for the professional practice of design. Additionally, since these are the most popular and cited documents of their kind, they are the ones most designers who search for them are engaging with.

This is reflected also in the fact that a significant portion of these documents often reference each other. AFD and AGDA both cite the ICoD proposal as inspiration [12, 13], and GDC mentions both AIGA and ICoD [16].

AIGA's incontrovertible sway over the design landscape of design [21] also makes it worthy of especially attentive inspection. In fact, AIGA's code of conduct is unique in that it is the only one of the analysed texts to feature a section addressed directly to the client. It begins like this: "if you represent a corporation, institution, advertising agency, investor or public relations firm, or you are an individual in need of graphic design, you've landed exactly where you need to be. Welcome" [11] (p. 13).

It then goes on to provide the reader with a brief overview of the field and business of design and is followed by a section on the "Standards of professional practice" [11] (p. 32). This section, however, is largely addressed to the designer. While it does offer some useful insight, it exclusively mentions the designer's responsibilities to other designers, to the audience, to society, and to the client, while neglecting to even allude to any responsibilities that the client might have. This is made even worse in the context of a chapter specifically intended for the client, which suggests to those who read this—be they clients, designers, or members of the public—by omission that the client is exempt from any responsibility. Even the topic of "wage fairness," which is indeed covered by all organizations, is framed as a responsibility of the designer, who is the one who should not accept underpaid work. That the client should not propose low wages in the first place is never even raised as an issue.

This is also a broad trend across all the documents. The designer's responsibilities toward the client and toward the profession of design are significantly overrepresented in detriment of those to the public and wider society. Indeed, at the AIGA 2002 Voice Conference, Milton Glaser had this to say: "in the new AIGA's code of ethics there is a significant amount of useful information about appropriate behavior towards clients and other designers, but not a word about a designer's relationship to the public" [22].

Glaser is referencing a document that has since been updated—the one considered for this review. This iteration is more thoughtful, to be sure; however, as also argues Paul Nini, "[designers'] responsibilities to audience members and users has not been substantially addressed" [23] (p. 1). And this is an indictment that holds for most of the documents considered in this analysis.

As an example, AFD asks that designers "be righteous in order to create the proper appreciation of the client for the service provider's quality of work and his/her skills" [12] (Article 4)—an assertion which explicitly states that the reason one ought to be righteous is to pursue the client's approval. Additionally, the AFD also declares that designers should "[a]void situations where the judgment and loyalty towards the customer could become altered" [12] (Article 15). This wording employed here is noteworthy since it simply states that designers should not work with clients with whom they disagree, which carries the implication that this need not be a judgement based on whether those ethics are 'good.'

The ESD document is also quite interesting. For one, it is the only student-led project to gain relevant traction; but is also based in Singapore, making it the only document on this list to be based in a non-Western country (though, yes, one which is still, to this day, suffering the consequences of British colonial rule). It acknowledges that "design is a powerful tool for communication, behavioral change and manipulation" [15] (Principle 2) and is the only one to frame the designer/client relationship to be mutual, posing ethical responsibility as something that the designer should bring to the attention of the client rather than shoulder alone. The ESD also raises an interesting argument. It contends that an ethical code should be constructed around "facts first, research second and personal opinion last," while also being cognizant of the contingency which permeates both knowledge and circumstance [15] (Principle 14).

This idea is crucial in terms of solving ethical quandaries. Indeed, the purpose of these documents is to serve as guide for best practices—how to meet the needs of the client, the public and society; but that, of course, begs the question of what to do when these demands collide. In that regard, a proposal of note, put forth by most of these organizations is the grievance committee—in essence, panels comprised by local objective industry experts. AGDA and IDSA both introduce them as an ethical recourse to which one can resort in case of conflict or when in need of guidance regarding a particular situation [11, 18]. AFD and GDC mention the use of these panels as spaces for litigation [12, 16] and CSD raises these committees as a space for protesting the actions of the organization itself, should the need arise [14].

Another thing of note within the context of this discussion is a particular line in AIGA's code, expressing that designers should not overstep on the human rights of another individual or group "without permission of such other person or group" [11] (p. 35)—which is especially preposterous. On its face, this seems like a fine idea, a great one even. But its applicability is severely limited to an exclusively interpersonal context. One simply cannot ask permission from an entire ethnic group or cultural community, and statements such as these treat the public as unfirm blocks of users rather than diverse people with individual needs and desires, which further reveals the lack of concern cited by both Glaser [22] and Nini [23].

Additionally, it was also found that these documents tend not to be recent, which is, perhaps, why they do not communicate any sense of urgency. Most were introduced in the past decade and have undergone little to no revision.

AIGA's code was originally published in 2001 and its last iteration dates from 2009 [11]. AGDA's is from 1996 [13]. The CSD document was not dated, but since it was only available online, we were able to retrieve an earlier version using the Wayback Machine. Though we do not have access to any archive that has not been catalogued, the earliest available version is from 2016 and remains virtually unchanged [24]. AFD's was first published in 2009 and later revised in 2012 [12], which is the same year the ESD project was launched [15]. The most recent iteration of the GDC proposal is from 2019 but the earliest draft we were able to locate is also from 2012 and has undergone barely any changed [25]. ICoD's document originally dates back to 1983 and was amended in 1987, reviewed in 1997, and then amended again in 2011, which is the latest version [17]. IDSA's entry is also not dated; however, we were able to find a reference to it which lists it as having been published in 2010 [25]. Given the significant technological and cultural development we have witnessed in the past few years alone, this is, demonstrably, inadequate.

Furthermore, these texts are generally quite broad. This is intentional, to some extent, since codes of this nature are expressly intended to "state the principles for an international basis of ethical standards related to the practice of design" [17] (p. 3). This vagueness, however, also works against them. They ultimately lack the nuance of a more comprehensive grasp that a more local and restricted context could provide. Indeed, even when there are local proposals, they proclaim the goal of being internationally applicable. As an example, AGDA puts up a "nationally ratified" code, yet claims to espouse "internationally accepted standards of professional ethics and conduct" [13] (para. 1). Statements such as these necessarily beg the questions of who is accepting these standards, and how can they verify that.

This is also related to a key issue of provenance. These codes are, overwhelmingly, produced under Western democracies and reflect Western standards for an ethical practice of design, largely anchored in neoliberal priorities [26]. As such, they are generally failing to account for the distinct nuances in how the professional settings of design unravel in differing social and cultural contexts by describing a standardized practice.

Moreover, the language employed in these documents is far from assertive. They are encircled by conditional terms like "avoid," or "should", and phrases such as "[a] professional designer shall strive to be sensitive to cultural values and beliefs" [11] (p. 35). Indeed, a close reading of the latter phrase, highlights the implication that the attempt to be aware of differing values and beliefs, not that one must consider and respect them and uphold their right to be held. Much the same way, designers are expected to "favor quality and virtue in the designer profession" [12] (Article 3), rather than be virtuous and do good work. And regarding the potential for egregious consequences, assertions like "work in a manner so that as little harm (direct or indirect) as possible is caused" [13] (Sect. 2.1), "endeavour to minimize adverse impacts" [16] (Sect. 4.1.5), or "be informed about and specify or recommend goods, services, and processes that are the least detrimental to the environment and society" [16] (Sect. 4.2.1) are especially pernicious given that they imply that harm is unavoidable.

This language matters. It moulds the way we think [27], and, conversely, how we choose to act. Anyone reading in an ethical code of conduct that they must limit the harm they cause via their work will assume and ultimately accept that they will cause harm; which, of course, is not necessarily true.

As such, in gauging whether these proposals converge enough to be redundant or diverge enough to be ambiguous, one must draw from these results and discussion. Indeed, the documents are certainly similar in a number of key ways, prevalent especially in the very similar language and concern for the professional duties of the designer. However, they slightly diverge on a few other aspects, the most relevant of which is in the focus on the topics pertaining to the "social responsibilities" category.

The mention of these issues is not consistent among these documents, unless they are touched upon in a way that is vague enough to include a broad range of generalizations. In dealing with specifics, however, a number of important issues, as is the case with such topics as "accessibility" or "do not harm," are some of the least explicitly covered—the former being mentioned by GDC [16] and IDSA [18] and the latter only by GDC [16]—which leads us to conclude that points of divergence of this nature are relevant enough to merit coexisting.

Finally, another relevant point of divergence are the topics contained in the "responsibilities to the designers" category. As relayed already, this is the least covered category, yet it provides a very important perspective to a discussion heavily biased towards what designers owe. This is significant to include because it affords the conditions in which designers are actually able to act as ethical agents with an informed sense of agency. An illustrative example is the issue of education, covered only in the ESD [15] and IDSA [18] documents. As per the latter, members should "strive to advance design education by holding as one of [their] fundamental concerns the education of design students" [18] (Article VI). Additionally, ESD asks "educators to take it upon themselves to discuss these issues with their students" [15] (Foreword, para. 6).

6 Conclusion and Future Work

A comparative analysis was conducted of eight documents from high profile institutions in design, which provide ethical guidelines for the exercise of the design profession. From this study, some relevant conclusion can be drawn.

Perhaps the biggest gap we were able to identify, as well as one of the most critical points derived from this investigation, is that the professional practice guidelines for design are overwhelmingly eschewed toward the responsibilities of the designers—be it to other designers, the client, the public, and society—even omitting any of the responsibilities of the clients. This is a trend among documents. Indeed, only one—the ESD's—frames the relationship between client and designer as somewhat mutual, proposing that designers bring ethical concerns to the client rather than shoulder them alone.

The idea of the grievance committee is also one that stood out. It is generally accepted as a good practice among these organizations, and it could indeed be a step in generating more space for accountability.

Another important point is that these codes are not recent. Most were written in the last decade and, have undergone very few changes or none at all. This could be a contributing factor in the lack of urgency displayed in the language, and could also aggravate the larger issue of delayed legislation of significant technological developments which often present a major potential for societal shakeup.

Indeed, we also verify that the language used in these documents is not assertive, often employing terms with conditional connotations. This matters because, especially regarding issues of maleficence or unintended consequences, a code that does not exert an assertive stance against them will ultimately create the perception that harm is inevitable.

This issue of language carries also in the tone of general vagueness present in the texts. Moreover, they purport to state the principles for an international basis of ethical standards related to the practice of design, yet are predominantly the product of Western democracies and therefore reflect mainly Western standards. Thus, for the most part, they do not take into account how the profession differs in distinct socio-cultural contexts.

In summary, the analysed set of documents share many traits. They include, for example, the overrepresentation of the designer's professional responsibilities, the lack of responsibilities aimed toward the designer, or the wanting language. However, they diverge in important points related to mainly social concerns—largely the topics mentioned in the "social responsibilities" category—deemed significant enough to merit coexistence.

Considering these findings, it should still be said that the format of the ethical code of conduct is a very valuable resource. Even these documents, despite the limitations, are productive efforts in the pursuit of ethics for the practice of design. Their existence, in addition to the content they display, shows that there is indeed a concern for all these assigned categories of responsibilities, which is a great step in a better direction.

In that regard, we see two productive directions for future work. The first would see a more comprehensive study would be conducted on how the prevalence of ethical codes of conduct which ignore the needs of the designers and the responsibilities they are owed impacts designers. The other would be to build on the criticism already dealt in this paper to propose some guidelines for the redaction of these types of documents that are cognizant of the identified gaps.

References

1. Manzini, E.: Design, When Everybody Designs: An Introduction to Design for Social Innovation. MIT Press, Cambridge (2015)
2. Simon, H.: The Sciences of the Artificial. MIT Press, Cambridge (1996)
3. Frede, D.: Plato's Ethics: An Overview. Stanford Encyclopedia of Philosophy (2017). https://plato.stanford.edu/entries/plato-ethics/. Accessed 15 Sept 2021
4. Ethics Resource Center: Creating a Workable Company Code of Ethics: A Practical Guide to Identifying and Developing Organizational Standards, 2nd edn. Ethics Resource Center, Washington, D.C. (2003)
5. Moor, J.H.: Why we need better ethics for emerging technologies. Ethics Inf. Technol. **7**, 111–119 (2005)
6. Luppicini, R.: The emerging field of technoethics. In: Luppicini, R., Adell, R. (eds.) Handbook of Research on Technoethics, Hershey, PA, pp. 1–19. IGI Global (2009)
7. Massumi, B.: The Politics of Affect. Polity Press, Cambridge (2015)
8. Bunge, M.: Towards a technoethics. Philos. Exch. **6**(1), 69–79 (1975)
9. Luppicini, R.: The knowledge society. In: Luppicini, R. (ed.) Technoethics and the Evolving Knowledge Society: Ethical Issues in Technological Design, Research, Development, and Innovation, Hershey, PA, pp. 1–23. IGI Global (2010)
10. AIGA: Design Business + Ethics. AIGA, New York, NY (2009)
11. AFD: Code of Ethics for Professional Designers. Alliance Française des Designers (2012). http://www.alliance-francaise-des-designers.org/code-of-ethics-for-professional-designer.html. Accessed 4 Nov 2020
12. AGDA: Code of Ethics. AGDA (1996). https://agda.com.au/member/code-of-ethics. Accessed 4 Nov 2020
13. CSD: Code Of Conduct. CSD (n.d.). https://www.csd.org.uk/about/code-of-conduct/. Accessed 4 Nov 2020

14. Goh, D.: Ethics for the Starving Designer. Ethics for the Starving Designer (2012). http://www.starvingforethics.com/. Accessed 4 Nov 2020
15. GDC: GDC Code of Ethics. GDC (2019). https://gdc.design/code-of-ethics. Accessed 4 Nov 2020
16. ICoD: Model Code of Professional Conduct for Designers. ICoD (2011). https://www.ico-d.org/database/files/library/icoD_BP_CodeofConduct.pdf. Accessed 4 Nov 2020
17. IDSA: Code of Ethics. IDSA (2020). https://www.idsa.org/code-ethics. Accessed 4 Nov 2020
18. Hudson, W.: Card sorting. In: Soegaard, M., Dam, R. F. (eds.) The Encyclopedia of Human-Computer Interaction, 2nd edn. Interaction Design Foundation (2014)
19. Few, S.: Data visualization for human perception. In: Soegaard, M., Dam, R. F. (eds.) The Encyclopedia of Human-Computer Interaction, 2nd edn. Interaction Design Foundation (2014)
20. Heller, S., Finamore, M.: Design Culture: An Anthology of Writing from the AIGA Journal of Graphic Design. Allworth Press, New York (1997)
21. Glaser, M.: This Is What I Have Learned. Voice: AIGA National Design Conference (2002). http://voiceconference.aiga.org/transcripts/ presentations/milton_glaser.pdf. Accessed 7 Nov 2020
22. Nini, P.: In search of ethics in graphic design. Voice: AIGA J. Des. **16** (2004)
23. CSD: Code of Conduct. CSD (2016). http://web.archive.org/web/*/https://www.csd.org.uk/about/code-of-conduct/. Accessed 4 Nov 2020
24. GDC: Code of Ethics. GDC (2012). https://www.gdc.net/sites/default/files/attachments/static-pages/1_3_ethics_2012.pdf. Accessed 7 Nov 2020
25. Miller, C.: Lost in translation? Ethics and ethnography in design research. J. Bus. Anthropol. **1**(1), 62–78 (2014)
26. Fiedlschuster, M.: Neoliberalism and European democracy promotion. In: Ness, I., Cope, Z. (eds.) The Palgrave Encyclopedia of Imperialism and Anti-Imperialism. Palgrave Macmillan, Cham (2019)
27. Moore, J.: AI for not bad. Front. Big Data **2**(32) (2019)

Situation-Aware Adaptations for Individualized User Experience and Task Management Optimization

Christian Herdin[1(✉)] and Christian Märtin[2]

[1] University of Rostock, Albert-Einstein-Str. 22, 18059 Rostock, Germany
Christian.Herdin@uni-rostock.de

[2] Faculty of Computer Science, Augsburg University of Applied Sciences, An der Hochschule 1, 86161 Augsburg, Germany
Christian.Maertin@hs-augsburg.de

Abstract. The SitAdapt system is an architecture and runtime system for building adaptive interactive applications. The system is integrated into the PaMGIS framework for pattern- and model-based user interface construction and generation. This paper focuses on the different types of adaptations and the timeslots for controlling the options for changing the user interface and the interactive behavior. During sessions the system is monitoring the user and collecting visual, bio-physical, and emotional data that may vary over time. Based on these data situations can be recognized and adaptation rules that activate the PaMGIS models and resources can be triggered at runtime. The operation of the system is demonstrated with examples from an adaptive travel-booking application. The paper also discusses, how task accomplishment can be controlled by mapping real user activities during a session to the task models that are made available through the PaMGIS model repositories.

Keywords: Adaptive user interface · situation awareness · model-based user interface development · situation-aware adaptations · task accomplishment

1 Introduction and Related Work

The work presented in this paper discusses the SitAdapt approach for exploiting user monitoring data in real-time to improve user experience (UX) and task accomplishment for responsive interactive web applications.

SitAdapt can be seen as an integrated component within the PaMGIS framework [3, 5]. The system provides a platform for observing users in their working environment and allows for emotion-recognition, situation awareness and rule-based decision-making for adapting the target application. The adaptation process is based on the observed user-characteristics, user-behavior, user actions and real-time meta-information from the target application. The paper focuses on the different types of adaptations and the timeslots for controlling the changing options as well as on the mechanisms that are triggering the situation rules.

M. Kurosu and A. Hashizume (Eds.): HCII 2023, LNCS 14011, pp. 108–118, 2023.
https://doi.org/10.1007/978-3-031-35596-7_8

The current version of the PaMGIS framework architecture was discussed in [4]. It provides pattern- and model-based user interface construction tools and resources like HCI-patterns, user interface models, and code fragments for the integrated SitAdapt situation analytics platform to build runtime-adaptive interactive applications that react to context changes in the user's environment as well as situational changes. Such changes include the user's task management behavior and emotional state. In this section we discuss user interface adaptation mechanisms in general. Three different categories of user interface adaptations were distinguished in [1, 10]:

- *Adaptable user interfaces.* The user customizes the user interface to his or her personal preferences.
- *Semi-automated adaptive user interfaces.* The user interface provides recommendations for adaptations. The user must decide whether he or she wants to accept the recommendation or not.
- *Automated adaptive user interfaces.* The user interface automatically reacts to changes in the context-of-use.

2 Adaptation Types in SitAdapt

Real-time adaptations that are controlled and generated by our runtime environment are mainly used to raise the individual user experience of a user when she interacts with a target web application. However, we also use situation-awareness and adaptation to offer intelligent assistance for task accomplishment. In the final paper we will give an example, how SitAdapt can be applied to relieve the user from a part of the task management burden [9] omnipresent in most complex environments, e.g., in e-commerce platforms that are in the focus of our research.

With SitAdapt the above mentioned three different categories of adaptations can be modeled by the developer and generated at runtime. The SitAdapt system allows different adaptation types within the category of automated user interface adaptations and combinations of the various types. The adaptations were inspired by the Cameleon Reference Framework [2].

- *Changes of media and interaction object types.* Such changes modify the way of the information presentation. Different types of charts (mosaic or a bar charts), personalized areas or functions (areas with functions frequently used by the individual) can be chosen by situation-aware adaptations. Other possibilities for adaptations can, e.g., be the replacement of a form with a wizard or the change of the input media from text to speech.
- *Changes in content.* The system can adapt the content presented to the user. Thus, it is possible to change button labels or offer help texts and even chatbot-assistance. In the e-commerce domain, specific advertising and offers, as well as additional elements or pop-ups such as vouchers can be presented to the user. Different users can also be offered different content, e.g., variably detailed text information or product images, or variably detailed content presentations, by adding or removing content attributes.
- *Changes in design and layout.* SitAdapt can adapt the design of the interface, e.g., colors, background colors, images and the contrast or change text layout and font size and type. The system can also change the layout of the user interface objects.

- *Changes in structure.* SitAdapt can change the number of objects displayed in the interface, e.g., the number of input fields of a form, or the navigation objects from the interface.
- *Personalized information.* The system can change the content of the text. For example, more formal or easier language.

The actors responsible for adapting a system depend on the phase of the development process [1]. At the design stadium of an interface, multi-targeting is possible with the knowledge of system designers and programmers. At the installation stadium, the system can be personalized for the first installation by IT system managers. At runtime, while the user interacts with the interface, the adaptation may be triggered by the user and/or the system. Depending on the adaptation types and the available data about the user in a situation, the SitAdapt system can modify the user interface at runtime, before the first display of the user interface, while the user interacts with the interface, or when the user revisits the interface a second time.

3 The Different SitAdapt Adaptations

Within the SitAdapt project a dedicated travel portal (see Fig. 1) was developed as a testbed for demonstrating the different adaptation options.

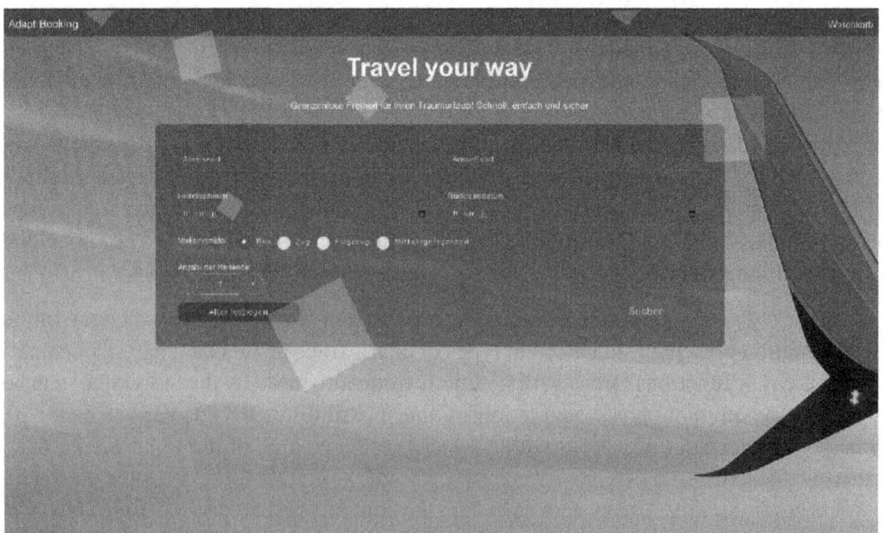

Fig. 1. Different start pages of the travel portal depending on the emotion user state.

3.1 Changes in Design and Layout

An adaptation type from the "Changes in design and layout" area could be to present different background pictures in the application depending on the emotional state of the user. The emotional state of a user can be analyzed in real-time by the FaceReader software[1]. If the system recognizes that a user is for example currently angry, the SitAdapt system tries to calm the user down with a color-matched background (see Fig. 2) with calming colors and images.

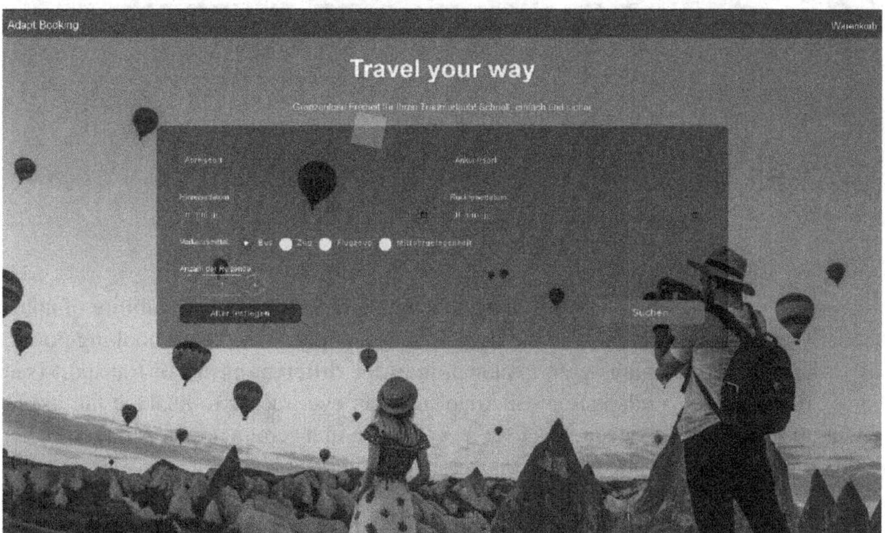

Fig. 2. Different start pages of the travel portal depending on the user's emotional state.

3.2 Changes in Content

An adaptation type from the "Changes in content" area could be the additional display of information for a specific target group. The following scenario is intended to explain, why the display of a utilization graph can represent an optimization of the user interface from the user's point of view. From the older person's point of view, it could be an advantage to know, how busy the respective means of transport are at a certain time (see Fig. 3). The risk of contracting Covid-19 on public transport during the pandemic is also very high. With the use of the utilization graph, contact encounters can be avoided.

[1] https://www.noldus.com.

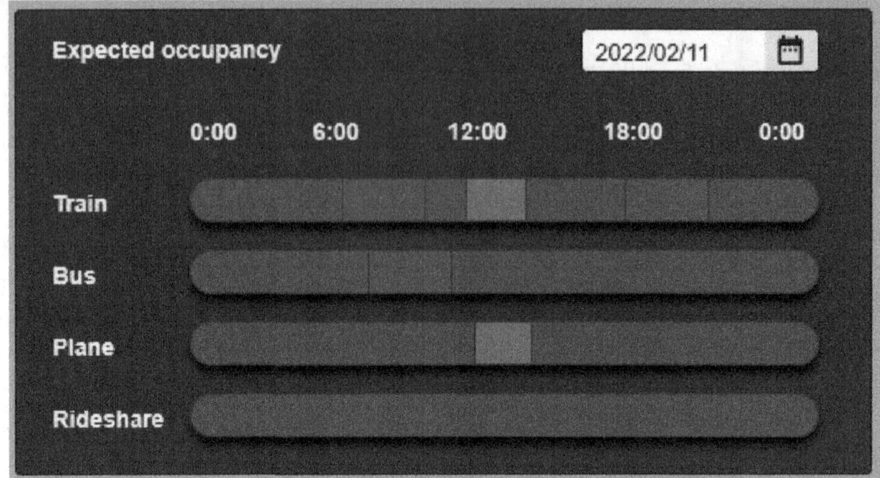

Fig. 3. Display of travel options with utilization chart.

Another example of an adaptation of the content changes is the possibility of automatically displaying a help text to the user. In the example of the travel booking portal, this is the option of displaying an explanation of the different means of transport (see Fig. 4). To enable this adaptation, SitAdapt uses an eye tracker to analyze the user's viewing position on the screen. If a user's eyes move in a certain area for longer than a specified period of time, the help text is automatically displayed.

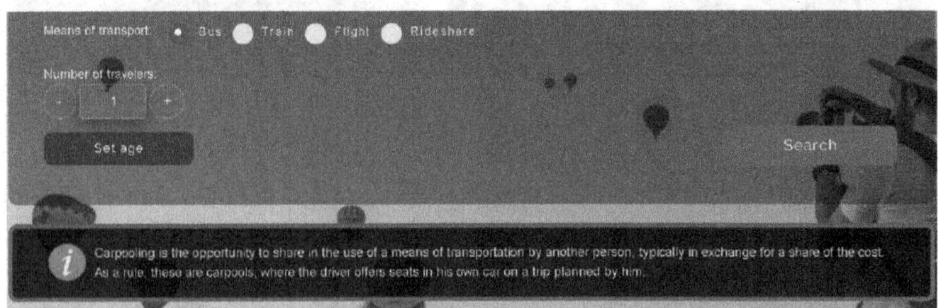

Fig. 4. Help text for the rideshare.

3.3 Changes of Media and Interaction Object Types

An adaptation from the "Changes of media and interaction object types" area could be to enable the entry of the personal data of the travelers instead of using a form (see Fig. 5) via a wizard (see Fig. 6). This adaptation is also possible if, e.g., a mobile phone is recognized instead of a large screen.

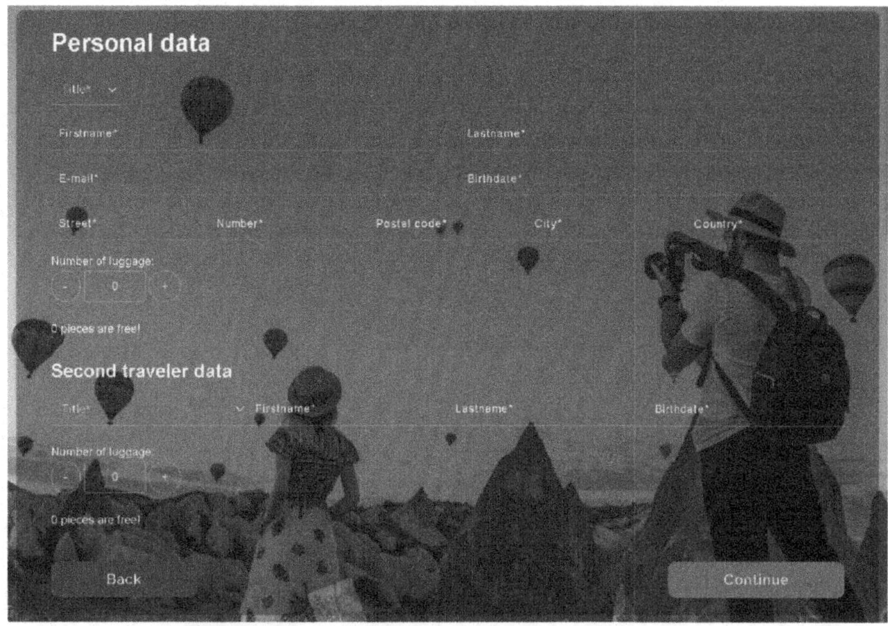

Fig. 5. Form for the personal data of the travelers.

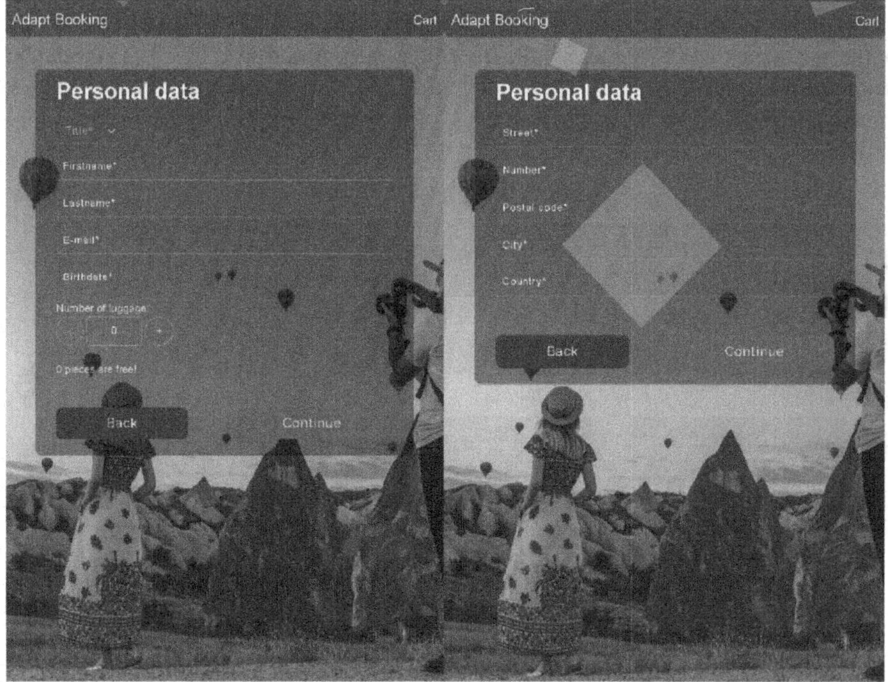

Fig. 6. Wizard for the personal data of the travelers.

3.4 Technical Realization of the Adaptation Process

A JavaScript function was used here to display the additional items or structural changes. Such graphics or structures are already known to the web application because they were modeled and coded in the development phase. They are made visible to the user at runtime by changing a variable in the HTML file after the travel portal has received the information from the rule editor to display the graphics (see Fig. 7). The decision to fire a specific rule, however, is made, because SitAdapt has observed the user in a specific situation, where the rule is applicable.

```
function show(){
  document.getElementById('label').style.display= 'block'
;
}
```

Fig. 7. Function show.

To make this different types of adaptation possible, it must be created at development time using the Rule Editor. The rule editor (see Fig. 8) allows the definition and modification of rules, e.g., for specifying the different user states and the resulting actions. The left-hand side of a rule can make use of all the observed situational and personal data. The right-hand side can access the resources of the PaMGIS repository or make direct use of pre-defined characteristics of the web application, like in this case. In the example of the occupancy graph, the age of the traveler is entered as a criterion. The age can be determined using the Noldus FaceReader software in combination with a webcam or via the application itself by entering the age of the traveler in the first step of selecting a trip.

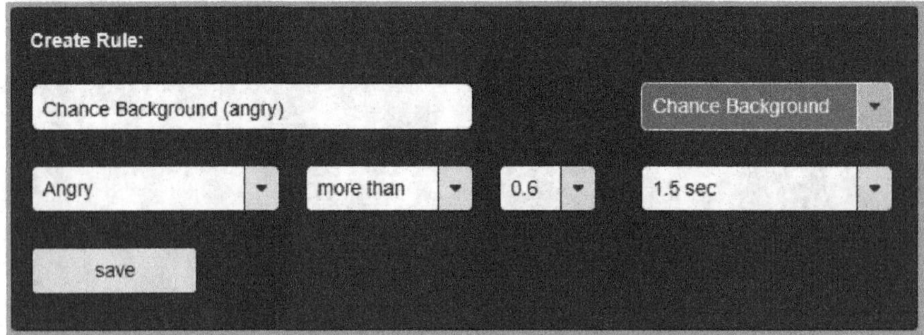

Fig. 8. The Rule Editor.

4 Task-Management Optimization and Adaptation Control

Since we are using a model-based approach that combines the PaMGIS MBUID-framework with the SitAdapt adaptation component, we do not only have access to the various modeling and generation tools and their model and pattern repositories during the interactive development phase of web applications. Applications can also access the repositories and the models of the currently running applications, e.g., task models, user interface models or user models at runtime. This opens possibilities for controlling task accomplishment and the success of dynamic individual adaptations. This can be especially helpful when prototypical implementations of the web applications are tested and optimized. For finally deployed commercial end-user applications, this can be an interesting feature that can lead to improved individualized user experience. However, it must always be clear for the user that he or she is observed by SitAdapt to allow for such advanced service capabilities. Broad acceptance will only be reached, if the recorded monitoring data are securely stored on the client devices and not accessible by the service provider. The commercial end-user must be able to decide, whether the client application can re-access recorded observational data in the next user-session or not.

For prototyping complex safety-critical interactive systems, very fine-grained task modeling notations and tools for testing the resulting human-in-the-loop systems, e.g., [6, 7] have been developed. Although these comprehensive approaches have also inspired our work, we are striving for easy to implement, but nevertheless powerful control structures that can be used in less critical system environments, e.g., e-commerce, entertainment web applications or tools for monitoring individual well-being.

Successful and rapid user task accomplishment creates a win-win situation for both, users, and service providers, because user satisfaction and user experience will rise and at the same time the business goals implicitly planned on the provider side by the contents of the task models, will lead to higher conversion rates and customer loyalty.

In our environment it is possible to map the key interaction objects in the FUI model to the elements of the task model that represent the actions that are necessary to successfully finish each sub-task, i.e., to reach each sub-goal of the planned business process. These mappings generate links between each activated user interface action, e.g., a button, and the respective sub-task of the task model. At the same time SitAdapt is monitoring all user actions together with eye-tracking and emotional behavior. What happens, when a user does not interact with the system in the way intended by the task model, will be demonstrated with the example shown in Fig. 8 that is part of the task model of our travel booking testbed web-application and is written in the CTT notation [8].

On the lowest level of the model each of the first three subtasks passes information to enable the execution of the next subtask. In the user interface each subtask is represented by a dialog box. When the user leaves one of the enabling subtasks before the trip summary is displayed, i.e., before the ticket purchase is completed, and arrives elsewhere in the web application or is even exiting the website, this is noticed by the system, because a different interaction object than the one intended by the task-model is activated. If the user is still within the application, SitAdapt can activate a pop-up message, informing the user about the unfinished subtask. If the application has been left altogether, SitAdapt can send a message to the user with the respective information. By analyzing the emotional state and the eye-tracking behavior recorded just before the deviation from the intended path, SitAdapt can adapt the message content with respect to the detected emotion and gazing behavior or decide whether such a message is necessary or not. For instance, no message is necessary, when the application window is left without finishing the task sequence, the detected emotional state is neutral or positive, and the user is only checking e-mails. If the emotional state is negative or surprised and the current dialog is left before finishing the subtask, the message content could remind the user of the unfinished subtasks, give some helpful information, and present a link back to the unfinished dialog.

By recording all deviations from intended task sequences, SitAdapt can also gather information about the quality of user interface adaptations. The number of such deviations, the emotional state, and the eye-tracking behavior prior to a deviation in situations with or without adapted user interfaces can be compared. Also, statistical information can be obtained, about whether individual adaptations can lead to more effective task accomplishment, e.g., by guiding the user towards her or his planned actions within the application, or by making it easier for the user to follow the sequence of actions modeled in the task model of the application (Fig. 9).

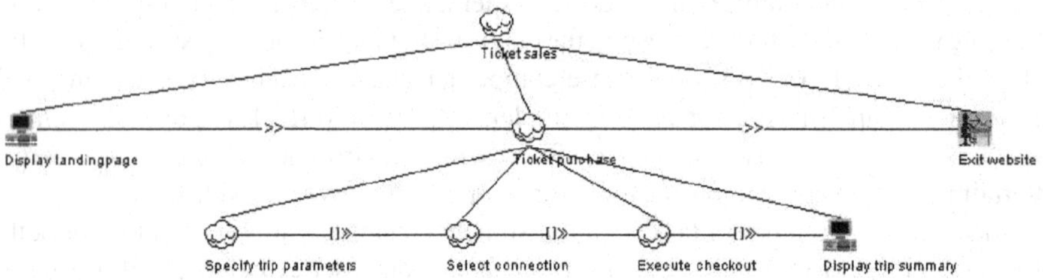

Fig. 9. Task model of the ticket sales task with sub-tasks.

5 Conclusion and Future Work

In this paper we have described and demonstrated the various possibilities for automated adaptations that are available when a web-application has been developed with the PaMGIS framework and the integrated SitAdapt system. In several earlier papers we have discussed the advantages of model-based design for interactive systems and especially the tools and mechanisms for generating parts of the user interface automatically from the models and patterns available in the PaMGIS repository. In other papers we have also presented the structure and functionality of the SitAdapt system in detail.

With the current paper we primarily aimed at giving realistic examples of the capabilities of the SitAdapt system in an e-commerce related testbed environment. We chose to build a travel-booking application that we modeled after existing travel-booking portals. Currently we are evaluating all available types of adaptations and the various adaption rules for the testbed environment in a user study in our usability lab with $N = 12$ participants. The results will give us valuable feedback concerning the quality of the adaptations and our applied adaption rules and will be presented in one of our next papers.

PaMGIS and SitAdapt are flexible enough to be used for designing and implementing real world client applications. However, because we make heavy use of visual user monitoring, we still operate testbed applications only in our usability lab. We started our work on situation-aware interactive systems six years ago. Since this time, we not only have modified and improved the SitAdapt architecture; we also have added new monitoring hardware and software components, e.g., different brain-computer interfaces and software for vocal emotion classification, that have been integrated into our observation platform.

Since we have started to work with situation analytical software systems, we have gained great experience in using the results of our prototypical work in the lab as input for modeling and building commercial applications in the e-commerce sector. One of the most important fields for prototyping is the study of task-accomplishment of our test users and to use the generalization of our findings in the modeling and design of real-world end-user applications. With the model-based resources available at runtime, as shown in this paper, we have a broad spectrum of opportunities to study both, the user side, and the provider side of web-applications, and to search and design for guidance and individual adaptations that can raise user experience and task-accomplishment at the same time.

Acknowledgements. The authors would like to thank Erwin Hrschitza and Daniel Beck, who implemented the travel-booking web-application in their bachelor theses and provided part of the figures for this paper.

References

1. Akiki, P.A., et al.: Integrating adaptive user interface capabilities in enterprise applications. In: Proceedings of the 36th International Conference on Software Engineering (ICSE 2014), pp. 712–723. ACM (2014)
2. Calvary, G., et al.: The CAMELEON Reference Framework, Document D1.1 of the CAMELEON R&D Project IST-2000-30104 (2002)
3. Engel, J., Märtin, C., Forbrig, P.: A concerted model-driven and pattern-based framework for developing user interfaces of interactive ubiquitous applications. In: Proceedings of the First International Workshop on Large-Scale and Model-Based Interactive Systems, Duisburg, pp. 35–41 (2015)
4. Herdin, C., Märtin, C.: Modeling and runtime generation of situation-aware adaptations. In: Kurosu, M. (ed.) HCII 2020. LNCS, vol. 12181, pp. 71–81. Springer, Cham (2020). https://doi.org/10.1007/978-3-030-49059-1_5
5. Märtin, C., Engel, J., Herdin, C.: A model-based environment for building and running situation-aware interactive applications. In: Human Interaction and Emerging Technologies (IHIET 2022), vol. 68, pp. 365–373. AHFE International (2022). https://doi.org/10.54941/ahfe1002754
6. Martinie De Almeida, C., et al.: Analysing and demonstrating tool-supported customizable task notations. Proc. ACM Hum.-Comput. Interact. **3**(12) (2019). ISSN 2573-0142
7. Palanque, P., Ladry, J.-F., Navarre, D., Barboni, E.: High-fidelity prototyping of interactive systems can be formal too. In: Jacko, J.A. (ed.) HCI 2009. LNCS, vol. 5610, pp. 667–676. Springer, Heidelberg (2009). https://doi.org/10.1007/978-3-642-02574-7_75

8. Paternò, F., et al.: Concur Task Trees (CTT), W3C Working Group Submission, 2 February (2012). https://www.w3.org/2012/02/ctt/
9. White, R.W.: Intelligent futures in task assistance. Commun. ACM **65**(11), 35–39 (2022)
10. Yigitbas, E., Sauer, S., Engels, G.: A model-based framework for multi-adaptive migratory user interfaces. In: Kurosu, M. (ed.) HCI 2015. LNCS, vol. 9170, pp. 563–572. Springer, Cham (2015). https://doi.org/10.1007/978-3-319-20916-6_52

Barrier-Free Design Leaf Vein Model for People with Disabilities

Nuoxi Li[1], Xiaoli Zhou[1], Lei Xue[1](✉), and Mohammad Shidujaman[2]

[1] School of Art and Design, Beijing Forestry University, Beijing, China
xuel0222@bjfu.edu.cn

[2] Department of Computer Science and Engineering, Independent University, Dhaka, Bangladesh
Shantothusets@iub.edu.bd

Abstract. The objective of this study was to explore the barrier-free design process and design thinking models for people with disabilities. As a design proposition, barrier-free design has continued to evolve in the direction of diversification and humanization in conjunction with human-computer interaction technologies in recent years. Our research experiments were conducted by user demand, combined visualization and data statistics methods, conducted big data research on the current situation of people with disabilities. We also conducted a quantitative survey and analysis of their design needs, built virtual user models and virtual scenarios. By using sampling and data analysis methods, we collected the views of over 80 professional designers about the barrier-free design and investigated the most important factors that designers need to consider in relevant design process. Therefore, these design characteristics were summed as the leaf vein model of barrier-free design based on HCI. By analyzing relevant design examples, we have qualitatively assessed the feasibility of the leaf vein model. The results show that a more functional, inclusive and standardized design product can be achieved in this design area by using the leaf vein model. These results can serve as a reference for forward-looking design and research directions for the application of HCI in the field of barrier-free design.

Keywords: Barrier-free design · Design model · People with disabilities · Human-computer interaction

1 Introduction

Nowadays, with the development of the economy and society, more and more attention is being paid to the living conditions of people with disabilities. This has led to a richer and more diverse range of theories and examples of barrier-free design for the disabled. Therefore, there has been a great deal of interest in how to provide more accessible and humane solutions for people with disabilities through design in recent years.

M. Kurosu and A. Hashizume (Eds.): HCII 2023, LNCS 14011, pp. 119–134, 2023.
https://doi.org/10.1007/978-3-031-35596-7_9

1.1 Research Background

As an integral part of our society, the disabled community is facing increasing attention and care. According to the Global Report on Health Equity for People with Disabilities, released by the World Health Organization in early December 2022, the number of people with severe disabilities worldwide is approximately 1.3 billion or 16% of the global population [1]. The study figures highlight the importance of achieving the full and effective participation of people with disabilities in all aspects of society and incorporating the principles of inclusion, accessibility and non-discrimination in the health sector. At the same time, according to the data website statista, there is now a social consensus for the care and support of people with disabilities [2]. And this is reflected in the development of barrier-free design in all areas based on user needs.

1.2 Research Status

As a design concept, the core proposition of barrier-free design is to create a safe, convenient and comfortable environment for people with different degrees of physical disabilities and reduced mobility (people with disabilities, the elderly). The main target group is people with disabilities. And the design directions include visual accessibility, auditory accessibility, behavioral accessibility and cognitive accessibility. In the current academic research related to barrier-free design, most of the papers focus on the application of barrier-free design in the fields of interior design, product design, interaction design and public design, or simply on the design elements.

For example, there has been relevant research that innovatively proposes the barrier-free design for multimodal communication systems based on remote collaboration systems in real-world scenarios by combining augmented reality technology with accessible design [3]. Also, in another study, the authors highlight the importance of inclusive design elements in the field of interior accessible design by analyzing the current state of inclusive design development in India [4]. However, few studies have been able to systematize and standardize a complete set of barrier-free design models from a top-level design perspective, providing designers with more convenient and comprehensive design ideas.

1.3 Research Objective

In response to this situation, this study combines user research, expert designer sampling, data analysis and theoretical research to deduce and build a systematic leaf vein model of barrier-free design by summarizing the design elements that have a greater impact. In conclusion, the ultimate goal of the leaf vein design model is not only to optimize the current barrier-free design system, but also to fill in the gaps and blanks in the relevant design fields. Thus, the result will also provide more standardized design ideas for barrier-free design in the future.

2 Research Method

2.1 Barrier-Free Design Questionnaire for Professional Designers

The objective of this study is to provide design elements and data to support the construction of the barrier-free design model, as well as to provide a basis for the next step in the analysis and development of a strategy. And on this basis, we will explore more influential elements of barrier-free design to optimize the user experience, etc. Our experiment was implemented through a questionnaire distributed randomly to professional designers on the internet and was designed using sampling and data research methods. The task of the experiment was to answer a series of questions related to barrier-free design and to provide examples of some specialist questions. Finally, the results and data of the experiment were recorded and analyzed in order to summarize some important design elements.

Questionnaire Design and Experimental Procedure. Through the questionnaire design process, a number of single choices, multiple choices, specific gravity selection and subjective questions were set up to investigate designers' views on barrier-free design. And a table was used to present the questions in the questionnaire (Table 1). Question 1 is a survey of basic information about the respondents and their basic understanding of barrier-free design. It is worth noting that questions 2 and 3 are the focus of the entire questionnaire. Several possible design elements of accessibility, such as emotionalization, functionality and balance elements, were pre-defined and the participants were asked to quantitatively assess the importance of each of them in numerical detail. In addition, the participants were asked to add necessary design elements based on their own experience.

In contrast to questions 1–3, which aimed to investigate the designer's perception of the accessibility process, questions 4 and 5 aimed to assess the designer's evaluation of the existing design in question. In answering questions 4 and 5, it was expected that the participants could recall barrier-free design projects they had seen or even been involved in. Furthermore, question 5 also included a quantitative assessment of issues related to the frequency of use of accessible design to allow for a refined analysis. In addition, the order of the questionnaire questions was optimized in order to sequence the questions in a logical way and to guide the participants' thinking in a progressive manner.

Participants. The experiment was mainly carried out by dividing the questionnaire on the internet, especially in the online community of professional designers. After a period of filling them out, we ended up with a sample of more than 80 questionnaires. The participants were professional designers of all ages from all over the world. Compared to non-professional designers and other professional groups, professional designers have more design experience and related theoretical knowledge. Besides, they are also able to provide stronger and more comprehensive support for the development of design models from a professional perspective.

Table 1. Questionnaire questions.

Question	Option1	Option2	Option3	Option4	Option5	Option6
1. Have you ever learned about barrier-free design? (single choice)	Nothing	Shallow understanding	Very familiar with and have done relevant cases			
2. Which elements do you think designers need to consider most in the process of barrier-free design? (Specific gravity selection)	Emotionalization. (0–100)	Functionality. (0–100)	Human-computer interaction ergonomics	Balance. (0–100)	Applicability. (0–100)	Else. (0–100)
3. Other elements that you consider important						
4. Which scenarios do you think barrier-free design is more suitable for? (Multiple choice)	Public place	Home	Medical field	Others		
5. Do you observe a high frequency of barrier-free design in your daily life?	0–20	20–40	40–60	60–80	80–100	
6. What barrier-free designs have you observed and can you give examples?						

2.2 Virtual User Models and Virtual Scenarios

Throughout the design thinking process innovation, virtual user models and user contextualization provide an in-depth understanding of the user behavioral motivations and needs, and can assist designers in making effective design decisions.

The experiments (Fig. 1) are based on a virtual travel process for people with disabilities and are combined with multidimensional data mining analysis to describe the process [5]. People with disabilities have individual functional limitations and often make effective use of their able-bodied functions (Fig. 2) to assist them in their daily lives. The following experiments are conducted with people with disabilities who are fully independent in their daily travels [6]. Firstly, they are trained to make a directional travel route and to summarize the pattern according to their personal perception [7]. At the same time, they were not only asked to judge walking distances and identify routes based on their personal memories, but were also trained to avoid obstacles to guide their travels with the help of aids such as the voice of an intelligent navigation system [8]. During the travel process, the continuity of the travel route and the unknown dangers are the focus.

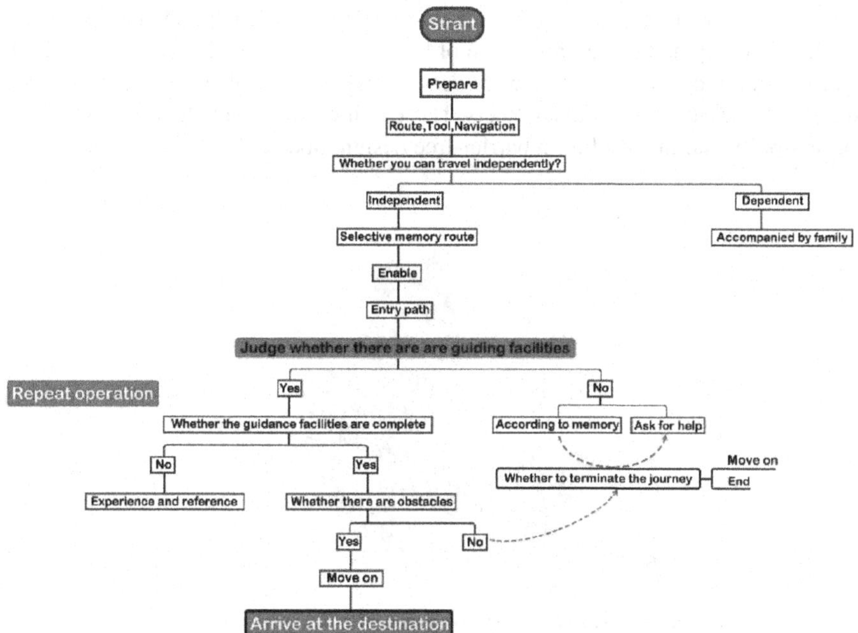

Fig. 1. Virtual user models and virtual scenarios flow chart.

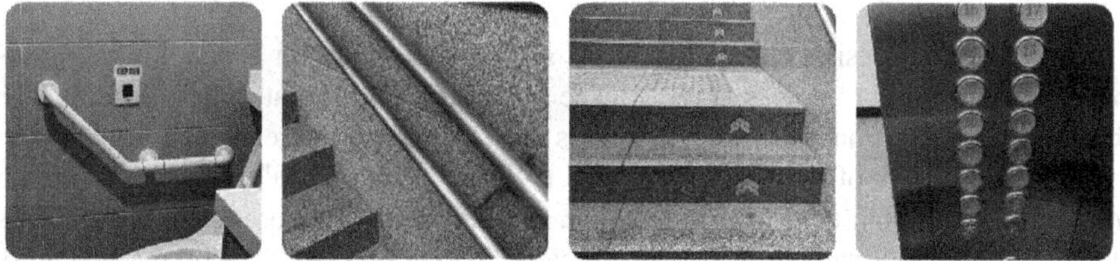

Fig. 2. The able-bodied functions in daily life.

3 Research Results

By comparing the proportion of different options selected in the questionnaire and creating a virtual user map, we have discovered which design elements are essential to the construction of the barrier-free design model. Analyzing and summarizing these findings can also help to identify the connections and causal relationships between the elements in the design model and thus refine the model. In addition, the results can be used as a reference for designers in the future.

3.1 Questionnaire Results

With regard to the six questions in the questionnaire, the responses of the participants were recorded and compared. As shown in Fig. 3, 38.1% of the respondents indicated that they had not been aware of barrier-free design and 47.62% of the participants indicated that they had some knowledge of barrier-free design. However, only 14.29% of participants indicated that they were very knowledgeable about barrier-free design and had been involved in related projects. These figures, therefore, demonstrate the lack of accessibility and the need for a barrier-free design model.

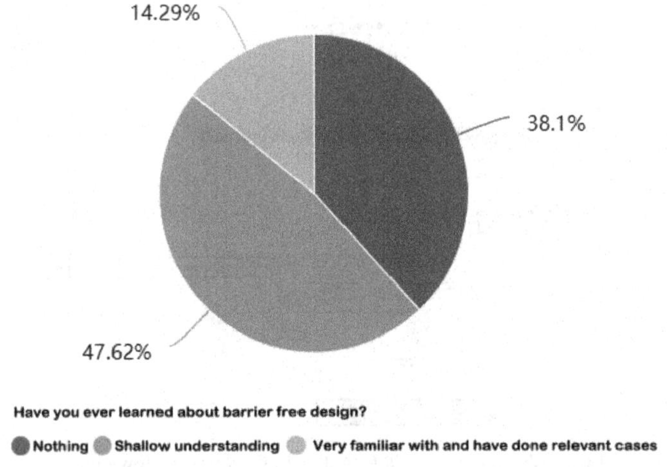

Fig. 3. Analysis of survey results for Question 1.

Out of several design elements that we set up in advance for accessibility, participants made different choices (Fig. 4). The fan charts reveal that 26.6% and 20.76% chose emotionalization and functionality as the most important elements to consider. In contrast, 18.14% of the total number of participants chose balance. 14.55% chose ergonomics or human-computer interaction, and only 14.11% chose applicability. This indicates that emotionalization and functionality are the two more important indicators for barrier-free design, while the other elements are closer to being secondary indicators. Furthermore, the results suggest that it is important to pay attention to the relationship between the priority and position of the elements when constructing a barrier-free design model.

Figure 5 shows the percentage of choices of applicable scenarios for barrier-free design in the eyes of designers. The majority of participants chose public spaces, the healthcare sector and the home as suitable locations. Of these, the percentage of participants who chose public places reached 79%. Meanwhile, according to the results of question 5 (Fig. 6), the frequency of the occurrence of barrier-free design observed by the participants in their daily lives was concentrated between 21 and 80, indicating that there is currently a social consensus on barrier-free design, but it still needs to be developed. Figure 7 shows an example of barrier-free design in everyday life in the form of a word cloud diagram. These data reflect the widespread application and need for barrier-free design models within various scenarios.

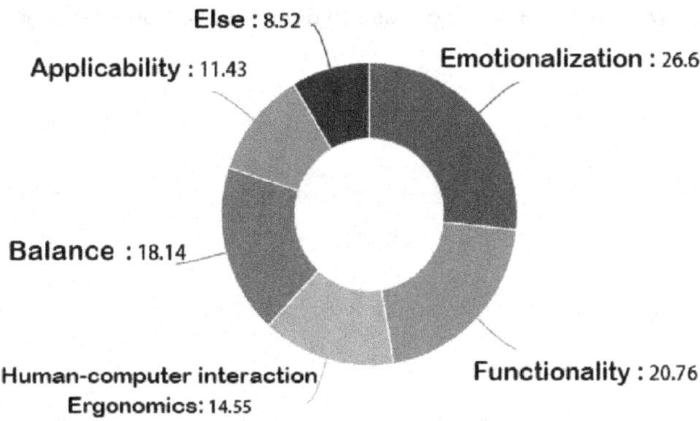

Fig. 4. Analysis of survey results for Question 2.

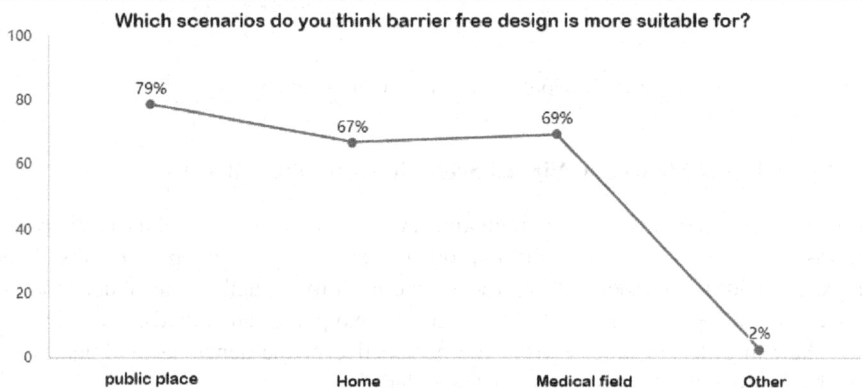

Fig. 5. Analysis of survey results for Question 4.

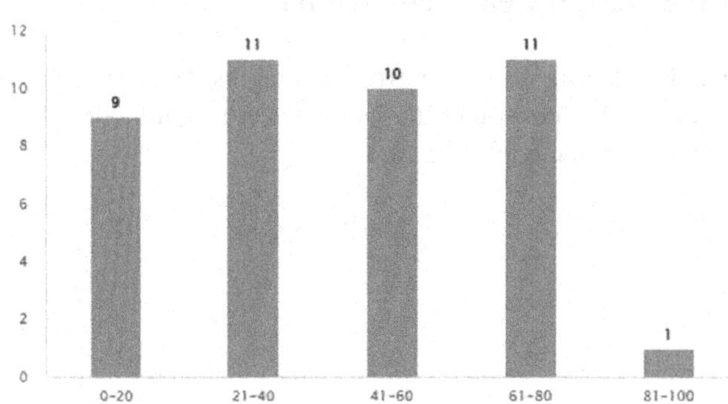

Fig. 6. Analysis of survey results for Question 5.

Fig. 7. Word cloud diagram for Question 6.

3.2 Virtual User Model and Virtual Scenario Experiment Results

Through virtual scenarios and user simulations, we identified the needs of the participants in terms of design, as well as the current problems that exist. To sum up the results of the analysis, in addition to social inclusiveness, we need to strengthen our understanding that barrier-free design thinking should constitute an organic and unified cycle, thinking about the entire design process from the perspective of the demander and achieving empathy between the designer and the demander.

4 Barrier-Free Design Leaf Vein Model

After recording and analyzing the above experimental results, we have summarized the six important elements that constitute the barrier-free design model and obtained the barrier-free design leaf vein model (Fig. 8).

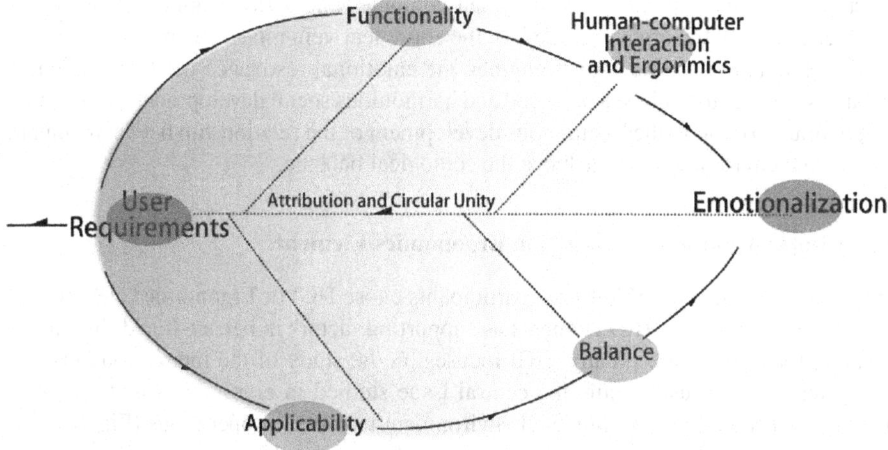

Fig. 8. Barrier-free design leaf vein model.

4.1 Functionality Element

The relationship between form and function has long been discussed by designers [9]. But in the field of barrier-free design, where design is designed to solve people's practical problems from a practical point of view, the element of functionality is said to be of great importance. In the qualitative research mentioned above, the reason why the participants placed the second most important weighting on functionality in the whole leaf vein model is that accessibility is primarily for people with disabilities and some elderly people. The design approach is also to take countermeasures to their problems, to ensure accessibility, operability and safety of the environment for people with disabilities, and to compensate for their lack of functionality with design features that remove certain barriers. The reason is that the functional element is for people and is designed to work for equality, safety, convenience and comfort.

4.2 Applicability and Balance Element

Barrier-free design is not only applied to public occasions, but also to the living space in daily life, including various appliances used for food, work and entertainment, and is a comprehensive design theme. With the development of society and technology, design needs to set a higher level of ideal goals. The leaf vein model makes the design product more reasonable and humane by integrating the two elements of applicability and balance from the perspective of the group with barriers.

In our questionnaire experiment, a significant number of subjects chose the elements of applicability and balance as the most important elements of barrier-free design, and in the next examples of additional elements, some subjects filled in the elements similar to the concepts of applicability and balance, as well as the extraction of relevant scenario words. We also found that the elements of applicability and balance complement the other elements in the leaf vein model and are applicable to the design The balance between the functionality, emotionalization, and human-computer interaction engineering elements is achieved so that the organic content of the entire leaf vein model can be circulated. To sum up, the main purpose is to strengthen the emotional resonance between designers and users in order to achieve a balanced and harmonious social development, from which we continue to explore the harmonious development of the relationship between human, society and environment and achieve the ecological balance.

4.3 Human-Computer Interaction Ergonomics Element

In the questionnaire, 14.55% of the participants chose HCI or Ergonomics elements. It has proved the need for HCI elements as supporting factors in barrier-free design models and processes. Conceptually, HCI focuses on the study of the interaction between the system and the user, while the central issue studied in ergonomics is the coordination between human, machine and environment in different operations (Fig. 9) [10]. In previous research, scholars have investigated how to combine ergonomics with age-appropriate and barrier-free design [11]. In line with this, the importance of human-machine interaction and ergonomic elements is also mentioned in the virtual user model [12]. In the barrier-free design process, designers should make effective design decisions after a thorough understanding of the user's behavioral motivation needs.

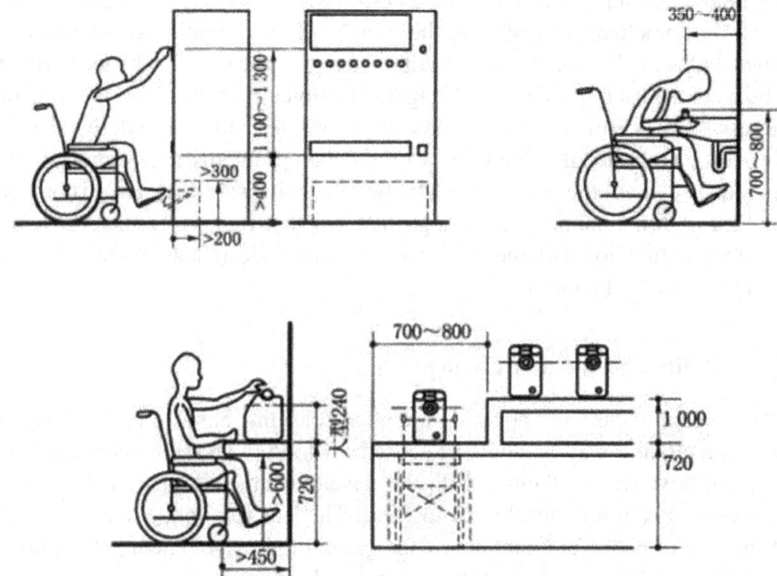

Fig. 9. Ergonomic diagram.

4.4 Emotionalization Element

Emotional design was proposed by Donald A. Norman, author of the Psychology of Design series (Fig. 10) [13]. "Cognition gives meaning to matters and emotion gives value to matters." Emotional design looks at the emotional and spiritual needs of the user and is an important element in barrier-free design. According to the results of the questionnaire, designers generally consider the emotional element to be the most important factor, as people with disabilities often have a strong sense of inferiority, anxiety and depression in psychological and spiritual terms compared to the general population, and exhibit abnormalities in cognition and behavior. The leaf vein model attempts to put itself in the shoes of people with disabilities, consider their psychological factors, establish an emotional connection between the user and the design, and relatively eliminate their sense of psychological disparity [14]. From the keyword extraction of the word cloud, it is found that close to life and caring content are the key issues to be considered in barrier-free design, and it can also be said that as the lack of psychological and physical aspects of people with disabilities is the most important user pain point and need in the whole design. Therefore, the process of barrier-free design needs to focus on emotional design elements from the instinctive level, behavioral level and reflective level.

The need for emotional elements has also been demonstrated in the above experiments from both the designer and user perspectives. Thus, in the leaf vein model, the emotional element occupies an important place in the leaf vein and is integrated into the other elements as the organic matter of the leaf vein circulates.

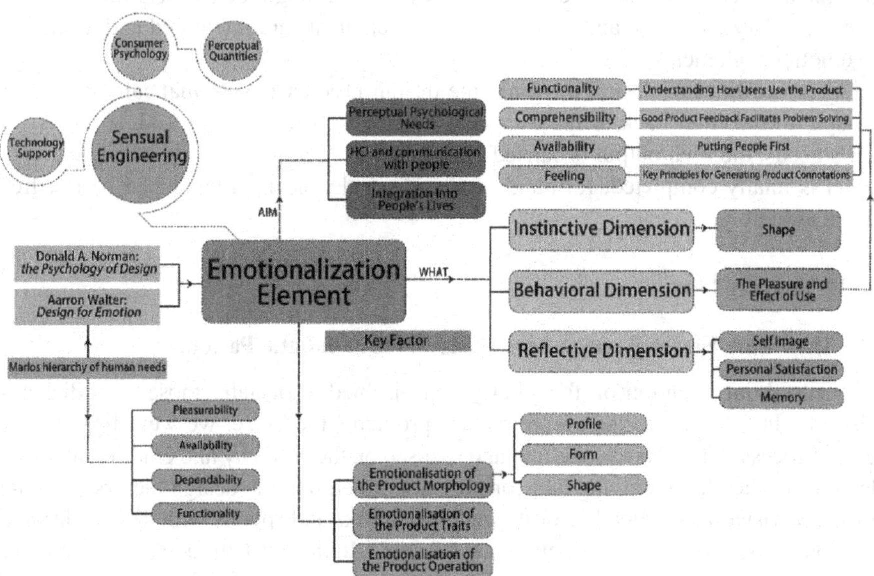

Fig. 10. The emotional design concept analysis diagram.

4.5 Attribution and Circular Unity Elements

The system theory of the leaf vein model is based on the shape and set of characteristics of a barrier-free design ecosystem. Therefore, the elements of the leaf vein model of design innovation and their primary and secondary relationships affecting design are derived by combining the elements of system and cycle unity.

The leaf vein model of barrier-free design innovation is characterized by a closed-loop leaf vein structure of the design process, which includes both primary and secondary vein lines of barrier-free design thinking. The overall design vein based on the system concept acts as the skeleton of the leaf, circulating through the entire design model and supporting the entire design process. Therefore, in the leaf vein model of accessible innovative design, the design elements at the two ends of the leaf are referred to as primary design elements and the design elements at the top and bottom are referred to as secondary design elements. The linear vein in the middle is referred to as the main design line, which coordinates all design elements in the accessible design process in a systematic and circular way.

As the design starting point for the whole model, the user needs element is on the far left and acts as the primary design element. Based on the perspective of persons with disabilities, design issues and design needs are the starting and ending points of accessible design.

The core point of the leaf vein model is the emotional element, which is located on the far right of the model. For people with disabilities, it is important to consider their emotional experiences and psychological elements. Therefore, in the barrier-free design model, from the design requirements, upwards through the functional and human-machine interaction secondary elements, downwards through the applicability and balance secondary elements, and finally the design elements are integrated and unified in the emotional elements.

After two lines of design thinking, the design product is systematically evaluated through a flow chart back to the user needs element. If the design product meets the user's needs, the final output is carried out to the left. The whole cycle of the leaf vein model is finally completed, forming a systemic cycle and interconnected barrier-free design system.

5 Research Cases

5.1 Tableware Series Barrier-Free Designed for Diabetic Patients

We focused our attention on the elderly and disabled, especially those with diabetes (Fig. 11). In response to the severe dietary problems they face, we went through the design process of leaf vein modelling and focused on the empathy and emotional design elements of the elderly, giving due consideration to ergonomic design factors to create graduated visualization bowls, portioning bowls, forks and spoons with thermochromic functions under different usage situations (Fig. 12). In the attribution and circular unity design stage, we used a series of formulas to calculate the proportion of each type of food that is suitable for consumption by elderly people of different age groups who are ill. And we took out the average of the data through user research and so on, to accurately grasp the bowl diameter opening and diameter depth.

The bottom of the bowl was designed in the form of a flower, and the undulations of the flower were used to specify the intake of each compartment, reflecting the functionality and applicability elements of the leaf vein model.

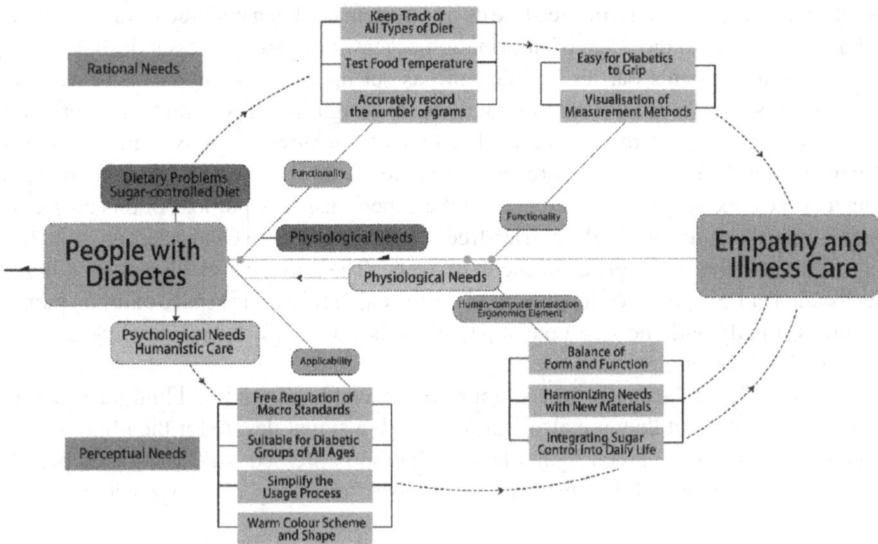

Fig. 11. Design Flow Chart.

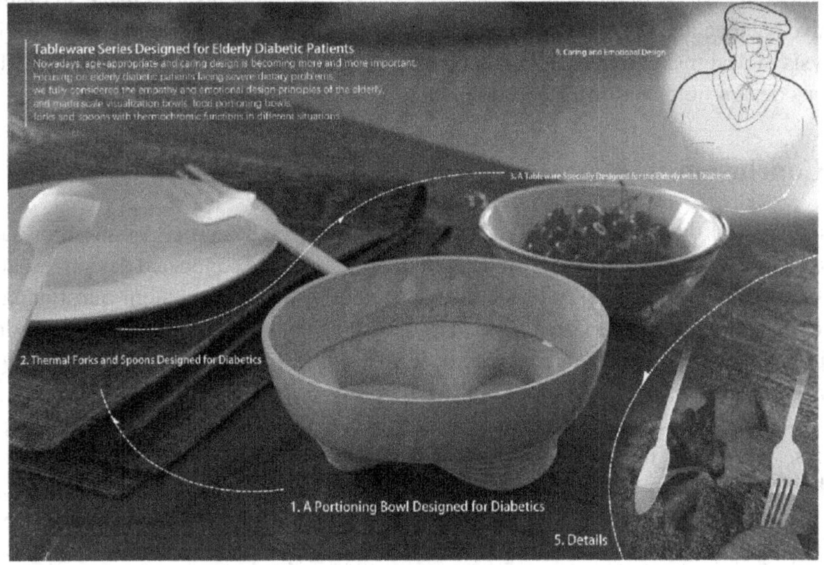

Fig. 12. The Conceptual Design Rendering.

5.2 Designing for Special Groups - Accessible Urban Public Service System

The leaf vein model is validated by the Japanese accessible urban public space service system, and it is found that the design model fully matches the basic design process required for accessible human-computer interaction. Based on the needs of the current social development, Japan's barrier-free design system has been matured in various fields and has developed to the stage of information accessibility and universal design.

First of all, Japan's barrier-free design has set up a very comprehensive vertical extension system, from laws and regulations to design systems, which can correctly predict the behavior of the action sender, so as to achieve the maximum efficiency of barrier-free design. Furthermore, it also achieves the balance of functionality and enhances the experience of "coherence" of the experience. The purpose of this project is to maximize the efficiency of the barrier-free design, to achieve a balance of functionality and to enhance the "coherence" of the experience. The construction also aims to make the disabled or transportation handicapped people enjoy the service space of urban public resources equally with the able-bodied people in the social life and it is applicable to all citizens of the society.

For example, in Japanese streets, not only are wide and guiding blind lanes set up on a regular basis, but they are also equipped with a signal device for the blind, which extends the time of the green light when the button is pressed. And it reminds people with visual impairment of their behavior with a clear "bird song". It also provides a sense of security.

It is necessary to fully consider the ergonomic human-computer interaction elements and their connection; the setting of counter height, the relationship between the passage space and human scale, and the consideration of safety and comfort are all necessary to fully deliberate with the human-computer interaction elements to achieve a comprehensive balance and apply to the corresponding situation. Finally, through comparative analysis of design solutions, testing and iteration, the whole design process is applied to various design fields to form a certain circular design system.

6 Conclusion

As society and the design discipline develop, barrier-free design is gaining more and more attention and is being widely practiced. In this study, we conducted design research and experiments through a series of design methods such as a random questionnaire survey for designers and a virtual user map for users. The experimental results and data findings were used to summarize the six key design elements of barrier-free design. Then, a systematic leaf vein model of accessibility design was constructed based on this. Finally, the feasibility of this model is evaluated and verified through relevant case studies. The design model has now been successfully applied to design areas such as product conceptualization to provide care and attention to people with disabilities.

The objective of the leaf vein model mentioned in this paper is to balance the relationship between barrier-free design and the needs of people with disabilities and to scientifically assess the design elements that designers should consider. More quantitative and qualitative research will be conducted, using a variety of research methods on a larger sample, in order to optimize the overall barrier-free design leaf vein model. We will also refine the functions of the secondary and primary vein lines. At the same time, we realize that more in-depth exploratory work is still needed to verify the feasibility with real-life examples. The main focus of this research is on visual accessibility and behavioral accessibility, but in the future the research will be extended to include auditory accessibility and cognitive accessibility such as autistic people. We hope that in the future, designers will use the leaf vein model to create more diversified and humanized barrier-free designs or concepts that meet the needs of the public and the principles of human-computer interaction. Finally, we are convinced that the use of the leaf vein model for barrier-free design will also make life easier for more people with disabilities and contribute to the development of society as a whole and to sustainable human development.

Acknowledgment. We gratefully acknowledge the effort made by Beijing Forestry University for providing us experiment condition. Special thanks to Xue Lei for giving us useful and important advice. Also, thanks to Li Yixuan and all the participants of the survey for giving us valuable help.

References

1. Global report on health equity for persons with disabilities. Geneva: World Health Organization (2022). Licence: CC BY-NC-SA 3.0 IGO
2. Statista Industries Health, Pharma & Medtech Care & Support. https://www.statista.com/markets/412/topic/455/care-support/#overview. Accessed 10 Jan 2023
3. Lee, G., Jang, H., Jeong, H., Woo, W.: Designing a multi-modal communication system for the deaf and hard-of-hearing users. In: 20th IEEE International Symposium on Mixed and Augmented Reality Adjunct, pp. 429–434. Institute of Electrical and Electronics Engineers Inc., Italy (2021)
4. Arora, S., Deshpande, A.: Inclusive design—designing barrier-free public spaces. In: Chakrabarti, A., Poovaiah, R., Bokil, P., Kant, V. (eds.) ICoRD 2021. SIST, vol. 221, pp. 133–146. Springer, Singapore (2021). https://doi.org/10.1007/978-981-16-0041-8_12
5. Mu, J., Zhu, F.: Study on the design of public facilities for visual impairment people. Creativity Des. (04), 45–51 (2018)
6. Lyu, Y.: Research on accessibility design of city bus. Changchun University of Technology (2018)
7. Wang, Y.: Research and design research on visually impaired traffic travel based on double diamond analysis model. Central Academy of Fine Arts (2021)
8. Pan, Y.: Travel research and navigation product design for visually impaired people based on interpretive structural model method. South China University of Technology (2021)
9. Wang, T., Guan, Y.: The relationship between the form and function of the product. West. Leather **40**(14), 85–86 (2018)
10. Yulan, D.: Ergonomics, 4th edn. Beijing Institute of Technology Press, Beijing (2011)
11. Butlewski, M., Tytyk, E., Wróbel, K., Miedziarek, S.: Heuristics in ergonomic design of portable control devices for the elderly. In: Stephanidis, C., Antona, M. (eds.) UAHCI 2014. LNCS, vol. 8515, pp. 24–33. Springer, Cham (2014). https://doi.org/10.1007/978-3-319-07446-7_3
12. Ker-Jiun, W., Caroline, Y.Z., Mohammad, S., Maitreyee, W., Mariana V.M.: Jean Joseph v2.0 (REmotion): make remote emotion touchable, seeable and thinkable by direct brain-to-brain telepathy neurohaptic interface empowered by generative adversarial network. In: 2020 IEEE International Conference on Systems, Man, and Cybernetics, pp. 3488–3493. IEEE, Canada (2020)

13. Donald, A.: Norman: The Psychology of Design. CITIC Press, Beijing (2003)
14. Arruda, L.M., Silva, L.F., Carvalho, H., Carvalho, M.A.F., Ferreira, F.B.N.: Somatic senses required for the emotional design of upper limb prosthesis. In: Ahram, T., Karwowski, W., Pickl, S., Taiar, R. (eds.) IHSED 2019. AISC, vol. 1026, pp. 489–494. Springer, Cham (2020). https://doi.org/10.1007/978-3-030-27928-8_74

Research on the Design of Online Participatory Design Workshop Platform Under Metaphor Design

Renxuan Liu[1], Qi Qi[2], and Duan Wu[1](✉)

[1] College of Design and Innovation, Tongji University, Shanghai 200092, China
wuduan@tongji.edu.cn

[2] Department of Architecture, Aalto University, Otakaari 1, 02150 Espoo, Finland
qi.qi@aalto.fi

Abstract. Participatory design workshops first emerged in Scandinavia in the 1970s to achieve a more democratic design by inviting users to participate in the design process. With the advent of COVID-19, many offline participatory design workshops had to use collaboration platforms, such as Miro and Conference table. However, such online collaboration design software often has a digital challenge for ordinary users. This study proposed a new design through the thinking of metaphor design—a "Card + Desktop" online participatory workshop platform. The platform uses cards as the carrier of information interaction, including four interactive forms: Card playing, Card flipping, Card adsorption, and Card grouping. At the same time, four modes are designed for different stages of the workshop: the Lobby mode of the main venue, the Round table mode in the ice-breaking stage, the Room mode for group discussion, and the Spotlight mode for group reports. Through the user test of participants, the study concluded that the card-based workshop platform could promote communication, inspire creativity, and increase engagement. It can also provide some references for the future design of online workshop platforms.

Keywords: Card-based Design Tool · Metaphor Design · Online Participatory Design Workshop

1 Introduction

In traditional design workshops, only designers participate in discussions to better iterate the product or service. In contrast, participatory design workshops invite product users to participate in the design process democratically [1], during which users and designers discuss the topic together. Moreover, many studies have shown that user participation is a key factor in product development and innovation [2]. With the advent of COVID-19, more and more online collaboration software, such as Zoom for online meetings, Google form for online document collaboration, and Miro for team brainstorming, have begun to appear. However, in participatory design workshops, people still use general online collaboration software for discussions. This type of software overemphasizes specific use scenes and increases the cognitive cost to ordinary users [3].

M. Kurosu and A. Hashizume (Eds.): HCII 2023, LNCS 14011, pp. 135–147, 2023.
https://doi.org/10.1007/978-3-031-35596-7_10

Physical cards have always been a popular design tool for designers because they are simple and efficient. Cards can visualize the entire design process and avoid abstraction. At the same time, cards, such as the famous Oblique Cards, can also stimulate the user's creative thinking and improve their creativity [4]. Previous studies have shown that using card-based design tools can improve communication between design team members and users [5]. However, the current card-based design tools are still mainly based on physical cards, and there are only a few studies on virtual card-based design tools. This study's hypothesis is to optimize digital card-based design tools and integrate them into online participatory workshops to improve the efficiency and engagement of the participants significantly.

The study first explored the design of a card-based workshop tool based on the metaphor design method. In order to integrate it perfectly into the online participatory design workshop platform, we also creatively propose four "Desktop" modes for different stages of the workshop. After prototyping, the overall user experience of the design was evaluated by inviting users to conduct a usability test. The results showed that the card-based online participatory design workshop platform can effectively increase users' engagement, communication, and immersion. Furthermore, it is also superior to other similar software in terms of efficiency. Finally, the study conducted semi-structured interviews with participants to explore how specific design features affect user experience. We believe that this discovery of interaction can give a reference for the future design of the online workshop platform.

2 Related Work

2.1 Card-Based Design Tools in Participatory Design Workshop

Previous studies have shown that using card-based design tools can improve creativity between design team members and users. One of the earliest examples of card-based design tools is The House of Cards, created in 1952 by the acclaimed American designers Charles and Ray Eames. Each of the 54 cards shows a different object. It aimed at helping inspire designers with their loved images [6]. Besides, cards are more than tools to generate creation; they can also provide structural information between different contents [6]. According to Christiane Wölfel1 and Timothy Merritt's study, there are mainly three kinds of existing card-based design tools: general purpose cards, customizable cards, and context specific cards [7]; they can be used for different needs and goals. Oblique Cards have been mentioned in the first chapter as a tool that can be engaged in any context to increase lateral thinking in general [4]. That is to say; it is static and unchanged. While the Ideation Deck is another tool that has to be created beforehand and therefore is applicable to the specific project and is adaptable to multiple themes [8]. In summary, various card-based design tools already have diverse and interesting physical features and rules.

There are already many card-based design tools that are specifically used in participatory design. Kim Halskov and Peter Dalsgård from the University of Aarhus created three kinds of physical cards used in the Inspiration Card Workshop. They are the Technology card, Domain card, and Inspiration card, which are applied in different stages with specific rules in the design process. The cards maximize participants' creativity by giving them flexibility and constraints during the workshop [5]. Although the card is of great significance to participatory design, it is still often used offline, and there are only a few studies on digital card-based design tools. For example, IDEO METHOD Card released its digital version of the card in the iPhone application, but just a virtual duplication of the physical one [7].

2.2 Metaphor Design in Human-Computer Interface

In rhetoric, the metaphor is a figure of speech in which one thing refers to another [9]. In 1980, Lakoff and Johnson published "Metaphors We Live By. " In the book, Lakoff's point of view, "metaphor is the main way for us to understand abstract concepts and express abstract reasons. This mechanism allows metaphor to become a research object in non-linguistics, so it has gradually been applied in related research in the field of design [10]. In layman's terms, metaphors can present complex, difficult, or too abstract concepts more intuitively and understandably. This feature coincides to some extent with the essence of good design that designers want to pursue.

In the early stage of interaction design, metaphors were applied in the user interface design, such as the classic recycle bin and the desktop icon in the graphical user interface (GUI). For interaction design, the most apparent advantage of metaphor is that it can reduce the cognitive burden of users [11] and promote efficient communication between designers and users [12]. At the same time, it can also make the information interaction of the graphical interface smoother and enhance the product's learnability. In Xu's research, metaphors can be divided into conceptual, behavioral, and functional [13]. On this basis, this paper discusses the design of online workshop platforms based on metaphorical thinking.

Research Approach

This study summarized the characteristics of card-based design tools in daily use and workshops, which can be divided into the following three parts:

1. Card-based design tools can promote equal communication between participants, including communication between designers and users.
2. Improve the creativity of users during participation. Card-based design tools with diverse gameplay and features can improve users' creativity in various ways, such as image association, design keyword extension, etc.
3. Card-based design tools visualize the complex design process or concept, reducing users' cognitive costs and improving the sense of immersion when participating in the workshop.

In order to better reflect the characteristics of the card-based design tools mentioned above in the design of the online workshop platform, this study introduced three types of metaphor thinking in the design process: concept metaphor, function metaphor, and behavior metaphor. The card-based design tool combined the characteristics of different metaphors in different parts. We also invited users to conduct usability tests and continuous product iterations during the prototyping process, targeting the improvements of

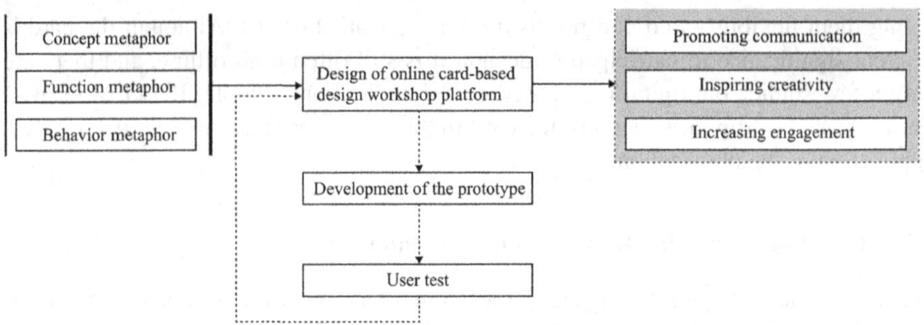

Fig. 1. Research method and procedure.

the participants' sense of communication, creativity, and engagement (see Fig. 1). Based on this, the research questions of this study are:

R1: How to design a card-based design tool through metaphorical design methods and improve the user's equal communication?
R2: How to design a card-based design tool through metaphorical design methods and stimulate users' creativity?
R3: How to design a card-based design tool through metaphorical design methods and increase the sense of immersion?

3 Design

3.1 Concept Metaphor Design

The participatory workshop requires a lively, inquiring mind and high engagement of participants. However, the tools used in current online workshops, such as Miro and Zoom, often reduce the effectiveness and the learnability due to their monotonous mode and lack of fun. This study attempts to establish a brand-new conceptual metaphor for online participatory design workshops so that users can build a new mental model with more engagement and fun.

Participatory workshops are usually aimed at collecting insights from participants. It is a process of participants outputting information. We connect this feature with card games, where cards are used to transfer information and bring the fun. Traditional card games are played with a card deck that is identical in suit and content. It usually has a set of rules that can be learned quickly, making them accessible to people of all ages and skill levels. Besides, the game can be modified and adjusted to suit different players and preferences, making them adaptable to different situations. This study uses the features of fun, structuring, and adaptability to metaphor a new card-based tool for the participatory design workshop.

We architected the new online participatory workshop tool with the card game feature. The tool includes sets of rules beforehand, and participants use cards with multiple colors to show their views on a virtual desktop. The cards are designed for two sides with different functions on each side. Besides, there are a series of interesting but easy interactions between cards, which makes the process more like a game. Furthermore, we built a series of virtual desktop modes to adapt different scenes so the participants could play the game immersively. A familiar mental model was built for the users: the workshop is like a card game, and users can imagine the workshop as a card game, which makes the tool more interesting and easier to learn.

3.2 Function Metaphor Design

Through functional metaphor design, participants' needs can be combined with desired functional points. Information input, feedback, and other common workshop functions are essential in the card-based design workshop platform. Combining the "cards + desktop" participation environment, we propose card playing, thumbs-up, collection, and four desktop modes for different scenarios.

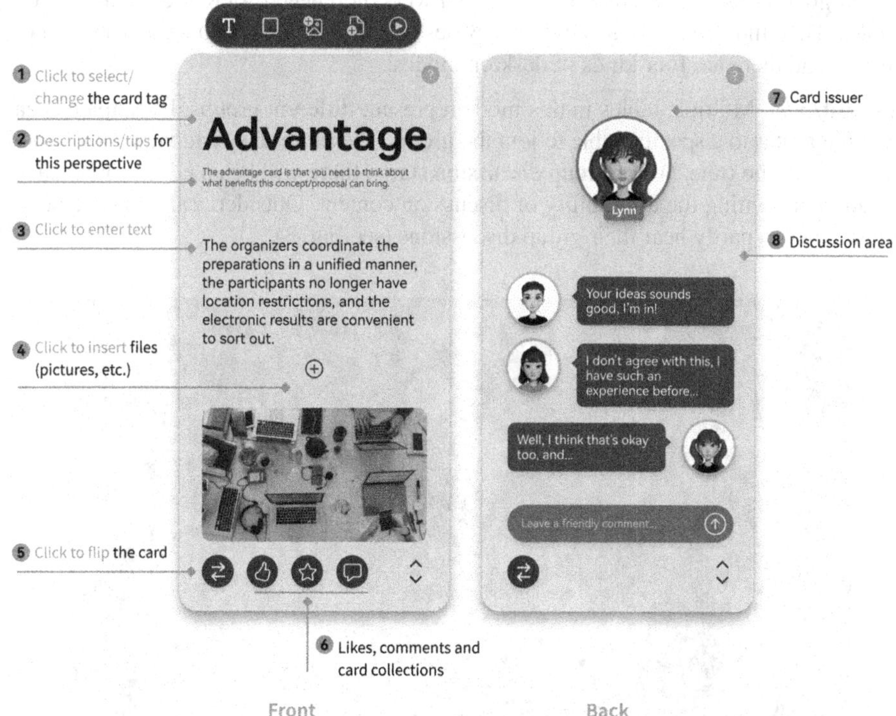

Fig. 2. Card-based design tool (use advantage card as an example)

Cards. Cards replaced post-it notes as the carrier of expressing information in the new tool. The design follows the suit rules of the card game, in which cards are with different top labels and the corresponding colors showing the recommended thinking angles (see Fig. 2). The organizer can also customize the types of cards, such as advantages, risks, costs, and distribution methods, for example, the number of cards per person) before the workshop so that the cards can be used in various kinds of workshops. More importantly, in order to follow the basic interactive operation of the card game and make the online card tool no longer a simple copy of the physical cards, the study also proposed the following four card-based interactions:

Card Playing. Workshop participants can select the type of card they want to play from the toolbar at the bottom of the platform, drag the card to the desktop and click to edit. They can choose to add text, graphics, images, files, and videos to the card to describe their views.

Thumbs-up & Collection. Participants can click the like icon at the bottom of the card when they agree with the views of the card. At the same time, they can collect them in their gallery. During the workshop, they can check the collected cards and discover and establish connections between them in their gallery at any time.

Desktop Mode. A desk in an online participatory workshop is a gathering place for participants to come together, organize information, and work collectively towards a shared goal. Different co-creation stages in a workshop need different communication modes. This study conceptualized these key desktop scenes through functional metaphor design, and there are four kinds of desktop modes:

Lobby Mode. Multiple tables in this mode represent different groups. Participants can drag the avatar to a specific table to join the group. Therefore, they can view the overall grouping all the time. When group discussion starts, there will be an edge around each group, representing the availability of discussion content. Outsiders can move close to other tables to partly hear their group discussions (see Fig. 3).

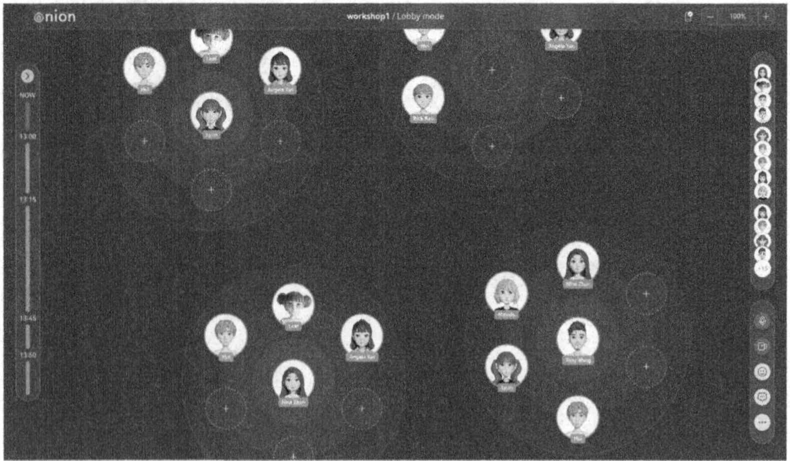

Fig. 3. Lobby mode

Round Table Mode. The icebreaker session hopes to establish an active atmosphere and encourage everyone to communicate and get acquainted with each other before the discussion. Therefore, in this mode, there is an irregular round table with avatars on the seats representing users. They can see each other directly and interact randomly, attributed to this continuous and centripetal desk shape (see Fig. 4).

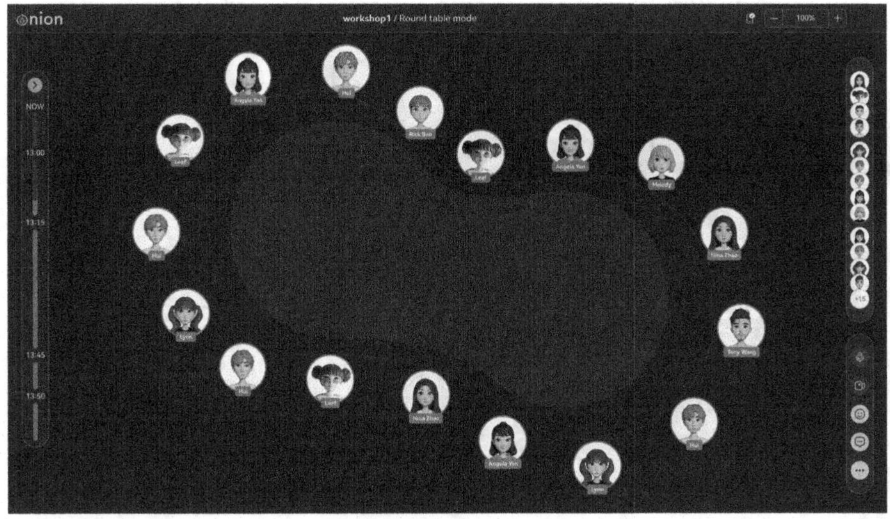

Fig. 4. Round table mode

Room Mode. This mode is used in group discussions, and the infinitely extended whiteboard allows group members to focus more on information and input (see Fig. 5).

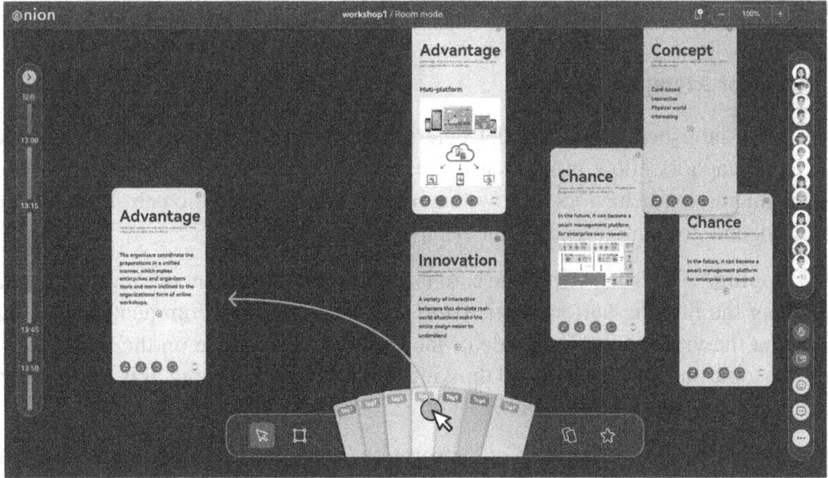

Fig. 5. Room mode

Spotlight Mode. Breaking the screen-sharing mode of the previous online workshop presentation. Spotlight Mode combines the shared screen with the auditorium and uses avatars to show the audience and the speaker. In this mode, all people can see each other's status, like in a real-life reporting hall, to enhance the presence of online participation (see Fig. 6).

Fig. 6. Spotlight mode

The gamified cards are a new mental model used in participatory design tools, while desktop modes adapt various co–creation scenes during a workshop. By combining the two features, there is huge space for the following functional design for the workshop tool.

3.3 Behavior Metaphor Design

The user's established mental model determines the priority of the user's behavior. Behavior metaphors allow users to use a new product more easily by mapping their previous interaction behaviors to how they use it. We designed the card flipping, card adsorption, and grouping based on the behavior metaphor.

Card Flipping. The front side of the card is mainly about the point of view (see Fig. 2). By clicking the flipping button, participants can check relevant comments and discussions about the view on the back side of the card. The discussion on the back helps to clarify the topic and promotes lateral thinking about the specific topic. It is also available for quick review after the workshop.

Card Adsorption & Grouping. Card adsorption (see Fig. 7) is adding cards to another one with the same label. Users can click the "plus" button below to adsorb or drag the card near the "plus" button to absorb automatically. In this way, cards are organized in a vertical layout. Card Adsorption (see Fig. 8) is different from Card flip. Adsorption is tidying the given perspective, while the Card Flip is more like a free discussion based on existing viewpoints. Unlike Card Adsorption, Card Grouping is a secondary induction of cards with all kinds of labels. The selected and grouped cards are arranged in a horizontal layout.

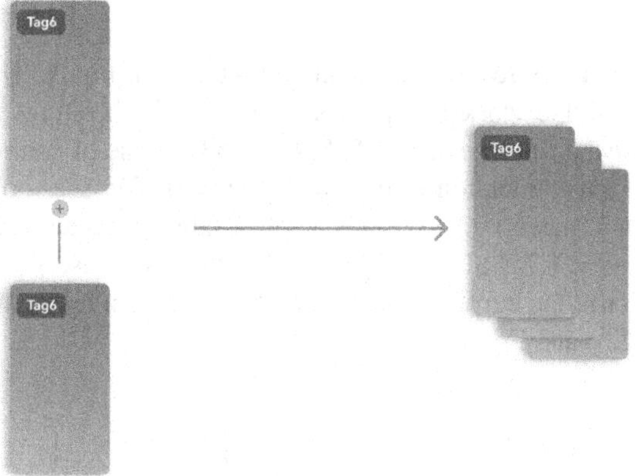

Fig. 7. Card adsorption

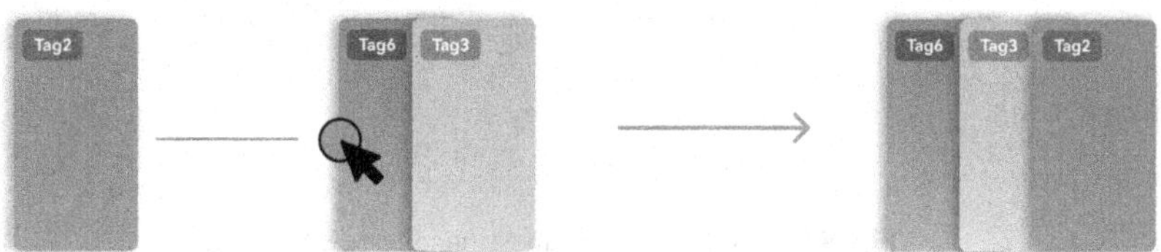

Fig. 8. Card grouping

4 Usability Test

It is universal that usability can be defined as a specific satisfaction goal achieved by users using a specific product in a specific situation, and it can be evaluated from three aspects: effectiveness, efficiency, and satisfaction [14]. The famous interaction design expert Nielsen also proposed five dimensions of usability design, which are efficiency, learnability, rememberability, frequency and seriousness of user errors, and user satisfaction [15]. The usability of a product is the basis of good user experience and human-computer interaction [16]. Therefore, it is necessary to test the overall user experience of the tool and also whether the card-based workshop tool can improve the participants' sense of communication, creativity, and engagement.

4.1 Participants

We conducted usability tests on seven typical users, including four males and three females aged 22–28. The objective of the usability test can be divided into subjective and objective. Therefore, this research combined the usability test questionnaire and semi-structured interview. We also redesigned the usability test questionnaire, in which the objective is divided into six indicators: usability, fun, creativity, sense of communication, immersion, and efficiency. Besides, the semi-structured user interview can help to obtain further design insights.

4.2 Results

The results of the usability test questionnaire are shown in Fig. 9. The results showed that the card-based online workshop platform received high ratings from users in the following three aspects: fun (mean = 2.5, SD = 0.53), sense of communication (mean = 2, SD = 0.76), and immersion (mean = 2, SD = 0.93). The tool is also affirmed by users in efficiency (mean = 2.13, SD = 0.83), usability (mean = 1.88, SD = 0.64), and creativity (mean = 1.75, SD = 0.71). Finally, the tested users expressed that they are more willing to use the current online workshop platform than online collaboration software such as Miro and Figma.

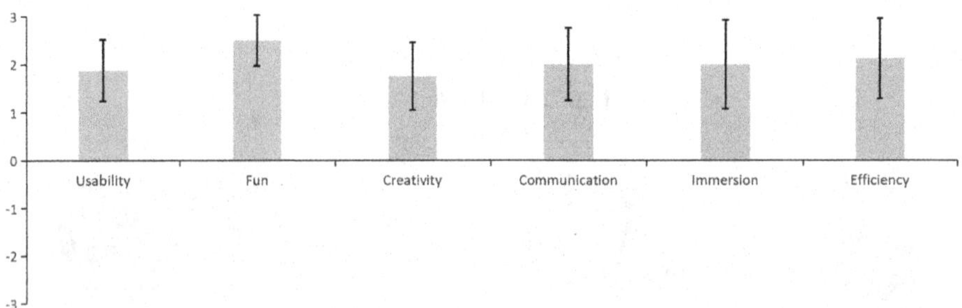

Fig. 9. Usability testing questionnaire results

It is found that the card-based online workshop platform can bring users a better experience in terms of overall usability. However, we still need specific design insights about the experience, such as how it improves the user's sense of presence when participating in the workshop, etc., so this study conducted a more in-depth semi-structured interview with the users after the questionnaire.

5 Discussion

Based on the user interviews, we summarised the design features that can improve the user experience and developed them into three categories: promoting communication, inspiring creativity, and increasing engagement.

5.1 Promoting Communication

The card interaction through metaphor design is from the user's experience in real life. It can improve usability to a certain extent and make communication more efficient. At the same time, improving communication initiatives is also what this study has aimed at, so we have summarized the following design features that can improve communications:

Card Flipping. Cards are the carrier of information, and efficiency is the key indicator. The comments area on the back of the card allows users to discuss the content or opinions of the card quickly. Currently, in most online collaboration software such as Miro, Figma, etc., the discussion is usually dissociated from the information, and the connection is made in the form of arrows or secondary annotations, which seem irrelevant to the information itself. Moreover, card flipping is more targeted, and the discussion data is stored in the background for data review.

Virtual Dynamic Avatar. Participants will be displayed as dynamic virtual avatars when they enter the digital lobby. Users can set the virtual avatar according to their preferences before the workshop starts, such as hair color, face shape, personalities, and keywords. On this platform, users are no longer the anonymous creators of text messages or pictures in the interface but individual characters with distinct personalities in the virtual world. By turning on the camera, the real-time avatars that replace faces give users a higher willingness to communicate. Additionally, the interesting interactions between avatars also allow users to feel like they are interacting with people in the real world.

5.2 Inspiring Creativity

Workshop organizers always consider improving users' creativity when participating in the workshop. Researchers have confirmed that card-based design tools can improve users' thinking activity. In this study, card labeling and card-based interactions can also assist users in sharing more opinions and inspirations.

Label. Labeled cards reduce the user's thinking cost and focus the user's limited energy on a fixed-angle topic to maximize everyone's creativity. At the same time, cards of different colors make it easier for participants to identify different themes on the whiteboard.

Card Adsorption and Grouping. This secondary content creation from the same or different viewpoints through card adsorption or secondary grouping of different cards increases the efficiency of the workshop's information output to some extent. This new interactive method encourages users to continuously inspire and integrate ideas during discussions, significantly improving the group's co-creation ability.

5.3 Increasing Engagement

The most significant distinction between online and offline participation is the surrounding environment, which will lead to completely different experiences for users. In this case, the sense of immersion during participation is vital for the workshop because online discussions lack sensual presence, which can result in low participation. To deal with this, the proposed platform can improve user experience in the following aspects:

Multi-scene Desktop Display. Users can enter different desktop scenes at different stages of the workshop, which can bring them a better sense of immersion. For example, in the Round table mode in the ice-breaking stage, users feel more engaged in the workshop through face-to-face communication. People who participated in the test said, "it is exciting to use the Round table mode to break the ice. People can see each other's status and expressions." Different workshop desktop scenes restore the spatial experience and socialization when participating in offline workshops.

Card Flipping. Utilizing the typical setting of the front and back of the card, the flipping operation simulates the natural movement when playing a physical card game. At the same time, the different information displayed on the front and back also prioritizes the information more reasonably. When users are interested in the information, they can choose to flip the card for further communication. More than one user has stated that "the flipping interaction of the cards is fascinating, like playing a game."

Avatar Movement. The avatar not only represents the digital image of the participants but also reflects the participants' physical actions and emotional expressions when moving and interacting on the whiteboard. The participants can feel the emotions of other participants and the organizers when they are in online status, not just the cursors. After using the prototype, many users said: "It is fascinating to interact with the participants on the desktop by tapping their avatars as if you are participating in an offline workshop and having a cordial conversation with others."

6 Conclusion

Participatory design workshops invite users to participate in the product design and development process, and users' opinions and ideas become key considerations for the products. This kind of workshop is an essential embodiment of user-centered design thinking. Metaphor Metaphorical design is about using people's experiences in the real world to rethink user behavior when the interaction environment is transformed into an online one. The proposed platform in this study cleverly applied card-based design tools to the online workshop scene through metaphor design and adapted it to specific scene modes in different stages of use. The concept of "card + desktop" can bring users a higher sense of engagement, and novel interactions can attract users' attention during participation and avoid distraction. All users' behaviors during the participation process happen in the real world. This blurred sense of online and offline boundaries can also help users better discuss and output.

References

1. Harrington, C., Erete, S., Piper, A.M.: Deconstructing community-based collaborative design: towards more equitable participatory design engagements. In: Proceedings of the ACM on Human-Computer Interaction, pp. 1–25. Association for Computing Machinery, New York (2019)
2. Wilkinson, C.R., De Angeli, A.: Applying user centred and participatory design approaches to commercial product development. Des. Stud. **35**(6), 614–631 (2014)
3. Ellis, R.D., Kurniawan, S.H.: Increasing the usability of online information for older users: a case study in participatory design. Int. J. Hum. Comput. Interact. **12**(2), 263–276 (2000)
4. Burns, A.: Oblique strategies for ambient journalism. M/c J. **13**(2) (2010)
5. Halskov, K., Dalsgård, P.: Inspiration card workshops. In: Proceedings of the 6th conference on Designing Interactive systems, pp. 2–11. Association for Computing Machinery, New York (2006)

6. Roy, R., Warren, J.P.: Card-based design tools: a review and analysis of 155 card decks for designers and designing. Des. Stud. **63**, 125–154 (2019)
7. Wölfel, C., Merritt, T.: Method card design dimensions: a survey of card-based design tools. In: Kotzé, P., Marsden, G., Lindgaard, G., Wesson, J., Winckler, M. (eds.) INTERACT 2013. LNCS, vol. 8117, pp. 479–486. Springer, Heidelberg (2013). https://doi.org/10.1007/978-3-642-40483-2_34
8. Golembewski, M., Selby, M.: Ideation decks: a card-based design ideation tool. In: Proceedings of the 8th ACM Conference on Designing Interactive Systems, pp. 89–92. Association for Computing Machinery,New York (2010)
9. Liao, H.: Conceiving the metaphor in UI design. J. Tongji Univ. (Soc. Sci. Sect.) **21**(03), 76–82 (2010)
10. Lakoff, G., Johnson, M.: Metaphors We Live By. University of Chicago press, Chicago (2008)
11. Carroll, J.M., Thomas, J.C.: Metaphor and the cognitive representation of computing systems. IEEE Trans. Syst. Man Cybern. **12**(2), 107–116 (1982)
12. Saffer, D.: The role of metaphor in interaction design. Inf. Architect. Summit **6** (2005)
13. Xu, Y.: Metaphorical study in graphic user interface design. The University of Suzhou, MA thesis (2017)
14. Frøkjær, E., Hertzum, M., Hornbæk, K.: Measuring usability: are effectiveness, efficiency, and satisfaction really correlated?. In: Proceedings of the SIGCHI conference on Human Factors in Computing Systems, pp. 345–352. Association for Computing Machinery, New York (2000)
15. Nielsen, J.: The usability engineering life cycle. Computer **25**(3), 12–22 (1992)
16. Rusu, C., Rusu, V., Roncagliolo, S., González, C.: Usability and user experience: what should we care about? Int. J. Inf. Technol. Syst. Approach **8**(2), 1–12 (2015)

Research on Elements of Physical Interaction Design and the Information Channel

Long Liu(✉) and Xiaoshan Wang

Tongji University, Siping Road 1230, Shanghai, China
2031991@tongji.edu.com

Abstract. Physical interaction, as an interaction occurring within the physical world, is a vital aspect of daily life. As digitization has progressed, more and more information and media have changed traditional physical interactions. Digital interaction is gradually becoming more prevalent. However, in some cases, the absence of physical operating equipment prevents the user from getting a timely and effective response, which may result in life-threatening situations. Additionally, some physical interactions that were retained degraded functionality and user experience. Therefore, it is necessary to explore the factors affecting physical interaction design and the elements of physical interaction design. In fact, there are not many theoretical studies on physical interaction, and the exploration of the nature of physical interaction is relatively lacking. In this study, qualitative data collection and analysis methods such as interviews, observations, and coding techniques are used to uncover the influencing factors and design element models of physical interaction design, and further explain the meaning of "interaction channel" from the standpoint of the interaction interface. The interaction channel represents the three-dimensional interaction space created by a physical interface and it can serve as a reference for design practice. Moreover, clarifying the concept of physical interaction and exploring the elements of physical interaction design will assist us in understanding physical interaction as well as digital interaction, and will allow us to complete the design in a reasonable manner, which in turn will inspire designers to create future interactions.

Keywords: Information of Presentation · Physical Interaction · Interaction Design · Information Channel

1 Introduction

1.1 Research Background

Physical interaction is accompanied by human creation practice and creation history. Since then, people have been constantly studying how to use tools and how to adapt tools to people [1].

Once upon a time, we were familiar with such a scene: Whether it is an airplane, a train, or a passenger car, the driving control area is lined with various buttons. However, with the advent of the digital age, more and more information and diverse media

M. Kurosu and A. Hashizume (Eds.): HCII 2023, LNCS 14011, pp. 148–162, 2023.
https://doi.org/10.1007/978-3-031-35596-7_11

have begun to change traditional physical interactions, such as typewriters evolving into keyboards (see Fig. 1) and mice evolving into touchpads, etc. More diverse digital interaction methods are also emerging. Digitization and intelligence have become the current mainstream design trends. However, when the physical buttons for interaction in the car gradually disappear and more and more touch screens replace them, new problems also arise. Since there are no physical operation buttons, the driver's stress response cannot be adequately handled in emergency situations, resulting in driving accidents. In previous interviews, drivers generally mentioned the "safety", "intuitive" and "accurate" advantages of physical interaction. Sometimes users can get some physical feedback immediately, which makes the basic logic of interaction design easier to understand [2].

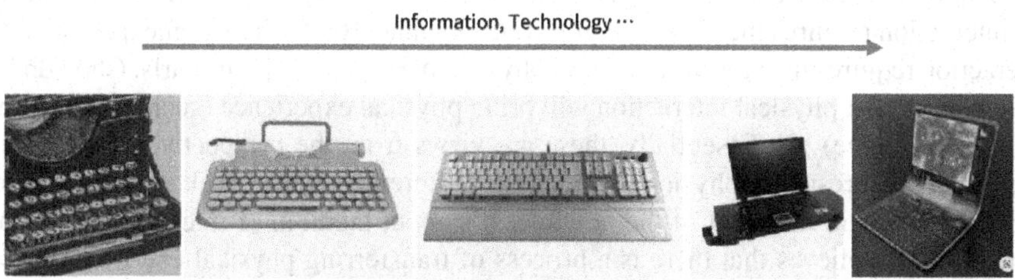

Fig. 1. The evolution of the keyboards (The pictures are from the website).

Physical interaction is an essential way of interaction in daily life. In our lives, some physical interactions are better preserved and designed, some are replaced by digital ones and continue to evolve. And in some cases, the combination of physical interaction and digital interaction forms a composite interaction, resulting in a better experience. Tangible interaction is a typical interaction that establishes the connection between the physical world and the digital world. It is dedicated to the fusion of physical interaction and digital interaction. Hiroshi Ishii and Brygg Ullmer mentioned that we live in two worlds [3]: one is the physical environment in which we live [4], and the other is untouchable cyberspace or digital space. They are parallel but independent of each other [5]. When digital and physical information are combined in an interaction between people and products, information transmission in that interaction becomes complex and diverse. Therefore, it is necessary to regard physical interaction as a fundamental interaction. Physical interaction and digital interaction do not need to be independent of each other but should be better integrated. Clarifying the concept of physical interaction and exploring the elements of physical interaction design will help us understand physical interaction and digital interaction, and reasonably complete the design. It will also allow designers to create more composite interactions in the future.

1.2 Problem Statement

This study aims to explore the factors that affect physical interaction design and the elements of physical interaction design, providing a theoretical basis for interaction design. Designers relying solely on intuition and experience to make design decisions may produce irrational designs. A poorly designed product may have a poor interaction experience for users or have low interaction efficiency for products in achieving certain functions. For example, for interactive operations that require fast and precise control, users often need to directly control and perceive devices. Hence, our aim is to find the general laws of physical interaction and interaction design through theoretical research in order to guide design practice and realize the intended applications.

2 Related Work on Physical Interaction

What is the nature of physical interaction? Is it merely the interaction between the physical world and humans?

Scholars have different views on physical interaction. Galán et al. believe that physical interaction requires the existence of physical contact [6]. Li et al. argue that physical interaction requires the presence of direct physical perception [7]. Similarly, Chowdhury et al. believe that physical interaction will bring physical experience (such as visual and tactile experience) [8]. Essentially, these are views from the perspective of the user's perception as a result of physical interaction. Differently, Sonar et al. equate the concept of "physical" with that of the tangible. It's about medium of interaction [9]. And Bert Bongers believes that there is a process of transferring physical energy in physical interaction [10]. This point of view involves information transfer in the interaction process. In fact, most of these perspectives come from applied research on physical interactions. These studies did not directly clarify the concept of physical interaction, but the researchers' demonstrations reflect different understandings of the concepts of "physical interaction" and "physical", and reflect the essential attributes of physical interaction from different perspectives.

In addition to applied research, theoretical research on physical interactions focuses on the properties of physical interactions. Campenhout et al. emphasize the different properties of people and artifacts in the physical and digital environments, and physical interaction is based on behavior [3]. Michelle Chandra abstractly described physical interaction as "a mind that is separated from the body cannot be perceived [2]." This emphasizes the physicality of physical interaction in the physical world. Dix et al. carefully and comprehensively deconstruct the behavior process of physical equipment in physical interaction, identify two types of physical interaction (See loop A and B in Fig. 2), and clarified the physical interaction process starting with physical manipulation [11]. However, this research focuses on the behavior of the physical device during the interaction and reduces the human part to an abstract "physical manipulation input".

Generally speaking, there are not many theoretical studies on the complete behavior process of physical interaction, and the exploration of the nature of physical interaction is relatively lacking. Also, it is rare for applied research to discuss the concept of physical interaction. Therefore, scholars' understanding of "physical interaction" is inconsistent or even contradictory.

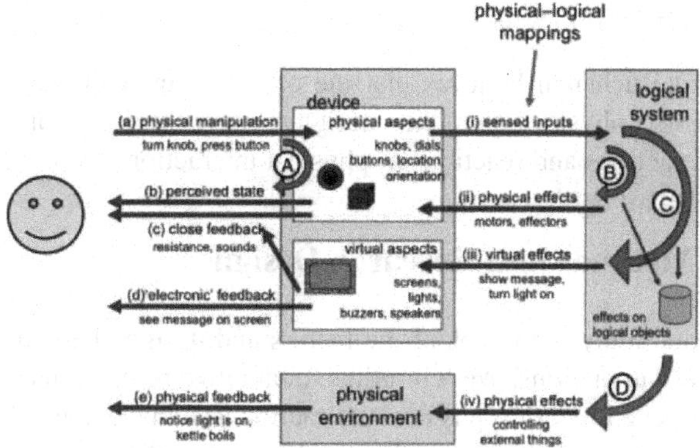

Fig. 2. Multiple feedback loops [11]. A and B are physical interaction loops.

3 Concept Definition

Physical interaction is a form of basic interaction that is related to human-computer interaction, interaction design, ergonomics, and other areas of study. Thus, based on the understanding of "physical interaction" in relevant literature in related fields, this study uses linguistic description to define the concept of "physical interaction" in order to avoid ambiguity.

3.1 Physical

"Physical" has multiple interpretations in English. Based on the background and problems of this research, in order to avoid ambiguity, the word "physical" adopts the following definition:

> "Having material existence: perceptible, especially through the senses and subject to the laws of nature [12]."

3.2 Interaction

"Interaction" is formed by "action" and "reaction" that lead to a round of interaction [13]. Therefore, interaction refers to a complete behavioral process consisting of a series of actions and reactions.

3.3 Physical Interaction

Based on the vocabulary, we define the concept of physical interaction as "a round of interaction that can be perceived through the senses and subject to the laws of nature". In spite of the similar wording, it should be noted that "physical interaction" in this study should be clearly distinguished from the concept of physical process or physical change in physics.

3.4 Physical Interaction Design

Professor Richard Buchanan believes that the object of interaction design is human activities [14]. Hence, physical interaction design refers to the design of human activities that consist of the actions and reactions of physical interaction.

4 Research Methods and Research Design

The purpose of our study is to explore the factors and design elements that affect the design of physical interactions. We will utilize qualitative research methods to explore factors and construct a model for physical interaction design elements. Considering the lack of research on physical interaction design, this study will make reference to related research and concepts in the fields of human-computer interaction, interaction design, and ergonomics in order to assist with the planning, analysis, and construction of the model based on the original data from the field study.

4.1 Research Methods and Tools

The research methods used in this study are as follows:

Literature Research.
Use relevant research materials to collect, analyze, and discuss data.

Purposive Sampling.
Used as a secondary sampling method in this study. Based on previous studies, a few representative samples are selected through initial judgment in order to increase the probability of discovering valuable information. Once the data has been analyzed, the sampling method is changed to theoretical sampling.

Theoretical Sampling.
Collection, analysis, and coding of data should be carried out simultaneously. With the results of the analysis, we can determine the next sample in the process in order to reach theoretical saturation [15].

Semi-structured Interview.
As the main method of first-hand data collection in this study, the interview outline is drawn up according to the research questions, and the user is asked to describe in detail the physical interaction process of using the product and the factors that affect the interaction. Details of the interaction, such as obstacles or confusion encountered, how to resolve them, etc.; help users recall details, do not restrict interviews excessively; continuously revise the outline content as the research progresses.

The Non-participatory Observation.
Used as a secondary method of first-hand data collection in this study. Observation

records, pictures, and videos are used to document the natural process of users using products in daily environments, and outcomes are documented objectively and truthfully.

Coding.
The method is used to generate concepts and categories and then form theories, so it is applicable to the induction of the influencing factors of physical interaction design. Images, videos, and texts are coded and analyzed. As we determine, describe, and compare codes continuously, we are able to derive concepts through induction and identify the factors that influence physical interaction design.

Mind Map and MAXQDA Software.
We used Xmind and MAXQDA software for coding, classification, and code organization. As a result, some illustrations in this article are based on screenshots taken from software.

4.2 Research Design

The research path is mainly divided into three stages: preparation, data collection and analysis, and discussion of the results.

During the preparation stage, we clarified the research questions, sample range, sampling method, and data collection plan, sorted out relevant literature, and identified possible related concepts for coding references. Lastly, we designed observation record sheets, interview outlines, and other materials necessary for the collection of data.

The data collection and analysis phase included conducting in-depth interviews with the respondents to understand their feelings and motivations for physical interaction, and collecting video materials of the physical interaction of the users through observation. A second-hand data source is gathered to augment and verify the results. On the one hand, data collection and data analysis are carried out simultaneously in the research process, such as organizing and coding the interview content after the interview and selecting the next sample to conduct the interview based on the coding situation. On the other hand, the three types of data collection and analysis were carried out sequentially in the order of "interview analysis-observation analysis-secondary data analysis", which will assist with the triangulation verification of coding. The reliability of the core categories can be verified due to similar coding performances across different types of data. After that, merge the data in order to complement one another. Finally, theoretical models of concepts, categories, and core categories are developed.

In the results stage, the coded results are checked for saturation. Upon saturation, the results of the research are sorted, and finally, the influencing factor model of physical interaction design is established.

5 Procedures and Results

5.1 Preparation

Define the Research Question.
Firstly, the research question of this study is clarified: what factors will affect the physical interaction design?

Determine Sample Range.
As researchers cannot do endless sample analyses for a specific problem, it is very important to establish the overall sample range at an early stage in order for the research to be of high quality and efficient.

In this study, participants will be adults who are in the good physical condition and don't suffer from any illnesses that significantly affect their daily lives. The study will include males and females aged 18–60 and 18–55 in accordance with the basic data indicated in my country's adult body size measurement standards in GB10000–88 in ergonomics, in order to conduct further research [16].

In order to avoid too large data sets, this study focuses on driving interactions of basic cars and selects normal and safe driving situation to begin data collection. The main reasons for this decision are: (1) There are various forms of in-vehicle interaction, so in addition to facilitating the comparative analysis between physical interactions, it is also easy to compare physical interactions with digital interactions, so as to obtain more valuable information; (2) In the field of vehicle interaction, many original data and research materials exist, which provide additional references for qualitative research on physical interaction and enhance its reliability. It should be noted that the conclusion of data processing will serve as a substantive theory of driving interactions, that needs to be abstracted further to generate a general theory that can explain a wider range of physical interactions.

In this study, samples are examples of physical interactions (see loops A and B in Fig. 1) in a vehicle. This study aims to gain a deeper understanding of physical interaction. Hence, a wide range of physical interaction samples can assist in increasing the efficiency of research. Further, combined interaction (including tangible interaction) offers a number of unique physical interaction forms, which makes it an excellent analysis sample.

Define the Sampling Method.
We used both purposive sampling and theoretical sampling in this study. Early in the research process, the sample was based on the age group of users, and after a round of data analysis, the sample was based on theoretical direction. The data should be used to explain as many phenomena within the sample as possible and the purpose of data collection is to achieve theoretical saturation [17].

Design the Data Collection Plan.
In order to ensure that the research results are explanatory, this study uses semi-structured interviews and observation methods to obtain first-hand data, as well as industry reports and consultations, public meeting records, expert forums, and other sources as second-hand data in order to achieve triangulation.

5.2 Data Collection and Analysis

This study uses the combination of first-hand and second-hand data to strengthen the triangular test. The data types, sources, and quantities are shown in Table 1.

Table 1. Type, source and quantity of the data.

Type	Source	Quantity	Detail
First-hand	In-depth interview	13 people	About 12k words, 750min
First-hand	Non-participatory observation	25 people	About 300min
Second-hand	Industrial reports, Forum Records, Web Articles	14 copies	400 + pages

Due to the lack of existing research, this study uses the open coding and selective coding techniques of classical grounded theory to analyze data and generate theories from raw data.

The data were imported into MAXQDA and coded jointly by two researchers. To ensure the validity of the coding, the researchers agreed on the research questions and their understanding of related concepts. One researcher coded the data, and the other analyzed and verified them, marked and recorded new or controversial codes, supplemented missing codes, and compared them with the original codes. A consensus is reached after coding discussions. After no new codes appeared, interviews were conducted with four new respondents as a saturation test in order to ensure coding saturation. The saturation test did not reveal any new codes, and the result was saturated.

Open Coding and Selective Coding.
In open coding, phenomena are named and classified based on careful analysis, which involves the process of inductive and comparative analysis, inspection, and conceptualization of data [15]. In this study, open coding is divided into three steps. The first step is to import the data into MAXQDA software. Second, the corpus is extracted sentence by sentence and paragraph by paragraph, as well as browsing pictures and videos to identify relevant information that affects the design of physical interactions. Our final step was to combine and summarize the obtained concept codes to form categories.

Selective coding of data is a process of highlighting core categories and discovering their relationships with other categories using targeted data coding [17]. At the selective coding stage, core categories such as "interaction channel", "interaction resources", "interaction costs", "user needs", and "context" gradually emerged.

Due to space limitations, we show part of the coding process here as an illustration in Table 2.

In this study, 1217 codes and 123 open codes were generated. As a result of coding, five core categories are identified, namely influencing factors, as shown in Table 3. "Interaction channel" is related to other core categories, making it a key factor in the design of physical interactions.

Table 2. An abstracting process for open coding.

Part of Data	Concept Connotation	Category	Core Category
I don't think it's a good idea to change the buttons from three-dimensional to flat. In this way, the dimension of tactile sensation is weakened, otherwise I would not be sure whether I clicked it, especially when I didn't see it	Displacement changes during interaction	Information Flow	Interaction Channel
	Tactile information feedback, visual information feedback	Information Content	
	Accessibility of different sensory feedback	Accessibility	Interaction Cost
	Whether the part is accurately controlled	Medium Resources	Interaction Resources
	The control ability of the user	Individual Resources	

Table 3. Five core factors of physical interaction design.

Core Categories	Concept connotation
Interaction Channel	The information channel generated during the interaction process
Interaction Resources	Resources held during the interaction
Interaction Costs	Resources consumed during the interaction
User Needs	The thoughts or desires that drive the user to physically interact
Context	The scene in which the interaction takes place

As shown in Fig. 3, the influencing factors and main aspects will be explained in detail below:

(1) Interaction channel: The definition of the word "channel" in the field of communication is very suitable for this study. There is a process of information transfer in the interaction process. Therefore, the interaction channel in this study refers to the channel generated by information transfer in the interaction process. There are four specific aspects to it.

Information content. It refers to the substantive content of information transmitted in an interaction, including the range and time of the action, the visual and tactile information in feedback, etc. Functional information also represents the physical information that needs to be transmitted during the process of implementing the function.

Communication for information. It refers to the correlation between different pieces of information. Synergistic functions are common in interaction processes, which can be explained by the high degree of correlation between functional content.

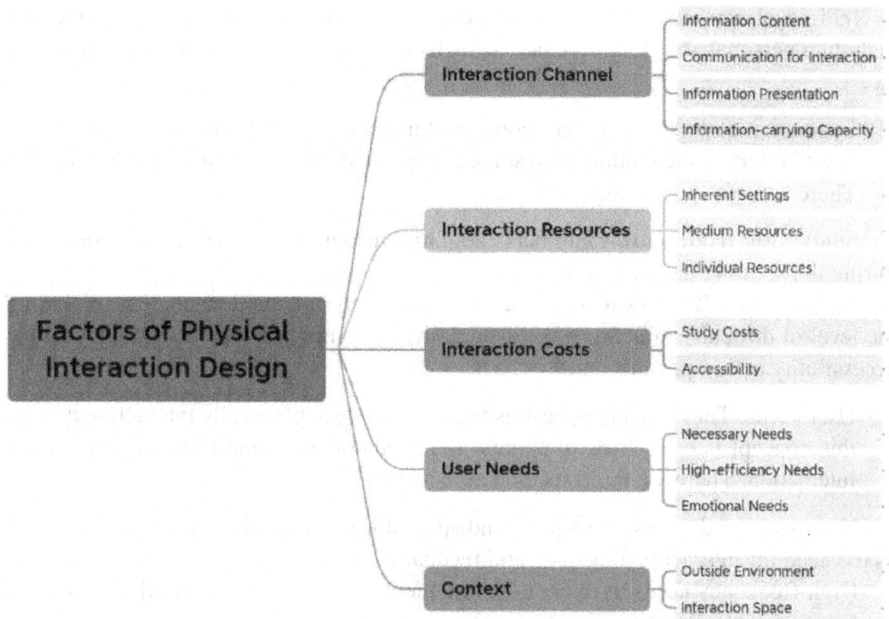

Fig. 3. Five core factors and their specific aspects.

Information presentation. In this context, it refers to the visual presentation of information, which may include the presentation of information architecture or design performance of information transmissions, such as the aesthetics of actions or the sense of interface design.

Information-carrying capacity. During information transfer, it refers to the amount, rate, and capacity of information that is transmitted. It is primarily that the information-carrying capacity determines the performance of information transmission during the interaction process.

(2) Interaction resources: resources held during the interaction process. The interaction resources refer to the "substance" of the interaction, on which the interaction is based. There are three specific aspects to it.

Inherent settings. In this context, inherent settings remain unchanged throughout the interaction process. This includes basic characteristics, such as age, gender, user familiarity, proficiency, physical characteristics of users and components, and spatial characteristics.

Medium resources. An interaction medium has resources, such as controllability and problem-solving ability, that are used in the interaction.

Individual resources. It refers to the user's own resources used in the interaction, including personal ability, experience, knowledge range, body and body activity range, etc.

(3) Interaction costs: the resources consumed in the interaction process. In economics, "cost" refers to the number of resources expended. Therefore, it is suitable for use. There are two specific aspects to it.

Study costs. It refers to the number of cognitive resources, time, and energy consumed during the learning interaction process.

Accessibility. It refers to the ease of realizing the interaction process, including the level of difficulty of actions, the availability of components and functions, and the accessibility of components and feedback.

(4) User needs: The thoughts or desires that drive users to physically interact. In design, this concept is often used to express the needs of users and to reflect the aim of interaction. There are three specific aspects to it.

Necessary needs. This refers to the indispensable and important needs of users, such as the need for interactive functions and feedback, etc.

High-frequency needs. It refers to the frequent needs of users, primarily referring to the functional requirements they prefer to use most frequently.

Emotional needs. An individual's subjective feelings, including their physical and mental feelings and emotions, are considered.

(5) Context. It refers to the context where the interaction takes place. In this study, they are mainly divided by the interaction space and outside environment. There are two specific aspects to it.

Interactive space. It refers to the space where interaction occurs, including traffic space and adjacent auxiliary space.

Outside environment. The environment outside the interactive space includes the natural environment as well as the social environment.

6 Discussion and Conclusion

The interaction channel, the interaction resources, the interaction costs, the user needs, and the context are all contributing factors to physical interaction design. Therefore, taking the five factors as elements to be considered in physical interaction design will play an important role in design (See Fig. 4).

The interaction channel is the key element of physical interaction design and is related to a number of other factors. The importance of this element can be attributed to the fact that it has a close relationship with the nature of physical interaction to some extent.

In order to gain a deeper understanding of the interaction channel element of physical interaction, we explored it further. Finally, we gained a better understanding of the nature of physical interactions and how they occur.

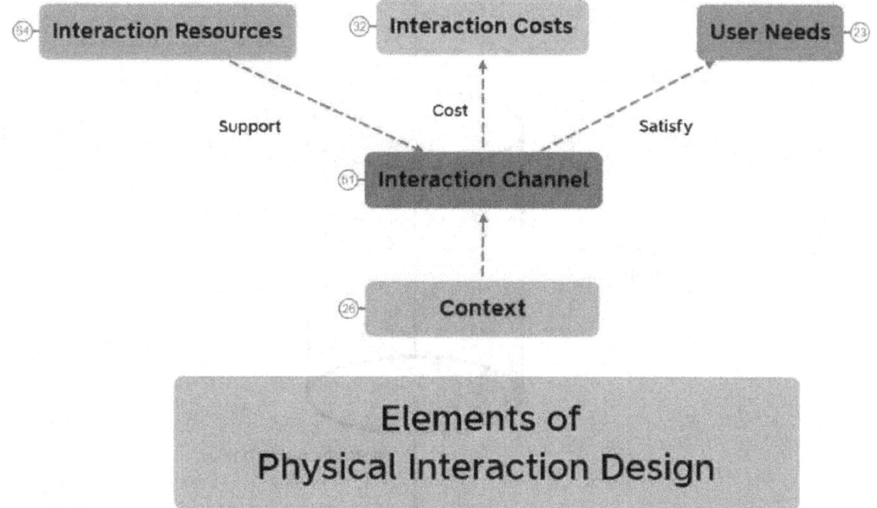

Fig. 4. Elements and Relationships of Physical Interaction Design

In this study, the interaction channel is further interpreted by the four concepts of information-carrying capacity, information content, information exchange, and information presentation, with information-carrying capacity encompassing information flow, information capacity, and information transmission rate. However, when the concept of "interaction channel" is considered within the context of the sub-level concept, a three-dimensional model emerges describing the "interaction channel" and what occurs during physical interaction (See Fig. 5).

The three aspects of information-carrying capacity have become the most influential attributes of an interactive channel's flow of information. Content is a real substance, and presentation is a means of expressing the content. Furthermore, this graph represents our understanding of "information communication" (see Fig. 6).

This communication symbolizes the convergence of multiple interactions. When two interactions meet, the original channel will change, which will result in the original attributes changing as well. The reason an interaction behaves differently when it is performed collectively versus alone is also because of this. In the physical world, this interaction between channel spaces is exclusive to physical interactions.

Interfaces serve as a means for transmitting information during the interactive process and are formed when users interact with physical devices. However, physical interaction actually leads to the creation of a three-dimensional space because of the movement of the interface. As with the interface, the channel is the process product of the physical information transfer process. Therefore, the interaction channel in physical space is a critical element in completing physical interaction. In contrast to the abstract concept of "channel" used in digital interaction such as screen interactivity, the interaction channel in physical interaction is real. With the description of the physical information transmission process through the attributes of the channel, we can explicitly visualize the physical information flow in physical interaction. For instance, we can clearly visualize

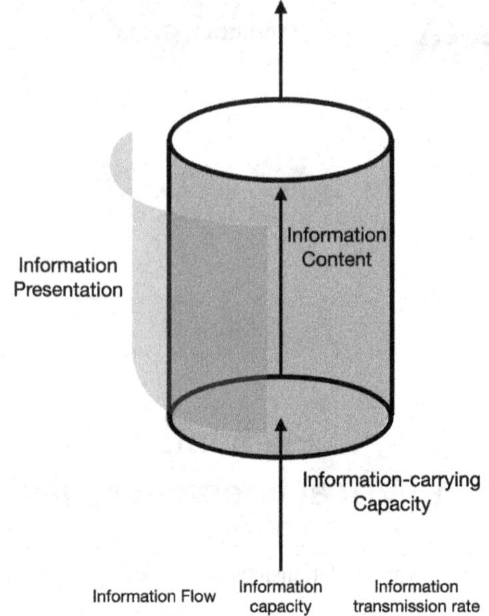

Fig. 5. Physical interaction channel

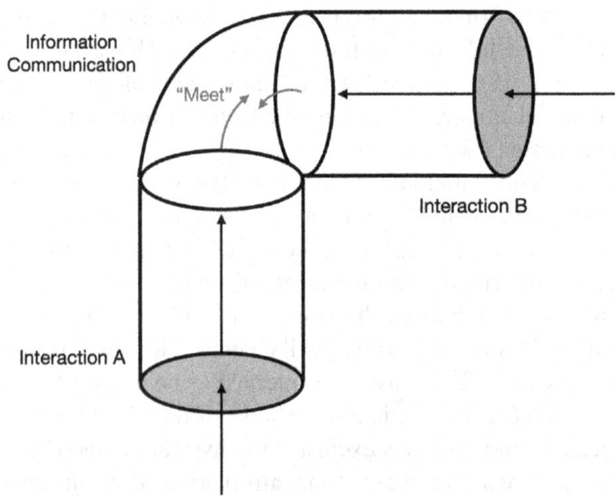

Fig. 6. A schematic diagram describing the information communication

the interaction channel of pressing the button or rotating the steering wheel. It is also this characteristic that distinguishes physical interaction from digital interaction. The creation of this channel requires the cooperation of both people and media in the physical environment. With the help of the interaction channel model, we can better explain and analyze the process of all physical interactions through visualization, evaluate the rationality of physical interaction design by establishing an interaction channel space, and optimize physical interaction design. In addition, this may allow for a more parametric, intelligent approach to interaction design.

In sum, the interaction channel is the key to physical interaction. It conveys information about the physical state of the interface during the physical interaction process, explains the transmission of physical information, and embodies the essence of physical interaction.

7 Future Work

In this study, we explore the factors affecting physical interaction design through qualitative research methods and further summarize it into a five-element model with the interaction channel as the core element. There are, however, some limitations to this study. In this study, we focused on the driving interaction in a car. It is triangulation that verifies the saturation of the data, but it does not imply a broader interpretation in other contexts. In order to ensure the reliability of the theory, more data collection and verification work is required. As well, the expression of codes and concepts still holds the potential to explain the phenomena more accurately. This research is still being followed up, so it will continue to be revised and optimized.

References

1. Marmaras, N., Poulakakis, G., Papakostopoulos, V.: Ergonomic design in ancient Greece. Appl. Ergon. **30**, 361–368 (1999)
2. Chandra, M.: What is Physical Interaction?. https://www.michellechandra.com/physical-computing/physical-interaction/
3. van Campenhout, L.L., Frens, J.W., Overbeeke, C., Standaert, A., Peremans, H.: Physical interaction in a dematerialized world. Int. J. De. **7**(1), 1–18 (2013)
4. Gibson, J.J.: The Ecological Approach to Visual Perception, Classic Psychology Press, New York (2014)
5. Ishii, H., Ullmer, B.: Tangible bits: towards seamless interfaces between people, bits and atoms. In: Proceedings of the ACM SIGCHI Conference on Human Factors in Computing Systems, pp. 234–241. ACM, Atlanta Georgia USA (1997)
6. Galán, J., Felip, F., García-García, C., Contero, M.: The influence of haptics when assessing household products presented in different means: a comparative study in real setting, flat display, and virtual reality environments with and without passive haptics. J. Comput. Des. Eng. **8**, 330–342 (2021)
7. Li, W., Alomainy, A., Vitanov, I., Noh, Y., Qi, P., Althoefer, K.: F-TOUCH sensor: concurrent geometry perception and multi-axis force measurement. IEEE Sens. J. **21**, 4300–4309 (2021)
8. Chowdhury, A., Karmakar, S., Reddy, S., Ghosh, S., Chakrabarti, D.: Usability is more valuable predictor than product personality for product choice in human-product physical interaction. Int. J. Ind. Ergon. **44**, 697–705 (2014)
9. Soft Touch using Soft Pneumatic Actuator–Skin as a Wearable Haptic Feedback Device - Sonar - 2021 - Advanced Intelligent Systems - Wiley Online Library. https://onlinelibrary.wiley.com/doi/full/https://doi.org/10.1002/aisy.202000168. Accessed 11 Feb 2023
10. Bongers, B.: Physical Interfaces in the Electronic Arts, vol. 30 (2000)
11. Dix, A., Ghazali, M., Gill, S., Hare, J., Ramduny-Ellis, D.: Physigrams: modelling devices for natural interaction. Form. Asp. Comput. **21**, 613–641 (2009)

12. Definition of PHYSICAL. https://www.merriam-webster.com/dictionary/physical. Accessed 11 Feb 2023
13. X, X.: Interaction design: from logic of things to logic of behaviors. Art Des. **1**, 58–62 (2015)
14. Buchanan, R.: Design as inquiry: the common, future and current ground of design. In: FutureGround: Proceedings of the International Conference of the Design Research Society (2005)
15. Flick, U.: Doing Grounded Theory
16. Ma, G.: Ergonomics and Design Application. Chemical Industry Press (2013)
17. Glaser, B., Strauss, A.: The Discovery of Grounded Theory: Strategies for Qualitative Research (1967)

Work Characteristics as Determinants of Remote Working Acceptance: Integrating UTAUT and JD-R Models

Nicoletta Massa(✉), Ferdinando Paolo Santarpia, and Chiara Consiglio

Department of Psychology, Sapienza University of Rome, Rome, Italy
{nicoletta.massa,ferdinandopaolo.santarpia, chiara.consiglio}@uniroma1.it

Abstract. The spread of remote working exponentially increased in recent years. Since remote working is by definition ICT-enabled, it seems important to identify which organizational and ICT-related factors may influence employees' attitudes towards remote working and remote productivity.

With this aim, we integrated the Unified Theory of Acceptance and Use of Technology model (UTAUT) with technostress literature, using Job demands-resources model (JD-R) as main conceptual framework.

Therefore, we proposed and tested a model of remote working acceptance in which predictors are operationalized in terms of techno-job demands (namely techno-complexity, techno-invasion and techno-overload) and techno-job resources (namely technical support and remote leadership support), to explore their distinctive influence on attitude towards remote working and, in turn, on remote working-enabled productivity.

Data from 836 remote workers from different organizations were collected and analyzed through structural equation modeling.

Results supported empirically the proposed model: both techno-job demands and techno-job resources affected attitude towards remote working which completely mediated the effect of the predictors on remote working-enabled productivity. Practical and theoretical contributions, along with limitations and future research direction, are presented and discussed.

Keywords: Remote working · Technostress · Remote productivity · JD-R Model

1 Introduction

In the last decades, the diffusion of Information and Communication Technologies (ICTs) has led to profound changes in organizational contexts and in the way work is performed by employees [1].

ICT brings several advantages to organizations, such as reducing company costs and fostering productivity [2]. Moreover, technology enables greater autonomy and flexibility so that employees can contribute to business goals anywhere and anytime [3]. However, empirical evidence has shown that it may also have detrimental effects on

M. Kurosu and A. Hashizume (Eds.): HCII 2023, LNCS 14011, pp. 163–180, 2023.
https://doi.org/10.1007/978-3-031-35596-7_12

people's psychological and physical health as well on job performance [4, 5]. Indeed, employees have to deal with increasingly complex work environments, new skills to be learned and blurred boundaries between work and personal life. This "dual nature" of technology calls for deeper understanding in the new ways of working [6], since technologies are not only devices used to achieve a task but also the main channel that connects workers with their job role and the organizational context.

In the field of work and organisational psychology, the Job Demands-Resources Model (JD-R [7]) provides a sound theoretical framework to acknowledge the demanding and beneficial aspects of technology.

This framework posits that every organizational context is characterized by two distinctive sets of work features, namely job demands and job resources. On the one hand, job demands include those work-related and organizational factors that entail costs on employees and, thus, activate an energy depletion process. On the other hand, job resources comprise those work-related and organizational factors that facilitate a positive motivational process. As such, job demands and resources are expected to exert opposing effects on employees' health and performance [8]. All in all, the JD-R represents a comprehensive and feasible model to explain the impact of the organizational context on job attitudes (i.e., engagement and burnout) and in turn, on individual and organizational outcomes.

Due to the widespread use of technologies and remote working, some studies have adapted the JD-R model to study the influence of technology-related job characteristics and their negative effects on employees [9, 10]. More specifically, these studies focused on the influence of technostress creators on well-being and performance [11, 12], such as the necessity of keeping up with constant technological updates, the intensification of work pace and the invasiveness of work in one's private life due to technological tools [13]. Although technology fosters remote working, our understanding of how techno-related demands and resources shape workers' attitudes towards it and the perceived benefits on one's own productivity is still limited. Indeed, understanding what determines the attitude towards remote working and its consequences represents a pivotal issue from both theoretical and practical points of view [14].

From a different perspective, the study of the determinants of attitude towards technological tools has been extensively investigated by technology acceptance models [15]. Those theories are aimed to understand how and why people accept or reject technological tools or systems. As such, aspects referring to the technology's characteristics (e.g., ease of use [16]) or individuals' traits (e.g., personal innovativeness [17]) have been taken into account as predictors of attitudes and intention to use. Nevertheless, the role of contextual and organizational variables, which may influence employee adoption of technological tools, has been to date neglected [18].

Among technology acceptance models, the Unified Theory of Acceptance and Use of Technology model (UTAUT [19]) is the most comprehensive framework to understand the predictors that shape a positive attitude towards technology. It suggests that technology usage depends on the perceptions and expectations that people have on technological tools, as well as the facilitating conditions that contribute to the behavioural intention to use it and to the actual adoption of the system.

However, a recent meta-analysis [20] has challenged technology acceptance and UTAUT models claiming that the literature on the topic has reached its peak, and therefore there is a need to investigate new theoretically relevant predictors and outcomes, new application contexts and new theoretical backgrounds aimed at understanding the processes behind technology acceptance.

Based on the assumption that remote working is ICT-enabled, emergent studies have been employing predictors from acceptance models to explore what determines a positive attitude towards remote working [21, 22].

The present cross-sectional study tries to answer the call for further theory-driven research on the topic [23–25], by proposing a conceptual systematization of predictors and outcomes of attitudes towards remote working that integrates JD-R and UTAUT models.

Specifically, the present research aims to contribute to the literature in several ways:

1. Emphasizing the role of organizational context and job characteristics for the acceptance of remote working, operationalizing predictors in terms of (techno) job demands or (techno) job resources;
2. Contributing to the technostress literature by exploring the influence of key technostress creators (namely "techno-job demands") on attitude towards remote working and in turn, on remote working-enabled productivity;
3. Expanding the contribution of the JD-R model to explain new outcomes, moving from traditional attitudinal dimensions (i.e., engagement/burnout) to attitude towards remote working and remote working-enabled productivity;
4. Exploring the mediating role of attitude towards remote working between (techno) job demands and (techno job resources) and remote working-enabled productivity.

1.1 The Present Study

As mentioned above, the idea behind the Job Demands-Resources model is that each job has characteristics that can be classified as demands or resources, that may influence employees' well-being and job attitudes, as well as organizational outcomes [26].

In the case of remote working and technology adoption, some ICT-related job features may represent a job resource whereas others may represent a job demand.

In this regard, previous studies have identified several technostress creators which are responsible for a variety of negative outcomes such as fatigue, lower job satisfaction, work overload and reduced productivity [27]. Among them, Techno-complexity (TCOM) refers to those ICT's characteristics that make the user feel inadequate regarding their digital skills. In fact, employees are required to constantly refresh their skills due to frequent updates that characterize technology systems. In the long term, this can lead to increased frustration and stress [28]. Techno-overload (TOV) deals with the overexposure to information channelled by ICT tools that must be managed. It also compels employees to work longer and faster, challenging their ability to handle workload and maintain an adequate level of efficiency [29]. Techno-invasion (TINV) refers to the invasiveness that technology brings outside of work, leading the person to always stay connected to job-related tasks. Being "always on" leads to negative health outcomes and ultimately, to an impairment of individual performance [30]. As such, technostress literature suggests that these inherent aspects of ICTs systems may influence their acceptance and adoption beyond the usage potential of technological artefacts (e.g., usefulness [31]; performance expectancy [32]). From this standpoint, we claim that techno-job demands may have an influence on the attitude towards remote working, since technology represents the *conditio sine qua non* this working modality can be implemented. To be sure, when employees perceive technologies as creators of demanding experiences like higher work overload, the erosion of work-life boundaries and the urgency to tune their skills to more complex technological tools, they may be less likely to enjoy working remotely or less likely to experience such a solution as comfortable and effective. The higher the techno-job demands (TJD), encompassing TCM, TOV and TIN, the more negative will be the attitude towards remote working. Therefore, we formulated the following hypothesis:

H1: Techno-job demands are negatively related to Attitude towards remote working.

However, there are some organizational characteristics that go in the opposite direction and act as important job resources. In fact, since companies are also affected by the opportunities and challenges of technological innovations, they are called to create the contextual facilitating conditions to make remote working sustainable, productive and a desirable solution for employees [33]. We believe that remote leadership support and technical support are likely to represent crucial organizational factors in this process. In the first case, leadership processes are transforming due to the diffusion of technology within work contexts, thus leaders play an increasingly decisive role in technology acceptance and usage [34, 35]. As such, we believe the same applies to remote working adoption. In this context, technology mediates the employer-employee relationship that must be reframed in accordance with the worker's characteristics and needs. According to how this turns out, we believe that the experience of working remotely can be facilitated. At the same time, the literature has outlined other crucial resources in dealing with technology and the stress it generates, named technostress inhibitors [36], such as literacy facilitation, innovation support and technical support. Specifically, technical support is defined as the assistance provided to employees in the context of their use of ICTs tools, which is also considered a facilitating condition in the UTAUT model in determining technology adoption and usage behaviour [37]. For this reason, we claim that the availability of both technical support given by the organization as well as the perceived support from the leader when working remotely, promotes a better work experience for employees, fostering a positive attitude towards remote working. Indeed, when employees are facilitated in using remote tools (e.g., timely support in solving technical problems) and perceive that the leader is supportive and engaged in make remote working effective, they may be more aware of the advantages of this working arrangement, as well as the resources to manage it if necessary. Taken together, the higher the techno-job resources (TJR) encompassing technical support and remote leadership support the more positive will be attitude towards remote working. As such, we formulated the following hypothesis:

H2: Techno-job resources are positively related to Attitude towards remote working.

The relationship between attitudes and behaviour is well-known [38]. Indeed, having a positive disposition toward a target situation can help to understand the consequent behaviours. For instance, recalling the technology acceptance model literature, people with a more positive attitude towards technology (e.g., ease of use, useful) are more likely to actually use the system [6, 16, 19]. Extending those results to remote working, we argue that when employees present a positive attitude towards working remotely (e.g., they think it is a good, comfortable and enjoyable working solution) they may perceive an increase of their productivity due to remote working, that is, achieving their goals more effectively and efficiently. Hence, the following hypothesis was investigated:

H3: Attitude towards remote working is positively related to Remote working-enabled productivity.

Moreover, since the type of perception people have of technologies affects the frequency and quality of ICT use as a function of the degree of acceptance [6, 9], we claim that the same applies for remote working. Indeed, being embedded in a supportive environment from both a technical and relational perspective in the use of technologies or being exposed to a technologically demanding context, may shape the perception of productivity in remote working in opposite ways, depending on the attitude people have toward this working arrangement. Specifically, when employees perceive that they have more TJR at their disposal to work remotely, they may be likely to experience this arrangement as positive and thus, draw performance advantages. Instead, the perception of higher TJD may be associated with a lower positive attitude towards working remotely, thereby perceiving it as hindering their performance.

Specifically, we assume that the attitude towards remote working may act as a mediating mechanism able to link techno-job demands and techno-job resources with remote working-enabled productivity.

Based on this, the following research hypotheses were investigated:

H4a: Attitude towards remote working mediates the effect between Techno-job demands and Remote working-enabled productivity.

H4b: Attitude towards remote working mediates the effect between Techno-job resources and Remote working-enabled productivity.

Specifically, we expect a total mediation, since we claim that the influence that TJD and TJR have on the considered outcome is via ATRW.

Figure 1 represents the overall hypothesized model which characterizes the present study.

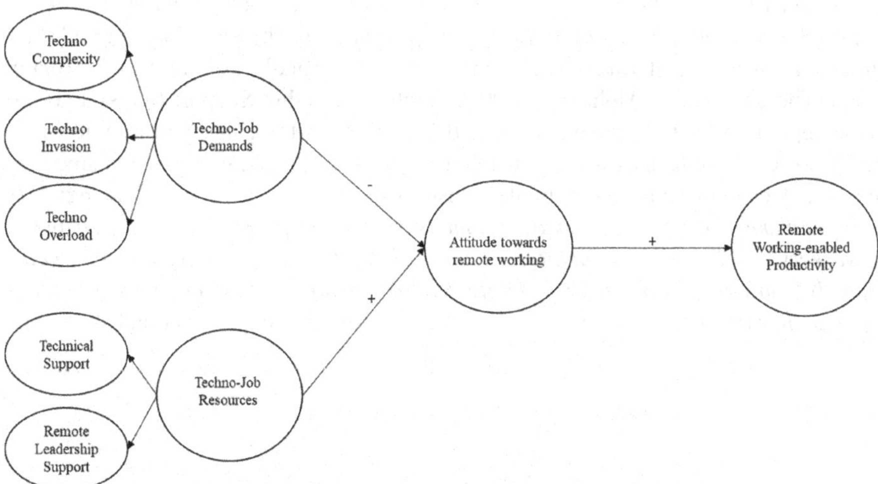

Fig. 1. The hypothesized model. *Note*: Solid lines are used to represent hypothesized direct effect.

2 Materials and Methods

Sample and Procedure. A total sample of 836 remote workers from different organizations took part in the study, of which 456 (54.5%) were females and 380 (45.5%) were males. Regarding age, 50.4% were at least 30 years old while 45.5% ranged from 31 to 60 years old. Few participants (4.2%) were older than 60 years old. Concerning the level of education, most of the sample (32.4%) had a high school diploma, 31.2% had a master's degree, 24.5% had a bachelor's degree, 10% had a post-graduate degree and 1.8% had a junior high school diploma. Most of the sample (60.6%) had a permanent contract and worked in the manufacturing industry sector (30.3%). The study was conducted via an anonymous online self-report questionnaire. Participation in the study was completely voluntary.

2.1 Measures

Techno-Job Demands. Techno-job demands (TJD) were measured with 9 items, using the Italian translation of the technostress creators scale [39]. Specifically, techno-complexity (TCOM) measured the individual's difficulties in dealing with the complexity associated with ICTs; Techno-invasion (TINV) measured the degree to which one's job invades one's private life through technology; Techno-overload (TOV) measured the perception of working longer and faster due to ICTs.

An example item for each dimension includes: "I do not find enough time to study and upgrade my technology skills"; "I have to stay in touch with my work even during holidays, evenings and weekends because of technology"; "Technology requires me to work much faster". Scales were measured through a 5-point Likert scale ordered from 1 (Totally disagree) to 5 (Totally agree). Cronbach's Alpha for TCM, TIN and TOV was respectively 0.79, 0.77 and0.83. The total techno-job demands scale reliability was 0.85.

Techno Job Resources. Techno-job resources (TJR) assessed technical support and remote leadership support. Technical support (TSUP) was measured using 3 items adapted by Tarafdar et al. [40] and Fisher et al. [41]. The dimension measures employee support activities to solve users' ICT related problems (e.g. *"Our organization offers support for the solution of any technological problem"*). The participants rated their agreement on a 5-point Likert scale ranging from 1 (Totally disagree) to 5 (Totally agree). The Cronbach's Alpha was 0.90. Remote Leadership Support (RLS) assessed the perception of leader's behaviours aimed at facilitating the efficacy of remote working. All of the 3 items used were generated ad hoc for this research context, since the literature does not provide any reliable measures to date. Items are the following: *"My manager makes the best use of remote channels and tools to promote exchanges between co-workers"*; *"My manager facilitates teamwork to effectively achieve common goals remotely"*; and *"My manager keeps motivated their remote co-workers by acknowledging their characteristics and needs"*. Items were measured through a 5-point Likert scale from 1 (Totally disagree) to 5 (Totally agree). The Cronbach's Alpha was 0.87. The total techno-job resources scale reliability was 0.83.

Attitude Towards Remote Working. Attitude towards remote working (ATRW) was measured by using 3 items from Venkatesh et al. [19] and adapted to the specific context of remote working.

They assessed the individual's positive feelings about performing the target behaviour as exemplified by items such as: *"Working remotely is a good idea"*. A 5-point Likert scale from 1 (Totally disagree) to 5 (Totally agree) was used and the Cronbach's Alpha was 0.93.

Remote Working-Enabled Productivity. To measure the perceived increase of productivity due to remote working (RWEP), 3 items adapted by Tarafdar and colleagues [42] were used. Each item assesses the perception of individual productivity through working remotely by a 5-point Likert scale from 1 (Totally disagree) to 5 (Totally agree). An example item is *"Working remotely helps me to accomplish more work than would otherwise be possible"*. Cronbach's Alpha was 0.90.

2.2 Data Analysis

As preliminary analysis, a Confirmatory Factor Analysis (CFA) was conducted on Mplus 8.4 [43] to verify the factorial structure of predictors (TJD and TJR) as latent dimensions, using the Maximum Likelihood (ML) as estimator.

In line with the literature on JD-R model [44], we hypothesized a second-order structure for techno-job demands and techno-job resources dimensions.

To determine whether the hypothesized second-order model (M5) showed the best fit to the data, the following five alternative models were tested.

More precisely, we compared the hypothesized model (M5) with the followings:

1. A first alternative model (M1) with a single factor structure. This model implements Harman's single factor test [45], where all predictor items load on a single factor. This test allows the determination of whether most of the variance can be accounted for by one general factor, representing the influences of method bias on observed item covariances [46].
2. A model with two first-order factor model (M2) representing techno-job demands (TJD) and techno-job resources (TJR), where all the techno-stressors items loaded on the first factor while items related to technical support and remote leadership support loaded on the second factor.
3. An alternative model with four correlated factors (M3) where TCOM, TINV and TOV items loaded on their respective factors (namely TJD) while TSUP and RLS items loaded on the same latent variable.
4. A competing alternative model with five first-order correlated factors (M4) where TCOM, TINV, TOV, TSUP and RLS items are treated as separate factors.
5. The hypothesized model (M5) with five first-order correlated factors (TCM, TINV, TOV, TSUP, RLS) and two second-order factors (TJD and TJR).

The best measurement model was evaluated through fit indices and significant differences in chi-square values [47]. Then the hypothesized measurement and structural models were tested via Structural Equation Modeling (SEM) and a mediation analysis was performed.

To examine the goodness of it, different fit indices were used: the $\chi 2$ goodness-of-fit statistic; the root mean square error of approximation (RMSEA), the standardized root mean square residual (SRMR), the Tucker–Lewis index (TLI) and the comparative fit index (CFI). The appropriateness of the model fit was established with (1) $\chi 2$ statistic values; (2) TLI and CFI values greater than .90 [48]; (3) RMSEA values lower than .08 [49]. Since the $\chi 2$ statistic is dependent on sample size and larger samples tend to result significant (i.e. if the $\chi 2$ is significant at $\rho < .05$ we accept the alternative hypothesis that there is a significant difference between the model and the data), additional fit statistics were used [50]. In order to statistically compare the alternative models, fit indices and significant differences in $\chi 2$ values ($\Delta\chi 2$; p. $< .001$) were evaluated [51]. To test the mediation hypothesis, specific indirect effects procedure was used as implemented in "Model Indirect" in Mplus 8.4. In addition, to evaluate the statistical significance of direct and indirect effects, bootstrapping method was performed, employing 5.000 bootstrap samples with the replacement from the full sample to construct bias-corrected 95% Confidence Intervals (CI) [52]. In particular, the mediation model is significant if zero is not contained within the intervals.

Gender, education, and age were included as control variables within the model, in accordance with previous technostress studies [e.g. 27, 36].

3 Results

As displayed in Table 1, the CFA clearly demonstrated that M1-M2-M3 models did not adequately fit the data. On the other hand, M4 (e.g., with five correlated first-order factors) was the first model to have a good fit, resulting as statistically better than the previous nested models and supporting the factorial distinctiveness of each dimension.

The M5, which relates the first-order factors (TCM, TINV, TOV, TSUP and RLS) to the second-order factors (TJD and TJR), fit the data adequately. According to $\Delta\chi 2$, there was no significant deterioration of the fit, thus, although more conceptually complex, the hypothesized model turned out to be empirically tenable.

The factor loadings of M5 were all statistically significant from zero and greater than 0.30, confirming the appropriateness of the hypothesized measured model. Specifically, the first-order factor loadings ranged from 0.48 to 0.93, while the second-order factor loadings ranged from 0.48 to 0.79.

Table 1. Results of confirmatory factor analysis and alternative model comparisons

Models (M)	χ^2	df	RMSEA	CFI	TLI	CI 95%	SRMR	$\Delta\chi^2$
M1: one-factor model (all 15 items)	3800.45**	90	0.22	0.40	0.30	0.21 0.23	0.17	
M2: two-factors model	2435.64**	89	0.18	0.62	0.55	0.17 0.18	0.12	1364.816 (df = 1) p. < .001
M3: four-factors model	1674.20**	84	0.15	0.74	0.68	0.14 0.16	0.11	761.435 (df = 5) p. < .001
M4: five-factors model	236.23**	80	0.05	0.97	0.96	0.04 0.06	0.03	1437.971 (df = 4) p. < .001
M5: hypothesized two second-order factors model	237.99**	84	0.05	0.97	0.96	0.04 0.05	0.03	1768.00 (df = 4) p. = 0.77

Notes. ** $p < 0.001$; $\chi 2$ = chi-square statistic; CFI = comparative fit index; TLI = Tuker–Lewis fit index; RMSEA = root mean square error of approximation; CI = confidence interval; df = degrees of freedom.The $\Delta\chi 2$ shows comparison of nested models in progressive order from M1 to M5

Table 2. Shows the correlations, means, standard deviation and internal consistencies of the study variables. The associations between the constructs were significant and in the expected direction. In particular, techno-job resources showed a positive correlation with attitude towards remote working and remote working-enabled productivity, while techno-job demands presented a negative relation with attitude towards remote working and remote working-enabled productivity.

Finally, attitude towards remote working showed a positive and significant relationship with remote working-enabled productivity.

Table 2. Descriptive statistics and zero-order correlations

	M (SD)	(1)	(2)	(3)	(4)	(5)	(6)	(7)
(1) Age	2.11 (1.30)	–						
(2) Sex	1.55 (.49)	−.17**	–					
(3) Edu	3.15 (1.04)	.13**	.64**	–				
(4) TJD	2.28 (0.70)	−.08*	−.01	−.04	(0.85)			
(5) TJR	3.52 (.70)	.02	−.03	.06	−.21**	(0.83)		
(6) ATRW	3.95 (.94)	.11**	−.01	.01	−.32**	.33**	(0.93)	
(7) RWEP	3.57 (.93)	.12**	.00	.07*	−.21**	.26**	.62**	(0.90)

Notes. * $p < 0.05$ ** $p < 0.01$; M = mean; SD = standard deviation; coefficient alpha reliability estimates are presented in brackets along the diagonal; TJD = techno-job demands; TJR = techno-job resources; ATRW = attitude towards remote working; RWEP = remote working-enabled productivity; Edu = education

3.1 Model Results

The hypothesized measurement model showed an adequate fit to the data ($\chi 2$ 606.18 $p < .001$; CFI = 0.97, TLI = 0.97, RMSEA [95% CI] = 0.04 [0.04 0.05], SRMR = 0.04), as well as the structural mediational model fit ($\chi 2$ 606.18 $p < .001$, CFI = 0.96, TLI = 0.95, RMSEA [95% CI] = 0.04 [0.04 0.05], SRMR = 0.04). As displayed in Fig. 2, techno-job demands were negatively associated with attitude towards remote working ($\beta = -.24$ $p < .001$), while techno-job resources presented a positive relation with attitude towards remote working ($\beta = .41$ $p < .001$), confirming respectively H1 and H2. Techno-job demands and techno-job resources were negatively correlated (β = -.36 $p < .001$). Hypothesis H3, concerning the direct effect between attitude towards remote working and remote working-enabled productivity was also supported. Indeed, ATRW was positively ($\beta = .67$ $p < .001$) related with RWEP.

The model explained 29% of the variance in attitude towards remote working and 48% in remote working-enabled productivity. The indirect effect for techno-job demands to RWEP was -.16 (bootstrap CI 95% = −.23 and −.08), while for techno-job resources to RWEP was .27 (bootstrap CI 95% = .19 and .36) confirming both H4a and H4b. To ascertain that the relationships between TJD, TJR and RWEP were fulling mediated by ATRW, we tested an alternative partial mediation model including the direct effects of techno-job demands and techno-job resources on RWEP. However, the relations were not statistically significant, therefore the model positing a total mediation of ATRW seems to be a more parsimonious picture of the data. Along with the presented variables, age, gender and education were included as covariates within the model. In particular, age was negatively related to techno-job demands ($\beta = -.15$ $p < .001$), while education was positively related to techno-job resources ($\beta = .11$. $p = .018$).

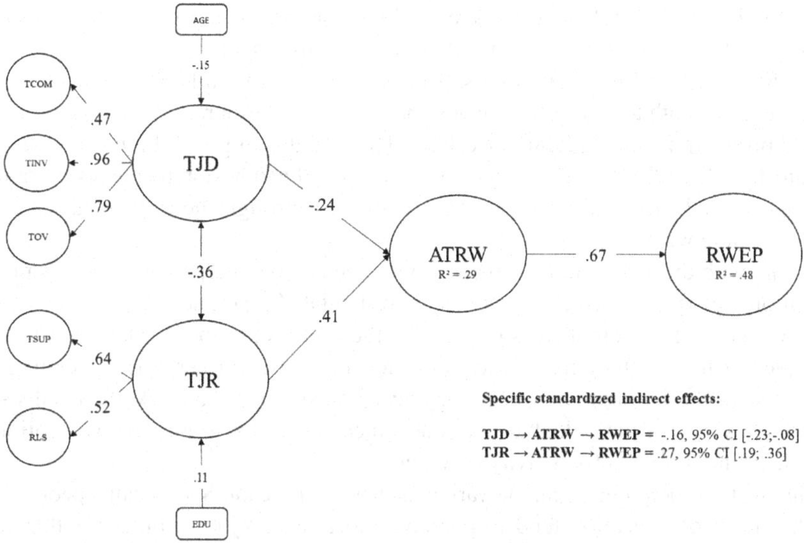

Fig. 2. Figure reports the standardized regression coefficients and the variance explained of the hypothesized structural model, controlled for gender, age and educational level. *Note*: All structural paths were significant, $p < 0.001$. TCOM = Techno-complexity; TINV = Techno-invasion; TOV = Techno-overload; TJD = Techno-job Demands; TSP = Technical support; RLS = Remote leadership Support; TJR = Techno-job resources; ATRW = Attitude towards remote working; RWEP = Remote working-enabled productivity; Edu = Education. R^2 = r-square.

4 Discussion

Overall, the results confirmed the hypothesized relationships between techno-job demands (techno-complexity, techno-invasion, techno-overload), techno-job resources (technical support and remote leadership), attitude towards remote working and remote working-enabled productivity.

In accordance with the JD-R model, techno-job demands and techno-job resources showed opposite associations with attitude towards remote working. More specifically, the higher the perceived techno-job demands, the more negative the attitude towards remote working. On the other hand, the higher the perceived techno-job resources, the more positive the attitude towards remote working.

We explain this result because high techno-job demands, such as being invaded during leisure time by e-mails or perceiving to be obligated to handle more work in a shorter period of time or forced to acquire new technological skills to work, may reduce the likeability and comfort of remote working. This is in line with previous studies underlining the impact of technostress creators on remote workers' performance and well-being [53].

On the contrary, perceiving high techno-job resources provided by the organization, such as the availability of technical support when problems arise as well as the support and encouragement of leaders when working remotely, may facilitate a positive employee experience of such ways of working. This result extends previous findings which emphasizes the role of the leader and the support given by the organization in facilitating effective performance in virtual work environments [54, 55].

Furthermore, we found that this resulting attitude is a key explanatory mechanism of the influence of both techno-job demands and techno-job resources on remote working-enabled productivity due to remote working. This result is of particular interest because it means that the influence of techno-job demands and techno-job resources on remote working-enabled productivity is uniquely conveyed through the individual's attitude towards remote working.

In line with the JD-R model [56], this outcome can be interpreted as the result of a motivational process in which the degree of ICT-related hindrance demands and facilitating resources leads employees to perceive themselves as more (or less) productive, consequently to how they experience working remotely. Furthermore, extending the predictions of the literature on technology acceptance to remote work, the results support the relevance of individual attitudes as a mechanism for turning the perception of technology into remote productivity outcomes.

Finally, two socio-demographic variables were significant. Specifically, people with a higher level of education tend to perceive more techno-job resources within their work context. We can hypothesise that people with a high degree of specialization are likely employed in work contexts that offer more support both technically and in the professional and digital development of the worker. Furthermore, younger people feel the impact of techno-job demands more strongly than older individuals. This result is in contrast with most of the literature that showed that older people are more exposed to technostress [57, 58]. However, other evidence in the literature has shown the contrary [59, 60] and others have observed that there is no generational difference [61, 62]. It should be noted, however, that in our study, the interpretative significance of the second-order factor of techno-job demands is mainly connoted by the invasion dimension. We can hypothesise that this component is more influential on the younger generations, for whom there is a higher need to define work and private life boundaries [63].

4.1 Practical and Theoretical Implications

From a theoretical perspective, the present research tested a conceptual model of remote working acceptance framed in the organizational context. As the latter is enabled by the use of technology, our model accounted for the perceptions of ICT-organizational and job-related factors to understand how employees approach remote working and perceive themselves as more or less productive under such an arrangement.

To this end, we used the JD-R model as main theoretical framework to define the predictors of remote working acceptance, namely, techno-job demands and techno-job resources. In particular, to specify the content of techno-job demands and techno-job resources, we started from Tarafdar's research on technostress creators (e.g., techno-complexity, techno-invasion, techno-overload) and inhibitors (e.g., technical support). Indeed, while the former refers to the hindering characteristics of technology, the latter concerns organizational factors that can help employees dealing with technostress. Furthermore, we used the UTAUT model to understand the process underlying the emergence of remote working acceptance. Indeed, the UTAUT suggested that technology acceptance is a process in which technology usage is determined by how people perceive and approach ICTs systems. In line with the UTAUT model and Tarafdar's contributions, this model posits that the behavioural intention and the effective usage of technology increases as a function of the available facilitating conditions. As such, we applied such assumptions in remote working settings with attitude towards remote working as a mechanism that channels the perceptions of technology in remote productivity outcomes.

To the best of our knowledge, this is the first contribution proposing an integration among these theoretical frameworks, applying it specifically to remote working.

Moreover, in doing this we extended the range of considerable predictors in these theoretical perspectives. With respect to the UTAUT, we extended the facilitating conditions beyond technical support (e.g., by considering remote leadership as a form of social support) and also considered the potential hindering factors (e.g., techno job demands), shaping the model's application to organizational contexts.

Regarding the JD-R model, we considered a new job attitude from those usually investigated [64] which in this case refers to a positive attitude towards remote working and the resulting perceived remote productivity.

From an applicational standpoint, our results offer relevant insights for designing interventions aimed at supporting the viability of the increasing use of remote working in organizations. Indeed, according to our study, organizations are called to promote an optimal balance between techno-job resources (i.e., technical support and remote leadership) and techno-job demands (i.e., techno-overload, invasion and complexity) to which workers are exposed to in remote working. Such a balance, in which the perceived techno-job resources exceed the demands, seems to be important in maintaining employees' positive attitude toward remote work, thereby helping them to perceive themselves as more productive in this working arrangement. First, the organization may primarily invest in developing techno-resources, given their greater association with attitude and perceived remote productivity. This could be concretely accomplished by activating organizational actions aimed at designing or at strengthening the technical systems to support the remote worker, ensuring technical feedbacks as timely and effectively as possible in resolving technological problems that the remote workers may encounter. Furthermore, leaders may be targeted with training and development paths designed to develop a variety of skills in managing employees remotely. On the one hand, training could focus on increasing the skills of leaders in adapting to the technological medium to effectively manage remote collaboration and feedback processes. On the other hand, leaders could be trained in learning how to recognize employees digital and work needs and coach them to face remote working challenges.

Second, organizations may take action to reduce perceptions of techno-job demands.

Regarding the perceived complexity of using and learning new technologies, organizations could improve the technological experience of employees, such as by implementing user-friendly work tools, as well as by providing periodic training sessions to update remote workers in terms of digital knowledge and skills [65]. Moreover, to reduce techno-overload and invasion (indicative of work intensification at the expense of recovery time on and off the job, as well as a deconstruction of work-life boundaries; [66]), organizations and managers may foster a culturally sensitive approach to employees' needs and human sustainability in order to keep them motivated and productive. For example, by discouraging formal and informal practices or expectations towards remote employees of working beyond negotiated hours due to their higher job flexibility [67, 68].

4.2 Limitation and Future Direction

The study presents several limitations that deserve consideration.

First of all, the cross-sectional nature of the data, requires us to be careful in interpreting influence relationships among variables of the study. To ascertain the direction of the observed effects, longitudinal research designs are needed and should be the objective of future studies.

Second, all measures were self-reported. However, they refer to perceived work characteristics and individual attitude that only the employee may evaluate. On the other hand, our outcome, namely remote working-enabled productivity, measuring the perceived increase of productivity due to remote working could be biased. Future studies should include an objective or other-report indicator of employees' remote productivity.

Third, we did not collect information on the intensity of remote working. Future studies could investigate to what extent the number of days or hours in remote working affect the tested model.

Fourth, although we developed a model with a focus on the organizational and techno-related components, we did not include other important predictors that should be investigated further. In particular, it is necessary to examine the role of (techno) personal resources (e.g. e-work self-efficacy [33]) and its specific effects on the attitude towards remote working and in turn on performance.

Finally, we focused only on remote working technology. Further investigations should explore the applicability of the model with other types of technological artefacts (e.g. collaborative robotics, artificial intelligence).

5 Conclusion

By integrating the JD-R and UTAUT models, this paper investigated how techno-related facilitating and hindering factors on the job are related to attitudes towards remote work and remote working-enabled productivity. In particular, the present research highlighted the mediating role of employee's attitude towards remote working in the relationships between perceptions of positive and negative job characteristics associated with technologies, as facilitating or demanding factors, and remote working-enabled productivity. These results provide useful insights on the implications of techno-job demands and techno-job resources in influencing the acceptance of remote working, which could be of particular interest for future research and practical application within organizations.

References

1. Boell, S.K., Campbell, J., Cecez-Kecmanovic, D., Cheng, J.E.: The transformative nature of telework: a review of the literature (2013)
2. Akinci, B., Kiziltas, S., Ergen, E., Karaesmen, I.Z., Keceli, F.: Modeling and analyzing the impact of technology on data capture and transfer processes at construction sites: a case study. J. Constr. Eng. Manag. **132**(11), 1148–1157 (2006)
3. Melville, N., Kraemer, K., Gurbaxani, V. Information technology and organizational performance: an integrative model of IT business value. MIS Q. 283–322 (2004)
4. Charalampous, M., Grant, C.A., Tramontano, C., Michailidis, E.: Systematically reviewing remote e-workers' well-being at work: a multidimensional approach. Eur. J. Work Organ. Psy. **28**(1), 51–73 (2019)
5. Perry, S.J., Rubino, C., Hunter, E.M.: Stress in remote work: two studies testing the demand-control-person model. Eur. J. Work Organ. Psy. **27**(5), 577–593 (2018)
6. Venkatesh, V.: Impacts of COVID-19: a research agenda to support people in their fight. Int. J. Inf. Manage. **55**, 102197 (2020)
7. Demerouti, E., Bakker, A.B., Nachreiner, F., Schaufeli, W.B.: The job demands-resources model of burnout. J. Appl. Psychol. **86**(3), 499 (2001)
8. Bakker, A., Demerouti, E., Schaufeli, W.: Dual processes at work in a call centre: an application of the job demands–resources model. Eur. J. Work Organ. Psy. **12**(4), 393–417 (2003)
9. Wang, W., Daneshvar Kakhki, M., Uppala, V.: The interaction effect of technostress and non-technological stress on employees' performance. In: AMCIS (2017)
10. Mahapatra, M., Pati, S.P.: Technostress creators and burnout: a job demands-resources perspective. In: Proceedings of the 2018 ACM SIGMIS Conference on Computers and People Research, pp. 70–77 (2018)
11. Brummelhuis, L.L.T., Hetland, J., Keulemans, L., Bakker, A.B.: Do new ways of working foster work engagement?. Psicothema (2012)
12. Ragu-Nathan, T.S., Tarafdar, M., Ragu-Nathan, B.S., Tu, Q.: The consequences of technostress for end users in organizations: conceptual development and empirical validation. Inf. Syst. Res. **19**(4), 417–433 (2008)
13. Weil, M.M., Rosen, L.D.: Technostress: Coping with Technology@ Work@ Home@ Play, vol. 13, p. 240. Wiley, New York (1997)
14. Ayyagari, R., Grover, V., Purvis, R.: Technostress: technological antecedents and implications. MIS Q. **35**, 831–858 (2011)
15. Marangunić, N., Granić, A.: Technology acceptance model: a literature review from 1986 to 2013. Univ. Access Inf. Soc. **14**(1), 81–95 (2014). https://doi.org/10.1007/s10209-014-0348-1
16. Davis, F.D.: Perceived usefulness, perceived ease of use, and user acceptance of information technology. MIS Q. 319–340 (1989)
17. Agarwal, R., Karahanna, E.: Time flies when you're having fun: cognitive absorption and beliefs about information technology usage. MIS Q. 665–694 (2000)
18. Venkatesh, V.: Adoption and use of AI tools: a research agenda grounded in UTAUT. Ann. Oper. Res. **308**(1–2), 641–652 (2021). https://doi.org/10.1007/s10479-020-03918-9
19. Venkatesh, V., Morris, M.G., Davis, G.B., Davis, F. D.: User acceptance of information technology: toward a unified view. MIS Q. 425–478 (2003)
20. Blut, M., Chong, A., Tsiga, Z., Venkatesh, V.: Meta-analysis of the unified theory of acceptance and use of technology (UTAUT): challenging its validity and charting A research agenda in the red ocean. J. Assoc. Inf. Syst. Forthcoming (2021)

21. Donati, S., Viola, G., Toscano, F., Zappalà, S.: Not all remote workers are similar: technology acceptance, remote work beliefs, and wellbeing of remote workers during the second wave of the COVID-19 pandemic. Int. J. Environ. Res. Public Health **18**(22), 12095 (2021)
22. Pérez Pérez, M., Martínez Sánchez, A., de Luis Carnicer, P., José Vela Jiménez, M.: A technology acceptance model of innovation adoption: the case of teleworking. Eur. J. Innov. Manage. **7**(4), 280–291 (2004)
23. Bélanger, F., Watson-Manheim, M.B., Swan, B.: R A multi-level socio-technical systems telecommuting framework. Behav. Inf. Technol. **32**(12), 1257–1279 (2013)
24. Allen, T.D., Golden, T.D., Shockley, K.M.: How effective is telecommuting? assessing the status of our scientific findings. Psychol. Sci. Publ. Interest **16**(2), 40–68 (2015)
25. Golden, T.D., Gajendran, R.S.: Unpacking the role of a telecommuter's job in their performance: examining job complexity, problem solving, interdependence, and social support. J. Bus. Psychol. **34**(1), 55–69 (2019)
26. Taris, T.W., Schaufeli, W.B.: The job demands-resources model. The Wiley Blackwell handbook of the psychology of occupational safety and workplace health, pp. 155–180 (2015)
27. Tarafdar, M., Tu, Q., Ragu-Nathan, T.S.: Impact of technostress on end-user satisfaction and performance. J. Manag. Inf. Syst. **27**(3), 303–334 (2010)
28. Nelson, D.L.: Individual adjustment to information-driven technologies: a critical review. MIS Q. **14**(1), 79–98 (1990)
29. Weil, M.M., Rosen, L.D.: Don't let technology enslave you: learn how technostress can affect the habits of your employees and yourself. Workforce **78**(2), 56–59 (1999)
30. Clark, K., Kalin, S.: Technostressed out? How to cope in the digital age. Libr. J. **121**(13), 30–32 (1996)
31. Fenech, T.: Using perceived ease of use and perceived usefulness to predict acceptance of the World Wide Web. Comput. Netw. ISDN Syst. **30**(1–7), 629–630 (1998)
32. Chang, A.: UTAUT and UTAUT 2: a review and agenda for future research. Winners **13**(2), 10–114 (2012)
33. Tramontano, C., Grant, C., Clarke, C.: Development and validation of the e-work self-efficacy scale to assess digital competencies in remote working. Comput. Hum. Behav. Rep. **4**, 100129 (2021)
34. Avolio, B.J., Sosik, J.J., Kahai, S.S., Baker, B.: E-leadership: re-examining transformations in leadership source and transmission. Leadersh. Q. **25**(1), 105–131 (2014)
35. Van Wart, M., Roman, A., Wang, X., Liu, C.: Integrating ICT adoption issues into (e-) leadership theory. Telematics Inform. **34**(5), 527–537 (2017)
36. Tarafdar, M., Tu, Q., Ragu-Nathan, T.S., Ragu-Nathan, B.S.: Crossing to the dark side: examining creators, outcomes, and inhibitors of technostress. Commun. ACM **54**(9), 113–120 (2011)
37. Venkatesh, V., Brown, S.A., Maruping, L.M., Bala, H.: Predicting different conceptualizations of system use: the competing roles of behavioral intention, facilitating conditions, and behavioral expectation. MIS Q. 483–502 (2008)
38. Ajzen, I.: The theory of planned behavior. Organ. Behav. Hum. Decis. Process. **50**(2), 179–211 (1991)
39. Molino, M., et al.: Wellbeing costs of technology use during Covid-19 remote working: An investigation using the Italian translation of the technostress creators scale. Sustainability **12**(15), 5911 (2020)
40. Tarafdar, M., Qrunfleh, S.: Examining tactical information technology—business alignment. J. Comput. Inf. Syst. **50**(4), 107–116 (2010)
41. Fischer, T., Reuter, M., Riedl, R.: The digital stressors scale: development and validation of a new survey instrument to measure digital stress perceptions in the workplace context. Front. Psychol. **12**, 607598 (2021)

42. Tarafdar, M., Tu, Q., Ragu-Nathan, B.S., Ragu-Nathan, T.S.: The impact of technostress on role stress and productivity. J. Manag. Inf. Syst. **24**(1), 301–328 (2007)
43. Muthén, B., Muthén, L.: Mplus. In: Handbook of Item Response Theory, pp. 507–518. Chapman and Hall/CRC (2017)
44. Bakker, A.B., Demerouti, E., De Boer, E., Schaufeli, W.B.: Job demands and job resources as predictors of absence duration and frequency. J. Vocat. Behav. **62**(2), 341–356 (2003)
45. Harman, H.H.: Modern Factor Analysis. University of Chicago press (1976)
46. Podsakoff, P.M., Organ, D.W.: Self-reports in organizational research: problems and prospects. J. Manag. **12**(4), 531–544 (1986)
47. Putnick, D.L., Bornstein, M.H.: Measurement invariance conventions and reporting: the state of the art and future directions for psychological research. Dev. Rev. **41**, 71–90 (2016)
48. Hoyle, R.H. (Ed.): Handbook of Structural Equation Modeling. Guilford press (2012)
49. Mulaik, S.A., James, L.R., van Alstine, J., Bennet, N., Lind, S., Stilwell, C.D.: Evaluation of goodness-of-fit indices for structural equation models. Psychol. Bull. **105**, 430–450 (1989)
50. Brown, M.W., Cudeck, R.: Alternative ways of assessing model fit. In: Bollen, K.A., Kenneth, A., Long, S.J., (Eds.), Testing Structural Equation Models, pp. 136–162. Sage, Newbery Park (1993)
51. Byrne, B.M.: Structural Equation Modeling with Mplus: Basic Concepts, Applications, and Programming. Routledge, Milton Park (2013)
52. MacKinnon, D.P., Lockwood, C.M., Williams, J.: Confidence limits for the indirect effect: distribution of the product and resampling methods. Multivar. Behav. Res. **39**(1), 99–128 (2004)
53. Borle, P., Reichel, K., Niebuhr, F., Voelter-Mahlknecht, S.: How are techno-stressors associated with mental health and work outcomes? A systematic review of occupational exposure to information and communication technologies within the technostress model. Int. J. Environ. Res. Public Health **18**(16), 8673 (2021)
54. Lilian, S.C.: Virtual teams: opportunities and challenges for e-leaders. Procedia Soc. Behav. Sci. **110**, 1251–1261 (2014)
55. Contreras, F., Baykal, E., Abid, G.: E-leadership and teleworking in times of COVID-19 and beyond: What we know and where do we go. Front. Psychol. **11**, 590271 (2020)
56. Bauer, G.F., Hämmig, O., Schaufeli, W.B., Taris, T.W.: A critical review of the job demands-resources model: implications for improving work and health. Bridging Occup. Organ. Public Health: Transdisc. Approach 43–68 (2014)
57. Syvänen, A., Mäkiniemi, J. P., Syrjä, S., Heikkilä-Tammi, K., Viteli, J.: When does the educational use of ICT become a source of technostress for finnish teachers?. In: Seminar. Net, vol. 12, no. 2 (2016)
58. Jena, R.K., Mahanti, P.K.: An empirical study of Technostress among Indian academicians. Int. J. Educ. Learn. **3**(2), 1–10 (2014)
59. Şahin, Y.L., Çoklar, A.N.: Social networking users' views on technology and the determination of technostress levels. Procedia Soc. Behav. Sci. **1**(1), 1437–1442 (2009)
60. Hsiao, K.L.: Compulsive mobile application usage and technostress: the role of personality traits. Online Inf. Rev. **41**(2), 272–295 (2017)
61. Maier, C., Laumer, S., Eckhardt, A.: Information technology as daily stressor: pinning down the causes of burnout. J. Bus. Econ. **85**, 349–387 (2015)
62. Krishnan, S.: Personality and espoused cultural differences in technostress creators. Comput. Hum. Behav. **66**, 154–167 (2017)
63. Kossek, E.E.: Managing work-life boundaries in the digital age. Organ. Dyn. **45**(3), 258–270 (2016)
64. Bakker, A.B., Demerouti, E., Sanz-Vergel, A.I.: Burnout and work engagement: the JD–R approach. Annu. Rev. Organ. Psychol. Organ. Behav. **1**(1), 389–411 (2014)

65. Venkatesh, V., Speier, C.: Creating an effective training environment for enhancing telework. Int. J. Hum. Comput. Stud. **52**(6), 991–1005 (2000)
66. Kubicek, B., Paškvan, M., Korunka, C.: Development and validation of an instrument for assessing job demands arising from accelerated change: the intensification of job demands scale (IDS). Eur. J. Work Organ. Psy. **24**(6), 898–913 (2015)
67. Derks, D., van Duin, D., Tims, M., Bakker, A.B.: Smartphone use and work–home interference: the moderating role of social norms and employee work engagement. J. Occup. Organ. Psychol. **88**(1), 155–177 (2015)
68. Mazzetti, G., Schaufeli, W.B., Guglielmi, D., Depolo, M.: Overwork climate scale: Psychometric properties and relationships with working hard. J. Manage. Psychol. **31**, 880–896 (2016)

User-Device-Interaction Model: A Multimodal Interaction Evaluation System Based on Analytic Hierarchy Process

Jian Peng and Xuepeng Wang(✉)

School of Design, Hunan University, Changsha, China
{jianpeng,wxpwxp}@hnu.edu.cn

Abstract. The evaluation of interaction system is an important step to guiding the iterative optimization of the interaction product. However, with the development of emotional, naturalistic and multi-channel HCI, there are some emerging problems, such as mere superposition of interaction modes and imbalance between efficiency and cost. In this study, we proposed a model called User-Device-Interaction Model (UDI). The goal is to establish an interaction evaluation system that takes into account the cost of interaction and quantifies the evaluation metrics. Interaction system was decomposed into measurable indicators from seven dimensions, including user perceived usability and user fatigue perception. Then, Analytic Hierarchy Process (AHP) is used to calculate the weights of the indicators at each level of evaluation, and the validity of the evaluation system was demonstrated through empirical research. We believe that this result can provide guidance and suggestions for the optimal design and evaluation of various types of interaction system.

Keywords: Human-computer interaction · Interaction evaluation · Analytic Hierarchy Process · Interaction usability · System evaluation

1 Introduction

The trend towards naturalization, emotionality and multi-channelization of interaction modalities is significant. The interaction effectiveness of single-modal inputs is easily influenced by factors such as interaction complexity and working conditions. Conversely, the more complex the task, the better the usability of multimodal interaction [1], as multimodal HCI can combine the advantages of single-modal interaction to achieve the complementary advantages of multiple input modalities [2–5]. However, multimodal interaction is not a mere overlay of interaction modules, since too many interaction modalities being integrated into one device may lead to problems such as information overload and increased interaction costs. Therefore, the evaluation of multimodal interaction for augmented reality (AR) devices is a key issue for improving user experience and balancing interaction effectiveness and interaction cost. However, current research on the evaluation of multimodal interaction systems is not sufficient, and a widely accepted standard evaluation system has not yet been formed at this new stage of interaction development.

M. Kurosu and A. Hashizume (Eds.): HCII 2023, LNCS 14011, pp. 181–199, 2023.
https://doi.org/10.1007/978-3-031-35596-7_13

1.1 Emerging Interaction Modalities

In recent years, new interaction modalities such as eye tracking [6, 7], gesture [8, 9] and voice [10, 11] have become common in smart devices, and the integration of these new interaction modalities in smart devices has improved the efficiency and naturalness of interaction to a certain extent.

The correctness and real time of gesture recognition is a key technical challenge in human-computer interaction. In early gesture recognition systems, the user mostly needed to wear sensors or special gloves [12]. Currently, advances in computer vision technology have made it possible for cameras to recognize gestures, for example using Time of Fight Camera (Tof Camera) [13], motion sensors [14], depth sensors [15], etc. to enable bare hand interaction. Gesture-based interaction provides a relatively intuitive and natural interaction experience [16], but prolonged use can lead to arm fatigue [17], in addition, is relatively expensive to apply, as gesture interaction requires multiple sensors to work with.

The boundaries of browsing, tapping and swiping in eye-tracking are not clear and may suffer from unconscious triggering (Midas-Touch) [7]. Therefore, it is difficult to use as the only interaction input modality, but eye-tracking can be used as a natural interaction modality to quickly locate a target and accomplish other interactions in conjunction with other modalities.

Voice interaction, which controls devices through verbal commands from a person [11], is relatively well developed and previous research has found that the efficiency of voice-only is comparable to gesture-only [18]. Meanwhile a study by Whitlock et al. evaluated voice, gesture and handheld devices in terms of objective (completion time, accuracy) and subjective (difficulty) and found that voice interaction had better performance and stability [19].

1.2 Multimodal Interaction Evaluation

Gesture-plus-speech input is widely used in current smart devices. The earliest research can be traced back to Bolt's 'Put-that-there' [20]. The combination of eye-tracking and gestures provides a more natural interaction experience, while outperforming single gesture interactions in terms of accuracy of interaction selection [21]. Using Fitts' Law, Chatterjee et al. compared the combination of eye-tracking and gesture with five other interaction types and found them to be highly complementary and close to the performance of the 'gold standard' (mouse, button or trackpad), which is evaluated on the basis of accuracy and completion time [22]. Roider et al. evaluated and improved the pointing accuracy of the interaction and found that gesture plus eye tracking had higher accuracy than a single modality [23]. Irawati et al. similarly conducted a comparison between multimodality and unimodality, where speech plus gesture improved the efficiency of interaction [24]. Tao et al. investigated the effects of body posture, interaction distance and target size on interaction with a large display and evaluated the interaction by three metrics: task performance, perceived usability and workload [25]. Wang et al. evaluated multimodal interactions in an AR environment based on objective (completion time, accuracy) and subjective experimental results (task load, user preference, system usability) and found that gaze + gesture + voice had the highest interaction efficiency and gesture + voice had better user satisfaction [26].

Most current evaluation metrics for multimodal interaction have been developed based on usability as defined in the standard ISO 9241–11 [27], which defines three evaluation dimensions: effectiveness, efficacy and satisfaction. However, the optimization of interaction systems should meet these three evaluation dimensions while controlling the costs of interaction in terms of economy and user effort in practical applications. The current interaction evaluation does not have an adequate selection of indicators, so it is difficult to effectively guide the optimal design and empirical evaluation of interaction. At the same time, most current research has only verified usability, but interaction cost as an important metric has rarely been considered. Therefore, this paper will propose a multimodal interaction evaluation system including interaction cost based on AHP.

2 Evaluation Indicator

The strengths and weaknesses of interactive systems cannot be directly measured. Although many studies have carried out interaction evaluation work, most of them were simply validated based on the design of the interactive system, so there might be problems of biased evaluation results due to the absence of a metric system to refer to. Therefore, we turned complex and not directly measurable systems into analyzable and measurable metrics to assist in the design and evaluation of interactive systems.

2.1 Evaluation Elements

The three components involved in an interactive system are the user, the interactive device and the input and output of the interactive product itself, so this paper will establish an evaluation index system from three levels: user, device and interaction. This paper will establish a structural framework for interaction evaluation with reference to relevant interactive system evaluation studies and expert panel discussions in order to justify the evaluation metrics and to analyze the impact of each metric at the user, device and interaction layers. The expert panel consisted of experts in interaction design, systems engineering, user experience design and consumer research. After analysis, discussion and combing through existing research, the panel selected its system elements and drew up a detailed list of elements, as shown in Table 1.

A total of 35 elements were discussed and identified for the interactive system evaluation, expressed in a set as:

$$S = \{s_i | i = 1, 2, \ldots\ldots, 35\}$$

2.2 Interpretative Structural Modeling

After analyzing and discussing, the group describes the interrelationships of the 35 elements in the set S and represents them in a directed graph, as shown in Fig. 1.

Based on the interrelationship of the elements to their regional division, it is known that all elements belong to the same region. On this basis, the hierarchy of elements is divided. The hierarchical analysis structure of complex problems is generally divided

Table 1. Evaluation elements of interaction system.

No	Elements	No	Elements	No	Elements
1	Perceived usability [25]	13	Electro cardiac activity(ECG) [28]	25	Accuracy of device [29]
2	Relevant background/experience [28]	14	Electrodermal activity [28]	26	False alarm rate [30]
3	Task-unrelated thought [31, 32]	15	Facial thermography [33]	27	Device response speed [34, 35]
4	Interactive behavior logic [36]	16	Respiratory rate [28]	28	Perceived workload [25]
5	Adverse effects of interaction [28]	17	Ocular measures [28]	29	Interaction hardware cost [37]
6	User cognitive load [38, 39]	18	Instantaneous self-assessment [40]	30	Interaction device performance [41]
7	Electroencephalogram (EEG) [28]	19	Task load index [42]	31	Interference from secondary tasks [43]
8	Interaction costs [37]	20	Interaction completion degree [25]	32	Interaction difficulty [43]
9	Software development costs [44]	21	User attention [45]	33	Number of interactive operations [25]
10	Willingness to use [46]	22	Multimodal interaction evaluation [47]	34	Interaction completion time [48]
11	Cognitive control degree [49]	23	User performance [25]	35	Extreme environment availability [37]
12	Error rate[25]	24	Accuracy of user operation [26]		

into three layers: the first layer is the target layer, which is to decompose the complex problem into objectives of different dimensions; the second layer is the criterion layer, which is the main direction to judge the completion of objectives and make optimization decisions; the third layer is the measurement layer, that is, some quantifiable factors that have effects on indicators of criterion layer. Based on this theory, we establish the accessibility matrix and complete the structural model, and finally we can get the division results of the target layer L_1, criterion layer L_2 and measurement layer L_3 as follows.

$$\pi(\mathrm{S})$$

$$= \{L_1, L_2, L_3\}$$

$$= \{\{22\}, \{1, 8, 23, 28, 30, 32\}, \left\{\begin{matrix} 2, 3, 4, 5, 6, 7, 9, 10, 11, 12, 13, 14, 15, 16, 17, 18, \\ 19, 20, 21, 24, 25, 26, 27, 29, 31, 33, 34, 35 \end{matrix}\right\}\}$$

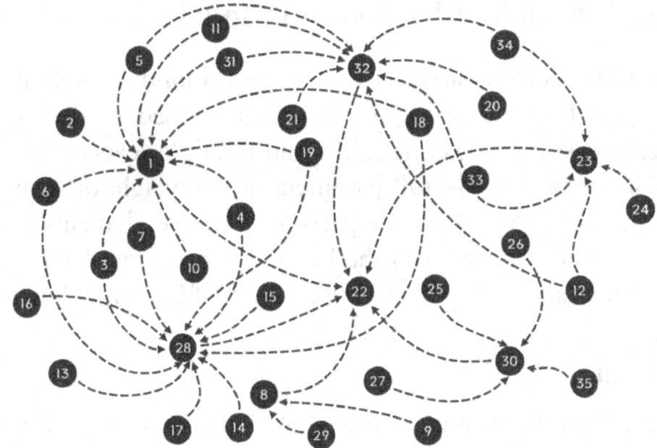

Fig. 1. Interrelationship of evaluation elements.

Hence, the interpretative structure model can be developed, as shown in Fig. 2.

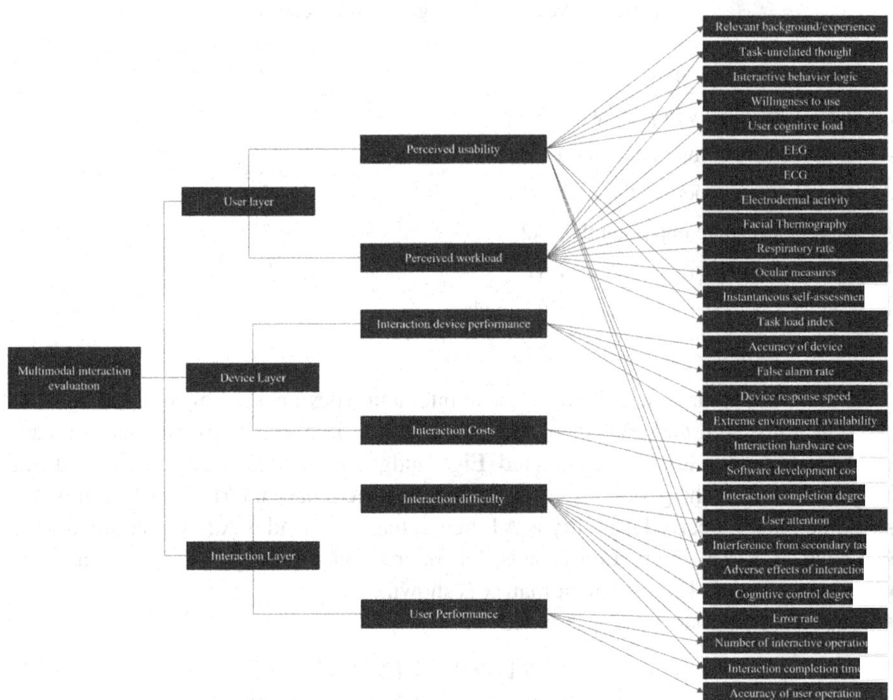

Fig. 2. Interpretative structural modeling.

3 AHP-Based Interaction Evaluation Model

AHP is a multi-criteria decision analysis method that combines qualitative and quantitative analysis proposed by TL Saaty [50]. It is mainly used for decision making and evaluation problems with complex structures and multiple levels of decision criteria. The basic idea is to replace the overall judgment of the weight of several elements in a complex problem with a "pairwise comparison" of these elements to determine the relative importance of each element in the hierarchy, and then determine the relative importance of decision factors through the integration of human judgment.

3.1 Indicator Weights

In order to compare the relative importance of the indicators, the evaluation indicators were compared in pairs by the expert consultation method and the relative comparison method, and a judgment matrix was established to describe the weights of each indicator more accurately and qualitatively, as shown in Table 2, where the numbers 1–9 and their reciprocals were used to define the importance levels among the indicators.

Table 2. Meaning of judgment matrix scale

Importance level description	Ratio scale
A1 and A2 are equally important	1
A1 is slightly more important than A2	3
A1 is much more important than A2	5
A1 is extremely more important than A2	7
A1 is definitely more important than A2	9
The degree is between two adjacent odd numbers	2,4,6,8

In this study, four experts in the fields of interaction design, system engineering, user experience research and consumer research rated the importance by geometric mean, and the judgment matrix was calculated. Eight judgment matrices were constructed and analyzed based on the geometric mean. Taking the secondary metrics as an example, it is assumed that perceived usability is A1, perceptual workload is A2, interaction device performance is A3, interaction cost is A4, interaction difficulty is A5, and the user performance is A6. The judgment matrix is shown in Table 3.

The judgment matrix is represented as:

$$A = \begin{pmatrix} 1 & 2.711 & 5.692 & 4.120 & 4.427 & 0.687 \\ 0.369 & 1 & 3.834 & 2.213 & 2.632 & 0.320 \\ 0.176 & 0.261 & 1 & 0.452 & 0.595 & 0.173 \\ 0.243 & 0.452 & 2.213 & 1 & 1.189 & 0.237 \\ 0.226 & 0.380 & 1.682 & 0.841 & 1 & 0.212 \\ 1.457 & 3.130 & 5.785 & 4.213 & 4.729 & 1 \end{pmatrix}$$

Table 3. Judgment matrix of the second level indicators

Indicators	A1	A2	A3	A4	A5	A6
A1	1	2.711	5.692	4.120	4.427	0.687
A2	0.369	1.000	3.834	2.213	2.632	0.320
A3	0.176	0.261	1.000	0.452	0.595	0.173
A4	0.243	0.452	2.213	1.000	1.189	0.237
A5	0.226	0.380	1.682	0.841	1.000	0.212
A6	1.457	3.130	5.785	4.213	4.729	1.000

3.2 Weight Vector

In order to distill effective information from the judgment matrix and achieve regularity, the weight vector of each judgment matrix and the synthetic weight vector of the whole judgment matrix are calculated using the square root method.

$$w_1^{'} = \sqrt[6]{1 \times 2.711 \times 5.692 \times 4.120 \times 4.427 \times 0.687} = 2.4044$$

$$w_2^{'} = \sqrt[6]{0.369 \times 1 \times 3.834 \times 2.213 \times 2.632 \times 0.320} = 1.1751$$

$$w_3^{'} = \sqrt[6]{0.176 \times 0.261 \times 1 \times 0.452 \times 0.595 \times 0.173} = 0.3587$$

$$w_4^{'} = \sqrt[6]{0.243 \times 0.452 \times 2.213 \times 1 \times 1.189 \times 0.237} = 0.6397$$

$$w_5^{'} = \sqrt[6]{0.226 \times 0.380 \times 1.682 \times 0.841 \times 1 \times 0.212} = 0.5431$$

$$w_6^{'} = \sqrt[6]{1.457 \times 3.130 \times 5.785 \times 4.213 \times 4.729 \times 1} = 2.8407$$

$$\sum_{i=1}^{6} w_i = w_1^{'} + w_2^{'} + w_3^{'} + w_4^{'} + w_5^{'} + w_6^{'} = 7.9619$$

Then normalize it to:

$$w_1 = \frac{w_1^{'}}{\sum_1^6 w_i} = 0.302$$

$$w_2 = \frac{w_2^{'}}{\sum_1^6 w_i} = 0.148$$

$$w_3 = \frac{w_3^{'}}{\sum_1^6 w_i} = 0.045$$

$$w_4 = \frac{w_4^{'}}{\sum_1^6 w_i} = 0.080$$

$$w_5 = \frac{w_5^{'}}{\sum_1^6 w_i} = 0.068$$

$$w_6 = \frac{w_6^{'}}{\sum_1^6 w_i} = 0.357$$

Therefore, the synthetic weight vector can be calculated as:

$$W = A \cdot w = \begin{pmatrix} 1 & 2.711 & 5.692 & 4.120 & 4.427 & 0.687 \\ 0.369 & 1 & 3.834 & 2.213 & 2.632 & 0.320 \\ 0.176 & 0.261 & 1 & 0.452 & 0.595 & 0.173 \\ 0.243 & 0.452 & 2.213 & 1 & 1.189 & 0.237 \\ 0.226 & 0.380 & 1.682 & 0.841 & 1 & 0.212 \\ 1.457 & 3.130 & 5.785 & 4.213 & 4.729 & 1 \end{pmatrix} \cdot \begin{pmatrix} 0.302 \\ 0.148 \\ 0.045 \\ 0.080 \\ 0.068 \\ 0.357 \end{pmatrix} = \begin{pmatrix} 1.836 \\ 0.903 \\ 0.275 \\ 0.486 \\ 0.411 \\ 2.180 \end{pmatrix}$$

$$\lambda_{max} = \frac{1.836}{6 \times 0.302} + \frac{0.903}{6 \times 0.148} + \frac{0.275}{6 \times 0.045} + \frac{0.486}{6 \times 0.080} + \frac{0.411}{6 \times 0.068} + \frac{2.180}{6 \times 0.357} = 6.082$$

3.3 Consistency Testing

We will test the consistency of the above results to ensure its credibility. Saaty suggested to take the ratio of consistency index CI to random consistency index RI, i.e. Consistency Ratio (CR), as the consistency test discriminant: CR = CI/RI. The CI discriminant is:

$$CI = \frac{\lambda_{max} - n}{n - 1} = \frac{6.082 - 6}{6 - 1} = 0.016$$

The RI is taken with reference to Table 4, and the matrix order is 6, so RI = 1.24.

Table 4. Random consistency RI

n	RI
3	0.52
4	0.89
5	1.12
6	1.24
…	…
20	1.63

The value CR can be obtained:

$$CR = \frac{CI}{RI} = \frac{0.016}{1.24} = 0.013$$

The smaller value of CR represents the better consistency of the judgment matrix, if CR < 0.1, the judgment matrix is considered to satisfy the consistency test, if CR > 0.1, the judgment matrix needs to be adjusted. CI = 0.016, RI = 1.24, CR = 0.013 < 0.1, therefore, the judgment matrix passes the consistency test.

Based on this method, other index weights are calculated, and the results are shown in Table 5.

Table 5. Index weights of interactive system evaluation

First-level indicators	Second -level indicators	Third-level indicators	Comprehensive weights	Weight order
User layer (A1, 44.959%)	Perceived usability (B1, 30.2%)	Relevant background/experience (C1, 11.235%)	3.393%	10
		Task-unrelated thought (C2, 6.21%)	1.875%	15
		Interactive behavior logic (C3, 15.464%)	4.67%	6
		Willingness to use (C4, 28.162%)	8.505%	5
		User cognitive load (C5, 38.929%)	11.757%	3
	Perceived workload (B2, 14.759%)	EEG (D1, 13.238%)	1.954%	13
		ECG (D2, 13.673%)	2.018%	12
		Electrodermal activity (D3, 11.497%)	1.697%	16
		Facial Thermography (D4, 9.334%)	1.378%	18
		Respiratory rate (D5, 5.736%)	0.847%	25
		Ocular measures (D6, 7.487%)	1.105%	23
		Instantaneous self-assessment (D7, 14.72%)	2.173%	11
		Task load index (D8, 24.315%)	3.589%	9

(*continued*)

Table 5. (*continued*)

First-level indicators	Second -level indicators	Third-level indicators	Comprehensive weights	Weight order
Device layer (A2, 12.54%)	Interaction device performance (B3, 4.505%)	Accuracy of device (E1, 30.399%)	1.369%	19
		False alarm rate (E2, 13.739%)	0.619%	27
		Device response speed (E3, 28.894%)	1.302%	20
		Extreme environment availability (E4, 26.968%)	1.215%	21
	Interaction costs (B4, 8.035%)	Interaction hardware cost (F1, 51.782%)	4.161%	7
		Software development costs (F2, 48.218%)	3.874%	8
Interaction layer (A3, 42.501%)	Interaction difficulty (B5, 6.822%)	Interaction completion degree (G1, 22.639%)	1.544%	17
		User attention (G2, 17.178)	1.172%	22
		Interference from secondary tasks (G3, 8.93%)	0.609%	28
		Adverse effects of interaction (G4, 10.386%)	0.709%	26
		Cognitive control degree (G5, 12.721%)	0.868%	24
		Error rate (G6, 28.146%)	1.92%	14
	User performance (B6, 35.679%)	Number of interactive operations (H1, 34.211%)	12.206%	2
		Interaction completion time (H2, 40.394%)	14.412%	1
		Accuracy of user operation (H3, 25.395%)	9.061%	4

4 Empirical Analysis

4.1 Experiment Design

The interaction system evaluation will be tested in two separate tasks, and the methodology refers to the USUS (Usability; Social Acceptance; User Experience; Societal Impact) HCI evaluation method and standard ISO 9241–11-2018 proposed by Weiss et al. The laboratory-based user study method recommended in the Weiss study was chosen. The test device will use the HiAR G200 and a gesture recognition module (Leap Motion Controller), which is a split optical see-through AR Head-Mounted Display (HMD) that integrates multiple interaction modal components.

In order to simplify the testing process, the experiment will combine the interaction characteristics of the device and the usage scenario to select the metrics with higher comprehensive weights among the metrics with equivalent relationships, and finally selected the following metrics: user cognitive load (C5), task load index (D8), accuracy of device (E1), interaction hardware cost (F1), error rate (G6), and interaction completion time (H2), and assigned secondary metric weights to them respectively. The metrics and their measurement methods are shown in Table 6, and the users will be asked to make a comprehensive rating of the whole interaction system after the experiment is completed.

Perceived usability and perceived workload are measured by questionnaires. The evaluation indexes of the usability perception questionnaire referred to the Computer System Usability Questionnaire (CSUQ), the Virtual Reality Disease Questionnaire (VRSQ), and the interaction study by Lou et al. The final perceived usability measurement questions were selected as accuracy evaluation (I can accurately select the interaction target), speed evaluation (I can quickly complete the interaction task), comfort evaluation (I have no discomfort such as dizziness, blurred vision, or nausea during the task), fatigue evaluation (I can complete the evaluation task effortlessly), and difficulty evaluation (the evaluation task is easy for me). User usability perceptions will be quantified after the task using the Likert-10 evaluation method (1 = completely agree, 10 = completely disagree); user workload perceptions will be quantified and calculated using the 10-point NASA Task Load Index (NASA-TLX), which has become a widely used subjective workload assessment tool for various HCI tasks. User usability perceptions will be quantified after the task using the Likert-10 evaluation method (1 = completely agree, 10 = completely disagree); user workload perceptions will be quantified and calculated using the 10-point NASA Task Load Index (NASA-TLX), which has become a widely used subjective workload assessment tool for various HCI tasks. Data for interaction hardware costs are sourced from the e-commerce platform Amazon.

Table 6. The metrics and their measurement methods

Criteria level (secondary indicators)	Measurement layer (three-level indicators)	Measurement method
Perceived usability	User cognitive load	Questionnaires (Likert-10)
Perceived workload	Task load index	NASA-TLX
Interaction device performance	Accuracy of device	Experimental data record
Interaction Difficulty	Error rate	Experimental data record
User performance	Interaction completion time	Experimental data record
Interaction Costs	Interaction hardware cost	Price statistics for components on Amazon

The task design refers to the AR interaction task classification study by Piumsomboon et al. and the task settings of related interaction evaluation studies. The tasks were finally determined as the light brightness adjustment task and the cube operation task. The light task and the cube task are common AR interaction tasks that represent a series of control operations in the AR environment. The specific tasks were set as follows.

Task 1 (T1): Virtual luminaire brightness adjustment task. Two lamps were placed on the floor and the table in the AR environment, and participants were required to operate the brightness control bar located on the right side of the lamps using different interaction methods, and the task was judged successful when participants adjusted the brightness value of the lamps to 6 ± 0.2.

Task 2 (T2): Virtual object movement task. A white cube and a colored cube were placed on the floor and bed in the AR environment. The task required participants to move the white cube to the colored cube and overlap it, with the white cube highlighted when selected.

For multimodal interaction, we considered the characteristics of each modality when designing the task process. (1) voice can trigger commands more quickly, such as "select", "confirm", "cancel" and other interactive input operations; (2) Both touchpad and gestures can be used to move or drag the position of virtual objects, but the machine feedback of touchpad is more accurate and rapid, suitable for moving the target position and controlling small targets, such as moving objects in parallel, dragging sliders and other similar operations; (3) The gesture input is more intuitive and natural, suitable for the position selection of virtual objects, and can be used for rotation and zooming operations.

The detailed operation is as follows: the user points his index finger to the operation target and uses the voice command "select" to select the target, and uses the voice command "finish" to end the task. In Task 1, the users slide their fingers up and down the touchpad sensing area to complete the brightness adjustment operation; in Task 2, the users use the touchpad to drag the virtual object to the target location.

The tasks were set up to ensure that each interaction modality interacted with the virtual objects in both Task 1 and Task 2, while participants were demonstrated and trained on device interaction before the test began and allowed to try out the operations to familiarize themselves with the device and the interactions.

4.2 Experiment Results

The subjective assessment data (user cognitive load and task load index) collected using the scales are shown in Tables 7 and 8, the objective assessment data (accuracy of device, error rate, and interaction completion time) collected using the experimental records are shown in Table 9, and the interaction cost statistics is shown in Fig. 3.

Table 7. Data of user cognitive load

	Accuracy		Speed		Comfort		Fatigue		Difficulty	
	Mean	SD	Mean	SD	Mean	SD	Mean	SD	Mean	SD
T1	5.95	1.73	5.85	1.69	5.35	1.46	4.5	1.32	5.2	1.36
T2	5.55	1.76	4.85	1.81	5.45	1.85	3.8	1.58	4.05	1.76

Table 8. Data of task load index

	Mental Demand		Physical Demand		Temporal Demand		Performance		Effort		Frustration	
	Mean	SD	Mean	SD	Mean	SD	Mean	SD	Mean	SD	Mean	SD
T1	5.35	1.14	5.15	1.09	4	1.12	5.15	1.18	5.75	1.16	4.9	1.17
T2	6.1	1.55	6.05	1.39	5.9	1.68	5.95	1.7	6.6	1.9	6.05	1.85

Table 9. Data of accuracy of device, error rate and completion time

	T1		T2	
	Mean	SD	Mean	SD
Accuracy of device	0.0325 lx	0.024	17.3 px	8.221
Error rate	4.69%	0.0659	8.24%	0.0936
Completion time	5.637 s	0.845	6.588 s	1.351

In order to ensure that the data can be calculated effectively, we standardize the data using the Min-Max normalization method. The multimodal interaction evaluation test has six indicators: user cognitive load, task load index, accuracy of device, interaction hardware cost, error rate, and task completion time, so the results are set as $x_1, x_2, \cdots, x_6$, the normalized results are set as $y_1, y_2, \cdots, y_6$. The calculation formula is as follows.

$$y_i = \frac{x_i - x_{min}}{x_{max} - x_{min}}$$

x_4 is taken from the existing experimental device price of 1200$, and the data of x_{max} and x_{min} are taken from the maximum and minimum cost of the AR devices with the combination of touchpad and voice, which are 2500$ and 299$ respectively.

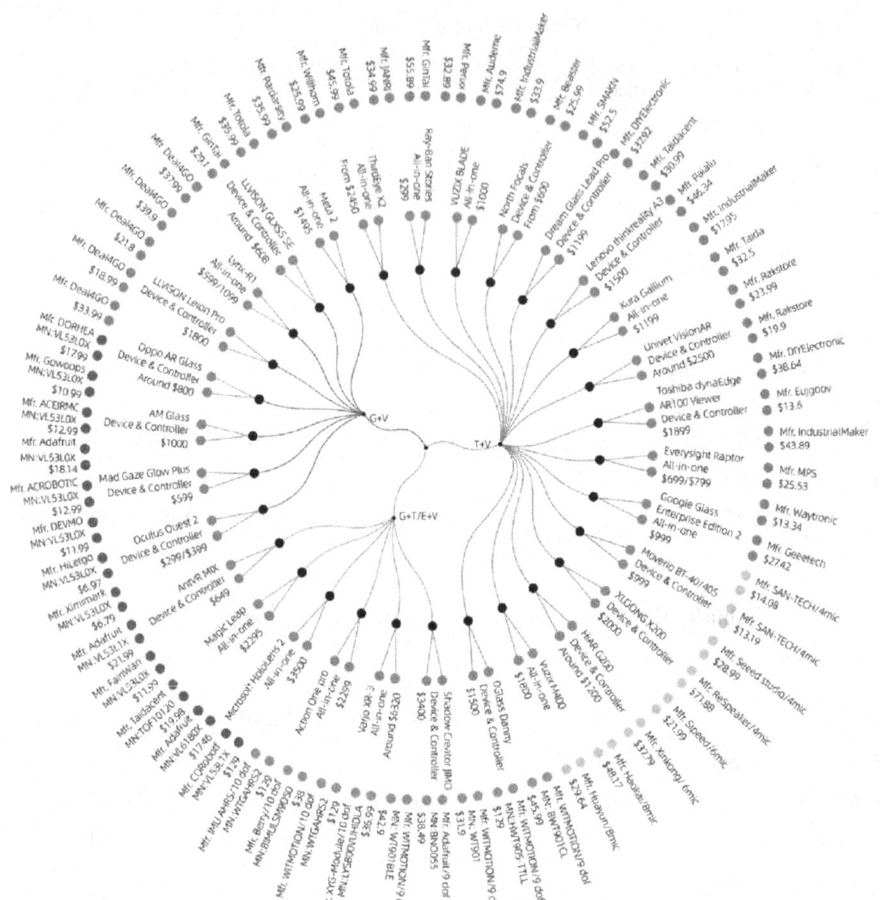

Fig. 3. Interaction cost statistics for selected products (Orange for voice recogniser, yellow for microphone array, green for IMU, blue for Tof, purple for touch component) and integration of the interaction modality in some AR/MR glasses (G + V: gesture + voice; T + V: touchpad + voice; G + T/E +: gesture + touchpad/eye tracking + voice)

4.3 Scale Data Reliability Testing

Reliability – Internal Consistency. Internal consistency tests were conducted on each question score of the 20 questionnaires by IBM SPSS 26 to obtain the value of Cronbach's Alpha. The results are shown in Table 10.

In T1, the Cronbach's Alpha value for user usability perception was 0.910 and the Cronbach's Alpha value based on standardized terminology was 0.915, both of which were above 90%. Similarly, the Cronbach's Alpha value for workload perception in T1 was 0.867 and the Cronbach's Alpha value based on standardized terminology was 0.864, both of which were above 80%.

In T2, the Cronbach's Alpha value for user usability perception was 0.902 and the Cronbach's Alpha value based on standardized terminology was 0.903, both of which were above 90%. Likewise, the Cronbach's Alpha value for user workload perception in T2 was 0.906 and the Cronbach's Alpha value based on standardized terminology was 0.908, both of which were above 90%.

Therefore, the scale data of the study had high internal consistency, i.e., high reliability.

Table 10. Results of internal consistency testing

	Cronbach's Alpha	Cronbach's alpha based on standardized items	N of items	N of cases
Perceived usability T1	0.910	0.915	5	20
Perceived workload T1	0.867	0.864	6	20
Perceived usability T2	0.902	0.903	5	20
Perceived workload T2	0.906	0.908	6	20

4.4 Model Validity Testing

To test the validity of UDI model, overall user ratings of the interaction system (only one question) were collected from 20 participants at the end of the experiment using the Likert-10 scale (1 = very poor, 10 = very good). The final comprehensive score (weighted mean), average comprehensive score (arithmetic mean), and interaction overall rating of the 20 participants were analyzed for correlation. The overall score of the individual question was used as a criterion to test the correlation between the comprehensive score and the criterion to indicate whether the UDI model accurately evaluated the interaction system.

The results of Pearson correlation analysis are shown in Table 11. The correlation coefficient between the overall score and the final comprehensive score is 0.495, and the correlation coefficient between the overall score and the average comprehensive score is 0.411, both of which are significant at the 0.01 level. The correlation coefficient calculated by the weighted mean is significantly higher than that calculated by the arithmetic mean, indicating that the scores calculated by the UDI model are closer to the real evaluation result of the interactive system. Therefore, the scores calculated based on the index system and the evaluation model weights have a high reliability.

Table 11. Correlation matrix of scores

Indicators	Overall user rating	Weighted average score	Arithmetic average score
Overall user rating	1	–	–
Final comprehensive score	0.495**	1	–
Average comprehensive score	0.411**	0.931**	1

5 Conclusion

In order to address the problem that the current multimodal interaction system evaluation is not well developed, we built a parsing structure model based on the system elements and their correlations, and then determined the index weights based on AHP and finally established the multimodal interaction evaluation UDI model. In addition, the model was empirically tested based on the results of the interaction experiment with 20 participants. The questionnaire data passed the reliability test and the experimental results passed the validity test, which verified that the UDI model is valid in evaluating the interaction system. Therefore, the method can be applied to the evaluation and optimization of interactive systems in various fields, with a view to providing theoretical suggestions for the establishment and improvement of interactive system evaluation. In this study, due to equipment limitations and simplified experimental procedures, some subjective data were collected and not all indicators were covered, which may have an impact on the objectivity and accuracy of the experimental results, and it is expected that more comprehensive and objective data will be used to further produce accurate systematic evaluation results in future work.

References

1. Jöst, M., Häußler, J., Merdes, M., Malaka, R.: Multimodal interaction for pedestrians: an evaluation study. In: Proceedings of the 10th International Conference on Intelligent User Interfaces, pp. 59–66. ACM, New York (2005)
2. 孙瀚: 基于多模态生物电信号人机交互技术研究. 东南大学,南京 (2019). Sun, H.: Research of human-computer interaction technology based on multi-modal biopotentials. Southeast University, Nanjing (2019)
3. Cohen, P.R., Dalrymple, M., Moran, D.B., Pereira, F., Sullivan, J.W.: Synergistic use of direct manipulation and natural language. In: Proceedings of the SIGCHI Conference on Human Factors in Computing Systems, pp. 227–233. ACM, New York (1989)
4. Oviatt, S.: Advances in robust multimodal interface design. IEEE Comput. Graph. Appl. **23**, 62–68 (2003)
5. Oviatt, S., Coulston, R., Lunsford, R.: When do we interact multimodally? Cognitive load and multimodal communication patterns. In: Proceedings of the 6th International Conference on Multimodal Interfaces, pp. 129–136. ACM, New York (2004)

6. Ware, C., Mikaelian, H.H.: An evaluation of an eye tracker as a device for computer input2. In: Proceedings of the SIGCHI/GI Conference on Human Factors in Computing Systems and Graphics Interface, pp. 183–188. ACM, New York (1986)
7. Jacob, R.J.: What you look at is what you get: eye movement-based interaction techniques. In: Proceedings of the SIGCHI Conference on Human Factors in Computing Systems, pp. 11–18. ACM, New York (1990)
8. Chaconas, N., Höllerer, T.: An evaluation of bimanual gestures on the Microsoft Hololens. In: 2018 IEEE Conference on Virtual Reality and 3D User Interfaces (VR), pp. 1–8. IEEE, New York (2018)
9. Satriadi, K.A., Ens, B., Cordeil, M., Jenny, B., Czauderna, T., Willett, W.: Augmented reality map navigation with freehand gestures. In: 2019 IEEE Conference on Virtual Reality and 3D User Interfaces (VR), pp. 593–603. IEEE, New York (2019)
10. Billinghurst, M.: Hands and speech in space: multimodal interaction with augmented reality interfaces. In: Proceedings of the 15th ACM on International Conference on Multimodal Interaction, pp. 379–380. ACM, New York (2013)
11. Goose, S., Sudarsky, S., Zhang, X., Navab, N.: Speech-enabled augmented reality supporting mobile industrial maintenance. IEEE Pervasive Comput. **2**, 65–70 (2003)
12. Olwal, A., Benko, H., Feiner, S.: Senseshapes: Using statistical geometry for object selection in a multimodal augmented reality. In: The Second IEEE and ACM International Symposium on Mixed and Augmented Reality Proceedings, pp. 300–301. IEEE, New York (2003)
13. Yu, C.-W., Liu, C.-H., Chen, Y.-L., Lee, P., Tian, M.-S.: Vision-based hand recognition based on ToF depth camera. Smart Sci. **6**, 21–28 (2018)
14. Marin, G., Dominio, F., Zanuttigh, P.: Hand gesture recognition with leap motion and Kinect devices. In: 2014 IEEE International Conference on Image Processing (ICIP), pp. 1565–1569. IEEE, New York (2014)
15. Rümelin, S., Marouane, C., Butz, A.: Free-hand pointing for identification and interaction with distant objects. In: Proceedings of the 5th International Conference on Automotive User Interfaces and Interactive Vehicular Applications, pp. 40–47. ACM, New York (2013)
16. Feiner, A.O.S.: The flexible pointer: an interaction technique for selection in augmented and virtual reality. In: Proceedings of the UIST, pp. 81–82. ACM, New York (2003)
17. Hincapié-Ramos, J.D., Guo, X., Moghadasian, P., Irani, P.: Consumed endurance: a metric to quantify arm fatigue of mid-air interactions. In: Proceedings of the SIGCHI Conference on Human Factors in Computing Systems, pp. 1063–1072. ACM, New York (2014)
18. Lee, M., Billinghurst, M., Baek, W., Green, R., Woo, W.: A usability study of multimodal input in an augmented reality environment. Virtual Reality **17**, 293–305 (2013). https://doi.org/10.1007/s10055-013-0230-0
19. Whitlock, M., Harnner, E., Brubaker, J.R., Kane, S., Szafir, D.A.: Interacting with distant objects in augmented reality. In: 2018 IEEE Conference on Virtual Reality and 3D User Interfaces (VR), pp. 41–48. IEEE, New York (2018)
20. Bolt, R.A.: "Put-that-there" Voice and gesture at the graphics interface. In: Proceedings of the 7th Annual Conference on Computer Graphics and Interactive Techniques, pp. 262–270. ACM, New York (1980)
21. Kytö, M., Ens, B., Piumsomboon, T., Lee, G.A., Billinghurst, M.: Pinpointing: precise head-and eye-based target selection for augmented reality. In: Proceedings of the 2018 CHI Conference on Human Factors in Computing Systems, pp. 1–14. ACM, New York (2018)
22. Chatterjee, I., Xiao, R., Harrison, C.: Gaze+ gesture: Expressive, precise and targeted free-space interactions. In: Proceedings of the 2015 ACM on International Conference on Multimodal Interaction, pp. 131–138. ACM, New York (2015)
23. Roider, F., Gross, T.: I see your point: integrating gaze to enhance pointing gesture accuracy while driving. In: Proceedings of the 10th International Conference on Automotive User Interfaces and Interactive Vehicular Applications, pp. 351–358. ACM, New York (2018)

24. Irawati, S., Green, S., Billinghurst, M., Duenser, A., Ko, H.: An evaluation of an augmented reality multimodal interface using speech and paddle gestures. In: Pan, Z., Cheok, A., Haller, M., Lau, R.W.H., Saito, H., Liang, R. (eds.) ICAT 2006. LNCS, vol. 4282, pp. 272–283. Springer, Heidelberg (2006). https://doi.org/10.1007/11941354_28
25. Tao, D., Diao, X., Wang, T., Guo, J., Qu, X.: Freehand interaction with large displays: effects of body posture, interaction distance and target size on task performance, perceived usability and workload. Appl. Ergon. **93**, 103370 (2021)
26. Wang, Z., Wang, H., Yu, H., Lu, F.: Interaction with gaze, gesture, and speech in a flexibly configurable augmented reality system. IEEE Trans. Hum.-Mach. Syst. **51**, 524–534 (2021)
27. Standardization, I.O.F.: ISO 9241–11: 2018—Ergonomics of Human-System Interaction—Part 11: Usability: Definitions and Concepts (2018)
28. Charles, R.L., Nixon, J.: Measuring mental workload using physiological measures: a systematic review. Appl. Ergon. **74**, 221–232 (2019)
29. Frutos-Pascual, M., Creed, C., Williams, I.: Head mounted display interaction evaluation: manipulating virtual objects in augmented reality. In: Lamas, D., Loizides, F., Nacke, L., Petrie, H., Winckler, M., Zaphiris, P. (eds.) IFIP Conference on Human-Computer Interaction, INTERACT 2019, vol. 11749, pp. 287–308. Springer, Heidelberg (2019). https://doi.org/10.1007/978-3-030-29390-1_16
30. Park, P.K., et al.: Low-latency interactive sensing for machine vision. In: 2019 IEEE International Electron Devices Meeting (IEDM), pp. 10.16.1–10.16.4. IEEE, New York (2019)
31. Mason, M.F., Norton, M.I., Van Horn, J.D., Wegner, D.M., Grafton, S.T., Macrae, C.N.: Wandering minds: the default network and stimulus-independent thought. Science **315**, 393–395 (2007)
32. Baror, S., Bar, M.: Increased associative interference under high cognitive load. Sci. Rep. **12**, 1–13 (2022)
33. Marinescu, A.C., Sharples, S., Ritchie, A.C., Sanchez Lopez, T., McDowell, M., Morvan, H.P.: Physiological parameter response to variation of mental workload. Hum. Factors **60**, 31–56 (2018)
34. Miller, R.B.: Response time in man-computer conversational transactions. In: Proceedings of the December 9–11, 1968, Fall Joint Computer Conference, part I, pp. 267–277. ACM, New York (1968)
35. Noguchi, O., Munechika, M., Kajihara, C.: A study on user satisfaction with an entire operation including indefinite-length response time. Total Qual. Sci. **2**, 70–79 (2016)
36. 邓力源, 蒋晓: 基于行为逻辑的隐式交互设计研究. 装饰 87–89 (2019). Deng, L.-Y, Jiang, X.: Research on implicit interaction design based on behavior logic. Zhuangshi 87–89 (2019)
37. 彭坚, 王雪鹏, 赵丹华, 李博雅: 单兵智能头盔在消防救援中的探索与应用. 包装工程 43, 1–14 (2022). Peng, J, Wang, X.-P., Zhao, D.-H., Li, B.-Y: Exploration and application of individual soldier intelligent helmet in fire rescue. Pack. Eng. **43**, 1–14 (2022)
38. Calvo, L., Christel, I., Terrado, M., Cucchietti, F., Pérez-Montoro, M.: Users' cognitive load: a key aspect to successfully communicate visual climate information. Bull. Am. Meteor. Soc. **103**, E1–E16 (2022)
39. Fishburn, F.A., Norr, M.E., Medvedev, A.V., Vaidya, C.J.: Sensitivity of fNIRS to cognitive state and load. Front. Hum. Neurosci. **8**, 76 (2014)
40. Hamann, A., Carstengerdes, N.: Fatigue Instantaneous Self-Assessment (F-ISA): development of a short mental fatigue rating. Institute of Flight Guidance, 1–13 (2020)
41. Elliott, S., Kukula, E., Sickler, N.: The challenges of the environment and the human/biometric device interaction on biometric system performance. In: International Workshop on Biometric Technologies-Special forum on Modeling and Simulation in Biometric Technology. (2004)

42. Cao, A., Chintamani, K.K., Pandya, A.K., Ellis, R.D.: NASA TLX: software for assessing subjective mental workload. Behav. Res. Methods **41**(1), 113–117 (2009). https://doi.org/10.3758/BRM.41.1.113
43. Gilbert, S.J., Bird, G., Frith, C.D., Burgess, P.W.: Does "task difficulty" explain "task-induced deactivation?" Front. Psychol. **3**, 125 (2012)
44. Rosson, M.B., Carroll, J.M.: Usability Engineering: Scenario-Based Development of Human-Computer Interaction. Morgan Kaufmann (2002)
45. Sutcliffe, A., Namoun, A.: Predicting user attention in complex web pages. Behav. Inf. Technol. **31**, 679–695 (2012)
46. Xia, J., Wang, Y., Fan, M.: Influence of using willingness of app with different initial interaction methods. In: 2020 International Conference on Innovation Design and Digital Technology (ICIDDT), pp. 278–285. IEEE, New York (2020)
47. Wechsung, I.: An Evaluation Framework for Multimodal Interaction. Springer, Cham (2014). https://doi.org/10.1007/978-3-319-03810-0
48. Vergel, R.S., Tena, P.M., Yrurzum, S.C., Cruz-Neira, C.: A comparative evaluation of a virtual reality table and a HoloLens-based augmented reality system for anatomy training. IEEE Trans. Hum.-Mach. Syst. **50**, 337–348 (2020)
49. Lavie, N.: Attention, distraction, and cognitive control under load. Curr. Dir. Psychol. Sci. **19**, 143–148 (2010)
50. Saaty, R.W.: The analytic hierarchy process—what it is and how it is used. Math. Model. **9**, 161–176 (1987)

Using Virtual Reality to Overcome Legacy Bias in Remote Gesture Elicitation Studies

Madhawa Perera[1,2(✉)], Tom Gedeon[1,3], Armin Haller[1], and Matt Adcock[1,2]

[1] Australian National University, Canberra, Australia
{madhawa.perera,tom.gedeon,armin.haller,matt.adcock}@anu.edu.au
[2] Commonwealth Scientific and Industrial Research Organisation, Canberra, Australia
{madhawa.perera,matt.adcock}@csiro.au
[3] Curtin University, Perth, Australia

Abstract. End-user Gesture Elicitation Studies (GESs) are the cornerstone of gesture design research and are used extensively when designing gesture-controlled interfaces. With the increasing accessibility of consumer-grade immersive devices, GESs are reshaping towards encapsulated studies using VR as a medium. These VR GESs appear to be effective in addressing the lack of ecological validity and systemic bias in typical GES designs. Yet, VR GESs often suffer from legacy bias, a phenomenon where elicited interactions are distorted by prior experiences and require study designs to mitigate them. In this study, we present a VR GES design that embeds three legacy bias reduction techniques: priming, partnering, and production (3Ps), and compare the impact of each technique with four between-group VR GESs. We discuss our design algorithms along with the results of the design evaluation. From the results, we postulate conducting VR studies outside the laboratory with legacy bias mitigation techniques is feasible and further discuss the implications and limitations of running GESs using VR as a medium for overcoming legacy bias.

Keywords: Gesture Elicitation · Legacy Bias Reduction · Virtual Reality · Remote User studies · Wizard of Oz

1 Introduction

Gesture interactions have captivated HCI researchers for a long time and continue to drive contemporary research as an emerging Natural User Interaction (NUI) technique. To design interaction for increasingly popular gesture-based systems, designers and developers need to understand how to identify and design "good" gestures that are discoverable, easy to perform, memorable, and reliable among the system users. For this purpose, Gesture Elicitation Studies (GESs) have been widely used in the development of gesture-based systems in HCI research [26].

M. Kurosu and A. Hashizume (Eds.): HCII 2023, LNCS 14011, pp. 200–225, 2023.
https://doi.org/10.1007/978-3-031-35596-7_14

Despite the popularity of GESs, one of the major concerns it inherits is "legacy bias", the impact of participants' prior experience on their gesture proposals [26]. In general, 'this bias limits the potential of end-user GESs to produce interactions that take full advantage of the possibilities and requirements of emerging application domains, form factors, and capabilities' [59]. Morris et al. [26] developed the 3Ps (Partners, Production, and Priming) method to counteract participants' legacy tendencies to help extract novel gestures, aiming to increase the usability of the new technologies. According to Morris et al. [26], 3Ps could be used alone or in combination. Yet, Vogiatzidakis et al's [51] systematic review shows only 32% of GESs have used legacy bias reduction techniques. Even those who attempted only used one of the 3Ps with no comparison to see the best technique. In search of the reason for this, we identified that one limitation of 3Ps is that they are designed to be conducted in a typical in-lab end-user gesture elicitation setting, which requires the presence of the investigator and is conducted in series (not in parallel). This design increases the time it requires proportional to the size of the population sample. Further, the majority of studies have utilized these techniques in an in-person or in-lab setting, making GESs highly susceptible to other types of biases, as discussed by Arendttorp et al. [3], named 'systemic bias', 'procedural bias' [48] and performance bias [42].

As shown in Vogiatzidakis et al. [51], the majority of GESs sample size was between 11–20. Thus, in search of alternative study designs, researchers leaned towards using immersive computing that precipitated transformations in social interactions, such as the Metaverse. For example, the increasing popularity of Virtual Reality (VR) [13] and its growing number of end-users have opened up new possibilities for empirical research such as GESs. With VR consumer devices' ability to track natural body movements (hands, head, eyes, etc.), researchers have attempted to use VR to study NUI. However, there is a dearth of work done in the area of utilizing VR for GES. Perera et al. [33] and Bellucci et al. [5] proposed using VR as a medium for remote GESs. While their works show a promising direction to attenuate systemic bias and procedure bias, embedding legacy bias mitigation techniques remains under-explored in these designs. To date, we have not found any VR GES that proposes an empirical study design to embed legacy bias reduction techniques. Additionally, according to Vogiatzidakis et al.'s [51] review, less than 1% papers that have used GES in VR have not used Morris et al. [26] 3Ps or any other method to reduce legacy bias. Therefore, in this paper, we propose a VR GES design to attenuate "legacy bias", based on a pragmatic research paradigm using the Research through Design (RtD) approach [63]. This, as evident from our exploration, is the first study that investigates the use of VR to implement legacy bias reduction techniques and discusses the required design guidelines aiming at encapsulated and remote GES design while comparing 3Ps in a single study.

The remainder of the paper is structured as follows. In Sect. 2 we review the 3P methods and existing designs and embed legacy bias reduction techniques in GESs. In Sect. 3.1 and Sects. 3, we illustrate the design approach and thecomposition of the VR applications. Then in Sect. 4, we discuss the GES we conducted with new VR designs that incorporated legacy bias reduction methods.

Finally, we present the results and our findings in Sect. 5 and discuss the challenges and opportunities in Sect. 6 and conclude in Sect. 7.

2 Related Work

2.1 Legacy Bias in Gesture Elicitation

Microsoft researcher Morris et al. [25] initiated the discussion on how proposals from participants in a GES could be affected by their previous experiences, coining the term "legacy bias". There are three main reasons identified by Morris et al. [27] for participants to suggest "legacy-inspired" gesture proposals, i) the explicit preference to use their previous experience with the new systems, ii) the desire to reduce the effort (physical and mental) when exposed to new technologies or form factors, and iii) the misunderstandings of the capabilities of the novel technologies [27]. As a result, a GES would potentially not be able to uncover gesture proposals that may be better suited for new technologies. Thus, Williams et al. [56] state, "legacy bias" is one of the main criticisms received by the GESs.

The impact of these biased gesture proposals can be seen in Ortega et al. [32] and Wittor et al. [58] elicitation studies, where they discuss how participants' gesture proposals for the referent 'zooming' were influenced by their use of smartphones. Additionally, Pisumsomboon et al.'s [35] end-user elicitation to identify user-preferred gestures to interact in Augmented Reality (AR) applications have observed that participants often resorted to using metaphors from their past experiences. For example, for deleting referent, participants imagined having a recycle bin where they could move objects, double tapping was proposed for the selection referent, and performed a scissor pose for the cut operation. Further, Arendttorp et al. [3] described how the use of pinch gestures for selection in commercial VR devices is an example of a legacy bias proposal inspired by the resizing gestures of Myron Krueger's Videoplace. These demonstrate the non-trivial number of gesture proposals that could potentially mitigate taking the full advantage of emerging technologies.

However, researchers have attempted not only to mitigate but in various ways to incorporate legacy bias in GESs due to the memorability and high agreement that it may bring [18,57]. Yet, Hoff et al. [16] postulate legacy bias gestures may benefit from their familiarity with the users, and may 'offer a tiny boost in learnability to first-time users' [10] yet, when the technology evolves, they may grow outdated and hard to guess [16], and do not scale well [10], when the metaphors fade away. For instance, the mid-air gesture of rotating a knob to increase and decrease volume might not bring a metaphoric connection to the majority of users in generation alpha [23]. Therefore, while acknowledging that legacy bias can be beneficial depending on the context, Morris et al. [26] argue that it still limits the potential of end-user elicitation studies, particularly GES, to produce interactions that take full advantage of the potential and requirements of emerging application domains. Hence, having a legacy bias reduction technique designed is important.

Researchers have recently tended to utilize immersive computing [36,38], for GESs. Perera et al. [33] work on the feasibility of using VR for GES studies along with 'Welicit', by Bellucci et al. [5] a Wizard of Oz (WoZ) tool for VR elicitation studies, shows a promising direction of reduction of 'systematic bias' [3] of GESs. However, these studies have not yet been designed to embed the 'legacy bias' reduction techniques in the GES designs. Therefore, inspired by these GES designs that use VR, we investigate a VR GES design that could be utilized in encapsulated end-user GESs in this paper.

2.2 Legacy Bias Reduction Designs

Further to the introduction of the concept, of legacy bias, Morris et al. [26] proposed three techniques to mitigate its effects, namely Production, Priming, and Partnering (abbreviated as 3Ps).

In ***Production*** technique, Morris et al. [26] suggested allowing participants to produce multiple gesture proposals for each referent used in GESs. This aimed to boost creativity [16], and let participants think beyond the legacy-inspired proposal if any. Hoff et al. [16] suggested that the implicit assumption here could be that participants may propose the legacy-inspired gesture in the initial proposal. This technique is utilized outside the domain of GESs as well [12]. While the production technique is the most frequently used legacy bias mitigation technique in GESs [55], it still requires further investigations to identify the appropriate number of production trials and how to maintain the illusion of system autonomy, which is vital to the results in a WoZ design. We observed that none of the studies discuss the referent presentation designs of production when combined with the WoZ method. This is important, especially when conducting remote GESs.

In ***Priming*** technique, Morris et al. [26] suggested letting participants be aware of the potential of new technology or form factor. This technique is widely used in psychology where a stimulus is used to non-consciously/sub-consciously influence participants on their current or future performance or behavior [45, 54]. While researchers have used different empirical study designs to utilize this technique in GESs, Morris et al. [26] have chosen to show a set of videos that include gesture interactions and communications. In addition, a subset of their participants was encouraged to carry out physical actions such as jumping jacks, pointing, etc., aiming to kinesthetically prime them. In terms of the time needed per participant and considering experiment logistics and participant fatigue, this is a facile technique to embed in in-lab GES. However, a common characteristic of all these methods is they are all conducted with investigator participation and within lab settings following the existing GES designs. Thus, there's a need to investigate a suitable empirical design for remote VR GES.

The third technique is ***Partnering***. The idea Morris et al. [26] suggest here is group brainstorming rather than individually proposing gestures. Again, inspired by the field of design as evinced in Dow's [12] work. In terms of experiment logistics, this is a difficult technique to embed into GES; hence there is a very low number of studies that use this technique compared to the other two techniques

(Priming and Production). For example, Morris et al. [26] have not incorporated these techniques in their introductory work. Yet, in a new study [25] they elicited gestures from participant pairs and indicated that participants would often improvise based on their partner's suggestions. In certain designs, this technique is referred to as *pairing* [9] or *paired elicitation* [55] because of the GES design, which places users in pairs and lets them work together to generate new gestures. Similar to the other two techniques, this also requires the presence of an investigator with its current empirical design. Thus, a change of design is required for remote and encapsulated VR GES.

3 VR Application Design

3.1 Design Approach

To investigate the suitable design and embed legacy bias reduction techniques to encapsulated GESs using VR, we utilized Research through Design (RtD) [64] methodology with a practical evaluation. Figure 1 shows the different research phases that we conducted following RtD methodology aiming to identify suitable designs that could embed Morris et al.'s [26] 3Ps into VR GES.

We started with the exploration phase and investigated GES designs that use VR as a medium. Out of the two options available in the literature; Perera et al. [33] and Bellucci et al. [5] we extracted the design ideas for our work. In addition, we explored VR application design guidelines discussed by Makela et al. [22] and Rivu et al. [41] for remote VR applications. Followed by the exploration phase, we designed and implemented four VR prototype applications following state-of-the-art VR design principles, and guidelines gathered during the exploration phase along with experts' advice. Once we had the initial design at hand, we conducted recursive pilot studies and qualitative interviews with a few participants and revised several design decisions to match and cater to change requests and fix bugs that were encountered during this iterative phase.

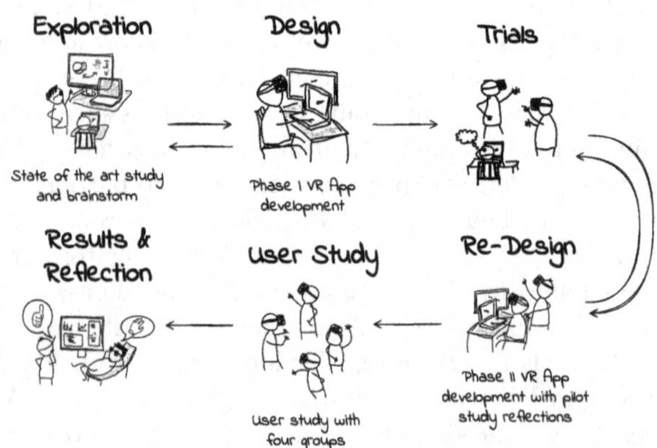

Fig. 1. Research through Design (RtD) Approach

This process is represented as the 'Trials' and 'Re-Design' phases. These iterations were important as we were designing for remote and encapsulated VR GES. Finally, with the results and learning from early phases, we amended and re-designed the VR GES prior to conducting the user study to evaluate the final design that aims to investigate the most practical techniques to reduce legacy bias in remote and encapsulated GESs. In Sects. 3.5, 3.6 and 3.4 below we discuss the final design that we followed.

3.2 Apparatus, Materials, and Setup

The VR application was developed using Unity Game Engine[1] and Normcore[2] (for partnering multi-user design) and all four VR applications could run in both Oculus Quest 1 and 2 VR Head Mounted Displays (HMDs). Oculus was chosen as it is widely used in many VR studies [5,33,36,37,40] and Steam statistics show that Oculus Quest has the highest VR user base [11]. Even though the implementations particularly aim for this VR HMD, designs are device agnostic. For this study, we selected a real-world office environment and created its digital duplicate in the VR as shown in Fig. 2. In VR GES, the environment is decoupled to easily replace it (e.g. to a vehicle, smart home, etc.). In our smart office setup, we used virtual models of the devices and allowed adding/removing them to suit the study requirements. This not only preserved the ecological validity [20,46] required for the elicitation study but reduced complications and safety issues that may arise in a physical setup.

Fig. 2. Chosen Office Space and its implementation in VR

All four VR applications welcome a participant and provide a textual and auditory introduction to the study, following the design guidelines from [33,36]. The audio guide is optional and participants can disable it. We followed an automated WoZ design without an investigator playing the wizard's role. All four VR designs were developed to run as encapsulated GESs [38]. Further, these four GESs were designed to protect participants' privacy, hence they only recorded skeleton data of participants' hands. No recording of the real-world

[1] https://unity.com/.
[2] https://normcore.io/.

or VR 'gameplay' is used. Referents were presented in balance order. It is also important to notice that certain referents must be presented to the participants after another. For example, the 'turn off' referent should be given to the participant after the 'turn on' referent as we started the experiment with all devices turned off for simplicity.

3.3 VR Training

Every participant enters a 'self-paced' training session. This training session aims to acquaint each participant with the features they are going to encounter in the main study. Training is mandatory in our design as it will greatly reduce the learning effect [19]. In the training session, features and design elements are labeled, and a participant interacts with two referents that are not presented in the main study. A VR capture of the production trial is shown in Figs. 3a and 3b.

During the training session, participants got acquainted with using a 'floating control panel' design and its features. Inspired from the 'waist pack tool kit' design[3], and the use of virtual panel design in several studies in the state of the art [3,33], we designed a 'floating control panel' (hereafter referred to as the 'c-panel') for participants. When a participant starts the VR application, they will see the c-panel in front of their waist (the c-panel will always adjust its position relative to the participant's height) with two main buttons with textual instructions as shown in Fig. 3d. This design element allows participants to freely move inside the space while interacting. After completing the training, the participant enters the main study, where they are given the time to familiarise themselves with the virtual environment shown in Fig. 2,3d. When they are ready to start, they press the main button as shown in Fig. 3d to start the study. This button can also be used if a participant wants to pause the study, which is required in an encapsulated user study [38].

3.4 VR GES with 'Production'

Once the participant starts the main study, the first referent will be displayed on the c-panel as shown in Fig. 3c. Referents will also communicate via voice if audio is enabled by the participant. The audio enable/disable button was introduced in the redesign phase as some participants mentioned they did not like the repetitive auditory instructions. The participant can first think of a gesture suitable for the given referent. In our pilot study, we limited the thinking time to 15 s by following the design guidelines in Hoff et al. [16] because Vatavu et al's [50] revealed a negative correlation between gesture agreement rates and thinking time and proposed maintaining an average time of less than 20.5 s. However, from the qualitative feedback received during the experiment 'trial' phase, the 15-second thinking time was sometimes insufficient for production, especially

[3] Waist packs, enable people to keep their tools/supplies close at hand at all times [2]. In our design, we use this as a metaphor to present the experiment's controllers to the participant.

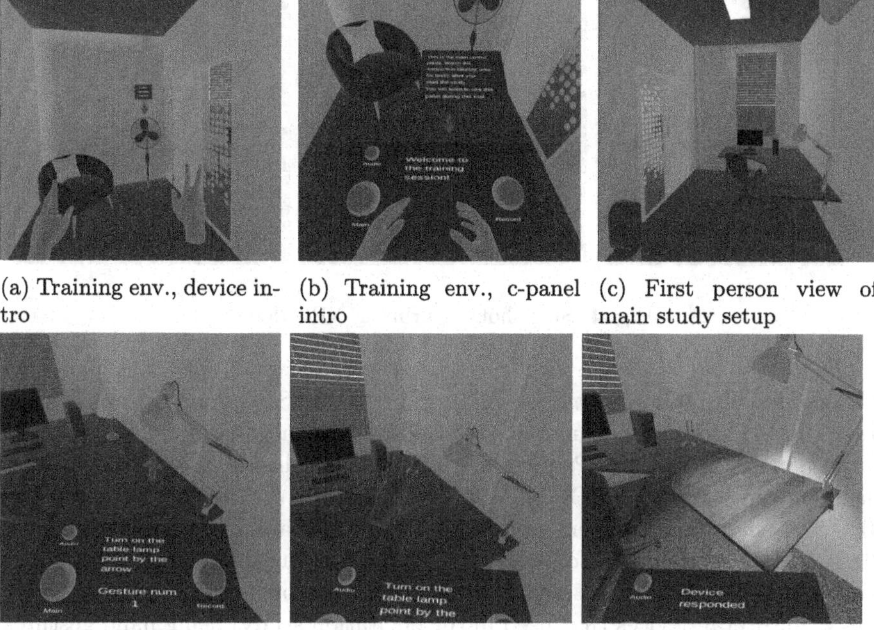

(a) Training env., device intro (b) Training env., c-panel intro (c) First person view of main study setup

(d) Instruction delivery, c-panel, and arrows (e) Gesture recording state; red hands (f) Device response after a gesture

Fig. 3. Snapshots of VR application for production technique

when proposing the second gesture for certain referents. This resonated with the finding of Chan et al. [9] where they mentioned some participants struggled to suggest multiple gestures in their production design. Hoff et al. [16] also noted in their production study that participants reported they needed to think more about further gestures for a given referent. Thus, we removed the thinking time limit and followed the simplified "1-to-2" design suggested by Wu et al. [60]. Once the participant is ready, they can press the 'Record' button (Fig. 3c). Then the virtual hands will turn red to indicate that their gesture is being recorded (Fig. 3d). Norman [29] noted that feedback is critical in action-based interaction, hence the hand color change. The recording time is set to 5 s as per Perera et al [33] and tested during the 'trial' phase, where participants rated this as sufficient time to perform a gesture.

3.5 VR GES with 'Priming'

In priming, we first let participants observe the 3D avatar behavior in the VR space. We borrowed the design of nonplayer characters (NPCs) from gaming research. We identified that NPCs are often used to advance the storyline of games and to make the players believe in certain aspects of the games [53] as a

Fig. 4. Snapshots of priming NPC demo

suitable design method to embed priming in VR GES. Uprooted from this, we created a 3D story (following the steps of building a game story [17]) for the purpose of priming users. Participants can navigate inside the virtual environment and observe the NPCs, similar to a game. In the story we created, the NPC will enter the VR scene and greet the participant first (See Fig. 4. Then the NPC follows a persona of a futuristic human living in a smart environment (similar to the ambient assisted living (AAL) concept), where the NPC interacts with several devices (not used in the elicitation study) using hand gestures. Participants can monitor how the devices react to the NPC's behavior. This is similar to Ali et al. [1] design, where they showed clips of Sci-Fi movies. The difference is the experience that 3D immersion brings, utilizing the capabilities of VR. Mcmahan et al. [24] noted that freedom of maneuver around the space and diegetic sounds will immerse a participant better compared to a 2D immersion. The reason we let users first experience this (even before the training session) is to avoid participants getting to know the purpose of this task. We did not intend to consciously make participants aware of the purpose of this immersive experience, as noted by Hoff et al. [16]. After priming, which is an average 1-minute experience, participants will be teleported into the training session. The training session of priming is similar to the production and is conducted in the same virtual environment where the participants are presented with the c-panel design. Instead of two gesture proposals, participants were asked to propose a single gesture for each referent in priming.

3.6 VR GES with 'Partnering'

We observed that partnering was the least used legacy bias reduction technique in GES. The current design of the partnering technique is impacted by the logistics and the number of participants required. Further, this technique is heavily dependent on the presence of an investigator. In an encapsulated VR GES, we realized that incorporating current partnering designs are a challenging task as it needs careful guidance and instructions. Thus, with the motive of reducing the required number of instructions, we followed Morris et al.'s [25,26] initial design. In the VR design, the user enters the VR setup and waits for their partner to

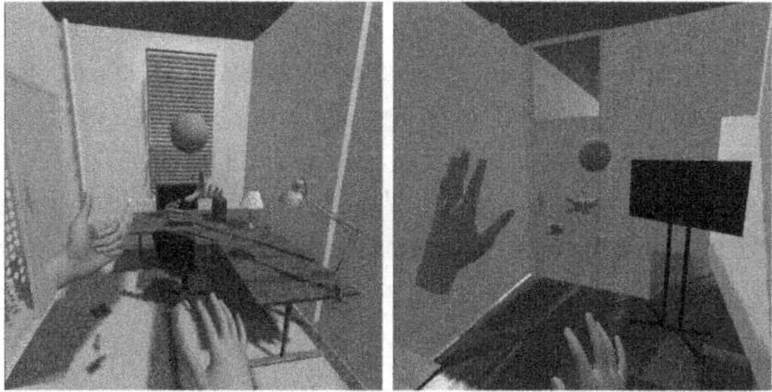

Fig. 5. Snapshots of partnering design (First person views)

join in. Once their GES partner joins in, they see an avatar figure representing them, as shown in Fig. 5. Both participants then teleport into an equal training environment, similar to Priming and Production designs, and follow the same training (See Sect. 3.3). Once they are in the tanning session, they can communicate via voice and get used to communication inside the app.

After completing the training session, participants will be teleported into the main study area. Both participants have their own c-panels. In the main study, both of them will be given the same referent simultaneously on the c-panel in balanced order. Participants record their gestures after brainstorming with each other. In our design, each participant could either agree on a single gesture or disagree and propose two different gestures via the c-panel operating procedure. In this way, participants were independent with their gesture proposals. We also limit the brainstorming time, which is visible to both the participants on the c-panel. This was aimed to maintain the standard HCI experiment time [28] to avoid unnecessary fatigue and to help keep the conversation focused. We made the partnering app simple in this way to avoid misunderstandings that could hinder the participant's attention to the main task.

3.7 Control Group Design

In the control VR app design a participant will enter the training session similar to the rest of the group, and after completing the training, they will enter the main study. In the control app, no legacy bias reduction technique is used. To maintain consistency with the experimental setup, we used the same environment and the same c-panel concept. All the participants went through the same number of referents related to the same set of devices.

4 Evaluating VR Design with Legacy Bias Reduction

We conducted a pragmatic evaluation of the Production, Priming, and Partnering VR designs discussed in the above sections along with a comparison of their effect on mitigating legacy bias. For this, we conducted a between-group study with four independent groups and compared and evaluated the designs from the end-user perspective and then the effects of legacy bias reduction techniques on the GESs. Three groups followed one legacy bias mitigation method each (one of the 3Ps [26]), and the control group followed the standard GES procedure. All 4 groups went through the same VR setup aiming to attenuate potential systematic errors due to the experimental environment [19].

4.1 Participants

The study involved a total number of 70 participants who originated from 16 countries. Their ages ranged from 21 to 61 (median = 33.1, SD = 9.4), with 28 females and 39 males, and 3 participants who did not disclose their gender. The participant composition among the four groups was counterbalanced. All the participants reported that they had a very good experience interacting with smartphones and home/office appliances, and 42.8% of all the participants had some VR experience prior to this experiment. 82.9% of the participants were right-handed. There were 2 ambidextrous participants, which was 2.9% of the overall sample.

4.2 Procedure

After a participant had given their informed consent to participate in the study, they starts the pre-questionnaire that covered the basic demographic and their previous experiences related to VR and smart devices. Following that, the participant either borrowed a VR HMD, or used their personal VR HMD if preferred. All the participants were given a VR safety guideline video and instructed to have at least 6.5×6.5 foot space when doing the experiment. Participants were free to withdraw from the study at any time, and none of the data will be collected in that case. Also, they could pause the study and come back and continue at a later time if preferred (with an exception for the partnering group, where even though the app allows this behavior, it is not appropriate).

In all four groups, participants went through a self-phased training as explained in the Sect. 3.3. During the main study, 20 referents spanning across 6 devices were presented in a counterbalanced order following the seemingly standard HCI user study procedure [19] and taking careful measures to attenuate systematic errors. We used two different types of table lamps to understand the influence of the signifiers [31] of a device. Since our design was developed for encapsulated GESs, the involvement of the experimenter during the experiment time was not required. Yet, our design made each device respond similarly to real life once the participant performed a gesture, safeguarding the illusion of system autonomy without the involvement of investigators. The experiment was conducted in various locations that were comfortable for participants. We made sure that each participant only went through one study group and only once, which made all the samples independent. Finally, participants filled out a post-experiment questionnaire and provided their qualitative feedback on the experiment.

4.3 Measures

Radiah et al. [36] and Perera et al. [33] showed that VR experiment design could affect the usability and the perceived participant experience. Therefore, in our post questionnaire, we investigated each design's usability and the participant experience from a quantitative and qualitative lens. All four groups received the same questionnaires. To evaluate the usability and experience, we used two standard questionnaires on 7-point scales, namely the System Usability Scale (SUS) [7], and igroup presence questionnaire (IPQ)[4] [47] which was used to measure the presence in VR. To assess the perceived workload in each design, we used the NASA TLX [15] with "Sources-of-Workload Evaluation" [14] where pairs of factors presented individually to each participant in a randomly selected order to obtain the weights of each scale. This allowed us to get a subjective measure of the workload of each design. Furthermore, we collected qualitative feedback from the participants related to the design and their gesture proposals. In addition, we collected the performance-based measures, i.e., task completion time (TCT) of each design. The composition of this data allowed us to investigate how well a participant completed a study, its efficiency, the amount of work it involved, and also how participants felt while completing the experiment. Furthermore, hand skeleton data of participants' virtual hands were collected for the gesture agreement analysis. We used Perera et al. [33] gesture visualization technique and remodeled the collected gestures prior to the binning process.

4.4 Gesture Binning

All groups produced a total number of 1680 gestures (280 in each category where the production method has two proposal rounds and the partnering group had 280 proposals in pairs) for 20 different referents. During the gesture binning process, we followed seemingly standard steps following previous research [8,16,35,43,55] and discussed among the researchers. The gesture proposals were given descriptive labels and numbers (to ease the binning process). During the gesture labelling process we instrumented a mix of Vogiatzidakis et al. [52] taxonomy, HDGI ontology by Perera et al. [34] and also Zhou et al.'s [62] gesture binning mechanisms. These include consideration of gesture elements such as flow, nature, finger states, palm direction, and the number of hands (uni-manual vs bi-manual) used, similar to Williams et al. [55]. Finally, the classification process was finalized with the help of an expert rater who was knowledgeable about the process. From the total of 1680 recorded gesture proposals, 94 bins were created.

4.5 Legacy Bias Classification

The 94 gesture bins were used in the analysis of legacy bias and gesture agreement among participants. In the process of categorizing gesture classes into

[4] http://www.igroup.org/pq/ipq/index.php.

legacy or non-legacy buckets, following Hoff et al [16], we looked at participants' qualitative post-questionnaire answers in which we asked them whether they have used the proposed gesture before, for each referent. Not all participants answered this question, hence we also used the consensus of three independent votes from knowledgeable raters in this categorization process similar to Williams et al. [55]. During this process, raters looked at the nature of gesture classes and the qualitative answers of the participants (when available). The criterion used, therefore, was 'if the gesture class could be identified with a known device in common usage, then the gesture proposal was classified as a legacy gesture' similar to previous studies [55]. For example, gestures that can be identified with known metaphors such as *Rotate volume knob clockwise, Pull down a cord, Turn on a wall switch, One hand swipe left or right, Finger swipe left or right, Mid air button press, pinch, and slide, remote controller use* are a subset of proposals that were categorized as legacy-inspired.

5 Study Results

5.1 Legacy Bias Reduction Design Analysis

In this section, we discuss the VR GES design evaluation and the impacts of embedding legacy bias reduction techniques into VR GES.

Usability Evaluation. Firstly we investigated, whether there were any significant differences between the usability of each VR design with the addition of legacy bias mitigation techniques. We started with the null hypothesis that there had been no differences between the means of usability score between the four groups. Figure 6a, shows the SUS scores for each VR design; Control (mean = 77.04, sd = 4.99), Priming (mean = 76.32, sd = 4.61), Partnering (mean = 78.67, sd = 3.65) and Production (mean = 73.77, sd = 5.91). With the normally distributed rating score in each group with nearly equal variances (supplemented by the Shapiro-Wilk normality test (p = 0.607) and Levene's homogeneity of variances test (p = 0.340), we conducted a univariate ANOVA on SUS ratings. Results show no statistically significant differences among the four groups' usability ratings (F = 2.89, p = 0.06). The returned F value is higher than the value at the 95% confidence interval; hence the null hypothesis is considered true, confirming each group performs more or less the same in each VR design. However, given the p-value is closer to the confidence interval, we conducted a post-hoc test to investigate which groups were different from each other. Out of all the contracts (pairs), we were particularly interested in the subset of them for simultaneous comparison, i.e., the pairs relative to the control group. Tukey's HSD post-hoc test for multiple comparisons found that the mean value of ratings of SUS were not significantly different between the control group and production group (p = 0.409), priming group (p = 979), and partnering group (p = 0.724). Therefore, according to the SUS questionnaire result analysis, we concluded that production, prime, and partner groups carry more or less similar and 'good' usability (closer to 'excellent'). This implies that embedding the legacy bias mitigation design in VR GES did not change the usability of the new GES empirical design.

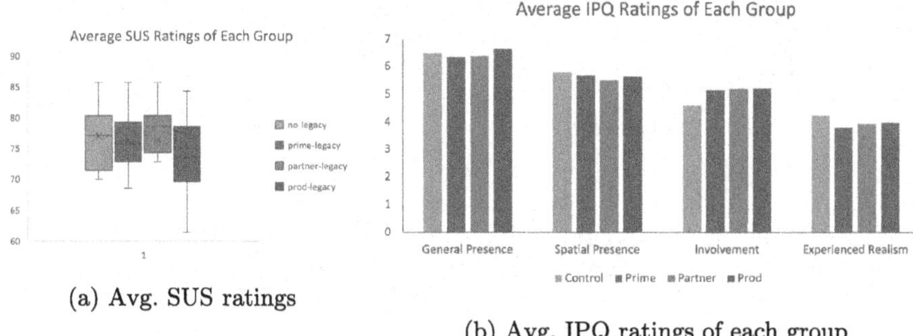

(a) Avg. SUS ratings

(b) Avg. IPQ ratings of each group

Fig. 6. System usability and VR presence analysis across all four groups

VR Presence Evaluation. After usability evaluation, we investigated whether VR presence is affected by the proposed VR designs to mitigate legacy bias in GESs. The ability to create the sense of presence [44] in VR GES helps to maintain the ecological validity required in GESs. Thus, we investigated whether our designs had an effect on the sense of presence using the IPQ questionnaire. We started with the null hypothesis that there had been no differences between the means of the sense of presence ratings between the four groups. With that, we looked into each category in the IPQ questionnaire, namely, general presence, spatial presence, involvement, and experienced realism. The mean IPQ ratings of each group with the sub-scales are shown in Fig. 6. We conducted a one-way ANOVA for each category across all four groups and found no statistically significant difference in mean ratings between the four groups for general presence ($F(3,66) = 0.985$, $p = 0.413$), involvement ($F(3,66) = 0.891$, $p = 0.458$) and experience realism ($F(3,66) = 2.36$, $p = 0.091$) but spatial presence ($F(3,66) = 4.04$, $p = 0.016$).

Since spatial presence mean rating is different between several groups, we further analyzed spatial presence rating using the post-hoc test to investigate which groups were different from each other. Again, out of all the contracts (pairs), we were particularly interested in the subset of them for simultaneous comparison, i.e., the pairs relative to the control group. The post-hoc Tukey test showed that the control group was not significantly different from the other three groups. This indicates that adding legacy bias reduction techniques to VR GES does not affect the ability to create the sense of presence [44] in VR GES.

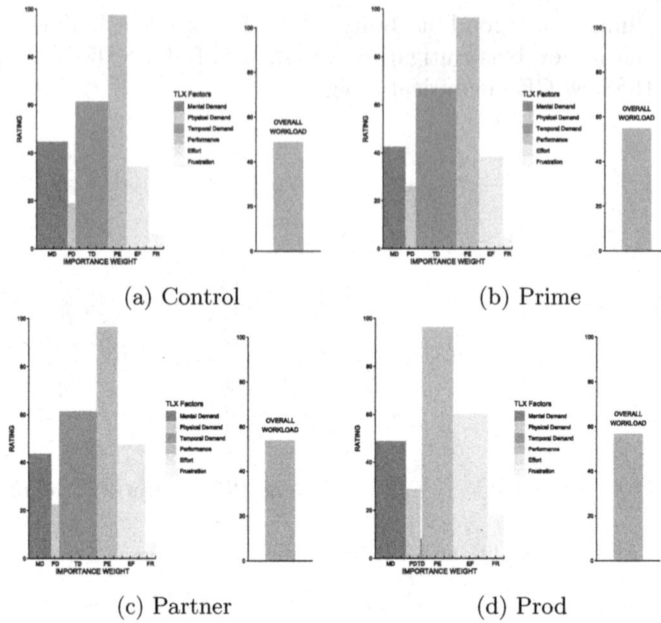

(a) Control (b) Prime

(c) Partner (d) Prod

Fig. 7. NASA TLX questionnaire ratings for each group

Task Load Evaluation. Since each group had to perform additional yet unique tasks compared with the control group, we investigated the task load using NASA TLX questionnaire ratings. Figure 7 shows the results of weighted sub-scales of NASA task load evaluation along with the overall workloads for each group. We started, with the null hypothesis that there had been no differences between the means of the task load ratings between the four groups. To test this hypothesis, we conducted a one-way ANOVA test. Assessed by the Shapiro-Wilk normality test on participant rating scores $p = 0.26$) and Levene's homogeneity of variances test ($F(3,66) = 0.338$, $p = 0.798$), we assumed that the distribution is normal and variances are equal. The results of the one-way ANOVA test showed that there is a significant difference in the average task load between the four groups ($F(3,66) = 5.18$, $p = 0.005$) where the test hypothesis was false. A post-hoc Tukey test revealed that the task load ratings in the control group (49 ± 5.88) were significantly lower compared to the other three groups: priming group (55.2 ± 5.02, $p = 0.03$), production group (57.1 ± 5.97, $p = 0.02$) and partner group (55.6 ± 6.04, $p = 0.05$). This implies that embedding the legacy bias mitigation design in VR GES has changed the task load of the participants.

Task Completion Time (TCT). We further investigated whether there was a difference between the task completion time (TCT) of participants who had some VR experience and those who did not. Out of all participants, 42.8% had some VR experience prior to this experiment. We used Welch's t-test to determine whether there was a statistically significant difference in recorded TCT between the two groups of participants. The results revealed that there was no statistically significant difference in mean TCT ($t = -0.730$, $p = 0.469$) between the two groups. Therefore, these designs can be conducted with both experienced and non-experienced VR participants.

Likewise, we conducted Welch's two-tailed t-test to investigate whether there are differences in the usability ratings, VR presence, and task load between experienced and non-experienced participants. Test results revealed that there were no statistically significant differences in mean scores for application usability ($t = 0.369$, $p = 0.714$), VR presence ($t = 0.330$, $p = 0.743$), and task loads ($t = -0.957$, $p = 0.343$) between the two groups. Therefore, these designs of legacy bias reduction techniques in VR GES can be conducted with both experienced and non-experienced filling encapsulated remote GES requirements.

5.2 Qualitative Analysis

The qualitative analysis focused on understanding participant experience of following these new empirical designs for GESs. We conducted a thematic analysis of the participant experience [6] and used open coding for the qualitative answers, mixed with rating questions. On average, Partnering and Priming showed the highest likelihood (80%) of recommending the experiment to another among all 4 groups. Overall, the participants have shown good motivation without the experimenter. This is particularly evident in statements such "*...didn't feel I was in an experiment*", "*...it was fund and futuristic*". Among the written feedback for Partnering, some participants mentioned they liked the "*group work nature*" of the study, and it was better to "*hear others' opinions*" when deciding on a gesture. Participants seemed to have positive responses to the use of NPC in the Priming study. Some participants mentioned "*like in a video game*", echoing our design inspirations. Overall, this indicates that proposed designs to conduct encapsulated and remote GESs using VR with legacy bias mitigation have not affected participant experiences or caused experiment fatigue due to increased task loads.

5.3 Legacy Bias Reduction Effect Analysis

In this section, we looked at the participants' gesture proposals to investigate how each legacy bias technique affects the frequency of legacy-inspired proposals.

Effect of 3Ps on Legacy Bias. During the analysis, we followed the procedure of Williams et al.'s [55] cost of production analysis and Hoff et al.'s [16] methodology of comparing Production and Priming in in-person GES to compare the effects of 3Ps towards mitigating legacy bias proposals. From overall gesture proposals, 26.6% were identified as legacy-inspired proposals. The legacy count percentages are, Control 32.14%, Priming Group 19.28%, Partnering Group 16.07%, Production Trial 1 34.28% Production Trial 2 31.07%. All 3P techniques seemed to reduce the tendency of proposing legacy-inspired gesture proposals in VR GES (except production trial 1). To further analyze this observation, with the null hypothesis that there has been no difference between the means of the legacy-bias gesture proposals between five elicitation study groups (considering production trial 1 and production trial 2), we conducted the Kruskal-Wallis H test. The test results revealed a statistically significant difference ($X^2(4) = 17.8, p = 0.001$) in legacy bias proposal score between the different GES design groups. In order to further analyze these differences, we conducted a post-hoc test by adjusting the significance values with the Bonferroni correction. This pairwise comparison indicated that the control group and the partner group have a significant difference with the legacy bias proposals with an adjusted significance value of p = 0.012. This shows embedding 3P techniques in VR GES can be used in encapsulated and remote GESs effectively and reduce legacy bias as in in-person and in-lab GESs.

Effect of Legacy Proposal on Referents. The analysis of the effect of the legacy bias proposal on each referent shows that *TL2_ON* elicited the most legacy proposals (i.e., 11.02% of all legacy proposals) with a count of 41 out of all the proposals, and it remains the highest in each category (3Ps) as well. The legacy counts for each referent are shown in Fig. 8. We observed that across the 4 conditions, the legacy-inspired proposal percentage for *TL2_ON* was declining in the order of Control (71.4%), Priming (64.4%), Production Trial 1 (64.2%), Production Trial 2 (50%) and Partnering (42.8%). While this does not represent the overall legacy bias mitigation pattern as in Sect. 5.3, it still reports the highest legacy-inspired gesture proposals in the Control group. In order to test whether there is a relationship between the type of the table lamps and the getting a legacy proposal for *TL_ON* referent, we conducted a within-group McNemar's chi-square test for the control group. When comparing the *Table Lamp 2* aesthetics with *Table Lamp 1*, the most pronounced signifier [30] is that *Table Lamp 2* has the pulling cord. We observed that many participants performed the gesture *Pull down a cord* and we considered it a legacy bias gesture, which was the most common proposal received for *TL2_ON* referent. The results of McNemar's test show that there is a significant statistical difference (X^2 (1, N=14) = 6.125, p = 0.01) between the participant proposing this legacy bias gesture for *Table Lamp 1* turn-on gesture compared with *Table Lamp 2* in the control group. We further observed this in other groups and it continued to be the same in Priming (p = 0.02), Partnering (p = 0.03), and Production Trial 1 (p = 0.02) but not in Production Trial 2 (p = 0.22).

Apart from *TL2_ON* the other referent that we observed to have a high legacy bias proposal was *TV_INCVOL*, *TV_DECVOL*, *BF_TMPINC* and *BF_TMPDEC*. Together, these referents carried 30.1% of the overall legacy bias proportion. However, a noticeable characteristic was the proposals for these referents were always symmetric and most often uni-manual [4]. For example, the participant who did *Right hand move up with palm facing upwards* for *TV_VOLINC* did the symmetrical opposite gesture *Right hand move down with palm facing down-*

wards. Similar to *TL2_ON*, these TV and BF referents also show attenuation of legacy proposals in priming, partnering, and production trial 1 compared to the control group. However, the production trial 2 count is higher than the control group legacy bias percentage for these proposals. i.e. for *TV_INCVOL*, Control 57.1% and Prod Trial 2 = 64.2% and *BF_INCTMP* Control 42.8% and Prod Trial 2 = 57.1%. As shown in Fig. 8a, all the referents had low legacy-inspired proposals in the partnering group compared to other conditions.

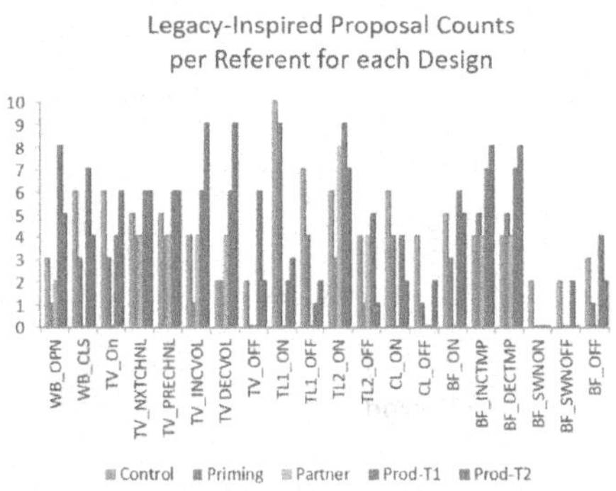

(a) Legacy-inspired proposal for each referent in four studies

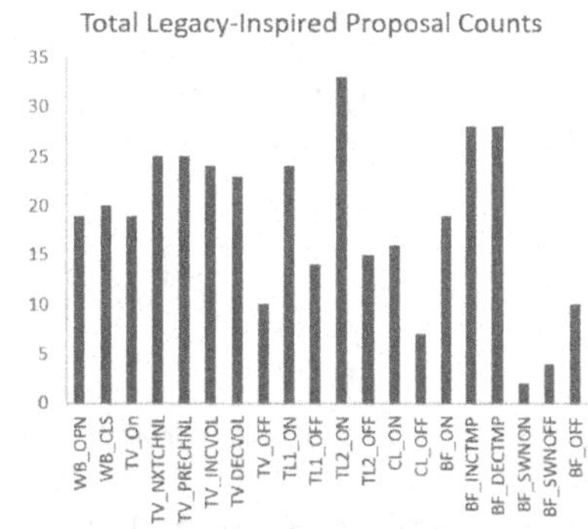

(b) Individual totals for legacy-inspired proposal for each referent

Fig. 8. Legacy-inspired proposal and referent across all four elicitation groups

Agreement Analysis with Legacy Bias. Lastly, we conducted a gesture agreement analysis using Agreement Rate AR introduced by Vatavu et al. [49] to observe the participant agreement on the gesture proposals. Calculated agreement rates for all the referents are shown in Fig. 9. Then we classified these referents as low, medium, high, and very high based on the AR interval magnitudes, which are $\leq .100$, .100 to .300, .300 to .500 and $> .500$ as proposed by Vatavu et al. [49]. Further, to observe the impact of the legacy bias gesture proposal on the agreement rates, we used the LAR metric introduced by Williams et al. [55].

From Fig. 9, we can observe that even for the same referent set in the same environment and for the same use case, different designs of GESs could fluctuate the agreement rates. This, of course, has an effect on the ubiquitous nature of human gestures, and another possible reason could be the different techniques followed in conducting each of these GESs. Compared with William et al.'s [55] cost production analysis, where they observed, 'production trials decrease the AR', resonates with our findings as well. We observed a 7.3% higher agreement in production trial 1 compared to trial 2. This further complements Wu et al.'s [61] 1-to-2 design which we incorporated. Wu et al. [61] have also observed a higher mean agreement rate than the second trial in their in-person GES. Furthermore,

Willimas et al. [55] finding shows that over their production trials, the contribution of legacy (LAR) remains consistent. We also received a mean $LAR = 0.056$ for both production trials 1 and 2 complementing Williams et al.'s [55] findings.

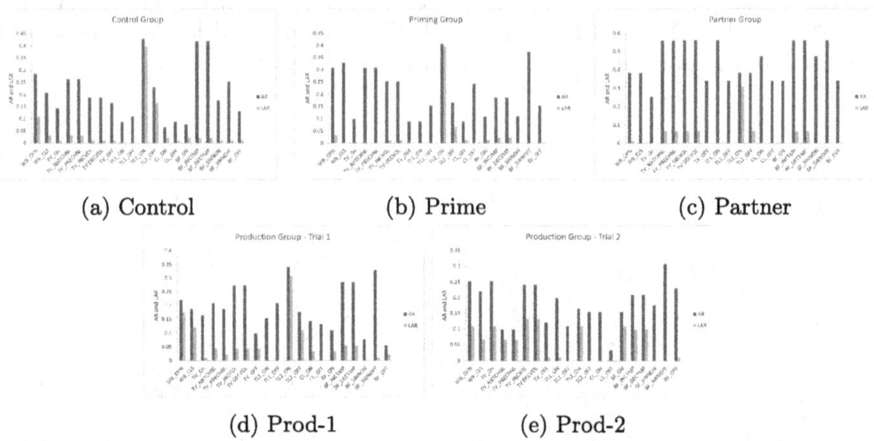

(a) Control (b) Prime (c) Partner

(d) Prod-1 (e) Prod-2

Fig. 9. Agreement Rates of all 4 groups with the relevant referents. As the legend indicates, blue color bars (on the left-hand side) represent the AR and yellow bars (on the right-hand side) represent the LAR value which shows the impact of legacy bias on the calculated AR. (Color figure online)

6 Discussion

The main objective of this work is to investigate the VR designs to incorporate legacy bias reduction techniques (i.e., priming, production, and partnering) in encapsulated [38] and remote GESs. In addition, we analyzed the fluctuations of legacy-inspired gesture proposals in each design when using different legacy bias mitigation techniques. To the best of our knowledge, this study is the first attempt to design, adapt, and experimentally test Morris et al's. [26] all 3P designs in a single study for the purpose of encapsulated and remote GESs. We selected VR as a medium due to its capabilities of collecting natural hand gestures, and its ability to immerse users by creating ecologically valid settings in contrast to web-based elicitation tools and to avoid common systematic errors in web-based GES tools [19].

Overall Outcomes. Our findings show that Priming and Partnering techniques can effectively reduce the possibility of legacy bias proposal from a participant. Furthermore, overall analysis shows that embedding legacy bias mitigation techniques with our proposed empirical design does not affect the usability of the VR GES design without legacy bias mitigation and its ability to create a sense of presence. The proposed design overcomes another major drawback of in-lab GESs with embedded legacy bias mitigation techniques - the experiment time. While it is common to increase the task load of a participant when the legacy bias mitigation techniques are incorporated in the GES, we observed that VR GESs with embedded legacy bias mitigation keep the experiments below the recommended HCI user study time threshold of 60–90 minutes [28]. In addition, we showed that VR GES with legacy bias reduction design does not reduce the participant involvement in the elicitation study even with the increased TCT. Therefore, we believe that our work will provide a good indication of how VR could be used with a well-developed empirical design as a medium for encapsulated and remote GESs with legacy bias mitigation. We expect this work will invite researchers to investigate more on the use of VR for other empirical studies in HCI and to bring practicality to the concept of "Remote XR Studies" discussed in Ratcliffe et al.'s [39] study.

Recommendations. Based on our findings we recommend the below points:

- On the design aspects, the majority of participants stated that the button-pressing mechanism to indicate the start of the gesture was useful. This allowed participants to control the flow of the GES and allowed them to propose gestures when ready. For example, participants mentioned that sometimes they attempted the gesture they wanted to perform prior to pressing the record button. We noticed this behavior during the pilot study phase as well, where participants tested how well the virtual hand gesture represented their real hand gesture before proposing it to command the device. On the other hand, as investigators, this helped to understand the start and end of the gesture and identify the phases [21] of the gesture proposal during the classification process.
- Include only the most important instructions and maintain a monotonous flow (fewer deviations) in the VR GES design when developing encapsulated and remote GESs with legacy bias mitigation techniques. Usually, GESs with a high number of referents tend to cause participant fatigue. This can reduce the potential of extracting useful gesture proposals. In our GESs we incorporated 20 referents, and observed that the frustration and effort ratings were higher compared to the control group. This is due to the additional tasks that participants had to perform in each of these 3P groups, which was inherent in the original 3P techniques design. Nevertheless, the sub-scale analysis of mental demand shows that there is no significant difference in the task load ratings between the 3P groups and the control group. This indicates that our design decisions of maintaining 'minimal instructions' and 'consistency with virtual environments and monotonous flow' have an effect on maintaining similar mental demands with VR GES and VR GES with legacy bias mitigation.
- When required to conduct GES with legacy bias mitigation, we recommend using VR, and Partnering or Priming techniques following the proposed empirical designs. Our VR design eases the logistical barriers that researchers face when they have to conduct in-person GESs with 3P techniques. Noting that the Partnering technique is used the least in the literature, yet performed the best in terms of reducing legacy bias (compared with other 2Ps and the

control group). Thus, embedding 3Ps with VR could ease the logistical difficulties compared to in-person, in-lab study steps and the reach for a diverse participant base.
- Plan ahead to identify the learning effects and different behavior types that participants may perform. For instance, no participant had recorded that they had run out of ideas for the gestures in the production in our study. Nonetheless, the descriptive investigation revealed that when participants realized that a certain gesture worked for similar types of referents, e.g., increasing volume and increasing temperature, they often proposed a similar gesture to all the devices that carry similar affordances. This can be further investigated via consistency rate (*CR*) introduced in [52] GES. This behavior was especially noticeable when conducting scenario-based elicitation studies, hence it is important to be aware and plan accordingly. Fuhrer participants acknowledged they repeated the same gesture for similar types of referents if they observed that the device previously responded to it.
- Consider developing an automated data-gathering mechanism, for remote and encapsulated GESs. For instance, in the trial phase, we asked participants to press a button to upload data at the end of the study and some participants missed attending it. Hence, informing participants early in the app that the data will be automatically uploaded once the study is completed helps not to lose data and participants' effort in helping the study. Thus, in our final design, we integrated functionality to automatically uploaded data to a secure server.

On a final note, legacy bias is a common observation of elicited interaction sets. While it is difficult to eradicate this bias, it is important to notice that some researchers have attempted to use legacy bias in their favor. Thus, this work does not emphasize that legacy bias is required to be mitigated at all costs but rather postulates that legacy bias proposals could appear in any GES; being aware of it and having a design to mitigate it when required is important. Therefore, researchers could follow these proposals when the need arises, to mitigate legacy bias and systemic bias from their GESs.

6.1 Limitation and Future Work

The use of emerging technologies such as VR for HCI empirical studies such as GESs started to proliferate with the recent advancement and the inclined popularity of the technology. Thus, future research should investigate the following directions to find answers to the open questions in this area.

In this research, we utilized Morris et al's [26] 3P methods for legacy bias mitigation. Apart from these techniques, there are other designs such as Ruiz et al. [43] 'soft constraints' approach to reducing legacy bias which we have not incorporated in this study. Further, we have investigated embedding each 3P technique individually yet did not investigate the effect of combing multiple techniques together. Thus, there is an opportunity for further explorations and new designs in improving encapsulated and remote VR GESs.

According to Vatavu et al.'s [50] there is a negative correlation between agreement rates for a gesture and thinking time. However, from the qualitative feedback received during the experiment's 'trial phase', the 15 s thinking time was reported as insufficient, especially when proposing the second gesture for certain referents. Thus, this creates an open question about whether it is good to limit the time, provide a trigger-based mechanism where participants can propose a gesture when they are ready, or a mixed method such as a first gesture will be proposed within a time limit and the second is trigger-based, etc.

7 Conclusion

In this study, we contribute to the still under-explored work in conducting encapsulated VR GESs with legacy bias mitigation techniques. We used three legacy bias reduction methods suggested by Morris et al. [27], compared and discussed the suitable VR design that could implement these methods in VR GESs. These designs were then evaluated with four elicitation studies, which contained 20 referents and 70 participants. We compared the use of each 3P method individually with a GES that used no legacy bias reduction design. This helped identify the significant changes these techniques brought in terms of designing GESs and the impact of embedding this legacy bias reduction technique along with its influence on the final gesture agreement rate calculation. We believe this work will encourage exploration and evaluation on improving remote and encapsulated empirical studies, particularly GESs, and hope to see more GESs use legacy bias reduction mechanisms with encapsulated VR GES design, furthering the reach for a more diverse participant sample and promoting design for the pluriverse.

References

1. Ali, A.X., Morris, M.R., Wobbrock, J.O.: I am iron man priming improves the learnability and memorability of user-elicited gestures. In: Proceedings of the 2021 CHI Conference on Human Factors in Computing Systems, pp. 1–14 (2021)
2. Allen, J.: Designing desirability in an augmentative and alternative communication device. Univ. Access Inf. Soc. **4**(2), 135–145 (2005)
3. Arendttorp, E.M.N., Rodil, K., Winschiers-Theophilus, H., Magoath, C.: Overcoming legacy bias: Re-designing gesture interactions in virtual reality with a san community in Namibia. In: CHI Conference on Human Factors in Computing Systems, pp. 1–18 (2022)
4. Balakrishnan, R., Hinckley, K.: Symmetric bimanual interaction. In: Proceedings of the SIGCHI Conference on Human Factors in Computing Systems, pp. 33–40 (2000)
5. Bellucci, A., Zarraonandia, T., Díaz, P., Aedo, I.: Welicit: a wizard of Oz tool for VR elicitation studies. In: Ardito, C., et al. (eds.) INTERACT 2021. LNCS, vol. 12936, pp. 82–91. Springer, Cham (2021). https://doi.org/10.1007/978-3-030-85607-6_6
6. Blandford, A., Furniss, D., Makri, S.: Qualitative HCI research: going behind the scenes. Synth. Lect. Hum.-Centered Inf. **9**(1), 1–115 (2016)

7. Brooke, J., et al.: SUS-A quick and dirty usability scale. Usability Eval. Ind. **189**(194), 4–7 (1996)
8. Buchanan, S., Floyd, B., Holderness, W., LaViola, J.J.: Towards user-defined multi-touch gestures for 3d objects. In: Proceedings of the 2013 ACM International Conference on Interactive Tabletops and Surfaces, pp. 231–240 (2013)
9. Chan, E., Seyed, T., Stuerzlinger, W., Yang, X.D., Maurer, F.: User elicitation on single-hand microgestures. In: Proceedings of the 2016 CHI Conference on Human Factors in Computing Systems, pp. 3403–3414 (2016)
10. Cooper, A.: The myth of metaphor. Visual Basic Programmer's J. **3**, 127–128 (1995)
11. Corporation, V.: Steam hardware and software survey: May 2022 (2022). https://store.steampowered.com/hwsurvey/Steam-Hardware-Software-Survey-Welcome-to-Steam
12. Dow, S., Fortuna, J., Schwartz, D., Altringer, B., Schwartz, D., Klemmer, S.: Prototyping dynamics: sharing multiple designs improves exploration, group rapport, and results, pp. 2807–2816 (2011). https://doi.org/10.1145/1978942.1979359
13. Gilbert, N.: 74 virtual reality statistics you must know in 2021/2022: Adoption, usage and market share (2022). http://financesonline.com/virtual-reality-statistics/
14. Human Performance Research Group NASA Ames Research Group: NASA TLX Paper and Pencil Version Instruction Manual. Moffett Feild, California (1988)
15. Hart, S.G., Staveland, L.E.: Development of NASA-TLX (task load index): results of empirical and theoretical research. In: Advances in Psychology, vol. 52, pp. 139–183. Elsevier (1988)
16. Hoff, L., Hornecker, E., Bertel, S.: Modifying gesture elicitation: do kinaesthetic priming and increased production reduce legacy bias? In: Proceedings of the TEI 2016: Tenth International Conference on Tangible, Embedded, and Embodied Interaction, pp. 86–91 (2016)
17. Jenkins, H.: Game design as narrative architecture. Computer **44**(3), 118–130 (2004)
18. Köpsel, A., Bubalo, N.: Benefiting from legacy bias. Interactions **22**(5), 44–47 (2015)
19. Lazar, J., Feng, J.H., Hochheiser, H.: Research Methods in Human-Computer Interaction. Morgan Kaufmann, Burlington (2017)
20. Lewkowicz, D.J.: The concept of ecological validity: what are its limitations and is it bad to be invalid? Infancy **2**(4), 437–450 (2001)
21. Madeo, R.C.B., Peres, S.M., de Moraes Lima, C.A.: Gesture phase segmentation using support vector machines. Expert Syst. Appl. **56**, 100–115 (2016)
22. Mäkelä, V., et al.: Virtual field studies: conducting studies on public displays in virtual reality. In: Proceedings of the 2020 CHI Conference on Human Factors in Computing Systems, pp. 1–15 (2020)
23. McCrindle, M.: Generation Alpha. Hachette, UK (2021)
24. McMahan, R.P., Gorton, D., Gresock, J., McConnell, W., Bowman, D.A.: Separating the effects of level of immersion and 3d interaction techniques. In: Proceedings of the ACM Symposium on Virtual Reality Software and Technology, pp. 108–111 (2006)
25. Morris, M.R.: Web on the wall: insights from a multimodal interaction elicitation study. In: Proceedings of the 2012 ACM International Conference on Interactive Tabletops and Surfaces, pp. 95–104 (2012)
26. Morris, M.R., et al.: Reducing legacy bias in gesture elicitation studies. Interactions **21**(3), 40–45 (2014)

27. Morris, M.R., Wobbrock, J.O., Wilson, A.D.: Understanding users' preferences for surface gestures. In: Proceedings of Graphics Interface 2010, pp. 261–268 (2010)
28. Nielsen, J.: Time budgets for usability sessions. Useit. com: Jakob Nielsen's web site 12 (2005)
29. Norman, D.A.: Design rules based on analyses of human error. Commun. ACM **26**(4), 254–258 (1983)
30. Norman, D.A.: The way i see it signifiers, not affordances. Interactions **15**(6), 18–19 (2008)
31. Norman, D.A.: The Design of Everyday Things. MIT Press, Cambridge (2013)
32. Ortega, F.R., et al.: Gesture elicitation for 3d travel via multi-touch and mid-air systems for procedurally generated pseudo-universe. In: 2017 IEEE Symposium on 3D User Interfaces (3DUI), pp. 144–153. IEEE (2017)
33. Perera, M., Gedeon, T., Adcock, M., Haller, A.: Towards self-guided remote user studies-feasibility of gesture elicitation using immersive virtual reality. In: 2021 IEEE International Conference on Systems, Man, and Cybernetics (SMC), pp. 2576–2583. IEEE (2021)
34. Perera, M., Haller, A., Rodríguez Méndez, S.J., Adcock, M.: HDGI: a human device gesture interaction ontology for the internet of things. In: Pan, J.Z., Tamma, V., d'Amato, C., Janowicz, K., Fu, B., Polleres, A., Seneviratne, O., Kagal, L. (eds.) ISWC 2020. LNCS, vol. 12507, pp. 111–126. Springer, Cham (2020). https://doi.org/10.1007/978-3-030-62466-8_8
35. Piumsomboon, T., Clark, A., Billinghurst, M., Cockburn, A.: User-defined gestures for augmented reality. In: Kotzé, P., Marsden, G., Lindgaard, G., Wesson, J., Winckler, M. (eds.) INTERACT 2013. LNCS, vol. 8118, pp. 282–299. Springer, Heidelberg (2013). https://doi.org/10.1007/978-3-642-40480-1_18
36. Radiah, R., et al.: Remote VR studies: a framework for running virtual reality studies remotely via participant-owned HMDs. ACM Trans. Comput.-Hum. Interact. (TOCHI) **28**(6), 1–36 (2021)
37. Ratcliffe, J., Ballou, N., Tokarchuk, L.: Actions, not gestures: contextualising embodied controller interactions in immersive virtual reality. In: Proceedings of the 27th ACM Symposium on Virtual Reality Software and Technology, pp. 1–11 (2021)
38. Ratcliffe, J., Soave, F., Bryan-Kinns, N., Tokarchuk, L., Farkhatdinov, I.: Extended reality (XR) remote research: a survey of drawbacks and opportunities. In: Proceedings of the 2021 CHI Conference on Human Factors in Computing Systems, pp. 1–13 (2021)
39. Ratcliffe, J., et al.: Remote XR studies: exploring three key challenges of remote XR experimentation. In: Extended Abstracts of the 2021 CHI Conference on Human Factors in Computing Systems, pp. 1–4 (2021)
40. Rey, A., Bellucci, A., Diaz, P., Aedo, I.: A tool for monitoring and controlling standalone immersive HCI experiments. In: The Adjunct Publication of the 34th Annual ACM Symposium on User Interface Software and Technology, pp. 20–22 (2021)
41. Rivu, R., et al.: Remote vr studies-a framework for running virtual reality studies remotely via participant-owned hmds. arXiv preprint arXiv:2102.11207 (2021)
42. Ruiz, J., Li, Y., Lank, E.: User-defined motion gestures for mobile interaction. In: Proceedings of the SIGCHI Conference on Human Factors in Computing Systems, pp. 197–206 (2011)
43. Ruiz, J., Vogel, D.: Soft-constraints to reduce legacy and performance bias to elicit whole-body gestures with low arm fatigue. In: Proceedings of the 33rd Annual ACM Conference on Human Factors in Computing Systems, pp. 3347–3350 (2015)

44. Sanchez-Vives, M.V., Slater, M.: From presence to consciousness through virtual reality. Nat. Rev. Neurosci. **6**(4), 332–339 (2005)
45. Schacter, D.L., Buckner, R.L.: Priming and the brain. Neuron **20**(2), 185–195 (1998)
46. Schmuckler, M.A.: What is ecological validity? a dimensional analysis. Infancy **2**(4), 419–436 (2001)
47. Schubert, T.W.: The sense of presence in virtual environments: a three-component scale measuring spatial presence, involvement, and realness. Z. für Medienpsychologie **15**(2), 69–71 (2003)
48. Tsandilas, T.: Fallacies of agreement: a critical review of consensus assessment methods for gesture elicitation. ACM Trans. Comput.-Hum. Interact. (TOCHI) **25**(3), 1–49 (2018)
49. Vatavu, R.D., Wobbrock, J.O.: Formalizing agreement analysis for elicitation studies: new measures, significance test, and toolkit. In: Proceedings of the 33rd Annual ACM Conference on Human Factors in Computing Systems, pp. 1325–1334 (2015)
50. Vatavu, R.D., Zaiti, I.A.: Leap gestures for tv: insights from an elicitation study. In: Proceedings of the ACM International Conference on Interactive Experiences for TV and Online Video, pp. 131–138 (2014)
51. Vogiatzidakis, P., Koutsabasis, P.: Gesture elicitation studies for mid-air interaction: a review. Multimodal Technol. Interact. **2**(4), 65 (2018)
52. Vogiatzidakis, P., Koutsabasis, P.: Frame-based elicitation of mid-air gestures for a smart home device ecosystem. In: Informatics, vol. 6, p. 23. Multidisciplinary Digital Publishing Institute (2019)
53. Warpefelt, H., Verhagen, H.: A model of non-player character believability. J. Gaming Virtual Worlds **9**(1), 39–53 (2017)
54. Wentura, D., Degner, J.: A practical guide to sequential priming and related tasks (2010)
55. Williams, A.S., Garcia, J., De Zayas, F., Hernandez, F., Sharp, J., Ortega, F.R.: The cost of production in elicitation studies and the legacy bias-consensus trade off. Multimodal Technol. Interact. **4**(4), 88 (2020)
56. Williams, A.S., Garcia, J., Ortega, F.: Understanding multimodal user gesture and speech behavior for object manipulation in augmented reality using elicitation. IEEE Trans. Visual. Comput. Graph. **26**(12), 3479–3489 (2020)
57. Williams, A.S., Ortega, F.R.: Evolutionary gestures: when a gesture is not quite legacy biased. Interactions **27**(5), 50–53 (2020)
58. Wittorf, M.L., Jakobsen, M.R.: Eliciting mid-air gestures for wall-display interaction. In: Proceedings of the 9th Nordic Conference on Human-Computer Interaction, pp. 1–4 (2016)
59. Wu, H., Fu, S., Yang, L., Zhang, X.: Exploring frame-based gesture design for immersive VR shopping environments. Behav. Inf. Technol. **41**(1), 96–117 (2022)
60. Wu, H., et al.: Understanding freehand gestures: a study of freehand gestural interaction for immersive VR shopping applications. Hum.-Centric Comput. Inf. Sci. **9**(1), 1–26 (2019)
61. Wu, H., Wang, Y., Qiu, J., Liu, J., Zhang, X.: User-defined gesture interaction for immersive VR shopping applications. Behav. Inf. Technol. **38**(7), 726–741 (2019)
62. Zhou, X., Williams, A.S., Ortega, F.R.: Towards establishing consistent proposal binning methods for unimodal and multimodal interaction elicitation studies. In: Kurosu, M. (eds.) International Conference on Human-Computer. Interaction Theoretical Approaches and Design Methods, HCII 2022, vol. 13302, pp. 356–368. Springer, Cham (2022). https://doi.org/10.1007/978-3-031-05311-5_25

63. Zimmerman, J., Forlizzi, J.: Research through design in HCI. In: Olson, J.S., Kellogg, W.A. (eds.) Ways of Knowing in HCI, pp. 167–189. Springer, New York (2014). https://doi.org/10.1007/978-1-4939-0378-8_8
64. Zimmerman, J., Forlizzi, J., Evenson, S.: Research through design as a method for interaction design research in HCI. In: Proceedings of the SIGCHI Conference on Human Factors in Computing Systems, pp. 493–502 (2007)

Design Guidelines Towards 4.0 HMIs: How to Translate Physical Buttons in Digital Buttons

Elisa Prati(✉), Giuditta Contini, and Margherita Peruzzini

Department of Engineering "Enzo Ferrari", University of Modena and Reggio Emilia, Modena, Italy
elisa.prati@unimore.it

Abstract. The fourth industrial revolution (known as Industry 4.0) has simplified the access to new smart technologies, which are even more adopted by companies in their manufacturing machines. These technologies (e.g., Internet of Things) open new evolutionary scenarios for industries and the whole production process, such as the use of big data for production process optimization. At the same time, also a Human-Machine Interface (HMI) evolution is required to manage and effectively exploit the new machines advantages. Currently, different industrial HMIs are still physical based (e.g., buttons, levers) and do not properly respond to the new opportunities offered by the 4.0 technologies, limiting the whole production evolution. The HMIs' evolution requires a proper design approach that considers the new machine possibilities (e.g., real time data analysis), the new interaction requirements and the users' needs in the new work scenario. However, a lack of indications to guide this redesign process emerged. In this paper is presented a list of design guidelines conceived during a project regarding the HMI redesign of an automatic production line. Specifically, the project focuses on the translation of physical buttons to digital ones in a graphic interface. The case study brought out that there are many aspects to consider during the design process toward new 4.0 HMIs, and specific methodologies are necessary to develop intuitive and clear HMIs. Providing this applicative example, the paper aims to fill the current gap of indication to face the HMIs evolution and redesign. In particular, the developed guidelines are described to make clear how to adopt them to solve similar use cases and as a support for the design teams.

Keywords: Digital pushbutton design guidelines · 4.0 HMI · Atomic design · User Centered Design (UCD) · Industry 4.0

1 Introduction and Research Context

The advent of Industry 4.0 (I4.0) has brought about widespread adoption of numerous new technologies, solutions, and concepts in many industries. Among the technologies associated with I4.0, the Internet of Things (IoT), the Internet of Services (IoS), and Cyber Physical Systems (CPS) have had a greater impact on the revolution of machines and production processes. The integration of such technologies enables the creation of a network between manufacturing resources and services, resulting in the development

M. Kurosu and A. Hashizume (Eds.): HCII 2023, LNCS 14011, pp. 226–242, 2023.
https://doi.org/10.1007/978-3-031-35596-7_15

of cyber-physical production systems (CPPS) [1], i.e. the integration of physical production processes with digital technologies and data exchange. This enables a real-time monitoring and control of production processes using sensors, actuators, and computing devices, thus increasing the machines' potentiality and modality of use. This results in a more efficient, flexible, sustainable, and safe manufacturing environment [2]. In essence, it is the use of technology to enhance and optimize traditional manufacturing methods [3].

The machines' evolution has also a significant impact on the Human-Machine Interfaces (HMIs), and thus on the interaction modality between humans and machines. The term HMI is often associated with Graphic User Interfaces (GUIs), however the HMI, or user interface, encompasses all means of interaction between users and machines, including physical interfaces (e.g., buttons and levers), GUIs (e.g., on monitor or smartwatch), and Natural User Interfaces (NUIs) such as vocal or gesture commands. In the industrial field, HMIs play a crucial role in informing users about the machines' status and production activity, ultimately supporting users in their tasks, such as supervision and maintenance [4]. Therefore, the success of machines' operations heavily depends on the characteristics and design quality of the HMIs. Consequently, a well-designed HMI is essential for creating intuitive interfaces that do not impede the production process. However, the machines' evolution has increased the complexity and inadequacy of the current HMIs. Although physical HMIs are technologically outdated [5, 6], they are still widely used in industry. Such outdated physical HMIs are no longer suitable to handle the new flexible functions of the 4.0 machines, thus hindering their evolution and making the user's tasks unnecessarily complicated. Subsequently, to effectively exploit the advantages of 4.0 technologies, the industrial HMIs must evolve alongside the machines. However, this redesign process does not consist only in a newer device choice, but it requires a proper consideration of the new interaction conditions, opportunities, and the impact on the whole User eXperience (UX). To this aim, the HMIs redesign should leverage the new interaction opportunities, such as AR (Augmented Reality) [7] and adaptive interfaces [8], to avoid the creation of unnecessarily difficult-to-use interfaces.

Despite the growing importance and demand for industries to update the previous HMIs to the new 4.0 machines' functions, there is a lack of indications to guide this HMI redesign process. Specifically, there have been no studies focused on the transition from physical pushbuttons to digital buttons on a graphical HMI. General purpose design pillars, such as the Nielsen's Heuristics [9], the Norman's Design Principles [10], and the Dimensions of Interaction Design [11], are universally applicable to any HMI design, as well as HMI studies in industrial or different domains (e.g., [12–14]) can be considered as starting point. More practical guidance can be found in regulations and ISO standards. The latter, for example, define symbols, colors, wording for control elements, and clear specifications for safety-related functions [15]. Indeed, their final aim is to minimize the risk of operators' errors or unintended actions and for this reason they must be strictly adhered to. In particular, the Machinery Directive 2006/42/CE [16] defines some internationally recognized symbols (see Fig. 1) for general functions to be used instead of words so that all operators, coming from different countries, can be able to understand the command. The ISO 13850:2015 [17] deals with the safety requirements and specifies that the emergency stop button must be easily accessible, easily identifiable, and regularly tested to ensure its correct functioning. At the same time, the EN 60204-1 [18] establishes the principles, recommendations and requirements to be applied during the design of control centers. Specifically, it deals with the safety of electrical devices in machines, regulating the general requirements for the type of protection for buttons, displays and illuminated buttons, as well as the colours that can be used for certain functions. As reported in Fig. 2, the standard defines the meaning of the colours and their use in industry, specifying that:

- the *Start/On* button cannot be red;
- the *Emergency off* and *Emergency stop* buttons must be red;
- the *Stop/Off* button cannot be green;
- when the same color is used for several functions, it is necessary to provide additional information (e.g., shape, position, symbol);
- the rotating operating elements must avoid unwanted rotations;
- the starting devices must prevent unintentional commissioning;
- the *Emergency shutdown* disconnects the power supply in case of emergency (comparable to the *Emergency stop* button). It must be a palm or mushroom pushbutton or pull cord switch.

These standards are precious indications for the design of any interface, both physical and digital. Infact, it is important that also the GUIs are in line with the symbols, colours and rules applied to the other HMIs (e.g., physical) and in general in the environment. All these aspects have been considered during the HMI redesign project described in the Sect. 2, and consequently includes in the proposed guidelines, as discussed in Sect. 3.

Symbols used on buttons and indicator lights and their meaning (according to EN 60204-1)

Symbol	Meaning
|	START or ON
 ○	STOP or OFF
 ⏼	Button used for ON and OFF
	Press and hold to operate: button pressed -> ON, without pressing -> OFF

Fig. 1. Symbols defined by the Machinery Directive 2006/42/CE.

Button colors and their meaning (according to EN 60204-1)

Color	Meaning	Typical use
	Emergency	• STOP/EMERGENCY STOP • Fire extinguishing
	Anomaly	Intervention to stop abnormal situations or to prevent unwanted changes
	Obligatory	Reset function
	Normal	Safe start
	No specific meaning assigned	• START/ON (preferably) • STOP/OFF
		• START/ON (preferably) • STOP/OFF
		• START/ON (preferably) • STOP/OFF

Indicator colors and their meanings (according to EN 60204-1)

Color	Meaning	Explanation	Typical use
	Emergency	Warning of potential danger or conditions that require immediate action	• Lack of system lubrication • Temperature outside the expected (safety) limits • Shutdown due to the intervention of a safety organ
	Anomaly	Imminent critical situation	• Temperature (or pressure) different from normal values • Overload (only allowed for a limited time)
	Obligatory	Requires operator intervention	• Remove obstacles • Stop to continue
	Normal	Shows safe operating conditions or the green light for continued operation	• Circulating refrigerant • Automatic boiler control in operation
	Neutral	No specific meaning: can be used when it is not clear which color (RED, YELLOW or GREEN) is appropriate to use, or as confirmation	• Engine running • Visualization of operational data

Fig. 2. Colours' use for buttons and indicators defined by the EN 60204-1.

2 Case Study

2.1 Case Study Description

The case study concerned the redesign of physical pushbuttons of an automatic production line of plastic cups, produced by an Italian company which is world leader in this sector. In particular, the operators that work along the production line are in charge to set up the machine parameters, control the production activity and perform maintenance tasks. For all these operations, the users interact with the machine through an HMI positioned at the beginning of the line. The overall HMI (Fig. 3) includes a graphic interface on a touchscreen display of 21", and about thirty physical buttons below the screen. On one hand, through the display the user can set the machine, visualize the production parameters, and manage the functions (e.g., thermoregulator activation and deactivation). On the other hand, each physical button is linked to a command that can be used based on the current machine's condition or production mode (e.g., automatic, manual). The project focused on deleting some physical buttons and include them in the graphical interface. This request from the client was a consequence of a wider review and reorganization of the entire production line in accord with the I4.0 improvements. In particular, the current rigid configuration of the physical buttons did not answer anymore to the production progress of the machines. Based on this, the starting design questions were:

1. Which physical buttons can be shifted on the graphic interface?
2. How to translate the buttons' commands on the graphic interface?
3. How to reproduce the natural feedback (e.g., button tap, button pressed) on the graphic interface?

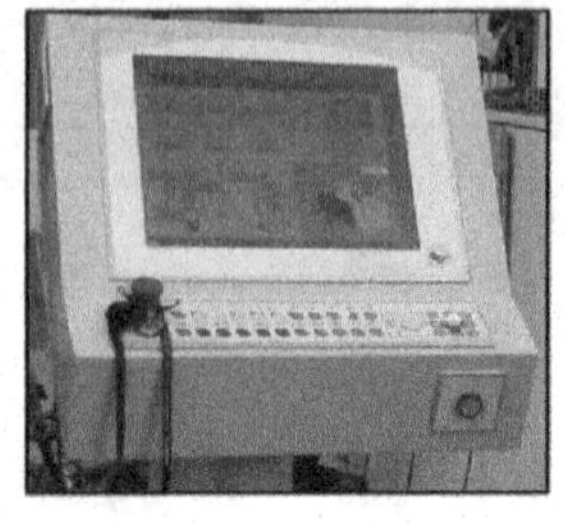

Fig. 3. Production line (on the left) and the HMI before the redesign (on the right).

2.2 Methods and Design Flow

The traditional User-Centered Design (UCD) approach was adopted to address the project. The UCD method puts the users' needs and wishes at the center of the design process and involves them during the design phases: (1) *Context and user research*, (2) *Design*, (3) *Prototype*, (4) *Test*. During the research phase, focus group, observation on field, and user interviews were conducted to understand the criticality during the interaction and define the precise design requirements. During the design and prototype phases, high fidelity prototype was developed and used for expert evaluation.

Research Phase. The context and user research started with focus group sessions, a technique used to gather qualitative data through group discussion under the guide of a moderator who encourages participation from all the group members. This technique can be adopted in different design phases with the aim to gain a deeper understanding of the attitudes, beliefs, and perceptions of the participants regarding the topic or the product being studied. In this project, the focus group sessions were fundamental to get inside the project and know the specific functions and use modality of each button. In particular, the buttons (Fig. 4) have been classified and subdivided in two categories, based on their interaction characteristics:

1. buttons with one function:
   - *buttons to launch a continuous operation:* the button launches an activity that has a prolonged duration;
   - *buttons to launch a start-end operation:* the button launches an operation that has a beginning and an end;
2. buttons with two functions: the button can activate or deactivation an operation.

Moreover, a list of feedback related to the interaction with the buttons was identified:

1. Feedback related to the buttons' condition of use:
   - *AbKey block:* it is required to hold down the AbKey physical button to enable the use of another button;
   - *User block:* the logged user does not have the permission to use the button and a higher level profile is required;

- *System block:* the machine's state does not allow to activate further action;

2. Interaction feedback:

- Button tap: give feedback that the button has been touched and the command has been received;
- Button's state: give feedback of the button's state (i.e., pressed, not pressed).

These feedbacks provide to the users the necessary information to understand the results of their actions and avoid errors (e.g., multiple sending of the command).

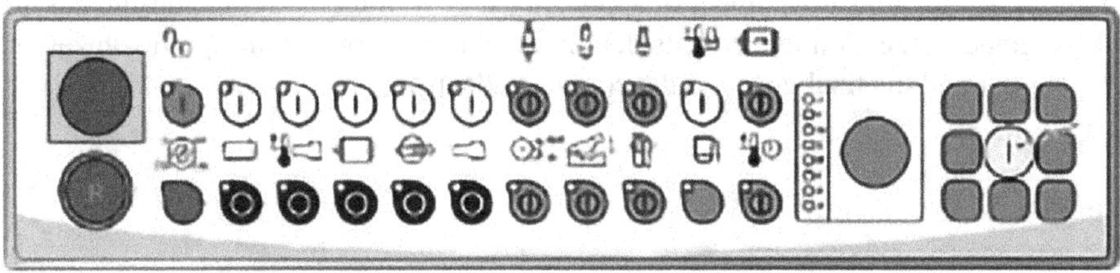

Fig. 4. Representation of the physical buttons before the redesign.

In order to deeply understand the interaction modality during a real scenario of use, observations on field and subsequent interviews with final users were conducted. Observations on field allow to observe the users in their natural environment without disrupting their normal task execution and collect qualitative information regarding the whole UX. At the same time, interviews are a means to gather implicit and explicit information from the users regarding their needs, motivations, opinions, experiences, and behaviour related to a specific product. Thanks to these activities it was possible to understand how the users interact with the display and the physical buttons, and mainly their problems during the interaction with the current HMI. Specifically:

- the high number of physical buttons causes difficulties in the memorization of the function associated to each button, therefore, first, it slows down the task execution, second, the users use to learn by heart the commands sequence, limiting their skills in case of unexpected or unusual task;
- the representation of the buttons' commands through icons and the buttons' status (with lights) are not immediate to understand;
- different commands can be done through the physical buttons and the graphic interface, confusing the users especially when the physical button's state does not match with the indication shown on the graphic interface.

Design and Prototype. The design phase was based on the research outputs. First, the buttons that could be shifted in the graphical HMI were selected. The choice was based on the consideration of the regulations and the company needs, trying to limit the fixed buttons as much as possible. Consequently, buttons such as the emergency and the AbKey ones remained physical, while the buttons with no exigence to remain physical (e.g., compressed air supply, unlock repairs, lamination start) were redesigned. Given the buttons' complexity, variety, and condition of use, a systematic approach was necessary to address the design. Based on this, the atomic and system design were adopted. The atomic design takes its idea by the chemistry and the matter composition. Indeed, it propose the use of 'atom elements' as building blocks to be combined to create even bigger elements, i.e. molecules and then organisms. As shown in Fig. 5, in the User interface (UI) design world, atoms are the smallest building blocks of the system (e.g., icons, labels, buttons), molecules are the combination of more atoms to create different bigger elements (e.g., components with a label, an icon, and a button) which in turn create interface section (i.e., organisms), such as the header of a website. At the same time, the system design is a collection of components, that guided by defined rules, can be assembled to build any number of applications. Therefore, the system design has the role to guide in the atomic elements definition and in the overall design organization, keeping in mind the final goal and the company identity.

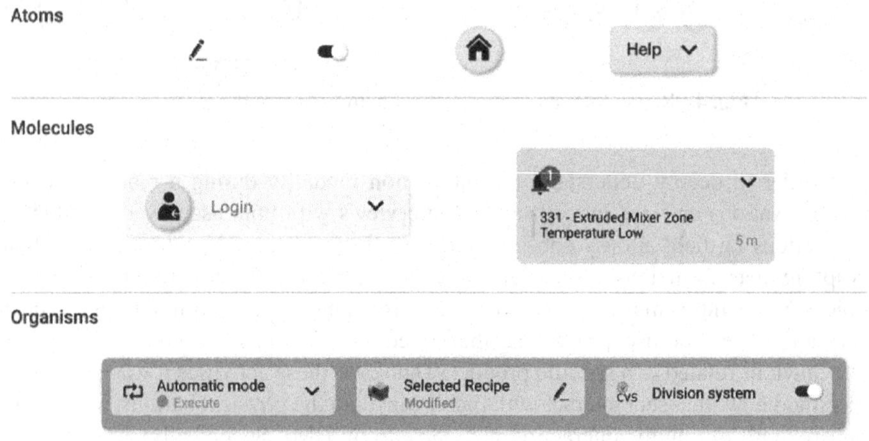

Fig. 5. Atomic design example.

The system design approach suggests starting each new design by building an inventory of all the different interface's elements. To this aim, a list of buttons and feedback typology has been done, identifying for each of them the aspects to be represented. Subsequently, it was started the study of how to represent each of those aspects. Table 1 summarizes these three phases: in the first column are listed the buttons and feedback type; for all of them in the second column are listed the related aspects to represents; and in the third column is reported how to represent the aspects in the new digital version of the buttons.

Table 1. Design requirements and representation choices.

WHAT REPRESENT		ASPECTS TO REPRESENT	REPRESENTATIONS CHOICES
Buttons		- Shape - Buttons' function - Action type	- Round and switch shapes - Function's description - Action icon change
One-function buttons	Continuous operation	- Ongoing activity - Activity completed - Error reporting	- Continuously moving bar - Use of colours green (completed), yellow (in progress), red (error detected) - Opacity to indicate that the button cannot be pressed if the activity is in progress
	Start-end operation	- Activity's progress - Activity completed - Error reporting - Stop operation	- Loading bar - Use of colours green (completed), yellow (in progress), red (error detected) - Action icon change
Two-function buttons		- Possible action (activate or disactivate) - Current modality	- Use of colours green (activated), red (non-activated)
Buttons' conditions of use	Abkey block	- Press the Abkey to enable the use of the button	- Opacity of the button's shape until the Abkey is pressed - Abkey icon - Short text description of the block reason
	User block	- The logged user is not authorized to use the button	- Opacity of the button and its icon - Short text description of the block reason
	System block	- The button cannot be used	- Opacity of the button and its icon - Short text description of the block reason

(continued)

Table 1. (*continued*)

WHAT REPRESENT		ASPECTS TO REPRESENT	REPRESENTATIONS CHOICES
Interaction feedback	Button tap	- Button touched	- Shadow - Haptic feedback with soft screen vibration
	State of the button	- Button pressed - Button non-pressed	- Strong shadow - Normal button visualization

Atom Elements Design. Following the atomic design approach based on the combination of singular aspects (i.e., atoms) to systematically compose bigger elements, the design phase started on the translation of each identified aspect, keeping in mind the final result to be obtained. The atom elements are listed as follow.

Buttons' Shape. Among the basic elements (i.e., atom), the first considered aspects was the button's shape. Considering the two buttons' categories, two different shapes have been defined. For the one-function button, a round shape was chosen to guarantee visual continuity with the buttons that, by law, will remain physical. Whereas for the two-function pushbuttons it was decided to adopt a 'switch button' because more appropriated for this kind of commands, also considering the best practices in graphic interfaces. Moreover, the shapes' choices (see Fig. 6a) have also considered the HMI's style and to sufficiently distinguish the pushbuttons from the rest of the digital interface's components.

Button's Function and Action. The second considered aspect regarded the communication of the button's function. Keeping as reference what was already done for the physical buttons, i.e. what is already know by the users, an icon positioned below the button's shape was chosen to represent the function (Fig. 6b). Exploiting the potential of digital interfaces, has also been chosen to provide more support to the users with a short text description: by clicking on the icon a pop-up will appear close to the pushbutton to provide more information related to the button and its function. Another support was introduced with the visualization of an action icon inside the button as further confirmation of the action that can be activated by clicking the button.

Buttons' Conditions. The different types of blocks were represented by an icon above the button which represent the type of block (Fig. 6c). Moreover, to immediate communicate the inability to use the button, an opacity is applied on the button's shape, leaving the icons visible in case of a simple block (i.e., AbKey block, User block) and applying the opacity also to the function's icon in case of System block.

Button Touch Feedback. To represent the effective touch of the button, it has been defined to show an opaque circle around the touched point in case of round buttons and around the circular shape in case of switch buttons (Fig. 6d). Moreover, a soft and short vibration is added as haptic feedback.

State of the Button Feedback. To represent the pressed and non-pressed state of the buttons, it has been decided to display it with the appearance of a shadow under the button itself (6e). It is a usual way in UI design to represent the state of the buttons.

Ongoing Activity. An ongoing activity is usually graphically represented with a movement, often circular or linear. For this reason, it has been chosen to represent the continuous activity by a circular movement of a line around the button (Fig. 6f). In this way, such information does not require more space inside the interface and it is strictly linked to the button, avoiding misunderstanding or that the users do not see the information.

Activity's Progress. Similarly to the ongoing activity, the feedback that an operation is started is marked by the appearance, around the button, of a loading bar which fills up until it is completed (Fig. 6g).

Activity Status. Another necessary feedback associated to both the previous cases (i.e., ongoing activity and activity's progress), is the activity status. The use of colours (green, yellow, red) was chosen to immediately communicate the activity status (Fig. 6h). In case of one-function button (round shape), the outline used to represent the activity varies color depending on whether the activity is ongoing (yellow) is finished (green) or an error has been detected and the operation has been stopped (red). While for the two-function button (switch shape) the color is applied to the button's internal area, changing between grey if the action is not activate, green when the button has been pressed and the function is active, red in case of error.

Molecules Elements Design. Once all the atom elements have been designed, they can be combined as layers (see Fig. 7) to create the bigger elements, i.e. the molecules. The latter correspond to the buttons' typologies summarized in Table 1, and on their variation of activity status (e.g., in progress, completed) and condition of use (e.g., AbKey block, System blocks).

One-Function Button - Continuous Operation. The continuous operation button is composed by the round shape, the functional icon, and the action icon at the center of the button, as shown in Fig. 8a. When the button is pressed the shadow for the button's status feedback appears together with the coloured outline, and the action icon change (e.g., play, stop) to communicate the beginning of the activity and give feedback on its status (Fig. 8b). If the button has some associated condition of use, the corresponding icon is added above the button (Fig. 8a). A practical example is the Jog Machine button which is used to carry out the machine's movements and for its activation the concurrent AbKey button pressing is required.

One-Function Button - Start-End Operation. As for the Continuous Operation button, the Start-End Operation button is composed by the round shape, the functional and action icons (Fig. 8a). When it is pressed the characteristic outline to communicate the activity's progress appears together with the shadow of the pressed-button feedback (Fig. 8c). Also in this case, if the buttons have some condition of use the corresponding icon is included

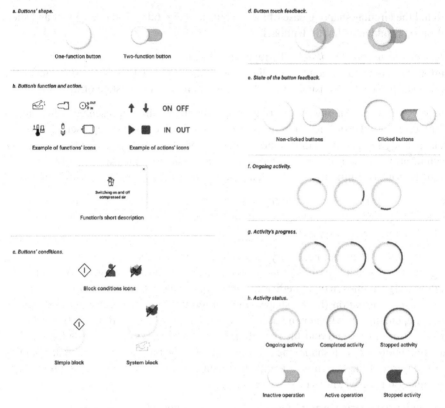

Fig. 6. Atom elements design. (Color figure online)

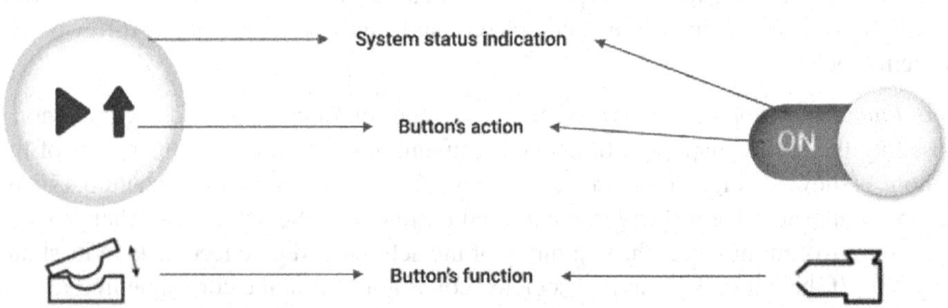

Fig. 7. Atoms combination structure to create the two digital buttons versions: one-function button (on the left), two-function button (on the right).

too (Fig. 8a). Example of this button are the Extruder Heating and the Machine Main Motion.

Two-Function Button. The two-function button is represented through the switch shape, the function icon and a label or an icon inside the button that represent the possible action (Fig. 8d). When it is pressed the characteristic round form moves from left to right, or vice versa, and the button's color and the activity icon respectively change. An example of this button is the Hydraulic Unit Pump, used to turn on or off the pumps of the hydraulic unit with the simultaneous pressure of the AbKey button.

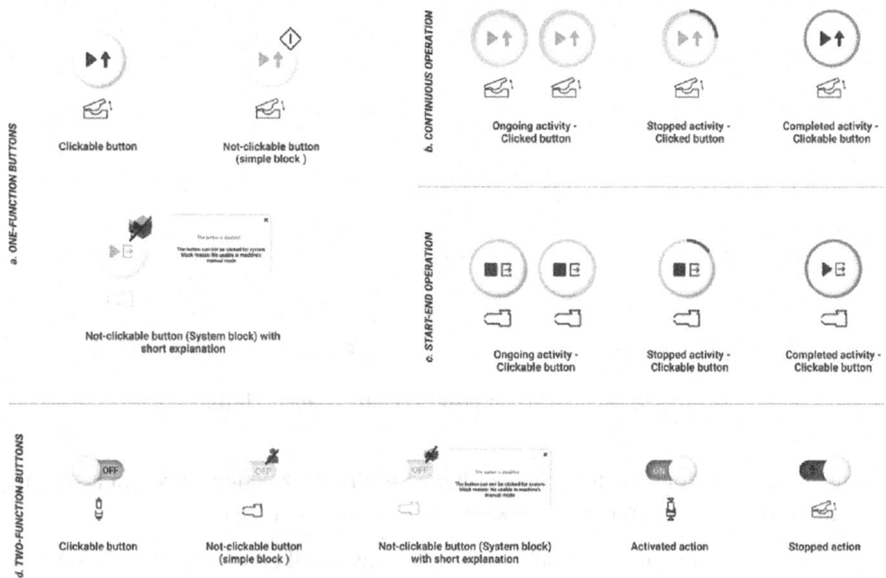

Fig. 8. Digital buttons (i.e., molecules) possible options.

Organism Design. Once the design of the buttons is completed, their position inside the graphic interface has to be studied since it plays a central role on the overall HMI's understanding and interaction. Referring to the atomic design language, the section where the buttons (i.e., molecules) are positioned corresponds to the organism. Different options have been considered during the design phase, such as displaying the buttons in an overlay layer or as an integrated part of the dashboard, both on the bottom and sides of the graphic HMI. An overlay layer positioned on the bottom (Fig. 9) has been chosen as the best option for the specific use case. The choice has been guided by the consideration of the graphic interface setup and the position of the physical under the display. On one hand, has been noticed that most of the pages' contents are positioned on the top, therefore the buttons' layer will not cover much information. On the other hand, it is possible to create a visual continuity with the physical buttons and also a continuity with the users' habit to have the buttons in the bottom part of the interface.

This configuration was then developed in more detail in view of the buttons' use during the tasks. In particular, the buttons have been organized into different section following their use modality, dividing them in:

- buttons that must always remain visible (i.e., mostly used by the operators);
- machine mode specific buttons: buttons that can be used just with a specific machine modality, so it is not useful to display them in case of others machine modes;

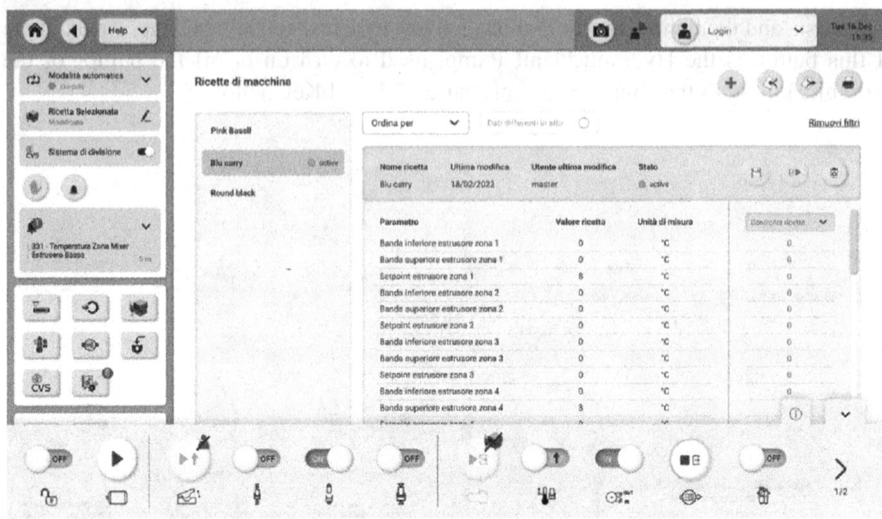

Fig. 9. Buttons' layer position on the graphic HMI.

– page specific buttons: buttons that are linked to the information shown in a specific page, therefore it is not useful to display them in the other pages.

Moreover, considering the number of the buttons and their organization in section, they have been subdivided in two pages easily accessible by clicking the chevron on side (Fig. 10).

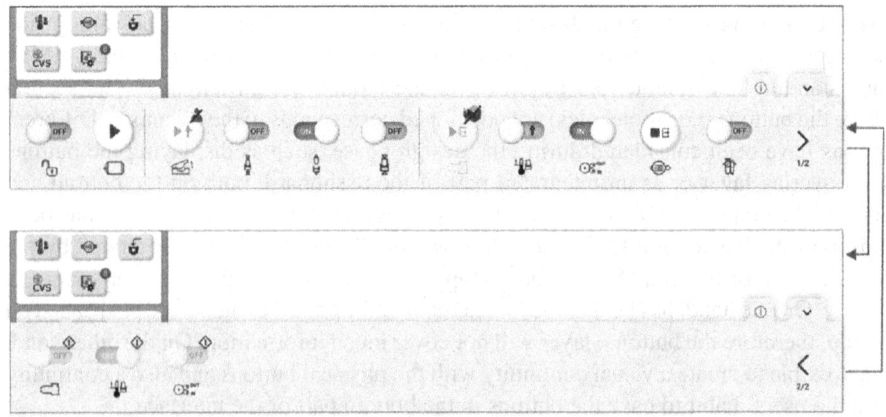

Fig. 10. Pages navigation of the buttons' layer.

Finally, also the close version of the buttons' layer has been designed. A tab with a keyboard icon has been located on the bottom-right corner of the graphic HMI and when it is clicked or dragged the layer will open (Fig. 11). While the layer can be closed clicking on the tab, this time containing a downward chevron instead of the keyboard icon. Figure 12 shows a mock-up of the final redesigned HMI, both with the remaining physical buttons and the new digital ones.

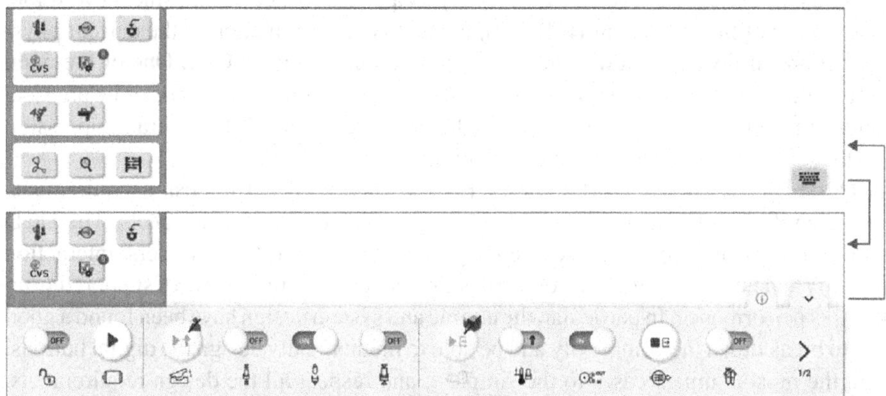

Fig. 11. Closed (above) and open (bottom) visualization of the buttons' layer.

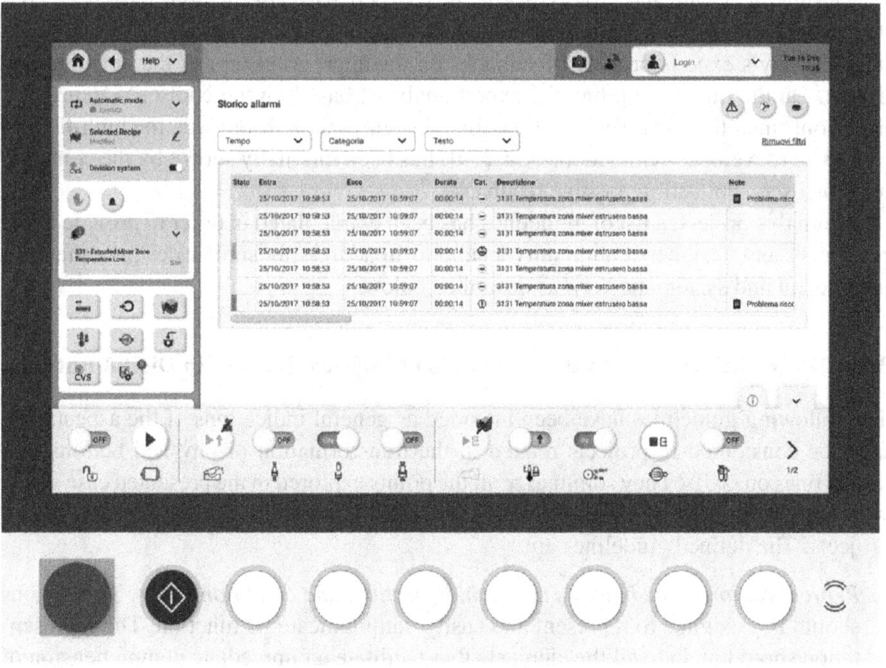

Fig. 12. HMI redesign mockup.

3 Discussion and Design Guidelines

The project described in the previous section faces one of the common design issues in I4.0 context, i.e. the HMI redesign necessity as a consequence of machines' evolution. An example of these frequent HMI readjustment is the elimination of the current physical buttons in favour of new digital ones, for example inside a GUI. One of the main motivations of the presented project was based on the idea that the shift of some physical buttons in the graphic interface will immediately improve the HMI's overall impression and the task performance, reducing execution time and errors.

During the research phase, the current HMI was analyzed and the design requirements were identified; subsequently, they have been translated into visual aspects. The UCD made it possible to face the project focusing since the beginning on the users' interaction modality and needs, therefore develop a design that results intuitive and of support during the tasks performance. In particular, the atomic and system design have been found a good way to break down the complexity and be able to methodically design the digital buttons, from the most complex cases to the simplest, and respect all the design requirements. Moreover, this approach allowed to offer to the company a design method suitable also for future changes such as additional or different buttons' characteristic, as well as to be applied to others HMI redesign as expressional asked from the company.

During the design and prototyping phases, expert-based evaluations have been conducted with both UX experts and company's production line experts. On one hand, the company's experts provided feedbacks on the appropriateness of the new buttons' design. On the other hand, the UX expert analysis, based on the Nielsen's Heuristics, have confirmed the intuitiveness of the final design version. Moreover, the high-fidelity prototype (developed with Adobe XD, [19]) has been internally shown by the company to some users, collecting positive feedback.

From this project, a list of guidelines has been extrapolated in order to provide to the researcher and designers community a support in addressing similar design issues in a methodical and systematic way, as described below.

3.1 Design Guidelines for the Translation of Physical Buttons in Digital Buttons

The following guidelines have been intended as general indications of the aspects that must be considered in projects related to the transformation of physical buttons into digital ones on GUIs. They summarize all the points explored in the presented case study, with the aim to guide in finding equally valid design solutions during new considered projects. The defined guidelines are:

1. *Representation of the button's function, operation, and condition of use:* The buttons should be designed to represent and easily communicate its function. The representation should include all the elements that facilitate an immediate comprehension of the buttons' operation (e.g., activate, disactivate) and conditions of use (e.g., block, not-clickable).
2. *Provide necessary feedback:* Include and properly represent all the feedback necessary to the users to understand the consequence of their actions, the buttons' status (e.g., clicked), and the action status (e.g., in progress, completed). Exploit the digital

interface opportunity (e.g., graphic effects, animations, sounds, haptic signs) to better transmit the necessary information.

3. *Provide support information:* The buttons' representation should provide all the necessary information that could help the user to better understand the buttons' functions and interaction modality (e.g., block clarification, function explanation).
4. *Visual aspect uniformity:* The button visual representation should be developed with a logic at their base to guarantee uniformity between the different buttons. The visual aspects of the buttons (e.g., shape, dimension, colours) must respect the industrial standards, and should be in line with the HMI style, both considering the graphic interface where the buttons are inserted, the used device, and the brand identity.
5. *Pushbuttons position:* The buttons should be placed in such a way that they do not interfere with the rest of the GUI's contents, and at the same time sufficiently distinguishable and accessible. The position should consider the users' habits, the use of the buttons during the tasks, and the position of any physical buttons in the HMI. The position choice should also consider the opportunity of the digital interfaces (e.g., no fixed positions, no binding spaces) in order to simplify the interaction with the buttons (e.g., subdivision of the buttons in section, hide buttons when not usable).

4 Conclusions

This paper deals with the necessary evolution of the industrial HMIs in the I4.0 context to meet the new opportunities and requirements of the 4.0 machines. The study focuses on translating physical pushbuttons into digital ones in GUIs. In this context, the absence of design guidelines has been identified as a critical issue, highlighting the need for the creation of such guidelines to ensure a consistent and effective design method. An industrial use case is presented as a real example of the topic, proposing an approach to face the issue. The project followed the UCD's phases and utilized the atomic and system design methods to create a modular language capable of managing the different buttons' functionality, from the simpler to the more complex. This project led to the development of a list of design guidelines that should be used as a general guide for design teams that face the translation of physical HMIs into digital components of GUIs. These guidelines cover all the aspects of the design process, such as buttons' visual aspect, interaction feedback representation and buttons' position into the interface. Future work will consider the application of these guidelines to different use cases for a more extended guidelines' validation.

In conclusion, this study contributes to the 4.0 HMI design research field by presenting a method for addressing the design challenges of transitioning physical pushbuttons to digital buttons into GUIs.

References

1. Xu, X.: Machine tool 4.0 for the new era of manufacturing. Int. J. Adv. Manuf. Technol. **92**(5–8), 1893–1900 (2017). https://doi.org/10.1007/s00170-017-0300-7
2. Contini, G., Peruzzini, M.: Sustainability and industry 4.0: definition of a set of key performance indicators for manufacturing companies. Sustainability **14**(17), 11004 (2022). https://doi.org/10.3390/su141711004

3. Peruzzini, M., Pellicciari, M., Grandi, F., Oreste Andrisano, A.: A multimodal virtual reality set-up for humancentered design of industrial workstations. Dyna Ing. E Ind. **94**(1), 182–188 (2019). https://doi.org/10.6036/8889
4. Kumar, N., Lee, S.C.: Human-machine interface in smart factory: a systematic literature review. Technol. Forecast. Soc. Change **174**, 121284 (2022). https://doi.org/10.1016/j.techfore.2021.121284
5. Papcun, P., Kajati, E., Koziorek, J.: Human machine interface in concept of industry 4.0. In: 2018 World Symposium on Digital Intelligence for Systems and Machines (DISA), Kosice, pp. 289–296 (2018). https://doi.org/10.1109/DISA.2018.8490603
6. Gorecky, D., Schmitt, M., Loskyll, M., Zuhlke, D.: Human-machine-interaction in the industry 4.0 era. In: 2014 12th IEEE International Conference on Industrial Informatics (INDIN), Porto Alegre RS, Brazil, pp. 289–294 (2014). https://doi.org/10.1109/INDIN.2014.6945523
7. Khamaisi, R.K., Prati, E., Peruzzini, M., Raffaeli, R., Pellicciari, M.: UX in AR-supported industrial human-robot collaborative tasks: a systematic review. Appl. Sci. **11**(21), 10448 (2021). https://doi.org/10.3390/app112110448
8. Nardo, M., Forino, D., Murino, T.: The evolution of man–machine interaction: the role of human in industry 4.0 paradigm. Prod. Manuf. Res. **8**(1), 20–34 (2020). https://doi.org/10.1080/21693277.2020.1737592
9. W. L. in R.-B. U. Experience: Nielsen Norman Group: UX Training, Consulting, & Research. Nielsen Norman Group. https://www.nngroup.com/. Accessed 07 Feb 2023
10. Norman, D.A.: The Design Everyday Things: Revised Expanded (2013)
11. Moggridge, A.: Designing Interaction, vol. 17 (2007)
12. Deng, L., Wang, G., Yu, S.: Layout design of human-machine interaction interface of cabin based on cognitive ergonomics and GA-ACA. Comput. Intell. Neurosci. **2016**, 1–12 (2016). https://doi.org/10.1155/2016/1032139
13. Villani, V., Sabattini, L., Loch, F., Vogel-Heuser, B., Fantuzzi, C.: A general methodology for adapting industrial HMIs to human operators. IEEE Trans. Autom. Sci. Eng. **18**(1), 164–175 (2021). https://doi.org/10.1109/TASE.2019.2941541
14. Grandi, F., Prati, E., Peruzzini, M., Pellicciari, M., Campanella, C.E.: Design of ergonomic dashboards for tractors and trucks: innovative method and tools. J. Ind. Inf. Integr. **25**, 100304 (2022). https://doi.org/10.1016/j.jii.2021.100304
15. Eaton: Concetti di interazione per le macchine di nuova generazione, p. 9 (2017)
16. Gazzetta ufficiale dell'Unione europea: DIRETTIVA 2006/42/CE DEL PARLAMENTO EUROPEO E DEL CONSIGLIO del 17 maggio 2006 relativa alle macchine e che modifica la direttiva 95/16/CE (rifusione) (Testo rilevante ai fini del SEE) (2006)
17. International Organization for Standardization (ISO). Emergency stop function - Requirements text. Geneva, Switzerland. Standard No. EN ISO 13850 (2015)
18. International Organization for Standardization (ISO). Machinery safety - Electrical equipment of machines - Part 1: General rules. Geneva, Switzerland. Standard No. EN 60204-1 (2018)
19. Adobe XD. https://helpx.adobe.com/it/support/xd.html. Accessed 08 Feb 2023

Meta-analysis Qualifying and Quantifying the Benefits of Automation Transparency to Enhance Models of Human Performance

Robert Sargent[1](✉), Brett Walters[1], and Chris Wickens[2]

[1] Huntington Ingalls Industries, 105 Technology Dr, Suite 190, Broomfield, CO 80021, USA
robert.sargent@hii-tsd.com

[2] Chris Wickens, 4303 Gemstone Lane, Ft. Collins, CO 80525, USA

Abstract. To enhance an existing human-automation interaction (HAI) framework associated with a human performance modeling tool, an extensive meta-analysis was performed on performance impacts of **automation transparency**. The main goal of this analysis was to gain a better quantitative understanding of automation transparency impacts on dependent variables such as trust in automation, situation awareness (SA), response times, and accuracy. The collective wisdom of multiple investigations revealed clear quantitative benefits of transparency in HAI, with the combined average effect sizes for response times, accuracy, SA, dependence, and trust ranging between 0.45 and 1.06 in performance improving directions. Mental workload was not significantly impacted by automation transparency.

These key findings indicate a need to consider automation transparency when evaluating the possible effectiveness of HAI on human-automation team (HAT) performance. The results will feed improvements to the existing HAI modeling framework, including more detailed transparency benefits caused by different moderator variables. Two of these main effects include; 1) when minimum transparency is imposed (and compared against a control condition), its benefit to accuracy is significantly less than when the level of transparency is increased (such as by adding confidence data), and 2) accuracy improvements are mostly applicable to normal task performance, while response time improvements are more applicable to automation failure response tasks.

Keywords: Automation Transparency · Human-Automation Interaction · Human Performance Modeling · Situation Awareness · Automation Failure

*The research was sponsored by the Army Research Laboratory and was accomplished under Cooperative Agreement Number W911NF-21-2-0280. The views and conclusions contained in this document are those of the authors and should not be interpreted as representing the official policies, either expressed or implied, of the Army Research Office or the U.S. Government. The U.S. Government is authorized to reproduce and distribute reprints for Government purposes notwithstanding any copyright notation herein.

M. Kurosu and A. Hashizume (Eds.): HCII 2023, LNCS 14011, pp. 243–261, 2023.
https://doi.org/10.1007/978-3-031-35596-7_16

1 Introduction

1.1 Background

In 2015, a team of Alion Science and Technology human factors engineers worked with NASA to create a Human-Automation Interaction (HAI) human performance modeling (HPM) framework and an associated algorithm (Sebok & Wickens, 2017). This framework included levels of automation assistance across different phases of automation, the expectancy of possible automation failures, the ability to script automation failures with different saliences during a modeled scenario, and an algorithm that applied an automation failure response time penalty to tasks based on these parameters. This framework and algorithm were built based on HAI research and new studies conducted with Colorado State University (Wickens, Clegg et al., 2015).

To enhance this HAI framework, new research* was conducted by the Alion (now HII Mission Technologies, Corp, a wholly owned subsidiary of Huntington Ingalls Industries, Inc., (HII MTC)) team to determine the effects of automation transparency on HAI team performance with a meta-analysis. The goals of this new research were two-fold; 1) to gain a better qualitative and quantitative understanding of possible automation transparency impacts on dependent variables such as trust in automation, task response times, and potential task errors, and 2) to add to the previously developed HAI HPM framework to include these possible automation transparency impacts.

1.2 Existing HAI HPM Framework and Algorithm

The current HAI HPM framework has several components that allow a modeler to represent an automated system and the human operator's use of that system. In addition to defining the system and possible automated modes of operation, the framework allows a modeler to add associated code in their model and apply an algorithm to modify task times for responses to automated system failures.

At the highest level, the modeler first defines the automated system, its function (or functions), and its modes of use. A notional example for an automobile system and driving function is shown in Fig. 1.

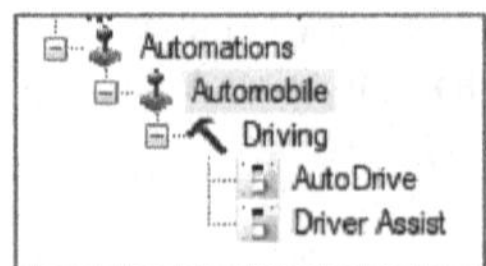

Fig. 1. Automated system, function, and mode of operation definition.

Next, for each possible mode of operation, the HAI framework allows the modeler to determine the level of automation (high, low, or manual) associated with each possible phase of automation assistance (Alert, Diagnose, Decide, Control; Parasuraman, Sheridan & Wickens, 2000). An example for possible Driving modes is shown in Fig. 2.

Automation Name: Automobile

Function Name: Driving

Mode	Alert	Diagnose	Decide	Control	Selected
AutoDrive	High Automation	High Automation	High Automation	High Automation	☑
Driver Assist	High Automation	High Automation	Low Automation	Manual	☐

Fig. 2. Levels of automation for phases of assistance.

This is also where a user selects which mode is being used for a particular set of model runs. The "AutoDrive" mode is selected in the example.

Subsequently, the HAI framework allows the user to define the expectancy for each possible automation system failure that may occur. The types of possible automation failures are pre-defined for each phase of automation assistance. The expectancy for the failures is either Unexpected or Expected. Unexpected failures may represent more reliable automation, more trust in automation, or both. Expected failures are those which result from inputs processed by automation known to be uncertain, like future weather conditions, sensing operations in visually degraded environments, or the use of automation by a user who has experienced its previous failures. In the example shown in Fig. 3, the only "Expected" failure associated with the different modes of operation and phases is a Wrong Decision associated with the AutoDrive mode. The gray cells represent manual operations, so automation failures do not apply.

Automation Name: Automobile

Function Name: Driving

Mode	Reliability									
	Alert			Diagnosis		Decision		Control		
	Gone	False Alarm	Miss	Gone	Wrong	Gone	Wrong	Gone	Catastrophic	Slow Failure
AutoDrive	Unexpected	Unexpected	Unexpected	Unexpected	Unexpected	Unexpected	Expected	Unexpected	Unexpected	Expected
Driver Assist	Unexpected	Unexpected	Unexpected	Unexpected	Unexpected	Unexpected	Unexpected	Unexpected	Unexpected	Unexpected

Fig. 3. Expectancy of possible automation system failures.

Finally, the user can script different automation failures to occur. Every possible failure for the mode selected is available to script. In the example in Fig. 4, a Wrong Decision is scripted to occur 10 min into the simulation. Another key component of the HAI framework is the **salience** of the scripted failures. It can be None, Low, or High (as in the example shown).

Mission Criteria | SPRINT Properties

Automation Failures

Automation Mode	Activate Failure	Failure Start Time	Failure Type	Failure Salience
Automobile / Driving / AutoDrive	True	00:10:00.00	Decision Making - Wrong	High

Fig. 4. Interface to script automation failures.

Most logic associated with the HAI components defined above is input into a human performance model with tasks and code logic (such as decision path logic) mapped to the interfaces above. For example, an operator may perform fewer tasks when high levels of automation across different phases are applied. They may also have different task recovery paths that need to be taken when automation failures occur. Each input entered into the interfaces above can be accessed by a modeler with code to build necessary model tasks and logic to represent the use of any automation mode and responses to different automation failures.

There is one built-in algorithm in the HAI HPM that impacts task performance for tasks as selected by the modeler, the automation failure cost. This cost is computed based on 3 factors; 1) the level of automation associated with the failed mode across every phase (higher automation, higher cost, greater time degradation), 2) the level of trust in the automation based on how expected or unexpected each possible automation failure is (high trust, or more "Unexpected" failures, higher cost, greater time degradation), and 3) the level of salience of the scripted automation failure that occurred (lower salience, higher cost, greater time degradation). These three factors result from numerical values derived from each HAI setting, divided by constants that make each factor equally impactful. These values are also based upon human-in-the-loop simulations and reviews of HAI research (Sebok & Wickens, 2017; Onnasch et al., 2014).

The primary goal of the current project was to find statistically significant data to inform an expansion of the HAI HPM modeling framework and associated algorithm described above to include impacts of **automation transparency (ATP)**. In the following section, we address the impacts of transparency specifically to understand what transparency is and does. We first present a more general influence-model of human-automation interaction, within which automation transparency influences can be represented.

1.3 An Influence Model of Human-Automation Team (HAT) Performance

Humans are interacting with increasingly complex and powerful automation tools, on the battlefield (Mercado, Rupp et al., 2016; Warden et al., 2022; Mifsud et al., 2022) as well as in other complex, safety critical environments (Chiou & Lee, 2021). Multiple factors determine the efficacy of what we here label the HAT, of which we argue that the actual **performance** (speed and accuracy of the team on the specific automation-supported task) is most important. Other cognitive factors such as workload and situation awareness (SA) are vital as well, as are mediating variables such as trust and dependence. In the following, we lay out the causal influences of these variables, as influenced by three vital properties of any automated system; its **reliability**, its **degree of automation (DOA)** and, the focus of the current research, its **ATP**. These causal influences are shown by blue solid and the red dashed arrows in Fig. 5, where blue represents a positive (i.e., increasing) effect, and red a negative (i.e., decreasing) one. In the figure, the three key automation properties are shown on the left. Human cognitive components are depicted by the green ovals in the center of the figure, and performance outcomes, for both routine tasks associated with an automated system and failure recovery tasks, are shown in the purple box to the right.

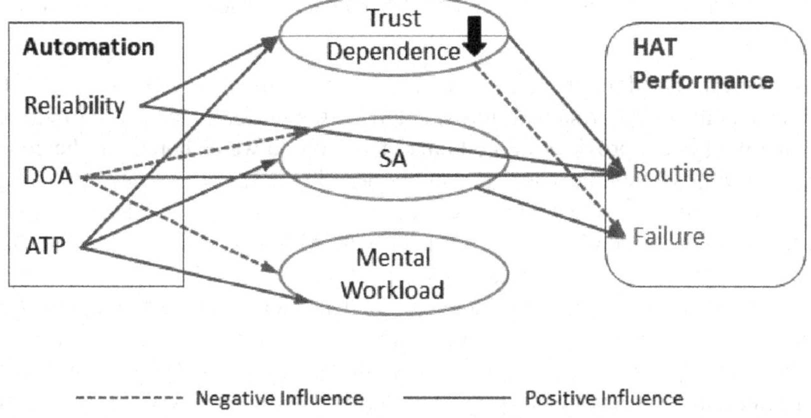

Fig. 5. Influence of 3 key automation properties on human cognition and HAT performance.

Reliability. Automation reliability is a critical attribute of any automation tool. Most artificial intelligence (AI) tools, like decision, detection or diagnostic aids will commit occasional errors when asked to perform in complex uncertain environments. These errors may be described as "expected" failures in the context of the model presented earlier. Its most direct effect is on increasing the trust in/dependence on the automation system (trust and dependence are related but not identical). Reliability then has two influences on HAT performance. First, to the extent that automation performance is better than that of the unaided human, greater reliability will directly improve HAT performance. Second, to the extent that a more trusting human will depend on and therefore use the automation more frequently, routine HAT performance will also increase with increased dependence on the automated system. But with more dependence, through a combination of less monitoring and loss of skill, the human will deal **less fluently** with an automation failure.

Degree of Automation. DOA is a concept that was developed concurrently by Kaber, Onal, and Endsley (2000), and Parasuraman, Sheridan and Wickens (2000) that describes the degree of cognitive and motor "work" supported by, or sometimes replaced by, automation systems. The formal influences of a higher DOA described here are based on a meta-analysis conducted by Onnasch et al. (2014). Assuming that the automation is well designed, reliable, and therefore used (depended on) by the human, then a higher DOA should produce better HAT performance when automation is functioning well (routine). Also, by doing more "work," a higher DOA will, almost by definition, reduce (negative influence) human mental workload. But at the same time, a higher DOA will also decrease SA, because, with a higher DOA, the human can pay less attention to what the more powerful automation is doing (Sebok & Wickens, 2017). Thus, effects of higher DOA on both SA and mental workload are indicated by the red dashed arrows in Fig. 5. It is at this point we note, and experimental data bear out (Onnasch et al., 2014) that increased SA will improve the fluency of the human response in case of an automation failure. The human will be better able to jump back into the loop. Hence the **decrease** in

SA resulting from a higher DOA can have a negative influence on the failure response performance.

Transparency. The third property of automation, a feature of the interface, rather than the functionality of the system, and the focus of the current paper is the **degree of APT** that the system provides to the human user. While we elaborate on the concept in the following section, here we can simply describe it as the presented information that provides the user with a better mental model of what the automation is doing and why. As Fig. 5 shows, almost by definition, ATP will increase SA (and hence the fluency of failure response performance); but increased ATP is also assumed (and found) to raise the level of trust in, and therefore dependence on, the automation, hence degrading failure response as well. Note then the two offsetting effects of transparency on failure performance. Finally, transparency, almost always implemented by offering added information to read, or displays to interpret, will be likely to increase mental workload.

The net influences of these factors, the model proposed in Fig. 5, provides some important predictions. For example, the joint influences of DOA on performance that is both routine (mediated by dependence) and failure (mediated by SA) predicts a tradeoff between these two types of performance as DOA is increased. This phenomenon referred to as the "Lumberjack effect" (Sebok & Wickens, 2017), meaning the higher the "tree" (higher DOA), the harder it falls when the "trunk" breaks (representing the automation failure in this analogy). A second important joint effect involves the counteracting influences of automation transparency and DOA on mental workload. The third effect is the offsetting influences of transparency on failure response. When such offsetting influences exist, it is difficult to predict in advance which one may dominate.

2 Focus on Automation Transparency

In this paper, we summarize a meta-analysis of the benefits of automation transparency to human-automation interaction, evaluating a set of 81 studies encapsulated in 49 reports that have either compared transparency to a control condition without it, or have compared higher levels of transparency with lower levels.

Many definitions have been offered of transparency, and we use here definitions offered by Lee and See (2004); transparency *communicates information about the automated system to allow operators to form an appropriate mental model and develop appropriate levels of trust.* More recently, Bhaskara et al. (2020) propose that transparency may allow operators to use automation more accurately and efficiently by facilitating their understanding of the reasoning underlying automation recommendations, and what they should expect to happen if they were followed.

In the past two decades of research on HAI, transparency has been proposed as a solution to the out-of-the-loop unfamiliarity problem, as transparency here has often been assumed to increase SA of what the system is doing and why. Hence, in the context of Fig. 5, it should increase trust in the automated system during all operations and, with better SA, and should also increase the fluency of human intervention should automation unexpectedly fail (Sebok & Wickens, 2017). It is also reasonable to assume that the increased trust should engender increased dependence on automation and, given that automation typically performs a task better than the human, such an increase would lead to better performance of the HAT. This would be applicable under both routine task and automation failure recovery circumstances and performance is expressed in both speed and accuracy measures.

While individual studies of transparency over the past few decades have generally revealed significant benefits, and recent reviews of the literature (e.g., Mueller et al., 2019; Van de Merwe et al., 2022; Wickens, Helton et al., 2021) have concluded its overall benefits to HAT performance and SA, to date there appears to be no meta-analyses that quantify these benefits across the various measures of the effectiveness of the human-automation system. Hence, the primary research questions driving our work reported here are that the meta-analysis will reveal the quantitative benefits of automation transparency for performance, failure recovery, SA, trust, dependence, and workload. As described above, such quantitative estimates can provide inputs to computational models that predict the benefits of automation.

3 Method

For this effort, a meta-analysis was used to assess research concerning the effects of ATP on HAT performance. We started our analysis by searching articles in the journals Human Factors and the Proceedings of the Human Factors and Ergonomics Society Annual Meeting with automation transparency as the key search term. After the initial list of articles was collected, the references for each article were reviewed to identify other appropriate studies. We also reviewed the studies that cited each of the articles in our list (as noted by the ResearchGate website) to identify additional relevant studies. A total of 224 articles were identified and reviewed. We initially identified 104 studies that had compared transparency with a control condition in which the same automation system was employed to assist human performance on the same task. We only included studies in our analysis that had assessed some measure of performance (speed/response time (RT) and/or accuracy/error rate (ER)), and for such studies we also included any data on SA, trust, dependence, and mental workload. In addition, articles were only included in our analysis if they reported effect sizes using Cohen's d or provided enough information from which to calculate effect sizes using Cohen's d. A total of 49 articles from our initial list met these criteria. Some of these articles reported on multiple experiments that were deemed relevant for our analysis, and a total of 81 studies were included in our analysis from these 49 articles. These articles are highlighted with an * in the Reference section of this paper.

Statistical data were extracted from each study to quantify an effect size (Cohen's *d*) for each independent comparison between a control and a transparency condition (either repeated measures or between-subjects), and these were then both aggregated and separated by key moderating variables as described below (Cohen, 1988). To be consistent with the sign of our effect sizes, those studies that reported results for accuracy were reversed to represent ER (although a reported decrease in ER had a negative statistical significance, it was a positive performance outcome). Similarly, a decrease in RT was also a positive performance outcome. For those studies that examined multiple levels of automation transparency (e.g., no transparency, low transparency, and high transparency), separate effect sizes were calculated when the data were available between adjacent levels of transparency (i.e., no transparency versus low, or "**imposed**" at some level, transparency; and low or imposed transparency versus **increased** levels of transparency such as explanatory information and/or confidence data). As data from each article was entered into our database, they were tagged based on when the ATP was presented to participants (offline, such as in training prior to system use, versus online or "real time" presentation during system use), how the ATP was presented (graphics, text), whether raw data were provided to the participant in the experiment, if an ATP explanation was provided to participants, if automation reliability (or confidence in data presented) was provided to the participants, and if the performance measured was related to routine task performance or an automation failure response. When a t-test was used to derive Cohen's *d*, we assured that 1-tailed t values were used and provided by the author. Finally, we did not implement any different weightings for the effect sizes across the studies.

Measures of SA were only included if they used more objective accuracy scales such as the situation awareness global assessment technique (SAGAT), rather than subjective self-rating scales, such as the situation awareness rating technique (SART).

4 Results

The combined effect sizes from all the studies were averaged to determine if ATP influenced the six dependent variables: accuracy (assessed ER, negative values indicate a positive impact on performance), speed (assessed by RT, negative values indicate a positive impact on performance), trust, dependence (transparency increases the chance that an automated system will be used effectively), mental workload (lower mental workload may be positive), and SA. If the mean effect sizes were at least two standard errors (2SE) away from 0, then the results were considered significant.

Table 1 provides the mean effect sizes, number of studies included (N), standard deviation (SD), standard error (SE), and 2SE values for these comparisons. For ER, the results revealed a significant transparency benefit ($p < .05$), with a large mean effect size of 0.99. For RT, a significant transparency benefit was obtained ($p < .01$), with a medium mean effect size of 0.53. For trust, there was a significant transparency benefit ($p < .01$), with a large mean effect size of 0.81. For SA, there was a significant transparency benefit ($p < .01$) with a large mean effect size of 1.06. No significant effect was found for ATP on mental workload (effect size was 0.15). The combined mean effect sizes are also shown in Fig. 6 for comparative purposes.

In deriving conclusions about the two moderator variables, there are two parallel paths that can be taken. One is to simply carry out *t*-tests between the two different levels of the moderator variable, using the effect size from each individual study as a raw data point for the *t*-test. This path has the disadvantage that if there are only a very small number of studies (e.g., two) contributing to one or both levels of the moderator variable, this will greatly diminish the statistical power of the comparison. Yet such a diminishing may be unwarranted, or unduly pessimistic, if this small number consists of studies with large differences between the two levels or a large number of study participants. Hence, the alternative approach is to simply compare the mean level of

Table 1. Descriptive statistics of the meta-analysis by dependent variable.

Dependent Variable	Mean Effect Size (MES)	N	SD	SE	2SE
ER	**−0.99** *	31	2.54	0.46	0.91
RT	**−0.53** *	48	1.22	0.18	0.35
Trust	**0.81** *	42	0.88	0.14	0.27
Dependence	**0.45** *	45	1.27	0.19	0.38
Workload	−0.15	28	1.25	0.24	0.47
SA	**1.06** *	18	1.57	0.37	0.74

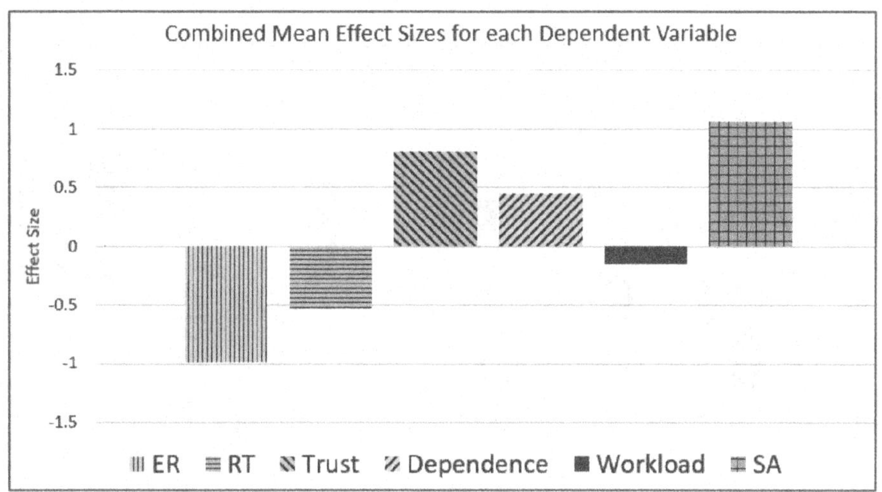

Fig. 6. Combined mean effect sizes for each dependent variable.

effect sizes between the two levels, and if this difference is large, we conclude that there remains strong evidence for a difference, regardless of the significance of the t-value of the difference between levels of the moderator variable. We adopt both approaches below.

Table 2 shows the effect sizes of transparency benefits for **routine** task performance as compared to situations in which automation unexpectedly **fails** (here note the small N for some of the dependent variables, such as ER). Similarly, Fig. 7 graphically compares the mean effect sizes for each dependent variable for routine tasks versus automation failure recovery tasks.

While the standard *t*-test comparisons revealed that there were no differences between routine and failure responses in any of the dependent variables, many of these null results reflected the low statistical power of the comparison as described above (e.g., for ER, there were only two such studies). If we take the second approach, considering the differences of the mean effect size, and use the standard classification of effect sizes as being small ($d = 0.2$–0.5), medium ($d = 0.5$–0.8) and large ($d > 0.8$) we see that, for

Table 2. Comparison of all dependent variables for routine tasks versus failure recovery.

Dep Var	Routine Tasks					Failure Recovery				
	MES	N	SD	SE	2SE	MES	N	SD	SE	2SE
ER	**−1.02**	29	2.53	0.47	0.94	**−.44**	2	0.79	0.56	1.12
RT	**−0.41**	36	1.07	0.18	0.36	**−0.90**	12	1.58	0.46	0.92
Trust	**0.72**	35	0.69	0.12	0.24	**1.12**	7	1.66	0.63	1.26
Dep	**0.22**	30	0.99	0.18	0.36	**0.92**	15	1.64	0.42	0.84
Wkld	**0.01**	23	1.11	0.23	0.46	**−0.92**	5	1.70	0.76	1.52
SA	**1.11**	14	1.75	0.47	0.94	**0.88**	4	0.78	0.39	0.78

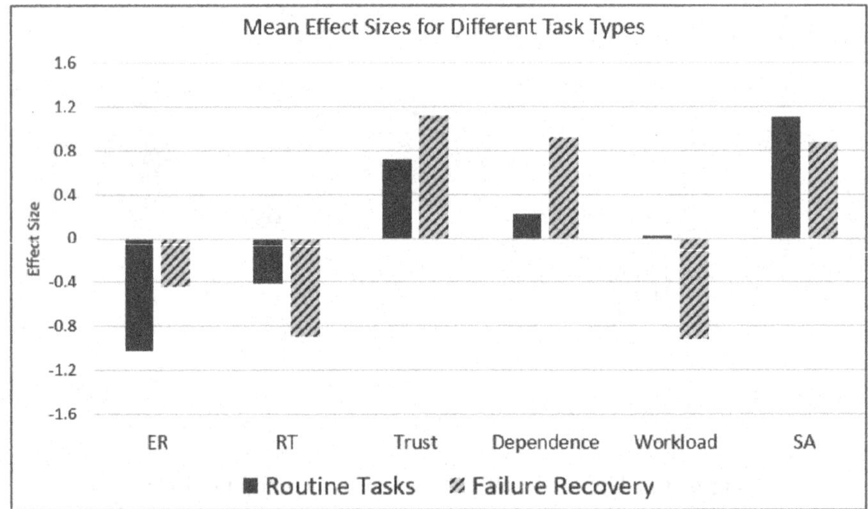

Fig. 7. Mean effect sizes for each dependent variable for different task types.

ER there is a large effect size benefit of transparency for routine performance, but only a small benefit for failure recovery performance. For RT the relationship is reversed; the transparency benefit for failure responses is large, and that for routine performance is small. A corresponding greater advantage of transparency in unexpected than routine conditions is also observed for trust, dependence, and workload reduction. For SA, the benefits of transparency are equally large for both task types.

Table 3 shows the equivalent data for the effects of the moderator variable that categorizes whether the transparency benefit was between a low transparency condition and a control, versus between a high and a lower transparency condition (i.e., level of transparency). Here it was found that, for ER, the benefits of transparency were significantly more with **Increasing** ATP ($M = -1.51$, $SD = 3.15$) than **Imposing** ATP ($M = -0.18$, $SD = 0.36$). Benefits of transparency were roughly equivalent for imposing and increasing ATP for RT, trust, and dependence. There were only small benefits for either comparison for workload. Prominently, for SA, there was a large benefit for imposing some form of transparency ($d = 1.4$), but only a small benefit for increasing its level. The data is summarized graphically in Fig. 8.

Table 3. Comparison of all dependent variables for imposing transparency versus increased levels of transparency.

Dep Var	Imposing Transparency					Increasing Transparency				
	MES	N	SD	SE	2SE	MES	N	SD	SE	2SE
ER	**−0.18**	12	0.36	0.10	0.21	**−1.51**	19	3.15	0.72	1.44
RT	**−0.45**	30	1.28	0.23	0.47	**−0.66**	18	1.13	0.27	0.53
Trust	**0.80**	19	1.07	0.24	0.49	**0.82**	23	0.72	0.15	0.30
Dep	**0.52**	33	1.29	0.22	0.45	**0.25**	12	1.24	0.36	0.72
Wkld	**−0.33**	13	1.52	0.26	0.52	**0.00**	15	1.01	N/A	N/A
SA	**1.40**	12	1.72	0.50	0.99	**0.36**	6	0.99	0.41	0.81

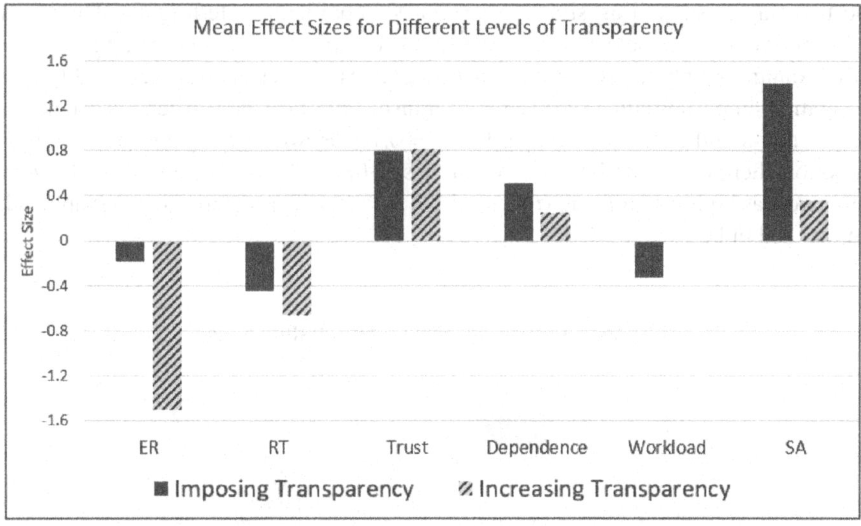

Fig. 8. Mean effect sizes for each dependent variable for different levels of transparency.

Our comparison between whether transparency was offered on-line, during HAT task performance versus off-line, via instructions of how automation worked, was thwarted because of very small (<3) N's in most variables for off-line studies versus very high N's associated with ATP online studies. Those variables that did have adequate N's in both groups yielded no difference in transparency benefits for either RT or dependence. For SA there was a very large benefit when transparency was offered offline, by way of instructions ($d = 3.5$), but only a medium benefit when offered online ($d = 0.74$). Offline versus online information data is summarized in Table 4.

Table 4. Comparison of all dependent variables for offline ATP information versus online APT information.

Dep Var	Offline Information					Online Information				
	MES	N	SD	SE	2SE	MES	N	SD	SE	2SE
ER	**−0.45**	1	0.00	0.00	0.00	**−1.08**	28	2.66	0.50	1.00
RT	**−0.49**	5	1.60	0.72	1.44	**−0.54**	40	1.25	0.20	0.40
Trust	**0.56**	1	0.00	0.00	0.00	**0.78**	40	0.94	0.15	0.30
Dep	**0.54**	7	0.61	0.23	0.46	**0.41**	37	1.37	0.23	0.46
Wkld	**N/A**	0	N/A	N/A	N/A	**−0.15**	28	1.25	0.24	0.48
SA	**3.56**	2	0.24	0.17	0.34	**0.74**	16	1.36	0.34	0.68

Our final comparison was based on the stage of information processing or system control assisted by automation, one of the two key components defining degree of automation, (the other being level of automation within a stage). To make this comparison we collapsed the original four phases proposed by Parasuraman et al. (2000) into two stages; supporting situation awareness (combining Alerting and Diagnosis) and supporting action selection and execution (combining decision making and control). Examining only the two performance variables, the RT analysis revealed that for automation supporting situation awareness, transparency provided no benefit, and indeed a small, non-significant cost of longer RT ($d = 0.18$). However, for automation supporting action, there was an RT benefit of medium size ($d = -0.50$). The difference between these two was highly significant ($t(42) = 3.39, p < .01$). This comparison is graphically summarized in Fig. 9.

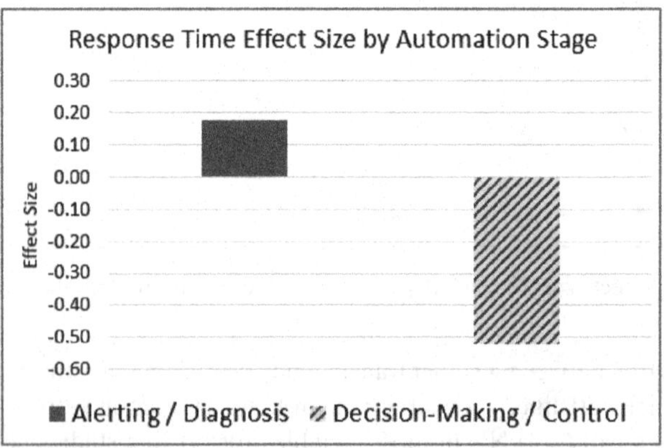

Fig. 9. Response time effect size by high level automation stage.

For ER, the difference in transparency support was even more dramatic. For automation phases supporting situation awareness, there was no benefit of introducing transparency (d = −0.08). But for action support automation the benefit was large ($d = -0.80$). This difference in benefit was also significant ($t(28) = 2.94$, $p < .01$). This comparison is graphically summarized in Fig. 10.

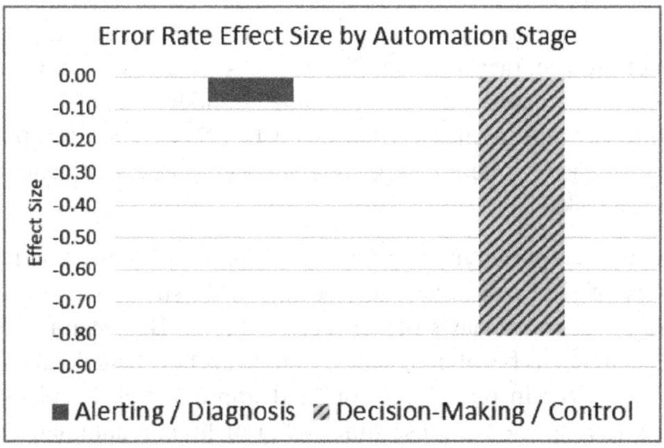

Fig. 10. Error rate effect size by high level automation stage.

In summary, independent of how much early versus late stage automation helps HAT performance as a whole, adding or increasing transparency to that automation is very beneficial for late stage automation, but less so for early stage automation.

5 Discussion

5.1 Review and Interpretation of the Effects

The collective wisdom of multiple investigations reveals clear quantitative benefits to transparency in HAI, with the combined average effect sizes for speed, accuracy, situation awareness, dependence and trust ranging between 0.45 and 1.06 in performance improving directions. Only the main independent variable of mental workload did not show a significant improvement, and this intuitively makes sense. Increasing transparency may increase workload required to process additional information, which may offset other mental workload reduction associated with the increased ability to perform tasks due to ATP assistance. All major dependent variable p values and combined effect sizes are summarized below:

- *Accuracy, assessed by ER*: The results revealed a significant transparency benefit (p < .05). Mean effect size = −0.99.
- *Speed, assessed by RT*. A highly significant transparency benefit (p < .01).
- Mean effect size = −0.53.
- *Dependence:* A highly significant transparency benefit (p < .01). Mean effect size = 0.45.

- *Trust:* A highly significant transparency benefit ($p < .01$). Mean effect size = 0.81.
- *Situation Awareness*. Highly significant transparency ($p < .01$). Mean effect size = 1.06.
- *Mental Workload*. No significant effect. Mean effect size = −0.15.

In addition to these main effects, two contrasts between the size of transparency benefits caused by different moderator variables revealed significant differences.

1. When minimum transparency was imposed (and compared against a control condition), its benefit to accuracy was significantly less ($p < .05$) than when the level of transparency was increased (such as by adding confidence data).
2. Accuracy improvements (as measured inversely by ER) were mostly applicable to normal task performance, while RT improvements were more applicable to automation failure response tasks.

The meta-analysis reported in the current study produced important results of value to the community of HAI researchers and designers. First, it confirms, quantitatively, assertions made in several reviews of the literature (e.g., Bakhshara et al., 2020) that automation transparency is beneficial, and also confirms how beneficial it is, as reflected by the large effect sizes in reducing errors and improving SA, and by the medium effect size in shortening the response times (RT) of human-automation transactions. Such quantification is important both to validate the importance of efforts to incorporate transparency in new automation aid designs, but also, as described below, to provide inputs to quantitative computational models, including those associated with models of human performance.

The benefits to increasing trust, and therefore often increasing dependence, may be seen as somewhat of a two-edge sword. On the one hand, increasing dependence will lead to increased performance (both speed and accuracy, the latter a large effect) to the extent that automation is highly reliable. However, on the other hand, it will degrade the automation failure response. In the context of the influence model presented in Fig. 5, we see this tradeoff played out; transparency is predicted to improve both kinds of performance as mediated by its large benefits to SA. But regarding automation failure recovery performance the benefits to ER are reduced (only a medium effect), because of the offsetting penalty of increased dependence when things go wrong – the so-called automation bias (Parasuraman & Manzey, 2010).

The influence model can also explain the only minimal benefits of transparency to decreasing workload. Here again, any online transparency will impose some level of added workload demands required to perceive and interpret the transparency information, an imposition which could, and apparently did, offset whatever benefits are conferred by making the task "easier," as transparency is designed to do. In this context it should be noted that extremely complex or poorly implemented transparency information may be ignored entirely, producing no benefit.

Finally, the influence model can predict the differential benefits of transparency by the phase or stage of automation to which it is applied (Figs. 9 and 10). With later stage automation, there is more that can go wrong (since late-stage automation also typically depends on the functioning of earlier stage automation) and hence transparency has a greater benefit in "cushioning the fall" of the taller tree, offsetting the effect of increasing transparency on increasing dependence.

5.2 Implications for the HAI Model

We will add interfaces to the human performance model HAI framework described in Sect. 1.2 that allow a user to represent the presence of automation transparency associated with different automated systems, functions, modes, and phases of automation assistance. This will range from "no transparency," to the display of raw data showing what the automation is doing, to a higher level of automation transparency that can include components explaining how and why the automation is performing its actions, as well as possible uncertainty data associated with its conclusions.

As we found while building the initial HAI plug-in, defining large, sweeping performance algorithms that impact tasks times and/or accuracies may not always be possible. Code will become available associated with the transparency inputs to allow a human performance modeler to uniquely build models representing transparency for a system they are modeling. For example, the presence of uncertainty data (a form of transparency) may cause an operator to be more likely to use the automation for decision making (or increase their dependence, or reliance and compliance, on the automation). This will be easier to model with the settings and variables provided by the automation framework.

Similar to the HAI framework automation failure cost algorithm already built-in to a HPM environment and discussed in Sect. 1.2, the results of this meta-analysis will help to inform more discrete human performance model task modification algorithms associated with automated systems and levels of automation transparency. For example, higher levels of automation transparency may improve the performance of some tasks in specified amounts (such as by percentage improvements over baseline values) in either times or accuracy. This could apply to normal HAT tasks being performed during an associated scenario or responses to automation failures.

References

Please note that references with an asterisk were included in the meta-analysis. Not all references included in the meta-analysis are explicitly called out in this paper.

* Antifakos, S., Kern, N., Schiele, B., Schwaninger, A.: Towards improving trust in context-aware systems by displaying system confidence. In: Proceedings of the 7th Conference on Human-Computer Interaction with Mobile Devices and Services, Austria, pp. 9–14 (2005)

* Bass, E.J., Baumgart, L.A., Shepley, K.K.: The effect of information analysis automation display content on human judgment performance in noisy environments. J. Cogn. Eng. Decis. Mak. **7**, 49–65 (2013)

* Bean, N.H., Rice, S.C., Keller, M.D.: The effect of gestalt psychology on the system-wide trust strategy in automation. Proc. Hum. Factors Ergon. Soc. **55**(1), 1417–1421 (2011)

* Beller, J., Heesen, M., Vollrath, M.: Improving the driver-automation interaction: an approach using automation uncertainty. Hum. Factors **55**(6), 1130–1141 (2013)

Bhaskara, A., Skinner, M., Loft, S.: Agent transparency: a review of current theory and evidence. IEEE Trans. Hum.-Mach. Syst. **50**(3), 215–224 (2020)

* Chen, T., Campbell, D., Gonzalez, L.F., Coppin, G.: Increasing autonomy transparency through capability communication in multiple heterogeneous UAV management. In: 2015 IEEE/RSJ International Conference on Intelligent Robots and Systems (IROS), Hamburg, Germany, pp. 2434–2439 (2015)

Chiou, E.K., Lee, J.D.: Trusting automation: designing for responsivity and resilience. Hum. Factors **65**(1), 137–165 (2023)

Cohen, J.: Statistical Power Analysis for the Behavioral Sciences, 2nd edn. Erlbaum (1988)

* Cramer, H., et al.: The effects of transparency on trust in and acceptance of a content-based art recommender. User Model. User-Adapt. Interact. **18**(5), 455–496 (2008)

* Detjen, H., Salini, M., Kronenberger, J., Geisler, S., Schneegass, S.: Towards transparent behavior of automated vehicles: design and evaluation of HUD concepts to support system predictability through motion intent communication. In: Proceedings of the 23rd International Conference on Mobile Human-Computer Interaction, vol. 19, pp. 1–12. Association for Computing Machinery, New York (2021)

* Dikmen, M., Li, Y., Ho, G., Farrell, P., Cao, S., Burns, C.: The burden of communication: effects of automation support and automation transparency on team performance. In: Proceedings of the 2020 IEEE International Conference on Systems, Man, and Cybernetics (SMC), Canada, pp. 2227–2231 (2020)

* Dorneich, M.C., et al.: Interaction of automation visibility and information quality in flight deck information automation. IEEE Trans. Hum.-Mach. Syst. **47**, 915–926 (2017)

* Du, N., et al.: Look who's talking now: implications of AV's explanations on driver's trust, AV preference, anxiety and mental workload. Transp. Res. Part C Emerg. Technol. **104**, 428–442 (2019)

* Forster, Y., Hergeth, S., Naujoks, F., Krems, J.F., Keinath, A.: What and how to tell beforehand: the effect of user education on understanding, interaction and satisfaction with driving automation. Transp. Res. Part F: Traffic Psychol. Behav. **68**, 316–335 (2020)

* Göritzlehner, R., Borst, C., Ellerbroek, J., Westin, C., van Paassen, M.M., Mulder, M.: Effects of transparency on the acceptance of automated resolution advisories. In: IEEE International Conference on Systems, Man, and Cybernetics (SMC), pp 2965–2970 (2014)

* Guznov, S., et al.: Robot transparency and team orientation effects on human–robot teaming. Int. J. Hum.-Comput. Interact. **36**(7), 650–660 (2020)

* He, D., Kanaan, D., Donmez, B.: In-vehicle displays to support driver anticipation of traffic conflicts in automated vehicles. Accid. Anal. Prev. **149**, 105842 (2021)

* Helldin, T.: Transparency for future semi-automated systems: effects of transparency on operator performance, workload and trust (ISBN 978-91-7529-020-1). Master's thesis. Örebro University, SE-70182 Örebro, Sweden (2014)

* Hussein, A., Elsawah, S., Abbass, H.: The reliability and transparency bases of trust in human-swam interaction: principles and implications. Ergonomics **63**(9), 1116–1132 (2020)

Kaber, D.B., Onal, E., Endsley, M.R.: Design of automation for telerobots and the effect on performance, operator situation awareness, and subjective workload. Hum. Factors Ergon. Manuf. **10**(4), 409–430 (2000)

* Kluck, M., Koh, S.C., Walliser, J.C., de Visser, E.J., Shaw, T.H.: Stereotypical of us to stereotype them: the effect of system-wide trust on heterogeneous populations of unmanned autonomous vehicles. Proc. Hum. Factors Ergon. Soc. Ann. Meet. **62**(1), 1103-1107 (2018)

* Koo, J., Kwac, J., Ju, W., Steinert, M., Leifer, L., Nass, C.: Why did my car just do that? Explaining semi-autonomous driving actions to improve driver understanding, trust, and performance. Int. J. Interact. Des. Manuf. **9**, 269–275 (2015)

* Krake, A., et al.: Effects of training on learning and use of an adaptive cruise control system (Technical Paper). SAE (2020)

* Kunze, A., Summerskill, S.J., Marshall, R., Filtness, A.J.: Automation transparency: Implications of uncertainty communication for human-automation interaction and interfaces. Ergonomics **62**(3), 345–360 (2019)

Lai, F., Macmillan, J., Daudelin, D., Kent, D.: The potential of training to increase acceptance and use of computerized decision support systems for medical diagnosis. Hum. Factors **48**(1), 95–108 (2006)

Lee, J.D., See, J.: Trust in automation and technology: designing for appropriate reliance. Hum. Factors **46**(1), 50–80 (2004)

* Loft, S., et al.: The impact of transparency and decision risk on human-automation teaming outcomes. Hum. Factors (2021)

* Mercado, J., Rupp, M., Chen, J., Barnes, M., Barber, D., Procci, K.: Intelligent agent transparency in human-agent teaming for multi-UxV management. Hum. Factors **58**(3), 401–415 (2016)

* Meteier, Q., et al.: The effect of instructions and context-related information about limitations of conditionally automated vehicles on situation awareness. In: Proceedings of the 12th International Conference on Automotive User Interfaces and Interactive Vehicular Applications (2020)

Mifsud, D., Wickens, C., Maulbeck, M., Crane, P., Ortega, F.: The effectiveness of gaze guidance lines in supporting JTAC's attention allocation. In: Proceedings of 66th Annual Meeting the Human Factors and Ergonomics Society. Sage Press (2022)

Mueller, S.T., Hoffman, R.R., Clancey, W., Emrey, A., Klein, G.: Explanation in human-AI systems: a literature meta-review, synopsis of key ideas and publications, and bibliography for explainable AI (Technical Report). Florida Institute for Human and Machine Cognition (2019). https://apps.dtic.mil/sti/citations/AD1073994

* Olatunji, S., Oron-Gilad, T., Markfeld, N., Gutman, D., Sarne-Fleischmann, V., Edan, Y.: Levels of automation and transparency: interaction design considerations in assistive robots for older adults. IEEE Trans. Hum.-Mach. Syst. **51**(6), 673–683 (2021)

Onnasch, L., Wickens, C., Li, H., Manzey, D.: Human performance consequences of stages and levels of automation: an integrated meta-analysis. Hum. Factors **56**(3), 476–488 (2014)

* Panganiban, A.R., Matthews, G., Long, M.D.: Transparency in autonomous teammates: intention to support as teaming information. J. Cogn. Eng. Decis. Mak. 14(2), 174–190 (2020)

Parasuraman, R., Manzey, D.H.: Complacency and bias in human use of automation: an attentional integration. Hum. Factors **52**(3), 381–410 (2010)

Parasuraman, R., Sheridan, T.B., Wickens, C.D.: A model of types and levels of human interaction with automation. IEEE Trans. Syst. Man Cybern. **30**(3), 286–297 (2000)

Rajabiyazdi, F., Jamieson, G.A., Guanolusia, D.Q.: An empirical study on automation transparency (i.e., seeing-into) of an automated decision aid system for condition-based maintenance. In: Black, N.L., Neumann, W.P., Noy, I. (eds.) IEA 2021. LNNS, vol. 223, pp. 675–682. Springer, Cham (2022). https://doi.org/10.1007/978-3-030-74614-8_84

* Rayo, M., Kowalczyk, N., Liston, B., Sanders, E., White, S., Patterson, E.: Comparing the effectiveness of alerts and dynamically annotated visualizations (DAVs) in improving clinical decision making. Hum. Factors **57**(6), 1002–1014 (2015)

* Roth, G., Schulte, A., Schmitt, F., Brand, Y.: Transparency for a workload-adaptive cognitive agent in a manned-unmanned teaming application. IEEE Trans. Hum.-Mach. Syst. **50**(3), 225–233 (2020)

* Rovira, E., Cross, A., Leitch, E., Bonaceto, C.: Display contextual information reduces the costs of imperfect decision automation in rapid retasking of ISR assets. Hum. Factors **56**(6), 1036–1049 (2014)

Sebok, A., Wickens, C.D.: Implementing lumberjacks and black swans into model-based tools to support human-automation interaction. Hum. Factors **59**(2), 189–202 (2017)

* Selkowitz, A., Lakhmani, S., Chen, J.Y., Boyce, M.: The effects of agent transparency on human interaction with an autonomous robotic agent. Proc. Hum. Factors Ergon. Soc. Annu. Meet. **59**(1), 806–810 (2015)

* Selkowitz, A.R., Lakhmani, S.G., Larios, C.N., Chen, J.Y.C.: Agent transparency and the autonomous squad member. Proc. Hum. Factors Ergon. Soc. Annu. Meet. **60**(1), 1319–1323 (2016)

* Seong, Y., Bisantz, A.M.: The impact of cognitive feedback on judgment performance and trust with decision aids. Int. J. Ind. Ergon. **38**(7), 608–625 (2008)

* Seppelt, B.D., Lee, J.D.: Making adaptive cruise control (ACC) limits visible. Int. J. Hum.-Comput. Stud. **65**, 192–205 (2007)

* Shull, E., Gaspar, J., McGehee, D., Schmitt, R.: Using human-machine interfaces to convey feedback in automated driving. J. Cogn. Eng. Decis. Making **16**(1) (2022)

* Skraaning, G., Jamieson, G.: Human performance benefits of the automation transparency design principle: validation and variation. Hum. Factors **63**(3), 379–410 (2021)

* Stowers, K., Kasdaglis, N., Newton, O., Lakhmani, S., Wohleber, R., Chen, J.: Intelligent agent transparency: the design and evaluation of an interface to facilitate human and intelligent agent collaboration. Proc. Hum. Factors Ergon. Soc. Annu. Meet. **60**(1), 1706–1710 (2016)

* Stowers, K., Kasdaglis, N., Rupp, M.A., Newton, O.B., Chen, J.Y., Barnes, M.J.: The IMPACT of agent transparency on human performance. IEEE Trans. Hum.-Mach. Syst. **50**(3), 245–253 (2020)

* Trapsilawati, F., Wickens, C., Chen, H., Qu, X.: Transparency and automation conflict resolution reliability in air traffic control. In: Tsang, P., Vidulich, M., Flach, J. (eds.) Proceedings of the 2017 International Symposium on Aviation Psychology. Wright State University, Dayton, OH (2017)

* unknown author. Trust in automation as a function of transparency and teaming. Proc. Hum. Factors Ergon. Soc. Annu. Meet. **63**(1), 78–82 (2019)

Van de Merwe, K., Mallam, S., Nazir, S.: Agent transparency, situation awareness, mental workload and operator performance: a systematic literature review. Hum. Factors 1–29 (2022)

* Verhagen, R.S., Neerincx, M.A., Tielman, M.L.: The influence of interdependence and a transparent or explainable communication style on human-robot teamwork. Front. Robot. AI (2022)

* Wang, N., Pynadath, D.V., Hill, S.G.: Trust calibration within a human-robot team: comparing automatically generated explanations. In: Proceedings of the 2016 ACM/IEEE International Conference on Human-Robot Interaction, pp. 109–116 (2016)

Warden, A.C., Wickens, C.D., Mifsud, D., Ourada, S., Clegg, B.A., Ortega, F.R.: Visual search in augmented reality: effect of target cue type and location. Proc. Hum. Factors Soc. Annu. Meet. **66**(1), 373–377 (2022)

* Westin, C., Borst, C., Hilburn, B.: Automation transparency and personalized decision support: air traffic controller interaction with a resolution advisory system. IFAC-PapersOnLine **49**, 201–206 (2016)

Wickens, C.D., Clegg, B.A., Vieane, A.Z., Sebok, A.L.: Complacency and automation bias in the use of imperfect automation. Hum. Factors **57**(5), 728–739 (2015)

Wickens, C., Helton, W., Hollands, J., Banbury, S.: Engineering Psychology and Human Performance, 5th edn. Taylor & Francis (2021)

* Wohleber, R.W., Stowers, K., Chen, J.Y.C., Barnes, M.: Conducting polyphonic human-robot communication: mastering crescendos and diminuendos in transparency. In: Cassenti, D., Scataglini, S., Rajulu, S., Wright, J. (eds.) Advances in Simulation and Digital Human Modeling. Advances in Intelligent Systems and Computing, vol. 1206, pp. 10–17. Springer, Cham (2020). https://doi.org/10.1007/978-3-030-51064-0_2

* Wright, J.L., Chen, J.Y.C., Barnes, M.J., Hancock, P.A.: Agent reasoning transparency's effect on operator workload. Proc. Hum. Factors Ergon. Soc. Annu. Meet. **60**(1), 249–253 (2016)

* Wright, J.L., Chen, J.Y.C., Barnes, M.J., Hancock, P.A.: The effect of agent reasoning transparency on complacent behavior: an analysis of eye movements and response performance. Proc. Hum. Factors Ergon. Soc. Annu. Meet. **61**(1), 1594–1598 (2017)
* Wright, J.L., Lee, J., Schreck, J.A.: Human-autonomy teaming with learning capable agents: performance and workload outcomes. In: Wright, J.L., Barber, D., Scataglini, S., Rajulu, S.L. (eds.) Advances in Simulation and Digital Human Modeling, vol. 264. Springer, Cham (2021). https://doi.org/10.1007/978-3-030-79763-8_1
* Zhang, W., Feltner, D., Kaber, D.B., Shirley, J.: Utility of functional transparency and usability in UAV supervisory control interface design. Int. J. Soc. Robot. **13**(7) (2021)
* Zhang, Y., Wang, W., Zhou, X., Wang, Q.: Tactical-level explanation is not enough: effect of explaining AV's lane-changing decisions on drivers' decision-making, trust, and emotional experience. Int. J. Hum.-Comput. Interact. (2022)

A Review of Human-Computer Interface Evaluation Research Based on Evaluation Process Elements

Xintai Song[1(✉)], Minxia Liu[1], Lin Gong[1,2], Yu Gu[3], and Mohammad Shidujaman[4]

[1] School of Mechanics and Vehicles, Beijing Institute of Technology, Beijing, China
1433626140@qq.com
[2] Yangtze River Delta Research Institute (Jiaxing), Beijing Institute of Technology, Beijing, China
[3] China Railway Test & Certification Center Limited, Beijing, China
[4] Department of Computer Science and Engineering, Independent University, Dhaka, Bangladesh
Shantothusets@iub.edu.bd

Abstract. As an important medium for human-computer information exchange, the human-computer interface (HCI) plays an important role in the human-computer-environment system that cannot be ignored. A friendly design of HCI not only enables operators to complete operation tasks efficiently, but also has the characteristics of simplicity, beauty, easy operation and low load. Therefore, how to evaluate the friendliness of HCI design and how to judge whether the evaluation process is scientific and reasonable has become an important issue in current HCI-related research. Starting from the elements of HCI evaluation process, this paper firstly summarizes and analyzes the representative evaluation purposes in HCI evaluation research, specifically including interface usability, visual performance, interface aesthetics, suitability for special people, mental load, and evaluation exploratory research, and points out the guiding role of evaluation purposes in HCI evaluation activities; Secondly, this paper categorizes and summarizes the construction of HCI evaluation index system, determination of evaluation index weights, and selection of evaluation methods involved in HCI evaluation research from the perspective of research methods, and analyzes the advantages and disadvantages of each method in conjunction with specific HCI evaluation research; Finally, by analyzing and summarizing the research literature, this paper finds that the following problems exist in HCI evaluation research: the evaluation indexes are too abstract, the objectivity and rationality of the evaluation process need to be improved, and the feedback guidance of evaluation results on HCI design needs to be improved. This paper also points out that the future research trends of HCI evaluation research are as follows: the research target will be more inclined to the HCI of mobile touch devices, the selection of evaluation indexes needs to be more specific, the evaluation process requires researchers to pay more attention to objectivity and rationality, and the evaluation results can be better used to optimize the HCI design.

M. Kurosu and A. Hashizume (Eds.): HCII 2023, LNCS 14011, pp. 262–289, 2023.
https://doi.org/10.1007/978-3-031-35596-7_17

Keywords: HCI Evaluation · Evaluation Purpose · Index System · Index Weight · Evaluation Method

1 Introduction

As an important medium for human-computer information exchange, the human-computer interface (HCI) plays an irreplaceable role in the human-computer-environment system. For the computer, the HCI provides a control vehicle to convey the manipulator's target intention, and also gives feedback to the controller on the result of the computer executing the manipulator's will; for the human, the controller has to manipulate the computer through the HCI on the one hand, and accept the information feedback from the computer to adjust the control content continuously on the other hand, so that both sides circle and repeat until the final goal of the controller is achieved. Therefore, the design of HCI has become an important content of ergonomic design. HCI design refers to the design of the controller, the display and the relationship between the two sides, including the design of the traditional physical interface with separate display and control, but also the design of the display and control of the interactive display interface, such as websites, mobile phone applications, etc. A well-designed HCI can provide a friendly and pleasant control environment to help users achieve their personal goals efficiently, and will also meet the needs of human emotional experience and provide a good user experience. However, there are still some unreasonable aspects in the existing HCI design, which have some influence on the HCI process. Therefore, how to evaluate whether the HCI design is scientific, reasonable, efficient and beautiful has become a problem worth studying.

This paper takes HCI evaluation as the main research object, summarizes and analyzes the content and research status of the evaluation objectives, evaluation index system, index weights, evaluation methods and other elements in the HCI evaluation process at home and abroad, and finally summarizes the problems and development trends of HCI evaluation.

2 Human-Computer Interface Evaluation Purpose

In HCI evaluation research, clear evaluation purpose is the beginning of conducting evaluation research work, and evaluation purpose directly affects the construction of the index system, the selection of evaluation methods, and other subsequent major evaluation process elements, so it is important to first clarify the evaluation objectives and make it clear which aspects of the research object are to be evaluated. In the existing HCI evaluation studies, the evaluation purposes (see Fig. 1) mainly include interface usability, visual performance, interface aesthetics, suitability for special people, mental load, and evaluation exploratory research, etc.

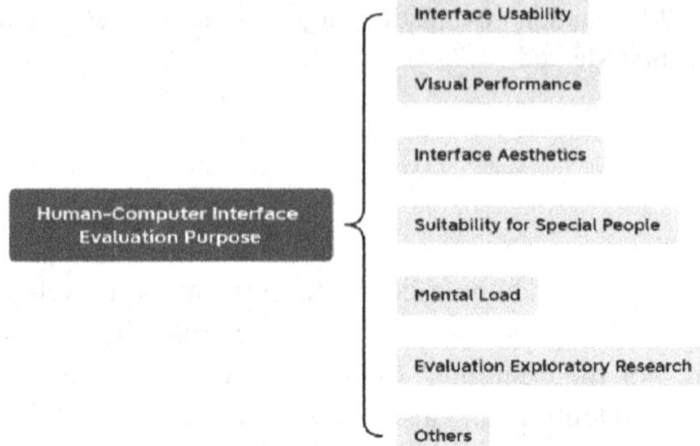

Fig. 1. Human-computer interface evaluation purpose relation figure.

2.1 Interface Usability

In 1998, the International Organization for Standardization (ISO) defined usability as "the effectiveness, efficiency and satisfaction of a product in specific use environment". Specifically, effectiveness can be measured by the accuracy and completeness of a given purpose; efficiency can be measured by the cost of resources (e.g., time and effort) required to achieve the purpose; and satisfaction can be measured by the consistency of the user's physical sensations, personal perceptions and emotional responses with personal needs and expectations [1–27]. The concept of usability has also been extended by different researchers, such as Nielsen, who extended usability to cover five characteristics: efficiency, satisfaction, learnability, memorability, and error rate [28].

In the research with usability as the main research purpose, different scholars have proposed various usability evaluation indexes and methods by combining the specific characteristics of the research object. Madureira et al. constructed the human-computer interaction flow by the GOMS model and applied it to the usability evaluation of adaptive web interface and fixed interface, and concluded that the adaptive user interface is more comfortable than the fixed interface, but the evaluation process was vague in its description of usability [19]. Zhu et al. addressed the problem of inefficient use of medical applications, took visual indexes, human-computer interaction indexes, and user behavior indexes as evaluation features from the perspective of user experience, and clearly proposed a usability evaluation index system covering 11 impact factors in combination with usability evaluation theory, and gave usability evaluation suggestions for medical applications [8]. Bessghaier et al. experimentally evaluated four hybrid applications for problems in performance, usability and security of hybrid mobile user interfaces, during which a predefined list of 13 structural usability defects aggregated from the literature was used, and finally created a usability defect library of hybrid application examples for better identification of hybrid application human-computer interaction with usability defects during human-computer interaction of hybrid applications [21]. At present, interface usability evaluation is the direction that scholars pay more attention to in HCI evaluation research, but at the same time, the fundamental research on interface usability lacks unified theoretical support, for example, the definitions of interface usability by different scholars are not exactly the same, and there are fewer usability-related empirical standards, which rely more on scholars' personal experience, and the overall research direction is more inclined to specific applications, and usability evaluation still needs further development.

2.2 Visual Performance

In human-computer-environment system, the vast majority of information to be conveyed is to be carried out visually. Therefore, many scholars in the field of HCI evaluation evaluate HCI from a visual perspective by studying the interface layout, interface color scheme, interface suitability, and visual characteristics of the human eyes [29–33].

Liu et al. established a visual information flow ergonomics evaluation system based on visual information flow ergonomics, and evaluated the interface suitability of the HCI [29]. Wang et al. established an ergonomics evaluation model based on the spatial characteristics of the human eyes from four aspects: visual distance, viewing angle, horizontal and vertical field of view, and evaluated the degree of matching between the HCI and visual characteristics, and then realized the evaluation of the operational efficiency of equipment operators [30]. Gao et al. constructed visual experimental samples by combining user research with the PCCS color system, and used gray clustering to cluster the samples and evaluate the color matching of the HCI [31]. Riegler et al. evaluated the visual complexity of mobile application interaction interfaces by performing analytical calculations on the visual appearance of applications, and concluded that there was a significant correlation between complexity calculation metrics and usability through user research. In these studies, although there are some differences in the specific research objectives, in general, they all take interface visual performance as the main research purpose, and compared to usability evaluation, it goes deeper into the object of study and provides a visual and perceptible analysis of the object of study in relation to its characteristics, which is an important feature that distinguishes HCI evaluation from other abstract contents evaluation such as system evaluation.

2.3 Interface Aesthetics

Along with the development of perceptual engineering, the aesthetic value of HCI begin to be gradually emphasized by research scholars, who begin to pay attention to the user's emotional experience and visual aesthetic brought by HCI, to study the influencing factors of interface aesthetics, and to link interface aesthetics with interface layout characteristics, and aesthetic measurement and evaluation become an important element in the study of interface aesthetics [34–44].

In terms of quantitative evaluation of interface aesthetics, Ngo et al. extracted 13 interface layout features to quantify the aesthetic value of the HCI and linearly weighted them to achieve the quantitative calculation of the overall aesthetic value of HCI, and obtained the conclusion that the degree of balance, continuity and overall degree contributed the most to the calculation of the aesthetic value of the HCI by T-testing the results of 57 different interface data, which became an important reference source for many aesthetic evaluation studies, but the quantitative calculation of the overall aesthetic value of the HCI is not very convincing due to the large number of extracted features, the complexity of the calculation, and the fact that only simple linear weighting is used between different feature relationships [34]. From the perspective of user experience, Zhou et al. extracted 12 aesthetic evaluation indexes with the balance, simplicity, proportion and echo of the interface as the main influencing factors of user aesthetic experience, and calculated the beauty of the design scheme by using gray correlation analysis, and achieved a comprehensive evaluation of the aesthetic value of the HCI, but the three indexes under each main influencing factor were assigned the same weight, which made the reasonableness of the comprehensive evaluation need to be further verified [35]. Zhang et al. extracted four aesthetic evaluation indexes, namely, balance, unity, simplicity and wholeness, and calculated the weights of the evaluation indexes by using hierarchical analysis, which realized a more reasonable distribution of index weights, and then achieved a comprehensive aesthetic evaluation of the layout of the HCI elements [36]. Li et al. analyzed the aesthetic value of the interface from the perspective of aesthetic cognition, extracted six influencing factors affecting the aesthetic value of the interface by using factor analysis, and used the variance contribution rate of each factor as the weight, and realized the calculation of the comprehensive aesthetic value of the HCI by combining with TOPSIS method [43].

2.4 Suitability for Special People

As an important part of the human-computer-environment system, people play an irreplaceable role in the process of Human-computer interaction. Therefore, the design of HCI should fully consider the user characteristics, pay attention to the user experience, and reflect the principle of human-centeredness. In the evaluation of HCI, besides studying whether the user experience of HCI is good and whether the interface design takes into account the user characteristics, we will also pay special attention to the special groups faced by HCI - elderly and sick groups, and study whether the interface design fully considers the use of special people [14, 23, 45–48].

Yang et al. addressed the problem of inefficient operation of the navigation interface of the intervention application for children with autism, and evaluated six navigation interfaces through a comprehensive evaluation method based on hierarchical analysis-entropy weight method, and screened out the optimal solution, which to some extent improved the intervention effect of enhancing the intervention application for children with autism, but the combination of the autistic children in the process of analysis was not sufficient and lacked the group of users' characteristics to be considered [45]. From the perspective of the special user group of elderly, Allah et al. analyzed the process of recording elderly in using the web search interface by means of systematic usability scale evaluation and user observation, and concluded through data T-test analysis that elderly preferred to use Google rather than Bing, and obtained some usability problems in the use process, which provided valuable feedback to designers [23].

2.5 Mental Load

With the continuous development of information technology and the increasing level of machine informatization, the amount of information conveyed in the process of human-computer interaction is gradually increasing. In the process of HCI design, if the information needs of manipulators are ignored or the information provided to manipulators is inconsistent with the human ability to process and use information, it may lead to excessive mental load on manipulators, which then has a negative impact on personnel manipulation performance or safety, etc. Negative effects.

Rakhra et al. used a user-centered design approach to redevelop a high-fidelity prototype of the farm machinery interface to address the problems in the design of the farm machinery interface, such as not focusing on user experience, and conducted a comparative evaluation with the original interface design through questionnaires and other means, and concluded that the mental load of the operators of the new interface was reduced by 19.7%, but most of the participants in the experiment of this paper were not experienced farm machinery operators, and the experimental conclusion was not so convincing [49]. Chen et al. developed a fuzzy comprehensive evaluation model of the user interface of nuclear power plants based on the mental load of the operators of nuclear power plants and achieved a valid comprehensive assessment of the mental load of the user interface design based on multiple factors, but again the experimental participants were all students and could not accurately reflect the changes in the mental load of the operators of nuclear power plants [50]. Li et al. used user performance, subjective ratings and EDA measurements to assess the mental load of smartphone users, and obtained the experimental conclusion that task duration, number of usability errors, psychological demands, effort and frustration were significantly related to mental load, and the experimental process divided the subjects into novice, average and skilled users, and the experimental participants were highly compatible with the group of smartphone users, which enhanced the persuasive power of the experimental findings [51].

2.6 Evaluation Exploratory Research

There is also a class of exploration of some fuzzy unknown findings related to interface design by means of interface evaluation in HCI evaluation, which can be broadly classified into two types: one studies the problem of HCI layout [52–55], the other studies the problem of the relationship between eye movement indexes and HCI evaluation [56].

By recording and analyzing the eye-movement data of 35 subjects performing the icon search task, Zhou et al. concluded that the interface laid out according to the principle of functional grouping has the shortest search time, the least number of fixation points and sweeps, the shortest scan path and the smallest fixation scatter, achieving the quantitative data support for the principle of functional grouping [54]. Wang et al. recorded the changes of eye-movement data of subjects in data search experiments in three different interfaces by an eye-movement instrument and compared them with subjective evaluations to obtain five eye-movement indexs that can be used for usability evaluation of HCI [56].

In addition to the six types of HCI evaluation objectives mentioned above, there are other studies with the objectives of interface reliability, etc. Although the objectives of the various types of studies are different, all of these studies clearly identify the evaluation purposes and determine the direction in which the evaluation work should be carried out. Therefore, for HCI evaluation, the first task must be to first identify clear evaluation purpose, which is a fundamental guideline for the evaluation work to be carried out [57].

3 Human-Computer Interface Evaluation Index System

When evaluating HCI, it is usually necessary to consider the influence of various factors, some of which are independent of each other and some of which are related to each other, and some of which have a great influence on the evaluation purpose while some of which have an average influence on the evaluation purpose. Therefore, evaluators need to screen multiple factors, analyze their degree of relevance to the evaluation objectives, and form a HCI evaluation index system that serves the evaluation objectives.

Due to the diversity of researchers' personal evaluation purposes and needs, the specific process of establishing the HCI evaluation index system usually has a strong subjective color. Many scholars will establish the HCI evaluation index system based on their own experience or literature analysis, but when faced with more complex problems relying on personal experience or existing literature will often fail to effectively solve them, so some scholars introduce mathematical methods to establish the HCI evaluation index system, such as factor analysis, cluster analysis, etc. In addition, due to the HCI evaluation research is oriented to the specific perceivable object of research, many scholars also establish the HCI evaluation index system through user research, HCI analysis, human-computer interaction analysis, etc. This has also become an important feature that distinguishes HCI evaluation research from other evaluation research (see Fig. 2).

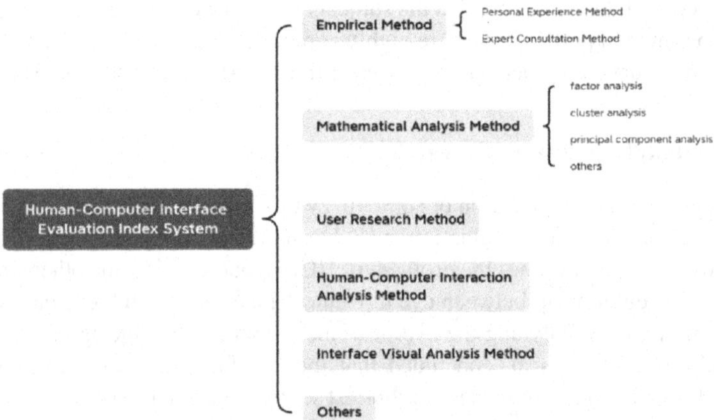

Fig. 2. Human-computer interface evaluation index system construction method relation figure

3.1 Empirical Method

Empirical method refers to the method that evaluators use relevant theoretical knowledge and personal or expert experience to construct the HCI evaluation index system according to the evaluation objectives, HCI characteristics, user characteristics, human-computer interaction process, etc. According to whether the evaluation process involves experts in the field other than the evaluator, the empirical method can be subdivided into the personal experience method and the expert consultation method.

Personal Experience Method. It refers to the method in which the evaluator personally uses personal practical experience combined with norms and related theories to determine the HCI evaluation index system, and in this process, the evaluator also draws on the ideas of some other methods for index analysis, such as commonly using the idea of hierarchical analysis in AHP to differentiate the indexes [32, 58, 59]. Ma et al. drew on the idea of hierarchical analysis to take the matching optimization of the human-computer interaction soft interface of the automobile cab as the target layer of the research content, and the matching optimization of the automobile instrument panel, central control display, functional equipment and the whole soft interface as the criterion layer of the judgment matrix to establish a reasonable HCI evaluation index system of the automobile cab [32]. Lin et al. used the idea of hierarchical analysis to divide the evaluation indexes into three categories of functional, technical and emotional indexs, and further refined and constructed a multi-level mobile game interface evaluation index system [58].

Expert Consultation Method. It is a method of constructing a HCI evaluation index system by consulting experts in the field and drawing on their considerable expertise and experience. In the 1950s, the American RAND corporation proposed the Delphi method in order to achieve better qualitative predictions by combining the process of consulting experts with multiple rounds of feedback and programming [60]. The essence of Delphi method is that the evaluator designs a questionnaire based on the HCI and user characteristics and evaluation purposes, consults several experts in the field and conducts statistical analysis, and gives the results to the experts anonymously until the experts' opinions converge and a stable HCI evaluation index system is obtained. Due to the features of Delphi method such as anonymity, inter-round feedback and statistical analysis of results, it has been more widely used in the process of complex system evaluation and analysis [20, 61–63]. Cui et al. used the classical Delphi method to invite 30 experts to conduct a questionnaire survey to establish a usability user interface evaluation system for mobile games in a simple and quick way [20]. Due to the different levels of experts, the classical Delphi method does not effectively distinguish, and it is easy to cause the opinions of experienced experts to be ignored, which leads to the reduction of the scientificity of the established evaluation index system, therefore, some scholars have improved the classical Delphi method and increased the weight of experts, which effectively makes up for the shortcomings of the classical Delphi method, for example, Song et al. selected 15 pilots with multiple aircraft flying experience as experts, based on the typical Delphi method, applied expert consensus, considered expert weights, and established a three-level evaluation index system for HCI in fighter aircraft cockpits, which effectively improved the shortcomings of the classical Delphi method [63].

3.2 Mathematical Analysis Method

Mathematical analysis method refers to the method of using mathematical methods to analyze the correlation between indexes in a known set of evaluation indexes, and then determine the HCI evaluation index system. Commonly used methods include factor analysis, cluster analysis, principal component analysis, etc.

Based on users' perceptual needs for HCI, Yuan et al. obtained a preliminary evaluation index set through user research, followed by Likert scale analysis of the interface samples, extracted four user perceptual demand influence factors using principal component analysis, and clustered the perceptual vocabulary around these four user perceptual demand influence factors to establish a HCI perceptual demand evaluation index system [64]. Zhu et al. screened 24 CNC machine tool interface samples through on-site research and literature review, conducted Likert scale analysis on the interface samples, extracted four immersion influence factors with eigenvalues greater than 1 using principal component analysis, and clustered the indexes based on the four influence factors to establish a CNC machine tool HCI immersion evaluation index system [65]. Li et al. extensively collected HCI of various products and screened them to obtain 33 words reflecting the aesthetic image characteristics of the interface, and then used Likert scale to obtain data and conduct factor analysis to extract six interface factors from the 33 image words and establish an evaluation index system of HCI aesthetics [43].

3.3 User Research Method

User research method refers to the method that takes users as the center, through questionnaires and user interviews, to familiarize with user operation habits and cognitive characteristics, clarify user needs, and then build a HCI evaluation index system. User research method embodies the user-centered design concept, emphasizes the user experience perspective, focuses on the embodiment of user needs in the design, and the research process is user-oriented and the evaluator is guided, which is direct and clear, so it has been favored by many scholars.

However, in the research process, the choice of users and the judgment of good or bad interface given by individual users are crucial, and users will be influenced by many subjective factors, which on the one hand requires the evaluator to have sufficient background research on the HCI before the user research, to filter out enough indexes for several users to choose or to ask questions that can fully explore the diverse needs of users, and on the other hand requires the evaluator to select representative high-quality users. Zhou et al. selected medical personnel with education level mainly of bachelor's degree who used this software for questionnaire survey and established medical HCI usability evaluation index system by combining emotional data analysis for medical software interface usability problem [12]. Zhao et al. took remote control clearing vehicle HCI experience metric as the evaluation purpose, divided user experience into three aspects of ease of use, emotional experience, and conveyance from the physical-emotional-cognitive perspective, selected a group of 30 people containing interface designers, operators, and engineers for questionnaire evaluation, and obtained the corresponding evaluation index system. Both of the above-mentioned scholars screened the HCI users and constructed a more reasonable HCI evaluation index system under the study of a small number of user samples [66].

3.4 Human-Computer Interaction Analysis Method

The human-computer interaction analysis method refers to the method of constructing a HCI evaluation index system by viewing the HCI evaluation from the perspective of human-computer-environment system and analyzing the human-computer interaction process involved in the research object by applying the basic theory of ergonomics about human, machine and environment. Ergonomic engineering is a discipline based on the physiological and psychological characteristics of human to study the interaction and interconnection of human, machine and environment to improve the human-computer-environment system, and the study of human physiological and psychological characteristics, environment and human-computer interaction can be used to construct a complete and scientific HCI evaluation index system [67–71].

Rao et al. decomposed the process of human-machine interaction between the driver and the train into two categories: normal driving and emergency handling, and decomposed each category from the interface device layer and the human action layer respectively, and established a train driving HCI evaluation index system based on human-machine interaction of the driver, but it ignored that the human-computer system is affected by environmental factors, and the integrity of the index system needs to be strengthened [69]. Li et al. studied in depth the respective performance of human, machine and environment in the human-computer-environment system in which the manned submersible is located, and established a HCI evaluation index system for manned submersible with human, machine and environment as the middle layer, but the interaction between the three and their coordination were ignored in the index system [71]. Song analyzed the human and computer factors involved in the software interaction process from the perspective of the human-machine-environment system as a whole, and took into account the coordination of the human-computer-environment, and established a more complete HCI evaluation index system, which effectively encapsulated each evaluation index [70]. In addition, the human-computer interaction analysis method can also be effectively integrated with other methods so as to meet the research focus of different research scholars. For example, Sun et al. combined the human-computer interaction analysis method with user research and divided the HCI evaluation index system into interface layer, operation layer, and demand layer, which both analyze the spacecraft software human-computer interaction process and reflect user needs, and after the completeness, dispersion and other index tests, the system also satisfies the evaluation requirements in a comprehensive and complete manner [67].

3.5 HCI Visual Analysis Method

The interface visual analysis method is a method to quickly construct an HCI index system by analyzing the visual elements of the computer HCI. Since the method only targets the interface for visual hierarchical analysis, without considering complex factors such as users and human-machine-environment system, which is relatively simple and fast, and requires relatively low knowledge reserve of the evaluator, and at the same time, specific perceptible HCI evaluation indexes can be obtained, it has also gained the attention of some scholars [72–75]. For example, Qiu et al. established a cab HCI evaluation index system based on the type of agricultural equipment cab components and characteristic parameters, realized a comprehensive evaluation of the cab HCI through fuzzy comprehensive evaluation and virtual interaction subjective evaluation, and developed a virtual ergonomics design and evaluation system for agricultural equipment cabs accordingly, and in this process since the development and implementation of the design and evaluation system is the main content, the process of evaluation model establishment only considers the visual model that can be calculated metrically, although the evaluation model is not complete, it does not need to consider some complex and difficult to collect and calculate factors such as the user's subjective feelings, human-machine-environment system, etc., and achieves a rapid evaluation of the agricultural equipment cab on the visual level [75].

In addition to the above methods, some scholars have introduced perceptual engineering [64], quality model [26, 40, 76, 77], information flow [29], IPO model [9], factor analysis [43] and other theories, all of which have also established a reasonable HCI evaluation index system and enriched the ways of establishing index system.

4 Human-Computer Interface Evaluation Index Weight

After the HCI evaluation index system is constructed, in order to reflect the degree of contribution of each index to the evaluation purpose in the overall context, each index must be assigned a certain weight factor, i.e. index weight. Index weight is a measure of the relative importance of each index in the set of indexes in the overall indexes [78]. For the same evaluation index system, using different weight coefficients, the evaluation results will often be very different or even completely opposite, so it is necessary to reasonably determine the HCI evaluation index weights.

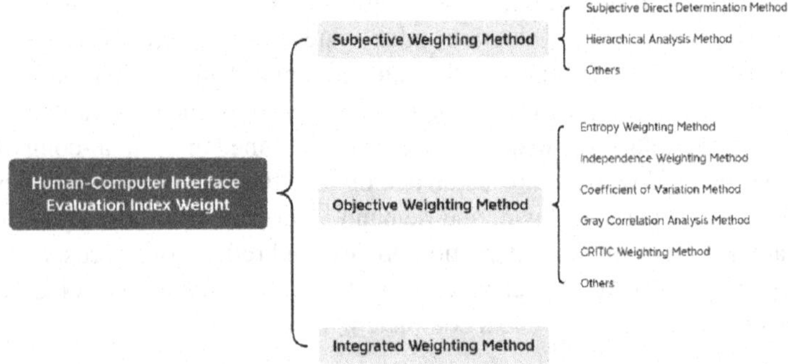

Fig. 3. Human-computer interface evaluation index weight construction method relation figure

In HCI evaluation, the methods for determining index weights can be broadly classified into three categories: subjective weighting method, objective weighting method, and comprehensive weighting method (see Fig. 3).

4.1 Subjective Weighting Method

Subjective weighting method refers to the method of determining the weight of indexes based on the evaluator's or expert's subjective judgment of the importance of evaluation indexes in relation to the evaluation objectives, including the subjective direct determination method and the hierarchical analysis method. The subjective weighting method can intuitively reflect the subjective judgment of the evaluator or expert and reflect the knowledge and needs of the evaluator or expert on the issue under study, but since the results are based on subjective judgment, there may be a certain degree of arbitrariness, and the reasonableness of the results may be limited by the lack of certain knowledge and practical experience of the evaluator or expert.

Subjective Direct Determination Method. In the subjective weighting method, the simplest method is to be determined directly by the evaluator or expert subjectively, and this method is mostly seen in the early stage of the HCI evaluation research where the index weight determination method is not perfect, for example, Zhang et al. set the weights directly for a management information system user interface evaluation index and used gray correlation analysis to get the advantages and disadvantages of three different solutions to verify the feasibility of using gray system theory in HCI evaluation, the paper is obviously not reasonable enough for the treatment of weights [79]. Wang et al. considered that the methods of determining index weight coefficients such as hierarchical analysis are too complicated and not convenient enough, and introduced the five-level scalar assignment method to determine HCI evaluation index weights, which is based on the qualitative judgment of evaluators or experts on the importance of indexes, transformed into fixed values, and normalized to obtain weight coefficients, and finally applied to HCI quality evaluation. Compared with the previous paper, this method reduces the subjective arbitrariness of the evaluator or expert and avoids the excessive intervention of some inexperienced evaluators on the index weights, but also limits the input of the expert's knowledge and practical experience on the importance of the indexes [80].

Hierarchical Analysis Method. Determining index weights by using hierarchical analysis method refers to the establishment of a system hierarchy, quantifying the importance of different indexes at the same level in terms of their impact on the evaluation purposes at the upper level to obtain a judgment matrix, and further determining the index weights. By decomposing the research object into the hierarchical structure of the system through hierarchical analysis and quantifying the subjective feelings of the evaluator or expert with a certain scale, it makes an initial combination of qualitative and quantitative methods, thus clearly and explicitly determining the weight coefficients [7, 13, 31, 36–38, 40, 44, 55, 59, 61, 63, 66, 70, 72, 76, 81–86]. Ding et al. compared the elements of the same level under a certain criterion in the established HCI evaluation index system two by two separately, used the 1–9 level scale method to construct the judgment matrix and calculate its maximum characteristic roots and orthogonal eigenvectors, and obtained the index weight coefficients after the consistency test [83].

However, the application of hierarchical analysis to arrive at reasonable index coefficients is based on the consistency of the judgment matrix meeting the requirements, but the actual situation is often not ideal, the judgment matrix is often not a consistency matrix, and the only criterion for applying the reasonableness test of hierarchical analysis is the consistency of the judgment matrix, in the actual application, there may be cases where multiple "reasonable" weighting factors are established for the same problem, and since the hierarchical analysis method needs to carry out two-by-two comparison of all indexes, the effect of the solution for multi-index problems is not ideal. Therefore, some scholars, in response to the above problem, changed the procedure of two-by-two comparison of all indexes to first sorting all indexes and then judging the importance of adjacent indexes, which avoids the problem of inconsistency in the judgment matrix and at the same time reduces the calculation volume and expands the scope of application [5, 87]. For example, Liu et al. ranked the importance of smart rice cooker ergonomics evaluation indexes and assigned values to adjacent indexes to obtain more reasonable index weight coefficients, and since the importance ranking between indexes was done in the first place, the process did not require further index consistency testing [5].

4.2 Objective Weighting Method

Objective weighting method refers to the method of determining the weight coefficients of indexes by calculating the degree of difference of each index in the HCI evaluation index system as a whole and the degree of influence on other indexes in the HCI evaluation index system, including entropy weighting method, independence weighting method, coefficient of variation method, gray correlation analysis method, CRITIC weighting method, etc. The objective weighting method no longer requires the evaluator or expert to judge the importance of index, and it determines the index coefficients directly according to the amount of information contained in the data of each index, which avoids the influence of the subjective arbitrariness of the evaluator or expert on the weighting, but sometimes the weight coefficients obtained may also be contrary to the subjective needs of the evaluator, and since it completely relies on the index data, for different data samples under the same index system, the output index coefficients may vary for different data samples under the same index system. Therefore, the objective weighting method is often used in combination with the subjective weighting method because it relies entirely on index data.

Entropy Weighting Method. Entropy weighting method is a method to calculate the information dispersion degree of each index through information entropy and then obtain the weight coefficient of the index. If the information entropy value of an index is smaller, the greater the degree of data dispersion it contains, the more information it contains, the greater its contribution to the whole HCI evaluation index system, and the higher the weight it takes up [10, 88–90]. Wang et al. obtained the index weight coefficients by calculating the information entropy value of engineering project organization interface evaluation indexes, which is applied to the multi-level gray evaluation of engineering project organization interface, which better fits the characteristics of small amount of data and uncertainty of engineering project organization interface evaluation [90]. Liu et al. determined the objective weights of HCI reliability evaluation indexes through the improved entropy weighting method and TOPSIS method, used the improved hierarchical analysis method to determine the subjective weights of HCI reliability evaluation indexes, and combined the two to comprehensively assign weights to the indexes, which not only effectively avoided the influence of too many subjective factors on the weighting, but also fully exploited the information in the evaluation data and improved the objectivity and accuracy of the weight data of evaluation indexes at all levels, reflecting the good combination of entropy weighting method and other methods [91].

Independence Weighting Method. Independence weighting method is a method to determine the weight coefficients of indexes based on the degree of co-linearity between each index and other indexes in the HCI evaluation index system. If the coefficient of complex correlation between an index and other indexes in the HCI evaluation index system is larger, the stronger the degree of co-linearity between it and other indexes, i.e., the easier it is to be represented by other indexes in the system, the smaller the contribution to the whole HCI evaluation index system, and the lower the weight it takes. He et al. calculated the objective weights of train passenger HCI satisfaction evaluation indexes by the independence weighting method and linearly integrated with the subjective weights obtained by the hierarchical analysis method to obtain the comprehensive weights, which realized the fuzzy comprehensive evaluation of train passenger HCI satisfaction, but its solution process for the subjective and objective index proportion coefficients in the linear integration process took the subjective and objective weight errors as the objective function, which did not reflect how to make the evaluation indexes show the maximum difference between them, which to a certain extent limits the embodiment of the objectivity of the independence weighting method [92].

Coefficient of Variation Method. The coefficient of variation method is a method to determine the coefficient of an index by calculating the ratio of the standard deviation to the mean of the sample data of each index to measure the degree of dispersion on the mean of the index. If the coefficient of variation of an index is larger, the greater the degree of difference of its sample data from each other, i.e., the different schemes can be better distinguished by this index, and it should be assigned a larger weight. Y et al. determined the index weight coefficients for nuclear power plants HCI evaluation by combining the coefficient of variation method and the entropy weighting method, avoiding the possible balance deficiency of the index weight distribution obtained by using the entropy weighting method only, and overcoming the adverse effect of outliers, the objective rationality of the index weights is further strengthened, but the issue of whether the index weights reflect subjective needs is ignored, and the determined index weights are highly likely to be contrary to subjective needs [50].

Gray Correlation Analysis Method. Gray correlation analysis method is a method of calculating the degree of association of factors by determining the degree of similarity in geometry between reference sample data and other comparison sample data. Some scholars consider the grayness of cognition in the judgment process and the cognitive and empirical bias of each expert, and introduce gray correlation analysis to further modify the subjective weighting method [64, 65, 93]. For example, Xia et al. construct confidence coefficients to reflect the credibility of each expert's evaluation information based on the gray correlation degree obtained from gray correlation analysis of expert evaluation data, and correct the weight coefficients obtained from the hierarchical analysis method to further improve the rationality of the evaluation results [93].

CRITIC Weighting Method. CRITIC weighting method is a method to analyze the volatility and correlation between indexes based on the volatility of sample data and then determine the coefficient of indexes. Volatility and correlation are expressed by the standard deviation of sample data and correlation coefficient respectively. If the standard deviation of sample data of an index is larger, the greater the volatility of sample data and the higher its weight, and if the value of correlation coefficient between indexes is larger, the smaller the conflict of sample data and the lower its weight. Wang et al. used CRITIC weighting method and hierarchical analysis method to determine the comprehensive weights of the visually impaired user HCI evaluation indexes, conducted a comprehensive HCI evaluation based on visually impaired user experience, and developed an HCI evaluation system, but the specific analysis and algorithm of the weight determination method were lacking, and the reasons for choosing the method and the applicability of the method in the comprehensive evaluation based on visually impaired user experience were not elaborated [94].

4.3 Integrated Weighting Method

The integrated weighting method is a method to determine the index weights by integrating the subjective weighting method and the objective weighting method, which simultaneously takes into account the advantages of the competent weighting method and the objective weighting method, and also makes up for the shortcomings of both sides, and is widely used in the HCI evaluation. In the application process of the integrated weighting method, in addition to selecting the competent and objective weighting methods suitable for the evaluation purposes, a reasonable combination of weighting methods should also be selected. In HCI evaluation, the commonly used combination assignment method is divided into two categories, one is linear combination [92]. For example, He et al. calculated the objective weights of train passenger HCI satisfaction evaluation indexes by the independence weighting method, and linearly combined with the subjective weights obtained by hierarchical analysis method to obtain the comprehensive weights, and then realized the fuzzy comprehensive evaluation of train passenger HCI satisfaction [92]. The other category is the product combination [45, 95, 96]. For example, Yan et al. used the improved hierarchical analysis method and entropy weighting method to calculate the subjective and objective weights of shopping-type application HCI evaluation indexes respectively, and multiplied the subjective and objective weights separately and normalized them to obtain the final weights, and then evaluated the advantages and disadvantages of different layout and color interfaces [96].

In addition, in addition to the above methods, some scholars have also introduced rough sets [97], fuzzy rough sets [69], genetic algorithm [26], artificial neural network [74] and other theories for the calculation of weight coefficients, all of which also provide more accurate and reasonable methods for solving uncertainty and incompleteness information problems.

5 Human-Computer Interface Evaluation Method

In modern comprehensive evaluation, there are various methods of comprehensive evaluation and different methods of classification. According to the evaluation information evaluation methods can be broadly classified into evaluation based on experience, data, models and fused information. In HCI evaluation, since the research object has been basically clarified, research scholars have selected some evaluation methods to evaluate according to their characteristics, such as physiological measurement method, user interview method, heuristic evaluation method, fuzzy comprehensive evaluation method, etc. Therefore, the content of this section will only describe the common use of these HCI evaluation methods (see Fig. 4) and their applications in HCI evaluation.

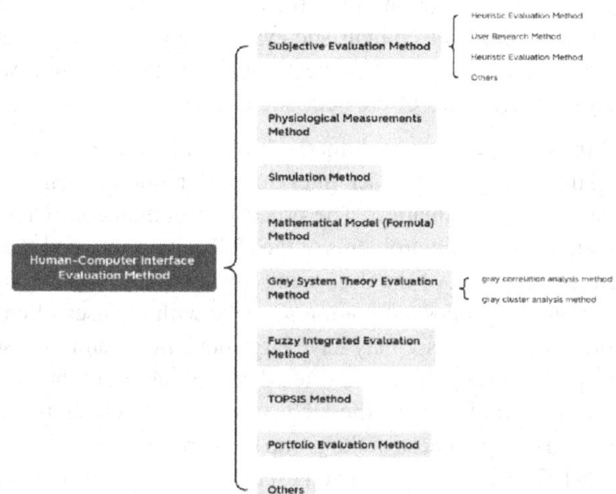

Fig. 4. Human-computer interface evaluation method relation figure

5.1 Subjective Evaluation Method

The subjective evaluation method is a method to evaluate the HCI mainly based on the subjective feelings of users, evaluators or experts. The general process is to get the overall or partial scores of HCI through questionnaires, interviews, etc., and then get qualitative conclusions after data processing [98]. In HCI evaluation, common methods include heuristic evaluation method, hierarchical analysis method, etc. Since users occupy a dominant position in HCI, there are also many scholars who conduct HCI evaluation through user research, user experience and other methods.

Heuristic Evaluation Method. Heuristic evaluation method is a method to find out interface usability problems by inviting several experts to simulate the human-computer interaction process and evaluate the usability of HCI according to the pre-agreed guidelines and personal experience and knowledge. The heuristic evaluation method is low cost to use, is not affected by the time period of machine development, does not involve user experience and user behavior analysis, is convenient, and has been favored by many companies and research scholars [18, 47, 99]. Maria et al. invited three evaluators to evaluate the usability and efficiency of five video websites using the Nielsen heuristic evaluation method, found problems in the search mechanism and content classification of these website interfaces, and gave corresponding suggestions, but the traditional

Nielsen heuristic evaluation method was proposed long ago, and the usability guidelines for today's new products may not be fully covered, so there may be part of usability issues being ignored [99]. David et al. proposed a generality heuristic evaluation method based on a generic classification method integrating usability attributes, contextual features and generic classification of UI elements into the technique, and applied it to usability research of mobile user interfaces, achieving the usefulness, ease of use and generality evaluation of the heuristic evaluation while increasing the depth and scope of evaluation, and compared with the Nielsen heuristic evaluation method, the usability range it contains is wider than that of the Nielsen heuristic evaluation method, while retaining the quick and easy characteristics of the heuristic evaluation method [18].

User Research Method. User research method refers to the method of obtaining user data through questionnaire survey, user interview, user observation, experiment and other ways to conduct HCI evaluation. The process of human-computer interaction is centered on the user, and the main problems of the HCI can be obtained at a low technical threshold through the feedback of the user using the computer, but due to the diversity of the user population, the process of communicating with the user often takes a lot of time, and the expression of the user may have large deviations, and the user research of a small scale or a specific group of people often does not represent the overall reflection of the users on the main problems of the HCI, so user research should emphasize the representativeness and completeness of the group being researched [6, 11, 12, 15–17, 25, 46, 51, 65, 85, 100–102]. Liu et al. conducted user research on 459 elderly users through a questionnaire and an experiment on the interface perceived usability evaluation of the elderly, and constructed an evaluation scale of the interface perceived usability of the elderly, which was tested to meet the requirements of reliability and validity and can effectively evaluate the interface perceived usability of the elderly in shopping websites, and provide a reference for the ageing-appropriate design of shopping websites [6]. Carl invited 20 subjects to evaluate the interface usability of an in-car touch device prototype through interviews and questionnaires, and no major usability problems were found, which verified that the HCI of the device was reasonably designed. In this HCI evaluation, although users' feedback can be used to find usability problems in the HCI design, the fact that users do not find problems does not mean that there are no problems, and it is not convincing enough to verify that the HCI design is reasonable only through users' feedback in this study [25].

Heuristic Evaluation Method. In the above section, a detailed description of the use of hierarchical analysis to determine the index weights was given, while the use of hierarchical analysis for the HCI evaluation is to determine the index weights and then carry out a weighted synthesis to calculate the total ranking weights of the lowest level relative to the highest level from top to bottom, so as to achieve the HCI evaluation. Since the calculation process is not very different, no example will be presented here.

5.2 Physiological Measurements Method

Physiological measurement method refers to the method of HCI evaluation by measuring the data changes of user's physiological indexes during the process of human-computer interaction. Since the physiological measurement method directly records the data changes of physiological indexes related to the evaluation content through various experimental instruments, it can reflect the physiological changes of users in the process of human-computer interaction more accurately, so this method is more objective and persuasive, and has a higher degree of credibility. In HCI evaluation studies, the commonly used metrics can be divided into two categories, one is measuring user eye movement data [10–12, 15, 17, 24, 53–56, 85, 91, 95, 96, 101]. For example, Li et al. used eye-movement heat map to indicate the overall effect, eye-movement usability index and information processing efficiency to indicate efficiency, and pupil size to indicate body satisfaction, and then established a usability evaluation model of mining machinery HCI through eye-movement experiments, and analyzed the usability problems of the rig based on observation method, performance measurement method, eye-movement analysis method and behavior analysis method, and proposed specific improvement measures [17]. Another category is recording user EEG data [103]. For example, Wang et al. studied the relationship between EEG indexes and operational efficiency by analyzing the differences between the number, difficulty and time required for different human-computer interaction tasks and EEG signal data, which provided a reference for HCI design and evaluation [103]. Compared with the acquisition and analysis of EEG signals, the acquisition and processing of eye-movement data are simpler and more convenient, and the research and application of eye-movement indexes in HCI evaluation are more adequate, the research on the correlation between EEG signals and HCI evaluation is still in the preliminary stage and needs further verification.

It is important to note that when evaluating HCI using physiological measures, it is important to try to select physiological indexes that have been widely validated and are relevant to the evaluation purposes, and to avoid using indexes that have not been validated by multiple parties to reduce the persuasiveness of the evaluation results.

5.3 Simulation Method

Simulation method refers to the method of evaluating the HCI by building a HCI model to simulate the human-computer interaction process. According to whether the simulation object is a physical entity or not, the simulation method can be further divided into hardware simulation method and virtual simulation method [98]. The hardware simulation method refers to the HCI evaluation by building a physical interface in the laboratory environment to simulate the human-computer interaction scene, which is commonly used in the HCI evaluation of automobiles, aircraft cabs, etc. The hardware simulation is highly reductive and immersive, but expensive, so it is not common in the HCI evaluation of common equipment, the virtual simulation method refers to the HCI evaluation through computer simulation software to build HCI scenarios, common simulation software such as JACK, CATIA, RAMSIS, virtual simulation is fast and easy to use, low cost, short test cycle, easy to obtain objective evaluation data of the HCI. For example, Qiu et al. proposed a comprehensive evaluation method for agricultural equipment cabs using virtual reality and hierarchical fuzzy analysis method, and developed a HCI evaluation system for agricultural equipment cabs based on VS.NET and Multigen Vega Prime simulation platform, but since the virtual simulation method cannot effectively obtain human subjective feeling data, the evaluation data obtained is also limited to objective data such as backrest tilt angle, and cannot be more complete for comprehensive evaluation, and it is because of this defect that the virtual simulation method is not used frequently in most HCI evaluations.

The use scenario of simulation method is mostly limited to some evaluation activities targeting visual ergonomics and comfort based on human physiological parameters in physical HCI, which is not commonly used in the evaluation of software HCI. In this aspect, many research scholars have created software interface prototypes as evaluation objects for HCI evaluation through prototype software such as Axure and Modao, for example, Zhang et al. used Modao software to create two prototype oilfield water injection system interfaces as an example of the proposed evaluation method to validate the practicality of the method [85]. The Software prototype method is also a kind of "simulation", but it is different from simulation method, and needs to be chosen reasonably by specific analysis.

5.4 Mathematical Model (Formula) Method

Mathematical model (formula) method refers to the method of evaluating by specifying evaluation indexes through mathematical models (formulas). In the HCI evaluation, some evaluation indexes such as viewpoint, field of view, operation domain, interface layout balance, etc. can be quantitatively calculated by mathematical models, and the evaluation data obtained through the calculation can be applied to the HCI evaluation to greatly improve the objectivity of evaluation activities, so it has been applied in the evaluation of interface computational aesthetics, interface layout evaluation, interface human-computer ergonomics evaluation, etc. The key to the application of mathematical model method is that the mathematical model introduced should be reasonable and complete, and can reflect the characteristics of evaluation indexes. In this regard, ANDREAS et al. quantified the user interface complexity indexes based on the research results of interface computational aesthetics for interface layout [34], the specific indexes include balance, density, color complexity, etc., covering a variety of factors affecting interface complexity such as color, typography, which is more reasonable and complete, and provides an effective means for evaluating the complexity of the early stage of mobile application user interface development [33]. Wang et al. calculated the degree of HCI and visual matching of missile launch equipment based on ergonomics on the visual characteristics of human eyes [104], and then assessed the effective operational efficiency of the manipulator, the calculation model reflects some problems of some equipment HCI in ergonomics, but the calculation only from the visual level does not fully reflect the overall operational efficiency of personnel, and it needs to be combined with human action and other aspects of research to achieve a more complete evaluation [30].

5.5 Grey System Theory Evaluation Method

In cybernetics, shades of color are used to indicate the certainty degree of information, with "white" indicating that the information is completely known, "black" indicating that the information is completely unknown, and "gray" indicating that the information is partially known and partially unknown. Gray system theory is based on the quantification, whitening and optimization of gray systems based on poor information, so as to realize the control and prediction of gray systems [105]. In the HCI evaluation, due to the fuzzy nature of human understanding, the randomness of dynamic changes of human-computer interaction system, data errors and other factors, the HCI evaluation process also has gray characteristics, therefore, gray system theory is also widely used in the HCI evaluation, among which the more common ones are gray correlation analysis method and gray cluster analysis method.

Gray correlation analysis method is a method to analyze the degree of correlation of factors according to the similarity or dissimilarity of the evolution trend of each factor in the gray system. The correlation analysis can reflect the closeness of the present state of each evaluation object to the ideal state, so as to realize the superiority and inferiority judgment of each evaluation object. Gray correlation analysis has no restriction on the number of samples, the calculation results are consistent with qualitative analysis, and it is practical in the HCI evaluation [70, 71, 79, 82, 89]. For example, Bao et al. calculated the correlation degree of user experience indexes of smart product interfaces for the elderly through gray correlation analysis, analyzed the reasons that easily cause misoperation in the elderly group and gave relevant suggestions [89].

Gray cluster analysis method is a method to classify each index or each research object according to the gray correlation matrix or whitening power function. Gray clustering analysis can also be specific gray correlation cluster method and gray whitening power cluster method. Gray correlation cluster method can be used to merge the evaluation indexes and select representative indexes through the calculation of correlation degree, which is of little significance to the discrimination of evaluation objects. Gray whitening power cluster method can classify different evaluation objects through the different values of whitening power function of each evaluation index to achieve the discrimination of superiority and inferiority, which has been used in the HCI evaluation [31, 72, 73, 76, 90, 106]. For example, Gao et al. conducted gray clustering analysis on the color matching samples of applications user interfaces for the elderly, and obtained excellent and average classes of interface color matching samples, which provide a reference for the color matching of applications user interfaces for the elderly [31]. Restricted by the intention of gray cluster analysis method to achieve object classification, many HCI evaluation studies using gray cluster analysis method only classify multiple evaluation samples into several classes, lacking discussion between each sample of the same kind, and some of the study conclusions for the cluster values of several samples in one class to distinguish the advantages and disadvantages of the scheme need to be further explored and studied.

In summary, grey correlation analysis is more widely used than grey clustering analysis, both in the determination of index weights and in the differentiation of evaluation schemes.

5.6 Fuzzy Integrated Evaluation Method

Fuzzy integrated evaluation method is an evaluation method based on fuzzy mathematics theory, which describes fuzzy boundary through membership degree, synthesizes qualitative and borderless factors by fuzzy relation to achieve quantification, and obtains the membership level of each factor. The mathematical model of fuzzy integrated evaluation method is simple, can better deal with complex uncertainty problems of multi-level and multi-indexes, and the obtained results are accurately described and informative, which are widely used in the HCI evaluation with strong fuzzy attributes [4, 13, 20, 32, 50, 61, 63, 69, 75, 80, 81, 84, 87, 92, 107]. For example, Cui et al. used the Delphi method to analyze each evaluation item of mobile game user interface, determine its weight, obtain the distribution of the weight level of mobile game interface usability indexes, and use fuzzy integrated evaluation to evaluate them comprehensively, and finally verified the applicability of the method by example [20]. However, when the evaluation index system involves more factors, the weight coefficients of each factor are small relative to the total target, and the results obtained after partial operator calculation will be meaningless, therefore, the research scholars also proposed the multi-level fuzzy comprehensive evaluation method, which divides each factor into multiple levels and judges the low level first, and then proceeds to the high level layer by layer, for example, Rao et al. used the hierarchical analysis method with the fuzzy rough set method to obtain the weights of the HCI evaluation indexes of train driving, and combined with the multi-level fuzzy integrated evaluation method to judge multiple driving interface layout schemes, which better solved the problem of multiple index evaluation of the complex systems interface [69].

5.7 TOPSIS Method

TOPSIS method is a method to rank each research object based on its closeness to the ideal target. TOPSIS finds the positive ideal solution and negative ideal solution by normalizing the normalized matrix, and calculates the Euclidean distance between each research object with the positive ideal solution and negative ideal solution to get the closeness of each research object to the ideal target, the closer the posting progress is to 1, the closer the study object is to the optimal level, thus allowing for a comprehensive ranking of each study object. TOPSIS can better reflect the comprehensive influence of multiple indexes on the total target, has no restriction on the number of indexes and evaluation data, has no objective function, and does not require follow-up testing, which has been applied in the HCI evaluation [41, 43, 65, 66, 88, 108]. For example, Wang et al. used Cogtool to predict the completion performance of interface human-computer interaction tasks based on the theory related to human cognitive model predicting user cognitive process, and established a fuzzy evaluation system, and used TOPSIS method to rank each sample interface, and proposed an HCI evaluation method based on Cogtool [108].

5.8 Portfolio Evaluation Method

The single evaluation methods covered above have evaluated the research object based on different perspectives, which are more or less deficient, therefore, it is natural for research scholars to try to combine different methods to achieve complementary advantages and make the evaluation results more reasonable. For example, Xiao et al. used the correlation degree obtained from gray correlation analysis method to correct the fuzzy evaluation results of the bottom-level indexes of HCI ease of use, and then used the evaluation results of the first level to obtain the top-level evaluation results by analogy, which more objectively responded to the interface situation [26]. However, the paper only shows that the combined method is more reasonable in a simple way, and lacks comparison with the pre-combination method, which is also a problem in many studies using the combined evaluation method, and is a concrete manifestation of the unresolved problem of "the rationality of the comprehensive evaluation" in the comprehensive evaluation, and it is still worthwhile for research scholars to go deeper.

6 Current Problems and Trends in HCI Evaluation Research

In Terms of Evaluation Objects. The mainstream of current research focuses on interfaces of special equipment, fixed equipment, and display-controlled separated equipment, such as nuclear power plant control rooms, automobile cabs, and machine tool manipulation interfaces, etc. In recent years, more research related to mobile application interface evaluation has also emerged. With the popularity of smart phones, tablets and other devices, touch mobile devices have gradually become the development trend of devices, and the research on the HCI evaluation of touch mobile devices will also become a major research content in the HCI evaluation research.

In Terms of Evaluation Indexes. Some studies select such as interface operation comfort, interface visual aesthetics, etc. directly as evaluation indexes, which are abstracted and not specific enough, leaving the process of evaluation completely to the user and not fully reflecting the value of the evaluator in the evaluation activity. The research object of HCI evaluation consists of controller and display, which are composed of various buttons and display components, and the process of human-computer interaction is also image-concrete. For such a concrete and knowable research object, the evaluator need to combine theoretical knowledge and practical experience to reflect them in evaluation indexes, and get more specific indexes such as interface layout balance, interface layout uniformity, interface information density, perspective, etc., so that users can just interact as much as possible without making too much of their own fuzzy and arbitrary judgment. In addition, the evaluation index system established by some studies is only based on a certain aspect, such as visual information flow, visual element composition of the interface, etc., which cannot reflect the meaning of the evaluation purpose in a more complete way. Therefore, how to construct a complete HCI evaluation index system is also a research problem worthy of in-depth study.

In Terms of Evaluation Process. Researchers have adopted many mathematical methods to improve the objectivity and rationality of the calculation process in order to improve the objectivity and rationality of the HCI evaluation. However, if HCI evaluation is considered as a system, research scholars hope that the output results of the system are objective and reasonable, but most of the current research scholars carry out various optimizations of the process, over-emphasizing mathematical methods and paying little attention to the source of the input (evaluation data) of the system, resulting in the evaluation results obtained are still not reasonable even though the calculation process is objective and reasonable. Therefore, the sources of HCI evaluation data must be given enough attention, and the evaluation data must be objective and reasonable for the subsequent evaluation activities to be meaningful. In addition, at present, the problem of "reasonableness of comprehensive evaluation" proposed by Guo et al. [109] is still not well solved, and it is still a challenging research problem to verify the rationality of the evaluation process in a more scientific way.

In Terms of Evaluation Results. The most results of the current partial HCI evaluation studies are presented in the way of ranking the advantages and disadvantages of different solutions only, with insufficient feedback on the problems in the HCI, which cannot well reflect the guiding role of HCI evaluation for HCI design. As the two functions of comprehensive evaluation, merit evaluation is the most basic function, and finding problems and improving reference for decision makers is a deeper function [57]. How to dig more useful information for HCI design from the process of HCI evaluation will definitely become an eternal topic in HCI evaluation research.

References

1. Wu, C., Zhang, K.: Diagnostic user interface usability evaluation (IM) (Part 1) – introduction and evaluation. Chin. Ergon. **03**, 54–57 (2000)
2. Wu, C., Zhang, K.: Diagnostic user interface usability evaluation (IM) (Part 2) – comparison and suggestion. Chin. Ergon. **04**, 35–38 (2000)
3. Wu, C., Zhang, K.: Human-computer interface usability evaluation method. Psychol. Sci. **06**, 727–728 (2001)
4. Liang, H.: Based on AHM and fuzzy comprehensive evaluation of interval number in the evaluation of mobile phone interface. Packag. Eng. **33**(16), 67–71 (2012)
5. Liu, S., Li, Y.: Study of evaluation on display interface ergonomic evaluation for intelligent electric cooker. J. Jilin Univ. (Inf. Sci. Ed.) **34**(02), 266–270 (2016)
6. Liu, C., Guo, F., Liu, W.: The evaluation scale of the perceived usability of the elderly shopping website interface was constructed. J. Inf. Syst. **01**, 49–71 (2017)
7. Xu, F., Zhang, L.: Research on human-factor fitness evaluation system of smart phone APP interactive interface. Chin. J. Ergon. **24**(03), 77–81 (2018)
8. Zhu, R., Yao, J., Tang, X.: Evaluation and reaserch of app interface for user experience optimization of doctors and patients. Dev. Innov. Mach. Electr. Prod. **32**(02), 45–47+92 (2019)
9. Liu, W., Li, L., Fu, G.: Research on usability evaluation index system of combat command software interface based on the IPO model. J. China Acad. Electron. Inf. Technol. **16**(10), 1060–1066 (2021)
10. Wu, J., Sun, J., Li, M.: Usability evaluation of WeChat program interface design based on entropy. Packag. Eng. **42**(12), 191–196+222 (2021)
11. Cigdem, A., Aycan, P., Mustafa, E., et al.: Usability evaluation of TV interfaces: subjective evaluation vs. objective evaluation. Int. J. Hum.-Comput. Interact. **38**(7), 661–679 (2021)
12. Zhou, M., Wang, Z., Zheng, Y.: Study on usability evaluation of medical software interface based on eye movement tracking technology. In: International Conference on Machine Vision (2020)
13. Wang, S., Li, B., Zhu, Y.: Comprehensive evaluation of usability at the mobile end interface. IOP Conf. Ser. Mater. Sci. Eng. **573**(1), 012–037 (2019)
14. Manoela, R., Rafael R.: User interface evaluation methods for elderly: a systematic review. In: 21st Symposium on Virtual and Augmented Reality (SVR), Rio de Janeiro, Brazil, pp. 84–91. IEEE (2019)
15. Nugraha, A., Rolando, Puspasari, M., et al.: Usability evaluation for user interface redesign of financial technology application. IOP Conf. Ser. Mater. Sci. Eng. **505**(1), 012–101 (2019)

16. Lestari, R., Muslim, E., Moch, B.: User interface evaluation of official store for FMCG (fast moving consumer goods) products in e-commerce website using user experience approach. IOP Conf. Ser. Mater. Sci. Eng. **505**(1), 012–079 (2019)
17. Li, H., Tian, S., Li, F., et al.: Usability evaluation of mining machinery interface based on eye movement experiment. In: Rebelo, F., Soares, M. (eds.) Advances in Ergonomics in Design. AHFE 2017: Advances in Intelligent Systems and Computing, vol. 588, pp. 591–599. Springer, Cham (2017)
18. Alonso, R., Mosqueira, R., Moret, B.: A systematic and generalizable approach to the heuristic evaluation of user interfaces. Int. J. Hum.-Comput. Interact. **34**(12), 1169–1182 (2018)
19. Rim, R., Mohamed, A., Adel, M., et al.: Evaluation method for an adaptive web interface: GOMS model. In: Madureira, A., Abraham, A., Gamboa, D., Novais, P. (eds.) ISDA 2016: Intelligent Systems Design and Applications, Advances in Intelligent Systems and Computing, vol. 557, pp. 116–124. Springer, Cham (2017)
20. Cui, M., Zhu, L.: Usability evaluation methods of user interface based on mobile games using fuzzy methods. In: Chen, Y., Christie, M., Tan, W. (eds.) Smart Graphics, pp. 124–131. Springer International Publishing, Cham (2017)
21. Bessghaier, N., Souii, M.: Towards usability evaluation of hybrid mobile user interfaces. In: 2017 IEEE/ACS 14th International Conference on Computer Systems and Applications (AICCSA), Hammamet, pp. 895–900. IEEE (2017)
22. Mator, J.D., et al.: Usability: adoption, measurement, value. Hum. Factors **63**(6), 956–973 (2021)
23. Allah, K.K., Ismail, N.A., Hasan, L., Leng, W.Y.: Usability evaluation of web search user interfaces from the elderly perspective. Int. J. Adv. Comput. Sci. Appl. **12**(12), 647–657 (2021)
24. Wu, Y., Cheng, J., Kang, X.: Study of smart watch interface usability evaluation based on eye-tracking. In: Marcus, A. (ed.) DUXU 2016. LNCS, vol. 9748, pp. 98–109. Springer, Cham (2016). https://doi.org/10.1007/978-3-319-40406-6_10
25. Normark, C.J.: Design and evaluation of a touch-based personalizable in-vehicle user interface. Int. J. Hum.-Comput. Interact. **31**(11), 731–745 (2015)
26. Xiao, G., Li, X., Xiao, M.: An ease-of-use evaluation of the human-machine interface. J. Southwest China Normal Univ. (Nat. Sci. Ed.) **34**(03), 98–102 (2009)
27. Wang, H., Xie, W., Zhao, Y.: Research on evaluation method about handing performance of man-machine interface of weapons. Command Control Simul. **35**(02), 68–70+84 (2013)
28. Nielsen, J.: Usability Engineering. Morgan Kaufmann (1994)
29. Liu, W., Yuan, X., Liu, Z., et al.: Comprehensive evaluation indexes and evaluation method for man-machine compatibility of display/control interface. China Saf. Sci. J. **04**, 36–39 (2004)
30. Wang, J., Cai, W.: Ergonomics evaluation of human-machine interface based on spatial vision characteristics. Tactical Missile Technol. **06**, 107–111 (2012)
31. Gao, S., Zhu, L., Li, Y.: Color matching evaluation of APP user interface for elderly based on grey clustering method. Packag. Eng. **42**(06), 198–205 (2021)
32. Ma, Y., Zhai, L., Wang, X., Liang, H.: Evaluation of the matching optimization of human-machine interface in the cab. In: 2020 5th International Conference on Mechanical, Control and Computer Engineering (ICMCCE), Harbin, China, pp. 152–156. IEEE (2020)
33. Riegler, A., Holzmann, C.: Measuring visual user interface complexity of mobile applications with metrics. Interact. Comput. **30**(3), 207–223 (2018)
34. Ngo, D.C.L., Teo, L.S., Byrne, J.G.: Modelling interface aesthetics. Inf. Sci. **152**, 25–46 (2003)
35. Zhou, L., Xue, C., Tang, W., et al.: Aesthetic evaluation method of interface elements layout design. J. Comput.-Aided Des. Comput. Graph. **25**(005), 758–766 (2013)

36. Zhang, N., Wang, J., Yang, Y.: Evaluation method of aesthetic image for man-machine interface form elements layout design. Mech. Sci. Technol. Aerosp. Eng. **34**(10), 1594–1598 (2015)
37. Dai, Y., Xue, C., Wang, H.: Research on interface beauty evaluation method based on AHP. Design **08**, 123–125 (2018)
38. Ren, X., Xue, C.: Evaluation of interface element layout of camera connect APP based on Meidu calculation. Design **04**, 142–143 (2018)
39. Li, H.: Overview of human-machine interface Meidu research. Ind. Des. **01**, 93–94 (2019)
40. Lv, J., Sun, W., Pan, W., et al.: Evaluation of information interface layout beauty based on cognitive characteristics. Packag. Eng. **40**(18), 220–226 (2019)
41. Zhou, A., Zhou, C., Ooyang, J., et al.: Model of synthetic evaluation on interface stylistic beauty based on moderately standardized of index. J. Zhejiang Univ. (Eng. Sci.) **54**(12), 2273–2285 (2020)
42. Pastushenko, O., Hynek, J., Hruška, T.: Evaluation of user interface design metrics by generating realistic-looking dashboard samples. Expert Syst. **38**(5) (2021)
43. Deng, L., Wang, G.: Quantitative evaluation of visual aesthetics of human-machine interaction interface layout. Comput. Intell. Neurosci. **2020**, 1–14 (2020)
44. Kong, Q., Guo, Q.: Comprehensive evaluation method of interface elements layout aesthetics based on improved AHP. In: Rebelo, F., Soares, M.M. (eds.) Advances in Ergonomics in Design, pp. 509–520. Springer, Cham (2019). https://doi.org/10.1007/978-3-319-94706-8_54
45. Yang, Y., Zhang, B., Li, X., et al.: Evaluation of navigation interface design of ASD children intervention APP based on AHP-entropy weight method. Packag. Eng. **43**(12), 165–173 (2022)
46. Susilo, F.F., Park, J.-H., Park, J.-M.: Evaluation of touch-based interface design for the elderly based on cultural differences. In: Stephanidis, C. (ed.) HCI 2018. CCIS, vol. 851, pp. 211–219. Springer, Cham (2018). https://doi.org/10.1007/978-3-319-92279-9_29
47. Krel, M., Kožuh, I., Debevc, M.: Heuristic evaluation of a mobile telecare system for older adults. In: Miesenberger, K., Kouroupetroglou, G. (eds.) Computers Helping People with Special Needs, pp. 391–398. Springer, Cham (2018). https://doi.org/10.1007/978-3-319-94274-2_56
48. Trilar, J., Sobo, T., Duh, E.S.: Family-centered design: interactive performance testing and user interface evaluation of the slovenian edavki public tax portal. Sensors **21**(15) (2021)
49. Rakhra, A.K., Mann, D.D.: Design and evaluation of individual elements of the interface for an agricultural machine. J. Agric. Saf. Health **24**(1), 27–42 (2018)
50. Chen, Y., Yan, S., Tran, C.C.: Comprehensive evaluation method for user interface design in nuclear power plant based on mental workload. Nucl. Eng. Technol. **51**(2), 453–462 (2019)
51. Li, M., Albayrak, A., Zhang, Yu., van Eijk, D.: Multiple factors mental load evaluation on smartphone user interface. In: Bagnara, S., Tartaglia, R., Albolino, S., Alexander, T., Fujita, Y. (eds.) IEA 2018. AISC, vol. 827, pp. 302–315. Springer, Cham (2019). https://doi.org/10.1007/978-3-319-96059-3_33
52. Li, F., Wang, B.: Evaluation methods of the relevance between PC and mobile terminal layout. Packag. Eng. **38**(20), 143–149 (2017)
53. Li, J., Yu, S., Liu, W.: Cognitive characteristic evaluation of CNC interface layout based on eye-tracking. J. Comput.-Aided Des. Comput. Graph. **29**(07), 1334–1342 (2017)
54. Zhou, Q., Cheng, Y., Liu, Z., Chen, Y., Li, C.: The layout evaluation of man-machine interface based on eye movement data. In: Bagnara, S., Tartaglia, R., Albolino, S., Alexander, T., Fujita, Y. (eds.) IEA 2018. AISC, vol. 824, pp. 64–75. Springer, Cham (2019). https://doi.org/10.1007/978-3-319-96071-5_7
55. Sun, L., Han, B., Zhang, W.: Evaluation of mobile APP interface design for english learning based on eye movement experiment. Chin. J. Ergon. **27**(02), 1–8 (2021)

56. Wang, J., Ma, J., Lv, S.: Evaluation of WinCC interface based on eye tracking technology. Exp. Technol. Manag. **36**(06), 53–57 (2019)
57. Du, D., Pang, Q., Wu, Y.: Modern Comprehensive Evaluation Methods and Selected Cases, 3rd edn. Tsinghua University Press, Beijing (2021)
58. Lin, H., Zhang, Y.: Quality evaluation of mobile game main interface design based on information entropy. Design **07**, 57–59 (2017)
59. Wang, M., Yu, S., Yang, Y.: Human-machine interface evaluation of aircraft cockpit based on Fuzzy AHP-GEM. J. Mach. Des. **34**(02), 105–109 (2017)
60. Baker, N.A., Redfern, M.S.: Developing an observational instrument to evaluate personal computer keyboarding style. Appl. Ergon. **36**(3), 345–354 (2005)
61. Song, H., Guo, M.: Study on methods and application of human-computer interface ergonomics evaluation for fighter cockpit. Aeronaut. Sci. Technol. **28**(05), 28–32 (2017)
62. Zhang, X., Yin, Y., Feng, Y., et al.: Study on ergonomics evaluation index system for display and control interface of automobile. Energy Conserv. Environ. Prot. Transp. **12**(04), 12–16 (2016)
63. Song, H., Xu, X.: Interface ergonomics evaluation methods and applied research for fighter cockpit. In: Long, S., Dhillon, B.S. (eds.) MMESE 2018. LNEE, vol. 527, pp. 333–340. Springer, Singapore (2019). https://doi.org/10.1007/978-981-13-2481-9_38
64. Yuan, S., Gao, H., Wang, W., et al.: Multi-image evaluation for human-machine interface based on Kansei engineering. Chin. J. Eng. Des. **24**(05), 523–529 (2017)
65. Zhu, S., Qu, Y., Wang, W., et al.: Evaluation model of human-machine interface of the CNC based on improved FAHP-TOPSIS. Mach. Des. Res. **35**(06), 144–148+156 (2019)
66. Zhao, H., He, L., Lin, L., et al.: Digital human-machine interface experience measurement based on TOPSIS. J. Mach. Des. **33**(01), 120–123 (2016)
67. Sun, J., Jiang, T., Wang, C., et al.: Research on ergonomic evaluation indicator and methodology for interactive interface of spacecraft software. Manned Spaceflight **26**(02), 208–213 (2020)
68. Zhao, J., Hao, J., Wang, S., et al.: Research on the human-machine interface evaluation of the tank. Microcomput. Inf. **25**(19), 243–244+224 (2009)
69. Rao, D., Chen, Y., Lv, W., et al.: Comprehensive evaluation of human-machine interface layout in ttrain driving cab based on the multi-level fuzzy theory. Packag. Eng. **42**(04), 61–69 (2021)
70. Song, H.: Application of the hierarchy analysis-grey ccorrelation in assessment of software interface. J. Donghua Univ. (Nat. Sci.) **03**, 318–321 (2008)
71. Li, B., Ji, X., Ye, C.: Evaluation of DSV man-machine interface based on fuzzy AHP & grey correlation. Manuf. Autom. **36**(23), 71–75 (2014)
72. Yan, S., Zhang, Z., Chen, N., et al.: Evaluation of human-machine interface based on human factor indicator. Chin. Ergon. **04**, 26–30 (2004)
73. Yan, S., Li, Q., Zhang, Z., et al.: Research on subjective evaluation method in human-machine-interface based on grey theory. J. Harbin Eng. Univ. **01**, 98–100+104 (2005)
74. Yan, S., Yu, X., Zhang, Z., et al.: Evaluation method of human-machine interface of virtual meter based on RBF network. J. Syst. Simul. **24**, 5731–5735 (2007)
75. Qiu, Y., Zhu, Z., Mao, E., et al.: Virtual ergonomics design and evaluation of agricultural equipment cab. Trans. Chin. Soc. Agric. Eng. **27**(03), 117–121 (2011)
76. Zhang, X., Li, K., Guo, J.: An evaluation method for software user interface. J. Shaanxi Normal Univ. (Nat. Sci. Ed.) **S1**, 185–187 (2005)
77. Xiong, S., Yao, Z.: An evaluation model for sonar ssoftware user interface. Ship Electron. Eng. **36**(03), 98–101 (2016)
78. Index weight. https://baike.baidu.com/item/%E6%8C%87%E6%A0%87%E6%9D%83%E9%87%8D?forcehttps=1%3Ffr%3Dkg_hanyu. Accessed 11 Apr 2022

79. Zhang, X., Guo, J., Zhang, F.: Software user interface evaluation based on grey incidence analysis. Comput. Eng. Des. **14**, 2661–2662 (2006)
80. Wang, B., Li, Y.: Five-level scale assignment-fuzzy comprehensive evaluation of huma-machine interface quality. Comput. Appl. Softw. **30**(02), 22–25 (2013)
81. Luo, A., Tan, D., Zeng, Y.: Fuzzy multi-level synthetic evaluation for human computer interface. Fuzzy Syst. Math. **04**, 80–86 (1999)
82. Yan, S., Li, Q., He, P., et al.: A comprehensive evaluation of software user interface. J. Harbin Eng. Univ. **05**, 653–657 (2004)
83. Ding, W., Yang, G., Fang, M.: Human-computer interface synthetical evaluation based on AHP. J. Nanyang Normal Univ. **12**, 72–73+85 (2007)
84. Zhao, C., Li, J., Ren, J., et al.: Research on evaluation method of human-machine interface of fitness equipment based on multi-factor fusion. J. Graph. **40**(05), 932–935 (2019)
85. Zhang, R., Wang, M., Guo, Y., et al.: Design and evaluation of man-machine interface of oil field water injection system platform. J. Mach. Des. **38**(07), 118–125 (2021)
86. Li, H., Wang, S., Li, J.: Research on human-machine interface evaluation method based on QFD-PUGH. J. Graph. **42**(06), 1043–1050 (2021)
87. Xiao, X., Wanyan, X., Zhuang, D.: Comprehensive evaluation model of multidimensional visual coding on display interface. J. Beijing Univ. Aeronaut. Astronaut. **41**(06), 1012–1018 (2015)
88. Zhang, R.: Evaluation of the user interface of university digital library based on the analysis of grey ideal relation. Value Eng. **33**(33), 231–232 (2014)
89. Bao, W., Hu, Y., Zhu, L.: Fuzzy comprehensive evaluation of interface design of elderly intelligent products based on grey correlation. Hunan Packag. **33**(04), 51–54 (2018)
90. Wang, Y., Wang, X.: Evaluation of organizational interface management of large-scale engineering projects based on entropy method and grey theory. Archit. Technol. **49**(02), 213–216 (2018)
91. Liu, X., et al.: Human reliability evaluation based on objective and subjective comprehensive method used for ergonomic interface design. Math. Probl. Eng. **2021**, 1–16 (2021)
92. He, S., Zhi, J.: Evaluation of train passenger interface design based on analytic hierarchy process with independent weight method. J. Southwest Jiaotong Univ. **56**(04), 897–904 (2021)
93. Xia, C., Jiang, K.: Weight assignment of evaluation indexes for human-machine interface based on reliability coefficient. J. Shenyang Univ. Technol. **35**(01), 53–57 (2013)
94. Wang, F., Zhou, X.: Research on APP evaluation based on visually impaired user experience. Sci. Technol. Innov. **02**, 103–104 (2021)
95. Wang, Y., Wang, X., Wu, T., et al.: Interface design evaluation of mobile phone music APP based on eye-tracking experiment. Sci. Technol. Eng. **18**(09), 266–271 (2018)
96. Yan, H., Wang, J., Wang, W.: Eye movement experiment analysis and evaluation of shopping app interface design. Ind. Des. Res. **00**, 206–211 (2018)
97. Li, X., Shou, Z., Zhang, T., et al.: Applicability evaluation model of customizable user interface based on rough set-FAHP. J. Guilin Univ. Electron. Technol. **38**, 279–284 (2018)
98. He, S., Zhi, J., Du, Y., et al.: A review of research on man-machine design evaluation of equipment driving interface. Mach. Des. Res. **35**(05), 97–103 (2019)
99. Eliseo, M.A., Casac, B.S., Gentil, G.R.: A comparative study of video content user interfaces based on heuristic evaluation. In: 2017 12th Iberian Conference on Information Systems and Technologies (CISTI), Lisbon, Portugal, pp. 1–6. IEEE (2017)
100. Wang, Y., Li, P.: Research on evaluation of digital man-machine interface of nuclear power plant based on personnel performance. Atomic Energy Sci. Technol. **55**(03), 534–543 (2021)
101. Hellianto, G.R., Iqbal, B.M., Komarudin: Ergonomics evaluation of game interface design provisions on various computer based monitor screens. In: Proceedings of the 2017 International Conference on Industrial Design Engineering-ICIDE 2017, Dubai, United Arab Emirates, pp. 38–44. ACM Press (2017)

102. Muslim, E., Lestari, R.A., Hazmy, A.I., Alvina, S.: User interface evaluation of mobile application KRL access using user experience approach. IOP Conf. Ser. Mater. Sci. Eng. **508**, 012110 (2019)
103. Wang, D., Qu, Y.: Research on human-computer interface evaluation of allegation system based on EEG indicators. J. Ordnance Equipment Eng. **42**(11), 196–203 (2021)
104. Guo, F., Qian, X.: Human Factor Engineering, 1st edn. China Machine Press, Beijing (2005)
105. Grey system theory. https://baike.baidu.com/item/%E7%81%B0%E8%89%B2%E7%B3%BB%E7%BB%9F%E7%90%86%E8%AE%BA/2262621?fr=aladdin. Accessed 22 Apr 2022
106. Xia, C., Li, Q., Liu, Y.: Research on evaluation method in human-machine interface based on grey interval clustering. J. Jiamusi Univ. (Nat. Sci. Ed.) **38**(02), 37–39 (2020)
107. Jin, X., Mao, E., Song, Z.: Study on qualitative classification evaluation method of vehicle cab human-machine interface. In: Advances in Man-Machine-Environment Systems Engineering, vol. 07 (2005)
108. Wang, Lu., Xue, Q., Hao, J., Yu, H.: Research of human-machine interface evaluation based on Cogtool. In: Yamamoto, S., Mori, H. (eds.) HCII 2019. LNCS, vol. 11569, pp. 371–391. Springer, Cham (2019). https://doi.org/10.1007/978-3-030-22660-2_27
109. Guo, Y.: Theory and Method of Comprehensive Evaluation, 1st edn. Science Press, Beijing (2002)

NUWA: Lifelike as a Design Strategy to Enhance Product's Hedonic Qualities

Yu-Sheng Tung and Wei-Chi Chien(✉)

Department of Industrial Design, National Cheng Kung University, No. 1, Daxyue Rd., Tainan 701, Taiwan, R.O.C.
P36104152@gs.ncku.edu.tw, chien@xtdesign.org

Abstract. Lifelike design is an approach trying to enrich the experience and strengthen the emotional bond between humans and artifacts. However, there is very little understanding of the design strategies that create lifelike experiences, and even less research has been done to understand the experience from a holistic perspective. In this project, a lifelike desk lamp, *NUWA*, was designed based on a systematic review of lifelike characteristics. Five participants were invited to use *NUWA* and a normal lamp for three days. Both quantitative measures and qualitative interviews were conducted to understand their perceived lifelikeness, user experience, human-artifact attachment, and social relationship. The results show the successful design of a lifelike artifact. The hedonic and pragmatic qualities of both lamps are exactly opposite. Participants scored higher on hedonic qualities and attachment to *NUWA*. Also, they reported a partnership-like experience with *NUWA*. The findings could inspire future lifelike design and its research.

Keywords: Lifelike Design · Hedonic Qualities · User Experience · Experience Design · Human-Robot Interaction · Human-Product Attachment

1 Introduction

In the last decade, more and more research has started to discuss lifelike features in design (e.g. [1–9]). For example, products with lifelike designs could suggest an intuitive interaction experience and unique experience [2]. While being inspired by the nature is essential in humans' learning practice, biomimicry designers, for example, accelerated room air circulation by imitating the arrangement of termites' nests [10]. Besides the functional aspects, the recreation and integration of natural elements in architecture are suggested by biophilic design to enhance humans' well-being of living [11–13].

Another major category that design learns from living nature to enhance user experience is social robots. The discussion on human-robot interaction has gone far beyond functional operation, which sees robots as "automatic workers," but now implies a holistic perspective on any interactive behavior between humans and robots [22]. To promote the interaction between humans and robots on this holistic and social-cultural level, the realism of robot design searches for sensors, motors, and other controlling techniques to make robots socially effective [14] – the richness of a robot's aesthesia and expressivity

M. Kurosu and A. Hashizume (Eds.): HCII 2023, LNCS 14011, pp. 290–301, 2023.
https://doi.org/10.1007/978-3-031-35596-7_18

is considered essential for non-living objects' imitated natural behavior and interaction [15–19]. For example, *Aibo*, a robotic dog pet, is designed to act as a real dog and to imitate various human-dog interaction patterns [20, 21].

The approach of sociable robots inspired the discussion about lifelike design, which has been proven effective in many aspects [6, 7, 21, 23, 24]. For example, *Knoby* [5] is an interactive door lock designed to be like a pet dog. When a user approaches, *Knoby* lights up in white and "wags its tail." Also, any attempt to unlock the door will trigger different responses from *Knoby* – a strong vibration against the wrong code and a tail wagging for the right code. When the user leaves the space and locks the door, *Knoby* wags his tail to indicate "goodbye." Its subsequent study suggests a better user experience and a better understanding of the product's function in the interaction with a life-like artifact [5].

Although researchers have started to explore the emotional effect on users aroused by lifelike artifacts, only a few have discussed what design features make a product lifelike [2]. This makes the lifelike design tend to imitate specific creatures and limits the imagination of new concepts in practical design projects. In most cases, designers have to orient to their personal experience – usually from humans or pets – to understand the lifelike characteristics (e.g. [5, 6, 25]). Some other lifelike design artifacts are designed using more natural materials, complex mechanics, and information technology to simulate a living organism [21, 26, 27]. A design attempt only oriented to lifelike strategies could break the ice.

Besides, when trying to summarize a systematic understanding of lifelike design strategies, we saw disarranged research interests. A more systematic research system is hard to clarify. Among these research gaps, we first designed a lifelike artifact beyond imitating any specific animal or pet but really grounded in the design features suggested by the existing research [2, 4]. Seconds, to gain systematic discussion about experience with the lifelike artifact, both quantitative and qualitative methods are conducted. The quantitative measurements include the evaluation of the lifelike features, the different experience qualities, and the social qualities so that we can explore the possibility of more referable research methods in the future.

2 The Lifelike Features and *NUWA*

There are many design cases [5–7, 9, 18, 21, 23, 26, 27] and some guidelines [2, 4, 28] discussing the key features of the design strategies of lifelike artifacts. We summarized four lifelike design features from these studies and used them as design guidelines to create our design of a lifelike desk lamp, *NUWA*. These characteristics are (i) appearance, (ii) responsive behavior, (iii) willingness to interact with humans, and (iv) autonomous goal (see the following). Based on these four categories, we designed a lifelike desk lamp, *NUWA* (Fig. 1). Inside the 3D-printed case of *NUWA*, there are controlling chips, sensors, motors, and LEDs for its lifelike behavior.

Lifelike Appearance

A user's perception of a product is strongly related to its appearance [29–31]. A good lifelike design product should be able to present its lifelike characteristics by the users' first impression. The current analogy for designing a lifelike appearance varies. It can be

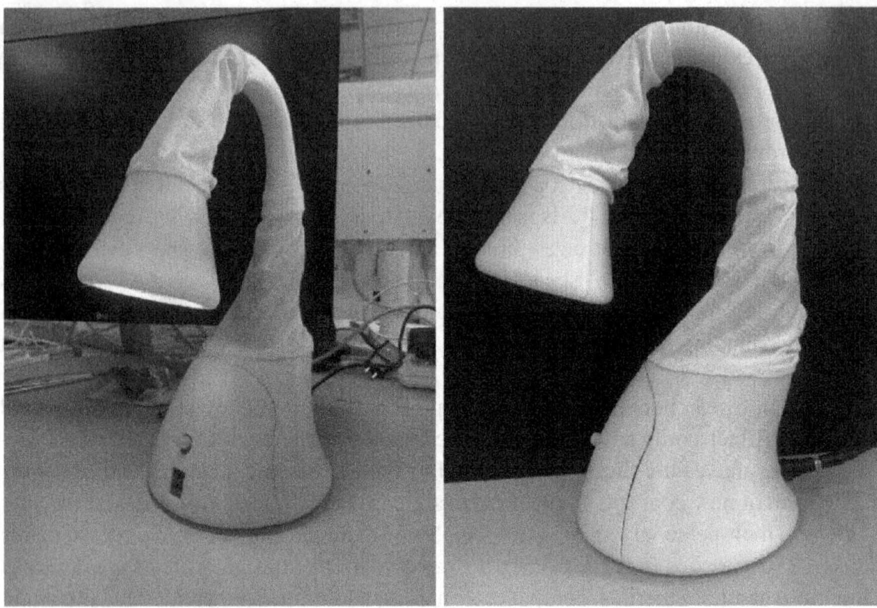

Fig. 1. NUWA, the lifelike-designed desk lamp.

a very concrete replication of one kind of specific species, such as the *iCub* robot with a humanoid body [27]. However, lifelike appearance can also be just a composition of soft, curved, or organic surfaces and shapes. For example, Clocky integrates the rounded display and pushbutton as its face [24], or *Furfur* appears just like a furry ball [39].

Unlike conventional desk lamps with "industrial" form and straight lines, *NUWA* has an exaggerated curved profile. *NUWA*'s neck is composed of smaller pieces of joints and wrapped with elastic clothes like the spine covered with skin. The form still fits a desk lamp's functional requirement. When the *NUWA* turns its head around, these clothes will form dynamic fold forms.

Responsive Behavior

The second characteristic is responsive behavior. The ability to perceive and respond is an essential phenomenon of natural life that "react to stimuli" [32]. Daily artifacts are "passive things" that work only when users purposely operate them. In contrast, lifelike things are "active." in which they present their activities as being seeing, hearing, or feeling to respond to the environment.

A pyroelectric detector and a capacitive sensor in *NUWA* enable it to be aware of the presence of the user's body. For example, when a user suddenly appears or moves in front of the lamp in a vast movement, the lamp may "look up" at the user. *NUWA*'s responsive behavior is expected to present a natural and intuitive response to the user's presence. The head-lifting mechanism differs from simple rotatory movement but moves like our spine. It is done by its segmented neck pieces driven by motors with two fishing lines. The frequency of responsive reactions is decreased (to 15 min per time on average) to avoid mechanical repetition and distraction when users are working at the desk.

Willingness to Interact with Human

A further step to present artifacts' activeness is to imitate social willingness. In Row and Nam's [2] lifelike category, dynamic behavior, they found the lifelike interaction should present the motivation of the artifact. Some lifelike-designed projects also adopted this feature, for example, a toaster that would start interacting with users without any outer trigger [7]. An artifact that appears perfunctory or disinterested when interacting with the user is in this feature category.

In our design, if the user tries to get the attention of *NUWA* by waving his or her hand, *NUWA* can respond with diverse results. For example, *NUWA* may refuse to respond to gestures. The different response results should inspire the interpretation of NUWA's moods and "personality."

Autonomous Goal

Unlike commercial products serving humans' goals, a lifelike artifact can have its own "purpose of life." Inspired by the biological understanding of animals [8, 33], the different response of lifelike artifacts should present their internal "goal." Users may interpret lifelike artifacts' properties, such as thoughts, personalities, experiences, or life stories. While this is driven by the artificial design of some random strategies, the ambiguous understanding or interpretation of interaction should enhance the lifelike experience.

In the current version of the design, *NUWA* lives between its explorative and sleep (idle) behaviors. When *NUWA* "wakes up," it starts its life journey and is interested in everything in its surroundings. In this status, *NUWA* looks around and reacts to the environment more often. After being active for over 2.5 h, it lowers its head and reacts to the surroundings only with weaker motions, just like it is getting tired.

3 Experiment Design

A lifelike artifact can allow rich imagination of interaction. While the connection between the input and output of the artifact is not fixed, we expect users to be engaged in understanding the object during the "unreliable" interaction. We are also interested in this alternative development of human-artifact relationships that developed in long-term usage, especially the correlation between the lifelike characteristics and the experience of an autonomous and lifelike thing.

Based on these two aspects, this study is conducted in a manner of *research through design* [48, 49]. *NUWA* was prototyped and used by our participants. Our goal is to package our understanding in design practice and unfold it in the field to observe users' understanding of the artifact. Besides the qualitative method, four measurement tools, *Godspeed*, *AttrakDiff*, *Product Attachment Scale*, and *Interpersonal Relationship Inventory*, were used to help profile users' experience. The four scales cover the evaluation of the design itself and users' subjective experience. Due to the limitation of space, we explain each tool briefly as follows.

The Godspeed questionnaire [14] is originally developed to measure users' anthropomorphic perception of humanoid robots. The questionnaire is a five-level semantic differential scale with 24 items in five constructs: anthropomorphism (ant), animacy (ani), likeability (lik), perceived intelligence (pi), and perceived safety (ps).

AttrakDiff [34] is a useful tool for profiling users' experiences from different perspectives. *AttrakDiff* is a seven-level semantic differential scale with 28 questions. It distinguishes hedonic quality from pragmatic quality (pq) and attractiveness (att). Besides, the hedonic quality is further categorized into two sub-categories. Identity (hqi) implies the social-cultural consequence, while stimulation (hqs) measures the perceptual pleasures.

Consumer-Product Attachment Scale [35] has 15 items measuring four essential aspects of consumers' attachment to the product. This scale is used to understand the relationship between humans and products, including emotional attachment (At), irreplaceability (Ir), indispensability (In), and the achievement of self-extension (SE). The last construct of self-extension is close to *AttrakDiff*'s hedonic identity.

The last questionnaire is the *Interpersonal Relationship Inventory – Short Form* [36] (see also [37, 38] for the original version). This questionnaire is usually used in psychology research to investigate the interpersonal relationships of a Participant and is borrowed to explore whether a social relationship could exist (beyond consumer attachment) in the usage of our lifelike lamps. The questionnaire is a seven-level Likert scale comprising 26 items, including social support and conflict, corresponding to positive and negative social relationships.

A total of five participants were invited. All participants were colleagues of the lab, including two females and three males, aged from 23 to 31. Each participant was given three days to use a normal desk lamp and another three days for the *NUWA* desk lamp in the lab or their rooms. Before they started to use *NUWA*, minimal instruction about its working principles was provided. Participants were asked to complete questionnaires after they used each lamp. After both lamps had been used, short interviews were conducted.

4 Results

In the experiment, all five participants finished the six-day tests and the self-reported questionnaires. In the following, we first report the quantitative result and then the interpretation of qualitative data.

4.1 Quantitative Result

The *Godspeed Questionnaire* (Table 1) helps us understand the level of lifelikeness perceived by users. The result is shown in Table 1. *NUWA* (mean = 3.32, SD = 0.36) scores significantly higher than a normal desk lamp (mean = 1.33, SD = 0.55) in the anthropomorphism (Z = −2.03, p = 0.042). Also, in animacy, *NUWA* (mean = 3.5, SD = 0.83) performs better (Z = −2.02, p = 0.043) than the normal lamp (mean = 1.42, SD = 0.79). The Perceived Intelligence of *NUWA* (mean = 3.44, SD = 0.80) is significantly higher (Z = −2.02, p = 0.43) than the normal lamp (mean = 2.2, SD = 0.53). The Likeability and Perceived Safety do not show significant differences.

While the significant differences in anthropomorphism, animacy, and perceived intelligence are evidence of *NUWA*'s lifelike character, the likeability is related to individuals' preferences. Our participants may not extremely desire the quality of *NUWA*'s prototypes. Besides, the perceived safety implies the emotional expression of the artifact (aggressive or less aggressive). In our case, *NUWA* is not designed to present such properties.

Table 1. Wilcoxon Signed Rans Test: Five Godspeed Questionnaire

	anthropomorphism_NUWA - anthropomorphism_normal	animacy_NUWA - animacy_normal	likeability_NUWA - likeability_normal	perceived intelligence_NUWA - perceived intelligence_normal	perceived safety_NUWA - perceived safety_normal
Z	-2.032[a]	-2.023[a]	-1.826[a]	-2.023[a]	-1.461[a]
Asymp. Sig. (2-tailed)	.042	.043	.068	.043	.144

a. Based on negative ranks.

Descriptive Statistics

	N	Mean	Std. Deviation	Minimum	Maximum
anthropomorphism_normal	5	1.4400	.55498	1.00	2.40
animacy_normal	5	1.4333	.78705	1.00	2.83
likeability_normal	5	2.8400	.92087	1.40	3.80
perceived intelligence_normal	5	2.2000	.52915	1.60	3.00
perceived safety_normal	5	2.6000	1.11555	1.00	3.67
anthropomorphism_NUWA	5	3.3200	.36332	3.00	3.80
animacy_NUWA	5	3.5000	.82496	2.50	4.50
likeability_NUWA	5	3.9600	.51769	3.20	4.60
perceived intelligence_NUWA	5	3.4400	.80498	2.60	4.60
perceived safety_NUWA	5	3.6667	.23570	3.33	4.00

The result of *AttrakDiff* informs relevant experience profiles of the lifelike design. The pragmatic quality of *NUWA* (mean = 2.80, SD = 0.67) is significantly lower (Z = −2.02, p = 0.43) than the ordinary lamp (mean = 5.77, SD = 0.42). A very possible reason is the unpredictability of *NUWA*. While we noticed that desk lamp is not a necessity on our desks nowadays, evaluating the perceived usefulness (pragmatic quality) can be interpreted as the controllability of the artifact.

However, *NUWA* has significantly higher scores (see Table 2) both in the stimulation (mean = 6.34, SD = 0.45) and identity (mean = 5.34, SD = 0.67) of the hedonic qualities. The high score in stimulation is not surprising since *NUWA* has more interactive capabilities by its design. What is interesting to us is that the *NUWA*'s lifelike characters also enhance participants' identity quality, in which personal values are related to the use of the artifacts. The result of attractiveness seems contradictory to *Godspeed*'s likeability, by which *NUWA* is considered to be more attractive. An explanation could be that *NUWA* can, due to its features, result in stronger emotional arousal, leading to high attractiveness. However, this did not lead to a higher likeability because the current version of *NUWA* had just a prototype quality and was not really desired by the participants – "*I try to ignore its material properties actually…because I knew it is a prototype*" (P3).

Table 2. Wilcoxon Signed Rans Test: *AttrakDiff* Questionnaire

	pragmatic qual._NUWA - pragmatic qual._normal	hedonic - stimulation_NUWA - hedonic - stimulation_normal	hedonic - identity_NUWA - hedonic - identity_normal	attractiveness_NUWA - attachment_normal
Z	-2.023[a]	-2.023[b]	-2.023[b]	-2.023[b]
Asymp. Sig. (2-tailed)	.043	.043	.043	.043

a. Based on positive ranks.

b. Based on negative ranks.

Descriptive Statistics

	N	Mean	Std. Deviation	Minimum	Maximum
pragmatic qual._normal	5	5.7714	.42378	5.29	6.43
hedonic - stimulation_normal	5	2.0857	.77328	1.14	3.29
hedonic - identity_normal	5	3.2857	.71429	2.57	4.29
attachment_normal	5	3.1556	.23040	2.89	3.44
pragmatic qual._NUWA	5	2.8000	.67461	1.86	3.71
hedonic - stimulation_NUWA	5	6.3429	.44721	5.86	7.00
hedonic - identity_NUWA	5	5.3429	.66701	4.29	6.00
attractiveness_NUWA	5	5.6286	.77328	5.00	6.86

Regarding the *consumer-product attachment*, participants reported a significantly higher score in using *NUWA* in all four aspects (Table 3), showing a stronger emotional attachment to it. However, we should note that both NUWA and the normal lamp have low scores on self-extension, although the difference is still significant. The desk lamp may not be a necessary tool for our participants. They were not really dependent on them.

The result of high attachment, irreplaceability, and indispensability is inspiring. While we believe that the resource of our planet is limited and our consuming behavior should be altered. This result suggests that what motivates users to keep using an artifact is not the functionality it presents but the intensive experience it creates.

The *interpersonal relationship inventory* borrowed from psychology is used for an explorative attempt. This relationship scale demonstrates the positive (supportive) and negative (conflicting) aspects. In our study, NUWA shows a significantly ($Z = -2.02$, $p = 0.043$) higher score ($m = 4.66$, $SD = 0.21$) than the normal lamp ($mean = 2.57$, $SD = 1.08$) on social support. The scores for social conflict have no significant difference (Table 4). Initially, we suspect a higher social conflict by NUWA because of the unpredictable performance of NUWA. However, the result suggests the opposite situation. The activeness of NUWA unfolded in users' experience as an inspiring companionship, which is consistent with our interview result in the following.

Table 3. Wilcoxon Signed Rans Test: Consumer-Product Attachment Questionnaire

	attachment_NUWA - attachment_normal	irreplaceability_NUWA - irreplaceability_normal	indispensability_NUWA - indispensability_normal	self-extension_NUWA - self-extension_normal
Z	-2.023[a]	-2.032[a]	-2.032[a]	-2.023[a]
Asymp. Sig. (2-tailed)	.043	.042	.042	.043

a. Based on negative ranks.

Descriptive Statistics

	N	Mean	Std. Deviation	Minimum	Maximum
attachment_normal	5	1.7200	.64187	1.00	2.60
irreplaceability_normal	5	1.8000	.76739	1.00	3.00
indispensability_normal	5	2.1000	.91173	1.00	3.25
self-extension_normal	5	1.3333	.40825	1.00	2.00
attachment_NUWA	5	5.6800	.90111	4.60	7.00
irreplaceability_NUWA	5	5.6000	1.06458	4.00	7.00
indispensability_NUWA	5	4.0500	.20917	3.75	4.25
self-extension_NUWA	5	2.8667	.80277	2.00	3.67

Table 4. Result of Interpersonal Relationship Inventory – Short Form Questionnaire

	social support_NUWA - social support_normal	social conflict_NUWA - social conflict_normal
Z	-2.023[a]	-.135[a]
Asymp. Sig. (2-tailed)	.043	.893

a. Based on negative ranks.

Descriptive Statistics

	N	Mean	Std. Deviation	Minimum	Maximum
social support_normal	5	2.5692	1.08322	1.46	4.00
social conflict_normal	5	4.7538	.93486	3.46	6.08
social support_NUWA	5	4.6615	.20783	4.46	4.92
social conflict_NUWA	5	4.9846	.43310	4.38	5.54

4.2 Interview Analysis

In addition to the qualitative analyses, interviews were conducted to understand participants' subjective interpretation of their feelings, interactions, and experiences with more details. Overall, we acquired three main findings from the quantitative result. We have found that the characteristics of *NUWA* attract more attention, drive the contrast between hedonic and pragmatic qualities, and lead users to develop a variety of personal interpretations of *NUWA*.

Caution of Attention

A significant difference between *NUWA* and the normal lamp lies in the attraction to the participants. For example, "[when using the normal lamp,] *I forget about its existence of it after turning it on or off*" (P1). "*In comparison* [to *NUWA*], *it never got my serious attention*" (P4). "It [*NUWA*] often grabs my attention" (P5).

When the features of *NUWA* attracted participants, it sometimes became annoying after a long time of usage. "*Sometimes it* [NUWA] *suddenly moved and interrupted my thought. I then forgot what I was thinking*" (P2). In fact, we foresaw this problem when we designed and tested the *NUWA*. A design improvement to reduce its interference with users could be reducing the frequency of *NUWA*'s activity and making it more intelligent. However, this distracting character of a lifelike artifact tends to be annoying due to its intensive presence as a desk lamp. This feature can be positive if we are designing an artifact only involving quick and short usage.

The Paradox of Hedonic Quality and Pragmatic Quality

Some users pointed out that the features associated with the lifelike design seemed to conflict with the essence of the lamp. "*A desk lamp is a very controllable thing, but NUWA... Finely adjusts its light, angle, height, color temperature, etc. NUWA's logic of its performance not predictable*" (P4). Besides, although the presence of *NUWA* is sometimes annoying, it also plays the role of a partner. "*It* [NUWA] *is less practical, but I like having it around*" (P1). While these narratives are related to negative experiences, participants also reported their positive ones. "*Having it* [NUWA] *on the table is a fresh, fun, and cool experience*" (P1). "*I love* NUWA *when it is moving*" (P3). "*I am excited to see it moving*" (P5).

Firstly, this is consistent with the quantitative result, where the lifelike *NUWA* has low pragmatic but high hedonic qualities. The changing and inconsistent performance of a lifelike artifact enriched the user experience. Secondly, the positiveness of the hedonic quality does not mean that the experience is always positive. We saw richness in the holistic. Therefore, it should be noted that lifelike design strategies do not always fit the requirement of a product. The desk lamp is an artifact that did not matter much in the participants' daily lives. An unrestrained room for *NUWA*'s presence allows users to accept it as a partner.

Interpretation of *NUWA*'s Motivation

The interpretation of the being of NUWA was diverse. "*It looks organic...like some kind of flower*" (P1). "*It looks like plants*" (P2). Or "*It looks like an alien creature from sci-fi movies*" (P4). It is also interesting that *NUWA's* users developed their own interpretation of what *NUWA* was doing. On the one hand, NUWA was interpreted as something with little intelligence. For example, "*I think it* [NUWA] *was trying to communicate with me.* [...] *It knows what the user is doing at a certain level*" (P1), "*It looks like it is sad... because its head is low*" (P3), or "*I think* NUWA *was trying to draw my attention*" (P3). On the other hand, some participants suggested their perception of an anthropomorphic object. "*It* [NUWA] *sometimes turns its head and looks at me*" (P4). "*I thought it* [NUWA] *want me to take a break*" (P5).

We suggest that the process of developing personal interpretation about unpredictable interactive devices results in not only a positive consequence in human-artifact attachment but also in the human-technology relationship.

Partnership
Finally, participants reported their social relationships to *NUWA*. In our case, NUWA is often perceived as a partner. "*It is a good partner when I am facing boring tasks. It made me feel having a partner around*" (P2). This is also associated with the interpretation of *NUWA*'s motivation. "*It was fun, just like having someone with me... Sometimes it tried to call you, sometimes it ignored you*" (P5).

5 Discussion and Conclusion

In this research, we try to answer whether the Lifelike strategy can enhance the hedonic qualities of products. We designed a desk lamp, *NUWA*. The concept was developed without imitating a real living creature but based on lifelike design strategies. The quantitative measurement of the five participants' experience shows an inspiring result. *NUWA* was found to be more lifelike from the perspective of anthropomorphism, animacy, and perceived intelligence. Besides, it has a higher score in the hedonic qualities but lower in the pragmatic quality. Participants also reported significantly higher attachment to *NUWA*, and *NUWA* created a kind of socially supportive relationship with our participants. The qualitative analyses suggest consistent results. Participants reported both pleasurable and unpleasant experiences with *NUWA*. However, the rich interpretation of the lifelike artifact created a stronger emotional bond to it.

In the implementation of lifelike design strategies, there should be a trade-off consideration. While lifelike brings strong emotional bound, the experience is a mixture of both positive and negative ones. The relational connection is apparently related to the space for free interpretation of what *NUWA* is doing. This should inspire our future design research about the hermeneutic understanding of the human-technology relationship.

Although this study provides inspiring results, the limited number of participants and time for field tests is a serious limitation. Our understanding of users' experience does not cover the experience in the long term. Besides, the artifact is of prototype quality, and the participants were from the college. The inherent perspective on interaction design and design research is a significant bias in user experience. Our future goal is to test the lifelike artifacts with better manufacturing quality and the real field in the long term.

References

1. Cakiroglu, I., Pazarbasi, C.K.: Critical design in daily life: Lifelike products. Des. J. **22**, 1227–1234 (2019)
2. Row, Y.-K., Nam, T.-J.: Understanding lifelike characteristics in interactive product design. Arch. Des. Res. **29**, 25–42 (2016)

3. Lee, D., Kim, M.: Reaction feedback as a lifelike idle interaction of human-robot interaction. In: Proceedings of International Conference on Kansei Engineering & Intelligent Systems. Springer, New York (2010)
4. Tan, H.: Lifelike design in robotic and interactive objects. Doctoral dissertation, Indiana University (2019)
5. Kim, Y.-K., Row, Y.-K., Nam, T.-J.: Knoby: pet-like interactive door knob. In: Proceedings of International Conference on Human Factors in Computing Systems, pp. 1685–1690, ACM Press, New York (2012)
6. Togler, J., Hemmert, F., Wettach, R.: Living interfaces: the thrifty faucet. In: Proceedings of Third International Conference on Tangible and Embedded Interaction, pp. 43–44. ACM Press, New York (2009)
7. Burneleit, E., Hemmert, F., Wettach, R.: Living interfaces: the impatient toaster. In: Proceedings of Third International Conference on Tangible and Embedded Interaction, pp. 21–22, ACM Press, New York (2009)
8. Jun, J.W.: Plant-like robots. In: Proceedings of Third Biennial Research Through Design Conference, Cambridge, UK, pp. 501–517 (2017)
9. Row, Y.K., Nam, T.J.: CAMY: applying a pet dog analogy to everyday ubicomp products. In: Proceedings of 2014 ACM International Joint Conference on Pervasive and Ubiquitous Computing, pp. 63–74 ACM Press, New York (2014)
10. Ahamed, M.K., Wang, H., Hazell, P.J.: From biology to biomimicry: using nature to build better structures – a review. Constr. Build. Mater. **320**, 126–195 (2022)
11. Kellert, S.R., Wilson, E.O., Benyus, J., Mador, M.L., Salingaros, N.A., et al.: Biophilic Design. Wiley, New York (2008)
12. Söderlund, J.: The Emergence of Biophilic Design. Springer, Cham (2019)
13. Mautner, M.N.: Life-centered ethics, and the human future in space. Bioethics **23**, 433–440 (2009)
14. Bartneck, C., Kulić, D., Croft, E., Zoghbi, S.: Measurement instruments for the anthropomorphism, animacy, likeability, perceived intelligence, and perceived safety of robots. Int. J. Soc. Robot. **1**, 71–81 (2009)
15. Sakuma, M., Kuramochi, K., Shimada, N., Ito, R.: Positive and negative opinions about living with robots in Japanese university students. In: 14th International Conference on Human-Robot Interaction, vol. 14, pp. 640–641. ACM Press, New York (2019)
16. Admoni, H., Scassellati, B.: Social eye gaze in human-robot interaction: a review. J. Hum.-Robot Interact. **6**, 25–63. ACM Press, New York (2017)
17. Tuomi, A., Tussyadiah, I.P., Hanna, P.: Spicing up hospitality service encounters: the case of PepperTM. Int. J. Contemp. Hosp. Manag. **33**, 3906–3925 (2021)
18. Yamaji, Y., Miyake, T., Yoshiike, Y., deSilva, P.R.S., Okada, M.: STB: child-dependent sociable trash box. Int. J. Soc. Robot. **3**, 359–370 (2011)
19. Saraiva, M., Ayanoğlu, H., Özcan, B.: Emotional design and human-robot interaction. In: Ayanoğlu, H., Duarte, E. (eds.) Emotional Design in Human-Robot Interaction. HIS, pp. 119–141. Springer, Cham (2019). https://doi.org/10.1007/978-3-319-96722-6_8
20. Weiss, A., Wurhofer, D., Tscheligi, M.: "I love this dog" – children's emotional attachment to the robotic dog AIBO. Int. J. Soc. Robot. **1**, 243–248 (2009)
21. Fujita, M.: AIBO: toward the era of digital creatures. Int. J. Robot. Res. **20**, 781–794 (2001)
22. Bartneck, C., Belpaeme, T., Eyssel, F., Takayuki, K., Merel, K., Selma, S.: Human-Robot Interaction. Cambridge University Press, Cambridge (2019)
23. Hart, E.: Breakaway: an ambient display designed to change human behavior. In: Proceedings of International Conference on Human Factors in Computing Systems, pp. 1945–1948. ACM Press, New York (2005)
24. Ofek, E., Avery, J.: Nandda home: preparing for life after clocky. Harvard Business School, no. 9, Case 511-134 (2011)

25. Yoshida, N., Yonezawa, T.: Investigating breathing expression of a stuffed-toy robot based on body-emotion model. In: Proceedings of 4th International Conference on Human Agent Interaction, pp. 139–144. ACM Press, New York (2016)
26. Pandey, A.K., Gelin, R.: A mass-produced sociable humanoid robot: pepper: the first machine of its kind. IEEE Robot. Autom. Mag. **25**, 40–48 (2018)
27. Metta, G., Sandini, G., Vernon, D., Natale, L., Nori, F.: The iCub humanoid robot: an open platform for research in embodied cognition. In: Performance Metrics for Intelligent Systems Workshop, vol. 9, pp. 50–56 (2008)
28. Tan, H., Sabanovic, S.: Designing lifelikeness in interactive and robotic objects. In: The Proceedings of 12th International Conference on Human-Robot Interaction, vol. 1, pp. 381–382. ACM Press, New York (2017)
29. Norman, D.A.: The Design of Every Day Thing. Basic Books, New York (1990)
30. Pieter, D., Paul, H.: Framework of product experience. Int. J. Des. **1**, 57–66 (2007)
31. Hassenzahl, M.: The thing and I: Understanding the relationship between user and product. Funnology **2**, 31–42 (2003)
32. McKay, C.P.: What is life: and how do we search for it in other worlds? PLoS Biol. **2**, 1260–1263 (2004)
33. Cantrell, B.E., Holzman, J.: Responsive Landscapes. Routledge, London and New York (2015)
34. Hassenzahl, M., Burmester, M., Koller, F.: AttrakDiff: Ein Fragebogen zur Messung wahrgenommener hedonischer und pragmatischer Qualität. In: Szwillus, G., Ziegler, J. (eds.) Mensch & Computer 2003, pp. 187–196. Springer, Cham (2003). https://doi.org/10.1007/978-3-322-80058-9_19
35. Schifferstein, H.N.J., Zwartkruis-Pelgrim, E.P.H.: Consumer-product attachment: measurement and design implications. Int. J. Des. **2**, 1–13 (2008)
36. Nayback-Beebe, A.M., Yoder, L.H.: Psychometric properties of the interpersonal relationship inventory-short form for active duty female service members. Res. Nurs. Health **34**, 241–252 (2011)
37. Kane, R.T., Chris, D.: The psychometric characteristics of the IPR inventory: data from rural Western Australia. Nurs. Res. **48**, 324–328 (1999)
38. Yarcheski, A., Mahon, N.E., Yarcheski, T.J., Hanks, M.M.: Psychometric evaluation of the interpersonal relationship inventory for early adolescents. Public Health Nurs. **25**, 375–382 (2008)
39. Chien, W.-C., Hassenzahl, M., Welge, J.: Sharing a robotic pet as a maintenance strategy for romantic couples in long-distance relationship: an autobiographical design exploration. In: Proceedings of the Conference Extended Abstracts on Human Factors in Computing Systems, pp. 1375–1382 (2016)

Rapid Prototyping Platform for Multi-stakeholder Involvement in the Design of User Interaction

Anjelika Votintseva(✉)

Siemens AG, Otto-Hahn-Ring 6, 81739 Munich, Germany
anjelika.votintseva@siemens.com

Abstract. Over the last couple of years, human oriented manufacturing, also called social manufacturing, became an ever more important aim in the transition into an industry 4.0. One of the best ways of doing that is to bring the end users, manufactures, and other participants from the production and design process closer together, so they can all make improved and socially sustainable products a reality. Prototyping, as a part of the design thinking process, plays a significant role in the physical and virtual implementation of a concept and is an essential phase during the collaborative design and search for new ideas. Depending on the project objectives and the collaborator skills and preferences, different forms of prototyping can be applied. This paper describes a prototyping platform that makes use of the combination of different prototyping techniques. The proposed approach for collaborative prototyping is illustrated with an example of the idea development for several interaction scenarios of different complexity.

Keywords: Collaborative Prototyping · Human-Computer Interaction · Remote Collaboration · Prototyping Platform

1 Introduction

This research was partially funded by the European Union's Horizon 2020 research and innovation program under Grant Agreement no. 870037 (iPRODUCE project [1]). During this project a prototype called Generative Design Platform (GDP) was developed to support both "makers" (engineers, designers, manufacturers) and consumers in their collaborative activities like co-design, collaborative prototyping, and testing [2]. In the current study, the GDP is extended via integration with external tools and components.

Over the last couple of years, human oriented manufacturing, also called social manufacturing, became an ever more important aim in the transition into an industry 4.0 [3]. Essentially, it puts the human being in the forefront when thinking about improving the manufacturing prosses. One of the best ways of doing that is to bring the end users, manufactures, and possibly other participants from the production and design process closer together, so they can all make improved and socially sustainable products a reality.

Design Thinking is a widely accepted user centric iterative process for the effective discovery of the user wishes, problem solving, and idea generation [4]. It is suited

M. Kurosu and A. Hashizume (Eds.): HCII 2023, LNCS 14011, pp. 302–313, 2023.
https://doi.org/10.1007/978-3-031-35596-7_19

for the objectives of social manufacturing. Design thinking consists of six main steps: empathize, define, ideate, prototype, test, and implement. Prototyping, as a part of the design thinking process, plays a significant role in the physical and virtual implementation of a concept for the early evaluation and selection of the proper solution. This paper focuses on the prototype phase by discussing different types of prototypes and proposing a methodology for their effective combination with an example of a prototyping framework and its application to a set of scenarios simulating a shopfloor with IoT features.

Transforming customer wishes into the final product is tricky and often goes a long way through different stages. One reason is because the end users lack technical understanding needed to specify requirements at the level, so that developers can proceed directly to implementation. During collaborative and co-creation sessions project stakeholders strive for different objectives. While low fidelity prototypes (as paper prototypes) are easily understandable and exploitable by non-technical stakeholders, they often cannot capture essential functionality details needed for developers. On the other hands, there are too many efforts implied for technical developers when implementing high fidelity prototypes. This coupled with the shortage on technical staff leads to a strong desire to shift as many tasks as possible away from the developers to other stakeholder often with less or no technical skills. Also, the rising standards on quality and usability of the applications request early involvement of the end users and other stakeholders in the design and prototyping of the applications.

The approach of this research aims to mitigate the hurdles for non-technical persons to participate in the feasibility study of interaction concepts during early prototyping phase. Our other target is to make the development of prototypes modular and easily extendable. To reach this, we propose to use resources that are simple enough to be quickly taught to different stakeholders and allow to build "executable" prototypes fast. Even technically skilled staff can benefit, as they can show very quickly several alternatives to the end customers to explain the possibilities of (new) technologies and details they need for the implementation. Our contribution illustrates how collaborative interaction can be prototyped fast and tested with several scenarios.

To apply rapid prototyping involving more stakeholders into the development of concepts for "collaborative interactions", we built a Rapid Prototyping Platform (RapPP). While Sect. 2 provides a general consideration about the existing prototyping methods, the implementation of our platform will be explained in Sect. 3 and exemplified with a use case for an "interactive" shopfloor prototyping in Sect. 4. Section 5 summarizes our experience during the prototyping of the platform and testing it with different user interaction scenarios.

2 Prototyping Methods

One main task during the user centric design is the identification of the user needs, which can be challenging as the end users often lack the technological understanding. This is especially a case in the new technology areas, where users may even have no idea what is possible to expect. It can be very difficult for them to discover requirements, what they can wish from the technologies they never heard before or from their combination or integration into existing tools.

Prototypes provide concrete representations of design ideas and give designers, users, developers, and managers an early insight into how the new system will look and feel. They have great potential because they can make it easier to express your thoughts, come up with new ideas, get valuable customer assessments, prove hypotheses and in addition to that they are cheap and expandable. Depending on the project objectives and the development state, different forms and types of prototyping can be applied [19, 20]. Moreover, each type of prototyping requires different skills (e.g., 3D modelling, additive manufacturing, hardware, or software knowledge) and may need an access to specific equipment, like additive/subtractive manufacturing devices (3D printer or laser cutter), or other resources (like licenses).

According to [20] the user prototypes are mostly created with a purpose to test a concept with customers and received direct feedback. Depending on the set objectives, engineers drive technical feasibility or improve data flows in live-data prototypes, therefore, this stakeholder group strives for either feasibility or life-data prototypes. For this reason, engineers often underestimate the importance of design principles. Feasibility prototypes are made to test the viability and functionality of the product. Live-data prototypes intend to test the digital features and functionalities of a program or a solution. Project managers have to take all three prototyping types into consideration. Thus, different prototyping techniques can help to bring end customers and technical developers closer to the mutual understanding.

Our contribution is devoted to a rapid prototyping example and illustrates how collaborative interaction can be tested for a selected case study. Rapid prototyping [6] is quick and inexpensive technique. On the other hand, it requires a more thought-out concept but can therefore evolve with further development into a finalized system. In addition to that, there is also iterative prototyping which is particularly attractive if the goal is to continuously improve ideas and learn from mistakes [5].

Figure 1 illustrates another dimension of the prototyping approaches and technologies used during our study to visualize and evaluate new ideas.

Paper prototyping [21] is an effective tool to visualize an idea in the shortest time. It belongs to the most common approaches for low-fidelity prototypes in the initial stage and requires no additional training or expensive specialized equipment. So, this approach is low-cost, which is an important factor for sustainable development. In our research, paper prototyping was applied to create a cardboard robot arm evaluating the range of motion, to simulate a shopfloor environment and working employees with the help of SAP Scenes [17]. Best practice includes usage of paper prototyping not only for user acceptance evaluation, but also for feasibility testing.

Virtual prototyping requires intermediate knowledge of 3D modelling. It may involve additional cost related to software licenses. In our research, Rhinoceros [11] with its plugin Grasshopper [12] was used to create and visualize parametric 3D models of smart products. This approach was useful to develop a movement simulation and design selection by means of visual scripting. Co-Spaces [18] were used to simulate the environment of a shopfloor and to test safety rules in potentially dangerous situations that may happen if humans will work together with different autonomously moving robots or other equipment. The best practice includes using virtual prototyping for initial concepts development and their simulation.

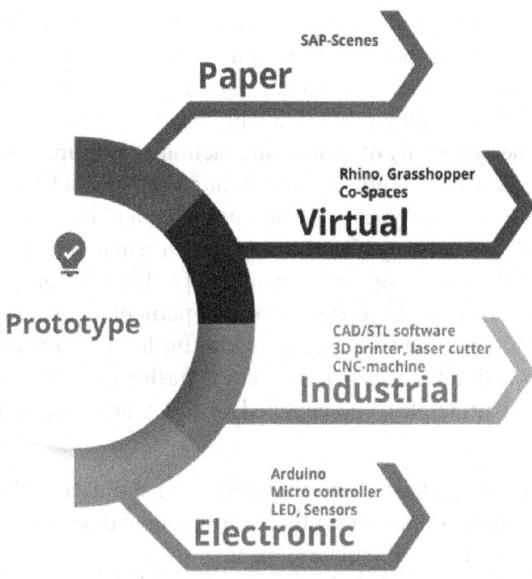

Fig. 1. Approaches and sample technologies considered in our Prototyping Framework.

Industrial prototyping involves advanced knowledge of 3D/2D modelling, CAD, and other software. It often involves additional cost caused by expensive software licenses and access to high-tech devices (3D printer, laser cutter, CNC machine). This type of prototyping drives innovation with additive and subtractive manufacturing approaches. In our study for the aim of rapid prototyping, we used ready 3D models from the 3D community Thingiverse [22] and printed them with Ultimaker [23], a 3D printer series. In this regard, the best practice involves feasibility testing but can also involve user acceptance testing.

Electronic prototyping requires knowledge in electronics and hardware (HW) programming. Moreover, it often involves additional costs needed for electronics, like microcontrollers, sensorics, motors, and other pieces of HW, but may also need a 3D printer or similar equipment to mount electronic components together. In our research project, Arduino [13] and micro:bit [14] microcontrollers with diverse sensors and actuators were used to check new interaction concepts including both human-machine (HMI) and machine-to-machine interaction (MMI). The best practice for this technique involves mainly feasibility testing.

3 Prototyping Platform

Different skills and backgrounds of stakeholders in combination with their different objectives in prototyping can have unpredictable consequences. Therefore, there is a strong need to combine collective efforts and improve stakeholder management during prototyping sessions.

In our case study we assume a situation we really faced in our project. The involved tools and components were originally designed as single-user applications. Our project partners reflected the wish for multi-player mode of the collaboration. This means they wanted that several persons participate simultaneously in one session to design 3D products. When asked for exact requirements and expectations on such collaboration, they only pointed to the existing online text editing tool.

To investigate the potentials of remote interaction of multiple users with a system of IoT devices we have built a prototyping framework – Rapid Prototyping Platform (RapPP) – combining several types of prototypes, UIs, and their connections. To keep the efforts low, we reused existing UIs, connecting different tools within this framework. Moreover, we applied visual scripting techniques ([7, 12, 15]) for quick modifications within different components of the framework, in particular for virtual and electronic prototypes. It is continuously being extended with further features needed to make the collaboration easier and more effective or to cover further collaboration scenarios.

There are several principles implemented in this platform that help to reach the targets:

- Integration of social platforms into the process of the user collaboration to reuse existing user interfaces (UIs) during the prototyping and to study the "natural" user interaction within their familiar environment.
- Different low-code/no-code techniques – like Visual scripting, graphical programming – to accelerate the creation of executable prototype for virtual and physical visualization of possible outcomes of the user interaction.
- Usage of the chat-bot technology by combining the social network applications with the GDP's component for natural language processing (NLP). This makes the human interaction effective in the prototyping phase because such interaction is flexible enough without the need to constantly update the interface.
- Integration of MQTT messaging [9] to capture the machine-to-machine communication and combine this with the human inputs.

One of the main achievements of the applied approach is the involvement of existing user interfaces (UI) into different steps of prototyping, which makes it easier for the users to participate in the prototyping activities by interacting over the familiar front ends, also remotely over the internet. This was discovered to be essential for collaborative prototyping. Another result of our research is the show case how to extend typical single player applications (like 3D modeling, NLP tool) to handle multi-player mode necessary for real collaborative user interaction, including different locations.

During this research, we studied different usage possibilities for our GDP. We have integrated it with other UIs and used it as Digital Twin connected to the physical prototypes.

Figure 2 below gives an overview of the overall structure of the RapPP and dependencies among its components as well as with other tools.

The collection of all inputs from different interfaces is performed within the RapPP server. The server is implemented with visual scripting tool Node-RED [7]. We decided to use Node-RED for the server prototyping, because it applies low code paradigm with a steep learning curve, contains many libraries for easy integration with other tools/interfaces (Slack, Twitter, Airtable, Alexa, and many other). For the current case study, we considered Slack [8] as an example of the social interaction interface. So, for the prototype we don't need to care about user management, security, and similar

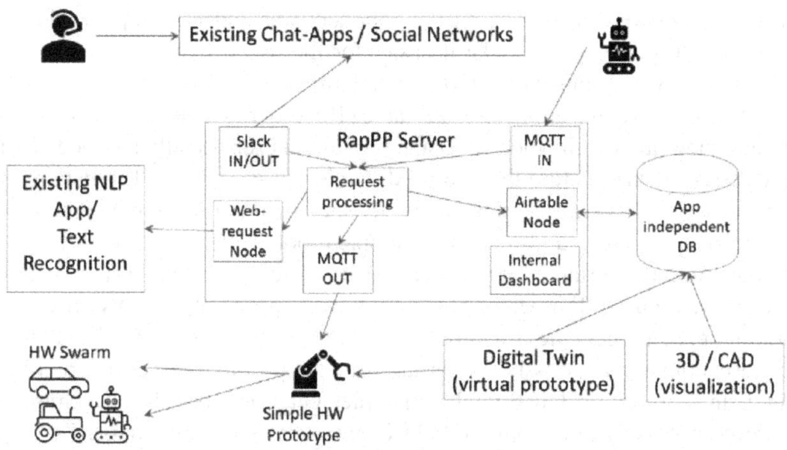

Fig. 2. RapPP overview.

features. Users can organize themselves in groups, called channels in Slack's workspaces, those identifying different projects or products. Users need only to configure a special chat-bot, an integration feature of Slack. The RapPP server communicates with this chat-bot listening for any textual inputs from the participants. It then processes these texts by calling external NLP (Natural Language Processing) application and saving the structured results on an external data base.

To allow potential algorithms, like other devices (including those from the internet) or artificial intelligence, to interact with the created HW prototype, we also integrated the MQTT communication within the RapPP server. To make it possible for humans to test this type of interaction, we constructed very simple dashboards on mobile devices that can be easily updated while concepts are evolving during the prototyping phase.

The server finally generates the reply to confirm the reception of the command or wish. In addition to the reply to the Slack's users, the server can send the reply as an MQTT message to be processed by any device subscribed to such messages. 3D/CAD/Digital Twin applications obtain the information directly from the external data base where structured information from all inputs is stored. The Slack interface was selected to add the multi-user interaction feature to our evaluation scenarios, as several participants can be invited to one channel and contribute to the same project simultaneously while observing the contributions of each other.

Currently, for the natural language processing we integrated our own tool Spatial Instructor, a component from the GDP, to understand commands from the collaborators. But any other can be also connected via the web-request node within the server implementation. The results from Spatial Instructor are structured texts with extracted parameter values that are mapped to the structure defined within the data base. The NLP component is optional one. The initial version of the RapPP was developed without the text analysis. The users needed to know the exact syntax of the command to control the digital twin and field devices. The NLP component was added to improve the usability of the RapPP prototype to make it easier for the users to specify their wishes in non-structural way and concentrate more on the interaction itself.

We selected an existing application Airtable [10] as our external data base, because it already has integration with Node-RED and provides a user-friendly no-code definition of the necessary data structure that we need within our case study. The data model of the current case study is simple, reflecting only spatial properties of the components of a 3D model and few commands to control simple robot prototypes.

The data from the Airtable data base can be accessed by existing 3D applications. In our case study, we used Rhinoceros [11] with Grasshopper [12] as tools for the digital twin definition, that access the structured data from Airtable over its REST API and perform the user commands. Grasshopper is another example of visual scripting tool within a 3D modeling application. Our digital twin implementation is based on the Grasshopper scripts developed as part of another GDP's component, 3D Configurator. These visual scripts contain the 3D model of a robot arm with the positioning information, different design options, and definition of the connection to the corresponding physical prototype. This allows to run user commands from Slack in the real world to check different possible scenarios of human interaction with different machines including simultaneous contributions.

The main physical prototype of a robot arm, developed with 3D printing and built based on a popular HW prototyping platform Arduino [13], was connected to its virtual presentation. This provided a real-time command execution, where the participants had an opportunity to test a collaborative interaction in nearly real-time, synchronously on the physical device and its digital twin.

We also built connections to further simple electronic examples developed on the basis of educational platform micro:bit [14] with the possibility for graphical programming [15]. The examples included an LED stripe attached to the paper prototype of a dashboard, small mobile robots running between SAP Scenes' objects, wearable electronics attached to "human" objects to capture the state of the human models. This swarm of the HW prototypes communicating wirelessly with each other can be extended at any point of time. The user commands from Slack are broadcasted to all participating devices, which may react on those commands or ignore them. This extendable HW swarm serves to check even more different scenarios of interaction among humans and machines.

4 Case Study: Prototyping an IoT Shopfloor

While developing the prototyping platform RapPP, we have designed a case study to check the feasibility of the following aspects, including their usability for non-technical stakeholders:

- Combination of different prototyping techniques in one system to be performed by different stakeholders with different skills.
- Application of low-code and low-cost paradigms with visual scripting, graphical programming, and educational HW platforms to involve more participants from different user groups into the prototyping process.

- Reuse of existing User Interfaces (UI) to allow a fast definition and check of new concepts but also to see possible challenges of the human-machine interaction before a specific application is implemented.

To cover these aspects, a team of different stakeholders with different skills and roles started to develop new concepts for the future shopfloors exploiting IoT technologies for an effective and safe interaction between humans and devices. In this shopfloor prototype, humans could interact directly with robots and other smart equipment and could command devices remotely, including the internet communication from remote locations, to correct the machines' behavior or to provide (new) tasks. The actual tests within real shopfloors are too expensive to perform, disturbing the work, and can be dangerous when introducing new devices/robots among humans. So, the initial tests for possible challenges in the interaction between multiple agents in a shared room were designed with small robots and human models on a small surface.

We have started with the paper prototype with SAP Scenes to set up environment and to define basic movements for the problem statement. After that, we added simple electronics of the following four types simulating different interactions with different hazard potentials:

- LED Dashboard (no real hazard for human),
- Robot arms (partially fixed, restricted hazards for humans),
- Fully mobile robots (the most potential for hazardous situations),
- Wearables for the human objects, interacting with other electronics to check different safety treatments.

Each device type got its own simple program to react on different signals, either sent as commands from the users over the Slack interface or as indicators for specific situations within the shopfloor. All commands from Slack, stored in the Airtable data base as described in the previous section, were accessed by the Grasshopper scripts (developed as parts of the GDP) over the web-interface. As an example, one such script defines a parametric model with the state of the digital twin corresponding to the electronic prototype of a robot arm. This digital twin allows to modify both design and spatial positioning of the robot arm by a team of the Slack users. Because this digital twin was connected to the electronic prototype, they both reacted synchronously on the commands from the users. But, due to the digital nature of the digital twin, it was also possible for remote users to test different designs of the digital robot arm: color schemes, textures, lights. So, our first tested scenario (Fig. 3) was the internet user interaction for the decisions on the design presented digitally.

While testing this scenario for the feasibility of the technologies integration, we observed that the RapPP was able to capture all requests from a team members in a FIFO (first in first processed) manner. So, only the latest decision was visible in the collaborative result. The process of collecting and storing the inputs as well as the digital twin needed to be extended to keep and visualize the information about the contributors and all the results from all contributors to visualize all design proposals individually. The team members must then decide, which options to keep for the resulting device.

After the first simple scenario test, we extended the scene with more electronic elements to check more complex system behavior, where more devices reacted to the

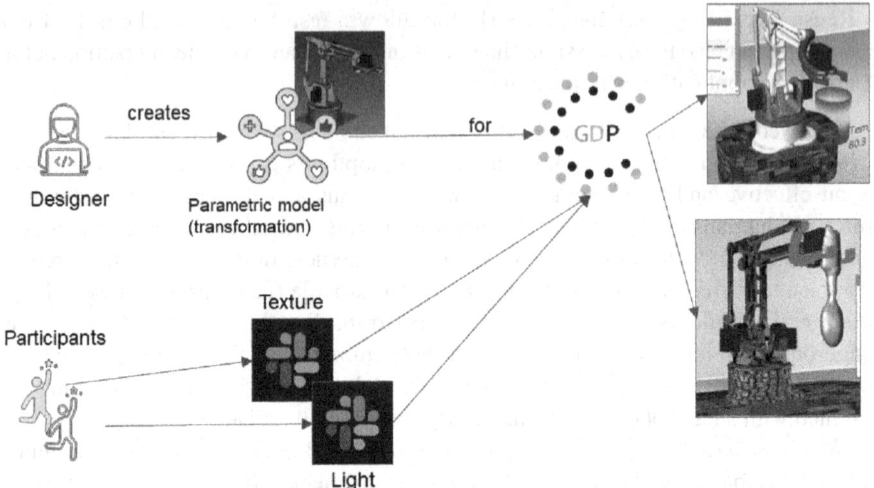

Fig. 3. Usage scenario I: user interaction for design definition.

commands from the Slack's users by starting or changing motion and lighting feedback (Fig. 4). During this experiment, we iteratively extended the electronic prototypes adding some micro:bit controllers to further elements on the scene. The objects from the paper prototyping phase, being extended with the electronics, provided a better and fast visualization for the target system functionality. New robots were 3D printed (corresponding to industrial prototyping) and added to the testbed to check collaboration effects among different types of robots. This gave us inputs for the further ideas about the possible needs for controls within shopfloor: setting up limits, feedback with lights and audio output on different devices, including wearable electronics attached to the human objects.

Parallel to all those digital and electronic tests for functional feasibility, a user with the role of safety engineer together with a designer developed a virtual and executable model illustrating cases that can happen when all those devices interact with humans within a shopfloor. So, the potential safety issues were modeled within an educational environment with virtual reality features [18] (virtual prototyping). This provided a quick spatial and dynamic visualization of new functionalities corresponding to the behavior observed during the incremental electronic tests. Then, new features were added to several elements within the electronic prototype to test the feasibility of new concepts for the safety control. These additional features included communication between the wearable electronics on the human object with the mobile robots and the dashboard. We tried and tested different alarm situations, defining how devices should react.

An example of prototype phases for the described IoT shopfloor use case is shown on Fig. 5.

Our project team tested the "executable" prototypes remotely over the internet operating HW and virtual prototypes collectively. This helped to analyze the robot arm operation in combination with other types of IoT devices. Due to the different levels of users' skills, the project required a solution with an easy and understandable interface

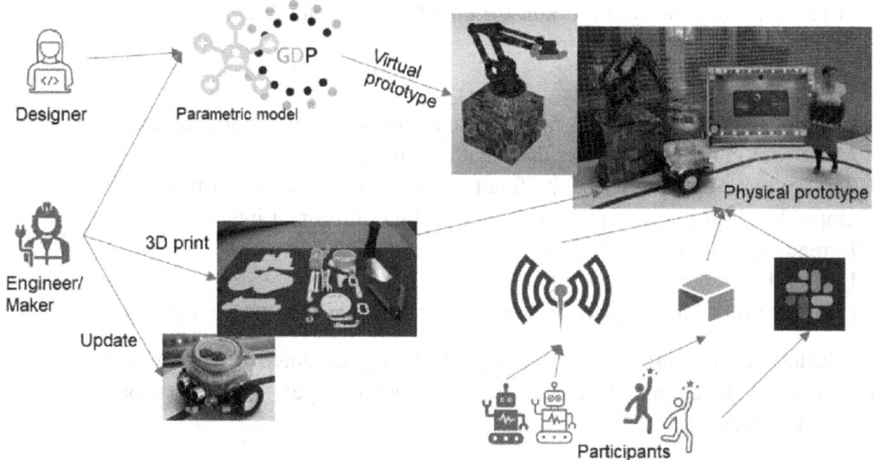

Fig. 4. Usage scenario II: user interaction with the IoT devices in a shopfloor.

Fig. 5. An example of prototypes for physical (paper + electronics) and virtual simulation of safety aspects (usage scenario III).

for a better communication among the team members. With the goal to make the prototype testing accessible and understandable for all participants, several intuitive user interfaces such as tabular interfaces (defined within Airtable) and textual inputs (within the social platform Slack) were used for commands to operate the prototypes remotely. This approach appears to be especially useful for project members without the necessary technical background.

As a result of our experiment, it was detected that multiple participants with different skills and different objectives can effectively collaborate during a multi-user session and develop new concepts together. The necessary condition is that each stakeholder participates in this process by means of a simple UI suitable for this person, his/her interests, skills, and preferences. For the better usability, the RapPP needed to be extended with more visualization features and feedback mechanisms.

The aspects that were important for collaborative interaction and being covered by the RapPP include the following:

- Several levels of prototyping,
- Combination of Machine-to-Machine and Human-to-Machine interaction,
- Multi-user collaboration over different channels,
- Testing spatial properties of the functioning devices and other objects,
- Unpredictability and, thus, complexity of the multi-agent interaction,
- Extendibility in the future,
- Low code / low costs,
- Combination of local interaction and global one over the internet.

The team participating in the RapPP prototyping contained different roles and skills – designers, SW developers, HW developers, project manager – thus, participants with and without technical skills.

5 Conclusion

During our study, we considered different prototyping techniques and tools. Because different stakeholders have different skill sets and prefer different tools according to the Jakob's law of UX from [16], it is often difficult to keep a clear communication as well as convey ideas to other team members. One approach would be to find a common prototyping tool with an easy-to-use interface. Another approach, considered in this paper, is to connect existing UIs familiar to the participants within one prototyping framework allowing people to continue using tools and views comfortable for them. Such connection of multiple UIs was implemented as a prototype with visual scripting, low-code, or no-code methods within the framework described in this paper.

A team of collaborators with different roles and skills, distributed in different locations, was able to perform effectively towards the concept development without compromising the completeness of the necessary features. The participants defined several interaction scenarios and checked their functional and technical feasibility providing guidance for their possible implementation. The usage of the RapPP platform was tested with the following selected scenarios: (a) design definition; (b) functionality identification; (c) safety cases analysis.

Next steps that will improve the functionality and usability of this prototyping platform shall include the integration of speech recognition in addition to the text recognition, integration of more existing user interfaces to check their compatibility, extend the understanding of more commands to cover more usage scenarios. Also, more visualization and feedback options should improve the usability of the platform, as it can be challenging to manage situations when too many participants interact simultaneously in one session. This also implies the need for the limitation definition during the interaction of multiple team members to make it better controllable.

References

1. iPRODUCE Homepage. https://iproduce-project.eu/. Accessed 05 Feb 2023

2. Votintseva, A., Johnson, R., Zabigailo, M., Cho, J.: Application of Generative Design in Social Manufacturing. In: Stephanidis, C., Antona, M., Ntoa, S. (eds.) HCI International 2022 Proceedings, Posters, Part IV, CCIS, vol. 1583, pp. 309–316. Springer, Heidelberg (2022)
3. Smit, J., Kreutzer, S., Moeller, C., Carlberg, M.: Industry 4.0: study for the ITRE committee (2016)
4. Razzouk, R., Shute, V.: What is design thinking and why is it important? Florida State University (2012)
5. Beaudouin-Lafon, M., Mackay, W.: Prototyping tools and techniques. Universite Paris—Sud, INRIA (2009)
6. Yan, X., Gu, P.: A review of rapid prototyping technologies and systems. Comput.-Aided Des. **28**(4), 307–318 (1996)
7. Node-RED Homepage. https://nodered.org/. Accessed 05 Feb 2023
8. Slack Homepage. https://slack.com/intl/de-de/. Accessed 04 Feb 2023
9. MQTT Homepage. https://mqtt.org/. Accessed 05 Feb 2023
10. AirTable Homepage. https://www.airtable.com/. Accessed 05 Feb 2023
11. Rhinoceros 3D Homepage. https://www.rhino3d.com/. Accessed 05 Feb 2023
12. Grasshopper 3D Homepage. https://www.grasshopper3d.com/. Accessed 05 Feb 2023
13. Arduino Homepage. https://www.arduino.cc/. Accessed 05 Feb 2023
14. BBC micro:bit Homepage. https://microbit.org/. Accessed 05 Feb 2023
15. Scratch Homepage. https://scratch.mit.edu/. Accessed 05 Feb 2023
16. Yablonski, J.: Laws of UX: Using Psychology to Design Better Products & Services. 1st edn. O'Reilly Media, Sebastopol (2020)
17. SAP Scenes. https://apphaus.sap.com/resource/scenes. Accessed 05 Feb 2023
18. CoSpaces Edu Homepage. https://edu.cospaces.io/. Accessed 05 Feb 2023
19. McElroy, K.: Prototyping for Designers: Developing the Best Digital and Physical Products. O'Reilly UK Ltd, Sebastopol (2017)
20. The Engineering Projects: what is prototyping? Meaning, types, process, tools and examples. https://www.theengineeringprojects.com/2021/05/what-is-prototyping-meaning-types-process-tools-and-examples.html. Accessed 06 Feb 2023
21. Snyder, C.: Paper Prototyping: The Fast and Easy Way to Design and Refine User Interfaces. 1st edn. Morgan Kaufmann, Burlington (2003)
22. UltiMaker Thingiverse Homepage. https://www.thingiverse.com/. Accessed 06 Feb 2023
23. Ultimaker Homepage. https://ultimaker.com/de/3d-printers. Accessed 06 Feb 2023

A Basic Study to Prevent Non-earnest Responses in Web Surveys by Arranging the Order of Open-Ended Questions

Ikumi Yamazaki(✉), Kenichi Hatanaka, Satoshi Nakamura, and Takanori Komatsu

Meiji University, Nakano 4-21-1, Nakano-Ku, Tokyo, Japan
yama1225iku@gmail.com

Abstract. Although web surveys are convenient and allow easy collection of a large number of survey responses, there is a significant issue that some people give non-earnest responses such as "nothing in particular" in open-ended questions because they want to cut corners. We aim to realize a questionnaire system that could improve a quality of web surveys to gather better responses from respondents. In this study, we focused on the order of open-ended questions in a survey. Then, we experimented using crowdsourcing to examine the effect of the order of open-ended questions on the non-earnest response rate. As a result of the experiment, we found that there were fewer non-earnest responses when the open-ended questions were presented firstly than when the open-ended questions were presented at last.

Keywords: Web surveys · Non-earnest Responses · Order of questions

1 Introduction

Web surveys are often used to collect responses on social research and services and to collect preliminary data for research purposes. Compared to paper-based surveys, web surveys can gather many answers, more easily. The number of people registering for crowdsourcing services is rapidly increasing because of easy participation and easy incomes. Researchers often use open-ended questions in surveys because they provide answers from various perspectives [1]. However, some respondents answer "nothing in particular" and "abcdefghij" in the open-ended questions and give non-earnest responses (abbreviated as NERs). Such NERs are influenced by the anonymous response format [2] and the ease of copying and pasting. These NERs in web surveys have become a problem.

Our laboratory asked 20,000 people to participate in web surveys and web-based experiments using *Yahoo! crowdsourcing* [3] in 2020. In these surveys, many people responded even though they were not the survey's target, and many answered "nothing in particular," "I don't know," and "asdfasdf" in the open-ended questions, where all respondents must write their opinions. Therefore, it takes time and effort to determine and remove NERs from the analysis and to register the persons in the block list. In addition,

M. Kurosu and A. Hashizume (Eds.): HCII 2023, LNCS 14011, pp. 314–326, 2023.
https://doi.org/10.1007/978-3-031-35596-7_20

this process reduces the number of responses for analysis. To solve this problem of NERs, we aim to clarify how to reduce NERs and realize a system that offers suggestions for improving the ability of a web survey to gather quality responses.

One of the reasons for NERs is that the respondents become bored with completing the task in the latter half of the survey. If they become bored, they may answer "nothing in particular" or "I don't know" in the open-ended questions. Schmidt et al. [4] found that the later the open-ended questions were asked, the lower the number of interpretable responses. However, these studies have not shown that changing the position of the open-ended questions improves the quality of the responses or affects the response text. We thought that if people faced the open-ended questions at an early stage of a survey, they might answer the questions more seriously because they would not feel bored. In addition, people who are not the survey's target would leave this survey quickly due to the presence of open-ended questions at an early stage. Then, researchers would be able to gather quality answers.

In this study, we investigate the effect of the position of open-ended questions on the number of NERs, aiming to realize a system that offers suggestions for improving a web survey to gather better quality responses. In particular, we hypothesize that people would give better answers to open-ended questions when they encounter them early in the process rather than when they encounter them later. This hypothesis is because people are expected to gradually become bored. We compare the number of NERs and the response content between a study that asks the respondents to answer the open-ended questions first and a general type of study in which the respondents answer the open-ended questions last.

The contributions of this paper are as follows.

- We conducted an experimental test on the order of open-ended questions and clarified that the number of NERs (Non-Earnest Responses) was lower when the open-ended questions were asked first than when they were asked last.
- We found that the instant respondents did not spend much time answering the open-ended question compared with the basic respondents.

2 Related Work

Various studies have been conducted on points to keep in mind when creating surveys. Regmi et al. [5] noted that there are many items to consider when planning an online survey, such as the simplicity of the questions, whether the survey is suitable for online implementation, and whether cultural and ethical considerations are taken into account. Tobias et al. [6] state that when designing a survey, it is necessary to consider not only the number and format of questions, but also how participants will respond to the survey design. Thus, it is believed that situation and response consideration are important when structuring the survey.

There have been many studies on open-ended questions. Reja et al. [1] compared the responses to online surveys in both close-ended and open-ended questions and found more missing data in the open-ended questions than in the questions with a close-ended format. Zhou et al. [7] experimented using a survey containing two types of questions: a single open-ended question and an open-ended question asking the respondents to give reasons for the selected question. More than 75% of the respondents did not answer either open-ended question. Holland et al. [8] investigated how the level of interest in a survey topic affects the responses. They found that people with a high level of interest in the case had a high quality of responses, while people with no or low interest had more non-responses to open-ended questions. Thus, it is difficult to obtain many good-quality answers to open-ended questions.

There have been many studies on the order of responses. However, although it is said to be better to place questions that require time to answer, such as open-ended questions, in the latter half of the survey, placing them there may be disadvantageous. Galesic et al. [9] found that if a question was asked later, the respondents responded in a shorter time and with a shorter text. This study investigates the effect of placing open-ended questions, which are considered difficult to answer, early in the survey.

There have been various studies on the relationship between the survey's medium and the open-ended responses. Denscombe [10] conducted a survey containing four open-ended questions on the web and on paper. As a result, although there was no significant difference between the web and paper surveys in three of the four open-ended descriptions, the responses in the web survey tended to be slightly longer than those in the paper survey. Rada et al. [11] conducted an online and paper survey for the citizens of Andalusia. The results showed that the online survey had fewer unanswered questions and more detailed responses to the open-ended questions. Sara et al. [12] compared the content of open-ended questions in email and paper surveys. They found that emails received more socially undesirable responses than paper, with longer responses and more information disclosed. These studies compared web-based and paper-based surveys and found that web-based surveys collected better responses. However, the relationships between the position of open-ended questions in the web survey and the quality of the answers were not clarified.

3 Experiments

3.1 Outline of the Experiment

The objective of this experiment is to investigate whether the number of NERs is affected by the position of the open-ended question in the web survey.

This experiment divided participants into two groups. One group faced the open-ended questions first (hereafter referred to as Group-FIRST). The other faced the open-ended questions last (referred to as Group-LAST). The survey for Group-FIRST first asked participants to answer open-ended questions (hereafter referred to as the open-ended questions phase). Then, it asked them to answer close-ended questions (hereafter referred to as the close-ended questions phase) and finally demographic information such as gender, age, and profession (hereafter referred to as the basic information phase) in that order (see Fig. 1). The order was reversed for Group-LAST (see Fig. 2). The order of the questions in each phase was the same: four questions in the open-ended questions phase, nine questions in the close-ended questions phase, and four questions in the basic information phase.

The survey topic in this experiment was for people who had engaged in teleworking and working from home. The contents and order of the four questions in the open-ended

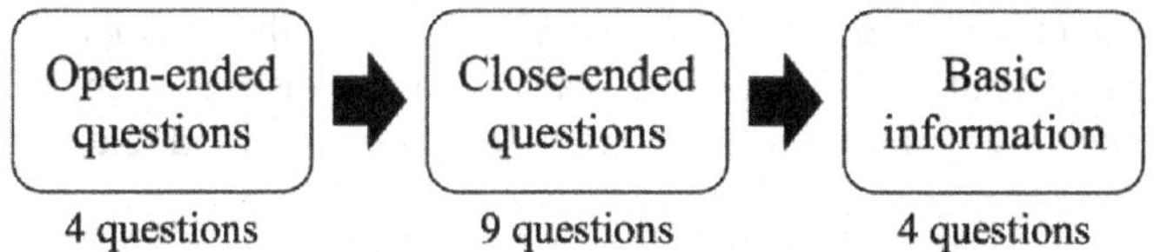

Fig. 1. Phase order for the group with the open-ended questions first (for Group-FIRST).

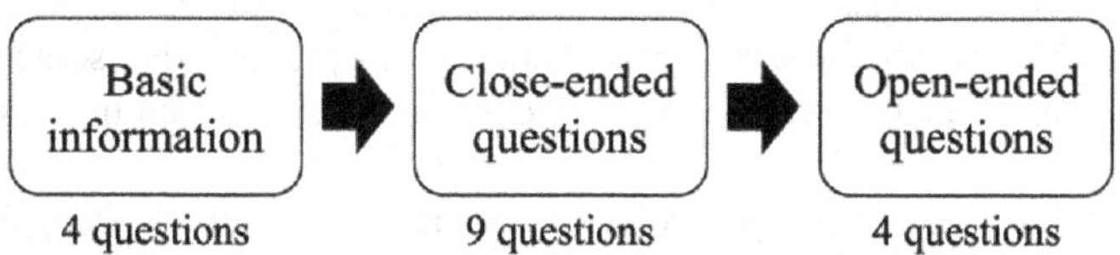

Fig. 2. Phase order for the group with the open-ended questions last (for Group-LAST).

questions phase were as follows. The phrase "even if it is a trivial matter" was added to encourage the respondents to answer each question.

- Q-a: What are the advantages of teleworking and working from home?
- Q-b: What are the disadvantages of teleworking and working from home?
- Q-c: What are the advantages of teleworking and working from home other than work (personal life, family, and so on)?
- Q-d: What are the disadvantages of teleworking and working from home other than work (personal life, family, and so on)?

Our experiment system displayed one question per page to control the order of answers. When a participant answered a question, the system showed the next question.

We conducted this survey on *Yahoo! Crowdsourcing* [3] and Google Form with different responses to verify whether the order of the open-ended questions affected the quality of the responses.

3.2 Experimental Procedure

We recruited 1,000 participants (500 males and 500 females) for this experiment. The experiment was conducted on *Yahoo! Crowdsourcing* [3], and the participants were divided into two groups by their gender to avoid gender variation. The start time of each request was 8:00 am.

First, the system showed the flow of investigations and the precautions. Then, the system asked participants to check the checkboxes of each description after reading that description. The precautions indicated that the experiment was intended for people who had teleworked or worked from home and that they should not press the back button or the reload button on their browsers. After that, the system randomly divided the participants into two groups, Group-FIRST and Group-LAST, and displayed the link to the Google Form for each group. The order of the survey phases was as indicated in either Fig. 1 or Fig. 2. The system showed a progress bar to let the participants know how many questions remained to complete the survey. When a participant completed the survey, the system presented a code at the end. As a reward, the participants received 10 Paypay-points (a popular point program in Japan), which was equivalent to 10 Japanese yen (0.08 US cents) after returning to the crowdsourcing screen and selecting the correct code.

3.3 Results

We obtained 1,101 responses (515 males, and 586 females) except for illegal responses in this survey. The reason for over 1000 responses was possible that some experiment participants answered the survey but did not return to the crowdsourcing screen to enter the code.

In order to investigate the percentage of NERs in the survey, it is necessary to determine the criteria for NERs. Therefore, we asked two university students (evaluators) to classify the open-ended responses as earnest or not earnest. The classification standards for an NER are as follows.

- It was not accompanied by an answer to the question.
- Its meaning could not be captured by the answer itself.

Note that NERs such as "nothing in particular" and "I do not know" were removed in advance. After the classifications, we evaluated the degree of agreement between the classifications using the Kappa coefficient. The results showed that the Kappa coefficient was 0.623, indicating a high agreement. Examples of NERs are as follows.

- Q-a: A little easy. I don't have beneficial to an own business, but a side business is email and phone calls, so it does not matter too much.
- Q-b: I work in childcare, so telework is not a basic requirement.
- Q-c: I can work from home. I'm single, so no relationship.
- Q-d: Without distinction. Nothing really. Tiresome.

We annotated each response as earnest or not earnest based on the evaluators' classification. If their response classifications differed, we ourselves judged whether the response was earnest or not earnest.

Figure 3 shows the percentage of NERs for each open-ended question. This figure clarifies that the number of NERs was lower in Group-FIRST in all questions. We tested the difference in the proportions for each question and found significant differences for three questions (Q-a and Q-d: $p < 0.01$, Q-c: $p < 0.05$). In addition, the percentage of NERs increased sharply in the fourth question in both groups.

Table 1 shows the average length of answers for each open-ended question. In this table, the results include NERs. The table shows that the answer length was longer for Group-LAST. In addition, the answer length was the longest for both groups in the second question. Still, the answer length gradually decreased, and the fourth answer was the shortest.

In order to investigate whether the position of the open-ended questions affects the withdrawal rate of the survey, we calculated the withdrawal rate by dividing the number of surveys collected in Google Form by the number of people who accessed the survey system. The withdrawal rate for Group-FIRST was 23.7% and for Group-LAST it was 23.9%. This result shows that the attrition rate is almost the same for Group-FIRST and

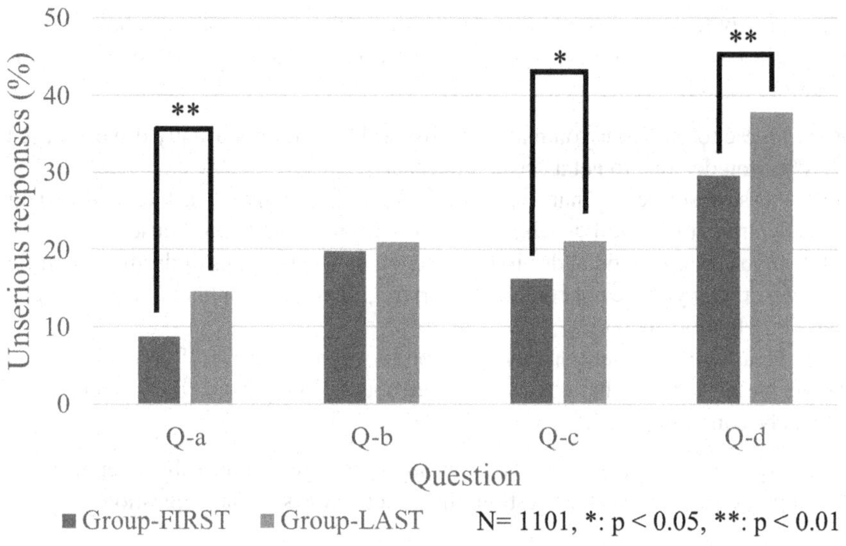

Fig. 3. Percentage of NERs in each question and group.

Group-LAST. However, this dropout rate is inaccurate because Google Form does not know how many respondents completed and left the survey. We will develop our survey system and conduct an additional experiment to clarify this withdrawal rate.

Table 1. The average length of answers (characters) in each question and group.

	Q-a	Q-b	Q-c	Q-d
Group-FIRST (N = 566)	13.2	13.5	12.5	10.8
Group-LAST (N = 535)	15.9	16.1	14.0	11.6

4 Additional Experiments Focused on Desertion Rate and Location

4.1 Outline of the Experiment

This additional experiment aimed to clarify the disengagement point by the presentation timing of the open-ended question in the web survey. In order to clarify this, we implemented a new survey system that recorded participants' behaviors, such as the answering time for each question and which questions they could not answer in the survey.

In this experiment, we also divided participants into Group-FIRST and Group-LAST. The number of questions in each phase was the same as in Sect. 3, and the questions in the open-ended questions phase were highly independent of those in the close-ended questions phase.

The survey topic in this additional experiment was for people who have a driver's license. The contents and order of the four questions asked in the open-ended questions phase were as follows.

- Q-e: Please tell us what you mainly drive for. If you do not usually drive, please tell us why you decided to get a driver's license.
- Q-f: Please describe the characteristics of the roads you mainly drive on. If you don't usually drive, please tell us what kind of roads are around your house.
- Q-g: If you are not good at driving, please tell us what aspects of driving are difficult for you or why you are not confident in driving. If you are confident in driving, please answer why you are so.
- Q-h: Please tell us what you pay attention to when you drive. If you do not usually drive, please answer what you were careful about when you got your driver's license. It can be something trivial.

Our experiment system displays one question per page to control the order of answers. When a participant answers a question, the system shows the next question.

4.2 Experimental Procedure

We recruited 1,000 participants (500 males and 500 females) for this additional experiment, as in Sect. 3. The requests were divided into those for males only and those for females only on *Yahoo! Crowdsourcing* [3].

In this additional experiment, the survey recorded the start time when a participant finished reading the explanation and proceeded to the next page. The order of the surveys was either Fig. 1 or Fig. 2. The system displayed the number of questions. After completing the survey, the system displayed a common code and ID. The participant was rewarded by money after returning to the crowdsourcing page, correctly selecting the code, and entering the ID.

4.3 Results

The number of participants who correctly entered their IDs was 979 (493 males and 486 females). We used them for the analysis of this experiment.

We also asked two university students (evaluators) to classify the open-ended responses as earnest or not earnest. The criteria for the classification of NERs were the same as in Sect. 3. The Kappa coefficient of the agreement was 0.75, indicating that the classifications were almost identical. Examples of NERs were as follows.

- Q-e: Because it is necessary. Because it's better to have it.
- Q-f: Ordinary Roads. Public roads.
- Q-g: I want to drive at my own pace. I just drive with caution.
- Q-h: I don't usually drive. It was interesting.

We annotated each response as earnest or not earnest based on the evaluators' classification. If their response classifications differed, we ourselves judged whether the response was earnest or not earnest.

Figure 4 shows the percentage of NERs for each question. In all questions, the number of NERs in Group-FIRST was lower than in Group-LAST. We tested the difference in the proportions for each question and found a significant difference in Q-e and Q-h (Q-e: $p < 0.01$, Q-h: $p < 0.05$). In the present experiment in Sect. 3, the percentage of NERs increased greatly for the last open-ended question (Q-d). However, in this experiment, the number of NERs did not increase for the last open-ended question (Q-h).

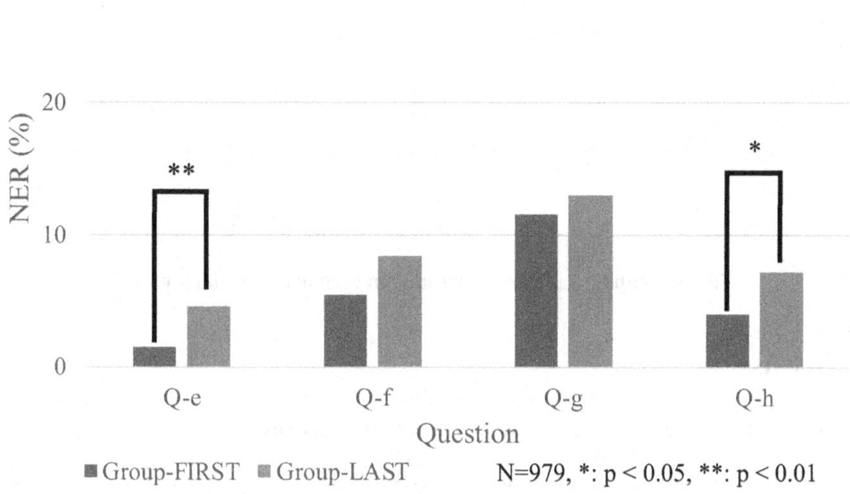

Fig. 4. Percentage of NERs in each question and group in the additional experience.

Table 2 shows the average length of answers, including the NERs, for each group and question. The answer length is longer in Group-LAST than in Group-FIRST in every question.

Table 2. The average length of answers in each question and group in the additional experience (characters).

	Q-e	Q-f	Q-g	Q-h
Group-FIRST (N = 484)	12.7	10.6	18.5	15.4
Group-LAST (N = 502)	14.0	11.6	20.1	16.8

The number of people who accessed the URL to this survey was 1,757 (883 for Group-FIRST and 874 for Group-LAST), and the number of participants who correctly entered their IDs was 979. This means that 778 people dropped out of this survey. Figure 5 shows the withdrawal rate for each question. The figure shows that the withdrawal rate of Group-FIRST increased from Q1 to Q4. On the other hand, in Group-LAST, there were few dropouts, and most of the respondents answered all questions.

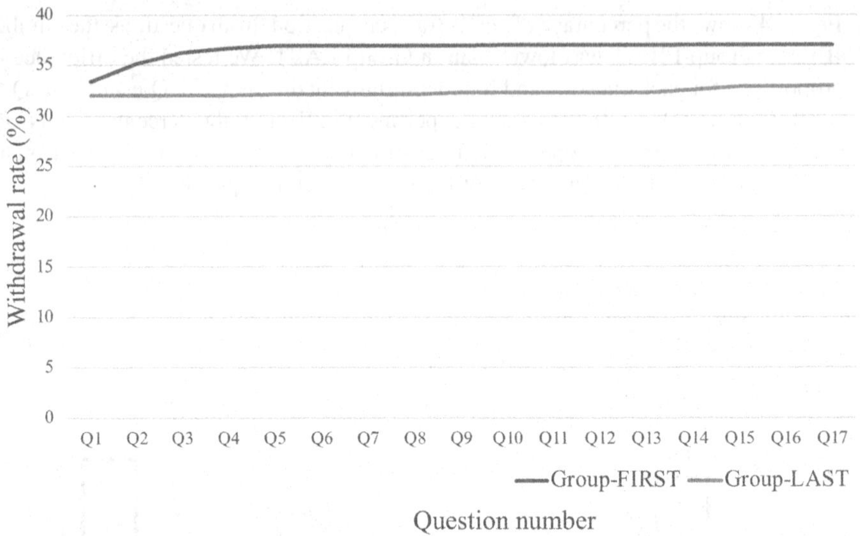

Fig. 5. Withdrawal rate per question in each question and group.

5 Discussion

5.1 Comparing Two Groups Based on Several Features

In the two experiments, the number of NERs was lower in Group-FIRST for all questions. This suggests that the position of the open-ended questions affects the quality of the responses. This result might have occurred because those in Group-FIRST did not feel bored answering the open-ended questions, but those in Group-LAST did feel bored answering these questions.

For both experiments, the trend differed only for the fourth open-ended question. Here, in the experiment in Sect. 3, all four open-ended questions were similar in that they asked about advantages and disadvantages. So, it is possible that the fourth question caused boredom. On the other hand, in the additional experiment in Sect. 4, the fourth question was not similar to the other three questions. So, it is possible that the difficulty of the questions was low. These findings suggest that asking similar open-ended questions may increase the number of NERs. In particular, open-ended questions that ask for the reason for the selected answer may increase the number of NERs.

In both experiments, the average length of answers was shorter for Group-FIRST. This may have been because the participants in Group-LAST answered the close-ended questions before the open-ended questions phase in detail, which made it easier for them to answer the open-ended questions, leading to an increase in the length of answers. On the other hand, although the participants in Group-FIRST did not feel bored, they answered the open-ended questions phase without answering the close-ended questions, which may have made it difficult for them to answer in detail.

To sum up, Group-FIRST had a lower percentage of NERs but a shorter length of answers, while Group-LAST had a higher number of NERs but a longer length of answers. This suggests a trade-off relation between the percentage of NERs and the answer length, depending on the position of the open-ended questions.

In the additional experiment, when analyzing at which point the respondents dropped out of the survey (Fig. 5), the results show that in Group-FIRST, a certain number of participants left the survey at the open-ended questions from Q1 to Q4. In Group-LAST, almost no participants left the survey in the middle. This suggests that some people left the survey because they thought it was troublesome due to the open-ended questions coming first. In addition, since the percentage of NERs was also small, it is highly likely that we could exclude from the survey people trying to answer it frivolously or who were trying to answer it even though they were not the target of the survey.

5.2 Comparison by Survey Start Time

The survey start time was adjusted to 8:00 am, although the dates answered were different by the gender. Therefore, we compared the percentages of NERs in the open-ended questions of those who accessed the website within 10 min of the start of the survey (hereafter referred to as instant respondents) and in the open-ended questions of those who accessed the website more than 10 min after the beginning of the survey (hereafter referred to as basic respondents) (see Fig. 6). The numbers for each group and the results are shown in Table 3.

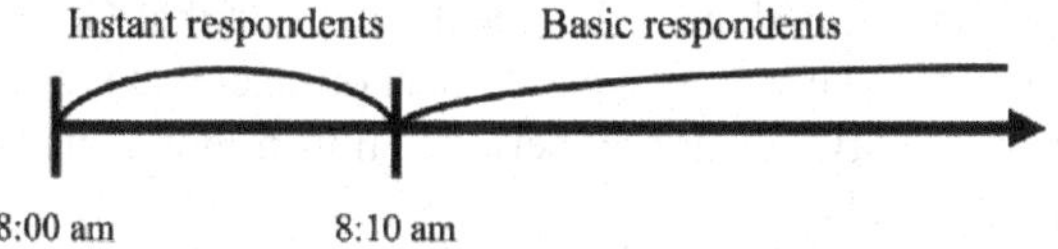

Fig. 6. Response time and the classification name of the respondent.

The table shows that NERs were lower for all questions in Group-FIRST and basic respondents. We conducted a chi-square test and found a significant difference ($p < 0.05$).

The comparison of the average length of answers is shown in Table 4. The results show that basic respondents gave longer responses in both groups than instant respondents.

Table 3. Percentage of NERs by survey start time (%).

	Q-e	Q-f	Q-g	Q-h
Group-FIRST and instant respondents (N = 256)	2.3	5.5	12.1	5.1
Group-FIRST and basic respondents (N = 221)	0.5	5.4	10.9	2.7
Group-LAST and instant respondents (N = 239)	3.8	8.0	13.4	6.7
Group-LAST and basic respondents (N = 263)	5.3	8.4	12.6	7.6

Table 4. The average length of answers by survey start time (characters).

	Q-e	Q-f	Q-g	Q-h	Total
Group-FIRST and instant respondents (N = 256)	12.2	9.9	16.6	14.3	53.0
Group-FIRST and basic respondents (N = 221)	13.3	11.5	20.6	16.8	62.2
Group-LAST and instant respondents (N = 239)	14.2	11.2	18.4	15.8	59.6
Group-LAST and basic respondents (N = 263)	13.8	12.1	21.7	17.6	65.2

Tables 5, 6, and Fig. 7 show the response time of each open-ended question in each group and respondent type. The two tables show that basic respondents took longer to complete all open-ended questions than instant respondents in both groups. Figure 7 also shows that the completion time of the survey tended to be longer for basic respondents than for instant respondents, regardless of whether they were in Group-FIRST or Group-LAST.

These results suggest that open-ended surveys of basic respondents are valid for analysis, and Group-FIRST is especially valid. Suppose that the order of the questions does not affect the content of the responses. In that case, it can be expected that dynamically changing the survey, for example, by presenting the free text first for respondents who accessed the site after 10 min, would be effective. The number of NERs was highest for Group-LAST and basic respondents. This result suggests that Group-LAST and basic respondents may be more likely to give not earnest or inaccurate responses. In addition, those who completed the survey in a short period of time might focus on getting rewarded and trying to finish it quickly.

Table 5. Open-ended questions response time for Group-FIRST (seconds).

	Introduction + Q1 (Q-e)	Q2 (Q-f)	Q3 (Q-g)	Q4 (Q-h)
Instant respondents (N = 256)	68.0	38.9	47.7	38.6
Basic respondents (N = 221)	69.0	44.9	58.9	47.2

Table 6. Open-ended questions response time for Group-LAST (seconds).

	Q14 (Q-e)	Q15 (Q-f)	Q16 (Q-g)	Q17 (Q-h)
Instant respondents (N = 239)	35.9	41.6	50.5	39.5
Basic respondents (N = 263)	40.6	43.1	61.6	48.4

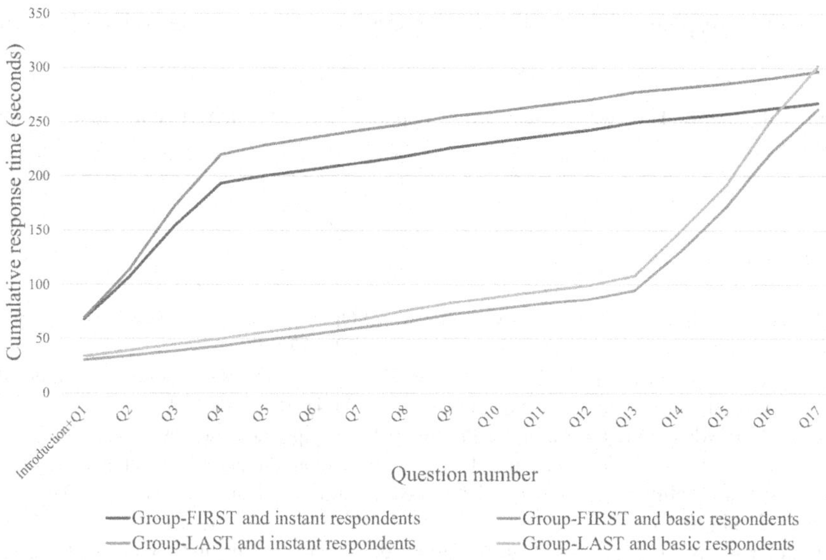

Fig. 7. Cumulative response time for each time period when the survey was accessed.

6 Conclusion

This study examined the relationship between NERs and the order of questions in open-ended questions in a web survey. We experimented by dividing participants into two groups, Group-FIRST and Group-LAST, based on the hypothesis that people would give better answers to open-ended questions when they encountered them early in the process compared to when they encountered them late in the process.

As a result of the experiment, we found a trade-off relationship between the number of NERs and the length of answers. In Group-FIRST, the number of NERs decreased. However, the length of answers also decreased, while in Group-LAST the number of NERs increased, but the length of answers increased too. In addition, it was suggested that placing the open-ended questions at the beginning would cause a certain number of people to leave the survey. Furthermore, we analyzed the percentage of NERs of those who accessed the website. We found that the NERs, the length of answers, and the response time were greatly affected by whether the respondent answered the survey within or after 10 min.

Before conducting the survey this time, the procedure and precautions were presented. However, the length of the explanatory text and the checkboxes that prevented people from skipping over the text may have significantly affected the response rate for the first question. In future experiments, we plan to use a system that starts the survey immediately after accessing the site, without setting up a page of instructions and precautions. Also, in the additional experiment, the response time of the first question was not accurate because it was obtained from the time when the website was accessed, not when the question was presented. We plan to experiment again to get the exact time. In addition, since it may not be appropriate to categorize the responses into only two types: earnest response and NERs, it is necessary to examine the method of classifying the responses.

Acknowledgement. This work was partly supported by JSPS KAKENHI Grant Number JP22K12135.

References

1. Reja, U., Manfreda, L.K., Hlebec, V., Vehovar, V.: Open-ended vs. close-ended questions in web questionnaires. Adv. Methodol. Stats. **19**(1), 159–177 (2003)
2. Dickinson, D.L., McEvoy, D.M.: Further from the truth: the impact of in-person, online, and mturk on dishonest behavior. J. Exp. Behav. Econ. **90**(4), 101649 (2021)
3. Yahoo! Crowdsourcing.https://crowdsourcing.yahoo.co.jp/. Accessed 09 Feb 2023
4. Schmidt, K., Gummer, T., Roßmann, J.: Effects of respondent and survey characteristics on the response quality of an open-ended attitude question in web surveys. Methods Data Anal. **14**(1), 3–34 (2020)
5. Regmi, P.R., Waithaka, E., Paudyal, A., Simkhada, P., van Teijlingen, E.: Guide to the design and application of online questionnaire surveys. Nepal J. Epidemiol. **6**(4), 640–644 (2017)
6. Tobias, G., Joss, R.: Explaining interview duration in web surveys: a multilevel approach. Soc. Sci. Comput. Rev. **33**(2), 217–234 (2015)
7. Zhou, R., Wang, X., Zhang, L., Guo, H.: Who tends to answer open-ended questions in an e-service survey? The contribution of closed-ended answers. Behav. Inf. Technol. **36**(12), 1274–1284 (2017)
8. Holland, J.L., Christian, L.M.: The influence of topic interest and interactive probing on responses to open-ended questions in web surveys. Soc. Sci. Comput. Rev. **27**(2), 196–212 (2009)
9. Galesic, M., Bošnjak, M.: Effects of questionnaire length on participation and indicators of response quality in a web survey. Public Opin. Q. **73**(2), 349–360 (2009)
10. Denscombe, M.: The length of responses to open-ended questions: a comparison of online and paper questionnaires in terms of a mode effect. Soc. Sci. Comput. Rev. **26**(3), 359–368 (2008)
11. de Rada, V.D., Domínguez-Álvarez, J.A.: Response quality of self-administered questionnaires: a comparison between paper and web questionnaires. Soc. Sci. Comput. Rev. **32**(2), 256–269 (2014)
12. Sara, K., Lee, S.S.: Response effects in the electronic survey. Public Opin. Q. **50**(3), 402–413 (1986)

Measurements of Complexity in Vehicle Dashboards: Revision and Validation of the Perceived Visual Complexity Scale

Chuyang Ye[1], Zhizi Liu[2], Sihan Dong[3], Xueying Shao[4], Hongyu Chen[1], Honghai Zhu[2], and Liang Zhang[1(✉)]

[1] Institute of Psychology, Chinese Academy of Sciences, Beijing 100101, China
zhangl@psych.ac.cn
[2] Chongqing Changan Automobile Co., Chongqing, China
[3] The University of Melbourne, Melbourne 3010, Australia
[4] McGill University, Montreal, Canada

Abstract. Perceived visual complexity is an important cognitive factor for the interface design. One-third of the world's automobile sales last year came from China, yet the Chinese version of perceived visual complexity scale for vehicle design has not been developed. Therefore, the current study aimed to examine the validity and reliability of the Chinese version perceived visual complexity questionnaire. One hundred and thirty-four participants were recruited online, aged between 18 to 44 ($M = 24.1$ years). Cronbach's alpha ($\alpha = 0.926$), confirmatory factor analysis, and OLS regression were used to examine the validity and reliability. These results demonstrated the practical reliability and validity of perceived visual complexity questionnaire and its availability in Chinese. Also, the study contributes to re-confirm the reasonability of the theoretical framework for the measurements of perceived visual complexity.

Keywords: Perceived visual complexity · Vehicle dashboards · Graphic user interface · Reliability · Subjective rating

1 Introduction

Visual information processing of vehicle dashboards takes up a large number of cognitive resources for drivers. Numerous studies showed that drivers' visual workload affects their driving performances [1–3]. Due to the limitation of the human capacity for information processing, an excess of visual stimuli presented during a driving task will significantly distract the driver which leads to risky driving behaviour [4–6]. Perceived Visual complexity is a crucial element of visual stimuli. Specifically, the vehicle dashboards provided important information regarding the vehicle itself as well as the driving conditions. It is often necessary for drivers to keep track of the interface to be able to perceive necessary information. Therefore, the design of the graphic user interface of the vehicle dashboards based on reasonably controlled visual complexity is crucial during the design process.

M. Kurosu and A. Hashizume (Eds.): HCII 2023, LNCS 14011, pp. 327–335, 2023.
https://doi.org/10.1007/978-3-031-35596-7_21

Perceived Visual Complexity (PVC) is the level of subjective awareness of the complexity of visual elements presented on a display [7]. Various studies on the interface design of vehicle dashboards attempted to measure the level of PVC by direct and indirect approaches. Direct measures are usually collected through subjective survey questionnaires. Apart from questionnaires, researchers also conducted behavioural experiments like visual search tasks or eye-tracking experiments that indirectly measure the performance change depending on a different level of PVC [7–10]. While previous study proposed the three basic factors used to evaluate PVC include the number of visual elements, the variety of visual elements and the spatial relation between visual elements [11]. And previous study suggested adding the overall PVC and preference into the developed framework for better predicting the perceived visual complexity [7].

To our knowledge, the proposed original PVC questionnaire has not been validated in the Chinese version environment. Therefore, the current study aims to examine the reliability and validity of the Chinese version PVC questionnaire with online recruited participants to use such a predictive framework in Chinese [7]. We hypothesized that the Chinese version PVC questionnaire is internally reliable by using Cronbach's alpha. We also hypothesized that the Chinese version PVC questionnaire has both good content and construct validity, which will be qualified in theory way and quantified by the statistical result of confirmatory factor analysis and OLS regression.

2 Methodology

In this experiment, we translated the PVC questionnaire into Mandarin and recruited 160 participants to rate a total of 100 instrument cluster interface images collected remotely, across various brands of vehicles. 134 participants (48.51% females, 51.49% males) were selected according to the result of lie detection and whether the scale was filled out abnormally (e.g., random answer), aged between 18 to 44 (M = 24.1 years, SD = 4.19 years). 96.27% of the participants received post-secondary education. All participants possessed a valid driver's license (61.94% driven less than 1000 km, 20.15% driven between 1000–10000 km, and 17.91% driven more than 10000 km). Each participant was asked to rate 25 instrument cluster interface images. Therefore, each interface image was rated by 40 different participants. The experimental stimuli set was standardized based on its size, luminance contrast, completeness and quality. 100 different PVC dashboard picture was used as experimental stimuli.

The original PVC survey questionnaire was translated and tested [7]. The questionnaire consists of 13 items in five categories, namely Quantity (Q, the number of visual elements), Variety (V, the similarity/dissimilarity among visual elements), Relation (R, the spatial arrangement of the visual elements), and Overall PVC (O, the overall visual complexity of the given instrument cluster image) and Preference (P, "I like this interface"). Each category includes 3 items, except Preference (P) contains only 1 item. Items were rated on a 7-point Likert scale (with 1 being the least agreed and 7 being mostly agreed), and two of the items were reverse-scored to avoid untruthful responses.

The data was collected online from participants' own devices. The experimenter was available via an online meeting platform to give instructions and provide assistance during the experiment.

Tests of reliability were performed in R studio, examining the reliability for each of the 4 categories of Quantity, Variety, Relation and Overall PVC. Further analysis for validity will be performed including the factor analysis and OLS regression in R studio.

3 Result

3.1 Internal Reliability

Internal reliability intends to measure whether the same construct in a questionnaire is consistent or at least correlated with one another [12]. For our proposed questionnaire, the corresponding Cronbach's alphas are generated for overall PVC and its three subdimension (quantity, relation, and variety). However, subdimension preference only included one item, indicating internal reliability analysis is not necessary for it. According to the rule of thumb, the internal consistency for Overall PVC was considered as excellent ($\alpha = 0.926$), Quantity are considered as excellent ($\alpha = 0.913$), Variety was considered as good ($\alpha = 0.853$), and Relation was considered as good ($\alpha = 0.881$) [13].

3.2 Validity

The validity of the proposed questionnaire was generated to measure the degree that the proposed questionnaire properly measures the intended attribute [14]. Content validity and construct validity were analyzed following.

Content Validity

Our Chinese version PVC questionnaire was translated from a previous study, which developed the original questionnaire from extensive literature and models that capture various aspects of PVC based on cognitive processing way [7].

Moreover, our translation had been revised multiple times, indicating very less possibility that the translation itself introduced poor validity due to semantic bias. Therefore, we have sufficient reason to believe that the PVC questionnaire can theocratically capture every aspect of PVC well.

Construct Validity

A common way to establish construct validity for one questionnaire is confirmatory factor analysis (CFA) [15]. From the rule of thumb, we have enough responses for each item to establish CFA; however, subdimension preference only included one item which cannot satisfy the minimum requirement for CFA, therefore, we will discuss its construct validity later [14]. The following figure is the visualization for the CFA result. f1 indicates to subdimension quantity (consists of items Q1, Q2, and Q3), f2 indicates to subdimension variety (consists of items Q4, Q5, and Q6), f3 indicates to subdimension relation (consists of items R7, Q8, and R9); 'R' indicates to reverse-scored item), f4 indicates to overall PVC (consists of items Q10, Q11 and Q12), and f5 indicates to preference with only one item Q13.

Based on the CFA result (see Fig. 1), we can generate corresponding statistical data to evaluate its validity. Construct reliability (CR) and average variance extracted (AVE)

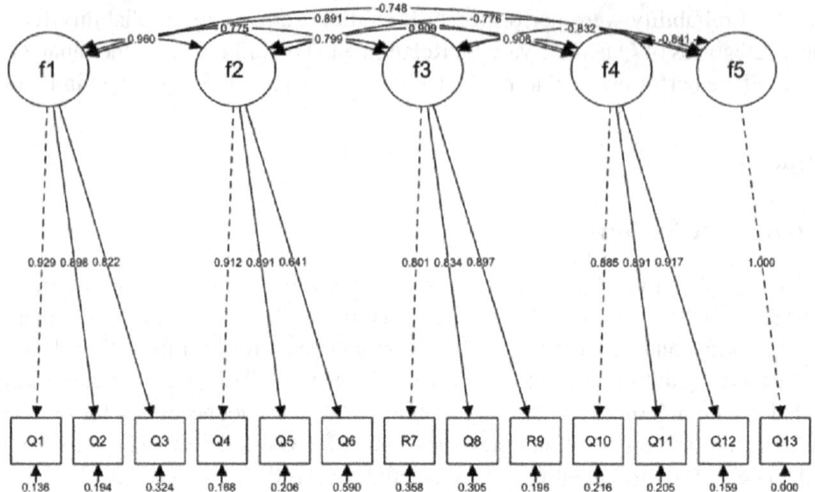

Fig. 1. Confirmatory factor analysis (CFA) for the proposed questionnaire

were calculated to estimate the convergent validity, which is one component of construct validity [16]. The chi-square goodness-of-fit, Standardized Root Mean Square Residual (SRMR), Comparative Fit Index (CFI), the (Adjusted) Goodness of Fit (GFI/AGFI), RMSEA, and incremental Fit Index (IFI) were used as indices of fit of model performance (see Table 1) which also are viable evaluation tool for construct validity.

Table 1. The indices for the CFA model

Measures	AVE	CR	SRMR	CFI	Chi-square (df), *p*-value	IFI	GFI/AGFI	RMSEA
Quantity	0.782	0.915	0.024	0.97	1364.320 (56), < 0.001	0.97	0.94/0.902	0.084
Variety	0.679	0.861						
Relation	0.714	0.882						
Overall	0.806	0.926						

According to previous studies, the recommended AVE value should be higher than 0.5 and recommended CR should be higher than 0.7 [17–19]. All AVEs and CRs could satisfy the above recommendation requirement. From statistical standards, both GFI and AGFI should be over 0.9 [20]. Our CFA result satisfied the above requirements. From the previous study, SRMR should be less than 0.08, CFI should be larger than 0.09, p-value of chi-square should be less than 0.05, and IFI should be higher than 0.09. All our results reached standards [21].

As mentioned above, for subdimension preference, we will use Ordinary Least Squares (OLS) regression to analyze the validity. We also use OLS regression on the other three subdimension to re-confirm their validity, which are presented below (see Fig. 2).

The low and acceptable multicollinearity of left regression in Fig. 2 was demonstrated by Variance Inflation Factor (see Fig. 3) [21].

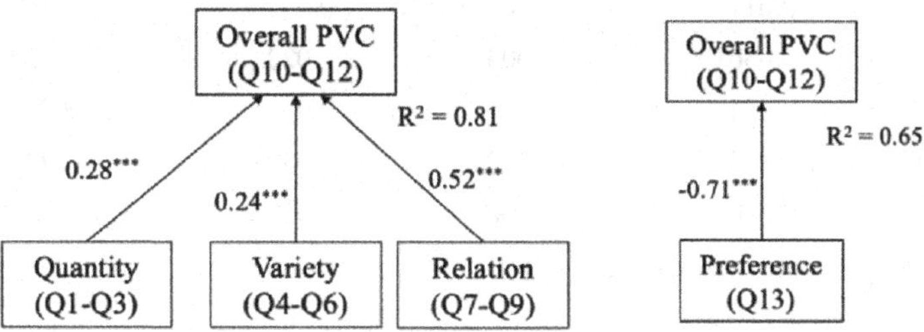

Fig. 2. Multiple regression results for our proposed questionnaire. Note: the number around arrow are the beta coefficients; $*p < 0.1$; $**p < 0.05$; $***p < 0.01$

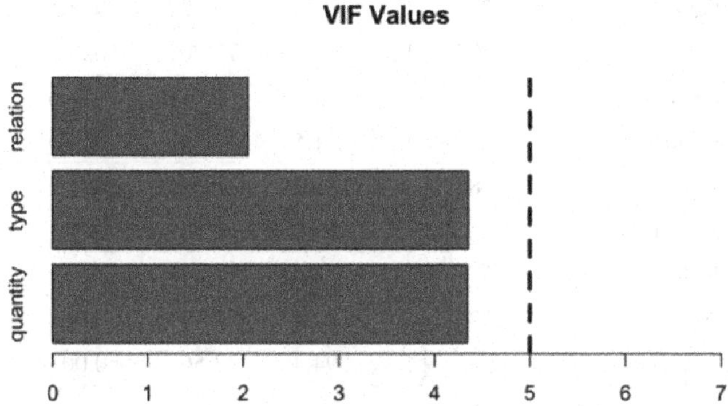

Fig. 3. Multicollinearity analysis operationalized by Variance Inflation Factor (VIF) for Left regression in Fig. 2.

Commonly, an R^2 that is significant and exceeds 0.5 is considered as evidence for strong construct validity [12]. For left regression, the R^2 (F (3, 3346) = 4650.44, $p <$ 0.01) satisfy the above requirement; for right regression, the R^2 (F (1, 3348) = 6252.83, $p < 0.01$) also satisfy the above requirement. Therefore, the proposed questionnaire has strong construct validity.

3.3 Correlation Analysis Between Variables

The correlation between gender, mileage, education, age, overall PVC and its each subdimension are shown in Table 2 (Table 3).

Based on previous correlation analysis, we use two-way ANOVA to further study the interaction effect of age and the other three variables. The results showed that only mileage has a significant interaction effect with age on PVC preference.

Table 2. Pearson correlation coefficient matrix

	Gender	Mileage	Education	Age
Quantity	0.017	−0.003	0.031	0.080***
Type	0.056**	−0.003	0.022	0.061***
Relation	0.004	−0.016	0.032	0.095***
Preference	0.028	−0.022	−0.047**	−0.144***
Overall	0.040*	−0.008	0.028	0.058***

* $p < 0.05$, ** $p < 0.01$, *** $p < 0.001$.

Table 3. Results of two-way ANOVA of the PVC preference

DV	Factors	*SS*	*df*	*MS*	*F*	*p*	η2
Preference	Gender	7	1	7.46	2.622	0.105	<0.001
	Age	205	1	204.83	72.001	<0.001***	0.021
	Gender × Age	4	1	3.67	1.290	0.256	<0.001
	Education	22	1	21.54	7.567	0.006**	0.002
	Age	186	1	185.58	65.192	<0.001***	0.019
	Education × Age	3	1	2.58	0.908	0.341	<0.001
	Mileage	5	1	4.61	1.64	0.2	<0.001
	Age	224	1	224.43	79.79	<0.001***	0.023
	Mileage × Age	94	1	94.40	33.56	<0.001***	0.010

* $p < 0.05$, ** $p < 0.01$, *** $p < 0.001$.

4 Discussion

The current study aimed to examine the reliability and validity of the Chinese version PVC questionnaire translated from a previous study [7]. Reliability was quantified by Cronbach's alpha. Validity was divided into two components: content validity and construct validity. Content validity was evaluated by reviewing the theoretical development way. Construct validity was established by using both CFA and OLS regression to properly analyze overall PVC and its subdimension. By using the rule of thumb from extensive literature, all our hypotheses that the Chinese version PVC questionnaire has good internal reliability, content validity, and construct validity were supported. This indicates that the PVC questionnaire from the previous study can be used in Chinese [7].

Our proposed questionnaire has consistent validity and reliability as previous study [7]. It indicated that the PVC questionnaire might have cross-language stability in terms of reliability and validity. It might indicate that language or culture has very little influence on the internal consistency and validity of the PVC questionnaire. However, the above logic deduction is out of the scope of the current study.

Moreover, we re-confirmed the reasonability of the four-factor model of overall PVC: quantity, variety, relation, and preference [7]. This four-factor model is concluded by reviewing and filtering potential factors related to PVC from and repeatedly examined by past studies [7, 11, 22, 23]. Therefore, it is theoretically established. The significant and good fitness of regression in the current study again verified that each factor can well predict the overall PVC. Therefore, the four-factor model still stands and is not influenced by language use.

Our study also contributed to the evaluation of PVC in Mandarin. To our knowledge, the PVC questionnaire is limitedly developed in only several languages, but not for Mandarin. The current study filled this gap with a new version of it that has good validity and reliability. It will give companies and future studies a practical evaluation tool to do a quick, reliable, and valid evaluation, which is vital for vehicle design, interface arrangement, or many other areas.

In addition to the validity and reliability of the scale, we also discovered that age might be a potential factor that negatively influences the preference for dashboard design. In other words, people like the instrumental display design more and more as they get older. However, other associations between variables are not strong enough. Moreover, age also has an interaction effect with mileage on preference.

Past studies showed that age is a factor that directly influenced people's preference for the design of website, urban buildings, and room configuration, despite older people having poorer perceptual, cognitive, and biological abilities (e.g., acuity) [24–27]. Based on these, we may conclude that there is a general tendency that the change in age is related to change in one's preference for certain design. To further explain, past study also found that the psychological developmental stage was a useful predictive factor for design preference which generally positively correlated with biological age [28]. Therefore, we may further imply that the potential underlying factor is one's psychological developmental stages. Similar pattern may apply to the effect of mileage on preference. Past studies also discovered that familiarity of certain product may potentially influence the use of it [29–31]. All in all, the psychological stage and familiarity of driving maybe the potential underlying factors that related to PVC preference.

In interpreting our study's findings, it is important to consider the impact of its limitations. First, our sample is relatively small with an uneven distribution of gender. And our sample mostly consisted of adults, therefore the transferability of our conclusion for older people is unknown. Second, this scale only used one item for PVC preference which may not be sufficient and overly simplified [7]. Last but not the least, the current study was an online study, indicating that we used pictures to simulate real dashboard. Hence, there may be differences between picture and real dashboard, leading to unclear bias. Therefore, based on all previous discussions, we first suggest future studies recruit a larger sample with a balanced gender and age distribution to further our conclusion. Secondly, future studies should focus on how to include more factors and adapt the current model to establish a more general PVC theory. At the same time, they can also think how to evaluate preference for PVC in a more detailed way. Third, future study should use driver simulators to increase ecological validity. Last, future studies parallelly replicate our study across different cultures, further discovering the stability of the PVC questionnaire across different languages and cultures. Meanwhile, future studies can use a consistent PVC questionnaire and control demographical variables, further discovering the relationship between different factors and PVC, including its sub-dimensions.

In conclusion, we found that the PVC questionnaire framework proposed by previous study is reliable and valid after validation with a large sample size and stimuli set [7]. The good reliability and validity also inform that the four-factor model from previous study is reasonable [7]. We encourage future studies to replicate our study in more language-speaking populations to increase the scope of application of the PVC questionnaire and review the theoretical model to further improve the accuracy of PVC evaluation. This translated version can be a practical and efficient evaluation tool for PVC among Chinese version populations in vehicle design, interface arrangement and other areas.

Acknowledgement. The study was supported by the National Natural Science Foundation of China (Grant No. T2192932) and the Scientific Foundation of Institute of Psychology, Chinese Academy of Sciences (No.E2CX4535CX). And the authors would like to thank Chongqing Changan Automobile Co., Ltd. for project support.

References

1. Engstroem, J., Johansson, E., Oestlund, J.: Effects of visual and cognitive load in real and simulated motorway driving. Transp. Res. F Traffic Psychol. Behav. **8**, 97–120 (2005)
2. Harbluk, J., Noy, Y., Trbovich, P., Eizenman, M.: An on-road assessment of cognitive distraction: impacts on drivers' visual behavior and braking performance. Accid. Anal. Prev. **39**, 372–379 (2007)
3. Horrey, W.J., Wickens, C.D., Consalus, K.P.: Modeling drivers' visual attention allocation while interacting with in-vehicle technologies. J. Exp. Psychol. Appl. **12**, 67–78 (2006). https://doi.org/10.1037/1076-898X.12.2.67
4. Horberry, T., Anderson, J., Regan, M.A., Triggs, T.J., Brown, J.: Driver distraction: the effects of concurrent in-vehicle tasks, road environment complexity and age on driving performance. Accid. Anal. Prev. **38**, 185–191 (2006)
5. Sagberg, F.: Accident risk of car drivers during mobile telephone use. IJVD **26**, 57 (2001). https://doi.org/10.1504/IJVD.2001.001929
6. Strayer, D.L., Johnston, W.A.: Driven to distraction: dual-task studies of simulated driving and conversing on a cellular telephone. Psychol. Sci. **12**, 462–466 (2001). https://doi.org/10.1111/1467-9280.00386
7. Lee, S.C., Hwangbo, H., Ji, Y.G.: Perceived visual complexity of in-vehicle information display and its effects on glance behavior and preferences. Int. J. Hum.-Comput. Interact. **32**, 654–664 (2016). https://doi.org/10.1080/10447318.2016.1184546
8. Dong, Y., Ling, C., Hua, L.: Effect of glance duration on perceived complexity and segmentation of user interfaces. In: Jacko, J.A. (ed.) HCI 2007. LNCS, vol. 4552, pp. 605–614. Springer, Heidelberg (2007). https://doi.org/10.1007/978-3-540-73110-8_66
9. Wang, J., Hsu, Y.: The relationship of symmetry, complexity, and shape in mobile interface aesthetics, from an emotional perspective—a case study of the smartwatch. Symmetry **12**, 1403 (2020). https://doi.org/10.3390/sym12091403
10. Yoon, S.H., Lim, J.H., Ji, Y.G.: Perceived visual complexity and visual search performance of automotive instrument cluster: a quantitative measurement study. Int. J. Hum.-Comput. Interact. **31**, 890–900 (2015). https://doi.org/10.1080/10447318.2015.1069661
11. Xing, J.: Measures of Information Complexity and the Implications for Automation Design 15 (2004)

12. Ling, C., Lopez, M., Shehab, R.: Complexity questionnaires of visual displays: a validation study of two information complexity questionnaires of visual displays. Hum. Factors Man. **23**, 391–411 (2013). https://doi.org/10.1002/hfm.20327
13. George, D., Mallery, P.: SPSS for Windows step by step: a simple guide and reference, 11.0 update. Allyn and Bacon, Boston (2003)
14. Nunnally, J.C.: Psychometric Theory. McGraw-Hill, New York (1978)
15. Thompson, B., Daniel, L.G.: Factor analytic evidence for the construct validity of scores: a historical overview and some guidelines. Educ. Psychol. Measur. **56**, 197–208 (1996). https://doi.org/10.1177/0013164496056002001
16. Arifin, W.N., Yusoff, M.S.B., Naing, N.N.: Confirmatory factor analysis (CFA) of USM Emotional Quotient Inventory (USMEQ-i) among medical degree program applicants in Universiti Sains Malaysia (USM). EIMJ **4** (2012). https://doi.org/10.5959/eimj.v4i2.33
17. Fornell, C., Larcker, D.F.: Evaluating structural equation models with unobservable variables and measurement error. J. Mark. Res. **18**, 39 (1981). https://doi.org/10.2307/3151312
18. Hair, J.F. (ed.): Multivariate Data Analysis. Prentice Hall, Upper Saddle River (2010)
19. Hüseyinoğlu, S., Aydın Doğan, R.: Labor Evaluation Information Scale (LEIS): development, validity and reliability. Int. J. Caring Sci. (2022)
20. Baumgartner, H., Homburg, C.: Applications of structural equation modeling in marketing and consumer research: a review. Int. J. Res. Mark. **13**, 139–161 (1996). https://doi.org/10.1016/0167-8116(95)00038-0
21. Lüdecke, D., Ben-Shachar, M., Patil, I., Waggoner, P., Makowski, D.: Performance: an R package for assessment, comparison and testing of statistical models. JOSS **6**, 3139 (2021). https://doi.org/10.21105/joss.03139
22. Xing, J.: Information complexity in air traffic control displays. In: Jacko, J.A. (ed.) HCI 2007. LNCS, vol. 4553, pp. 797–806. Springer, Heidelberg (2007). https://doi.org/10.1007/978-3-540-73111-5_89
23. Xing, J., Manning, C.A.: Complexity and automation displays of air traffic control: literature review and analysis (2005)
24. Li, L., et al.: Establishing a role for the visual complexity of linguistic stimuli in age-related reading difficulty: evidence from eye movements during Chinese reading. Atten. Percept. Psychophys. **81**(8), 2626–2634 (2019). https://doi.org/10.3758/s13414-019-01836-y
25. Chadwick-Dias, A., McNulty, M., Tullis, T.: Web usability and age: how design changes can improve performance. SIGCAPH Comput. Phys. Handicap. 30–37 (2002). https://doi.org/10.1145/960201.957212
26. Bogicevic, V., Bujisic, M., Cobanoglu, C., Feinstein, A.H.: Gender and age preferences of hotel room design. IJCHM **30**, 874–899 (2018). https://doi.org/10.1108/IJCHM-08-2016-0450
27. Herzog, T.R., Gale, T.A.: Preference for urban buildings as a function of age and nature context. Environ. Behav. **28**, 44–72 (1996)
28. Ozer, B., Baris, M.E.: Landscape design and park users' preferences. Procedia Soc. Behav. Sci. **82**, 604–607 (2013). https://doi.org/10.1016/j.sbspro.2013.06.317
29. Kim, A., Han, J., Jung, Y., Lee, K.: The effects of familiarity and robot gesture on user acceptance of information. In: 2013 8th ACM/IEEE International Conference on Human-Robot Interaction (HRI), Tokyo, Japan, pp. 159–160. IEEE (2013). https://doi.org/10.1109/HRI.2013.6483550
30. Tan, H.S.G., van den Berg, E., Stieger, M.: The influence of product preparation, familiarity and individual traits on the consumer acceptance of insects as food. Food Qual. Prefer. **52**, 222–231 (2016). https://doi.org/10.1016/j.foodqual.2016.05.003
31. Wicki, M.: How do familiarity and fatal accidents affect acceptance of self-driving vehicles? Transport. Res. F: Traffic Psychol. Behav. **83**, 401–423 (2021). https://doi.org/10.1016/j.trf.2021.11.004

Research on Design Method for Online Panoramic Tourist Website Based on AHP-QFD

Junnan Ye, Ziqiang Ren, Yue Fang, Yue Wu, Mengli Xu, and Chaoxiang Yang(✉)

East China University of Science and Technology, Shanghai, China
1143415567@qq.com

Abstract. Since the outbreak of the COVID-19 in 2019, the travel industry worldwide has been greatly affected. Although the epidemic has been largely controlled in various countries and society has steadily entered the post-epidemic era, social life is still affected by the epidemic. Meanwhile, a for the development of virtual reality, more and more people are turning their attention to the development of the travel industry to online virtual travel, and the design research of online panoramic travel websites is gradually becoming popular. However, the existing online panoramic travel websites has many problems such as imperfect functional modules, poor interface interaction experience and so on. How to use effective scientific means and methods to solve the above problems has high research value and significance.

Hierarchical analysis (AHP) and quality function development (QFD) theory can help to obtain important user requirements and translate them into specific design elements. The aim of this investigation was to combine AHP and QFD to develop the research of design methods of online panoramic travel website. In the study process, Firstly, users' requirements for the online panoramic travel website is determined through user interviews and questionnaire research, and the system requirement framework is established; secondly, AHP is applyed to analyze the weight of the system requirement framework and the hierarchical structure of users' requirements for the system is established; then, the relationship between users' requirements and platform design elements of websites is established through the QFD theory, and the key design elements will be obtained to provide innovative ideas for the design of panoramic online travel platform. Finally, this study will use a case study of the online tourism website based on panorama as an example to verify the feasibility and effectiveness of the design method. The result of this research provides methodological support and case reference for how to develop online panoramic tourism website design in the future.

Keywords: Panoramic · AHP · QFD · Online Tourism · Design Method

1 Introduction

With the COVID-19 outbreak worldwide, various industries have been greatly affected, among which the tourism industry has been more affected due to the rapid spread of the virus and the trauma it brings to the human body. As the epidemic was effectively controlled and society entered the post-epidemic era, the tourism industry gradually entered

M. Kurosu and A. Hashizume (Eds.): HCII 2023, LNCS 14011, pp. 336–351, 2023.
https://doi.org/10.1007/978-3-031-35596-7_22

a transformation phase after the impact. Nowadays, many people combine tourism with the Internet model, and online tourism has become an new direction for the development of the tourism industry [1].

The study for online tourism is more inclined to the field of panoramic technology, such as c imaging technology, 3D panoramic technology, etc. [2]. The existing design process lacks AHP of design requirements for users and weighting analysis of requirements, which cannot effectively provide decisions for innovative design; therefore, the study will combine QFD and AHP to design innovation for panoramic online tourism website to provide better experience and service for users.

QFD is a multi-level deductive analysis method that translates user or market requirements into design requirements, component characteristics, process requirements, and production requirements. In recent years, foreign scholars' research has also applied QFD methods to product quality analysis, product service systems, and product development collaboration at the level of product development. Therefore, the use of QFD method for online panoramic travel website design is to ensure that the system design is based on the technical guarantee to achieve the comprehensive requirements of function, interaction and aesthetics.[3] In the specific design practice, QFD theory can assist to realize the online panoramic online tourism website design requirement analysis, and then through the use of quality house, the relevant element relationship and comparison can be obtained. The main problem to be solved in this paper is the website interaction and functional design, which involves more design elements and complex relationships, so the introduction of AHP method as a means to calculate the weights among design elements on the basis of the completion of functional unfolding will be able to improve the scientific nature of the design process.

2 Design Status of Online Panoramic Travel Website

2.1 Introduction of Online Panoramic Travel Website

The method of scene simulation in online virtual tourism websites is mainly based on two technologies: three-dimensional technology and panoramic technology.

Three-dimensional simulation, using three-dimensional modeling to simulate the actual scene, can build a display screen with three-dimensional effect. In terms of interactive experience, it is better than flat panoramic simulation, but 3D simulation has disadvantages such as low authenticity, high cost and long development cycle, so it cannot be applied to the market on a large scale so far. And panoramic simulation, with the help of 360° panoramic virtual environment, combined with virtual reality helmet display, can restore the full picture of the tourism scene more realistically and completely, so that people can get a three-dimensional, panoramic viewing experience. Because the output of this technology has a strong sense of realism and the advantages of low R&D cost and high output efficiency, it is highly favored in the exchange of tourism scene display [4].

Panorama technology is a new type of virtual reality multimedia technology that can present the user's surroundings through 360 panoramic images and videos, taking images and videos of different locations through multiple perspectives and then connecting them together to create a panoramic spatial environment. The final presentation effect can realize a 360-degree all-round spatial experience, enabling users to visit scenes in the virtual environment and feel the actual far more realistic environment than the virtual one. Due to the low cost, high authenticity and high output efficiency of the technology itself, the panoramic technology is also widely used to establish online tourism websites, which can enhance the effect of virtual tourism by enabling people to get an immersive viewing experience without leaving home. Therefore, the in-depth study of this technology, the design and application of online tourism websites based on this technology, and the active search for more effective design and use of online panoramic tourism websites can enrich the service system of the tourism industry and promote the optimal construction of the tourism and leisure industry [5].

2.2 Current Status of the Advantages of Online Panoramic Travel Websites

According to the data obtained from expert interviews and user research, combined with market research, it can be found that the advantages of the panoramic tourism industry compared to 3D technology-related products on the market are:

(1) Real scenario experience delivery. Panorama technology analyzes, adjusts and splices adjacent floor plans after shooting multi-angle floor plans at selected points to create panoramas, and finally presents real scenes in the form of 360 panoramas to meet the demand of browsing scene images in all directions. Since the materials composing the panorama are all from the real shot floor plans, the panorama technology is more suitable for the display of tourism scenes than the 3D technology [6].
(2) Low-cost panoramic image production. Compared with 3D technology, panoramic technology does not require model design, model construction and rendering work of the model. Panoramic images can be stitched together after multi-angle shooting by cameras or directly shot by panoramic cameras such as insta360 and Ricoh, so the cost in terms of manpower and capital is greatly reduced, lowering the threshold of the industry.
(3) Abundant resources of panoramic tourism scenes. Compared with 3D technology, panoramic technology obtains panoramic images without design, modeling and rendering work, which can be completed by simple production after shooting, so the output of panoramic images is highly efficient, which can bring abundant image resources, and well-known online panoramic tourism websites often have abundant image resources.

2.3 Current Status of the Disadvantages of Online Panoramic Travel Websites

Compared with 3D technology, panoramic technology has higher realism, lower cost and higher output efficiency, and also has certain advantages in the online virtual tourism industry, which can be realized in scale and volume. However, due to the limitations of the technology, there are still some disadvantages:

(1) Poor simulation experience caused by low interactive forms. Compared with the model form of 3D technology, the image form of panoramic technology lacks more free, flexible and rich interaction experience. The online travel website can only

provide basic interaction forms such as panoramic scene display, panoramic scene switching and point-and-touch, so it cannot experience a more realistic travel scene, which reduces the user's experience.

(2) Users' needs for different viewpoints cannot be met by panoramic images. Since the panoramic image is obtained by shooting and the shooting point is fixed, it cannot flexibly meet the user's demand of wishing to view the landscape from different perspectives, and can only adjust the shooting point after shooting the panoramic image for several times and meet the demand by switching scenes [7].

(3) Design limitations exist in panoramic online tourist websites. They mainly meets the users' demand for browsing and communication of tourism scenes, and the existing website generally lacks the system attributes of evaluation and socialization, which creates a certain obstruction to the users' demand for displaying and communicating tourism scenes and needs to be improved in the user demand experience.

2.4 Design Status Summary of Online Panoramic Travel Website

Panoramic photo is a 360 panoramic picture stitched together from a combination of real shot flat photos, and the virtual tourism scene formed by this form of processing is far more realistic than the virtual scene created by 3D technology. In addition, due to its low cost and small output efficiency, there is less resistance in the scale production of the product. However, there are also disadvantages such as simple forms of interaction and poor immersion experience. These shortcomings are caused by the technology itself, and it is difficult to solve them fundamentally. However, it is found in the market research that the existing products do not do more design on other attributes of the website to improve user experience and alleviate the defects caused by technical problems of panoramic online travel products. Therefore, this paper will combine QFD and AHP to innovate the design of panoramic online tourist to provide better experience and service for users.

3 Analysis of User Needs

After analyzing the experience and research of existing online panoramic travel websites worldwide and reviewing related literature, the target user needs become more clearly the research objects mainly include 720yun, Airpano, Wanos and so on. In this study, we focus on feeling the user's experience of using panoramic and the interactive experience of users using the online panoramic tourism website. The task portraits of 10 users in different age groups were drawn, and the user requirements of online panoramic travel websites were obtained through comprehensive analysis of the interactive experience feelings of the above user portraits [8].

Through the collation of existing panoramic technology-related products and related literature, evaluation criteria for a total of five demand levels of price, function, interface, interactive experience and immersion experience are obtained; the five demand levels are used as guideline layers (A1–A5), and 20 specific indicators (a1–a20) of panoramic online travel platform are obtained by summarizing the needs of target users, as shown in Fig. 1.

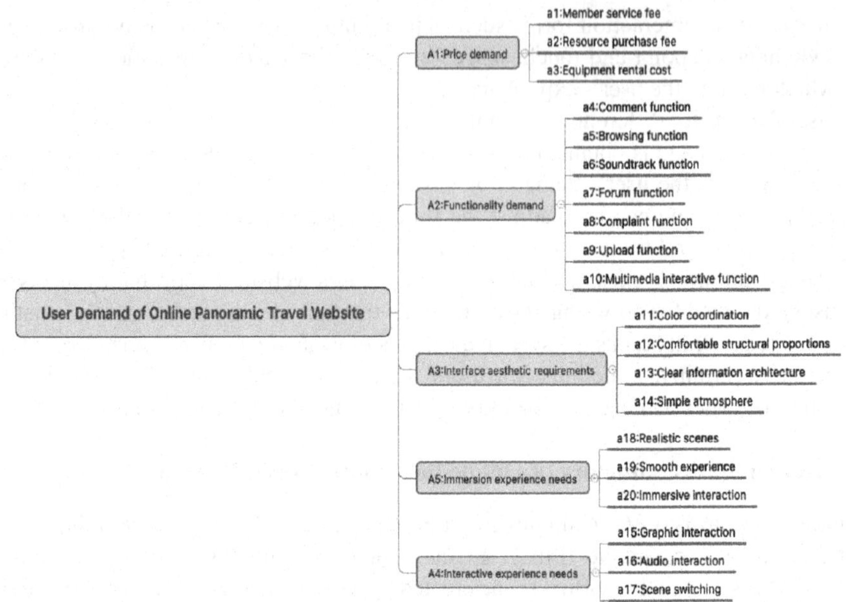

Fig.1. Online panoramic travel website user demand map

4 Online Panoramic Tourism Website Design Process Based on AHP and QFD

4.1 AHP-Based User Requirement Weighting Analysis

AHP is a method of decomposing the factors related to a decision problem in a hierarchical manner and analyzing the decision on this basis. Then, the eigenvectors and maximum eigenvalues of the judgment matrix are solved, and the weights of the factors in each level and the combined weights of the factors in each level to the total objective are obtained.

The characteristic of this method is that on the basis of in-depth research on the nature of complex decision-making problems, influencing factors and their intrinsic relationships, etc., the thinking process of decision-making is mathematized by using less quantitative information, thus providing an easy decision-making method for complex decision-making problems with multiple objectives, multiple criteria or no structural characteristics. It is a model and method for making decisions on complex systems that are difficult to fully quantify.

According to the nature of the problem and the total goal to be achieved, the AHP method decomposes the problem into different constituent factors, and gathers and combines the factors at different levels according to their interrelated influences and affiliations to form a multi-level analysis structure model, so that the problem finally boils down to the lowest level (solutions, measures, etc. for decision) relative to the highest level (the total goal) The determination of the relative importance weights or the ranking of relative advantages and disadvantages.

The steps of AHP, when using AHP to construct a system model, can be broadly divided into the following four steps: building a hierarchical structure model, constructing a judgment (pairwise comparison) matrix, single ranking of levels and its consistency check, and total ranking of levels and its consistency check [9].

4.2 AHP-Based User Requirement Weighting Analysis Process

AHP constructs a comparison judgment matrix based on the importance level between related requirements and performs a consistency test to derive the weight values corresponding to different requirement layers. Professor Saaty compares the criterion layer and the indicator layer of target user requirements with each other and proposes nine importance levels. According to the relative importance degree of the indicator layer, the indicators of the same layer are compared with each other and assigned values by the binary comparison method, and the relevant importance comparison values are composed of 1 to 9 and non-zero values corresponding to the inverse [10].

In this study, the AHP questionnaire was designed for the above established target user requirements indicators. A number of design-related practitioners and experts in the field of panoramic technology were invited to make a two-by-two comparison of the collated requirements, and they were asked to score the above panoramic online related requirements in comparison and construct the relevant judgment matrix as follows.

$$B = (bij)n \times n = \begin{bmatrix} b11 & b12 & \cdots & b1n \\ b21 & b22 & \cdots & b2n \\ \vdots & \vdots & \ddots & \vdots \\ bn1 & bn2 & \cdots & bnn \end{bmatrix} \tag{1}$$

According to the AHP method, we set the design of panoramic online tourism platform as the target layer, five demand levels as the criterion layer, and 20 specific indicators of panoramic online tourism wensite as the sub-criteria layer, and constructed a AHP model.

Based on the AHP model, a scientific and reasonable judgment matrix is constructed to compare the mutual importance of the user demand indicators of the same level, and the weights of the demand indicators of the criterion layer and sub-criterion layer are calculated by using the geometric mean method, and the general operation procedure is as follows.

(1) Calculate the scalar product of each row.

$$Mi = \prod_{j=1}^{m} bij \, (i = 1, 2, ..., 3) \tag{2}$$

where: bij indicates the demand indicator in the i-th row and j-th column,m represents the demand indicator volume.

(2) Determine the geometric mean of the product of scalars in each row.

$$ai = \sqrt[m]{Mi} \, (i = 1, 2, ..., 3) \tag{3}$$

(3) Calculate the relative weights.

$$Wi = \frac{ai}{\sum_{i=1}^{m} ai} \tag{4}$$

(4) Calculate the maximum characteristic root.

$$\lambda\max = \frac{1}{n}\sum_{i=1}^{n}\frac{B_{Wi}}{Wi} \tag{5}$$

where: B_{Wi} denotes the *i*-th component of vector B_W, *n* represents the order.

(5) Result consistency test.

$$CI = \frac{\lambda\max - n}{n - 1} \tag{6}$$

$$CR = \frac{CI}{RI} \tag{7}$$

Table 1. Judgment matrix RI value

n	1	2	3	4	5	6	7	8	9	10	11
RI	0.00	0.00	0.58	0.90	1.12	1.24	1.32	1.41	1.45	1.49	1.52

where: *n* indicates the number of orders corresponding to the evaluation scale of the judgment matrix; *RI* represents the average random consistency index, each order has a corresponding value, as shown in Table 1; *CR* indicates the consistency ratio, when $CR \leq 0.1$, indicating that the consistency test passed; if $CR > 0.1$, it means that the consistency test did not pass, the judgment matrix needs to be checked and corrected and adjusted and then calculated and analyzed again.

4.3 AHP-Based Online Panoramic Travel Website User Demand Weighting Analysis

In this stage, we collected the user demands of the panoramic online tourism platform through field user interviews and the collation and analysis of the panoramic online tourism platform, and applied the AHP hierarchical analysis method to analyze the weighting of the user demands of the panoramic online tourism platform. Firstly, several relevant experts are invited to conduct comparative evaluation of 9 importance levels of the relevant demands of the panoramic online tourism platform, and the evaluated results are used to construct the relevant judgment matrix, and the first and second level indicators of the panoramic online tourism platform are obtained through normalization, by which the weight values of the user demands of the judgment matrix are calculated, as shown in the following Table 2, 3, 4, 5, 6, 7.

Table 2. Primary indicator judgment matrix

Demand target	Price demand	Functional demand	Interface demand	Interaction experience demand	Immersive experience requirements	Weight ω1i
Price demand	1.000	0.200	0.500	0.333	0.333	6.617%
Functional demand	5.000	1.000	2.000	3.000	2.000	38.214%
Interface demand	2.000	0.500	1.000	0.333	0.500	12.162%
Interaction experience demand	3.000	0.333	3.000	1.000	2.000	24.704%
Immersive experience requirements	3.000	0.500	2.000	0.500	1.000	18.303%

Table 3. Judgment matrix for secondary indicators of price requirements

Price Demand	Member service fee	Resource purchase cost	Equipment rental fee	Weight ω2i
Member service fee	1.000	0.500	4.000	31.786%
Resource purchase cost	2.000	1.000	6.667	59.762%
Equipment rental fee	0.250	0.150	1.000	8.452%

Calculate the maximum characteristic value λmax1 - 6 and Consistency ratio,to test the consistency of the judgment matrix, after checking Table 1, the *CR* was calculated by the formula, and the relevant values are shown in Table 8.

From the table, it can be seen that $CR1 - 6$ all less than 0.1. Therefore, the judgment matrix is consistent and the weights are valid. Normalize the weights $\omega 1$ - 6i. The comprehensive weight value of user requirements is obtained, and the user requirements weight priority is shown in Fig. 2.

Table 4. Judgment matrix for secondary indicators of function requirements

Functional requirements	Comment function	Browsing function	Soundtrack function	Forum function	Complaint function	Upload function	Multimedia interactive function	Weightω3i
Comment function	1.000	0.250	2.000	0.500	2.000	0.333	0.500	7.999%
Browsing function	4.000	1.000	6.000	2.000	5.000	1.333	2.000	28.758%
Soundtrack function	0.500	0.167	1.000	0.333	1.000	0.200	0.250	4.449%
Forum function	2.000	0.500	3.000	1.000	4.000	0.500	1.000	14.827%
Complaint function	0.500	0.200	1.000	0.250	1.000	0.200	0.250	4.422%
Upload function	3.000	0.750	5.000	2.000	5.000	1.000	1.000	22.515%
Multimedia interactive function	2.000	0.500	4.000	1.000	4.000	1.000	1.000	17.040%

Table 5. Judgment matrix for secondary indicators of interface requirements

Interface requirements	Color coordination	Comfortable structural proportions	Clear information structure	Simplicity	Weight ω4i
Color coordination	1.000	2.000	0.500	3.003	27.318%
Comfortable structural proportions	0.500	1.000	0.333	1.499	14.678%
Clear information structure	2.000	3.000	1.000	5.000	48.491%
Simplicity	0.333	0.667	0.200	1.000	9.513%

Table 6. Judgment matrix for secondary indicators of interactive experience requirements

Interaction experience requirements	Graphic interaction	Audio interaction	Scene switching	Weight ω5i
Graphic interaction	1.000	3.003	0.500	30.923%
Audio interaction	0.333	1.000	0.200	10.954%
Scene switching	2.000	5.000	1.000	58.122%

Table 7. Judgment matrix for secondary indicators of immersive experience requirements

Immersion experience demand	Scene realistic	Experience fluency	Immersive interaction	Weight ω6i
Scene realistic	1.000	2.000	5.000	59.489%
Experience fluency	0.500	1.000	2.000	27.661%
Immersive interaction	0.200	0.500	1.000	12.850%

Table 8. Maximum characteristic value

Maximum characteristic value	λ_{max1}	λ_{max2}	λ_{max3}	$\lambda max4$	λ_{max5}	λ_{max6}
Numerical value	5.228	3.004	1.360	4.008	3.004	3.006
Consistency ratio	**CR1**	**CR2**	**CR3**	**CR4**	**CR5**	**CR6**
Numerical value	0.057	0.002	0.007	0.003	0.002	0.003

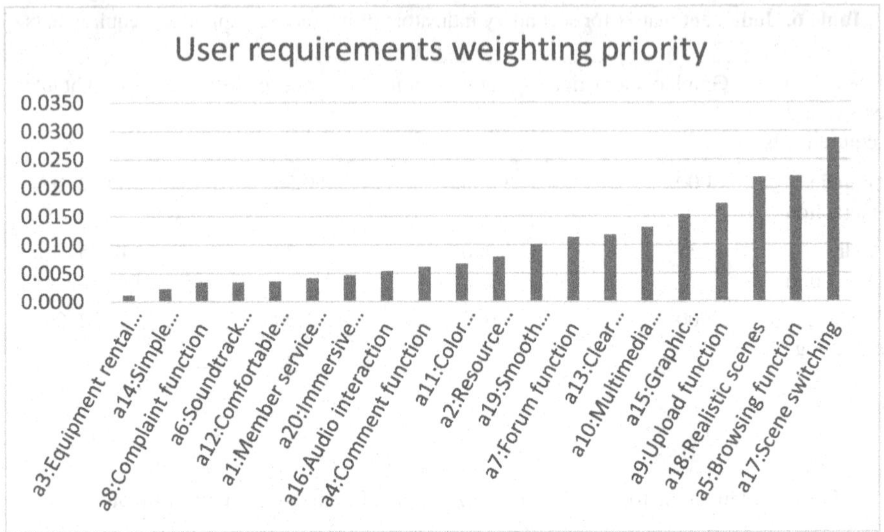

Fig.2. User requirements weighting priority

4.4 QFD-Based User Requirements Transformation

QFD was proposed by Japanese scholars Mizuno and Akao in the late 1960s as a method to develop design quality for satisfying customers. QFD is market-oriented and driven by user needs, and can reasonably and effectively translate user needs into technical objectives at each stage of product development. QFD consists of user requirements, engineering characteristics, customer requirements-engineering AHP-based User Requirement Weighting Analysis characteristics relationship matrix, autocorrelation matrix between engineering characteristics, planning matrix of customer requirements and design matrix of engineering characteristics, etc. Through the construction and decision making of quality house, QFD can effectively plan product design and ensure that the product design process is always in line with user requirements [11].

4.5 QFD-Based Design Requirements Approach

In the QFD method, design requirements are the core component of building the quality house model [12]. Based on the user requirements and the product characteristics of the panoramic online travel platform, the design requirements related to the panoramic online travel platform are analyzed comprehensively, and the design requirements of the panoramic online travel platform are obtained from four aspects: functional requirements E1, interface requirements E2, experience requirements E3, and interaction requirements E4. The design requirements of the panoramic online travel platform are shown in Table 9.

Table 9. Design requirements

First-level design requirements	Second-level design requirements
Functional requirement E1	Panoramic travel scene display functional requirement e1 Panoramic travel scene upload function requirement e2
Interface requirements E2	Interface appearance color matching requirements e3 Interface information architecture integrity requirements e4
Experience requirements E3	Immersion experience requirements e_5 Smooth operation experience requirements e6
Interaction requirements E4	Multimedia interaction requirements e7 Scene switching interaction requirements e8

4.6 QFD-Based Online Panoramic Travel Website User Demand Transformation

Through the target user requirement weight values obtained by hierarchical analysis, a panoramic online travel bottle body ah requirement quality house was established, and the design requirement relationship matrix E was derived based on the expert group's analysis of the relationship between user requirements (UR) and design requirements (DR), as shown in Table 10.

F_j is used to denote the importance of the design requirement DR_j, f_j denotes the relative importance, w_i is the weight of the i-th user requirement, and E_{ij} is the value of the relationship corresponding to both [13].

$$Fj = \sum_{i=1}^{n} wi \times Eij(i, j = 1, 2, ..., n) \tag{8}$$

$$fj = \frac{Fj}{\sum_{j=1}^{n} Fj}(j = 1, 2, ..., n) \tag{9}$$

The calculated related design requirements are ranked in order of importance after normalization, and the functional requirement model is constructed according to the priority of the functional requirements of the panoramic online travel platform. The main functional requirement model consists of panoramic travel scene display function, panoramic travel scene upload function, immersive experience, smooth operation experience, and scene switching interaction function.

Table 10. Target user needs-design demand relationship matrix

		E_1		E_2		E3		E_4		用户
		e1	e2	e3	e4	e5	e6	e7	e8	需求权重
A	a			△	△	□		△		0.0
1	1	■								042
	a		△					△	△	0.0
A	a									0.0
2	4	■	△	△		■	□		△	061
	a									0.0
	5				□					220
	a									0.0
	6		■		□		□		□	034
	a			△			□			0.0
	7									112
A	a			■		□				0.0
3	11									066
	a		△		■				□	0.0
	12			■		□	□			036
A	a	□	□							0.0
4	15		□			□				153
	a	□	□			□	■		■	0.0
A	a	■				■			□	0.0
5	18			□	△	□	■		■	218
	a	■			□	■		■	■	0.0
Design requirement weighting		0.4 140	0.2 691	0.1 140	0.1 729	0.3 841	0.3 575	0.0 288	0.3 276	

Note: ■, □, △ correspond to the degree of relationship between user requirements and design requirements, where "■" represents a strong correlation, the value is 5; "□" represents a medium correlation, the value is 3; "△" represents a weak correlation, the value is 1, no correlation between the two needs is not marked, the value is 0.

5 Design and Evaluation of Online Panoramic Travel Platform

According to the above approach, the design direction and design focus of the panoramic online travel platform is obtainable. After compiling existing panoramic technology-related products and related literature, 20 specific indicators of the panoramic online travel platform were obtained at five demand levels, including price, function, interface, interactive experience and immersive experience. Among them, the weighting analysis shows that at the user demand level, they mainly include the clear information architecture of the interface, the multimedia interactive function of panoramic pictures. Graphic interaction function, uploading panoramic tourism scene function, and panoramic tourism user needs mainly include clear information architecture of the interface, multimedia interaction function of panoramic images, graphic interaction function, uploading panoramic tourism scene, authenticity of panoramic tourism scene, and panoramic tourism scene switching function. Through the study of quality function unfolding method, the main functional demand model consisting of panoramic tourism scene display function, panoramic tourism scene upload function, immersive experience, smooth operation experience, scene switching interaction function is obtained, and the design drawing of online panoramic tourism website is shown in Fig. 3–4.

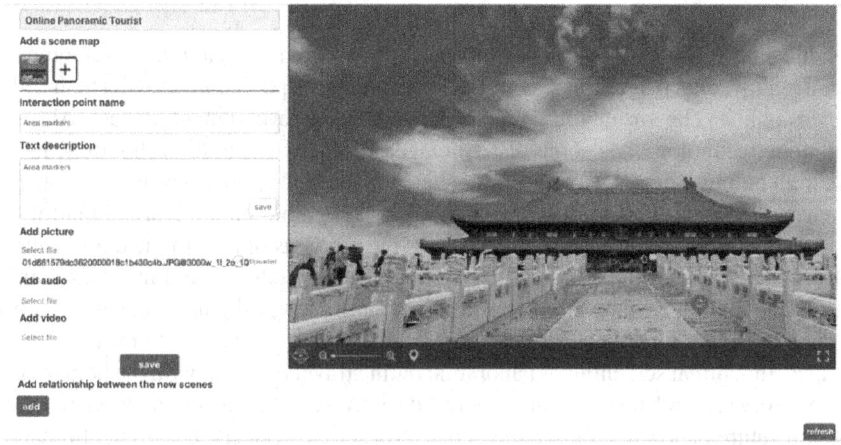

Fig. 3. The design drawings of the online panoramic tourist website (1)

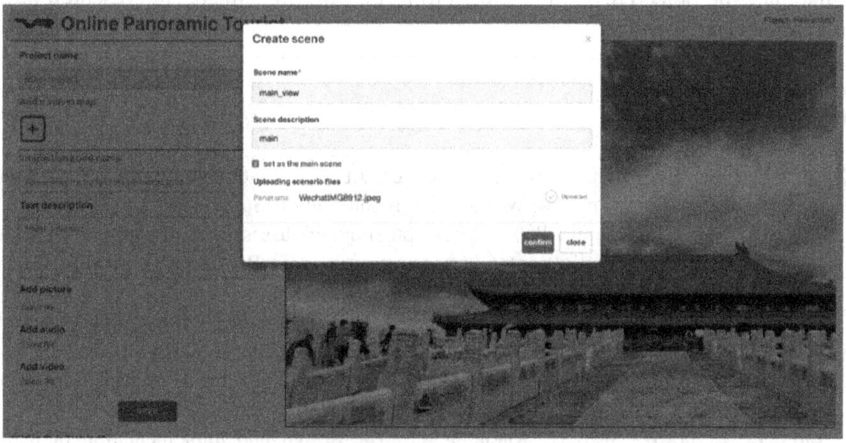

Fig. 4. The design drawings of the online panoramic tourist website (2)

The innovative research methods of AHP and QFD are introduced to derive the importance weights of user needs and product functions, and finally output the design recommendation directions. The panoramic online travel platform should make further improvements in the direction of panoramic scene uploading and scene switching that are conducive to enhancing user experience. For instance, optimizing the scene uploading and scene switching process can improve the efficiency and enthusiasm of users in supporting the platform resources and greatly enhance the content richness of the platform. In addition, optimizing the multimedia interaction function and graphic interaction function of panoramic images can enhance the virtual immersion experience of users and improve the user experience.

6 Conclusion

With the emergence of social issues such as new coronaviruses and the development of virtual reality concepts such as metaverse, more and more people are moving their offline services online. The virtual tourism industry requires a development process. Although panoramic technology has some disadvantages compared with 3D technology, its low cost, high output efficiency and realism make it favored in the pre-development stage of the virtual tourism industry. The research takes panoramic online tourism platform as the research target, comprehensively analyzes the products of panoramic online tourism platform and clarifies the design gaps, excavates user needs by field interviews, introduces AHP and QFD innovation research methods, derives the importance weights of user needs and product functions, and outputs design suggestion directions. Researchers conducts functional screening of panoramic online travel platform with the help of innovation theory research methods, and the final design direction provides a certain reference basis for future panoramic online travel platform series products. Due to the limitations of objective factors, the number of personnel will be expanded in the subsequent user interviews and expert panel evaluation process, and more research data will be added to guarantee the objectivity of the results to further improve the design research of the panoramic online travel platform.

References

1. He, Y.F., Jiang, Z.G., Wu, N., Bian, N. and Ren, J.L.: Correlation between COVID-19 and hepatitis B: a systematic review. World J. Gastroenterology **28**(46), 6599–6618 (2022)
2. Hayat, U., Sitara, A., Imran Ullah, K.: Perceptual quality assessment of panoramic stitched contents for immersive applications: a prospective survey. Virt. Real. Smart Hardware (English and Chinese) **4**(03), 223–246 (2022)
3. Fargnoli, N., Fargnoli, M., Sakao, T.: Integrating QFD for product-service systems with the Kano model and fuzzy AHP. Total Q. Manage. Bus. Excellence **31**(9–10) (2020)
4. Guo, X.-D.: Research on DSO vision positioning technology based on binocular stereo panoramic vision system. Def. Technol. **18**(04), 593–603 (2022)
5. Yabo, Z., Lixia, W., Wei, L., Xiaofeng, C.: The design and implementation of harbor panoramic browsing system based on image based rendering technology. In: Proceedings of 2017 16th International Symposium on Distributed Computing and Applications to Business, Engineering and Science(DCABES 2017), pp. 190–193 (2017)
6. Magadán-Díaz M., Rivas-García J.I.: Residents' perception of sustainable tourism in protected mountain areas: the case of Asturias. J. Mount. Sci. **19**(12), 3597–3614 (2022)

7. Witmer, B.G., Singer, M.J.: Measuring presence in virtual environments: a presence questionnaire. Presence **7**(3), 225–240 (1998)
8. Yiannakopoulou, E., et al.: Virtual reality simulators and training in laparoscopic surgery. Int. J. Surg. **13**, 60–64 (2015)
9. Zhang, W.Y., et al.: Product design evaluation of home appliances based on fuzzy-AHP. Adv. Mater. Res. **3530**(1044–1045), 1855–1858 (2014)
10. Hsieh, H.T., Chen, J.L.: Using TRIZ methods in friction stir welding design. Int. J. Adv. Manuf. Technol. **46**(9–12), 1085–1102 (2010)
11. Matzler, K., Hinterhuber, H.H.: How to make product development projects more successful by integrating Kano's model of customer satisfaction into quality function deployment. Technovation **18**(1), 25–38 (1998)
12. Li, L., et al.: Computer-aided 3D human modeling for portrait-based product development using point- and curve-based deformation. Comput. Aided Des. **45**(2), 134–143 (2013)
13. Salahuddin, M., Lee, Y.A.: Identifying key quality features for wearable technology embedded products using the Kano model. Int. J. Clothing Sci. Technol. **33**, 93–105 (2020)

Incorporating Design Thinking Approach to the Mutual Learning Process: A Case Study of Participatory Design with Senior Daycare Workers

Tzu-Hsuan Yu and Wan-Ling Chang(✉)

National Cheng Kung University, No. 1, University Road, Tainan City 701, Taiwan (R.O.C.)
{p36104021,WanLingChang}@gs.ncku.edu.tw

Abstract. Participatory Design (PD) originated in Scandinavia in the 1970s. Then it shaped the approaches of striving for power balance in the decision-making process within the Human-Computer Interaction (HCI) design field for decades. Mutual learning played an essential role in PD to fulfill democratic equality during the design process. The multi-disciplinary communication was a nature of PD to achieve the ideal equality. Nowadays, solving complex human issues needs collaboration across different fields. Design Thinking (DT) has become popular in the problem-solving process. This paper describes our PD workshop experience, which integrated DT methods and tools as mutual learning approaches. We conducted three PD workshops and invited the workers from the dementia daycare center as the end-user and information engineers and industrial designers in a multi-disciplinary team to ideate solutions for the problems from senior daycare workers' daily experience with natural language processing (NLP) technology. We conclude the discourse between daycare workers, engineers, and designers. The results are positive in applying DT methods and tools to PD. Finally, we discuss how to improve for better genuine participation through the DT approach.

Keywords: Participatory Design · Mutual Learning · Design Thinking

1 Introduction

When contemporary human living issues became complex, the diverse discussions on dealing with the challenge of complexity opened in the design field. Bjögvinsson et al. [4] mentioned that design activities no longer happened on an isolated object within a limited time. The concept of 'design-after-design' describes an evolution process according to the social developing context in progress. It involves multiple stakeholders to improve the design objects while interacting with these objects. The discussion happens not only between designers but also with multi-disciplinary experts. Another theory from Kimbell [27] suggested considering the roles that human and non-human play in constituting design activity. The various actors involved in the design activities shape the quality of unfolding design practice and the de-center of designers as the main agent in designing.

M. Kurosu and A. Hashizume (Eds.): HCII 2023, LNCS 14011, pp. 352–369, 2023.
https://doi.org/10.1007/978-3-031-35596-7_23

It presents the demand for collaboration between various actors since designers are not the autocrat of the design process anymore. Nowadays, as the work style has radically changed by the internet, Manzini [33] described the 'connected world' and the barrier of the design works were gone, and all designing processes were, in fact, co-designing processes. Also, he introduced that designers and non-designers could use 'new design knowledge' produced by design research in their co-designing process, and the knowledge must be explicit, discussable, transferable, and accumulable [31]. He normalizes non-designers as a part of the design actions. It implies when we develop the professional knowledge of design, at the same time, we need to consider a more friendly and accessible interface for the design operation to invite non-designers to join in the design process. These design arguments indicate a common feature: it needs more multi-disciplinary collaboration to keep communicating during the dynamic change of the time. This also means the boundary between the different professions is getting blurred.

On the other hand, the demands of multi-disciplinary discourse have brought Design Thinking (DT) to greater visibility since 2005 since the design is a subject that overlaps into different fields [24]. DT concept was originally from the academic design term of Designerly Thinking and has been translated into a more simplified version [23]. With this background, DT has begun to wide-spread to Business Management and prove that the DT concept is workable to the designer and non-designers discourse as a communicating tool [13, 24, 35]. It has been applied to organizations, companies, and schools as a co-design tool in multi-disciplinary team collaboration. With the help of DT tools as an accessible interface to interact with non-designers in multi-disciplinary team collaboration, our PD research can invite more diverse backgrounds of participants in the design process to share their own experiences and communicate more fluently.

Moreover, co-design is a concept that has been introduced previously in the design field. This practice of creating ideas collectively has been performed in Participatory Design (PD) field for more than 50 years [38]. Reviewing the PD research project's history, it started in Scandinavia in the 1970s for collective bargaining working rights in trade unions. The PD researchers claimed to have workers' voices be heard and increase workers' power when making decisions in workplaces [25]. Genuine participation is the core of PD, which emphasizes that people who own less power in a group should participate in the decision-making processes. Also, to empower the weaker participants to make decisions equally, mutual learning between all participants is necessary and is the other core notion of PD [36]. Employing PD as the framework in our research provides the advantage of examining our design practice if reciprocal and reasonable collaboration is carried out between designers and non-designers in a design process. Mutual learning will contribute to this reciprocal and reasonable collaboration by comprehending other participants' circumstances and knowledge, then make participants gain the ability to supply effective information to the collaborators in the discussion.

This paper describes the experience of combining DT tools with mutual learning practice in PD workshops. We invited workers from the dementia daycare center, information engineers, and industrial designers to work together in a co-design process. The workshops began with finding problems from daycare workers' experiences and applying NLP technology to solve the problems. With the structure of PD, we coordinate the designers (industrial designers) and non-designers (daycare workers and information engineers) in cooperative teams to make sure the voices of each participant can be heard in the problem-framing and decision-making process. Mutual learning provides a medium to empower participants who own less knowledge when making decisions and DT tools equip participants to communicate with comprehensible quality. We aim to use the DT tools as a scaffold of mutual learning in order to achieve the goal of genuine participation during the co-design process.

2 Background

2.1 Genuine Participation Through Mutual Learning in Participatory Design

The initial projects of PD strived for labor right in the 1970s [25]. These experiences of early PD projects supported the circumstance that shifted from local unions to computer science workplaces by the 1980s to build on workers' own experience and provided them with the resources to be able to act in their current situation [5]. The 1980s was the era of micro-computer development for individual use. This context made the concept of 'user' begin to merge into the design process. At the same time, it also revealed the management problems in a 'waterfall model' production. Even though the 'user' was presumed in Human-Computer Interaction (HCI) design, the users were still playing the role of informant to be observed during the working process rather than participating in the design work in the early 1980s [25]. A well-known Florence project demonstrated a successful setting of mutual learning by building a computer system prototype with users cooperatively through their daily work [3]. The mutual learning process presents the evolving change of ideas and visions through a design project. It is a pragmatic rationale of genuine participation, which is referred to bringing the users' role from being informants to being legitimate and acknowledged participants in the design process [36]. To support the practice of cooperation with others, the ethnographic approaches have been introduced into PD by the researchers in Xerox Palo Alto Research Center (PARC). PACR researchers devoted themselves to advocating 'situated action' to understand how people use their circumstances to achieve intelligent action rather than abstracting the action away from its circumstances [25, 42]. PD has been led by the computer science field for a long period of time, continuing to develop the PD methods, techniques, and tools to interact with users and provide a way of mutual learning to empower users to participate in the design process more equally. The design-by-doing method creates the interplay between two language games of designer and user by using prototyping, mock-ups, and scenarios are recommended. It emphasizes the language-game of its qualities in the social aspect. Game is a term playful, but more important is for interacting and cooperating purposes [17]. The telling-making-enacting framework formulates other typical techniques of PD. The framework aims to conduct the co-design process of designers and non-designers with a sufficient grounding for whatever participatory actions they joined in [7]. Some typical telling-making-enacting frameworks of technique and tools design, such as diaries, 2D mapping, 3D mock-ups, improvisation, etc., will prompt participants to mutual learning through genuine participation [39]. This paper suggests using the DT method/tools as the mutual learning approach. DT method/tools are presented in visual components that would help participants to clarify their thought. The advantage is to involve participants in a more profound user experience with design communication. In PD research, methods, and techniques provide a channel for non-designers to express their own knowledge which is usually not spoken out consciously by themselves. Through the process of operating the methods and techniques, it is also a platform for participants to shape mutual learning with each other for better equality of decision-making. By well engaging in the decision-making process, it makes participants in genuine participation during the design activities.

2.2 A Current Practice of Design Thinking

Kimbell has reported a practical analytical taxonomy of DT theory [26]. Firstly, DT as a cognitive style was identified in a more traditional designer's approach from academic design history. Some representative theories include 'reflection-in-action' by Schön [41] and 'designerly way of knowing' by Cross [15]. To this cognitive style notion, the purpose of the design was problem-solving. Secondly, while DT is a general theory of design, Buchanan considered the design of taming 'wicked problems' [9]. Thirdly, the DT as an organizational resource, focused on Business innovation by advocators like Brown [8] and Martin [34]. The current popular version of DT that apply to organizations, companies, and schools comes from the third type of Kimbell's taxonomy, which is translated from the academic Designerly Thinking in a simplified way. There may have two left out in DT from the translation of the academic works: One considers DT equated to creativity, and the other considers DT equated to a toolbox and ignores the ability to operate the tools [23]. As Cross mentioned, design knowledge resides in three perspectives: in people, in processes, and in products [16]. Design can be a more comprehensive thought and competence in nature. However, when DT has diffused in the translated version, it provides non-designers an understandable method to have an opportunity to leave the ingrained patterns of thinking and have a holistic understanding of the ambiguous or subjective emotion behind the problems [19]. Although the current popular DT tools may streamline some aspects of design, designers who are equipped with the design knowledge and know how to adjust to the shortage of these tools, DT tools still can be considered efficient instruments when collaborating with non-designer partners. One of the well-known DT frameworks is from Stanford d.school [1], it built a 5-stages model, which included empathize, define, ideate, prototype, and test. On the other hand, some of the DT tools are developed maturely. They are available such as in Lewrick et al.'s work [30] and the publication of TU Delft [43]. In our research, we follow the model of Stanford d.school and utilize several DT tools from Lewrick et al.'s work.

2.3 Design Thinking Methods and Tools in Participatory Design

Several researchers have contributed to merging DT methods/tools and PD practice. Planning the PD research with the 5-stage DT model of Stanford, even though the end-user might not fully participate yet in the DT stages, is a kind of strategy [18]. Also, considering numerous and different DT tools in PD research is a typical proposal in social innovation PD activities [32], such as interviews, storyboards, mock-ups, etc. Additionally, most PD researchers have implemented a single DT method or tool to improve PD outcomes. Brainstorming is a favorite tool for ideation. It is used for community-based PD discussion [21], children's education for the art programs in the museum [37], and bully issue discussion [44]. Culture Probe is a usual academic DT method [43], and PD researchers have applied it to sensitize participants to the topics [22]. Reflection is a concept of reflective practice by Schön [41] and has been used to facilitate PD education in the university [14]. In this paper, we incorporate multiple DT methods/tools and tools under the first three stages of the Stanford model to PD workshops in multi-disciplinary team collaboration with full participation for all participants.

3 The Workshop Design

3.1 Recruitment

We invited four computer science engineers who were specialists in NLP technology, four daycare workers, and two industrial designers to collaborate in order to create better solutions for the problem that was found in the daily routine of the daycare center by using NLP technology. The daycare workers came from the senior daycare center, which has specialized in caring for old people with dementia since 2009 in Tainan City. The engineers were master's students from the department of computer science and information engineering. At the same time, two designers were master's students from the department of industrial design of a National University in south Taiwan. We divided all participants into two groups: two engineers, two daycare workers, and one designer. Two authors of this paper who were researchers also played the role of designers and worked within separate groups. Three workshops took place in the classroom of the National University in November and December 2020. The workshops were held on weekday nights and lasted for 4–5 h each time.

3.2 Workshop Format and Schedule

The first workshops started with introducing NLP technology as a part of mutual learning and background knowledge (Table 1). The engineers gave a lecture on Speaker Recognition and Speech Synthesis (see Fig. 1-a). Then, the engineers demonstrated the prototype of the APP of their development that applied the technology of Speaker Recognition and Speech Synthesis in the Taiwanese language, as well as invited all participants to have a try-out of the APP on pad devices (see Fig. 1-b). After a short break, a group discussion activity was led by designers in each group, discussing 'How can we use the technology of Speaker Recognition and Speech Synthesis in the Taiwanese language in the real context of caring for old people with dementia' (see Fig. 1-c).

The second workshop was executed by the empathize stage of the Stanford DT model. The working distribution was that the designer led interviews with the daycare workers, and the engineers helped to write down the answer on the Post-it note. We used two DT tools: Stakeholder Map and User Journey Map to explore the daily work experience of the daycare workers. Researchers briefly introduced the Stakeholder Map, then the first task was to figure out the stakeholders involved in each group's daycare workers' work (see Fig. 2-a). This warm-up session expected the daycare workers to recall more of the details of their working procedure and think about how the stakeholders influenced their work. At the same time, all non-designer participants could get familiar with the

Fig. 1. The first workshop: (a) a lecture on Speaker Recognition and Speech Synthesis; (b) a try-out of the APP on the devices; (c) the group discussion of the application of the NLP technology.

operation of the DT tools. Later, the researcher presented another DT tool, the User Journey Map, and invited daycare workers to provide the information under two different persona scenarios: the yellow notes represented old people with dementia, and the blue notes represented daycare workers. Each group established a typical day through the two personas' perspective on User Journey Map (see Fig. 2-b). The User Journey Map results were the build-up to discover the problems and seek insights that could be designed (see Fig. 2-c).

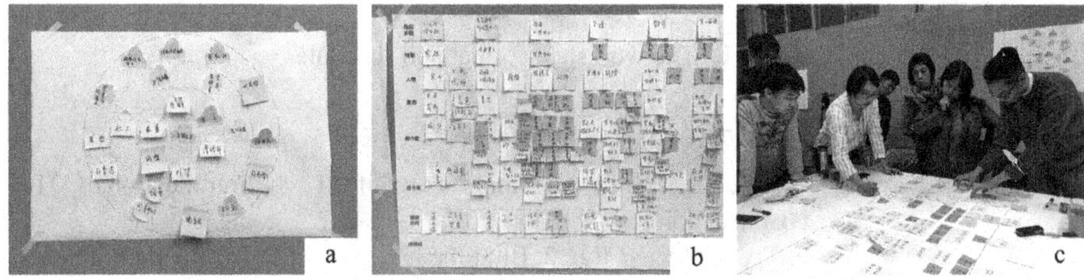

Fig. 2. The second workshop: (a) The Stakeholder Map; (b) Two persona scenarios on the User Journey Map; (c) the group discussion of the insights from the User Journey Map.

The third workshops were in the define and ideate stages of the Stanford DT model. The workshop began with the How Might We method to define the context of the problems from different points of view, situations, and background conditions. The Problem Statement Card was a tool that helped participants to formulate the insights into the problems and prepared for getting started in the ideation stage. Due to the two personas' perspective on User Journey Map, each group laid out two problem statements (see Fig. 3-a, b). According to the problem statement, Technology Card which represented 'Speaker Recognition' and 'Speech Synthesis' respectively, was used with every Problem Statement Card (see Fig. 3-c). Designers in each group guided the participants to think about whether this problem statement will be solved by Speaker Recognition and Speech Synthesis technology. After a short group discussion, in the final stage, each group selected one problem statement with the relevant Technology Card to proceed with the Brainstorming activity and ideating the solutions. The participants wrote down or drew the ideas of the solution on an A6 size sheet with a blank format (see Fig. 3-d). The workshop ended with an overall discussion to summarize the solutions of the ideation (see Fig. 3-e, f).

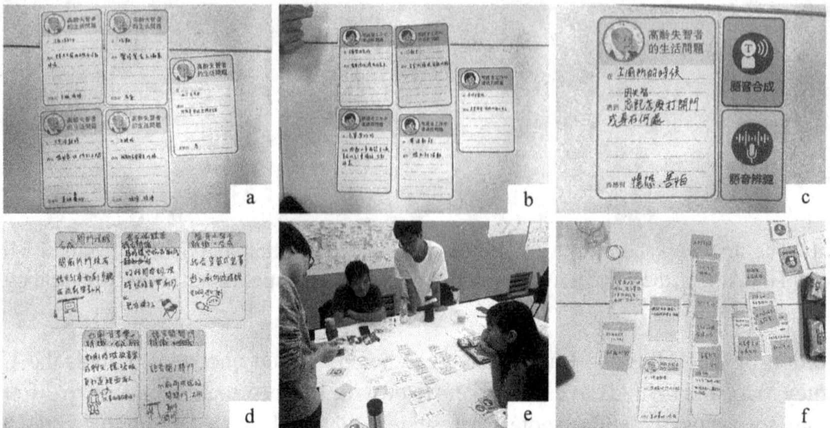

Fig. 3. The third workshop: (a) the problem statements of the old people with dementia scenario; (b) the problem statements of daycare worker's scenario; (c) using the Technology Card (on the right side) with every Problem Statement Card; (d) Brainstorming sheets. (e) the overall discussion to summarize the solution of the ideation; (f) the classification of the Brainstorming sheets with titles (the blue Post-it note) (Color figure online).

Table 1. The workshop format and schedule

	Workshop 1	Workshop 2	Workshop 3
Activity	1. Introduction of NLP technology 2. Try out the NLP APP 3. Discussion	1. Introduction of DT tools 2. Built the Stakeholder Map and User Journey Map of the daycare workers' working experience	1. Introduction of DT tools 2. Wrote the Problem Statement Card 3. Discussed the problem statements with the Technology Card 4. Selected one problem statement to ideate the solutions 5. Discussion
Mutual learning	Learn from the engineers	Learn from the designers and the daycare workers	Learn from the designers
Stage of Stanford DT model	–	Empathize	Define, Ideate
DT method & tools	–	1. Stakeholder Map 2. User Journey Map	1. How Might We 2. Problem Statement Card 3. Technology Card 4. Brainstorming

3.3 Data Collection and Analysis

The semi-structured interview with individual participants was conducted before the first workshop and after the third workshop with audio records. We also recorded the audio and video data of the discussion process during the three workshops. All the written working sheets of the DT tools including the Stakeholder Map, User Journey Map, Problem Statement Card, and Brainstorming sheet, were collected. Two researchers who fully participated in the three workshops analyzed their field observation and their notes of audio records from the semi-structured interview and compared the notes to the video records and all the written data.

4 Findings

In the semi-structured interviews, we collected the conversational discourse between designers, daycare workers, and engineers. The discussion followed three sections: 'the operation of design tools', 'mutual learning between daycare workers and engineers,' and 'the feeling of participation'. In each section, we discussed an overall perspective and three different points of view from designers, daycare workers, and engineers.

4.1 The Operation of Design Tools

An Overall Perspective

Nobody Mentioned Problem Statement Card and Technology Card. We organized four design tools during the workshops to conduct the mutual learning purpose. Daycare workers and engineers talked about the Stakeholder Map and User Journey Map, but the Problem Statement Card and Technology Card were not mentioned at any time. In the observation from designers who acted as the facilitator, the design method concept of How Might We was too complicated to understand in such a short time for the daycare workers, so they could not give feedback on action to fill the Problem Statement Card. Although we prepared the Technology Card and tried to remind them about the technology that we used in a visual (graphic image) way, it seemed like they did not aware of the help of the Technology Card when they were busy in figuring out the How Might We process.

View of Designers

The Role of Stakeholder Map and User Journey Map. The original idea of using Stakeholder Map as the first operating design tool was to widely explore daycare workers' working experiences, which might reveal more detailed information about their daily work in the User Journey Map. For the daycare workers, it was not easy to connect the experiences between these two design tools the first time. Designers should consciously remind them to think further about people who might be involved in their work procedure according to the Stakeholder Map when doing the User Journey Map. Moreover, by exercising with the aid of the designers, daycare workers could gradually illustrate their daily work in the User Journey Map that involved three (of the four) levels of stakeholders from the Stakeholder Map.

Both Groups Selected the Old People with Dementia's Problems to Solve. In the User Journey Map, we considered two personas to describe a typical day in the daycare center. One was an old people with dementia, and the other was a daycare worker. In the How Might We activity, we used a Problem Statement Card to define problems both in the view of old people with dementia s and daycare workers. For the final activity, we asked each group to pick up one problem to ideate the solutions. Rather than focusing on the view of daycare workers from themselves, both groups chose to solve the problems caused by the 'negative emotion of old people with dementia.' We supposed that the negative emotion of old people with dementia might be a more severe problem that the daycare workers encounter in daily work, or they thought the NLP technology was more suitable for solving this kind of problem.

View of Daycare Workers

The Stakeholder Map and User Journey Map were Useful. One of the four daycare worker referred to the Stakeholder Map might be useful for her routine at work:

> *"When learning or working, the concentric circle format of Stakeholder Map is better for noting and memorizing…, I can write down my new clients in the center of the note, then record main works about him and add note by dates."*

Moreover, two daycare workers noticed that User Journey Map was an excellent tool to examine the logic of the work and clarify the goal of the work, and could be contributed to communicating with old people with dementia and their family members:

> *"The detail information of User Journey Map helps me to connect each work together with logic…, it also helps me to understand what I can do when I have problems guiding and communicating with the old peoples or with their family members."*

> *"User Journey Map helps to understand my entire day of work and know how to distribute my workload and time... it helps to know better what I am doing so that I will not work to work. For example, I will know the old peoples' emotion, what the old peoples do, what my dilemma is, and what I should do. It provides me with the goal of my work."*

View of Engineers

How Engineers Understanding and Interpreting Design Tools. Despite providing design tools in a graphic edited style diagram, the engineers still considered the tools to be presented by a 'linear planning.' However, the engineers thought the situation in the daycare center and the problems they faced were more 'human-oriented,' which were usually NOT linear circumstances. Sometimes when chatting with the daycare workers without using design tools, they responded to more emotional or human reactions, which were interesting and useful. This also indicated an opposite expectation of the designer's intention: designers considered a 'graphic map' style tool should arouse more memories and thoughts. The understanding of the design tools was influenced by people's professional backgrounds instead of completely accepting designers' guidance and intention.

The User Journey Map were Useful But Lack of Some Information. As we mentioned above, although three of four engineers noticed the User Journey Map was a practical tool, but two of them insisted that the tools could not provide all the information from reality:

> *"The map style format does help to recall user's memory, but it may not be the most impressive experience. I mean, if they can think of something, what will be the problem of it? They can remember some problems which are usual, but the most impressive one may probably not be seen under this tool. This is a kind of emotional part and cannot be evaluated by a 'linear planning' ... if we map the most impressive experience to the User Journey Map, it may work. Because what the user feels impressively is not a point in the timeline. It is actually cause-and-effect'. It may related to people or something on the User Journey Map. And if we can figure out this cause-and-effect, we may find more entry points of the insights. I feel sometimes an unreasonable old people is with his cause-and-effect reason. Maybe he was too tired in the morning, so that caused his unreasonable reaction later. If we help to examine the extreme cases and their reaction, it will probably solve more problems."*

> *"Because we only picked one typical morning and afternoon of their weekdays, but actually they have different activities in their everyday lives, we cannot know the days of the other activities. We still miss some information."*

The engineers suggested the importance of observation in the field. For example, a video of how daycare workers work or visit the daycare center would supplement the detailed information that daycare workers should have provided during the interview in the workshop. Additionally, an assumption was raised by an engineer. If the situation was a huge problem but did not speak out from daycare workers' interviews, then the problem would be missed. However, this was a kind of thinking bias that if the daycare workers did not think the situation was a problem, then the assumption from the engineers was not valid actually. This was a valuable discourse that should be prompted designers and engineers to believe in the actual experience of the user interview instead of sticking to the logical assumption.

The Problems of Learning Design Tools. One of the engineers who were in the second time to participate workshop that used design tools still did not know how to interact with the daycare workers (user). Although User Journey Map was a good tool for collecting information, he found that asking further questions when interviewing the daycare workers was difficult. The engineer also mentioned his experiences using different design tools. Due to lacking the capacity of any design skills, most of the time, he just played a subsidiary role in the activities and did not feel confident when operating the design tools by himself. We thought the problem was the depth of the learning in using design tools. It revealed that insufficient training in interview techniques might cause the failure of operating the User Journey Map. A similar situation might happen in using other design tools when lacking some critical capacities.

4.2 Mutual Learning Between Daycare Workers and Engineers

View of Daycare Workers

Learning Technology Knowledge. Three of the four daycare workers thought they had learned the new technical knowledge, and one of them believed that NLP technology was workable for the daycare industry. She was looking forward to the massive production of the NLP technology products being applied to the daycare center in the future.

View of Engineers

Gaining the First-Handed Information from Daycare Workers. All engineers agreed that the first-hand information from the daycare workers in the User Journey Map was useable. It helped to build the actual circumstance of a typical day in the daycare center. For example, engineers could never imagine that old people with dementia s would like to go home so eagerly. Besides, the first-hand information broke down the stereotype of the daycare workers who were not always patient and had emotional reactions. Moreover, it might assist in correcting the technical development by knowing what the difficulty of their jobs was or something engineers considered difficult, however, daycare workers did not feel like a problem. Or something engineers viewed as a need, but daycare workers did not need indeed.

Only Part of Problems Could Be Solved by Technology. By having an in-depth interview with the daycare worker in User Journey Map, one of the engineers realized that some problems of old people with dementia s could not be solved by NLP technology, such as mental level issues or severe dementia patient problems.

The Divergence Between the Expecting of Technology and the Actual Need. Two engineers described how they felt about the NLP technology being adopted in the daycare industry. The NLP technology was expected to serve a high technical level demand and should act like Siri to respond to more complicated communication performance. However, solving the problems caused by the 'negative emotion of old people with dementia,' for example, designing a chatting robot for accompanying purposes without being accurate in NLP performance, could indeed achieve by a low-level technique of programming. One of the two engineers kept a positive attitude toward applying NLP technology in the daycare center. He thought considering the chatting robot idea as a control system of monitoring and reporting for multi-space management in the daycare center was worthwhile. Another engineer mentioned that NLP technology might not be suitable for daycare centers since the NLP technology and the chatting robot were not at the same technical level, or so far, it was hard to apply NLP technology in a chatting robot on 'non-logical conversation' performance for the old people with dementia.

4.3 The Feeling of Participation

View of Daycare Workers

Expecting of Concrete Outcomes. Three of the four daycare workers noticed they desired to test the ideas in the daycare center. One worker said that even if the idea was made in a mock-up or simulation (do not have to be the final product), that would be great.

We supposed that a concrete outcome might visualize the idea's imagination and fulfill their sense of accomplishment.

Too Rushed to Learn Design Tools and Discuss. One daycare worker thought the time was not enough to discuss and make a comprehensive presentation of the idea. The workshop focused on finding problems, and the final solution was still in a large scope of concept that needed to be revised. She suggested extending the time duration of the workshop and having more ideas iterations. Another daycare worker mentioned that the schedule was in such a hurry, and she could not stay calm and think carefully, especially on the third day of the workshop, where every step needed to write down and make the connection.

View of Engineers

Hardly Engaged in Using Design Tools. The reason was rooted in the learning depth of design tools, as we described in the last section. One engineer felt they only had a superficial knowledge of design tools. During the User Journey Map interview for daycare workers, all he could do was ask questions, but he was not able to help. The discourse with the daycare workers became a one-way direction, not mutual. Besides, he knew nothing about the profession of daycare, which made the interview more difficult since he was lack of interview skills and did not know how to ask questions about an unfamiliar subject. That made him feel like a supernumerary. He suggested that the workshop should share some preliminary knowledge of the daycare profession.

The Suggestion of Inviting Senior Management Workers. The engineers were enthusiastic about the market feasibility of their technical development. One of them suggested that in the future, we could invite senior management workers to participate when doing the Stakeholder Map to share their experience in cost management and business operation. The ideal manipulation of the work procedure might invite the senior management workers at the early stage of ideation. This could bridge the gap between the ideal concepts and the practical needs.

5 Discussion

5.1 Designer as a Facilitator

A remarkable difference of the workshops is the role of the designer. In the traditional PD researches, the engineers who are usually researchers also played the role of designers during the developing process [6]. In the past two decades, the User Centered Design (UCD) concept was widespread and accepted in HCI field [11]. Despite the profession in engineering, the UCD concept has turned the PD spirit towards an equal mindset to consider the user's voice in the developing process rather than concentrating on a technology-oriented thought. In this paper, we distinguish the role of 'designer' from 'engineer.' This also discloses the mediated view of industrial designers who are experts in bridging technical solutions and human needs together. We incorporate DT tools as the approach to conducting PD workshops. While the designers are facilitators to share the design knowledge of defining problems, ideating solutions, and interacting with users, on the other hand ensures all participants can understand and communicate at the same level. There are some advantages of having designers as facilitators. First, it provides an objectiveness of considering technical solutions and human needs more equally. Besides, the traditional PD researchers are 'engineers' and 'designers' at the same time. It is hard to discover the thinking bias. When the engineers try to learn the DT tools which are not familiar to them as usual, they always compare to their experience and describe how their thinking logic was. We find that engineers sometimes believe in logical assumptions rather than accepting a simple fact that is presented by the users. Another advantage is that the designers who are facilitators help better 'telling' [7]. Designers with a sensibility of UCD perspective can be more quickly aware of users who are usually with less power to make decisions in a typical developing process and guide the users to speak out their feeling. Also, the discourse with engineers may prevent the process from jumping into a design decision too fast. Creating conversations with all participants would help the PD process be conducted more effectively [12].

5.2 The Effects of Mutual Learning

Our research is concerned with genuine participation in a mutual learning level between designers and users [20]. By having a series of workshops, we empowered the technicians (engineers) and users (daycare workers) with design skills to frame the users' problems and carry out the technological solutions to accomplish the product design ideations. With the lecture on NLP technology and prototype testing as a piece of background knowledge, we concentrated on using DT tools as the mutual learning approach, as well as the Technology Card to remind all participants of the application of NLP technology during the workshop. Participation through the DT tools and mutual learning process is practiced by stringing the knowledge collaboratively and making decisions. We consider DT tools with a more ethnographic mindset to learn the patterns from users' everyday settings [2]. It allows technicians and users with a starting point for collaborating inquiry (especially User Journey Map) to investigate 'what might be' of the real problems from a collaborative perspective, rather than a designer's view of 'what the user wants' [10], also the collaborating inquiry encourage to make the decision more equally between all participants in the Problem Statement Card activity.

For the Brainstorming outcomes of the ideation, it is still hard at the beginning of the Brainstorming activity. As the designer demonstrated how to unfold the ideas with imagination, the engineers and the daycare workers generally have become to think outside of the box freely, and the discussion between all participants was getting exciting. More and more ideas have been provided in technological applications but beyond NLP technology by the end of the workshop. For example, one of the ideas is about 'considering a conveyor belt near the gate to transport the old people back to the center once the sensor detects the voice of the old people who was eager to go home and lingering near the gate.' It seems to be digressed and unrealistic, but it presents a condition of creating an idea to solve the situation. This observation aligns with the previous research that the users began to think more 'designerly' in the training process of the workshop [29]. However, we still can not claim the way of operating the DT tools in this series of workshops is the ideal manners to applying DT tools to those non-design participants since the daycare workers felt that it was difficult to identify the problems and carry out the solutions in such a short time, as well as the engineers were not fully engaged in using the DT tools due to lacking key capacities of design skills.

5.3 Using the DT Tools as a Co-design Method

We implemented the first three stages of the Stanford DT model, which included empathizing, defining, and ideating. Compared to the PD, which uses telling-making-enacting techniques to envision the new possibilities of the future [7], the DT tools in our workshops provide telling techniques in depth. Stakeholder Map and User Journey Map are useful tools to recall memories and unfold incisive descriptions of daily experiences. Also How Might We method is a scaffold to draw up the statement of the problem findings and give a starting point for the ideation of the solutions. However, as we only focus on the 'telling' part without a tangible 'making' process, the users' (daycare workers) imaginations are hardly convergent into a narrow scope to 'enact' the possible future through participation. Besides, if we regard the point of view in the creativity level of people's lives during the co-design process [40], when we treat both the daycare workers and the engineers as the recipients of the DT tools knowledge, they actually are at different levels, while the daycare workers are acting like 'adapting level' and the engineers are more similar to 'making' level. When it comes to how the different roles (user, researcher, and designer) are intertwined in the co-designing process [45], we researchers supply DT tools as the scaffold which is aimed to support people in the 'making level,' but indeed we face the participants in mixed levels (both adapting and making level), so that most of the time, we deal with leading and guiding works rather than serving the needs for creative expression during the workshops. This is perhaps the reason that we have encountered some difficulties in operating DT tools through the PD workshops. The other role of the researchers in the co-designing process is designers, who shall be integral to the creation and exploration of new tools and methods for generative design thinking [38]. Although DT tools are efficient in some ways, considering how to adapt the tools to different types of non-designer is significant. This will also enhance engagement for participation in mutual learning.

5.4 Limitation and Further Works

In this research, we planned three PD workshops to accomplish the mutual learning goal by using the DT approach. One limitation was that we organized the activities that were framed by the first three stages of the Stanford DT model, which were empathizing, defining, and ideating. We excluded prototype and test stages which would supposedly support the co-design process. According to the feedback of the daycare workers, a concrete simulation was expected for the workshop. Furthermore, the frequency and time duration of each workshop was not enough for learning through every design tool and bringing out the effort of the ideation.

In the future, we have several recommendations for improving the PD workshop with the DT approach for mutual learning purposes. Firstly, prepare some activities for increasing the key capacity of design skills for those who are not from the design field, for example, a brief lecture and pre-exercise of interview skills before User Journey Map. It will help them to engage in the workshops more comfortably and confidently. Secondly, provide preliminary knowledge of each expert member equally before starting to use the design tools. Although the design tools are for mutual learning, the preliminary knowledge will guide the participants to immerse into the topic more quickly. Thirdly, cross-disciplinary discourse should be prompted more frequently during the workshop. Not only to focus on demonstrating the expertise of the method but also to share the thought behind the method, especially for the people who take the responsibility of being facilitators. Be more sensitive to the differential background of the participants. In this research, the designers who are the facilitators can consciously discuss with the engineers their logical assumption of the missing part in the User Journey Map, while design tools actually mean to learn things from the fact to avoid the bias of human thought.

Some tips from the 'sensitizing packages' [45] may be a sort of inspiration when exploring the improvement of the DT approach in PD workshops. Plan some short sessions at the beginning of the workshops as a 'sensitization stage.' The sessions can cover a broader range of subjects than the workshops and include some exercises for the key capacities or preliminary knowledge. These will also be able to build the communication channel between the researcher and participants in a warm-up and more relaxed atmosphere, at the same time empowering the participants to speak more of their own thought. The purpose is to increase their confidence in 'being an expert of their experiences' [38] in the following activities in co-designing with DT tools.

6 Conclusion

By standing with the spirit of PD in genuine participation of the users [36], a series of PD workshops that combined the DT approach to carry out the mutual learning identity was held in 2020. The three workshops were organized by the empathize-define-ideate stages of the Stanford DT model and used design methods and tools to co-design with the engineers and daycare workers. We started the problems from two perspectives: old people with dementia s and daycare workers. Based on the premise of solving the problem by using NLP technology, both groups of participants in the workshops regarded the problems caused by the negative emotion of old people with dementia as the most important to solve, as well as the final discussion was concentrated on it.

The workshops have successfully delivered the usage of the design tools in some aspects as a mutual learning approach. Both the daycare workers and the engineers mentioned they considered the Stakeholder Map and User Journey Map practical to their jobs, especially the latter one. At the end of the Brainstorming in the ideation stage presented a tendency of 'designerly' thinking, which corresponded with the previous research [29]. Although some engineers thought these DT tools were not comprehensive tools, they took advantage of using the tools to understand the user better. However, there are still some deficiencies while we implemented the design methods and tools as a mutual learning approach to the participants who are not from the design background. First of all, we should be aware that some tacit knowledge which might be easy for designers, is difficult for a novice without any design training. For example, the How Might We method is too complicated to learn in a short time. The written words in the Problem Statement Card by daycare workers have been presented in a vague statement generally. This proves that they have difficulties using these tools. Also, the engineer struggled to ask questions during the User Journey Map interview with the user. It reveals that they need aid with the extra exercise of interview skills and preliminary knowledge of the daycare profession. Another reason for the failure to deliver the DT tools is adopting a set of DT tools to the participants at different creativity levels [40]. Furthermore, the situation of learning design tools links to another core issue: the engagement of the participants. The engineer noticed that his superficial knowledge of design tools made him feel like a subsidiary member in the workshops. The daycare workers have expected more operating time to get a deeper understanding of the How Might We method and a concrete outcome of the ideation, as well as some tangible outcomes to envision and narrow down the scope of the imagination of the solutions.

Nevertheless, a valuable discovery is also found in the mutual learning process, which is the divergence between the expectation of technology and the actual need from the perspective of the engineers. While we devote the endeavor to collaborate with the daycare workers and the engineers through empowering them with operating the design tools to mutual learning with each other, thinking about 'what the designer, who is also a facilitator, should do to communicate in the divergence' was essential. It is crucial to help all participants find a way to represent their contribution in a way that makes sense in their own community in the negotiated participation [10]. For future work, we have to keep awareness when we operate the method and tools that we are masters of them. Keep reflecting on not falling into the trap of being 'design elite' [21]. Raising more discourse among all participants will prevent the decision from inclining towards one-sided and advance the PD achievement more successfully. The purpose of incorporating DT into PD workshops is to support the co-design process in order to empower the user to switch the role from informant to partaker [28], which means the voice of the user can be considered as a more crucial notion. Considering how to make DT tools workable for the different backgrounds of non-designers, such as applying the concept of 'sensitization' to organizing the PD workshops in the future, will be a positive attitude to propel PD to a compatible quality of inviting the diversity of participants. Despite the fact that the engineers have some expectations of what the technology can apply in, we should commit ourselves to communicating with them to find out if there are any better solutions that can possibly meet users' needs and technical fulfillment more closely.

References

1. An Introduction to Design Thinking Process Guide. https://web.stanford.edu/~mshanks/MichaelShanks/files/509554.pdf. Accessed 8 Feb 2023
2. Blomberg, J., Karasti, H.: Ethnography: positioning ethnography within participatory design. In: Routledge International Handbook of Participatory Design, pp. 86–116. Routledge (2012)
3. Bjerknes, G., Bratteteig, T.: The memoirs of two survivors: or the evaluation of a computer system for cooperative work. In: Proceedings of the 1988 ACM Conference on Computer-Supported Cooperative Work, pp. 167–177 (1988)
4. Bjögvinsson, E., Ehn, P., Hillgren, P.-A.: Design things and design thinking: contemporary participatory design challenges. Des. Issues **28**, 101–116 (2012)
5. Bødker, S.: Creating conditions for participation: conflicts and resources in systems design. DAIMI report series (1994)
6. Bodker, K., Kensing, F., Simonsen, J.: Participatory IT Design: Designing for Business and Workplace Realities. MIT Press, Cambridge (2009)

7. Brandt, E., Binder, T., Sanders, E.B.-N.: Tools and techniques: ways to engage telling, making and enacting. In: Routledge International Handbook of Participatory Design, pp. 145–181. Routledge (2012)
8. Brown, T., et al.: Design thinking. Harv. Bus. Rev. **86**, 84 (2008)
9. Buchanan, R.: Wicked problems in design thinking. Des. Issues **8**, 5–21 (1992)
10. Buur, J., Binder, T., Brandt, E.: Taking video beyond 'hard data' in user centred design. In: Participatory Design Conference, pp. 21–29. Citeseer (2000)
11. Carroll, J.M.: Encountering others: reciprocal openings in participatory design and user-centered design. Hum.-Comput. Interact. **11**, 285–290 (1996)
12. Cederman-Haysom, T., Brereton, M.: A participatory design agenda for ubiquitous computing and multimodal interaction: a case study of dental practice. In: Proceedings of the Ninth Conference on Participatory Design: Expanding Boundaries in Design, vol. 1, pp. 11–20 (2006)
13. Chasanidou, D., Gasparini, A.A., Lee, E.: Design thinking methods and tools for innovation. In: Marcus, A. (ed.) DUXU 2015. LNCS, vol. 9186, pp. 12–23. Springer, Cham (2015). https://doi.org/10.1007/978-3-319-20886-2_2
14. Christiansson, J., Grönvall, E., Yndigegn, S.L.: Teaching participatory design using live projects: critical reflections and lessons learnt. In: Proceedings of the 15th Participatory Design Conference: Full Papers, vol. 1, pp. 1–11 (2018)
15. Cross, N.: Designerly ways of knowing. Des. Stud. **3**, 221–227 (1982)
16. Cross, N.: From a design science to a design discipline: understanding designerly ways of knowing and thinking. In: Michel, R. (ed.) Design Research Now, pp. 41–54. Springer, Basel (2007). https://doi.org/10.1007/978-3-7643-8472-2_3
17. Ehn, P.: Scandinavian design: on participation and skill. In: Participatory Design, pp. 41–77. CRC Press (2017)
18. Fabri, M., Andrews, P.C., Pukki, H.K.: Using design thinking to engage autistic students in participatory design of an online toolkit to help with transition into higher education. J. Assist. Technol. **10**, 102–114 (2016)
19. Interaction Design Foundation, Dam, R.F., Siang, T.Y.: What is design thinking and why is it so popular? (2021)
20. Halskov, K., Hansen, N.B.: The diversity of participatory design research practice at PDC 2002–2012. Int. J. Hum.-Comput. Stud. **74**, 81–92 (2015)
21. Harrington, C., Erete, S., Piper, A.M.: Deconstructing community-based collaborative design: towards more equitable participatory design engagements. Proc. ACM Hum.-Comput. Interact. **3**, 1–25 (2019)
22. Hemmings, T., Crabtree, A., Rodden, T., Clarke, K., Rouncefield, M.: Probing the probes. In: Proceedings of the Participatory Design Conference (2002)
23. Johansson-Sköldberg, U., Woodilla, J., Çetinkaya, M.: Design thinking: past, present and possible futures. Creativity Innov. Manag. **22**, 121–146 (2013)
24. Julier, G.: The Culture of Design. Sage (2014)
25. Kensing, F., Greenbaum, J.: Heritage: having a say. In: Routledge International Handbook of Participatory Design, pp. 41–56. Routledge (2012)
26. Kimbell, L.: Rethinking design thinking: part I. Des. Cult. **3**, 285–306 (2011)
27. Kimbell, L.: Rethinking design thinking: part II. Des. Cult. **4**, 129–148 (2012)
28. Laura Ramírez Galleguillos, M., Coşkun, A.: How do i matter? A review of the participatory design practice with less privileged participants. In: Proceedings of the 16th Participatory Design Conference 2020-Participation(s) Otherwise, vol. 1, pp. 137–147 (2020)
29. Lee, H.R., et al.: Steps toward participatory design of social robots: mutual learning with older adults with depression. In: Proceedings of the 2017 ACM/IEEE International Conference on Human-Robot Interaction, pp. 244–253 (2017)

30. Lewrick, M., Link, P., Leifer, L.: The Design Thinking Toolbox: A Guide to Mastering the Most Popular and Valuable Innovation Methods. Wiley, Hoboken (2020)
31. Manzini, E.: New design knowledge. Des. Stud. **30**, 4–12 (2009)
32. Manzini, E., Rizzo, F.: Small projects/large changes: participatory design as an open participated process. CoDesign **7**, 199–215 (2011)
33. Manzini, E.: Design, When Everybody Designs: An Introduction to Design for Social Innovation. MIT Press, Cambridge (2015)
34. Martin, R., Martin, R.L.: The Design of Business: Why Design Thinking is the Next Competitive Advantage. Harvard Business Press (2009)
35. Pratomo, L.C., Wardani, D.K., et al.: The effectiveness of design thinking in improving student creativity skills and entrepreneurial alertness. Int. J. Instr. **14**, 695–712 (2021)
36. Robertson, T., Simonsen, J.: Participatory design: an introduction. In: Routledge International Handbook of Participatory Design, pp. 21–38. Routledge (2012)
37. Roussou, M., Kavalieratou, E., Doulgeridis, M.: Children designers in the museum: applying participatory design for the development of an art education program. In: Proceedings of the 6th International Conference on Interaction Design and Children, pp. 77–80 (2007)
38. Sanders, E.B.-N., Stappers, P.J.: Co-creation and the new landscapes of design. Co-design **4**, 5–18 (2008)
39. Sanders, E.B.-N., Brandt, E., Binder, T.: A framework for organizing the tools and techniques of participatory design. In: Proceedings of the 11th Biennial Participatory Design Conference, pp. 195–198 (2010)
40. Sanders, E.: Design serving people. In: Copenhagen Cumulus Working Papers, pp. 28–33. University of Art and Design Helsinki (2006)
41. Schon, D.A.: The reflective practitioner, New York (1968)
42. Suchman, L.A.: Plans and Situated Actions: The Problem of Human-Machine Communication. Cambridge University Press, Cambridge (1987)
43. Van Boeijen, A., Daalhuizen, J., Zijlstra, J.: Delft Design Guide: Perspectives, Models, Approaches, Methods. BIS Publishers (2020)
44. Ventä-Olkkonen, L., et al.: Nowhere to now-here: empowering children to reimagine bully prevention at schools using critical design fiction (2021)
45. Visser, F.S., Stappers, P.J., Van der Lugt, R., Sanders, E.B.: Contextmapping: experiences from practice. CoDesign **1**, 119–149 (2005)

Interaction Methods and Techniques

Eye Tracking Auto-Correction Using Domain Information

Parviz Asghari[1(✉)], Maike Schindler[1], and Achim J. Lilienthal[2,3]

[1] University of Cologne, 50923 Cologne, Germany
parviz.asghari@uni-koeln.de
[2] Technische Universität München, 80333 München, Germany
[3] Örebro University, 701 82 Örebro, Sweden

Abstract. Webcam-based eye tracking (wcET) comes with the promise to become a pervasive platform for inexpensive, easy, and quick collection of gaze data without requiring dedicated hardware. To fulfill this promise, wcET must address issues with poor and variable spatial accuracy due to, e.g., participant movement, calibration validity, and the uncertainty of the gaze prediction method used. Eye-tracking (ET) data often suffer particularly from a considerable spatial offset that reduces data quality and heavily affects both qualitative and quantitative ET data analysis. Previous works attempted to mitigate the specific source of spatial offset, e.g., by using chin rests to limit participant movement during ET experiments, by frequent re-calibration or by incorporating head position and facial features into the gaze prediction algorithm. Yet spatial offset remains an issue for wcET, particularly in daily life settings involving children. It is currently unclear (1) if spatial offset can be automatically estimated in absence of ground truth; and (2) whether the estimated offset can be used to obtain substantially higher data quality. In response to the first research question, we propose a method to estimate the spatial offset using domain information. We estimate the spatial offset by maximizing the ET data correlation with Areas of Interests (AOIs) defined over the stimulus. To address the second research question, we developed a wcET system and ran it simultaneously with a commercial remote eye tracker, the Tobii Pro X3-120. After temporal synchronization, we calculated the average distance between the gaze points of the two systems as a measure of data quality. For all tasks investigated, we obtained an overall improvement of the raw data. Specifically, we observed an improvement of 1.35°, 1.02°, and 0.92° in three tasks with varying characteristics of AOIs. This is an important step towards pervasive use of wcET data with a large variety of practical applications.

Keywords: Eye tracking · Webcam-based eye tracking · Spatial Offset · Spatial offset correction · Data quality

1 Introduction

Webcam-based eye tracking (wcET) is a rapidly growing field of research and development, with numerous applications in fields such as human-computer

M. Kurosu and A. Hashizume (Eds.): HCII 2023, LNCS 14011, pp. 373–391, 2023.
https://doi.org/10.1007/978-3-031-35596-7_24

interaction, psychology, and marketing [20,25]. The main advantage of wcET is its accessibility and affordability. Unlike traditional eye-tracking methods that require specialized hardware and software, wcET can be performed with costumer grade webcams and open-source software. This makes it a cost-effective and widely accessible solution for researchers, developers, and businesses looking to incorporate eye tracking into their work. However, there are also several limitations to wcET that need to be taken into consideration. One of the key limitations is accuracy. In comparison to traditional eye-tracking methods that rely on dedicated hardware (dhET), wcET is typically less accurate, which can make it challenging to obtain reliable and valid data for the intended applications. Additionally, the accuracy of wcET is often more strongly influenced than traditional eye-tracking methods by factors such as lighting conditions and user movement. It is further subject to unstable calibration validity and, generally, the performance of the gaze prediction algorithm used. As a result, the accuracy of wcET data is limited and this could negatively affect subsequent data processing.

Determining the sequence of gaze points a participant is looking at generally comes with inaccuracy due to various factors. In addition to what was mentioned above, it depends crucially on eye-tracking technology, the quality of the particular eye-tracking device being used, the user (who may wear glasses, for example) and on proper calibration.

The uncertainty that determines eye tracking accuracy can be decomposed into several different components (see Fig. 1), including:

- Spatial offset: Systematic error in the gaze data that causes the gaze location to be shifted compared to the true gaze location.
- Spatial noise: Random variations in the estimation of the gaze location.
- Spatial scaling: Systematic error in the gaze data that affect the scale of the distances between gaze points depending on their spatial location.

Fig. 2 shows an example of strong spatial offset as it is often observed for wcET data. It can be seen that the gaze distribution is *not* well aligned with the contextual information. In this paper, we suggest an auto-correction method to compensate for the spatial offset that makes use of domain information about the visual stimulus.

The presence of spatial offset can affect the data quality in several aspects. First, it makes it more difficult or impossible to associate gazes to relevant AOIs, which is essential for researchers and practical applications. Second, it can increase the data variance by introducing different amounts of bias for different participants. This often results in lower performance of downstream AI-based methods.

Most methods to improve accuracy, e.g., to restrict head movements by using a chin rest [24], are ineligible for wcET given that the goal is to facilitate ubiquitous eye tracking in daily life settings.

Gaze estimation from web-camera video streams is currently a very active field of research [14,19,22,25] and may lead to gradually more accurate wcET

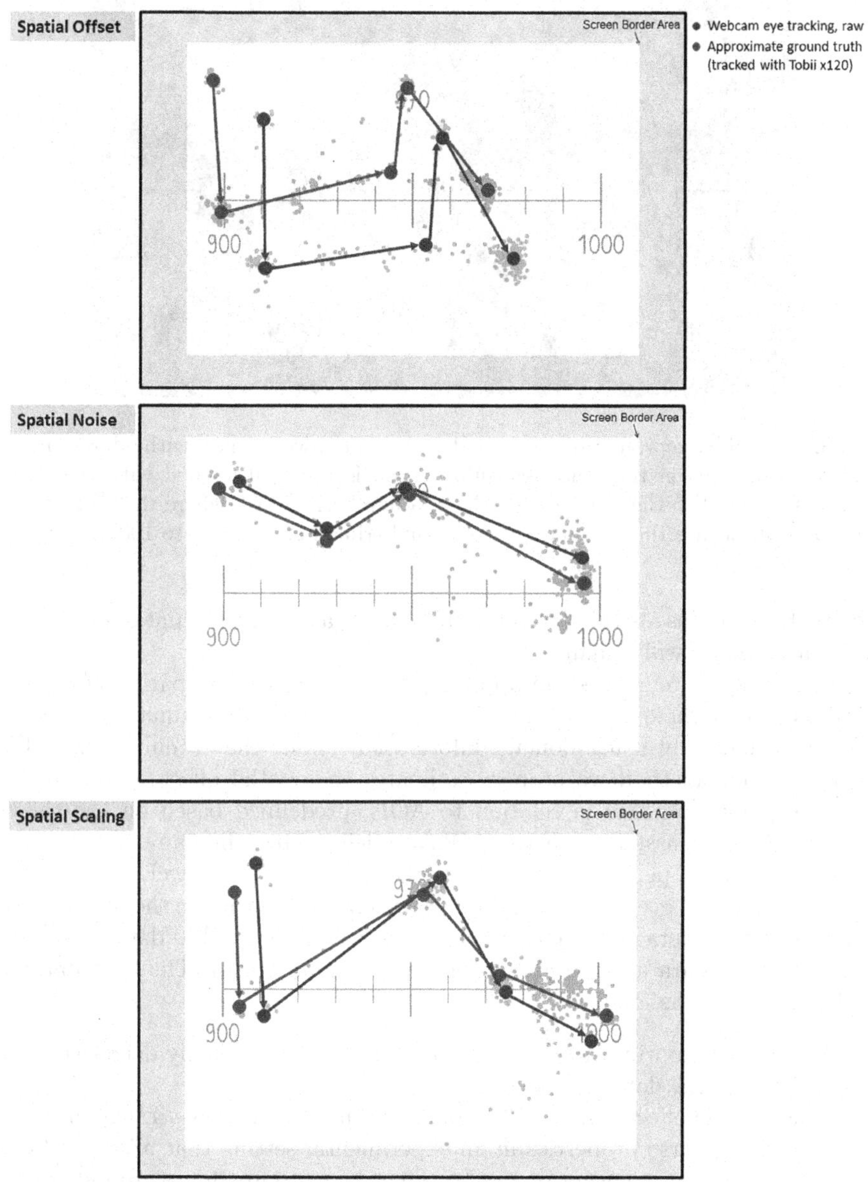

Fig. 1. Visualization of three different components that affect eye tracking accuracy. Each of them is shown with two vector sequences based on gaze data recorded simultaneously with very accurate eye-tracking data, which can be achieved with dedicated hardware (light red) and less accurate wcET data (light blue) in the same scenario. The vector sequences (red and blue) represent possible scan paths selected to clarify the concepts of spatial offset, spatial noise, and spatial scaling [4]. This paper suggests a method to compensate for the spatial offset. (Color figure online)

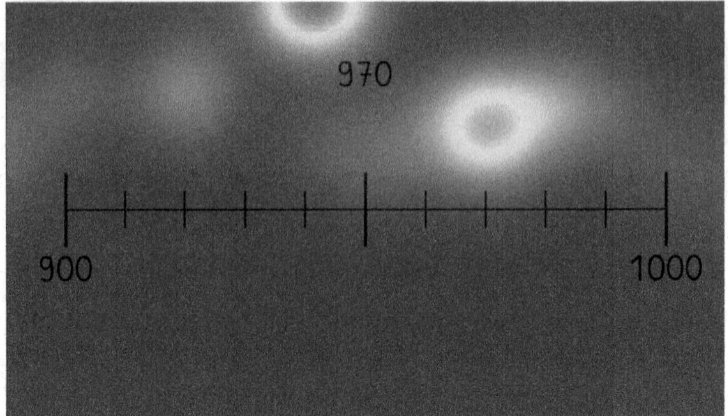

Fig. 2. Exemplary representation of the distribution of wcET data with a large spatial offset. It can be seen that the gaze information is not well aligned with the visual context presented to the participants (here, a numberline task where the participants were asked to locate the number 970 on a numberline between 900 to 1000).

results. However, as also observed for dhET data, a certain amount of inaccuracy and spatial offset will remain.

In this paper we suggest an approach to compensate for spatial offsets and thus to enhance the quality of raw ET data. We attempt to estimate the spatial offset automatically using domain information about the stimuli shown. The auto-correction method we propose estimates the spatial offset by optimizing the gaze point positions in relation to AOIs, predefined based on the shown stimulus (here we assume that the AOIs are defined by a human expert).

To evaluate the performance of our method, we developed a wcET system and used a commercial eye tracker (dhET) as a reference to measure the data quality in terms of the average distance between the wcET and dhET data (assuming that the dhET data approximately represent ground truth). The contributions of this article are as follows:

- We suggest an optimization-based approach to automatically detect the spatial offset in ET data, see Sect. 3.
- We assess the effectiveness of the proposed method across a range of visual tasks with diverse properties in an experimental setting that allows a direct comparison to more accurate eye tracking data (approximate ground truth), see Sect. 4.

2 Experimental

2.1 Webcam Eye Tracking (wcET)

The wcET system [1] that we used is composed of three distinct blocks. First, the participant's image is captured by the webcam. In this paper we used the model

Logitech Brio 60 Hz webcam as the imaging device. Second, a deep learning, appearance-based gaze estimation model uses the pre-processed and normalized raw images from the webcam to estimate a 3D gaze vector. We used resnet 18 trained on the MPIIgaze data set. Finally, based on the calibration for each participant, the 3D gaze vector is mapped to a 2D point on the screen. To this end, we use a modified version of the hybrid screen calibration technique discussed in [6].

2.2 Participants

The sample size for our study consisted of 170 fifth-grade school students. Of these, 14 students' data were excluded, since for them it was not possible to temporally synchronize the wcET and dcET data. As a result, 156 students were included in the analyses of this study.

2.3 Initial Calibration/Validation (wcET)

For the initial calibration and a subsequent validation, we asked the participants to move the mouse to calibration points shown on the screen. In this way we realized a fast calibration method (on average our calibration method required approximately 40 s) and made sure that the participants fixated the points. For each calibration point, first, a red circle with a 1.58° diameter (60 pixels) was displayed around the central calibration point on the black screen. As soon as the users hovered over the circle with the mouse, we assumed that they looked at the circle; and the system recorded the related gazes. We did this for six different calibration points twice in order to obtain a stable calibration. Then we validated the calibration result with nine points and the same procedure. Six of these nine points were at the same points as in calibration, and three additional points were chosen.

2.4 Reference Eye Tracker, Computer, and Screen

For comparison to wcET, we used the Tobii Pro x3-120 screen-based (IR) eye-tracker 120 Hz sampling and screen refreshing rate. The experiment was run on a desktop computer (Intel Core i7-11700k @ 3.60 GHz, 32 GB RAM, Windows 11) and the task stimuli were presented on a screen (24", 53 x 30 cm, 60 Hz refresh rate, 1920×1080 pixels).

2.5 Experiment

In our experiment, we ran both ET systems at the same time. We first launched the Tobii eye tracker, followed by the wcET system after the calibration phase. We used the calibration start point timestamp and the start time of dhET as a general offset between the two systems since both were measured to the global clock. For improved accuracy in synchronization, we determine a specific time offset using ET information in relation to the general offset. In certain scenarios, it was not possible to calculate the specific time offset as either the wcET or dhET failed to gather participant ET data.

3 Proposed Method

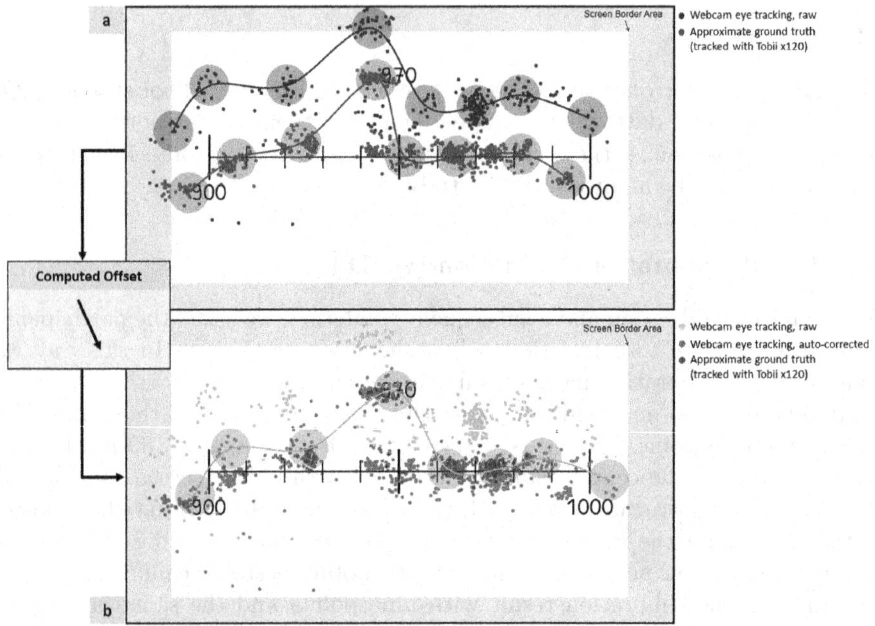

Fig. 3. Illustration of the proposed method for an example of real gaze data, recorded with two independent eye-tracking systems, the Tobii Pro X3-120 eye tracker and our wcET system. Plot (a) shows the participant's eye movements recorded with the accurate Tobii eye tracker as red dots, and the wcET data as blue dots. To make it easier to appreciate the substantial spatial offset in the wcET data, we encircled regions with high gaze density and connected them to a possible eye movement sequence. Plot (b) shows the same gaze data after subtraction of the estimated spatial offset with light green dots. It is evident that the correlation between the contextual information and the gaze points substantially increases. In this example it is also apparent that the auto-corrected wcET data are much better aligned with the approximate ground truth (dhET) gaze points. (Color figure online)

The method we proposed entails leveraging domain information to auto-correct spatial inaccuracies that may occur in an individual's ET data. Figure 3.a shows that the performance of our wcET is often fairly good when compared to the more accurate dhET data, but for a substantial spatial offset that causes many wcET predicted gaze points to fall into areas that are not relevant in the stimulus.

The underlying idea of this paper is to estimate the spatial offset based on the assumption that participants look at areas that contain relevant information more often and that the gaze distribution therefore tends to be denser in these areas compared to arbitrary other areas. The proposed auto-correction method consists of two stages. First, assisted by a human expert, we identified Areas of Interest (AOIs) in the stimulus that contain task-relevant information (Fig. 4-b). Given the AOIs, we then determine the spatial offset by maximizing the correlation between the gaze points and the AOIs (Fig. 4-c). This is achieved by maximizing the number of gaze points that fall into the AOIs for a given offset (Δ_x, Δ_y):

$$N^*_{AOI} = \max_{\Delta_x, \Delta_y} \left(\sum \{(x, y) \in P | (x - \Delta_x, y - \Delta_y) \in A\}\right) \tag{1}$$

where Δ_x and Δ_y indicate the horizontal and vertical components of the spatial offset, P is the set of gaze points and A describes the AOIs, respectively. Finally, the gaze point coordinates are updated based on the estimated offset. To establish a reliable spatial distance metric between wcET and dhET, it is imperative to identify the gaze points that exhibit the least temporal discrepancy. This is crucial because participants may exhibit repetitive eye movements towards similar areas at different time intervals. Subsequently, calculating the spatial distance between such points can enable the assessment of the precision of gaze point measurements in relation to spatial accuracy. This metric can then be employed to evaluate the quality of wcET data, based on its proximity to the reference system provided by dhET. It is important to note that, while we use the dhET gaze data obtained with the Tobii Pro X3-120 eye-tracker as approximate ground truth, we do not use the dhET data in any way when estimating the spatial offset of the wcET data.

4 Evaluation

4.1 Visual Tasks

The experiment involves various well-established visual tasks in mathematics education, which are important with respect to basic mathematical competencies. We used a task on the number line, where numbers are to be regarded in their ordinal arrangement; a task on the 100-dot field, where multiplicative thinking is involved; and a task with place value material, where understanding of the place value system is decisive. In our project, these tasks are used to assess and to support students' mathematical abilities of the participants. The three tasks differ from each other, among others, with regard to the number of areas of interest (AOIs), their distribution in horizontal and vertical direction, and their size. Human experts have identified the areas that are likely to hold the most relevant information for the participant to complete each task, as depicted in Fig. 5, which displays each task and its pre-defined AOIs.

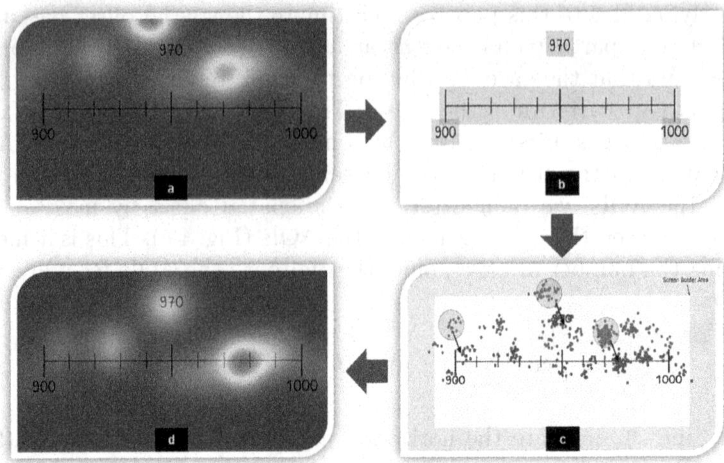

Fig. 4. Comparison of a gaze distribution before and after applying the auto-correction method proposed in this paper demonstrating the effectiveness of our approach.

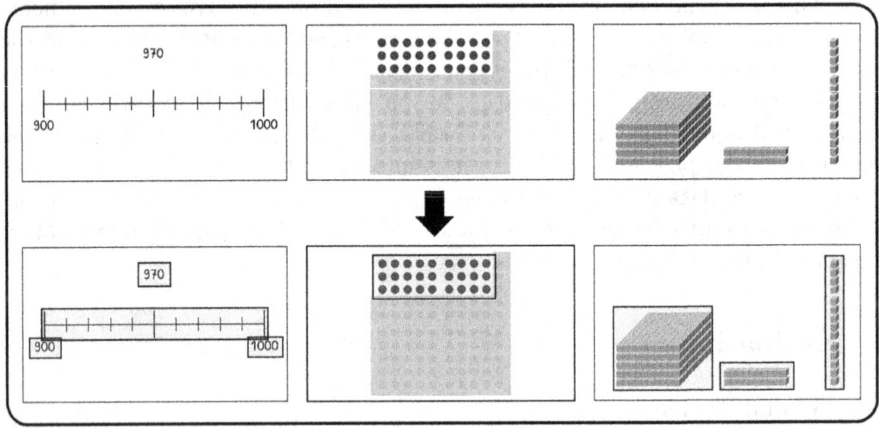

Fig. 5. Visual tasks used in this study (number line task, 100-dot field task, and place value material task) and their assigned specific areas of interest (AOIs), indicated with light yellow color. The AOIs have been pre-determined by human experts and vary in number, size, and distribution, both in vertical and horizontal direction. (Color figure online)

For our evaluation, we computed the median distance between gaze points obtained with the dhET [23] and our wcET system (Eq. 2).

$$d_{median} = median(d_1, d_2, ..., d_m), d_i = \sqrt{(x_i^{wc_{t_i}} - x_{i*}^{dh_{t_{i*}}})^2 + (y_i^{wc_{t_i}} - y_{i*}^{dh_{t_{i*}}})^2} \quad (2)$$

Here, d_{median} is the median distance and m is the number of gaze data points from the wcET. wc and dh indicate gaze data from the webcam and the Tobii eye tracker, respectively. t_{i*} indicates the time stamp of the dhET gaze point corresponding to the wcET gaze point time stamp t_i.

4.2 Results

Table 1. The table compares the median distance (in degrees) between dhET and wcET gaze points for three tasks: Numberline (NL), 100-dot field (100-DF), and Place value material (PVM). The results are divided into three categories: Improved samples, Non-Improved samples, and all samples combined. The median distances are reported for both wcET raw data and wcET auto-corrected data.

Task	type	# samples	wcET raw	improvement°	wcET auto-corrected
NL	Improved	130	5.20°	1.76°	3.44°
	Non-Improved	26	3.95°	−0.22°	4.17°
	All	156	4.90°	1.35°	3.55°
100-DF	Improved	114	4.74°	1.81°	2.93°
	Non-Improved	29	3.85°	−0.76°	4.61°
	All	143	4.42°	1.02°	3.40°
PVM	Improved	119	5.69°	1.43°	4.26°
	Non-Improved	37	4.19°	−0.57°	4.76°
	All	156	5.31°	0.92°	4.39°

Table 1 shows the results of our assessment using the eye movement information obtained from 156 participants in the tasks involving the number line, 100-dot field, and place value material. The data is categorized into three groups: Improved, Non-Improved, and All, based on whether the median distance to the dhET data (approximate ground truth) was reduced or increased after applying the proposed auto-correction technique. The table presents the median distance before and after auto-correction and the degree of improvement or decline for each category. It should be noted that the total number of data samples varies based on the number of individuals who completed each task. Example figures, demonstrating the Improved (Fig. 6) and Non-Improved (Fig. 7) categories, are included.

On the whole, the use of auto-correction technique has enhanced the quality of the data. However, the extent of this improvement appears to vary and may be influenced by the specific characteristics of the AOIs. Out of 156 samples in the number line task, 130 have improved by 1.76°. In the number line task, there were several distinct areas of interest (AOIs) mainly located in the center of the screen. The auto-correction method has substantially improved the data accuracy by 1.35°. Moreover, the number of samples that did not show improvement (26 samples) and the decline in data quality (−0.22°) were less compared to other tasks. Despite the fact that the 100-dot field task only had one AOI positioned in the top middle of the screen, our approach showed satisfactory results by enhancing the data quality by 1.02°. Of the 143 samples analyzed, 114 showed improvement with a median value of 1.81°. However, the drop in the sample (29 samples) quality by −0.76° was greater than that of the number line task. This can be attributed to the fact that the AOI's restricted coverage of the screen may not have been able to precisely represent all gaze points, thereby leading to an inadequate estimation of the spatial offset. The most challenging task was dealing with the place value material, which had various AOIs with unique characteristics. These AOIs were located in areas where the webcam-based eye tracking had difficulty determining gaze points accurately, such as the bottom of the screen, where the participant's eye region was not clearly visible. As a result, less precise gaze points were recorded in these areas. Moreover, scaling offsets were observed in the far left and right areas on the screen, which had been reported in previous eye-tracking studies. Despite these challenges, the knowledge of the domain helped to enhance the data accuracy by 0.92°. Specifically, out of 156 samples, 119 experienced an enhancement of 1.43° in data quality, while 37 showed a decline of −0.57°.

Figure 7 shows two failure cases of the proposed method from the 100-DF task. Figure 7.a illustrates that, in violation of our key assumption, sometimes the participant completes the task without focusing on the area of interest much. Another case where our auto-correction method was registered in the evaluation as not having improved the accuracy of the ET data is shown in Fig. 7.b. The reason in this case is that the approximate ground truth obtained from the dhET was corrupt. Remote eye trackers such as the Tobii Pro X3-120 used in this study suffer from data degradation if the participants gesture and block the line of sight between the eye tracker and the participant's pupil.

Figure 8 shows the obtained results in two histograms for all three tasks. The histogram of the distance between raw webcam ET data and auto-corrected webcam ET data from Tobii ET data was plotted to evaluate the performance of our proposed method Fig. 8. The larger histogram compares the distance between the wcET data and the corresponding gaze data from the Tobii eye tracker (approximate ground truth) before and after applying our auto-correction method. It is clearly visible that the distribution after auto-correction (in pink) shifted towards lower errors for all three tasks, indicating that our auto-correction method improved the data quality. The smaller histogram in the inner panel on the top right shows a histogram of the distribution the improvement/degradation through our auto-correction per sample (in green). This distribution is clearly skewed to the right and only a few samples experience small degradation.

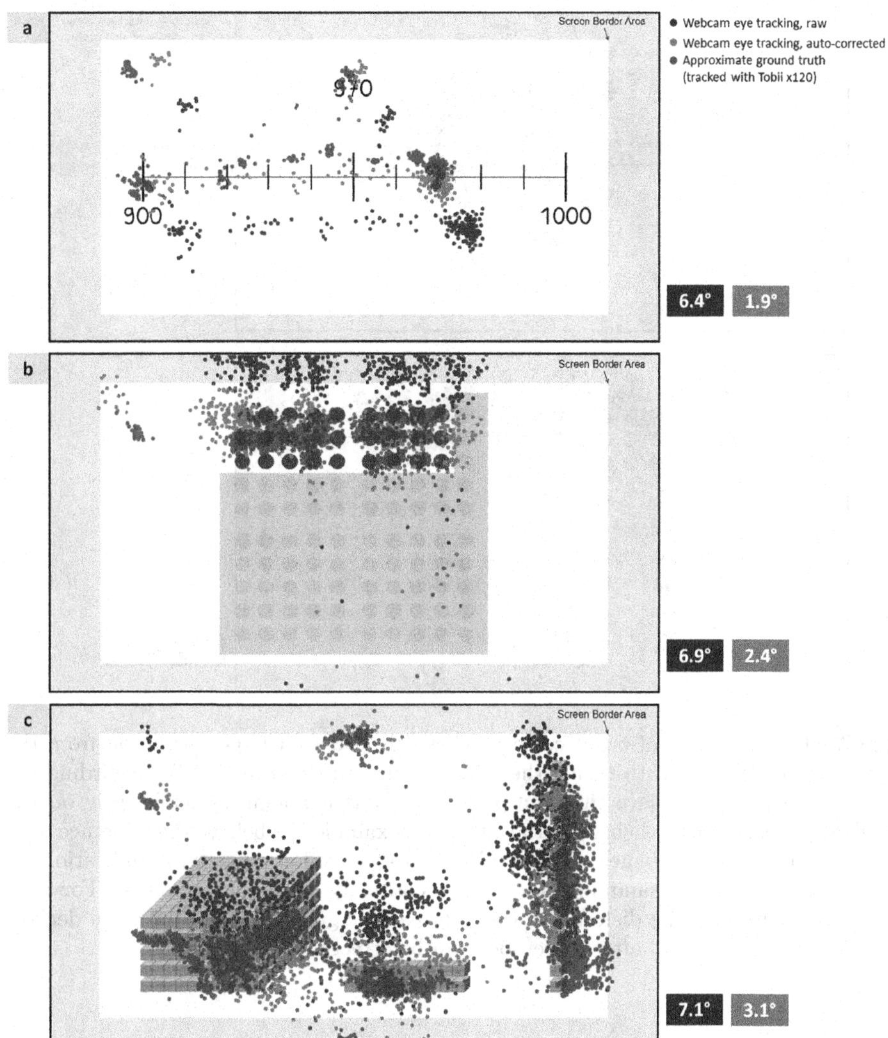

Fig. 6. Examples of successful auto-correction. In plots a and b, a significant discrepancy is observed between the gaze points recorded with wcET (purple dots) and the respective approximate ground truth (dhET, red dots). In plot a, the spatial offset of the gaze points shifted them to areas outside the stimulus. Plot b shows an even more critical situation where most of the gaze points were shifted outside of the screen border. However, our proposed auto-correction method is able to improve the data quality (light green dots). We can see this also in plot c where the gaze points are spread across a wide range in both horizontal and vertical direction. Even in such scenarios the proposed auto-correction method is able to utilize domain information to improve the data quality. For each example we provide the distance to the approximate ground truth (dhET) in degrees before (purple box) and after (green box) auto-correction. (Color figure online)

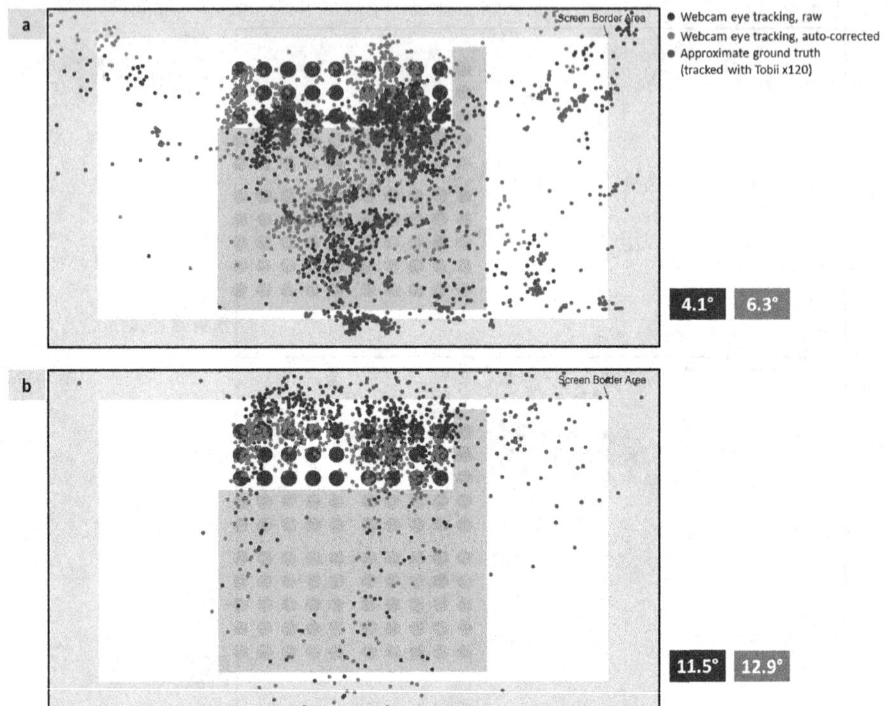

Fig. 7. Two examples of offset corrections which lead to a larger deviation from the approximate ground truth (using the same colour coding as in Fig. 6). Regarding the example in (a), we believe that the participant was not focusing sufficiently on the AOIs while completing their task. In the second example, we believe the reference data were unreliable due to issues with the dhET data collection process (an indication for data loss is the lower sampling rate and, accordingly, sparse gaze points). For each example we provide the distance to the approximate ground truth (dhET) in degrees before (purple box) and after (green box) auto-correction.

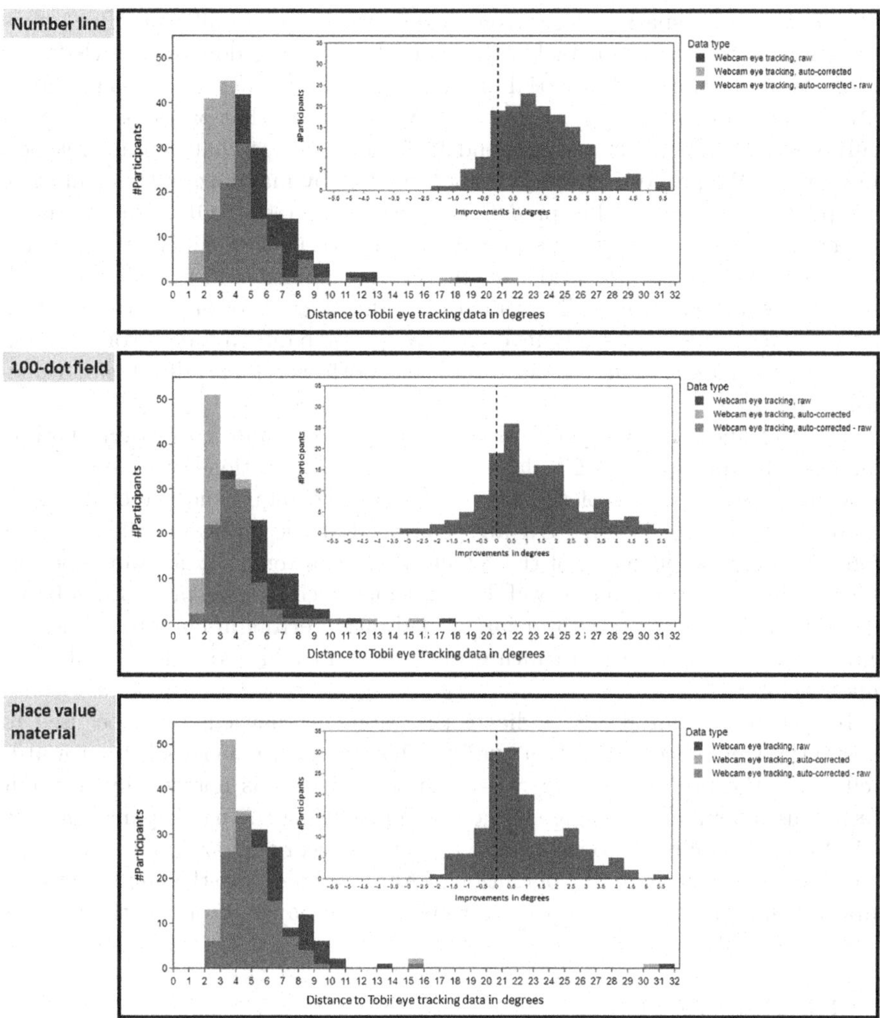

Fig. 8. Comparison between the distributions of the distances between wcET and their respective dhET gaze point, for raw and auto-corrected wcET data in three tasks: Number line, 100-dot field, and Place value material. The larger histogram compares the two types of wcET samples, with the auto-corrected samples shown in a lighter and the raw samples in darker shade of purple. The smaller histogram in the top right corner illustrates the improvement or degradation in each sample after the auto-correction process (shown in green). The black dashed line on the x-axis emphasizes zero, i.e., bars to the right of this line represent improvement. (Color figure online)

5 Discussion and Future Work

Eye tracking accuracy is often plagued by spatial offset, which decreases data quality and has a negative impact on subsequent analysis. Especially in real-life settings, spatial offset remains a significant challenge. Our auto-correction method aims to tackle this issue by utilizing domain knowledge to automatically estimate the spatial offset without having access to ground truth data. The proposed method is based on the assumption that participants - especially when they perform tasks - tend to focus on areas that contain relevant information. We propose to compensate the offset by maximizing the number of gaze points which fall within predefined areas of interest (AOIs). We evaluated our method by conducting experiments on three tasks with different AOI characteristics, such as size, location on the screen, number, and orientation (both horizontally and vertically). To evaluate the effectiveness of our auto-correction method, we conducted a study involving 156 participants in a real-world setting where we gathered eye movement data using both wcET and dhET simultaneously.

The obtained results show that, over all, our auto-correction method enhances the quality of wcET data. We also find indications of a dependency between the effectiveness of the auto-correction technique and the characteristics of the task AOI. When AOIs are positioned at the bottom of the screen or along the right or left edges of the screen, there is a tendency for worse performance, which could be due to wcET limitations such as gaze predictions based on the partial eye region data or larger calibration errors in close to the left or right border of the screen. In future work, we will look more deeply into this dependency.

In conclusion, our results indicate that domain knowledge can be used to substantially enhance wcET data quality. This constitutes a crucial step towards facilitating the use of wcET in real-world scenarios. It is noteworthy that our method uses domain knowledge without compromising the participants' privacy as it does not require video information - just the recorded gaze points. In future work, we aim to automate the definition of AOIs and decrease the number of non-improved samples to achieve a more robust performance of our method across various applications.

6 Related Work

In recent years, wcET technology has made its way into various fields such as psychology and digital learning [10,14,15,20,25]. With the advent of pervasive wcET applications, eye-tracking can now be used outside of lab settings and in real-world scenarios. This is a significant breakthrough as it allows researchers and practitioners to capture more data, which can lead to a better understanding of human behavior and cognition. One of the challenges of these systems is that they can be used to gather data from individuals who cannot be physically restrained, such as infants, children, and individuals with disabilities. Remote eye-trackers have been marketed as a solution to this problem, as they can capture gaze data without requiring participants to be in a chin rest position. However, previous studies and practical experiences have shown that even the quality of the dhET data recorded from unrestrained participants in non-optimal positions can be lower compared to participants who are trained and in a chin rest position. This can be a significant challenge for researchers and practitioners, as it can make it difficult to draw accurate conclusions from the data collected [16].

Studies have revealed that eye-trackers may experience difficulties in accurately tracking a participant's gaze, even if their eyes remain within the designated headbox, when conditions are not ideal for instance unconstrained gaze tracking settings. Unconstrained gaze tracking refers to calibration-free, subject-, viewpoint-, and illumination-independent gaze tracking using a remotely placed off-the-shelf camera. It allows for free head motion of the subject. However, they face numerous challenges, the most essential of which is spatial accuracy.

The main objective of this paper is to address the issue of automatic spatial offset correction in ET data as a post-processing step, regardless of the type of ET system or data acquisition method used. To achieve this, we begin by reviewing different approaches and algorithms for systemic ET offset correction. Subsequently, we provide a more detailed analysis of the wcET system.

6.1 Systematic Offset Correction

Spatial offset is a phenomenon that occurs in both dhET and wcET systems, and various studies have attempted to address this issue in different applications. Previous studies on dhET-based offset correction have mostly focused on improving text reading tasks by correcting the vertical shift that occurs during experiments [3]. These techniques aim to match eye movement fixations with text line details in a manner that is more consistent and in agreement with human-generated fixation annotations. The analysis conducted by Carr et al. evaluated the effectiveness of advanced ET correction algorithms using both simulated and real-world eye-tracking data. However, these algorithms require task-specific information, such as the location and number of lines, and word coordinates. One limitation of the analysis was that it relied on human-based annotations, which may not accurately reflect the true characteristics of participants' eye movements. Additionally, there were instances where human annotators disagreed in their interpretations of participants' eye movement patterns. The sampling rate of ET is an essential parameter that requires consideration. Typically, the dhET system employs a high sampling rate of 100 to 1000 Hz Hz to accurately identify saccades and fixations. However, using a low sampling rate 30 Hz, similar to the wcET system, may not allow for precise identification of saccades and fixations [21]. In this article, we aimed to utilize the unprocessed data without any fixation or saccade data to eliminate any complications, especially due to the limited sampling rate. Additionally, To ensure a more precise assessment of our performance, we compare our results to a reference eye tracker, in order to eliminate any potential errors that may arise from subjective human validation.

6.2 WcET

The first video-based eye-tracking study was conducted in the 1940s s to analyze pilot behavior [5]. Not least because of increasing computing power, real-time eye trackers became available in the 1990s.s. Baluja et al. [2] proposed an artificial neural network-based appearance-based eye tracker for non-intrusive gaze tracking in 1993, for example. Eye trackers differ among others along two dimensions: the imaging device and the gaze estimation method used. Accordingly, we will discuss various imaging devices and gaze estimation techniques below, followed by common eye-tracking applications and calibration techniques.

Imaging Devices. Various imaging devices such as RGB [12], RGBD [13], and IR cameras are used for ET. RGBD cameras use extra depth information ("D") to predict the gaze direction based on RGB images. The corneal reflection technique can be used with IR cameras to predict the gaze direction. Besides that, a variety of setups such as multiple cameras, different camera positions (near-eye, around the screen, on glasses), as well as active and passive light are used [8]. Most of works attempt to use a single RGB camera that is compatible with cameras integrated into laptops and mobile devices.

Gaze Estimation. The computation of the direction in 3D space or the area on a 2D screen the foveal area of the eye is directed to is known as gaze estimation. Gaze estimation techniques can be divided into three major groups: feature-based, model-based, and appearance-based. Feature-based methods extract eye region features such as eye corners and other eye landmarks to predict the gaze direction. In model-based approaches, gaze direction is determined using a 3D model of the eyeball and geometry calculations. These methods usually need a high-resolution image of the eye region to reach satisfactory results. Appearance-based models, try to find a mapping function between raw image input and gaze [8]. With progress in AI, appearance-based gaze estimation reached promising results with low-resolution camera inputs [11]. This has kick-started the use of low-resolution single RGB cameras also in ET research [9]. One of the interesting data sets to test these methods' performance is MPIIGaze [26], which has been captured with regular web cameras without restrictions of head movements and under naturally occurring different light conditions. Appearance-based methods can reach an accuracy of around 4° on this data set, which is promising for some real-world applications of ET.

Applications of WcET. Several wcET studies have recently been conducted in fields such as marketing [25], code development [22], and digital learning [14,15,17,18,20]. Yang et al. [25] conducted an online study with the WebGazer eye tracker to examine customer decision-making behavior. Thilderkvist and Dobslaw [22] used ET for visual processing of source code. They note that applications such as text reading with small AOIs (Areas of Interest), require more accurate gaze tracking. Another important point is temporal stability [7,22], i.e. that gaze estimates are delivered at an approximately constant rate. Sodoke et al. [20] used a webcam based intelligent tutoring system help reinforcing gradually the learning stages of novice clinicians with some cues from the behavioral implicit expert knowledge in terms of visual attention to perform a clinical reasoning in critical anesthesiology clinical case. in the [15,18] they used a webcam based system to predict student test performance based on their eye movement data. Lin et al. [14] use webcam in Chinese reading test and compare it result with a commercial eye tracker.

Calibration. With a less restrictive set up, one critical component of webcam eye-tracking during online experiments is the calibration routine. All gaze estimation methods need to determine a set of parameters through calibration. For 3D gaze-vector prediction some works use model-based ET to reduce calibration requirements. However, estimating the gaze point within the 2D coordinate system of a screen in front of the subject requires a second calibration layer (screen calibration) for each participant [8]. Traditional models use geometry calibration to map the gaze to a point on the screen. Also, some machine learning-based methods try to learn a regression function to calibrate the system. Gudi et al. [6] propose a hybrid approach that uses machine learning to learn geometry calibration parameters. Saxena et al. [19] suggest strategies to estimate calibration parameters such as distance from screen and screen calibration to perform personal gaze calibration.

Acknowledgement. This project has received funding by the Federal Ministry of Education and Research as a part of the program KI-ALF [01NV2123]. The responsibility for the content of this publication remains with the authors.

We also want to thank Han Fan for providing valuable feedback on this manuscript.

References

1. Asghari, P., Schindler, M., Lilienthal, A.J.: Can eye tracking with pervasive webcams replace dedicated eye trackers? an experimental comparison of eye-tracking performance. In: Stephanidis, C., Antona, M., Ntoa, S., Salvendy, G. (eds.) HCI International 2022 - Late Breaking Posters, pp. 3–10. Springer Nature Switzerland, Cham (2022). https://doi.org/10.1007/978-3-031-19679-9_1
2. Baluja, S., Pomerleau, D.: Non-intrusive gaze tracking using artificial neural networks. In: Proceedings of the 6th International Conference on Neural Information Processing Systems, pp. 753–760. NIPS 1993, Morgan Kaufmann Publishers Inc., San Francisco, CA, USA (1993). https://doi.org/10.5555/2987189.2987284
3. Carr, J.W., Pescuma, V.N., Furlan, M., Ktori, M., Crepaldi, D.: Algorithms for the automated correction of vertical drift in eye-tracking data. Behav. Res. Methods **54**(1), 287–310 (2022)
4. Fahimi, R., Bruce, N.D.: On metrics for measuring scanpath similarity. Behav. Res. Methods **53**(2), 609–628 (2021)

5. Fitts, P.M., Jones, R.E., Milton, J.L.: Eye movements of aircraft pilots during instrument-landing approaches. Aeronaut. Eng. Rev. **9**(2), 1–6 (1950)
6. Gudi, A., Li, X., van Gemert, J.: Efficiency in real-time webcam gaze tracking. In: Bartoli, A., Fusiello, A. (eds.) ECCV 2020. LNCS, vol. 12535, pp. 529–543. Springer, Cham (2020). https://doi.org/10.1007/978-3-030-66415-2_34
7. Gómez-Poveda, J., Gaudioso, E.: Evaluation of temporal stability of eye tracking algorithms using webcams. Expert Syst. Appl. **64**, 69–83 (2016)
8. Hansen, D.W., Ji, Q.: In the eye of the beholder: a survey of models for eyes and gaze. IEEE Trans. Pattern Anal. Mach. Intell. **32**(3), 478–500 (2010)
9. He, J., et al.: On-device few-shot personalization for real-time gaze estimation. In: 2019 IEEE/CVF International Conference on Computer Vision Workshop (ICCVW), pp. 1149–1158. Seoul, Korea (South) (2019). https://doi.org/10.1109/ICCVW.2019.00146
10. Lai, J., Asghari, P., Baumanns, L., Pihl, A., Lilienthal, A.J., Schindler, M.: A digital adaptive learning system for diagnostics and support of basic arithmetic competencies. In: Fernández, C., et al. (eds.) Proceedings of the 45th Conference of the International Group for the Psychology of Mathematics Education, p. 368. PME (2022). http://hdl.handle.net/10045/127020
11. Li, Y., Kumar, R., Lasecki, W.S., Hilliges, O.: Artificial intelligence for HCI: a modern approach, pp. 1–8. CHI EA 2020, Association for Computing Machinery, Honolulu (2020). https://doi.org/10.1145/3334480.3375147
12. Lian, D., et al.: Multiview multitask gaze estimation with deep convolutional neural networks. IEEE Trans. Neural Netw. Learn. Syst. **30**(10), 3010–3023 (2019)
13. Lian, D., et al.: RGBD based gaze estimation via multi-task CNN. Proc. AAAI Conf. Artif. Intell. **33**, 2488–2495 (2019). https://doi.org/10.1609/aaai.v33i01.33012488
14. Lin, Z., et al.: An eye tracker based on webcam and its preliminary application evaluation in Chinese reading tests. Biomed. Signal Process. Control **74**, 103521 (2022)
15. Madsen, J., Júlio, S.U., Gucik, P.J., Steinberg, R., Parra, L.C.: Synchronized eye movements predict test scores in online video education. Proc. Natl. Acad. Sci. **118**(5), e2016980118 (2021)
16. Niehorster, D.C., Cornelissen, T.H., Holmqvist, K., Hooge, I.T., Hessels, R.S.: What to expect from your remote eye-tracker when participants are unrestrained. Behav. Res. Methods **50**, 213–227 (2018)
17. Robal, T., Zhao, Y., Lofi, C., Hauff, C.: Webcam-based attention tracking in online learning: a feasibility study. In: 23rd International Conference on Intelligent User Interfaces, pp. 189–197. IUI 2018, Association for Computing Machinery, Tokyo (2018). https://doi.org/10.1145/3172944.3172987
18. Sauter, M., Hirzle, T., Wagner, T., Hummel, S., Rukzio, E., Huckauf, A.: Can eye movement synchronicity predict test performance with unreliably-sampled data in an online learning context? In: 2022 Symposium on Eye Tracking Research and Applications, pp. 1–5. ETRA '22, Association for Computing Machinery, New York (2022). https://doi.org/10.1145/3517031.3529239
19. Saxena, S., Lange, E., Fink, L.: Towards efficient calibration for webcam eye-tracking in online experiments. In: 2022 Symposium on Eye Tracking Research and Applications, pp. 1–7 ETRA '22, Association for Computing Machinery, New York (2022). https://doi.org/10.1145/3517031.3529645
20. Sodoké, K., Nkambou, R., Tanoubi, I., Dufresne, A.: Toward a webcam based ITS to enhance novice clinician visual situational awareness. In: Cristea, A.I., Troussas,

C. (eds.) ITS 2021. LNCS, vol. 12677, pp. 239–243. Springer, Cham (2021). https://doi.org/10.1007/978-3-030-80421-3_26

21. Špakov, O., Istance, H., Hyrskykari, A., Siirtola, H., Räihä, K.J.: Improving the performance of eye trackers with limited spatial accuracy and low sampling rates for reading analysis by heuristic fixation-to-word mapping. Behav. Res. Methods **51**, 2661–2687 (2019)
22. Thilderkvist, E., Dobslaw, F.: On current limitations of online eye-tracking to study the visual processing of source code. Available at SSRN 4051688 (2022). https://doi.org/10.2139/ssrn.4051688
23. Tobii: Tobii pro x3–120 eye tracker. computer hardware (2017). http://www.tobiipro.com/
24. Wisiecka, K., et al.: Comparison of webcam and remote eye tracking. In: 2022 Symposium on Eye Tracking Research and Applications, pp. 1–7. ETRA '22, Association for Computing Machinery, New York (2022). https://doi.org/10.1145/3517031.3529615
25. Yang, X., Krajbich, I.: Webcam-based online eye-tracking for behavioral research. Judgm. Decis. Mak. **16**(6), 1485–1505 (2021)
26. Zhang, X., Sugano, Y., Fritz, M., Bulling, A.: MPIIGAZE: real-world dataset and deep appearance-based gaze estimation. IEEE Trans. Pattern Anal. Mach. Intell. **41**(1), 162–175 (2019)

Incorporating Eye Tracking into an EEG-Based Brainwave Visualization System

Matheus Cavalcanti, Felipe Melo, Thiago Silva, Matheus Falcão, Daniel de Queiroz Cavalcanti, and Valdecir Becker(✉)

Laboratory of Interaction and Media, Informatics Center, Federal University of Paraíba, João Pessoa, PB, Brazil

contato@lim.ci.ufpb.br

Abstract. This article describes the incorporation of eye tracking into a brainwaves visualization and analysis system, based on electroencephalography (EEG), to map attention during fruition of audiovisual content. The visualization system was developed in Python, using an Emotiv Insight headset. During the tests, there was a need to identify whether the reactions mapped by the EEG were in fact related to the fruition of the content or whether they originated from elements external to the screen, with the individual looking away and, consequently, losing attention. Based on the Design Science Research methodology, eye tracking was incorporated into the system architecture. For validation, tests were performed with 10 users. Analyzing the generated data, it was possible to identify the correlation between the information presented by the EEG and the gaze of the individuals. In this way, it is possible to increase confidence about the origin of user's emotions during the fruition of audiovisual content.

Keywords: Eye Tracking · EEG · Audiovisual Fruition

1 Introduction

Eye tracking technology is well known and used in several areas of knowledge, such as usability research, marketing, cognitive psychology experiments, as well as in entertainment, and games. Its operation is based on detecting user's eyes movement during interaction. This can be done through different tools: webcams, infrared cameras, head-mounted displays. The collected data provides relevant information about users, such as their attention to a certain area or object on the screen, for example.

The technology is flexible and can be used with other tools, such as brainwave readers and viewers. In previous stages of this research, a brainwave visualization system based on electroencephalography (EEG) was developed [1, 2]. The objective was to map emotions during the fruition process of audiovisual content, based on changes in brainwave patterns. However, a problem that arose during the tests was related to the origin of some emotions, which in some cases came from outside the TV screen. As a specific example, at a certain moment the cell phone of one of the participants rang, generating attention and a state of stress, identified by the mapped brainwaves.

M. Kurosu and A. Hashizume (Eds.): HCII 2023, LNCS 14011, pp. 392–403, 2023.
https://doi.org/10.1007/978-3-031-35596-7_25

However, for the purpose of the system, only emotions arising from audiovisual fruition are relevant.

To solve this problem, eye tracking was incorporated into the system via webcam, which allows identifying which elements of a scene the user is looking at or if his attention has been diverted to another subject outside the screen. For the tests, a movie trailer was shown while measuring user's brainwaves through the EEG device Emotiv Insight. Thus, the objective of this article is to demonstrate how the use of eye tracking helped to identify the specific points on the screen that caught the user's attention, indicating what possibly caused the results observed through the visualization of the EEG waves.

2 Materials and Methods

In this article, eye tracking software for a webcam was used, with the aim of helping to identify the user's points of interest in scenes of a trailer displayed on the screen. Research development is based on Design Science Research (DSR). This methodological process legitimizes the development of problem-solving artifacts as an important way of producing scientific and technological knowledge [3–5]. DSR was considered relevant for this study after identifying gaps in technical and scientific production in the field of audiovisual systems. For DSR, a fundamental element is understanding external and internal environments that surround the artifact to be created. It was found that, in recent years, there has been no mention, either in the HCI or in media studies, about the creation of models, methods or structures capable of supporting graphic visualization of neural waves during fruition of contents of audiovisual systems with mapping of the user's gaze [6]. The stages of this method consist of six activities: 1: Identification and motivation of problems; 2: Defining the objectives of a solution; 3: Design and development; 4: Demonstration; 5: Evaluation; and 6. Communication.

This article describes the use of the GazeRecorder tool, a freemium online software for eye tracking experiments based on computer cameras. For the demonstration and validation steps, an experiment was set up with a movie trailer. An initial calibration step was carried out with the users, which consists of following, with the eyes, a red dot moving on the screen. After calibration, the trailer was displayed. The tool was able to identify regions of the video where the user had the greatest concentration. Finally, the software generated a heat map over the movie scenes, displaying the experiment results for later analysis. The software used has an accuracy of 1.05°, a precision of 0.129° and a sampling frequency of 30 Hz [7].

In the literature, the combination of EEG with eye tracking tools to improve emotion recognition techniques can be observed in [8], proving to be positive, with an accuracy of 87.59% using a fuzzy integral to perform data fusion. In [9] we see another application to improve emotion recognition based on EEG, eye tracking and other biometric signals. In the context of content recommendation systems, [10] uses data referring to user attention to items on an online platform of documents, images, and videos, obtained through eye tracking, to recommend new content in a personalized way. Eye tracking can also be seen in usability research [11] and in neuromarketing [12], as a tool to predict individual's usage/consumption pattern.

For a better understanding of how eye tracking technology works and how it can provide relevant data to analyze user's interest, enjoyment, or emotional state, it is important to understand some terms that will help to define what types of information will be observed when carrying out an eye tracking experiment (Fig. 1). The first term is the "gaze point", which refers to specific points of the image that the user looked at. A set of gaze points grouped in a certain space in a certain period is called "fixation" [13]. This region is of paramount importance for our study, as it is during its occurrence that the user's main cognitive processes occur, such as comprehension and memory.

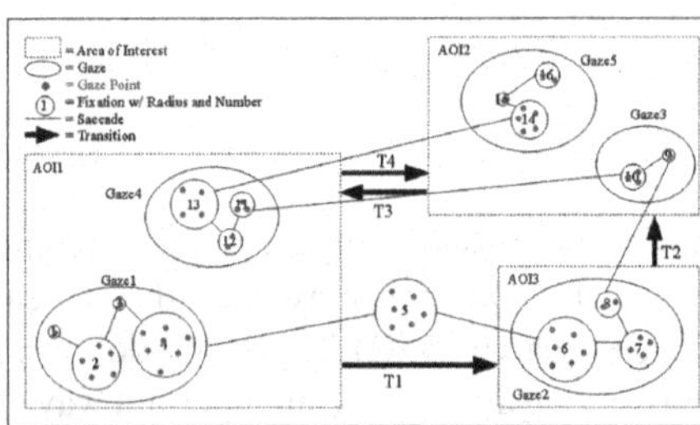

Fig. 1. Representation of terms related to understanding eye tracking. [7].

Fig. 2. Heat map obtained through eye tracking [8].

The rapid movement performed between the "fixation" areas is called a "saccade". During its occurrence, which corresponds between 30 and 80 ms, the visual information is suppressed. A set of "fixations" can be grouped by proximity in a gaze, which in turn is organized into "areas of interest" (AOI) [13]. The time spent on each AOI (dwell time) can be a factor that will define the user's interest in a given stimulus presented on the screen, and a longer time spent can mean a higher level of interest or attention. One way to observe this phenomenon, which was used in this work, is through heat maps, which will show on the screen the points that caught the user's attention [14], as shown in Fig. 2.

Using the information indicated above, associated with the data obtained through the EEG, it is possible to generate a diagnosis regarding the user's perception of visual stimuli. This allows for a better understanding of preferences and emotional and cognitive processes that naturally occur as content on a screen is consumed.

3 Definition of Objectives and Development of the Artifact

Considering Activity 2 of DSR and, based on the definition that the main problem of this research dwells in the identification of emotions during the visualization of audiovisual workpieces, the objectives of the artifact were established as: 1. based on non-invasive, easy-to-use and low cost devices; 2. reading and identification of brainwave patterns; 3. availability and access to data for processing in real time and on demand, using proprietary software; 4. data storage for later recovery; 5. data retrieval for the study and analysis of neural patterns; 6. graphical visualization of neural patterns; 7. integration with the focus of the eyes of individuals; 8. integrated analysis of emotions in front of audiovisual workpieces. An initial description of the architecture of this system is in [26]. Next, we describe how the artifact was designed, implemented, and tested, in addition to the lessons learned so far.

The device used in this stage, which fully meets objectives 1 and 2, and 3, in part, was the Emotiv Insight 2.0 headset, along with the development of a Python script for data processing and visualization (which completes objective 3). The Cortex API [15], developed by the headset manufacturer and available free online, was also used.

Emotiv Insight 2.0 [16] is an EEG measuring device with a wireless Bluetooth connection, with 5 channels for reading, located at positions AF3, AF4, T7, T8 and Pz of the international system 10–20. The headset has Right Driven Connections Leg (DRL) and Common Mode Sense (CMS) on the left mastoid, acting as a reference for the system. Sampling takes place sequentially, at a frequency of 2048 Hz, with subsequent filtering and reduction of the sampling rate to 128 samples per second, submitted to a 14-bit analog-to-digital converter (2 bits of instrumental noise floor are discarded), with 1 Least Significant Bit (LSB) representing $51\mu V$ and a dynamic range for inputs of $8400\mu V$. The headset also has a fifth order sync filter, digital notch filters for 50 Hz and 60 Hz and AC coupling, in addition to recognizing bandwidths for brainwaves in the range of 0.5–43 Hz. Another functionality of Emotiv Insight is its ability to detect movements, through the accelerometer, magnetometer and gyroscope present in the IMU ICM-20948 coupled to the headset.

Considering the system architecture, the user is exposed to audiovisual content using the Emotiv Insight device. While reading electromagnetic pulses is done by the headset, data interpretation takes place in a cloud server environment via constant exchange of information with the Cortex API.

The connection is made from Websockets Secure Protocol in a Websocket server, using the JSON-RPC 2.0 protocol. After the application's authentication process, through credentials validated by the Emotiv Launcher application, it is possible to extract different data streams from the readings. The records are immediately displayed on a graph, dynamically constructed in a Python language program through the Matplotlib library. The information is arranged in this research using power readings in $\mu V^{2}/Hz$ in the Alpha, Low Beta, High Beta, Gamma and Theta frequency bands, transmitted at a frequency of $8 Hz$, according to with the API specifications.

Simultaneously, a file in CSV format is built and fed with the information obtained. Aiming at the study and subsequent analysis of the recorded neural patterns, the application can be fed back with the generated files. Analogously to real-time visualization, it uses the graphics exploration features of the Matplotlib library to facilitate readings in greater detail of the extracted data. In this way, objectives 4 to 8 are also met, closing the cycle of this research, as provided by the stages of DSR method.

4 Test Description

Following the DSR method, which in Activities 4 and 5 presupposes demonstrations and evaluation of the artifact, tests were performed with 10 users, all male, mostly young adults and one middle-aged person. The environment was the Laboratory of Interaction and Media (LIM) at the Federal University of Paraíba, where a space was organized to receive users and allow usability testing in a private and monofocused way. The class of problems [3] for this artifact consists of identifying possible noises that may disturb the analysis of brainwaves. Inspired by artifacts previously generated in similar studies [17], a pre-test questionnaire with seven questions, five of which were based on a Likert scale, one binary question and one multiple-choice question, was used to collect data on emotional and physical state, level of sleep, hunger, and use of prescription drugs. These data may be relevant to identify possible noise and discrepancies in the obtained readings (Fig. 3).

Fig. 3. Tests performed to validate the artifact.

For the tests, the trailer of the horror movie "The Black Phone", by Scott Derrickson (2022), was chosen, lasting 2 min and 17 s. The movie tells the story of a 13-year-old boy, kidnapped by a sadistic killer, and trapped in a soundproof basement, where he has no use for screaming. When an unplugged phone in the wall starts ringing, the boy discovers he can hear voices of killer's previous victims. It is an engaging story, which already in the trailer generates fright and agony in those who watch. To view the trailer, the video was uploaded via a YouTube link on the GazeRecorder platform, and the duration of the experiment was adjusted based on the video. The evaluation started with the preview of the trailer in the player built into the platform itself. Before the trailer, a non-invasive EEG reader, the Emotiv Insight, was placed on the participants' heads, who relaxed for about a minute, calibrating the eye tracking. After the trailer, a post-test questionnaire with five questions was applied, with two binary questions and three on a Likert scale. Of these three, two are based on the Self-Assessment Manikin (SAM) [18], a non-verbal method to assess levels of valence, arousal, and mastery (Fig. 4). The post-test questionnaire aims to help in the analysis of brainwaves, since they obtain the report of how the participants felt emotionally before watched the content.

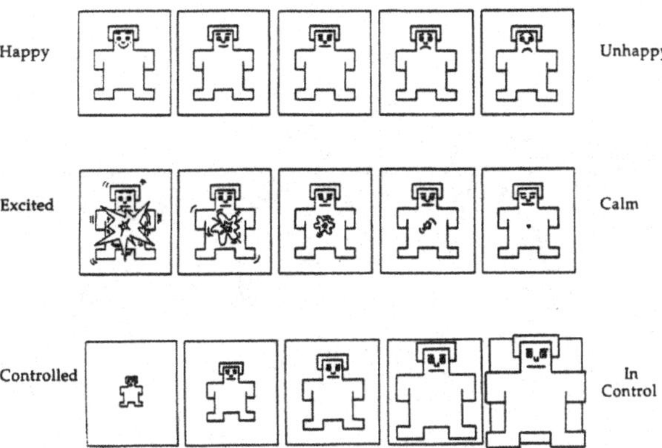

Fig. 4. Self-Assessment Manikin (SAM) [10].

5 Analysis of Test Results and Lessons Learned

The movie's trailer shows several moments that frighten or cause tension in the viewer, using a combination of scenes and sounds that can somehow impact who is watching, causing short-term emotions. It has several occasions of tension, caused by distressing moments, and sounds that gradually increase to the climax of the scene, and with several sudden scares, worked with a abrupt increase in sound effect. These moments can be identified both by the neural patterns read and by the attention in eye tracking. For example, in the frontal lobe region, represented by the AF3 and AF4 electrodes, it is possible to analyze, at the macro level [19], that there was a great stimulus of the low beta and high beta waves in moments of fright or tension, especially in events called jumpscares (a technique used in horror movies and electronic games, when something suddenly appears on the screen in order to scare). These beta spikes in the frontal lobe may indicate a large startle-related information processing, with a presence of fear and anxiety [20].

In addition, large alpha peaks are also observed in this region. As alpha waves are related to relaxation and meditation, we can infer, also on a macro level, that the brain processes the information received and realizes that the threat is not real. After the tension of the fright, the level of relaxation increases. This can be seen in Fig. 6, between four and five seconds. It is notable where alpha waves generate peaks after increased low beta and high beta activity.

Theoretically, in the temporal lobe, represented by electrodes T7 and T8, an expressiveness of gamma waves was expected, in comparison with other regions of the brain. This region is responsible for sensory processing. The gamma wave is correlated with visual, tactile, and auditory stimuli, which should be high when the individual is exposed to audiovisual content. However, from the readings performed, contrary to other studies, such as those carried out by [21–24], it was not noticeable major changes in this region (Fig. 6). This theme still lacks a deeper analysis to elucidate the causes of the non-deep alteration of gamma waves, including to identify elements of micro expressions, as identified by [19] and its relationship with emergentism [19], which presupposes an integration between the mental elements and the physical reactions of individuals (Fig. 5).

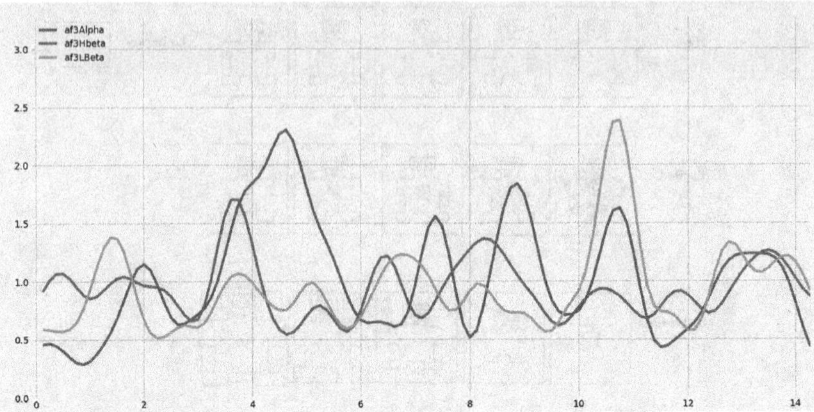

Fig. 5. Example of reading Alpha, High Beta and Low Beta waves on the AF3 electrode in the Frontal Lobe in a period of approximately 14 s.

To assess whether the individual enjoyed something, it is necessary to analyze the levels of valence (positive and negative) and excitement (provoked intensity), in relation to the stimulus provoked (images, sounds, touches, flavors, etc.) [25]. In the present study, valence levels were measured from alpha waves (related to relaxation and meditation), low beta (fear, negative anxiety), and high beta (positive fear, anxiety), and levels of excitation, by the intensity of those same waves. For this taste analysis, the moments of greatest activity were observed, which generate peaks in the waves. In theory, these moments are mainly related to the scenes of fear and tension in the trailer. There were no noticeable variations in the waves between people who reported that they liked and disliked the content. Comparing some participants, it is possible to see a minimal difference in the power of the low beta and high beta waves, where participants who said they did not like the content had a lower power in these waves. One possibility to explain this scenario is that people who don't like this genre of film are more inert to the surprise factor and feel more bored. Those who liked it had slightly higher levels of valence and arousal, which may indicate that they were more excited about the content they watched. As the differences were small, it is not possible to conclusively state whether there is indeed a relationship in the waves between people who liked and disliked the content. This is another topic to be further explored in future analyses.

Eye Tracking (Fig. 7) aimed to help in the analysis of waves and emotions to understand what might have generated that emotion or brain activity, based on where the participants were looking. It is possible to notice the gaze points and the fixations are almost always in what is in evidence on the scene, representing areas of interest. When something is not being presented with much evidence, the heat map is more dispersed, looking for points to focus on, noting the occurrence of scanpaths, that is, the user's search behavior for significant elements of the scene.

At 29 s into the trailer, it is possible to identify a fixation on the character that is in evidence. It is a dark scene, with an air of mystery and tension. Considering a specific user, when relating the eye tracking (Fig. 8) of this scene with the EEG (Fig. 9), it is possible to identify, in fact, a great wave activity at that instant, especially the low beta

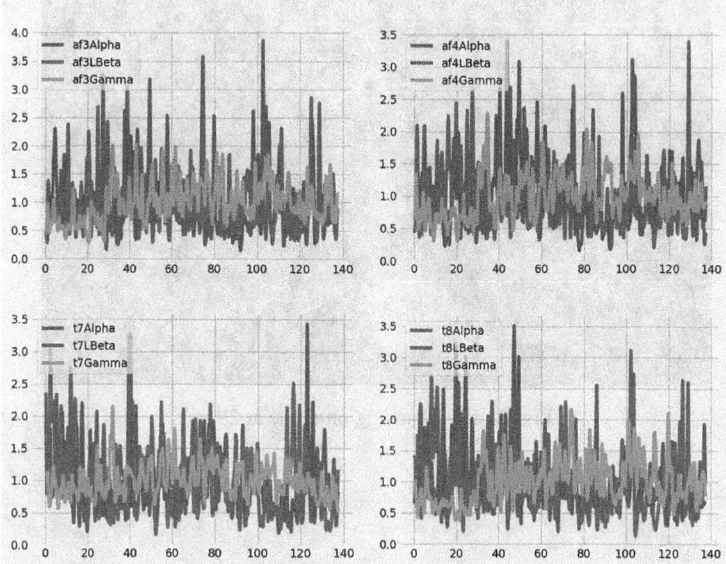

Fig. 6. Reading of the ratio between the power in the frequency bands relative to their average in channels AF3, AF4 (Front) and T7, T8 (Temporal).

Fig. 7. Eye Tracking heat maps obtained during tests.

and high beta waves. That is, it is possible to deduce that the participant was afraid, anxious because of this character in the scene. It is also noted that when there is text on the screen, either by subtitles or by the textual elements that make up the trailer, the user tends to momentarily divert his attention from the scene to read the texts, with the presence of saccades that indicate his reading.

Fig. 8. Eye Tracking on scene at 29 s.

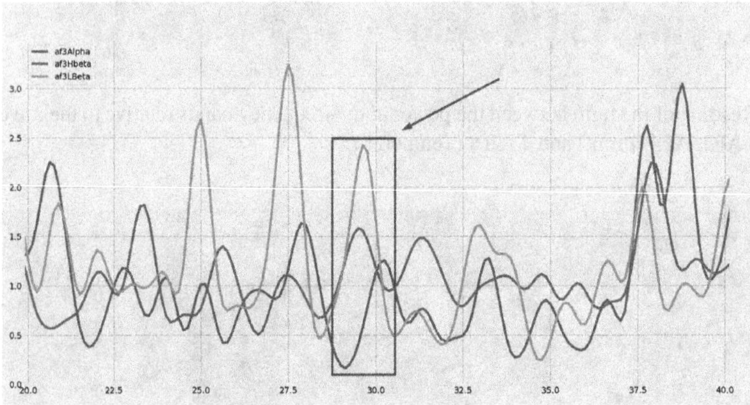

Fig. 9. Alpha, High Beta and Low Beta waves, with peak activity evident at 29 s.

6 Conclusion

This article described a brainwave visualization system using EEG and Eye Tracking to map the emotional relationship of individuals with audiovisual workpieces, especially attention and enjoyment. Applying the Design Science Research method, the artifact was specified, implemented, and tested with 10 individuals, using a horror movie trailer. A preliminary questionnaire and a post-test were presented to the participants. The results indicate patterns of emotional identification with the film, which can be interpreted as an inclination to watch the film in movie theaters or a revulsion towards the theme/genre of the film. It was also evident, both by reading the neural patterns and by focusing attention on the eye tracking, that moments of tension, fright and relaxation portray the main emotions related to the theme of the film and were manifested coherently with the answers to the questionnaires.

In conclusion, this research points to a breakthrough in the analysis and evaluation of audiovisual workpieces, contemplating unconscious emotional elements of subjective perceptions about the watched content. Possible immediate applications may include a more accurate assessment of audiovisual workpieces, considering the exact moments in which emotions were felt. In addition, advertising pieces can be evaluated and inferred the potential for sales or engagement in the advertised product.

Although the project and research objectives were achieved, limitations were identified and had to be mitigated throughout the process. As described in the text, the visual analysis of the results of the waves obtained through electroencephalography is still considered one of the main challenges encountered. As demonstrated by the experiment in this article, large variations in results are not noticeable between users who declared that they liked or disliked the type of content displayed. Since the differences between the analyzed graphs were small in this regard, it has not yet been possible to conclusively state the existence of a cognitive pattern that represents the relationship of affinity between viewer and content. One can only infer this in relation to specific moments in the film.

The Emotiv Insight device also has limitations that impacted the development of the described experiment. Although it has good portability, stable connection via Bluetooth and good coupling with the developed program, the device fails to obtain stable readings in people with voluminous hair or thick fiber, generating difficulty in stabilizing the flows of brainwave readings. During tests with unstable signal acquisition, an attempt was noted to normalize the results obtained, either by the device or by the API provided by the manufacturer, causing readings that were incompatible with the participant's real mental state. The type of results obtained, and the format of the output files are also limited by the manufacturing company's business model. In addition, some functionalities are blocked by the need to subscribe additional services, such as obtaining raw EEG data and exporting results in their own formats.

As with the use of EEG for the experiments, the eye tracking tool used has limitations. Because it is a tool that operates using webcam recordings, the result cannot be as accurate as with recordings made using an infrared camera, more suitable for TV environments, where the user is more in front of the screen. In addition, because the free version of the GazeRecorder software was used, there was a limitation in the number of tests that could be performed. As future works, we list the acquisition of an infrared camera, use and integration of open software for analysis of eye tracking results, together with the implemented software for analyzing of EEG waves. Regarding wave analysis, we point out the need for more powerful EEG readers, which do not suffer interference from the hair fiber. In addition, more data is needed, with a greater number of users, to deepen the analysis of issues related to standards of enjoyment and affinity with the workpieces.

Acknowledgments. This work was funded by the Public Call n. 03 Produtividade em Pesquisa PROPESQ/PRPG/UFPB proposal code PVL13414-2020.

References

1. Da Silva, T.H.C.T., Cavalcanti, M.D., Becker, V.: Desenvolvimento de um sistema para visualização gráfica de ondas neurais durante consumo de conteúdos midiáticos. IV Jornada Internacional GEMInIS (JIG 2021) (2021)
2. Becker, V., et al.: A system for graphical visualization of brainwaves to analyse media content consumption. In: Kurosu, M. (eds.) HCII 2022. LNCS, vol. 13303, pp. 319–328. Springer, Cham (2022). https://doi.org/10.1007/978-3-031-05409-9_24
3. Dresch, A., Lacerda, D.P., Júnior, J.A.V.A.: Design science research: método de pesquisa para avanço da ciência e tecnologia. Bookman Editora (2020)
4. Järvinen, P.: Action research is similar to design science. Qual. Quant. **41**(1), 37–54 (2007)
5. Hevner, A.R., March, S.T., Park, J.: Design research in information systems research. MIS Q. **28**(1), 75–105 (2004)
6. Toscano, R.M., de Souza, H.B.A.M., da Silva Filho, S.G., Noleto, J.D., Becker, V.: HCI methods and practices for audiovisual systems and their potential contribution to universal design for learning: a systematic literature review. In: Antona, M., Stephanidis, C. (eds.) HCII 2019. LNCS, vol. 11572, pp. 526–541. Springer, Cham (2019). https://doi.org/10.1007/978-3-030-23560-4_38
7. Simply User, User Experience Lab. The comparison of accuracy and precision of eye tracking: GazeFlow vs. SMI RED 250 (2013)
8. Lu, Y., et al.: Combining eye movements and EEG to enhance emotion recognition. In: Proceedings of the Twenty-Fourth International Joint Conference on Artificial Intelligence (IJCAI 2015) (2015)
9. López-Gil, J.M., et al.: Method for improving EEG based emotion recognition by combining it with synchronized biometric and eye tracking technologies in a non-invasive and low cost way. Front. Comput. Neurosci. (2016)
10. Xu, S., et al.: Personalized online document, image and video recommendation via commodity eye-tracking. In: RecSys 2008 (2008)
11. Poole, A., Ball, L.: Eye Tracking in Human-Computer Interaction and Usability Research: Current Status and Future Prospects (2010)
12. Santos, R., et al.: Eye tracking in neuromarketing: a research agenda for marketing studies. Int. J. Psychol. Stud. **7**(1), 32 (2015)
13. Blascheck, T., et al.: State-of-the-art of visualization for eye tracking data. In: Eurographics Conference on Visualization (EuroVis) (2014)
14. Farnsworth, B.: 10 Most Used Eye Tracking Metrics and Terms, iMotions (2020)
15. Emotiv. 2022. Cortex API Getting Started. https://emotiv.gitbook.io/cortex-api/. Accessed 30 Jan 2023
16. Emotiv. 2022. Insight Manual Technichal Specification. https://emotiv.gitbook.io/insight-manual/introduction/technical-specifications. Accessed 30 Jan 2023
17. Liao, D., et al.: Design and evaluation of affective virtual reality system based on multimodal physiological signals and self-assessment manikin. IEEE J. Electromagnet. RF Microwaves Med. Biol. **4**(3), 216–224 (2020)
18. Bradley, M.M., Lang, P.J.: Measuring emotion: the self-assessment manikin and the semantic differential. J. Behav. Ther. Exp. Psychiatry **25**(1), 49–59 (1994)
19. Dattada, V., Mohan, V., Jeevan, M.: Analysis of concealed anger emotion in a neutral speech signal. In: 2019 IEEE International Conference on Distributed Computing, VLSI, Electrical Circuits and Robotics (DISCOVER), pp. 1–5 (2019)
20. Fransworth, B.: EEG (Electroencephalography): The Complete Pocket Guide (2019). https://imotions.com/blog/eeg/. Accessed 30 Jan 2023

21. Gabert-Quillen, C.A., Bartolini, E.E., Abravanel, B.T., Sanislow, C.A.: Ratings for emotion film clips. Behav. Res. Methods **47**(3), 773–787 (2014). https://doi.org/10.3758/s13428-014-0500-0
22. Gross, J.J., Levenson, R.W.: Emotion elicitation using films. Cogn. Emot. **9**(1), 87–108 (1995)
23. Samson, A., Kreibig, S., Soderstrom, B., Wade, A., Gross, J.: Eliciting positive, negative, and mixed emotional states: a film library for affective scientists. Cogn. Emot. **30**(5), 827–856 (2015)
24. Schaefer, A., Nils, F., Sanchez, X., Philippot, P.: Assessing the effectiveness of a large database of emotion-eliciting films: a new tool for emotion researchers. Cogn. Emot. **24**, 1153–1172 (2010)
25. Gao, Z., Wang, S.: Emotion recognition from EEG signals using hierarchical Bayesian network with privileged information. In: Proceedings of the 5th ACM on International Conference on Multimedia Retrieval (Shanghai, China) (ICMR 2015), pp. 579–582. Association for Computing Machinery, New York (2015)
26. Becker, V., Silva, T., Cavalcanti, M., Gambaro, D., Elias, J.: Potencial das interfaces cérebro máquina para a recomendação de conteúdos em sistemas de vídeo sob demanda. In: 4o Congresso Internacional Media Ecology and Image Studies - Reflexões sobre o ecossistema midiático pós pandemia. Ria Editorial, pp. 145–167 (2021)

Research on Brain-Computer Interfaces in the Entertainment Field

Daniel de Queiroz Cavalcanti, Felipe Melo, Thiago Silva, Matheus Falcão, Matheus Cavalcanti, and Valdecir Becker(✉)

Laboratory of Interaction and Media, Informatics Center, Federal University of Paraíba, João Pessoa, PB, Brazil
contato@lim.ci.ufpb.br

Abstract. Brain-computer interfaces (BCI) have become commonplace in human-computer interaction. New forms of interaction were incorporated, innovating in the ways in which individuals exchange information with computational systems. A BCI that has become increasingly common is based on electroencephalography (EEG), that is, on the reading of brainwaves and the consequent generation of binary data to be used by computers. This type of interface is more common and widespread in the health field. Research has shown great potential in the treatment of trauma, both physical and psychological. However, few studies were identified on the use of EEG as BCI in other areas of knowledge, such as entertainment and fruition of audiovisual content. Although headsets are commercially available with a wide variety of formats and prices, there is a limitation of studies on the use of this technology for mapping emotions, tastes, and subjective relationships with audiovisual content. Within this context, a survey was carried out, in the form of a systematic literature review (SLR), to identify research and scientific projects in progress, with complete or partial results, on brain-computer interfaces in fields related to entertainment studies. The focus is to understand how the topic of emotion is addressed in research based on electroencephalography and if there is research that points to the use of EEG-based BCIs to identify emotions during the audiovisual enjoyment process. Analyzing the three most important databases for the area of human-computer interaction, ACM, Springer, and IEEE, and applying the inclusion and exclusion criteria, 56 articles on the subject were identified. A synthesis of these papers is presented in this article.

Keywords: RSL · EEG · Audiovisual Fruition

1 Introduction

Brain-machine interfaces (BCI) [1] will become common in human-computer interaction, which aims to connect the human brain to computers or electronic devices. By now, through the evolved BCI technology [7, 16], it is possible to deepen and implement records and markings of electrical, magnetic or functional activities of the brain. Furthermore, it is also possible to decode the neural code and through algorithms, therefore translate it into a machine language signal, so that it can then inspect electronic devices that may be around us, embedded in the human body or at the same time kilometers away.

M. Kurosu and A. Hashizume (Eds.): HCII 2023, LNCS 14011, pp. 404–415, 2023.
https://doi.org/10.1007/978-3-031-35596-7_26

Through this, a BCI that has become increasingly common is based on electroencephalography (EEG), or segue, on the identification of neural waves and the resulting development of a binary data base for use by computational tools. Emotion is treated as a natural feeling in living beings, according to the author Yang Li [1]. From the point of view of neuroscience, there are some regions of the cerebral cortex, for example, orbital frontal cortex, ventral medial prefrontal cortex and amygdala, that are surprisingly closely related to emotions. Those regions provide us with a potential way to decode emotions by recording the signals of the human brain to identify the best or real meaning of this feeling that is part of our lives. As an example, it is possible to place the EEG electrodes on the scalp, we can record the neural activities of the brain, which can be used to recognize the emotions of the human being.

By far, this type of interaction area is more shared and widespread in the health field. Research has received immense quality and mastery in the treatment of traumas, both physical and mental. Still, few studies have been reported on the use of EEG as BCI in different fields of knowledge, such as entertainment and use of audiovisual content. However, the headsets are commercially available with a wide abundance and assortment of aspects and prices, there is a gap of studies on the application of this technology for subjective relationships, tastes, mapping of emotions through audiovisual content.

For this research, were analyzed the three most significant databases for the field of human-computer interaction, ACM, Springer, and IEEE, and fulfilling the inclusion and exclusion criteria, resulting in 56 articles on the researched topic. A summary of these works is presented in this article. As a main conclusion, it follows that the identification of emotions in human beings plausibly leads to identification through magnetic resonance imaging, thus assenting to the proper investigation of emotions, which in turn exist levels with diversified foci, particularly macro and micro. Knowing this, not at the micro level, the analysis is based on a specific evaluation or a combination of evaluations, which vary between different individuals. Yet at the macro level the result is deterministic, like a standard emotion.

In close connection with this situation, a systematic review of the literature (SRL) was undertaken to review research on the subject area and answer two central questions: what is discussed about the development and use of EEG as a BCI in fields related to entertainment? What are the main technologies and methods used to map emotions and identify affinities with audiovisual content? In this way, it was possible to diagnose the importance of electroencephalography in consonance and connection with brain-computer interfaces (BCI), with a connection that aims at improving the lives of people, in the various areas of study in a clear and objective manner.

2 Methods

Systematic reviews (SRs) are considered a key research method to support evidence-based research [49]. This review includes articles from three different databases and classifies the results of the problems and solutions proposed by the analyzed articles. For this SR, we adopted the PICO (Population, Intervention, Comparison and Outcomes) protocol for initial organization. The population comprises primary studies on theories and methods of using EEG as a BCI and emotion analysis. The intervention indicates theories or reports on the use, development, and evaluation of BCIs. For Comparison and Outcomes, we sought to verify which studies were directly involved with the use or development of EEG as a BCI and emotion analysis or had potential contribution to the development of similar tools. From these topics, the following points were raised: what is discussed about the development and use of EEG as a BCI and what are the main technologies and methods used to map emotions and identify affinities with the content.

The search string was adapted according to the different search mechanisms of the libraries, encompassing the following keywords: affective computing, neuroscience, man-machine interaction, emotions, shape emotions, rendering emotions, emotion eracking, emotion recognition, EEG, emotion detection, electroencephalography, emotion detection using electroencephalography, affective computing, neuromarketing, artificial intelligence affective computing.

The inclusion criteria used in the mapping were: (i) containing the keywords of the search string in the title or abstract; (ii) having an available online version; (iii) in the case of articles that dealt with the same research, only the most recent was included. From the found articles, the exclusion criteria were defined to maintain the focus of the research: (i) articles whose main focus was not the analysis of emotions or the use of EEG as a BCI; (ii) specific articles on the health field; (iii) mappings and systematic reviews that only used EEG and BCI as examples. Applying the search string to the three databases, considering the period between 2013 and 2021, 151 articles were identified. Applying the inclusion and exclusion criteria in each article resulted in 56 articles, which make up this article. Of these, 37 are from the ACM Digital Library, 13 from the IEEE and 6 from Springer (Fig. 1). The survey was carried out throughout 2022.

For the analysis of the information and organization of the data, the Grounded Theory method [50] was used. That is, the research is grounded (or rooted) in the data, to develop analytical categories from the collected data, transforming empirical research into a strong theoretical reflection, facilitating the understanding of the phenomenon. This method examines phenomena seeking to theorize and not simply describe. A central part of the Grounded Theory is coding, a process in which theories are tested in different scenarios, which strengthens scientific validation in a very objective way.

At the beginning, the research was focused on the field of study that, in turn, we have been constantly working on and defined the research question, to know if the same line of research existed in evidence. Next, started the capturing data process (data collection). Then data was analyzed using the constant comparison method, coding methodologies and theoretical sampling. Once realized, theories were generated, with the help of interpretive procedures, before finally being written and presented.

The method of constant comparison helped to prepare the research follow-up methodology, in line with the research that was already being used, through systematic coding and analysis procedures. Firstly, the researcher compares the interviews (or other data) aiming at the emergence of the theory. The results of the comparison are coded (coding), identifying categories (equivalent to themes) and their properties (sub-categories). To codify, certain theoretical propositions show up. Those can be relationships between the categories or on the central category of the study. How to emerge from other categories and properties, or how they relate to the central category provides a theory. During this process, when the ideas and insights occur, the researcher makes notes for himself about the categories and properties and the relationships between them. These annotations are called memo. With the emergence of theory, the researcher compares the data with literature. Grounded Theory treats literature as another data source to be integrated into constant comparison analysis.

The categories emerge and the researcher seeks to add to his sample data that increases diversity aiming to develop and strengthen the emerging theory. This is known as theoretical sampling, which is a data collection process to generate theory, when researcher collects, codes and analyzes the data and decides which data will be next to be collected. Clearly, this data collection approach carried out jointly with the analysis is quite different from the classical qualitative methodologies that adopt a pre-planned and sequential approach. Once the researcher reaches a theoretical saturation of the categories, he proceeds to review, classify, and integrate closely related categories, their properties, and the relationships between them. This procedure is called sorting and is an essential procedure once you place fragmented dice together. We have classified them according to a conceptual framework with the main ideas and facts about what is being investigated. Likewise, the writing phase is simply a product of the sorting procedure.

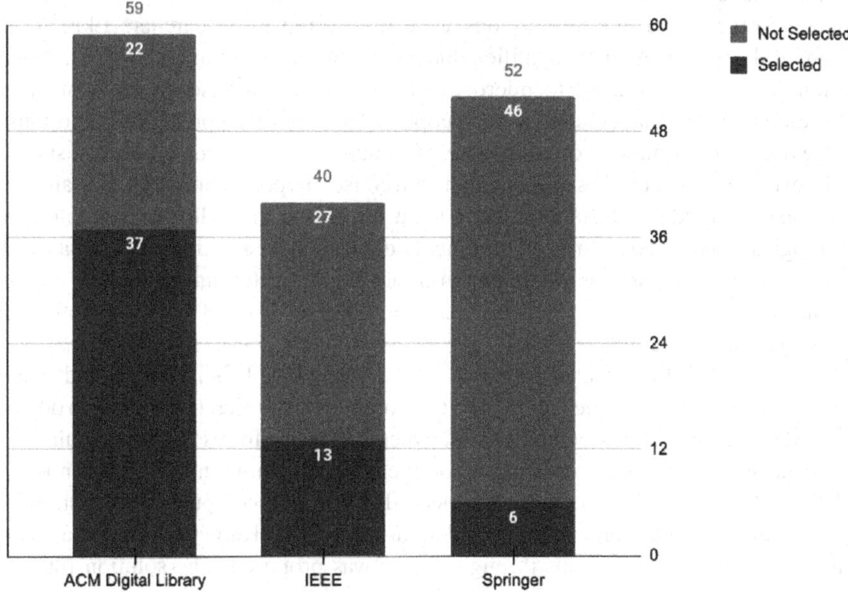

Fig. 1. Proportion of used articles in the SLR.

3 Results Analysis and Discussion

From the neuroscience point of view, there are regions of the cerebral cortex that are closely related to emotions [1]. This finding provides us with a potential way to decode emotion by recording the signals of the human brain from these regions. Consequently, in theory, it is also possible to identify meanings of emotion. One way to do this is by coupling EEG electrodes to the scalp for recording brain neural activities. Another common way is through functional magnetic resonance imaging, where variations in blood flow in response to neural activity are detected. The generated data can be used to recognize human emotions.

Within this perspective, scientists have carried out research on humor induction and language activation based on magnetic resonance imaging (fMRI), discovering that sadness and happiness are processed by each hemisphere [2, 3, 5, 7, 8, 15, 16, 22, 27, 31, 36]. Additionally, researchers [2, 5, 24–26, 31] have also proposed methods to measure the differences between the two hemispheres, which have been used for the detection of depression and EEG monitoring. However, it is still an interesting topic how to use the property of brain asymmetry to improve emotion recognition performance.

According to [2], the analysis of emotions can be divided into two levels, macro and micro. At the macro level, the result is deterministic, like a standard emotion. In addition, researchers [2, 15] defend emergentism, assuming that the combination of the evaluation of elements in the recursive process is unfolding over time. This resulting reaction will form emerging emotions that are more than the sum of their constituents and more than the instant of rigid categories.

On the other hand, micro emotions were discovered by researchers Ekman and Friesen in 1969, when they identified hidden emotions in individuals [46]. Micro emotions are directly related to micro expressions and comprise an involuntary, or unconscious, feeling that emerges when people try to hide or suppress their emotions.

The detection of micro expressions helps to understand the true emotional state of people, even if this detection is uncorrelated with conscious perception [46]. This analysis of true state or hidden information has a great impact on the fields of psychological, physiological, and interrogative environments diagnosis. In addition, it also has wide applications in healthcare for the treatment of autism and determining medical clients' state during healthcare. This motivated the study and analysis of hidden emotions in speech signals, for example.

The authors [47] conducted research on the detection of facial micro and macro expression in long video sequences using a temporal oriented reference frame. To do this, they used the leave-one-out method, that is, a method that performs N error calculations, one for each data. Despite presenting a complete investigation on the variation of the model in relation to the data used, this method has a high computational cost and is only indicated for situations where few data are available. Knowing this, an analysis of micro and macro expressions through videos was proposed. The solution found is based on deep learning, which, instead of tracking differential movement, compared each video frame using a convolutional model. In this way, with two temporal local reference frames, they were shown according to the duration of the user's calculated micro and macro expressions. However, there was better performance on a set of long high frame rate SAMM video data (200 fps) (SAMM-LV) than on a low frame rate (30 fps) (CAS(ME)2) and it was possible to achieve an F1-Score of 0.1531 as a baseline result.

Another relevant concept identified in this RSL is the component process model (CPM) [4]. This is a vision for explaining emotions as emergent results of underlying dimensions, adding a layer of mechanism at the base of emotional experience. This model assumes a series of cognitive evaluations at different levels of processing that introduces more flexibility and can explain individual and contextual differences in responses to the same stimuli. In addition, this model can accommodate non-prototypical and mixed/diffuse emotion. According to the component process model of emotion, changes in subsystems in an organism are driven by evaluations that reflect the subjective evaluation of an event and activate changes in other subsystems. In this model, each emotional experience arises from coordinated changes in five components: 1) the evaluation component, which involves evaluating the event/situation in relation to meaning, implications for goals, potential for coping, novelty, and compatibility with norms; evaluations are drawn from memory and goal representations and examine the relevance of the event and its consequences for the organism's well-being. Changes in this component trigger changes in the other four main components; 2) a motivation component that defines changes in action tendencies (e.g. fight, flee, or freeze) and prepares for appropriate responses; 3) a physiological component that encompasses changes in peripheral autonomic activity (e.g. changes in heart rate or respiratory rate) and occurs based on the results of evaluation and associated motivational changes; 4) an expression component that involves changes in expressive motor behavior, such as facial expression, gestures/body postures, and is also activated similarly to the physiological component as a result of evaluation and motivation components; and finally 5) a feeling component that reflects the conscious experience associated with changes in all other components, usually described by people with some categorical labels (such as anger, happiness, sadness, etc.).

This approach has been applied to the development of artificial agents, which are increasingly present in our social environment, with an increasing number of these agents appearing in contexts of hospitality, care, and education [5]. An example is the development of humanoid robots. Research has shown that, to maximize the quality of social interactions between humans and artificial agents, it is important that the artificial agent not only responds to the emotions expressed by the human agent, but also is able to express emotions itself. As interest and investment in social robotics continue to grow, developing artificial agents with this type of emotional capacity is a fundamental requirement for truly social robotics agents. While the emotional component of artificial agents has been neglected until recently, when empirical investigations began to shift the focus. Emerging research documents how robots are expressive and can be classified as more sympathetic and humanized, leading to increased engagement and more enjoyable interactions. Acceptance and cooperation with a robot depend on the match between the situation and its emotional behavior [5].

Over the past decades, emotion recognition has played a significant role in human interaction, increasingly drawing interest and attention [6]. However, much of the work in this area has focused on the analysis of represented or stereotyped emotions. In most studies [2, 6, 9] on emotions, there is a classification into some basic discrete emotions [9] (e.g., happiness, sadness, surprise, fear, anger, and disgust). Although many promising recognition results have been achieved recently, the current state of the art still does not meet all the needs of real life, as it displays subtle, complex emotional states that cannot be fully expressed or classified by a label or category of emotion [10].

Focused on this, researchers [2, 7–12, 29, 33, 35] argue that the dimensionality approach to emotion modeling is more suitable for expressing complex emotions. In this way, there is an attempt to learn emotion in a multidimensional space, rather than some discrete basic concepts. For example, the dimension of arousal refers to the emotion as excited or apathetic. The valence dimension refers to how positive or negative the emotion is. The dominance dimension refers to the degree of power or sense of control over the emotion [1–3]. Therefore, the various emotional states located at different positions and their similarities and differences can be expressed by their distances in this space. In view of this, other research [4, 9, 13, 14] on this topic has expanded the scope, not only detecting various prototypical emotions, but also recognizing the emotional states at each moment. In this way, it is possible to work in a subtle direction, generating continuous and specific interpretations of the context of monitors recorded in real world configurations.

Another relevant element identified in this SRL is the recognition of emotion in the auditory, visual, and physiological dimensions. Based on the Long Short-Term Memory Recurrent Networks (LSTM-RNN) architecture [9], which can be explained as the state-of-the-art classifier for dimensional emotion recognition [47, 48], two techniques are used in the dimensional emotion recognition: 1. ε-insensitive loss: the ε-insensitive loss is used as the loss function to train the neural network. Label noise is an inevitable problem for dimensional emotion. Compared with the squared loss function, which is the most widely used loss function for dimensional emotion recognition, the ε-insensitive loss is more robust to label noise. Additionally, the ε-insensitive loss can ignore small errors to better strong correlations between predictions and labels.

The LSTMRNN is one of the latest generation machine learning techniques in dimensional emotion recognition. It has the ability to incorporate knowledge about how emotions typically evolve over time, so that inferred emotion estimates are produced under consideration of an optimal amount of context [13]. In this way, the challenge posed by the regression problem for dimensional emotion is simplified into a positive and negative classification problem. By combining audio and visual modalities, [14] obtains the state-of-the-art performance.

For the regression problem, directly focused on dimensional emotion recognition, [7] also use LSTM-RNN to analyze the dimensional emotion recognition problem. Asynchronous data between continuous ratings and window size analysis data for emotion dimensions and multimodal fusion make up the center of the analysis in [4]. Damien Dupré et al. [4] also use LSTM-RNN to analyze the dimensional emotion recognition problem. Obtaining high inter-observer agreement is one of the main challenges in emotion data annotation, especially for dimensional emotion analysis [9, 10]. Therefore, label noise is an inevitable problem currently. [17] seek to minimize label noise to calculate the average ratings of all evaluators [18–20, 44, 45, 48] by centering the data from different evaluators according to the average value of all the inputs. The result was a combination of these ratings linearly weighted by their respective agreements among evaluators. Agreement is measured by the concordance correlation coefficient (CCC).

Additionally, [19, 21, 23] added other features to the label in certain time windows. By calculating the average of the labels in the window, the label is smoothed, and the noise is reduced to a certain extent. Researchers [2, 6, 9, 18–20, 44, 45, 48] have also sought to minimize annotation noise in various ways. However, when noisy labels are given, this problem is rarely considered from the loss function. Additionally, [28–30] have added temporal clustering, described as an emotional dimensional recognition technique using the function in the deep belief network. This technique allows for temporal modeling in the direct network, generating highly competitive results [32–34]. In this context, the temporal clustering function is used before the LSTM layer [35, 37, 38], short-term temporal modeling [39–41], aiming to increase the diversity of the resources fed to the forward prediction layers [42–45].

4 Conclusion

This article described the results of a systematic literature review (RSL) on the relevant concepts, mapping techniques, and analysis of individuals' emotions from brain-machine interfaces. The research was based on the PICO protocol, with data collection in the ACM, Springer, and IEEE databases, resulting in 56 articles. The research aims at two central points. The first sought to identify how emotion was broadly approached in research using BCIs in the enjoyment of audiovisual content. Different approaches were identified, considered relevant within the research context. The classification of emotions, their origins, and mapping based on fMRI are present in most of the 56 articles studied in depth. In addition, techniques based on artificial intelligence and machine learning were also identified. Such research points to an empirical approach aimed at developing and emulating emotions in computational systems.

In addition, a second aim of the systematic literature review was to identify research that used electroencephalography as a brain-machine interface to map emotions during the process of audiovisual enjoyment. Given the methodology adopted, the three scientific databases searched, and the time frame, no specific research on EEG as a BCI to identify or map emotions during the enjoyment of audiovisual content was identified.

One of the limitations and improvements for future work is the absence of results in the areas of affective computing and affective neuroscience. These are two areas with potential contributions to the topic, but with insignificant results in the methods used in this systematic review. It is possible that relevant studies have not been mapped due to the idiosyncrasies of these areas, especially in terms of the concepts and keywords used. Another limiting factor is the fact that some articles only have the summaries published online, leading to disqualification by the exclusion criteria. Finally, the number of researchers involved in the systematic review (three) was also a limiting factor, as more participants could help with decision-making, reducing some subjectivity still present in the application of inclusion and exclusion criteria.

For future work, it is suggested to carry out a systematic mapping (Scoping Review), a type of exploratory research that systematically maps the literature on a topic, identifying key concepts, theories, and sources of evidence that inform practice in the field. This is a broader approach than the SLR, allowing the inclusion of research outside of the central databases, while maintaining scientific rigor and the validity of data interpretation.

Acknowledgments. This work was funded by the Public Call n. 03 Produtividade em Pesquisa PROPESQ/PRPG/UFPB proposal code PVL13414-2020.

References

1. Li, Y., Zheng, W., Zong, Y., Cui, Z., Zhang, T., Zhou, X.: A bi-hemisphere domain adversarial neural network model for EEG emotion recognition. IEEE Trans. Affect. Comput. **12**(2), 494–504 (2021). https://doi.org/10.1109/TAFFC.2018.2885474
2. Dattada, V.V.M., Jeevan, M.: Analysis of concealed anger emotion in a neutral speech signal. In: 2019 IEEE International Conference on Distributed Computing, VLSI, Electrical Circuits and Robotics (DISCOVER), pp. 1–5 (2019). https://doi.org/10.1109/DISCOVER47552.2019.9008037
3. Alimuradov, A.K., Tychkov, A.Y., Churakov, P.P.: A novel approach to speech signal segmentation based on empirical mode decomposition to assess human psycho-emotional state. In: 2019 3rd School on Dynamics of Complex Networks and their Application in Intellectual Robotics (DCNAIR), pp. 9–12 (2019). https://doi.org/10.1109/DCNAIR.2019.8875525
4. Mohammadi, G., Vuilleumier, P.: A multi-componential approach to emotion recognition and the effect of personality. IEEE Trans. Affect. Comput. **13**(3), 1127–1139 (2022). https://doi.org/10.1109/TAFFC.2020.3028109
5. Hortensius, R., Hekele, F., Cross, E.S.: The perception of emotion in artificial agents. IEEE Trans. Cogn. Dev. Syst. **10**(4), 852–864 (2018)
6. Farahani, F.S., Sheikhan, M., Farrokhi, A.: A fuzzy approach for face emotion recognition. In: 2013 13th Iranian Conference on Fuzzy Systems (IFSC) (2013). It hurts. https://doi.org/10.1109/IFSC.2013.6675597
7. Rakshit, R., Reddy, V.R., Deshpande, P.: Emotion detection and recognition using HRV features derived from photoplethysmogram signals. In: Proceedings of the 2nd Workshop on Emotion Representations and Modeling for Companion Systems (ERM4CT 2016), pp. 1–6. Association for Computing Machinery, New York (2016). Article 2. https://doi.org/10.1145/3009960.3009962
8. Gjoreski, H., et al.: emteqPRO: face-mounted mask for emotion recognition and affective computing. In: Adjunct Proceedings of the 2021 ACM International Joint Conference on Pervasive and Ubiquitous Computing and Proceedings of the 2021 ACM International Symposium on Wearable Computers (UbiComp 2021), pp. 23–25. Association for Computing Machinery, New York (2021). https://doi.org/10.1145/3460418.3479276
9. Chao, L., Tao, J., Yang, M., Li, Y., Wen, Z.: Long short term memory recurrent neural network based multimodal dimensional emotion recognition. In: Proceedings of the 5th International Workshop on Audio/Visual Emotion Challenge (AVEC 2015), pp. 65–72. Association for Computing Machinery, New York (2015). https://doi.org/10.1145/2808196.2811634
10. Bryant, D., Howard, A.: A comparative analysis of emotion-detecting AI systems with respect to algorithm performance and dataset diversity. In: Proceedings of the 2019 AAAI/ACM Conference on AI, Ethics, and Society (AIES 2019), pp. 377–382. Association for Computing Machinery, New York (2019). https://doi.org/10.1145/3306618.331428411
11. Hassan, S.A., Akbar, S., Rehman, A., Saba, T., Kolivand, H., Bahaj, S.A.: Recent developments in detection of central serous retinopathy through imaging and artificial intelligence techniques–a review. IEEE Access **9**, 168731–168748 (2021). https://doi.org/10.1109/ACCESS.2021.3108395
12. Djavanshir, G.R., Chen, X., Yang, W.: A review of artificial intelligence's neural networks (deep learning) applications in medical diagnosis and prediction. IT Prof. **23**(3), 58–62 (2021). https://doi.org/10.1109/MITP.2021.3073665.10
13. Valenza, G., Citi, L., Lanata, A., Scilingo, E.P., Barbieri, R.: A nonlinear heartbeat dynamics model approach for personalized emotion recognition. In: 2013 35th Annual International Conference of the IEEE Engineering in Medicine and Biology Society (EMBC), pp. 2579–2582 (2013). https://doi.org/10.1109/EMBC.2013.6610067

14. Kim, D.H., Seo, D.S.: Vector based 3D emotion expression for emotion robot. In: Proceedings of the 5th International Conference on Mechatronics and Robotics Engineering (ICMRE 2019), pp. 113–117. Association for Computing Machinery, New York (2019). https://doi.org/10.1145/3314493.3314499
15. Faita, C., Vanni, F., Tanca, C., Ruffaldi, E., Carrozzino, M., Bergamasco, M.: Investigating the process of emotion recognition in immersive and non-immersive virtual technological setups. In: Proceedings of the 22nd ACM Conference on Virtual Reality Software and Technology (VRST 2016), pp. 61–64. Association for Computing Machinery, New York (2016). https://doi.org/10.1145/2993369.2993395
16. Menezes, M.L.R., et al.: Towards emotion recognition for virtual environments: an evaluation of eeg features on benchmark dataset. Pers. Ubiquit. Comput. **21**(6), 1003–1013 (2017). https://doi.org/10.1007/s00779-017-1072-7
17. Chao, L., Tao, J., Yang, M., Li, Y., Wen, Z.: Multi-scale temporal modeling for dimensional emotion recognition in video. In: Proceedings of the 4th International Workshop on Audio/Visual Emotion Challenge (AVEC 2014), pp. 11–18. Association for Computing Machinery, New York (2014). https://doi.org/10.1145/2661806.2661811
18. Jiang, H., Deng, Z., Xu, M., He, X., Mao, T., Wang, Z.: An emotion evolution based model for collective behavior simulation. In: Proceedings of the ACM SIGGRAPH Symposium on Interactive 3D Graphics and Games (I3D 2018), pp. 1–6. Association for Computing Machinery, New York (2018). Article 10. https://doi.org/10.1145/3190834.3190844
19. Horlings, R., Datcu, D., Rothkrantz, L.J.M.: Emotion recognition using brain activity. In: Proceedings of the 9th International Conference on Computer Systems and Technologies and Workshop for PhD Students in Computing (CompSysTech 2008), pp. II.1–1. Association for Computing Machinery, New York (2008). Article 6. https://doi.org/10.1145/1500879.1500888
20. Ma, J., Tang, H., Zheng, W.-L., Lu, B.-L.: Emotion recognition using multimodal residual LSTM network. In: Proceedings of the 27th ACM International Conference on Multimedia (MM 2019), pp. 176–183. Association for Computing Machinery, New York (2019). https://doi.org/10.1145/3343031.3350871
21. Zhao, M., Adib, F., Katabi, D.: Emotion recognition using wireless signals. Commun. ACM **61**(9), 91–100 (2018). https://doi.org/10.1145/3236621
22. Huang, Z., Dong, M., Mao, Q., Zhan, Y.: Speech emotion recognition using CNN. In: Proceedings of the 22nd ACM International Conference on Multimedia (MM 2014), pp. 801–804. Association for Computing Machinery, New York (2014). https://doi.org/10.1145/2647868.2654984
23. Liogienė, T., Tamulevičius, G.: SFS feature selection technique for multistage emotion recognition. In: 2015 IEEE 3rd Workshop on Advances in Information, Electronic and Electrical Engineering (AIEEE), pp. 1–4 (2015). https://doi.org/10.1109/AIEEE.2015.7367299
24. Wei, G., Jian, L., Mo, S.: Multimodal (audio, facial and gesture) based emotion recognition challenge. In: 2020 15th IEEE International Conference on Automatic Face and Gesture Recognition (FG 2020), pp. 908–911 (2020). https://doi.org/10.1109/FG47880.2020.00142
25. Sokolov, D., Patkin, M.: Real-time emotion recognition on mobile devices. In: 2018 13th IEEE International Conference on Automatic Face & Gesture Recognition (FG 2018), p. 787 (2018). https://doi.org/10.1109/FG.2018.00124
26. Keshari, T., Palaniswamy, S.: Emotion recognition using feature-level fusion of facial expressions and body gestures. In: 2019 International Conference on Communication and Electronics Systems (ICCES), pp. 1184–1189 (2019). https://doi.org/10.1109/ICCES45898.2019.9002175

27. Gonuguntla, V., Kim, J.-H.: EEG-based functional connectivity representation using phase locking value for brain network based applications. In: 2020 42nd Annual International Conference of the IEEE Engineering in Medicine & Biology Society (EMBC), pp. 2853–2856 (2020). https://doi.org/10.1109/EMBC44109.2020.9175397
28. Gümüslü, E., Barkana, D.E., Köse, H.: Emotion recognition using EEG and physiological data for robot-assisted rehabilitation systems. In: Companion Publication of the 2020 International Conference on Multimodal Interaction (ICMI 2020 Companion), pp. 379–387. Association for Computing Machinery, New York (2021). https://doi.org/10.1145/3395035.3425199
29. Gao, Z., Wang, S.: Emotion recognition from EEG signals using hierarchical Bayesian network with privileged information. In: Proceedings of the 5th ACM on International Conference on Multimedia Retrieval (ICMR 2015), pp. 579–582. Association for Computing Machinery, New York (2015). https://doi.org/10.1145/2671188.2749364
30. Yang, T., Huang, W., Toe, K.K.: Statistical modeling on motion trajectories for robotic laparoscopic surgery. In: 2017 39th Annual International Conference of the IEEE Engineering in Medicine and Biology Society (EMBC), pp. 4347–4350 (2017). https://doi.org/10.1109/EMBC.2017.8037818
31. Prajapati, S., Naika, C.L.S., Jha, S.S., Nair, S.B.: On rendering emotions on a robotic face. In: Proceedings of Conference on Advances In Robotics (AIR 2013), pp. 1–7. Association for Computing Machinery, New York (2013). https://doi.org/10.1145/2506095.2506151
32. Bekele, E., et al.: Multimodal adaptive social interaction in virtual environment (MASI-VR) for children with Autism spectrum disorders (ASD). In: 2016 IEEE Virtual Reality (VR), pp. 121–130 (2016). https://doi.org/10.1109/VR.2016.7504695
33. Gill, R., Singh, J.: A review of neuromarketing techniques and emotion analysis classifiers for visual-emotion mining. In: 2020 9th International Conference System Modeling and Advancement in Research Trends (SMART), pp. 103–108 (2020). https://doi.org/10.1109/SMART50582.2020.9337074
34. Schaat, S., et al.: Emotion in consumer simulations for the development and testing of recommendations for marketing strategies. In: Proceedings of the 3rd Workshop on Emotions and Personality in Personalized Systems 2015 (EMPIRE 2015), pp. 25–32. Association for Computing Machinery, New York (2015). https://doi.org/10.1145/2809643.2809649
35. Sivagnanam, S., Yoshimoto, K., Carnevale, N.T., Majumdar, A.: The neuroscience gateway: enabling large scale modeling and data processing in neuroscience. In: Proceedings of the Practice and Experience on Advanced Research Computing (PEARC 2018), pp. 1–7. Association for Computing Machinery, New York (2018). Article 52. https://doi.org/10.1145/3219104.3219139
36. Guzzi, J., Giusti, A., Gambardella, L.M., Di Caro, G.A.: A model of artificial emotions for behavior-modulation and implicit coordination in multi-robot systems. In: Proceedings of the Genetic and Evolutionary Computation Conference (GECCO 2018), pp. 21–28. Association for Computing Machinery, New York (2018). https://doi.org/10.1145/3205455.3205650
37. Garcia, D., Schweitzer, F.: Modeling online collective emotions. In: Proceedings of the 2012 Workshop on Data-Driven User Behavioral Modeling and Mining from Social Media (DUBMMSM 2012), pp. 37–38. Association for Computing Machinery, New York (2012). https://doi.org/10.1145/2390131.2390147
38. Saini,T.S., Bedekar, M., Zahoor, S.: Circle of emotions in life: emotion mapping in 2dimensions. In: Proceedings of the 9th International Conference on Computer and Automation Engineering (ICCAE 2017), pp. 83–88. Association for Computing Machinery, New York (2017). https://doi.org/10.1145/3057039.3057046
39. Kata, G., Poleszak, W.: Cognitive functioning and safety determinants in the work of a train drivers. Acta Neuropsychologica **19**(2), 279–291 (2021). https://doi.org/10.5604/01.3001.0014.9958

40. Madlenak, R., Masek, J., Madlenakova, L.: An experimental analysis of the driver's attention during train driving. Open Eng. **10**(1), 64–73 (2020). https://doi.org/10.1515/eng-2020-0011
41. Suzuki, D., Yamauchi, K., Matsuura, S.: Effective visual behavior of railway drivers for recognition of extraordinary events. Q. Rep. RTRI **60**, 286–291 (2019). https://doi.org/10.2219/rtriqr.60.4_286
42. Silversmith, D., et al.: Plug-and-play control of a brain–computer interface through neural map stabilization. Nat. Biotechnol. **39**(3), 326–335 (2021)
43. Zeng, Y., Sun, K., Lu, E.: Declaration on the ethics of brain–computer interfaces and augment intelligence. AI Ethics **1**(3), 209–211 (2021). https://doi.org/10.1007/s43681-020-00036-x
44. Wanga, C., Yi, H., Wang, W., Valliappan, P.: Lesion location algorithm of high-frequency epileptic signal based on Teager energy operator **47**, 262–275 (2019). ISSN: 1746-8094. https://www.sciencedirect.com/science/article/abs/pii/S1746809418302313
45. Saesa, M., Meskers, C.G.M., Daffertshofer, A., van Wegen, E.E.H., Kwakkel, G.: Are early measured resting-state EEG parameters predictive for upper limb engine impairment six months poststroke? **132**(1), 56–62 (2021). ISSN: 1388-2457. https://doi.org/10.1016/j.clinph.2020.09.031
46. Martin, C.W. (ed.): The Philosophy of Deception, 1st edn, pp. 3–11. Oxford University Press on Demand (2013). ISBN: 9780195327939
47. Yap, C.H., et al.: 3D-CNN for facial micro-and macro-expression spotting on long video sequences using temporal oriented reference frame. In: Proceedings of the 30th ACM International Conference on Multimedia (MM 2022), pp. 7016–7020. Association for Computing Machinery, New York (2022). https://doi.org/10.1145/3503161.3551570
48. Reddy, S.P.T., Karri, S.T., Dubey, S.R., Mukherjee, S.: Spontaneous facial micro-expression recognition using 3D spatiotemporal convolutional neural networks. In: 2019 International Joint Conference on Neural Networks (IJCNN), pp. 1–8 (2019). https://doi.org/10.1109/IJCNN.2019.8852419
49. Romero,K., Yumi, E., Camargo, S., Ferrari, F.: Systematic Review of Literature in Software Engineering Theory and Practice. 1st edn. LTC (2017). ISBN: 9788535286410
50. Tarozzi, M.: What is grounded theory? Research methodology and theory based on the data. Translation by Carmem Lussi. Petrópolis: Voices (2011)

Arrow2edit: A Technique for Editing Text on Smartphones

Mattia De Rosa(✉), Vittorio Fuccella, Gennaro Costagliola, Maria Giovanna Albanese, Francesco Galasso, and Lorenzo Galasso

Department of Informatics, University of Salerno, Via Giovanni Paolo II, 84084 Fisciano, SA, Italy
{matderosa,vfuccella,gencos}@unisa.it

Abstract. We present Arrow2edit, a technique for efficient text editing on smartphones, based on the use of arrow soft buttons. Arrow2edit, after the user touches the text to place the cursor, displays keys with directional arrows that allow the user to move the cursor. The technique also allows selection/cut/copy/paste/undo operations using additional dedicated buttons.

The technique was compared, in a first experiment, to the standard Android technique. The results show that the Arrow2edit is in general more efficient than the standard Android technique, especially when the font size is small, with a 24% advantage on the overall time required. In a second experiment, Arrow2edit was compared to two different input methods: a soft keyboard with arrow keys and keys for select/cut/copy/paste operations, and a popular soft keyboard-based method that allows the cursor to be moved after a long press on the space bar. Also in this case the experimental results show that Arrow2edit is advantageous in terms of efficiency, but not in user preference.

Keywords: Text editing · Smartphone · Mobile User Experience · Mobile User Interfaces and Interaction Technologies · Human-Computer Interaction · Human Factors

1 Introduction

The use of touchscreen devices, especially smartphones, has rapidly increased in the last few years. People use these devices for all sorts of purposes, such as web browsing, chatting, reading documents, etc. Nowadays, most of the tasks that used to be performed only on computers need to be performed quickly and intuitively on mobile devices too. The most recent mobile devices in particular have large screens that cover their entire frontal surface, making it easy to perform tasks that involve direct manipulation. However, not all functionalities had a proper transition from one environment to the other. One of these is text editing, which benefits more from an indirect control method via mouse and/or keyboard. A common text editing task can be divided into three main operations: cursor placement, text selection, and clipboard operations. In a traditional

M. Kurosu and A. Hashizume (Eds.): HCII 2023, LNCS 14011, pp. 416–432, 2023.
https://doi.org/10.1007/978-3-031-35596-7_27

mouse/keyboard environment, the first two operations can be easily performed using the mouse, which allows for rapid cursor movement or text selection, and through the arrow keys, which allow the cursor to be moved one character at a time. As for operations on the clipboard, they can be performed through buttons or menus with the mouse or, more efficiently, with keyboard shortcuts.

On touchscreen mobile devices, the same techniques cannot be translated in a similar way. The finger, with its size, cannot be as accurate as a mouse pointer and suffers from obstruction, and this is especially evident with smaller font sizes. In addition, there is no shortcut for clipboard operations, since on a soft keyboard it would be difficult to perform key combinations. For these reasons, complex text editing is not a frequent activity on these devices. Text is typically entered with a soft keyboard, and the user moves the cursor simply by touching the desired position in the text with their finger. The use of arrow buttons in this situation can facilitate this operation, for example by allowing the user to move the cursor without having to touch precisely the intended screen location.

The purpose of this paper is to present and evaluate Arrow2edit, a technique designed to allow text editing in a simple and intuitive way, and based on the use of soft buttons for arrows and the most common editing operations. The approach is also separate from text input methods, thus allowing the use of any input method, including different types of soft keyboards [5,8–10,13,19]. An earlier version of the technique has been presented in [1].

This paper is organized this way: Sect. 2 describes related work on text editing; Sect. 3 describes Arrow2edit, while Sect. 4 and Sect. 5 its experimental evaluation. Section 6 concludes the paper with a discussion of what has been observed and comments on future work.

2 Related Work

Text editing research evolved with the introduction of the first graphical interfaces, starting with cut-and-paste techniques created in the 1970s. The exploration of further functionality was prompted by the growth in the level of sophistication of text editors [2,22,23].

More recently, researchers started investigating novel forms of interaction as a result of the widespread use of touchscreen devices. One of the earliest metaphors utilized was to imitate the use of paper, while in recent years several works in the field have addressed the issue of text editing on mobile devices.

A more efficient method for cursor positioning, especially with smaller fonts, was proposed in [11] with simple gestures performed on top of the soft keyboard, which can also be used for selection and clipboard operations. In [16] a method based on shortcuts was proposed: after a long press on a key, the method extracts all the words containing the respective letter and places them on a list above the keyboard. By selecting the desired word, the cursor will automatically jump to that specific position, right before the letter corresponding to the initial key. With a one-handed use, this proved to be faster than Gboard [13] and as fast as the traditional handle method, while also being less prone to errors. In [24] the author proposed the use of a virtual stick, located on the bottom of the screen, to control a pointer. The overall results were slower than the traditional method, but with smaller fonts and short pointing distances there was no difference.

TextPin [14] allows text selection by presenting a handle that can be moved freely and locked in place at any time. After locking it, another handle appears, which can be used to control the other end of the selection. This method proved to be faster, but the overall accuracy was the same as the traditional one. A complementary method to use in addition to the traditional one is Gaze 'n Touch [21]. This method uses eye tracking to select the text to highlight. The selection begins when the user presses a button and ends when they release it. This proved to be more efficient with larger fonts.

Gestures are often proposed to facilitate clipboard operations. BezelCopy [4] is a cross-application copy-paste technique based on gestures that start on the bezel of the device and continue on the touch screen. Although the results proved that a full copy-paste operation is twice as fast as one with the traditional method, nowadays it can be incompatible with navigational gestures in the most recent Android versions. Gedit [28] relies on-keyboard gestures and is 17–24% faster when compared to the default interaction. TouchTap [12] allow gestures on the keyboard of multi-touch devices and showed a slight advantage in mean task completion time. A similar gesture-based technique was proposed in [6,7], but in this case, it was independent from the input method, with gestures performed directly on the text, making the task easier and more precise with bigger font sizes. In [17], instead, a study was conducted focusing on the execution of various shortcuts via gestures on the device surface. Although this only works on fully touch-sensitive smartphones, this proved to be as intuitive and faster than the most common methods used today. Eloquent [15] aims to improve the traditional method to make it more understandable and comfortable, with functions such as a permanent handle for cursor dragging, an inline text magnifier, and a non-hierarchical menu for operations. Finally, voice commands can also be used for text editing and/or text replacement, as shown in [29]. This method proved to be slightly better in completion time than the touch-only traditional method.

Commercial smartphones basically use the editing techniques of the two major mobile operating systems-Android and iOS. For cursor positioning, on Android, the user can tap on the text to move the cursor and cause a handle to appear, which can be used to adjust the position of the cursor by dragging it to the desired location; iOS offers a similar way to move the cursor, with the addition of a magnifying glass that shows the portion of text under the finger. In addition, on iOS the user can move the cursor by long-pressing the space key on the soft keyboard, and then, without raising the finger, moving it in the desired direction. Such functionality in Android depends on the soft keyboard. Some provide functionality similar to that of iOS (e.g. Samsung Keyboard, SwiftKey [19]) or are limited to horizontal (but not vertical) movement (e.g., Gboard [13] by Google), while others allow moving the cursor through arrow keys, placed either on the main keyboard layout (e.g. Hacker's Keyboard [26]) or on a separate layout (e.g. Technical Keyboard [20] or Samsung Keyboard). Regarding text selection, the traditional method on Android and iOS devices involves holding down or double-tapping on a word, after which the user can reposition the beginning and end of the selection by moving the provided handles. The iOS keyboard and some Android soft keyboards also allow users to select text in a manner similar to cursor movement. Finally, in the traditional method, cut/copy/paste operations are performed via the menu that appears after text selection. In addition, some soft keyboards also provide dedicated selection/cut/copy/paste keys, usually in a separate layout (e.g. Samsung Keyboard, AnySoftKeyboard [9]).

3 Arrow2edit

Arrow2edit was mainly designed to simplify the process of placing the cursor precisely within the text. With the touch of a finger on the text, directional arrow soft keys appear on the screen that can be used to move the cursor to the desired location, eliminating the need for multiple taps until the cursor is at the desired position. This can be particularly useful when dealing with small font sizes, which can make it challenging to accurately position the cursor (thick-finger problem). Arrow2edit is also immediately visible (and so discoverable by the user), unlike the cursor movement allowed by a long press of the space bar on some soft keyboard, and it is also closer to the text to be edited.

In addition to cursor positioning, Arrow2edit also enables basic editing operations. In fact, a button has been incorporated to make text selection easier. When pressed, it starts the selection process from the current cursor position, and the user can either tap elsewhere on the screen or use the arrow soft keys to move the cursor and select the desired text range between the starting and ending cursor positions.

Moreover, the copy and cut buttons are shown when text has been selected, and the paste button is available when there is text on the clipboard. This allows for quicker access to these functions, e.g. compared to the traditional Android method where one has to wait for a menu to appear or call it up by touching the cursor handle. Another button allows the user to hide the interface if it covers any portion of the text they want to access. Finally, in addition to the version presented in [1], buttons to undo the last operation and to move the interface have been added, and the initial positioning of the interface has been improved.

The technique is based on standard Android one and does not disable any existing functions. For instance, it remains possible to select a whole word with a long press. The technique is demonstrated in the screenshots of Fig. 1. We decided not to mandate a specific input method for deletion and text entry, but to use the system's default input method (in our tests a soft keyboard with the backspace key for deleting characters).

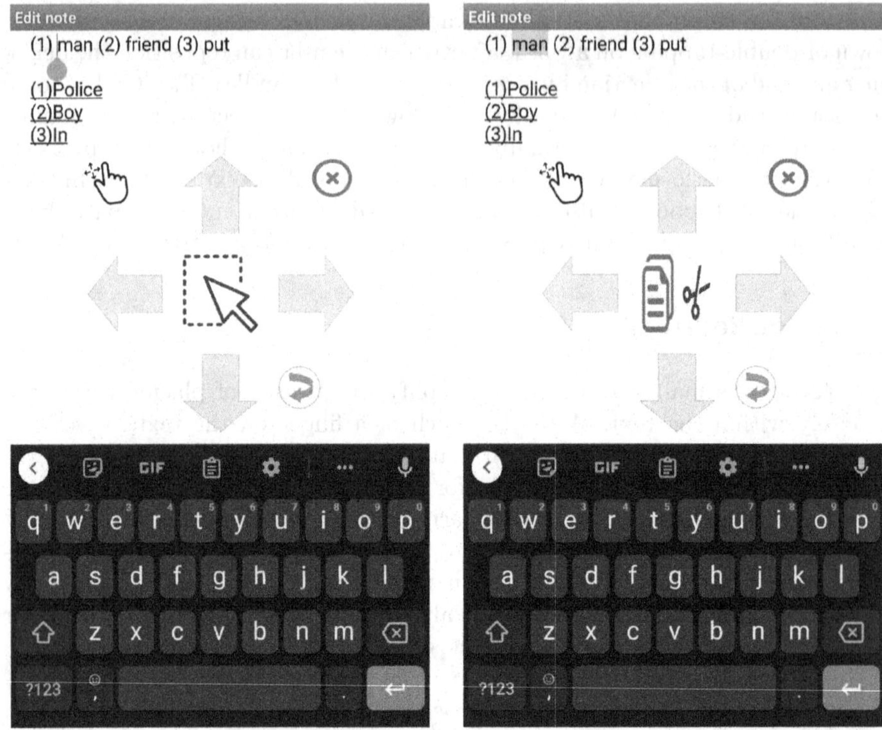

Fig. 1. The Arrow2edit interface: immediately after a touch on the left and after text selection on the right. The arrows allow the user to move the cursor, the hand to move the interface, the ⊗ to hide it, and the ⟲ icon to undo the last operation. In the center, buttons for selection, paste, copy, and cut operations are displayed based on the current state.

4 First User Study

To test the effectiveness of Arrow2edit, we first compared it with one of the standard mobile device text editing techniques and recorded information about participants' performance on various editing tasks. Specifically, we compared it with the standard Android text editing technique, implemented by the EditText widget, which allows to:

1. Move the cursor to the desired position with a single tap. Moreover, the cursor can be moved by dragging the handle that appears below it. Tapping on the handle displays a menu above it with the paste button.
2. Selecting a word by long-pressing or double-tapping on it. Once selected, the selection can be enlarged/reduced by dragging the handles at the left/right of the selection. Also, after selection, the cut, copy, and paste buttons become available in a menu that appears directly above the selected text

3. Delete the character that precedes the cursor (or the selected text) by using the backspace key on the soft keyboard.
4. Drag the selected text to the desired location to move it.

4.1 Methods

Participants. For the study, we recruited 16 participants (6 female) aged 20 to 56 years (mean 27.6 years, standard deviation 10.7). Fourteen were university students and two were senior workers, all of whom agreed to participate for free.

They all already had extensive experience with smartphones and used theirs daily. We asked them how often they perform text editing tasks on their smartphones and found that they rarely performed text editing, with most just performing occasional copy-paste. Moreover, all participants reported having at least average English knowledge. We considered this level sufficient to perform English text editing tasks.

Apparatus. The experiment was carried out on a Xiaomi Mi 10T Pro smartphone running Android 11. The touchscreen display is 6.67" in size with a resolution of 2340 × 1080 pixels.

The experimental software is an Android application that displays a list of tasks. Tapping on one of the list items starts the corresponding task in an editing view. After the user has completed the task, the item is highlighted in the list. The editing view uses either the classic editing technique (EditText Android Widget) or the Arrow2edit editing technique. A soft keyboard (with suggestions/autocompletion disabled and no editing functionalities) was used for text entry (allowing deletions with the backspace key). The task was considered not completed if the text still contained errors. However, the user had the option to abort the task (e.g. if they were no longer able to correct the text). In this case, the task was reset and restarted.

The software records all relevant user actions and records the completion time for each task. A task is considered completed when the current text is equal to the text defined in the task solution. When the task is completed, an *Android toast* with the completion time is displayed to the user.

Procedure. Before the start of the experiment, participants were asked to fill out a form with the following information: age, gender, experience in using smartphones and editing text on them, and English language proficiency. The experimental procedure was then explained to them.

Once the experimenter was satisfied that the subjects understood the experimental procedure, the experiment began. The experiment consisted of eight tasks in which the user had to correct the provided text; each task was repeated using both editing techniques. If a participant was unable to complete a task a failure was recorded and s/he had to repeat it. The experiment was divided into three blocks. The first block was used to train the user (not logged) and was

Table 1. Editing task list (in order to reduce table size, the task texts are only partially shown).

Task	Title	Description	Presented Text	Final Text
1	Delete character	Delete the X characters from the text	It was a lovely night, so warm that he threw his coat over his arm and did not evXen put his silk scarf round his throat. As he stroXlled home, smoking his ...	It was a lovely night, so warm that he threw his coat over his arm and did not even put his silk scarf round his throat. As he strolled home, smoking his ...
2	Delete word		It was a lovely night, so warm that he threw his coat over his arm and did not even put his silk scarf XXXXXX round his throat. As he strolled home, smoking his ...	It was a lovely night, so warm that he threw his coat over his arm and did not even put his silk scarf round his throat. As he strolled home, smoking his ...
3	Delete phrase		It was a lovely night, so warm that he threw his coat over his arm and did not even put his silk scarf round his throat. As he XXXXX XXXXX strolled home, smoking his ...	It was a lovely night, so warm that he threw his coat over his arm and did not even put his silk scarf round his throat. As he strolled home, smoking his ...
4	Move word	Move the highlighted words/phrases in the correct position (shown as a vertical bar)	It was a lovely night, so warm that he threw his coat over his arm and did not even put his silk scarf round his throat. As he strolled home, smoking his ...	It was a lovely night, so warm that he threw his coat over his arm and did not put even his silk scarf round his throat. As he strolled home, smoking his ...
5	Move phrase		He of them heard one whisper to the other, "That is Dorian Gray." He used to be when remembered how pleased he he was pointed out, or stared at, or talked about ...	He heard one of them whisper to the other, "That is Dorian Gray." He remembered how pleased he used to be when he was pointed out, or stared at, or talked about ...
6	Duplicate word	Copy the three words next to the words already there	(1) man (2) friend (3) put (1)Police (2)Boy (3)In	(1) man (2) friend (3) put (1)Policeman (2)Boyfriend (3)Input
7	Duplicate phrase	Copy the phrase between XXX at the bottom of the text	XXXIt was a lovely nightXXX, so warm that he threw his coat over his arm and did not even put his silk scarf round his throat. As he strolled home, smoking his ...	XXXIt was a lovely nightXXX, so warm that he threw his coat over his arm and did not even put his silk scarf round his throat. As he strolled home, smoking his ... It was a lovely night
8	Text correction	Fix the text	It was a lovely night, so warXm that he threw his coat over ... them whisper to the other, "That XXXX is Dorian Gray." ... Half the charm of the village where he had little been ...	It was a lovely night, so warm that he threw his coat over ... them whisper to the other, "That is Dorian Gray." ... Half the charm of the little village where he had been ...

done with the medium font size. Half of the users used the new editing technique first, followed by the classic editing technique, while the other half used the classic editing technique first. In the other two blocks, the actual experiment was carried out, each block with a different font size (small and medium).

The tasks are shown in Table 1. They were based on [7], an analysis of some works on the same topic [11,18,27], and considering the most important tasks related to the main editing operations that can be performed (at least partially) using Arrow2edit. The tasks can be divided into three main groups depending on the type of operations that are prevalent in them. The first group consists of intensive deletion tasks (1, 2, 3); the second group consists of intensive moving tasks (4, 5); the third group consists of intensive copy tasks; and task 8 is a mixed task.

At the end of the experiment, participants were asked to complete the System Usability Scale (SUS) questionnaire [3] for each of the two editing techniques. In addition, users' free comments and suggestions were also collected after the experiment. In fact, a free form field was provided where each participant could write their comments and suggestions about the techniques, as well as a checkbox where they could indicate if they would like to use the new technique.

Design. The experiment was a two-factor within-subjects design. The factors were text font size (small (7 pt) and medium (8.5 pt)) and editing technique (Arrow2edit, Classic). The font sizes were selected by choosing a comfortable size, and then adding a smaller size. The order of editing technique and font size was counterbalanced between participants as shown in Table 2.

The dependent variables were the overall task completion time (defined as the sum of the completion times of the eight tasks) and the number of failed tasks.

Table 2. Counterbalancing used during the experiment.

Participants	Font size order	Editing technique order
1, 5, 9, 13	small - medium	Arrow2edit - Classic
2, 6, 10, 14	medium - small	Arrow2edit - Classic
3, 7, 11, 15	small - medium	Classic - Arrow2edit
4, 8, 12, 16	medium - small	Classic - Arrow2edit

4.2 Results

All participants completed the experiment, which lasted approximately half an hour. Significance was tested using repeated measures analysis of variance (ANOVA) with alpha level set at 0.05.

Task Completion Time. The overall task completion times grouped by font size are shown in Fig. 2. Participants were faster with the Arrow2edit editing technique (129.9" vs 171.4"), with a bigger advantage for the small font (127.8" vs 176.1") compared to the medium font (132.0" vs 166.7"). The advantage decreases as the font size increases since in the classical technique it is easier to position the cursor when the font is larger.

ANOVA revealed a significant effect for the editing technique ($F_{1,15} = 12.519$, $p < .005$). The main effect of the font size on the overall task completion time was not statistically significant ($F_{1,15} = 0.195$, ns). The interaction effect between the two factors was also not statistically significant ($F_{1,15} = 1.174$, $p > .05$).

The overall mean completion times for each task are shown in Fig. 3. The Arrow2edit editing technique was almost always faster than the Classic technique, with task 2 (*delete word*) as the only exception (overall and for the small font size). In the case of the medium font instead, the classic technique was faster for tasks 2 and 3 (deletions) and task 6 (*duplicate word*), while the Arrow2edit technique was faster for the remaining five tasks (and especially the two move tasks).

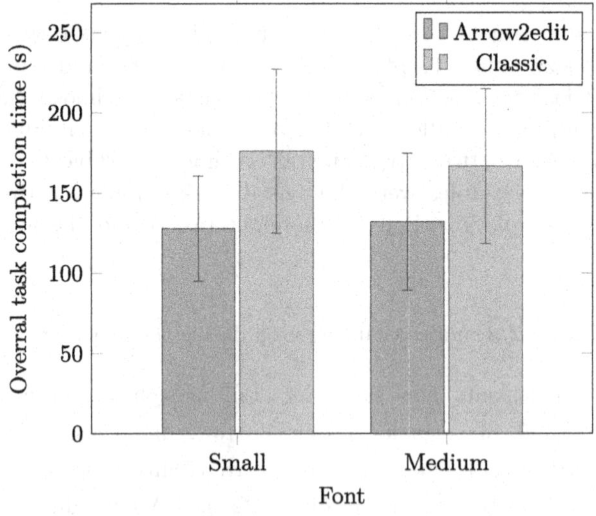

Fig. 2. First user study: mean overall task completion time for the two editing techniques, grouped by font size. Error bars show the standard deviation.

Failed Tasks. It resulted that participants failed slightly fewer tasks with the Arrow2edit editing technique than with the classic editing technique. In particular, the failed tasks were 3.1% (of the successful tasks) for the Arrow2edit technique (5.5% with small font size and 0.8% with medium font size), while 3.9% for the classic technique (3.9% with small font size and 3.9% with large

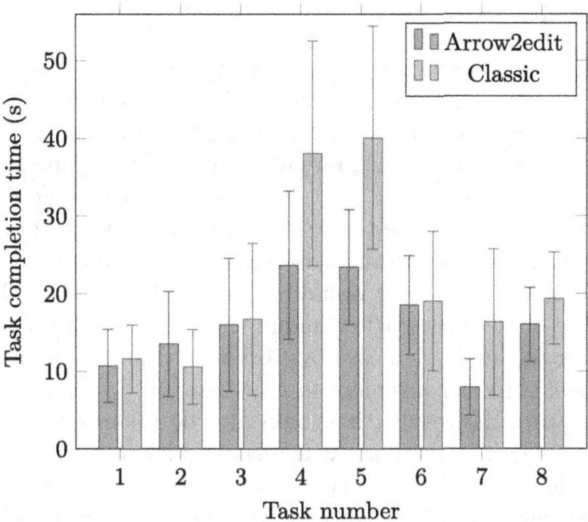

Fig. 3. First user study: mean task completion times (among both font sizes). Error bars show the standard deviation.

font size). Nevertheless, the ANOVA results showed no significant effects for the editing technique ($F_{1,15} = 0.111$, ns), the font size ($F_{1,15} = 1.709$, $p > .05$), or their interaction ($F_{1,15} = 4.355$, $p > .05$).

User Satisfaction and Free-form Comments. The average SUS score was 74.5 for the classic editing technique ($SD = 18.8$) and 72.7 ($SD = 20.5$) for the Arrow2edit editing technique. However, a Wilcoxon matched-pairs signed-ranks test [25] performed on SUS scores revealed no statistical significance between the two techniques ($z = -0.028$, $p > .05$). The difference in scores was mostly caused by two participants who gave very low scores to the Arrow2edit technique (in one case only 10 points out of 100, giving 100 to the classical technique instead), not liking the idea of not being allowed to use the classical technique anymore. When asked if they would like to use the Arrow2edit system, 11 participants said yes and 5 said no.

Among the things most appreciated by participants were the functionality for copy/cut-paste and the convenience of having the arrow buttons, although one would have liked the cursor to keep moving if one held down an arrow button, rather than having to press it multiple times. The most common criticism concerned the size of the buttons and icons, considered by some to be too large, with one participant not only asking for their size to be reduced but also suggesting that a text description be added for the buttons, rather than just the icons, for the sake of clarity.

4.3 Discussion

Participants noted that sometimes the technique interface occupies parts of the text that the user would like to tap on. In this case, the user can still hide or move the interface (or give up tapping and move the cursor with the arrows), but this requires an extra operation. Moreover, since, for example, in the classical technique it is possible to select a whole word with a single long press, some participants asked if it was possible to use the same functionality in the Arrow2edit technique. To make a proper comparison in our experiment we did not allow this possibility, but in real use it would be possible to allow simultaneous use of the functionality of the classical technique and the Arrow2edit technique, thus allowing the user to choose on a case-by-case basis which technique to use, based on what they feel is most convenient in that case.

When evaluating the results, it should also be taken into account that the participants were already familiar with classic editing techniques and had to learn the new one. With more experience, we expect even more favorable results for Arrow2edit. Nevertheless, all participants showed a rapid learning process.

5 Second User Study

Given the positive results of the first experiment, we performed a second similar experiment, in which we compared Arrow2edit to two other techniques:

1. a soft keyboard, that in the following we will call FunctKeyboard (Fig. 4), with arrow keys and keys for select/cut/copy/paste operations in an additional row of the keyboard, that is based on AnySoftKeyboard [9];
2. the SwiftKey [19] soft keyboard (Fig. 5), which allows the cursor to be moved, after a long press on the space bar, by moving the finger in both horizontal and vertical directions. This technique is quite similar to that offered by the default iOS keyboard.

Fig. 4. FunctKeyboard: a soft keyboard with arrow/function keys.

Fig. 5. SwiftKey soft keyboard.

5.1 Methods

Participants. For the study, we recruited 12 participants (1 female) between 22 and 55 years old (mean 26.4, standard deviation 9.6), who had not already participated in the first study. They reported a similar experience as the participants in the first study with respect to smartphone use and text editing, and also with respect to English proficiency.

Apparatus. The experiment was carried out on a device and with software similar to those in the first user study, except that in this case, in addition to Arrow2edit, two additional editing modes were provided, based on the use of the SwiftKey and FunctKeyboard soft keyboards, respectively (in both cases with the standard Android EditText widget).

Procedure. The procedure used is similar to that of the first user study, except that the three editing methods described above were tested. In addition, we decided to add an additional font size (large) and a ninth task, "delete all text", in order to compare that operation as well. Participants were asked to fill out a SUS questionnaire for each of the three editing techniques and indicate their preferred technique.

Design. The experiment was a two-factor within-subjects design. The factors were text font size (small (7 pt), medium (8.5 pt), large (11.3 pt)), and editing technique (Arrow2edit, FunctKeyboard, SwiftKey). The order of editing techniques and font sizes was counterbalanced between participants.

The dependent variables were the overall task completion time (defined as the sum of the completion times of the nine tasks) and the number of failed tasks.

5.2 Results

All participants completed the experiment, which lasted approximately an hour. Significance was tested using repeated measures analysis of variance (ANOVA) with alpha level set at 0.05.

Task Completion Time. The overall task completion times grouped by font size are shown in Fig. 6. Participants were faster with Arrow2edit (148.1"), followed by FunctKeyboard (160.5") and SwiftKey (182.1"). Also in this case Arrow2edit had the advantage with the small font and the medium font sizes, but with the larger font size FunctKeyboard was faster.

From the ANOVA, it resulted that the effect of the editing technique was statistically significant ($F_{2,22} = 5.794$, $p < .01$). The main effect of the font size on the overall task completion time was not statistically significant ($F_{2,22} =$

2.252, $p > .05$). The interaction effect between the two factors was instead highly significant ($F_{4,44} = 9.258$, $p < .0001$).

The overall mean completion times for each task are shown in Fig. 7. Overall, Arrow2edit has a clear advantage on three tasks. Analyzing the results by font size, they differ strongly based on it. In fact, Arrow2edit was the fastest technique for the majority of tasks (5) in the small font case, in the medium font case each of the three techniques was the fastest on three tasks, and in the large font case FunctKeyboard was the fastest technique for the majority of tasks (5).

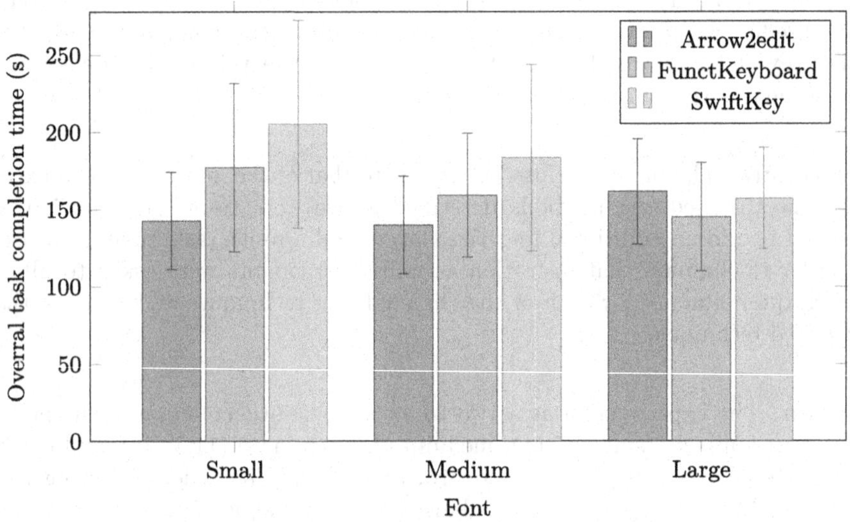

Fig. 6. Second user study: mean overall task completion time for the three editing techniques, grouped by font size. Error bars show the standard deviation.

User Satisfaction and Free-form Comments. The average SUS score was 76.9 for FunctKeyboard ($SD = 19.4$), 70.4 for Swiftkey ($SD = 20.1$), and 62.9 ($SD = 12.2$) for Arrow2edit ($SD = 12.2$). A Friedman test performed on SUS scores revealed statistical significance between the three techniques ($H(2) = 8.375$, $p < .05$). Post hoc tests (using Conover's F at $\alpha = .05$) revealed a significant difference between Arrow2edit and FunctKeyboard, and between Arrow2edit and SwiftKey. FunctKeyboard was also the most preferred technique, with 10 participants out of 12 choosing it, with most of them also stating that they would like to use it on their smartphone.

5.3 Discussion

Although Arrow2edit was the fastest technique among the three, some participants reported some problems while using it, especially because it covered part

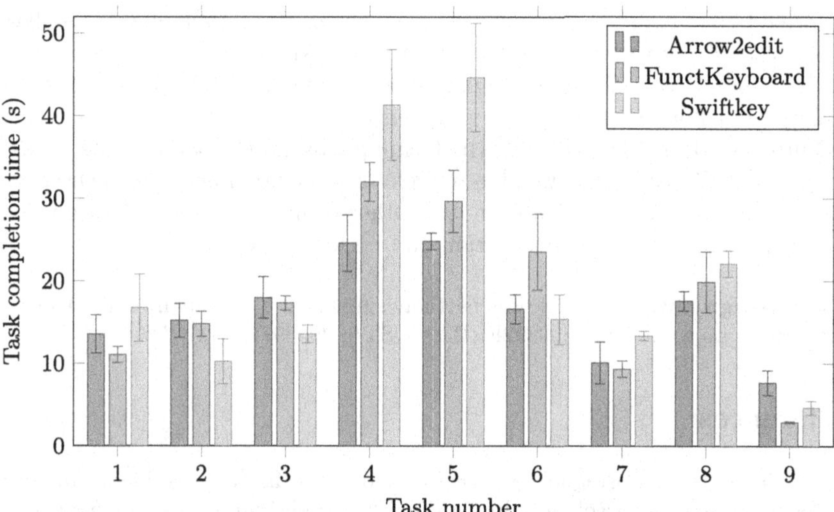

Fig. 7. Second user study: mean task completion times (among the three font sizes). Error bars show the standard deviation.

of the screen, in addition to the portion already covered by the soft keyboard, necessitating repositioning it or hiding it or the soft keyboard, especially with larger fonts. Nevertheless, the presence of soft keys to precisely adjust the position of the cursor was considered a very useful feature and a major advantage for Arrow2Edit and FunctKeyboard over the features of SwiftKey, which was considered less precise for selection operations and cursor placement, especially with smaller characters.

Regarding clipboard operations, we observed that, during the experiment, they proved to be more intuitive with Arrow2edit than with FunctKeyboard, mainly because the selection/cut/copy/paste operations were all shown in the center of the overlay and in sequence, following a familiar editing workflow. Instead, the fact that FunctKeyboard showed all possible operation buttons at all times confused some users (e.g., some tapped a cut/copy button without first activating the select operation). In addition, some users reported that although the presence of keys and buttons for text editing operations above the keyboard was a useful feature, they sometimes ended up mistakenly pressing nearby keys, failing the intended operation. For this reason, some users suggested adding an "undo" button, just like the one in Arrow2edit.

6 Conclusions and Further Works

This paper proposes Arrow2edit, a text editing technique that allows users to perform operations such as text deletion and copy/cut/paste more efficiently. A first user study was conducted to compare Arrow2edit with the classical technique. The results showed that the Arrow2edit editing technique generally outperformed the classic technique, especially when the text font was smaller. A second user study was also conducted, in which Arrow2edit was compared with FunctKeyboard and SwiftKey, again showing an advantage in terms of time required, but not in terms of user preference.

Future work includes refining the technique by taking participants' feedback into account. In particular, we plan to introduce the possibility for the user to use the features of both Arrow2edit and the other techniques to investigate whether this option improves user satisfaction and performance.

Acknowledgment. This work was partially supported by grants from the University of Salerno (grant numbers: 300392FRB20COSTA, 300392FRB21COSTA).

References

1. Albanese, M.G., Costagliola, G., De Rosa, M., Fuccella, V.: A technique to improve text editing on smartphones. In: 2022 IEEE Symposium on Visual Languages and Human-Centric Computing (VL/HCC), pp. 1–3 (2022). https://doi.org/10.1109/VL/HCC53370.2022.9833120
2. Borenstein, N.S.: The evaluation of text editors: a critical review of the Roberts and Morgan methodology based on new experiments. SIGCHI Bull. **16**(4), 99–105 (1985). https://doi.org/10.1145/1165385.317475
3. Brooke, J., et al.: SUS-a quick and dirty usability scale. Usability Eval. Ind. **189**(194), 4–7 (1996)
4. Chen, C., Perrault, S.T., Zhao, S., Ooi, W.T.: Bezelcopy: an efficient cross-application copy-paste technique for touchscreen smartphones. In: Proceedings of the 2014 International Working Conference on Advanced Visual Interfaces, AVI 2014, pp. 185–192. ACM, New York (2014). https://doi.org/10.1145/2598153.2598162
5. Costagliola, G., De Rosa, M., D'Arco, R., De Gregorio, S., Fuccella, V., Lupo, D.: C-QWERTY: a text entry method for circular smartwatches. In: The 25th International DMS Conference on Visualization and Visual Languages, pp. 51–57 (2019). https://doi.org/10.18293/DMSVIVA2019-014
6. Costagliola, G., De Rosa, M., Fuccella, V.: The design and evaluation of a text editing technique for stylus-based tablets. In: The 23rd International DMS Conference on Visual Languages and Sentient Systems, pp. 14–23 (2017). https://ksiresearch.org/seke/dms17paper/dms17paper_9.pdf
7. Costagliola, G., De Rosa, M., Fuccella, V.: A technique for improving text editing on touchscreen devices. J. Vis. Lang. Comput. **47**, 1–8 (2018). https://doi.org/10.1016/j.jvlc.2018.04.002
8. Costagliola, G., De Rosa, M., Fuccella, V., Martin, B.: BubbleBoard: a zoom-based text entry method on smartwatches. In: Kurosu, M. (eds.) HCII 2022. LNCS, vol. 13303, pp. 14–27. Springer, Cham (2022). https://doi.org/10.1007/978-3-031-05409-9_2
9. Danan, M.E.: Anysoftkeyboard. https://anysoftkeyboard.github.io
10. De Rosa, M., et al.: T18: an ambiguous keyboard layout for smartwatches. In: 2020 IEEE International Conference on Human-Machine Systems (ICHMS), pp. 1–4 (2020). https://doi.org/10.1109/ICHMS49158.2020.9209483

11. Fuccella, V., Isokoski, P., Martin, B.: Gestures and widgets: performance in text editing on multi-touch capable mobile devices. In: Proceedings of the SIGCHI Conference on Human Factors in Computing Systems, CHI 2013, pp. 1–10. ACM, New York (2013). https://doi.org/10.1145/2470654.2481385
12. Fuccella, V., Martin, B.: Touchtap: a gestural technique to edit text on multi-touch capable mobile devices. In: Proceedings of the 12th Biannual Conference on Italian SIGCHI Chapter, CHItaly 2017, pp. 21:1–21:6. ACM, New York (2017). https://doi.org/10.1145/3125571.3125579
13. Google: Gboard - the google keyboard. https://play.google.com/store/apps/details?id=com.google.android.inputmethod.latin
14. Huan, W., Tu, H., Li, Z.: Enabling finger pointing based text selection on touch-screen mobile devices. In: Proceedings of the Seventh International Symposium of Chinese CHI, Chinese CHI 2019, pp. 93–96. Association for Computing Machinery, New York (2019). https://doi.org/10.1145/3332169.3332172
15. Jenson, S., Bau, O.: Eloquent: improving text editing for mobile. In: Adjunct Proceedings of the 34th Annual ACM Symposium on User Interface Software and Technology, UIST 2021 Adjunct, pp. 92–94. Association for Computing Machinery, New York (2021). https://doi.org/10.1145/3474349.3480178
16. Lai, J., Rajabi, N., Javadi, E.: A shortcut for caret positioning on touch-screen phones. In: Proceedings of the 21st International Conference on Human-Computer Interaction with Mobile Devices and Services, MobileHCI 2019. Association for Computing Machinery, New York (2019). https://doi.org/10.1145/3338286.3340146
17. Le, H.V., Mayer, S., Weiß, M., Vogelsang, J., Weingärtner, H., Henze, N.: Shortcut gestures for mobile text editing on fully touch sensitive smartphones. ACM Trans. Comput.-Hum. Interact. **27**(5) (2020). https://doi.org/10.1145/3396233
18. Leiva, L.A., Alabau, V., Romero, V., Toselli, A.H., Vidal, E.: Context-aware gestures for mixed-initiative text editing UIS. Interact. Comput. **27**(6), 675 (2015). https://doi.org/10.1093/iwc/iwu019
19. Microsoft: Microsoft swiftkey keyboard. https://www.microsoft.com/en-us/swiftkey
20. NextApp: Technical keyboard. https://play.google.com/store/apps/details?id=nextapp.inputmethod.latin
21. Rivu, R., Abdrabou, Y., Pfeuffer, K., Hassib, M., Alt, F.: Gaze'n'touch: enhancing text selection on mobile devices using gaze. In: Extended Abstracts of the 2020 CHI Conference on Human Factors in Computing Systems, CHI EA 2020, pp. 1–8. Association for Computing Machinery, New York (2020). https://doi.org/10.1145/3334480.3382802
22. Roberts, T.L.: Evaluation of computer text editors. Ph.D. thesis, Stanford University, Stanford, CA, USA (1980)
23. Roberts, T.L., Moran, T.P.: The evaluation of text editors: methodology and empirical results. Commun. ACM **26**(4), 265–283 (1983). https://doi.org/10.1145/2163.2164
24. Scheibel, J.B., Pierson, C., Martin, B., Godard, N., Fuccella, V., Isokoski, P.: Virtual stick in caret positioning on touch screens. In: Proceedings of the 25th Conference on L'Interaction Homme-Machine, IHM 2013, pp. 107:107–107:114. ACM, New York (2013). https://doi.org/10.1145/2534903.2534918
25. Siegel, S.: Nonparametric Statistics for the Behavioral Sciences. McGraw-Hill, New York (1956)
26. Weidner, K.: Hacker's keyboard. https://github.com/klausw/hackerskeyboard

27. Wolf, C.G., Morrel-Samuels, P.: The use of hand-drawn gestures for text editing. Int. J. Man Mach. Stud. **27**(1), 91–102 (1987). https://doi.org/10.1016/S0020-7373(87)80045-7
28. Zhang, M., Wobbrock, J.O.: Gedit: keyboard gestures for mobile text editing. In: Proceedings of Graphics Interface 2020, GI 2020, pp. 470–473. Canadian Human-Computer Communications Society (2020). https://doi.org/10.20380/GI2020.47
29. Zhao, M., Cui, W., Ramakrishnan, I., Zhai, S., Bi, X.: Voice and touch based error-tolerant multimodal text editing and correction for smartphones. In: The 34th Annual ACM Symposium on User Interface Software and Technology, UIST 2021, pp. 162–178. Association for Computing Machinery, New York (2021). https://doi.org/10.1145/3472749.3474742

A Comparison of Finger, Stylus and Mouse in Trajectory Tracing Task Execution on Touchscreen Mobile Devices

Valentina Ecimovic[1], Luka Skitarelic[1], Alen Salkanovic[1,2], and Sandi Ljubic[1,2(✉)]

[1] Faculty of Engineering, University of Rijeka, Vukovarska 58, 51000 Rijeka, Croatia
{valentina.ecimovic,luka.skitarelic,alen.salkanovic, sandi.ljubic}@riteh.hr

[2] Center for Artificial Intelligence and Cybersecurity, University of Rijeka, R. Matejcic 2, 51000 Rijeka, Croatia

Abstract. In this paper, we empirically investigate the performance of trajectory tracing on mobile touchscreen devices. Our main goal is to compare three different tracing modalities, two of which rely on direct touch (finger and stylus) and one on indirect interaction (mouse). We conducted an experiment involving 25 users and a specially designed mobile application for managing trajectory tracing tasks and touch events logging. We describe the outcomes of this empirical study, with particular emphasis on tracing time and tracing error on a touchscreen tablet. In addition, we also discuss the associated interaction workload, specifically targeting the physical demand, perceived performance and effort, and level of frustration when using different ways to trace the given path. Finally, we show how the obtained data can be used to develop predictive models for trajectory tracing time.

Keywords: trajectory tracing task · steering task · index of difficulty · curved path · predictive model · touchscreens

1 Background

Fitts' law [4] has revolutionized the field of Human-Computer Interaction (HCI) by enabling predictive modeling of point-and-select operations and platform-independent comparison of input/pointing devices. Numerous device evaluation studies have been conducted under the Fitts' law paradigm, eventually leading to ISO standardization of pointing device evaluation and useful heuristics for constructing Fitts-based models and conducting appropriate experiments [11].

A huge amount of research has led to the validation of Fitts' law and its corresponding derivatives in many application domains, including the touchscreen context [3,6]. However, while Fitts' law only applies to a specific type of motion (directional pointing, target acquisition), pointing devices are used for a wide range of alternative operations, such as drawing, writing, steering, and trajectory

M. Kurosu and A. Hashizume (Eds.): HCII 2023, LNCS 14011, pp. 433–449, 2023.
https://doi.org/10.1007/978-3-031-35596-7_28

tracing. A much smaller part of the research focuses on modeling the aforementioned operations and analyzing the effectiveness of the pointing devices during their execution. This paper contributes to this body of research by addressing the trajectory-tracing tasks performed with different input devices on modern touchscreens.

We build our research on the seminal work previously done by Accot and Zhai [1], wherein a theoretical model that quantifies the difficulty in generalized trajectory-based tasks is derived. Namely, the index of difficulty is formalized as the integral of the inverse of the width along the path:

$$\int_{C} \frac{ds}{W(s)} \tag{1}$$

In Eq. 1, C represents a given curved path, and W represents a width of the "tunnel" in which the steering is allowed. Although the model allows this tunnel to be of variable width along the line, we can, for the purpose of this research, assume that W is constant (see Fig. 1).

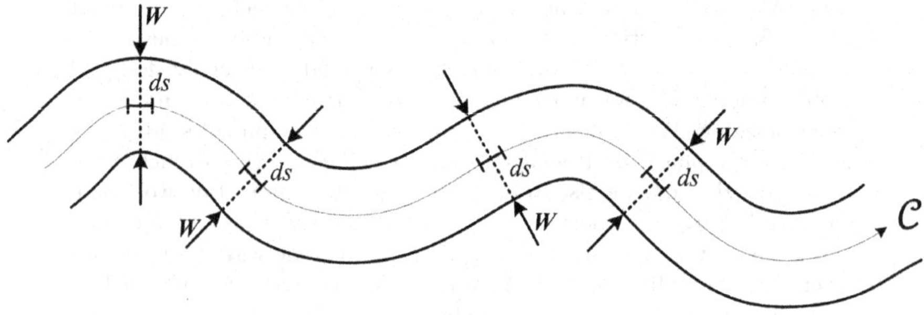

Fig. 1. A steering task with the given trajectory and a tunnel of constant width

Furthermore, we could further restrict the conditions of the steering task in such a way that we observe a tunnel with $W = 1$. This leads to a tunnel width equal to the nominal unit length of the screen on which the task is executed, e.g., one pixel. In this situation, the steering task essentially converts to a trajectory-tracing task (TTT), which requires reproducing the given trajectory without any deviations. At the same time, according to Eq. 1, the index of difficulty for such a task is directly determined by the length of the given trajectory, from the starting point a to the ending point b:

$$ID_{C} = \int_{a}^{b} ds = l(C) \tag{2}$$

Indeed, it is expected that more interaction time and effort should be invested in tracing a longer curve. In order to normalize the values of ID to a smaller range, we propose to introduce an additional constant c that appropriately scales the length of the given path. The value of the constant c can be chosen depending on the set of designed TTTs, the screen resolution, and the display density of the target device:

$$ID_{\mathcal{C}} = c \cdot \int_a^b ds = c \cdot l(\mathcal{C}) \tag{3}$$

We can use the polar coordinate system to formalize specific instances of tracing tasks. Namely, each point of a given trajectory is determined by a distance r from a reference point and an angle θ from a reference direction. The reason for using the polar coordinate system lies in the simpler mathematical representation of interesting tracing templates that can be utilized in empirical research. If the tracing task is determined by the curve $\mathcal{C}$, which in the polar system can be described by the function $r(\theta)$, then the length of that function is given by the following expression:

$$l(\mathcal{C}) = \int_{\varphi_1}^{\varphi_2} \sqrt{[r'(\theta)]^2 + [r(\theta)]^2}\, d\theta \tag{4}$$

To analyze the efficiency of performing a TTT, it is important to monitor and quantify the error that the user makes. Assume we have a given trajectory $r(\theta)$ that needs to be traced and a curved path $p(\theta)$ that the user actually drew. Using the polar coordinate system as a base, we can determine the tracing error in a particular part of the trajectory by calculating an offset for a corresponding angle θ_i (see Fig. 2).

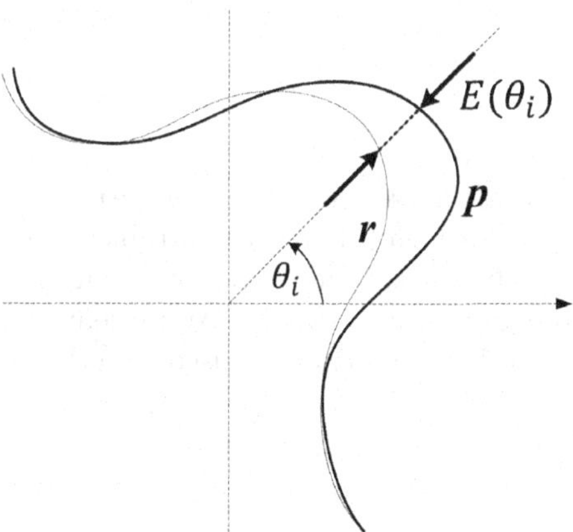

Fig. 2. Tracing error defined for a particular angle θ_i

The value of the tracing error corresponding to the specific angle θ_i is therefore calculated as:

$$E(\theta_i) = |r(\theta_i) - p(\theta_i)| \tag{5}$$

Assuming that altogether n points, making up the drawn trajectory $p(\theta)$, were registered during the execution of the tracing task, the average error can be obtained according to the following expression:

$$E = \frac{1}{n} \sum_{i=1}^{n} E(\theta_i) \tag{6}$$

The goal of this research is to empirically investigate the effectiveness of performing trajectory-tracing tasks on a touchscreen device, and, in doing so, to use the abovementioned TTT formalism in the corresponding experiment. We decided to compare a total of three tracing modalities: two of them being based on direct touch (finger and stylus), and one based on indirect interaction (mouse). Namely, each of the three mentioned devices (we call a finger a "device" here) provides a different level of occlusion, and thus a varying interaction burden and different speed-accuracy tradeoff [15] can be expected, when tracing is performed.

Regarding the related work in this context, Accot and Zhai evaluated five commonly used computer input devices, but the given tasks were from the steering domain (straight and circle tunnel), and no direct-touch modality was involved in their study [2]. On the other hand, Zabramski and coauthors [13,14] applied a similar idea using a touchscreen tablet, however in their research the trajectory-tracing tasks were not mathematically formalized, and the error calculation was based on a rougher discretization of the given shape. In our work, we wanted to explore the effect of trajectory ID in more detail, letting users try out tracing tasks of varying complexity. In doing so, we utilized trajectory templates of different shapes and lengths, defined by graphs of the corresponding polar functions.

2 Method

In this section, we describe a user study that empirically investigates the effectiveness of trajectory tracing on a touchscreen tablet. We conducted an experiment involving twenty-five users and a custom-built Android application for managing TTTs and logging touch events. We present full details of the tasks, participants, experiment design and devices used, and the procedure of the experiment.

2.1 Tasks

Regarding the experimental tasks, Table 1 summarizes TTT instances that were used in our research. Corresponding mathematical functions, as well as calculated ID values, are presented. Trajectory lengths were obtained using Eq. 4 and the $[0, 2\pi]$ angle domain, with the computations being performed utilizing the WolframAlpha platform [12]. ID values were calculated subsequently using Eq. 3, with a c value of 0.001.

Table 1. Formalization and classification of selected tracing tasks

$\mathcal{C}$	Polar function	$ID_{\mathcal{C}}$	Category
1	$r(\theta) = 250 - 100 \cdot sin(2\theta) \cdot cos(\theta)$	1.719	easy
2	$r(\theta) = 300$	1.885	
3	$r(\theta) = 150 \cdot (2 + 0.3 \cdot sin(2\theta))$	1.927	
4	$r(\theta) = 250 - 125 \cdot sin(4\theta) \cdot cos(\theta)$	2.195	medium
5	$r(\theta) = 300 - 80 \cdot sin(3\theta) \cdot cos(6\theta)$	2.490	
6	$r(\theta) = 200 + 200 \cdot sin(3\theta)$	2.899	
7	$r(\theta) = 85 \cdot (3 + 2 \cdot sin(6\theta) \cdot sin(3\theta)$	3.674	hard
8	$r(\theta) = 180 + 200 \cdot sin(6\theta)$	5.104	
9	$r(\theta) = 240 + 120 \cdot (sin(5\theta) + cos(10\theta))$	5.534	

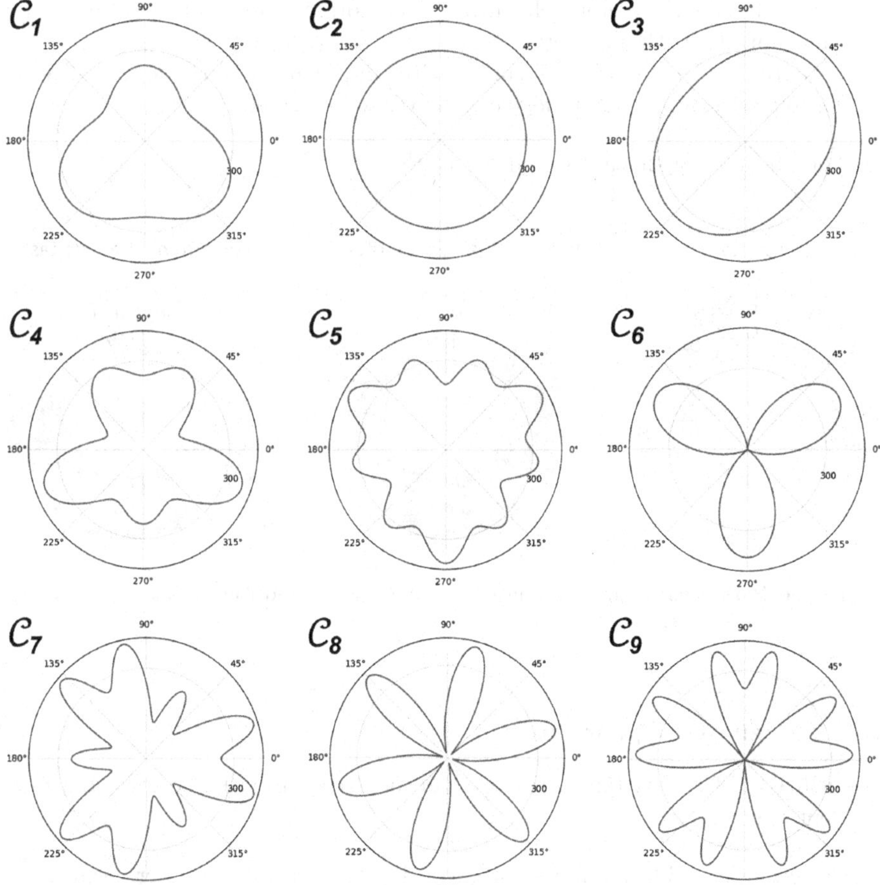

Fig. 3. Tracing tasks visualized in polar coordinate system. The three rows represent patterns from the easy, medium, and hard categories, respectively.

It can be seen that the selected TTTs are sorted by the increasing index of difficulty and distributed into three categories: easy ($ID < 2$), medium ($2 < ID < 3.5$), and hard ($ID > 3.5$). The layouts of all curves are shown in Fig. 3.

2.2 Participants

Twenty-five users have been involved in our empirical research (17 males, and 8 females). The participants' age varied from 21 to 44 years, with an average of 25.5 years ($SD = 7.5$). Only two of them were left-handed. The initial questionnaire revealed the following about the user sample:

- about one third of the participants own a tablet;
- there is no clear preference for a particular orientation (portrait, landscape) when working with a tablet;
- as many as 40% do not perform any drawing-related interaction at all when working with touchscreen devices (smartphone, tablet).

The above statistics are visualized in Fig. 4.

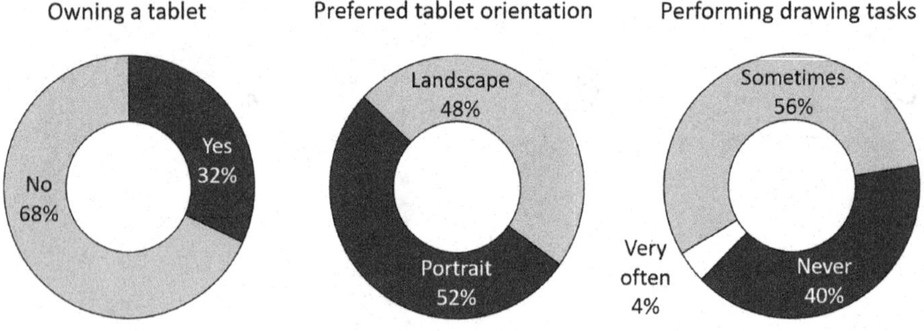

Fig. 4. Participant statistics related to tablet usage and touch-based drawing

2.3 Design and Apparatus

We utilized a 3×3 within-subjects experiment design with the following independent variables:

- *Device*: interaction modality for executing tracing tasks (finger, stylus, and mouse);
- *Complexity*: the tasks, i.e. trajectory templates come in three different levels, according to the corresponding ID values from Table 1 (easy, medium, hard).

The dependent variables were:

- Tracing time (i.e. task execution time): indicating how long does the user need for tracing the given trajectory;
- Tracing error: specifying how much the user deviates from the tracing template, according to the calculation in Eq. 6.

All experiment conditions were properly counterbalanced in order to avoid the learning effect [5]. The test application was implemented to randomly assign a cycle of nine trajectories with different ID values and record the corresponding metrics for each task execution in a log file. The automatic timing is based on monitoring the periods when contact with the touchscreen is active (or the mouse button is pressed). There are no additional distractions on the application screen, only the given trajectory template, so the user can easily focus her/his attention only on the unit task.

As for the testing hardware, we opted for a tablet device, namely the Lenovo Tab M10 HD running Android 10, with 10-inch IPS LCD display and a resolution of 800×1280. The physical dimensions of this device are $241.5 \times 149.4 \times 8.3$ mm, it weighs 420 g and has a display density of 149 ppi. The selected mouse was Trust GXT 108 RAVA, and the chosen stylus model was Adonit Jot Pro with a high-precision disc tip.

2.4 Procedure

After signing an informed consent form and completing the initial questionnaire (with general questions about tablet use and touch-based drawing), participants were briefed on the goals of the experiment. Participants were then shown an example of a typical trajectory-tracing task. To familiarize themselves with the physical devices (tablet, mouse, and stylus) as well as the experimental mobile application, participants were engaged in a practice session prior to the actual experiment. The practice session included three complete sequences of nine TTTs, each of which had to be performed with a different pointing device in no particular order.

In the actual experiment, users were instructed to complete a task cycle (i.e., the nine trajectories with different ID values) as quickly and accurately as possible and at a comfortable pace using the finger, stylus, and mouse. The order of pointing devices was predetermined for each participant to ensure appropriate counterbalancing. During the experiment, participants were seated at a desk with the tablet positioned on the desktop in front of them. The tracing tasks had to be performed with the dominant hand. All network-based services on the tablet were turned off during the experiment. Figure 5 shows an example of a participant performing the trajectory-tracing task with a stylus.

In addition to collecting quantitative data, we also wanted to obtain subjective impressions of the trajectory-tracing experience. Therefore, after completing all TTTs, participants were asked to complete a post-study questionnaire based on the rating part of the NASA-TLX [8]. In practice, many researchers skip the

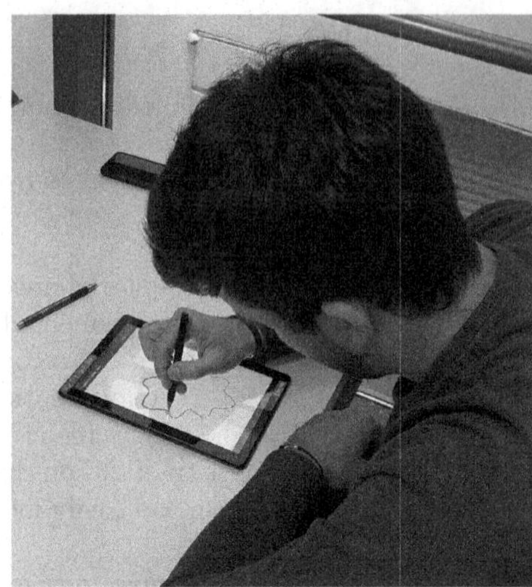

Fig. 5. A participant performing a trajectory-tracing task using a stylus

weighting step of the NASA-TLX standard, which reduces the time required to administer the test, and analyze the raw TLX responses only (Raw-TLX format) [10]. Since we did not conduct a longitudinal study, we opted for such a "quick-and-light" approach embodied by Raw-TLX. Moreover, we further deviated from the TLX standard by intentionally omitting two TLX factors (mental demand, and temporal demand) because they did not seem too important in our context. Therefore, individual opinions about perceived workload had to be estimated using standard 21-point rating scales for four TLX factors: physical demand, frustration, performance, and overall effort.

At the end of the experiment, participants completed a final questionnaire in which they provided their concluding remarks on the tasks and the devices tested in the context of trajectory tracing. The tests lasted approximately 40 min per user, including the practice session. The total number of trials (excluding practice session) was 25 participants $\times$ 3 devices $\times$ 3 difficulty categories $\times$ 3 task instances = 675.

3 Results and Discussion

In this section, results are presented for tracing time, tracing error, and the perceived interaction workload. Here we also show how the obtained data can be utilized for building predictive models for trajectory-tracing time.

To analyze the data obtained from the application log file, a 3 $\times$ 3 repeated measures ANOVA was used, with *Device* (finger, stylus, mouse) and *Complexity* (easy, medium, hard) being the within-subjects factors. The Greenhouse-Geisser ε correction for the violation of sphericity was applied when appropriate. In cases where a significant effect was found, post-hoc pairwise comparisons with Bonferroni adjustment were utilized.

3.1 Tracing Time

The tracing times obtained for three devices and three task complexity categories are shown in Fig. 6. Based on descriptive statistics indicators (mean values and corresponding standard deviations), it can be seen that tracing time tends to increase with task complexity and with the respect to the device used. As expected, more complex tasks with longer trajectories require more time. On the other hand, task execution seems to be fastest with the finger and slowest with the mouse.

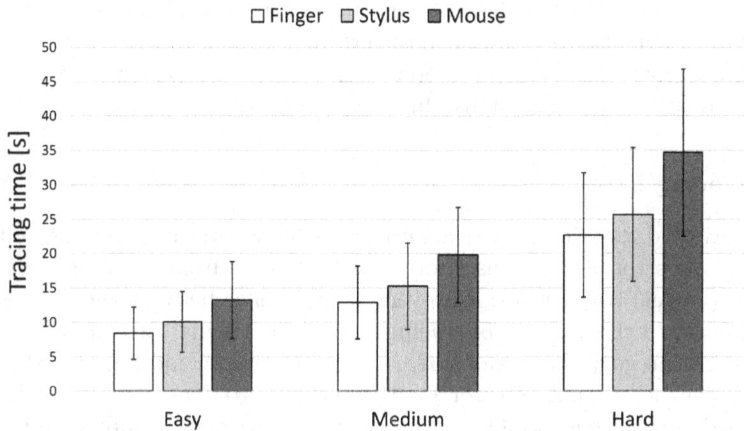

Fig. 6. Tracing times across three devices and three task complexity categories

Analysis using 2-way ANOVA RM revealed a significant effect of *Device* on trajectory-tracing time: $F(2, 48) = 41.735, p < .001$. The effect of *Complexity* was also found to be statistically significant: $F(1.121, 26.909) = 215.506, \varepsilon = 0.561, p < .001$.

For the pairwise comparisons, the time differences with respect to the devices used and with respect to the task categories are reported in the following. In addition to the grand means, the standard error values are given.

- Finger vs. Mouse: $(14.66 \pm 1.19\,s)$ vs. $(22.58 \pm 1.61\,s)$, $p < .001$
- Stylus vs. Mouse: $(17.00 \pm 1.33\,s)$ vs. $(22.58 \pm 1.61\,s)$, $p < .001$
- Finger vs. Stylus: $(14.66 \pm 1.19\,s)$ vs. $(17.00 \pm 1.33\,s)$, $p < .01$

- Easy vs. Hard: $(10.57 \pm 0.85\,s)$ vs. $(27.68 \pm 1.92\,s)$, $p < .001$
- Medium vs. Hard: $(15.99 \pm 1.13\,s)$ vs. $(27.68 \pm 1.92\,s)$, $p < .001$
- Easy vs. Medium: $(10.57 \pm 0.85\,s)$ vs. $(15.99 \pm 1.13\,s)$, $p < .001$

Not surprisingly, statistically significant differences in tracing times were found between all categories of task complexity. More complex trajectories are longer and take more time to trace. However, this also proves that the ID threshold values are correctly chosen to determine the three categories.

Regarding the interaction modality, the mouse proved to be clearly the slowest. This is likely due to the fact that the user is performing indirect tracing, where mouse control on the desktop must be carefully coordinated with visual tracking of the pointer on the tablet display. Furthermore, using a mouse in combination with a tablet is not typical, and for some users it was their first encounter with such a setup.

Finally, tracing the trajectory with the finger turned out to be significantly faster compared to both alternatives. It is particularly interesting that the finger outperforms the stylus, which seems to be the more natural device for such tasks, since it does not bring the problem of screen occlusion to the same extent as a finger does. However, this is a difference in tracing time, and to get a complete picture, tracing errors should also be analyzed.

3.2 Tracing Error

The descriptive statistics for tracing errors are shown in Fig. 7. Similar to tracing time, tracing error also increases for tasks that come from categories with more complex (longer) trajectories. However, the difference between the devices is not as obvious as in the analysis of tracing time. In particular, it can be noted that within each category the amount of error for the mouse and finger is almost the same, while the amount of error for the stylus is to some extent smaller. The mentioned difference is more pronounced in categories with more complex tasks.

The same statistical tests were used for the analysis of tracing errors. 2-way ANOVA RM revealed a significant effect of *Device* on trajectory-tracing error: $F(1.535, 36.832) = 13.452, \varepsilon = 0.767, p < .001$. The effect of *Complexity* was found to be statistically significant as well: $F(1.130, 27.113) = 613.061, \varepsilon =$

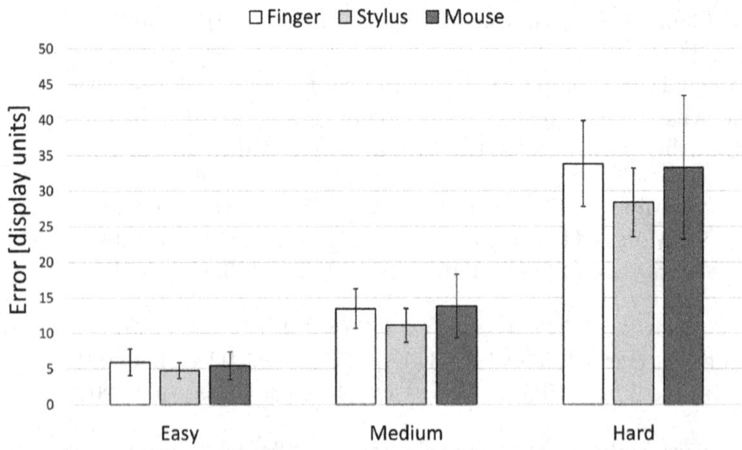

Fig. 7. Tracing errors across three devices and three task complexity categories

$0.565, p < .001$. Post-hoc pairwise comparisons are reported next. We consider a pixel as a unit of measurement for the tracing error.

- Finger vs. Mouse: $(17.7 \pm 0.6\,px)$ vs. $(17.5 \pm 1.0\,px)$, $p > .05$, ns
- Stylus vs. Mouse: $(14.7 \pm 0.5\,px)$ vs. $(17.5 \pm 1.0\,px)$, $p < .01$
- Finger vs. Stylus: $(17.7 \pm 0.6\,px)$ vs. $(14.7 \pm 0.5\,px)$, $p < .001$

- Easy vs. Hard: $(5.4 \pm 0.3\,px)$ vs. $(31.8 \pm 1.2\,px)$, $p < .001$
- Medium vs. Hard: $(12.8 \pm 0.6\,px)$ vs. $(31.8 \pm 1.2\,px)$, $p < .001$
- Easy vs. Medium: $(5.4 \pm 0.3\,px)$ vs. $(12.8 \pm 0.6\,px)$, $p < .001$

To put things in perspective, we can look at the values for the tracing errors in standard length units. Since the display density of the tablet used is 149 ppi according to the official specification, this means that a single dot on the screen has a physical size of about 0.17 mm. In this context, the average tracing errors for finger, stylus, and mouse are 3.02, 2.51 and 2.98 mm, respectively.

From the point of view of tracing error, the stylus proves to be the most effective for performing trajectory tracing. It has the statistically significant lowest error compared to both alternatives. This is a logical outcome, since tracing with a stylus is a form of direct interaction, as opposed to tracing with a mouse, where a small movement in an undesirable direction can lead to a larger deviation of the pointer on the tablet display. As for the relationship between the finger and the stylus, while both involve direct contact with the touchscreen, tracing with the stylus is superior to the finger due to occlusion issues and the well-known fat finger syndrome. Namely, when performing the tracing task with the finger, the user covers a certain part of the trajectory with a fingertip, and apart from not being able to see a certain part of the screen as a result, the precision of the touch is limited by the anatomy of the index finger itself. With the stylus, the problem of occlusion is much less, since there is a sufficient distance between the hand and the screen. In addition, the stylus used in the study has a specially designed tip - a transparent disc that allows more precise touches. The transparency of the stylus tip allows the user to see the exact point of contact with the screen, which is not possible when interacting with a finger.

The difference in tracing error between mouse and finger is not statistically significant. The disadvantages of these two tracing modalities seem to contribute equally to the error rate.

It is also interesting to note that the tracing error increases significantly with more complex or longer trajectories. This can be attributed to the difficulty of maintaining concentration while performing a tracing task of a longer duration. However, the error calculation presented here, based on the polar coordinate system geometry, is not advantageous for tasks that require longer tracing near the origin point. This is because the deviations from the given trajectory near the origin point may contribute more to the average error than the deviations on the parts of the curve farther from the origin. Since the trajectories of the *Hard* category have more points near the origin, this also contributes to a higher error in the corresponding tracing tasks, along with the greater effort that the user must exert. Therefore, an alternative way to calculate the tracing error can be considered.

3.3 Interaction Workload

Turning to the qualitative data collected in the Raw-TLX surveys, Fig. 8 shows a box-and-whiskers diagram with comparative ratings of perceived interaction workload associated with performing trajectory tracing with finger, stylus, and mouse. It can be seen that the ratings for finger and stylus interaction are quite similar, while the ratings for mouse interaction diverge in terms of a worse experience. The above applies to all observed TLX factors.

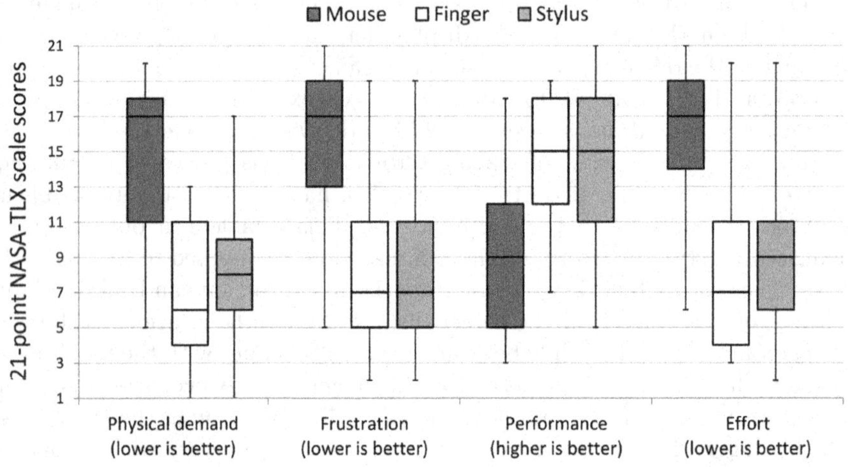

Fig. 8. Users' comparative ratings on perceived interaction workload between different trajectory-tracing modalities

For the statistical analysis of the obtained TLX results, we first used the Friedman test, which indicates whether there is a significant difference between the tested tracing modalities with respect to each TLX factor. The results of this test are presented in Table 2.

Thus, there is a statistically significant difference in physical demand, frustration, and perceived performance, as well as in overall effort, depending on how trajectory tracing was performed. Subsequently, post-hoc analysis with Wilcoxon signed-rank tests was conducted with a Bonferroni correction applied, resulting in a significance level set at $p < .017$. The results of the corresponding pairwise comparisons are presented in Table 3.

Table 2. The Friedman test results on observed TLX factors

Physical demand	Frustration	Performance	Effort
$\chi^2(2) = 18.694$	$\chi^2(2) = 28.170$	$\chi^2(2) = 19.474$	$\chi^2(2) = 29.771$
$\boldsymbol{p < 0.001}$	$\boldsymbol{p < 0.001}$	$\boldsymbol{p < 0.001}$	$\boldsymbol{p < 0.001}$

Table 3. Wilcoxon pairwise comparisons on observed TLX factors

Pairwise comparison	Physical demand	Frustration	Performance	Effort
Finger vs. Mouse	$Z = -3.971$ $\boldsymbol{p < 0.001}$	$Z = -3.974$ $\boldsymbol{p < 0.001}$	$Z = -3.257$ $\boldsymbol{p = 0.001}$	$Z = -4.292$ $\boldsymbol{p < 0.001}$
Stylus vs. Mouse	$Z = -3.650$ $\boldsymbol{p < 0.001}$	$Z = -4.017$ $\boldsymbol{p < 0.001}$	$Z = -3.508$ $\boldsymbol{p < 0.001}$	$Z = -3.976$ $\boldsymbol{p < 0.001}$
Finger vs. Stylus	$Z - 1.545$ $p = 0.122$	$Z = -0.703$ $p = 0.482$	$Z = -0.144$ $p = 0.886$	$Z = -0.850$ $p = 0.395$

The outcomes of the formal statistical analysis confirm what can be inferred from the diagram in Fig. 8. Participants rated trajectory tracing with the mouse as the significantly worst modality with respect to all observed TLX factors. The physical demand and overall effort are significantly higher when using a mouse due to the aforementioned need to constantly pay attention to simultaneously moving the device and monitoring the movement of the pointer on the tablet display. According to the users' comments, during tracing, the mouse was sometimes in such a position that it had to be moved to a more favorable position (for easier handling), which resulted in an unintentional deviation of the cursor from the given trajectory. In such cases, this led to a higher level of frustration.

When comparing finger and stylus, no statistically significant difference was found for any of the TLX factors, indicating that users found these two tracing modalities equally challenging. This may be related to previous results that showed that tracing with the finger is faster but also more error-prone than with the stylus. In addition, tracing a trajectory is very similar to drawing, which is usually done in a pen-and-paper setup. While this might suggest that the stylus might be the preferred device for TTTs on touchscreens, it should be taken into account that finger-based interaction is still the predominant way of operating mobile touchscreen devices.

We can conclude that the results of the TLX questionnaire corroborate the quantitative indicators obtained from the mobile application log. The answers from the final survey, visualized in Fig. 9, can be used in the same context.

Namely, 60% of the participants think that the stylus gives the best feeling of natural interaction when performing trajectory tracing. Not a single user considers a mouse to be such a device. Furthermore, given all the above, it is not surprising that most users feel that they made the most mistakes when using the mouse (80%) and the fewest when using the stylus (only 4%). Finally, the majority of participants (60%) believe that tracing longer trajectories is more difficult and that they had to exert considerably more interaction effort while performing tasks with a higher ID.

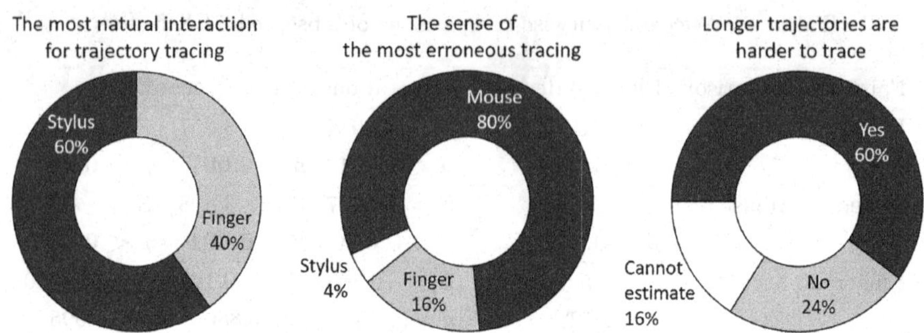

Fig. 9. Users' opinions on some trajectory tracing features observed during the experiment

3.4 Predictive Models

The data obtained from the application log file can also be used to build predictive models for trajectory-tracing time. In this case, the modeling is based on existing studies that show a linear relationship between the trajectory ID and the tracing time.

For each individual TTT, we averaged the tracing time and plotted it on a graph in relation to the corresponding ID value. A regression line was created for the generally increasing series of nine points thus obtained, for which the corresponding line equation and coefficient of determination (R^2) were calculated. The same was done for three different types of trajectory tracing, i.e. for finger, stylus, and mouse. The resulting models are shown in Fig. 10.

It can be seen that the regression models describe the empirical data well, with all R^2 values at a level of about 0.95. This proves the applicability of the steering law to the case investigated in this paper.

Although the obtained models are satisfactory, it should be noted that only the length of the trajectory was considered in the modeling process. In contrast to the general steering law, in our study the width of the tunnel is made constant and set to 1. However, the question arises whether, in addition to the length, the curvature of the trajectory itself has an effect on the tracing time. Indeed, it is to be expected that it is not the same to trace two trajectories of equal length, one of which contains many bends and the other of which has little curvature.

Pastel [9] has shown that 45° corners are easier to deal with than 90° or even 135° corners for biomechanical reasons, and even the mere presence of a corner increases the time required to complete a trajectory-based task. Not considering curvature as part of the model is not much of a problem when curvature is constant over a path, but can become a problem when curvature varies frequently. Therefore, there is further potential for a modeling procedure that incorporates the curvature property, similar to the work of Nancel and Lank [7].

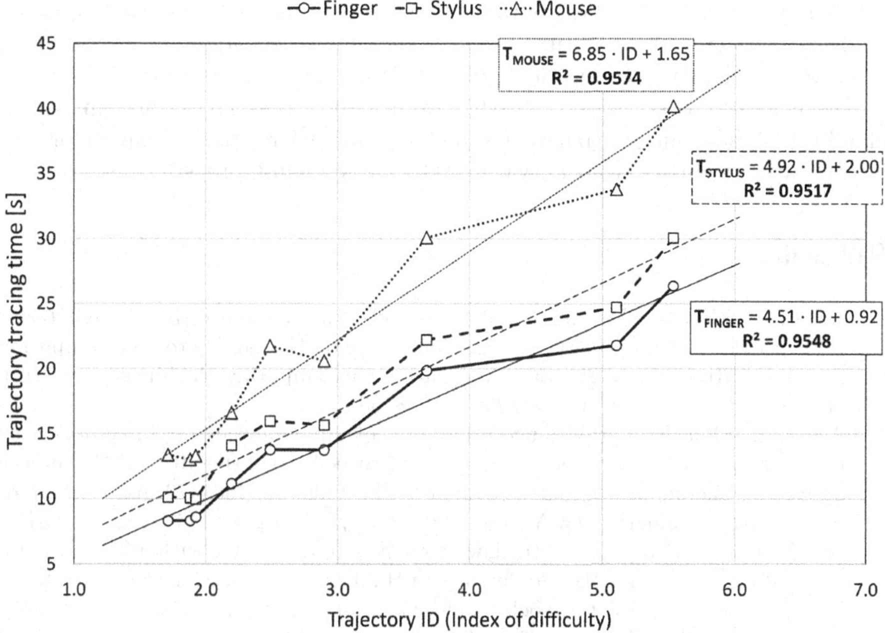

Fig. 10. Predictive models (linear regressions) for trajectory-tracing times

4 Conclusion

In this paper, the efficiency of trajectory tracing on a touchscreen device was investigated. Different tracing tasks were designed and mathematically formalized, with trajectories of different lengths, i.e. with varying ID values. The execution of the mentioned tasks with a finger, a stylus, and a mouse was tested in a controlled experiment.

Special attention is paid to the analysis of tracing time and tracing error. It is shown that both the time and the error increase with the complexity of the trajectory to be traced. In this context, tracing with a mouse is by far the slowest modality, with an error rate comparable to that of tracing with a finger. The stylus, while not the fastest, is significantly less inaccurate, and users find that it provides the best sense of natural interaction.

The above conclusions are supported by the results of the questionnaire examining the corresponding interaction workload. Participants rated trajectory tracing with the mouse as the significantly worst modality in terms of all observed TLX factors. No significant difference was found between finger and stylus in this regard, suggesting that users perceive these two modalities as equally demanding.

Finally, we showed how the obtained quantitative data can be used to develop models of trajectory-tracing time. All obtained models based on linear regression agree very well with the empirical data, with R^2 values above 0.95.

We have discussed ways to further improve the presented work, in particular by including an alternative method for calculating the tracing error and incorporating the trajectory curvature into the modeling procedure.

References

1. Accot, J., Zhai, S.: Beyond Fitts' law: models for trajectory-based HCI tasks. In: Proceedings of the ACM SIGCHI Conference on Human Factors in Computing Systems, CHI 1997, pp. 295–302. Association for Computing Machinery, New York (1997). https://doi.org/10.1145/258549.258760
2. Accot, J., Zhai, S.: Performance evaluation of input devices in trajectory-based tasks: an application of the steering law. In: Proceedings of the SIGCHI Conference on Human Factors in Computing Systems, CHI 1999, pp. 466–472. Association for Computing Machinery, New York (1999). https://doi.org/10.1145/302979.303133
3. Bi, X., Li, Y., Zhai, S.: FFitts law: modeling finger touch with Fitts' law. In: Proceedings of the SIGCHI Conference on Human Factors in Computing Systems, CHI 2013, pp. 1363–1372. Association for Computing Machinery, New York (2013). https://doi.org/10.1145/2470654.2466180
4. Fitts, P.M.: The information capacity of the human motor system in controlling the amplitude of movement. J. Exp. Psychol. **47**(6), 381–391 (1954)
5. MacKenzie, I.S.: Human-Computer Interaction: An Empirical Research Perspective. Morgan Kaufmann, Amsterdam (2013)
6. Scott MacKenzie, I.: Fitts' throughput and the remarkable case of touch-based target selection. In: Kurosu, M. (ed.) HCI 2015. LNCS, vol. 9170, pp. 238–249. Springer, Cham (2015). https://doi.org/10.1007/978-3-319-20916-6_23
7. Nancel, M., Lank, E.: Modeling user performance on curved constrained paths. In: Proceedings of the SIGCHI Conference on Human Factors in Computing Systems, CHI 2017, pp. 244–254. Association for Computing Machinery, New York (2017). https://doi.org/10.1145/3025453.3025951
8. NASA: Task Load Index (TLX). https://humansystems.arc.nasa.gov/groups/tlx/
9. Pastel, R.: Measuring the difficulty of steering through corners. In: Proceedings of the SIGCHI Conference on Human Factors in Computing Systems, CHI 2006, pp. 1087–1096. Association for Computing Machinery, New York (2006). https://doi.org/10.1145/1124772.1124934
10. Sauro, J.: 10 things to know about the NASA TLX (2019). https://measuringu.com/nasa-tlx/
11. Soukoreff, R.W., MacKenzie, I.S.: Towards a standard for pointing device evaluation, perspectives on 27 years of Fitts' law research in HCI. Int. J. Hum.-Comput. Stud. **61**(6), 751–789 (2004). https://doi.org/10.1016/j.ijhcs.2004.09.001
12. WolframAlpha: Computational intelligence. https://www.wolframalpha.com/
13. Zabramski, S.: Careless touch: a comparative evaluation of mouse, pen, and touch input in shape tracing task. In: Proceedings of the 23rd Australian Computer-Human Interaction Conference, OzCHI 2011, pp. 329–332. Association for Computing Machinery, New York (2011). https://doi.org/10.1145/2071536.2071588

14. Zabramski, S., Shrestha, S., Stuerzlinger, W.: Easy vs. tricky: the shape effect in tracing, selecting, and steering with mouse, stylus, and touch. In: Proceedings of International Conference on Making Sense of Converging Media, AcademicMindTrek 2013, pp. 99–103. Association for Computing Machinery, New York (2013). https://doi.org/10.1145/2523429.2523444
15. Zhou, X., Cao, X., Ren, X.: Speed-accuracy tradeoff in trajectory-based tasks with temporal constraint. In: Gross, T., et al. (eds.) INTERACT 2009. LNCS, vol. 5726, pp. 906–919. Springer, Heidelberg (2009). https://doi.org/10.1007/978-3-642-03655-2_99

On the Benefit of Independent Control of Head and Eye Movements of a Social Robot for Multiparty Human-Robot Interaction

Léa Haefflinger[1,2](✉), Frédéric Elisei[1], Silvain Gerber[1], Béatrice Bouchot[2], Jean-Philippe Vigne[2], and Gérard Bailly[1]

[1] Univ. Grenoble Alpes, CNRS, Grenoble INP, GIPSA-lab, 38000 Grenoble, France
{lea.haefflinger,frederic.elisei,silvain.gerber,gerard.bailly}@gipsa-lab.fr

[2] Innolab, ATOS, 38130 Echirolles, France
{beatrice.bouchot,jean-philippe.vigne}@atos.net

Abstract. The human gaze direction is the sum of the head and eye movements. The coordination of these two segments has been studied and models of the contribution of head movement to the gaze of virtual agents or robots have been proposed. However, these coordination models are mostly not trained nor evaluated in an interaction context, and may underestimate the social functions of gaze. Indeed, after analyzing human behavior in a three-party conversation dataset, we show that the contribution of the head to the gaze varies depending on whether the speaker is addressing two interlocutors or one of them: the conversational regime actually impacts the head/eyes coordination. We therefore propose an evaluation of different coordination policies in a social interaction context, using a Furhat robot to replay the human multimodal behavior from our data record. The verbal content and gaze targets are the same, but the robot uses four different head and eye coordination policies. (1) Furhat's default gaze control, whose eyes move faster and start before the head, but finally aligns both segments. (2) the robot head is fixed and only the eyes move. (3) the eyes are fixed and only the head moves. (4) Human-like control where the robot mimics the head movements of the human dataset, which naturally exploits independent eye and head control. Using an online crowdsourced test, we show that the human-like policy, which uses decoupled head and eye movements, is perceived significantly more natural than the others.

Keywords: Human-Robot Interaction · Head Orientation · Gaze · Multiparty Interaction · Multimodal Attention

Introduction

Non-verbal cues are an essential part of human conversation, and in particular gaze cues. The gaze has many functions in human face-to-face interaction, such

M. Kurosu and A. Hashizume (Eds.): HCII 2023, LNCS 14011, pp. 450–466, 2023.
https://doi.org/10.1007/978-3-031-35596-7_29

as giving feedback, complementing speech with emotional information, as well as regulating the conversation and turn-taking in particular [1,2]. In a multi-party conversation, the gaze is even more important to regulate the flow: it strongly contributes to addressee identification [3] or next speaker identification [4]. Conversely, social robots and virtual agents must also be able to generate gaze cues to interact smoothly with humans.

Gaze generation can be decomposed into two parts, the identification of where the robot should focus its attention, and the control policy that determines how body segments (from feet, trunk, and head to eyes [5]) direct and signal that attention. The gaze is essentially a combination of eye and head movements, and these two vectors have their own kinematics [6]. A realistic way to manage the attention of robots would be to control independently the eyes and the head of the robot. However, in Human-Robot Interaction (HRI) gaze is not always supported by these two vectors since some robots do not have the ability to reproduce human movements and cannot move their eyes freely – Nao robot [7] for example – or their neck – many telepresence robots for example [8]. In this case, gaze models only use the head or the eyes as attention vectors. In contrast, some robots are able to produce realistic eyes movements like the iCub [9] or Romeo [10] robots. More realistic kinematic models can be implemented on these robots.

Several bio-inspired control models that decouple eyes and head movements have been proposed, such as the model proposed by Itti [11] used by Zaraki et al. for their robot [12] and Peters et al. for the virtual agent Greta [13]. However, these control models are often tuned for the exploration of natural scenes and do not take into account the context of the interaction: the head orientation is determined by eye movements. However, the head should be considered as a vector of attention like the eyes [14], and each of them conveys redundant as well as complementary communicative information. A fixed coordination model that does not take into account the context seems to neglect the social functions of these two vectors. We therefore hypothesized that for a robot's gaze to be natural, it must use both the head and the eyes and the coordination of these two should take into account the context of the interaction.

The goal of our study is (a) to evaluate if gaze patterns with decoupled head and eye control are actually perceived as more natural than basic models with eye-only, head-only or eye-dependent head movements and (b) if certain eyes-head coordination strategies that depend on the interaction context could be identified.

To do so, we first analyzed an original dataset where the eye and head orientations of a human pilot were recorded in a multiparty conversation using immersive teleoperation of a robot. We evidence that independent head and eyes control makes a difference in such conversational situations. We then produced videos in which a virtual Furhat robot [15] mimics the recorded human attention behavior, with different eyes-head coordination strategies. A crowd-sourced comparative evaluation was then conducted to rank these strategies.

1 Background

Gaze is a widely studied nonverbal cue in both Human-Human Interaction (HHI) and HRI [16]. Two aspects of the gaze have been studied, mostly independently: its social functions during interaction and its kinematics. In multi-party conversation, gaze is an essential cue of the floor regulation between participants. Multu et al [17] showed that a robot can regulate the roles of participants in a conversation through appropriate gaze behavior, while Skantze et al [18] used gaze to impact turn-taking behavior. But in these studies, information about the chosen coordination strategy is not given. However, an appropriate eyes-head coordination can also impact speech distribution. Based on a talk time ratio, Gillet et al [19] adapted the robot's gaze behavior to balance participation between subjects, by controlling the distribution of head orientations of the robot. The dialogue role-based robot gaze control proposed by Shintani et al [20] is perceived as more natural when it combines head and eye movements especially for gaze aversions.

Beyond knowing where the robot should look, eyes-head coordination also plays a role in managing multi-party conversations. The coordination of the head and eyes in humans has been studied for a long time, but without really taking into account the interaction contexts. A lot of information about the kinematics of the human gaze is already known. The gaze is the addition of head and eye movements, whose kinematics are different. In particular, the eyes react before the head and move faster [6]. The head contribution in the gaze movement is roughly a linear function of the amplitude of the gaze [21]; but for small gaze shifts, only the eyes move [22]. Stiefelhagen and Zhu [23] show that in a multi-party conversation with four people, the contribution of the head varies among humans, but performs about 70% of the total gaze movement. Inspired by neurobiological observations, several models of gaze control have been proposed. The most cited model was proposed by Itti [11]. It is widely used for virtual agents and robots [12]. Note that this model was developed for screening natural scenes, and therefore doesn't take into account any interaction with human agents. Several studies try to evaluate the naturalness of this kind of neurobiological models depending on head contribution (from 0% to 100%) [13,24]. To evaluate the different coordination strategies, subjects watch videos of a virtual agent looking at objects on a table. They found that a head contribution of 0% is perceived as the least natural, while a contribution of 75% is perceived the most natural [24]. Unfortunately, no evaluation was performed in an interaction context such as a multi-party conversation. The social functions of the gaze are neglected and it is not known whether or not the context impacts the control and perception of head movements. The data that we will present and use in the next sections show that we should care about that.

2 Collection of Naturalistic HRI

2.1 Data Collection

The dataset used in this paper is the RoboTrio corpus [25]. The interaction takes part through a collaborative game (see Fig. 1) called Unanimo® and involves two human players and a robot teleoperated by a human (animator). The purpose of the game is to find the most popular words associated to a seed word. The animator spells the played theme out, e.g. "shrimp" and players deliberate on proposing their answers, maybe "pink", "seafood", ... The role of the animator is to motivate the dyad and to provide the rank of the scoring of the possible answers, displayed on a screen only available to him. Each session is composed of 9 seed words, with one for warming-up. The immersive teleoperation platform used in this study is the one proposed by Cambuzat et al [26]. The robot is an iCub robot [9] with extended communicative capabilities [27], such as speech generation with synchronized articulated lips and jaw. Thanks to the immersive teleoperation platform, the iCub reproduces the three degrees-of-freedom of head (pitch, roll, yaw), and eye (azimuth, elevation, vergence), lips and jaw movements of a human pilot while diffusing his voice through the mouth. The pilot perceives the subjects through the robot's sensors: the human pilot wears a virtual reality headset to hear and see the conversation captured by the robot's ears and eyes, as a pair of live video streams. Moreover, thanks to augmented reality, the pilot can see in front of him a tablet containing the various information of the game in progress (seed word, best answers and their scores). With this setup, the players usually think they interact with an autonomous robot endowed with a human-like behaviour. In return, the monitored animator behavior already takes into account HRI limitations. All the signals (input and output) are logged and can be replayed.

The corpus is composed of 22 sequences, each sequence lasts approximately 20 min. Between all the sequences, the pilot remains the same but the players are different and are composed of same-sex pairs.

2.2 Data Annotation

For this study only five sequences of men pairs were fully annotated and used for the experiment. The multimodal behavior of the robot pilot and the players has been annotated :

- **Verbal cues:** Verbal content as well as intention of players and animator have been manually annotated for each sequence using the ELAN [28] tool. The intentions of the pilot and the players are not similar due to their asymmetric roles in the interaction. In total, we have defined 24 intentions for the robot pilot ("Theme announce", "Ask for a proposition", "Ask for validation", "Give positive scoring", "Give null score"...) and 9 intentions for the players ("Proposition", "Positive Feedback", "Negative Feedback"...).

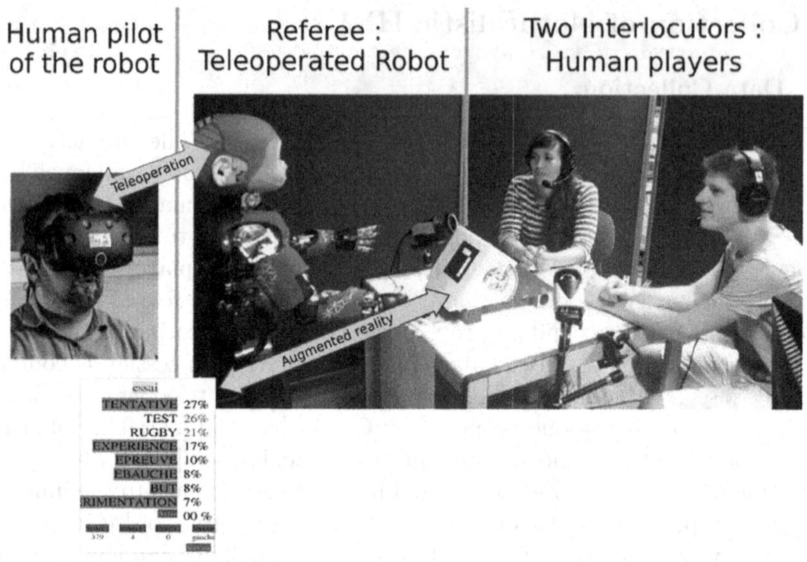

Fig. 1. Experimental setup for data collection of the RoboTrio corpus.

- **Pilot's gaze:** The recorded movement data of the pilot allowed us to compute the gaze focal points of the robot pilot in a virtual cylinder positioned at 1.2m from the robot (distance between the robot and the players). All the points corresponding to a fixation and not to a saccade have been automatically annotated with Gaussian Model Mixture (GMM). For the different classes, we have defined three regions of interest (RoI); "Left player", "Right player", and "Tablet", plus an "Elsewhere" class for gaze aversion. In addition to gaze focal points, we have also computed head focal points, corresponding to where the head is pointing on the same virtual cylinder. Head focal points have been classified in four classes with GMM; "Left", "Right", "Center", "Down".
- **Players' gaze:** We used Openface [29] to detect head and eyes orientations at each frame from the reference camera pointing to each player, from which we computed the corresponding focal point. If the focal point corresponds to a fixation, it is classified using GMM with one of the three labels: "Robot", "OtherPlayer", "Elsewhere".

3 Analysis of the Human Pilot's Eyes-Head Coordination

In this study, we are interested in the contributions of head and eyes orientations to the gaze. Before comparing different coordination strategies, we have analyzed the human behavior of the robot pilot in RoboTrio. We first compared the position of the gaze focal points and those of the head computed during the annotation phase of the corpus. Figure 2 shows the comparison of the distributions of the focal points of the fixations depending on the head orientation for one sequence. Several observations can be made showing that **the orientations of the gaze and the head are not always identical.** First of all, the distribution of head focal points is much more restricted than that of the gaze. The contribution of head movements in the gaze seems to be closer to 30–40% than 100%, as implemented on several robots. Another observation is that a gaze point corresponding to a rightward head orientation (yellow) is not necessarily positioned in the rightmost RoI, and conversely for a gaze point whose head orientation is classified as leftward (blue). In an even more pronounced way, when the head is positioned in the center (red), between the two players, the gaze is mostly positioned on one of the two players and not on the middle.

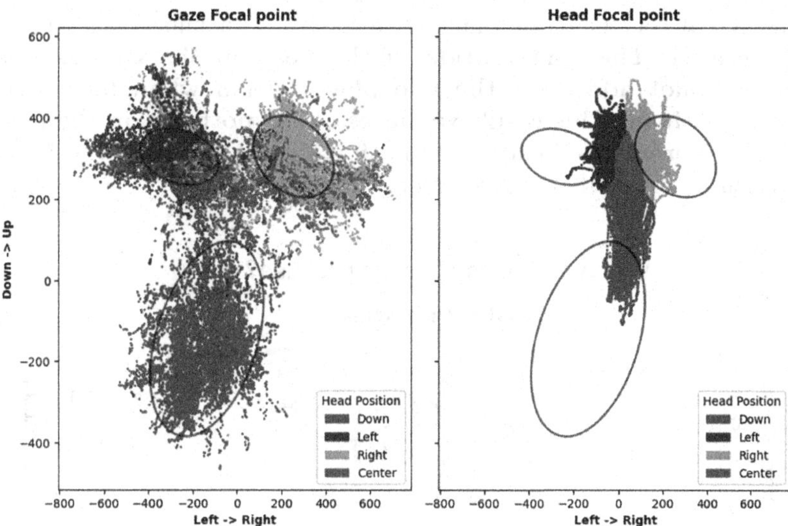

Fig. 2. Distribution of gaze and head focal points of the human pilot for one RoboTrio sequence. The colored point are obtained by a GMM classification of head focal points. The three ellipsoids show the Gaussians of the three ROIs (left player, right player, tablet) obtained with the GMM gaze classification.

We therefore try to better understand why at certain moments the pilot decides to position his head between the two players. **The hypothesis we made is that the head being a vector of attention, the pilot centers his head when he directs his attention on the two players, and directs it towards one player when he focuses his attention on only one.** To test this hypothesis, we decided to analyze and compare the orientation of the human pilot's head when addressing one or both players. To define the addressee, we detected in the utterances the use of the French pronouns "Vous" and "Tu". The "Vous" pronoun indicates that the pilot is addressing both players, while the "Tu" pronoun is used to address only one player. Of course, not all the utterances of the pilot contain one of these two pronouns, so we had to limit our analysis to those containing them. For all utterances where a "Tu" was detected, we then manually annotated whether the "Tu" was directed at the left or right player. Then, we computed the median yaw angles performed by the head and the gaze (sum of head and eyes) during each utterance of 5 RoboTrio sequences annotated with "Tu" and "Vous". Figure 3 shows the distribution of the median yaw angles of the pilot according to whether he pronounced a "Tu" or a "Vous" in the utterance. The left y-axis presents the bar plot distribution of the median angles, and the right y-axis shows the probability of the Gaussian distribution fitted on the median angles. We found that the distribution of head angles when the utterance contains a "Vous" is significantly more centered than when it contains a "Tu", which is not the case when we focus on the distribution of the gaze (combination of head and eye angles).

The verbal content of the interaction has thus an impact on the human pilot's behavior. **The contribution of the head in the gaze is weaker when the pilot addresses the two players than when he addresses only one of them. This result validates our hypothesis on the need to consider different eye-head coordination strategies in interaction, and in particular for multiparty conversations.**

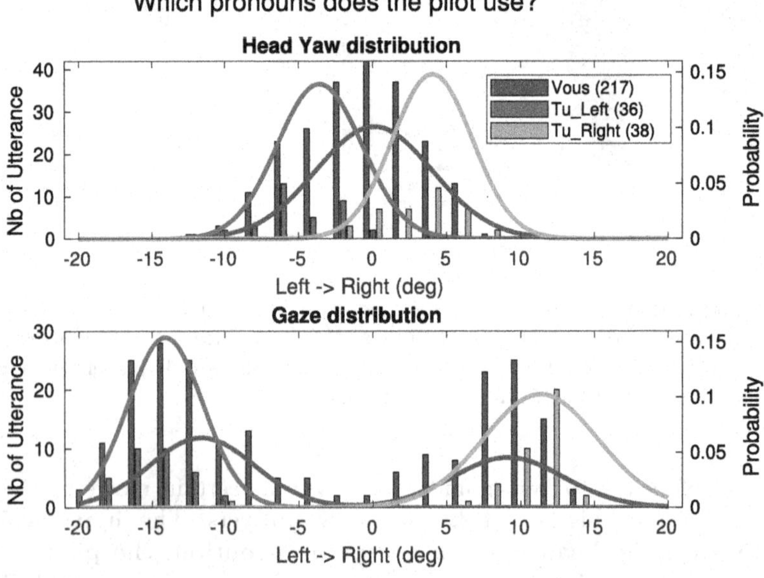

Fig. 3. Distribution of head and gaze median yaw angles according to who is/are addressed by the human pilot. The addressees are guessed thanks to the french pronouns, "Tu" for one player (left or right), "Vous" for both players. The left y-axis corresponds to the bar plot distribution, and the right y-axis to the probalility distribution after fitting a Gaussian distribution on the median yaw angles.

4 Subjective Evaluation

In this study we exploit the data collected with the iCub robot to control a Furhat robot. While we always impose the gaze target of the original data, we could keep or modify the head part. To do so, we used the annotated gaze fixations of the pilot and the original verbal content so that Furhat could synthesize speech and **always attend the original gaze targets**. To perform these gaze fixations, different controls can be used for Furhat's head by imposing – or not – head movements matching the groundtruth data. This process allows **to compare different head/eyes contributions strategies while imposing the same gaze targets.**

4.1 Policies and Hypotheses

In order to test the necessity to use and decouple head and eyes movements in attention management of Furhat, we decided to compare four policies.

- **EyesOnly policy:** Only the eyes of the robot move. The robot head is pointing to the center and is fixed. The trajectory of the eyes is computed by Furhat, according to the target that the robot must look at.
- **HeadOnly policy:** The head performs all the movement of the gaze. The eyes are enslaved to the head, as if they had no possibility to move freely. The pitch and yaw head angles are computed by adding eyes and head angles performed by the human pilot in our corpus. To smooth the trajectory and to avoid too fast movements for the head, a low-pass filter was applied on the eyes angles before the addition. The head roll of the head is kept as performed by the pilot.
- **Default Furhat policy (Baseline):** We used the default policy of Furhat. It computes eye and head movements from gaze targets. The eyes move first and faster than the head, but at the end of the movement both are aligned in the same direction.
- **EyesHead policy (Proposed policy):** This is the proposed policy, which is the closest to the pilot's behavior using the head and eyes. The three degrees of freedom of the head are kept identical to those performed by the pilot during the RoboTrio sequences. The eye trajectories to attend the imposed gaze targets are generated by Furhat.

From these four policies, we made two hypotheses:
(H1) The robot using EyesHead policy for attention management will be perceived as more natural than the others.
(H2) The preference between the other three policies will depend on the context of the interaction.

4.2 HEMVIP Evaluation

To evaluate these policies, we have decided to perform an on-line evaluation by third parties. We recorded video clips of Furhat (the way clips have been

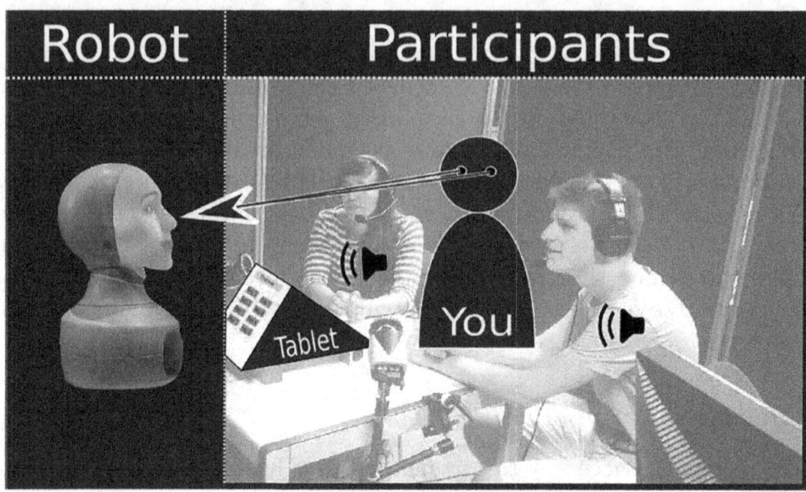

Fig. 4. Diagram presented in the introduction of the subjective evaluation to explain the perception context in the scoring interface: subject faces the robot, and can hear each player accordingly, i.e. on the right or on the left.

selected is explained in Sect. 4.3) replaying interaction passages from RoboTrio corpus, with the four control policies. For each interaction extract, four videos corresponding to the four policies were recorded. In these four videos, the verbal content and the robot's attention target are the same (left subject, right subject, tablet). Only the attention management are different according to the policy used. In order to keep environmental conditions identical, we recorded animations with the Furhat simulator. For all the clips, only the virtual robot is visible, the soundtracks of the RoboTrio's participants are broadcasted in stereo. In addition to explanations given in the experiment introduction, the context (see Fig. 4) is also shown to the subjects.

We used the HEMVIP[1] method [30] for the evaluation: evaluation is performed via several web pages; each page displays a panel with 4 sliders and "Play" buttons to score the 4 different video clips corresponding to the 4 different control policies for the same interaction extract. Subjects have to play each video clip at least once and give a score between 0 and 100 based on how natural they perceive the robot's behavior. The order of the control conditions is random. Each web page corresponds to a different extract of interaction, the order of the pages is also random: all subjects see and rate the same videos but not in a defined order. An example of the webpage is shown Fig. 5. At the end of the evaluation, subjects have to fill a general questionnaire about their familiarity with robots and can comment about the seen video clips.

[1] https://github.com/jonepatr/hemvip.

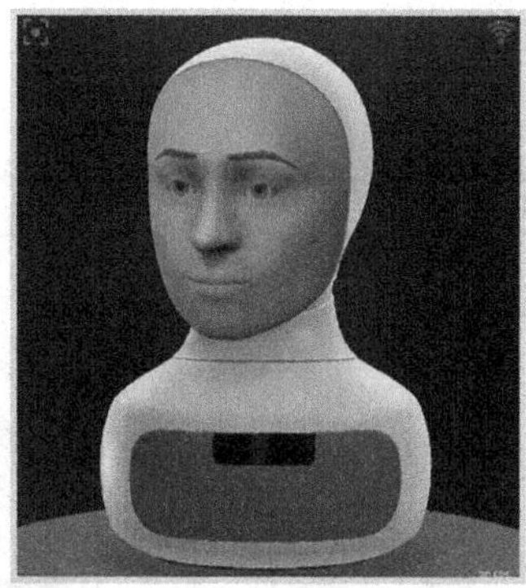

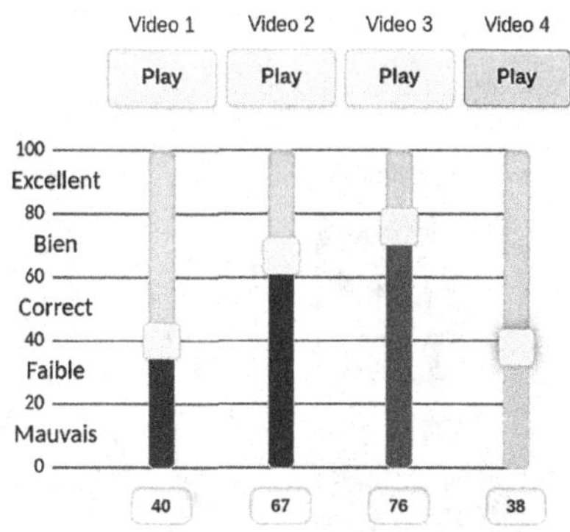

Fig. 5. Example of one of the fifteen web pages of the HEMVIP evaluation. The given instruction at the beginning means: "Rate the videos based on how natural the robot's behavior looks". Left area is used to display the video. Right area collects the evaluations with the four scales for the four videos, each having a dedicated play button.

4.3 Clips' Selection

Short clips of interaction had to be selected for the evaluation. In order not to make the experiment too long, a total of 15 interaction clips were chosen, 3 clips for each of the 5 annotated sequences of the corpus. The average duration of these clips is 10.5 s, no clip is shorter than 9 s nor longer than 12 s. In addition to these 15 clips, 1 more clip was taken as a training clip for the subjects. The selection of the clips is achieved in three steps. No control policy has been favorized:

1. A first selection is performed automatically by focusing on the interaction moments where the head movements in the 4 control policies are the most different. For this, the sum of the absolute differences between the head Yaw angles (left/right) of the HeadOnly, the EyesOnly and the EyesHead policies are computed. We further add a constant according to whether there is verbal activity or not. The time course of these behavioral differences is smoothed by a median filter with a 10 s window. Then, peaks of maximum difference were detected. From these peaks, a first group of potential interaction extracts was obtained (red points on Fig. 6).
2. Once the peaks are detected, it is necessary to check that they correspond to relevant moments of the interaction (e.g. not corresponding to the explanation of the rules for example) and that the on-going context is clear, without the previous seconds. As a result, some ambiguous passages are rejected.
3. To finalize the selection, the main purpose was to diversify the extracts. This was arbitrated by the content of the interaction, to not only have passages where the animator gives the score, but also to have moments where the players debate between them, or make a proposal, etc. Moreover, it was also

done on the context of the interaction, so that the themes of the game are varied, and that passages are selected at the beginning, middle and end of the game sessions.

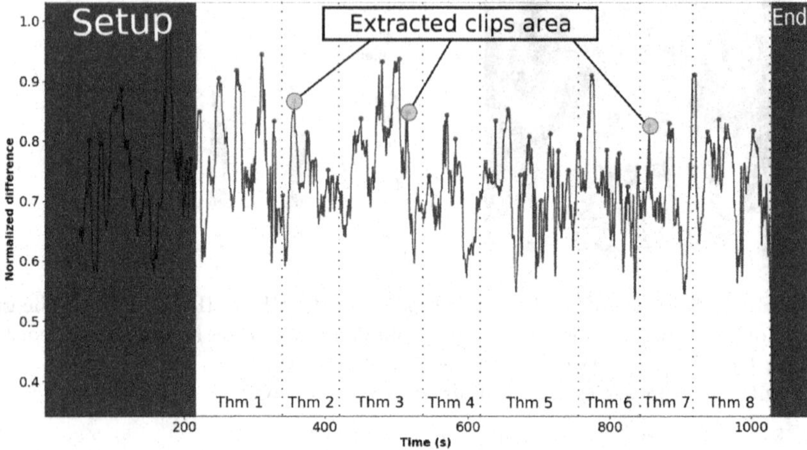

Fig. 6. Time course of the normalized difference between the head yaw trajectories of the different policies for one sequence. The position of the peaks of maximum differences are marked in red. The peaks corresponding to the three video clips finally selected for this sequence are marked with yellow dots. (Color figure online)

4.4 Participants

Participants were recruited via the Prolific[2] platform. Access to this experience was restricted to French speakers residing in France, Belgium or Switzerland, so that participants can fully understand the verbal context of the videos. A total of 51 people, aged between 18 and 60, completed the evaluation. One submission was rejected, the completion time being too short. In the end, 50 submissions are considered, with a balanced number of Female and Male.

5 Results

The result of the subjective experiment are shown Fig. 7 and Fig. 8. The statistical significance of the distributions of subjective ratings has been studied by a beta regression with *clips_Id* and *users_Id* as random variables using the glmmTMB package [31] of R software [32]. Using a likelihood ratio test, we found that the policy significantly impacts the rated score (chisq(3)=744.53,

[2] https://www.prolific.co/.

p<0.0001). We then conducted multiple pair-wise comparisons between the policies using the multcomp package [33] of R software; the Fig. 7 shows the adjusted p-value obtained. The EyesHead policy is significantly higher rated than the other policies. The closest coordination strategy from the human behavior is clearly perceived as more natural. The HeadOnly policy is the second highest rated policy, but strongly worst than the former. Ratings of Furhat and EyesOnly are not statistically different but significantly lower than the two preceding ones. With the beta regression, we found that familiarity significantly impacts the scores too (chisq(12)=197.84, p<0.0001). Nevertheless, for all the familiarity values, the EyesHead policy is the best rated. **The hypothesis (H1) is verified.** Moreover, we found that *clips_Id* significantly impacts the rated score too (chisq(9)=64.5, p<0.0001). But even if the rated score is not the same between the video clips, the EyesHead policy is always the highest rated (see Fig. 8). For the other policies, most of the time the HeadOnly policy is the second highest rated but it's not always the case. For example, for the "C" video clip, the EyesOnly policy scored higher than the two other policies, which probably means that smaller head movements are preferred for this interaction extract. For the "F" video clip, the Furhat policy obtained the second best score. **The (H2) hypothesis is also verified: depending on the extract of interaction the preference between the three other policies is different.**

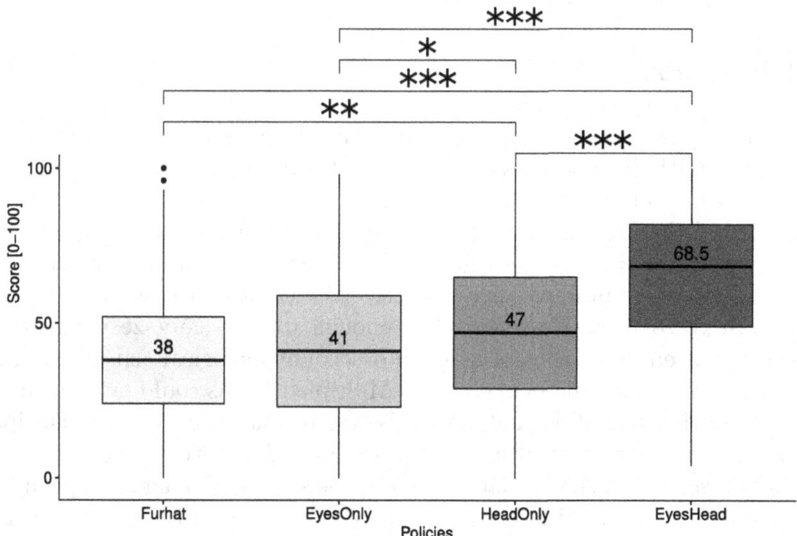

Fig. 7. Results of the subjective experience. Comparison of the reported naturalness-score, according to the policy. Each boxplot contains distributions of 50×15 points (number of subjects x number of clips). Significant p-values are indicated by * (<0.05), ** (<0.01) and *** (<0.001).

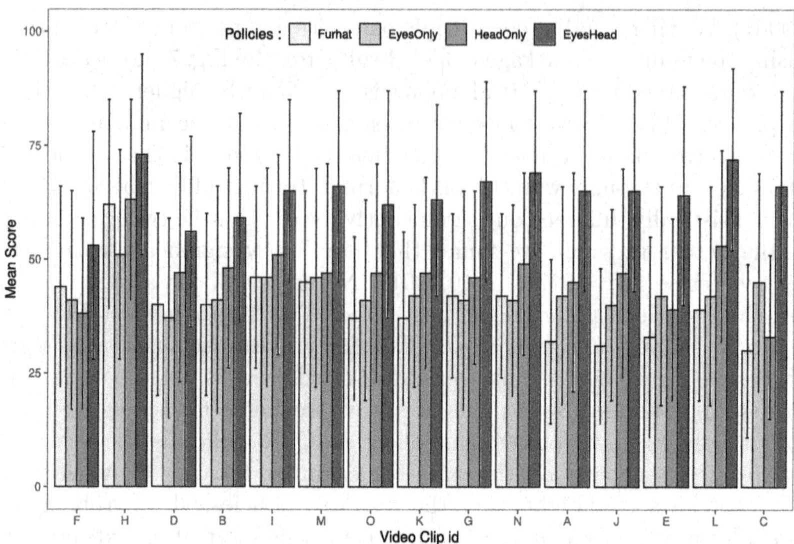

Fig. 8. Results of the subjective experience. Comparison of the average naturalness scores given for each policy according to the video *clip_Id*. Video clips are ordered by increasing difference between mean scores obtained by EyesHead and the mean of the other policies.

6 Discussion

In this study, we replayed multimodal human behavior recorded in multiparty conversation with different eyes-head coordination strategies for the robot's gaze. We show with a subjective online evaluation that driving only eyes or only head is less natural than the simulation of the original data involving both channels. Surprisingly, the Furhat policy using both eyes and head movements that align at the end doesn't obtained very good scores compared to the other policies. Using both vectors doesn't seem to be enough to manage gaze behavior in a natural way, even if the control takes into account biological aspects of human gaze, such as the vestibulo-ocular reflex. Multiple reasons could explain this low score. First, the default Furhat policy is not meant to cope with multiparty conversation, in particular with such context as collaborative games. Moreover, the head movement of the Furhat policy is quite slow, with a large amplitude. So when the pilot quickly shifts his gaze between two targets, the robot's behavior is not very natural. The better results obtained by the HeadOnly policy could be explained by the speed of the head which is much faster and so more natural than the default Furhat policy. Globally, the three policies (Default Furhat, EyesOnly and HeadOnly) have fixed coordination between head and eyes, and this lacks the variability that the multiparty context deserves. However, the results of Fig. 8 show different rating scores between the polices depending on the extract of the interaction. The preferred coordination between head and eyes depends on the context of the interaction. This result is consistent with the previous VOUS/TU analysis of the human pilot's behavior that we have conducted about the difference between head movements according to the pilot's addressee.

Nevertheless, a first limitation of our study is that, except the EyesHead policy, the three others have a head movement propensity fixed at 0% (EyesOnly) or 100% (Default Furhat, HeadOnly). There is no intermediate head contribution as is proposed in [13,24]. It would be interesting to compare EyesHead policy with policies with non extreme head movement contributions. Moreover, the different strategies were compared only on the naturalness of the behavior. Other questions could have been asked to the subjects concerning for example the personality of the robot, or the understanding of its intentions. Similarly, with the human behavior replay method, the subjective evaluation was performed with a third-person perspective. We therefore didn't have access to the feelings of a person who experienced the physical interaction with the robot. Note however that everything was done to allow the subject to understand the context of the interaction as well as possible. Pereira et al [34] showed that a third-person evaluation of gaze patterns in HRI provided similar results to a first-person evaluation.

Other limitations of this study have been identified for potential future improvements. For example, natural blinks were not transfered on the robot. We chose to use the model already implemented on the Furhat robot. So the blinks don't systematically occur at the same time between policies, but they are generated by the same model that is unaware of the cognitive activity of the robot nor it's communicative intentions. Similarly, the possible gaze targets for the robot are limited to the 3 RoI (left player, right player, tablet): there is no gaze aversion in the gaze replay nor gaze paths over the subjects' faces [35]. However, we hypothesize that for this evaluation in this interaction context, aversions are not paramount. The pilot never fixes at a player for very long time, and he can use the tablet to drop out of the ongoing conversation.

Another topic of discussion could be the use of Mixed Reality to collect groundtruth data on human behavior. Indeed, wearing a virtual reality headset could impact the behavior of the pilot. Pfeil et al [36] compared eyes-head coordination in physical and virtual environments and showed that subjects in virtual environments seemed to use their heads more, but in the study by Sidenmark et al [5] no significant difference was found. It is therefore difficult to conclude on some impact in our case, especially as we display real video streams rather than synthetic content.

Anyway, despite these possible limitations, our results show a strong preference for the coordination strategy combining head and eye movements in a very realistic way.

7 Conclusions and Perspectives

This study argues for the independent control of the head and eyes movements for the generation of the robot gaze. Both body segments provide redundant and complementary information about the conversational regime and communicative intentions throughout the interaction. Indeed, the orientation of the head seems to be a key element in the regulation of multiparty conversations, for example to communicate to whom we are addressing. We notably show that the head orientation may contribute to the identification of a message, delivering somehow the median direction of an "attention cone" in the assembly of attendees.

In the future, we will try to exploit the Robotrio corpus to train a multimodal gaze control model for our robot that takes into account its communicative intentions and the overt verbal and non verbal responses of the interlocutors.

The coordination between eyes, head and possibly other segments of the body depends on numerous factors such as the actual physical disposition of the interlocutors, their social roles and status (see the Multidimensional Dimensional Scaling analysis performed on gaze models in [37]) as well as the context of the interaction. We will see how a multimodal gaze control model can be biased by these physical and social settings.

Acknowledgements. This work is supported by the ANR 19-P3IA-0003 MIAI. The first author is financed by a CIFRE PhD granted by ANRT. The authors thank Juliette Rengot for the automatic gaze classification tool and Nathan Loudjani, who was invaluable in the RoboTrio corpus recording (CNRS SI2H PEPS funding).

References

1. Kendon, A.: Some functions of gaze-direction in social interaction. Acta Physiol. (Oxf) **26**(1), 22–63 (1967)
2. Sacks, H., Schegloff, E., Jefferson, G.: A simple systematic for the organisation of turn taking in conversation. Language **50**, 696–735 (1974)
3. Vertegaal, R., Slagter, R., van der Veer, G., Nijholt, A.: Eye gaze patterns in conversations: There is more to conversational agents than meets the eyes. In: Proceedings of the SIGCHI Conference on Human Factors in Computing Systems, pp. 301–308. Association for Computing Machinery, New York, NY, USA (2001)
4. Ishii, R., Otsuka, K., Kumano, S., Yamato, J.: Predicting who will be the next speaker and when in multi-party meetings. NTT Techn. Rev. **13** (2015)
5. Sidenmark, L., Gellersen, H.: Eye, head and torso coordination during gaze shifts in virtual reality. ACM Trans. Comput. Hum. Interact. **27**(1) (2019)
6. Freedman, E., Sparks, D.: Coordination of the eyes and head: movement kinematics. Exp. Brain Res. **131**, 22–32 (2000)
7. Gouaillier, D., et al.: Mechatronic design of Nao humanoid. In: 2009 IEEE International Conference on Robotics and Automation, pp. 769–774 (2009)
8. Kristoffersson, A., Coradeschi, S., Loutfi, A.: A review of mobile robotic telepresence. Adv. Hum. Comput. Interact. **2013**, 3–3 (2013)
9. Metta, G., et al.: The iCub humanoid robot: an open-systems platform for research in cognitive development. Neural Netw. **23**(8), 1125–1134 (2010)
10. Pateromichelakis, N., et al.: Head-eyes system and gaze analysis of the humanoid robot Romeo. In: 2014 IEEE/RSJ International Conference on Intelligent Robots and Systems, pp. 1374–1379 (2014)
11. Itti, L., Dhavale, N., Pighin, F.: Photorealistic attention-based gaze animation. In: 2006 IEEE International Conference on Multimedia and Expo, pp. 521–524 (2006)

12. Zaraki, A., Mazzei, D., Giuliani, M., de rossi, D.: Designing and evaluating a social gaze-control system for a humanoid robot. IEEE Trans. Syst. Man Cybern. Part A Syst. Hum. **44**, 157–168 (2014)
13. Peters, C., Qureshi, A.: Graphics for serious games: a head movement propensity model for animating gaze shifts and blinks of virtual characters. Comput. Graph. **34**, 677–687 (2010)
14. Hietanen, J.K.: Does your gaze direction and head orientation shift my visual attention? NeuroReport **10**(16), 3443–7 (1999)
15. Al Moubayed, S., Beskow, J., Skantze, G., Granström, B.: Furhat: A back-projected human-like robot head for multiparty human-machine interaction. Int. J. Human. Robot. (2013)
16. Admoni, H., Scassellati, B.: Social eye gaze in human-robot interaction: a review. J. Hum. Robot Interact. **6**, 25 (2017)
17. Mutlu, B., Shiwa, T., Kanda, T., Ishiguro, H., Hagita, N.: Footing in human-robot conversations: How robots might shape participant roles using gaze cues. In: Proceedings of the 4th ACM/IEEE International Conference on Human Robot Interaction, pp. 61–68. Association for Computing Machinery, New York, NY, USA (2009)
18. Skantze, G., Johansson, M., Beskow, J.: Exploring turn-taking cues in multi-party human-robot discussions about objects. In: Proceedings of the 2015 ACM on International Conference on Multimodal Interaction, pp. 67–74. Association for Computing Machinery, New York, NY, USA (2015)
19. Gillet, S., Cumbal, R., Pereira, A., Lopes, J., Engwall, O., Leite, I.: Robot gaze can mediate participation imbalance in groups with different skill levels. In: Proceedings of the 2021 ACM/IEEE International Conference on Human-Robot Interaction, pp. 303–311. Association for Computing Machinery, New York, NY, USA (2021)
20. Shintani, T., Ishi, C.T., Ishiguro, H.: Analysis of role-based gaze behaviors and gaze aversions, and implementation of robot's gaze control for multi-party dialogue. In: Proceedings of the 9th International Conference on Human-Agent Interaction, pp. 332–336. Association for Computing Machinery, New York, NY, USA (2021)
21. Zangemeister, W., Stark, L.: Types of gaze movement: variable interactions of eye and head movements. Exp. Neurol. **77**(3), 563–577 (1982)
22. Fuller, J.H.: Comparison of head movement strategies among mammals. In: The Head-Neck Sensory Motor System. Oxford University Press (1992)
23. Stiefelhagen, R., Zhu, J.: Head orientation and gaze direction in meetings. In: CHI 2002 Extended Abstracts on Human Factors in Computing Systems, pp. 858–859. Association for Computing Machinery, New York, NY, USA (2002)
24. Pejsa, T., Andrist, S., Gleicher, M., Mutlu, B.: Gaze and attention management for embodied conversational agents. ACM Trans. Interact. Intell. Syst. **5**, 1–34 (2015)
25. Prévot, L., Elisei, F., Bailly, G.: Robotrio (2020). https://hdl.handle.net/11403/robotrio/v1. ORTOLANG (Open Resources and TOols for LANGuage) – www.ortolang.fr
26. Cambuzat, R., Elisei, F., Bailly, G., Simonin, O., Spalanzani, A.: Immersive teleoperation of the eye gaze of social robots assessing gaze-contingent control of vergence, yaw and pitch of robotic eyes. In: ISR 2018–50th International Symposium on Robotics, pp. 232–239. VDE, Munich, Germany (2018)
27. Parmiggiani, A., Randazzo, M., Maggiali, M., Metta, G., Elisei, F., Bailly, G.: Design and validation of a talking face for the Icub. Int. J. Human. Robot. **12** (2015)

28. Wittenburg, P., Brugman, H., Russel, A., Klassmann, A., Sloetjes, H.: ELAN: a professional framework for multimodality research. In: Proceedings of the Fifth International Conference on Language Resources and Evaluation (LREC 2006). European Language Resources Association (ELRA), Genoa, Italy, May 2006
29. Baltrusaitis, T., Zadeh, A., Lim, Y.C., Morency, L.P.: Openface 2.0: Facial behavior analysis toolkit. In: 2018 13th IEEE International Conference on Automatic Face & Gesture Recognition (FG 2018), pp. 59–66 (2018)
30. Jonell, P., Yoon, Y., Wolfert, P., Kucherenko, T., Henter, G.E.: Hemvip: human evaluation of multiple videos in parallel. In: Proceedings of the 2021 International Conference on Multimodal Interaction, pp. 707–711. Association for Computing Machinery, New York, NY, USA (2021)
31. Brooks, M.E., et al.: glmmTMB balances speed and flexibility among packages for zero-inflated generalized linear mixed modeling. The R J. **9**(2), 378–400 (2017)
32. R Core Team: R: A Language and Environment for Statistical Computing. R Foundation for Statistical Computing, Vienna, Austria (2022). https://www.R-project.org/
33. Hothorn, T., Bretz, F., Westfall, P.: Simultaneous inference in general parametric models. Biometrical journal. Biometrische Zeitschrift. **50**, 346–363 (2008)
34. Pereira, A., Oertel, C., Fermoselle, L., Mendelson, J., Gustafson, J.: Effects of different interaction contexts when evaluating gaze models in HRI. In: Proceedings of the 2020 ACM/IEEE International Conference on Human-Robot Interaction, pp. 131–139. Association for Computing Machinery, New York, NY, USA (2020)
35. Bailly, G., Raidt, S., Elisei, F.: Gaze, conversational agents and face-to-face communication. Speech Commun. **52**(6), 598–612 (2010)
36. Pfeil, K., Taranta, E.M., Kulshreshth, A., Wisniewski, P., LaViola, J.J.: A comparison of eye-head coordination between virtual and physical realities. In: Proceedings of the 15th ACM Symposium on Applied Perception. Association for Computing Machinery, New York, NY, USA (2018)
37. Mihoub, A., Bailly, G., Wolf, C.: Social behavior modeling based on incremental discrete hidden Markov models. In: Salah, A.A., Hung, H., Aran, O., Gunes, H. (eds.) HBU 2013. LNCS, vol. 8212, pp. 172–183. Springer, Cham (2013). https://doi.org/10.1007/978-3-319-02714-2_15

Sticky Cursor: A Technique for Facilitating Moving Target Selection

Shunichiro Ikeno[1(✉)], Chia-Ming Chang[2], and Takeo Igarashi[3]

[1] Department of Computer Science, The University of Tokyo, Tokyo, Japan
ikeno-shunichiro730@g.ecc.u-tokyo.ac.jp
[2] Department of Creative Informatics, The University of Tokyo, Tokyo, Japan
[3] Department of Creative Informatics and Computer Science, The University of Tokyo, Tokyo, Japan

Abstract. There are many applications that consist of moving objects which require users to select them with a cursor, such as 3D simulations, video games, and air traffic control systems. However, selecting a moving target via a cursor is much more difficult than a static target. In this study, we introduced "Sticky Cursor", a technique that allows a cursor to stick to (i.e. moving together with) a moving target before selecting it. We believe this "sticky" feature can facilitate the process of moving target selection. We ran a user study to compare our proposed sticky cursor with a traditional "non-sticky" cursor in a moving target selection task. The results showed that the participants were able to select the moving targets and more correctly via the sticky cursor than the traditional cursor, while the completion time was comparable. In addition, most of the participants preferred the Sticky Cursor to the traditional cursor. We discussed the reasons and potential applications.

Keywords: Mouse Cursor · Pointing Technique · Moving Target Selection · Sticky Cursor

1 Introduction

Recently, personal computers obtain high performance that can deal with heavy tasks in real-time. The designs of computer applications has become complicated and require users to select (point and click) moving objects using pointing devices. Cursor pointing is an important task for users to interact intuitively with applications. As for an air traffic control system, operators can select a moving airplane in the display to view its flight plan, or as for 3D video games and 3D simulations, users need to select moving objects in the scene to manipulate them. However, the task to select a moving object via a mouse cursor is much more difficult than to select a static object. Unlike static objects, even if users once put the cursor on the target object, it always goes away from the pointing area, and they should keep adjusting the cursor position to track the target.

One idea to solve this problem is to pause the scene to make the target static. [7] But if the scene stops, users might miss some important information

M. Kurosu and A. Hashizume (Eds.): HCII 2023, LNCS 14011, pp. 467–483, 2023.
https://doi.org/10.1007/978-3-031-35596-7_30

[1], such as the velocity of the target or the possibility of going across the path of other objects. So selecting moving objects should be solved without pausing in real-time application.

Several studies [5,7,9] have proposed a concept to expand the selecting area of moving objects or a cursor. These techniques allow users to point and click the moving objects more easily with a larger selection area. However, expanding the selecting area may cause some problems. One is the overlapping issues. By expanding the selecting area, there occurs a larger overlapping area in the scene. If multiple targets are overlapping, it becomes difficult for users to distinguish which target they are pointing. Another issue is implementability. It may be difficult to implement the concept of expanding the selecting areas in some applications. It requires changes in the shape of a cursor or targets. For example, in 3D first-person view applications (e.g. video games, 3D simulations), the cursor is generally invisible. If such cursors are introduced to the applications, users may not understand the selecting area, or if the selecting area is visualized, it may spoil the visibility of the scene.

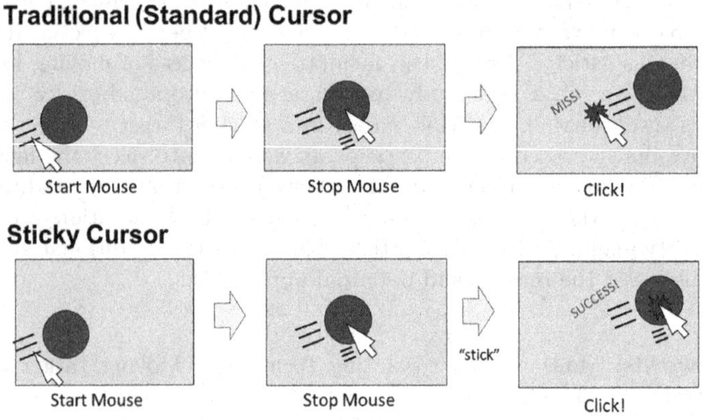

Fig. 1. Sticky Cursor.

In this study, we aim to provide an alternative solution without pausing the scene or changing the visual representation. We introduce, *Sticky Cursor*, a mousing pointer technique that allows a cursor to *stick* to moving targets in a scene. (i.e. move together with the target) By using a sticky cursor, users first move (point) the cursor onto a moving object, and then the cursor will automatically move together with the moving object unless the user intentionally moves the cursor away from the object. (Fig. 1 bottom) We expect this sticky feature helps users to select a moving object more easily and precisely.

We ran a user study (16 participants) to compare the proposed sticky cursor to a traditional non-sticky cursor in a 2D moving target selection task. The results showed that the rate of missing the target and the total number of error clicks were significantly lower in the sticky cursor condition than in the traditional non-sticky cursor, while the task completion time was comparable between the two conditions. Furthermore, the questionnaire results showed that more participants preferred the sticky cursor than the traditional non-sticky cursor in subjective ratings. In addition, more than half of the participants indicated that the sticky cursor was easy to use and easy to get used to.

Finally, we suggest possible applications of the sticky cursor technique. Three main contributions of this study are as follows:

- *Sticky Cursor*, a pointing technique for moving objects selection.
- A user study to compare *Sticky Cursor* to a traditional non-sticky cursor, demonstrated the benefits of the sticky cursor in a moving target selection task.
- Suggestions for further applications of the *Sticky Cursor* technique.

2 Related Work

2.1 Selection of Static Targets

Fitts' Law. Human behavior in the task of pointing a static target is generally described by Fitts' law. [3] A formula called Fitts' law describes the relationship between the movement time MT to point and select a target, the width W of the target, and the distance or amplitude A from the cursor to the target. One of the commonly used variations by MacKenzie [14,15] is as follows:

$$MT = a + b\log_2(A/W + 1)$$

where a and b are constants the value of which is determined through empirical observation. The log term $\log_2(A/W+1)$ is mentioned as the Index of Difficulty (ID) of the task. ID is expressed with bits since the base is 2. Assuming the unit of MT is second, the unit of the constant a is also second and that of b is second/bit. And the reciprocal number of b is referred to as the Index of Performance (IP) in the unit of bit/second, which is thought to be the rate of which a human can process the task to move a cursor and select a static target. Many research has been done on Fitts' law and it has been extended into a 2-dimensional version by MacKenzie [16], different shapes of targets by Grossman, Kong, and Balakrishnan [6], and an error model on it by Wobbrock, Cutrell, Harada, and MacKenzie [17]. According to these works, the wider or larger the target is, and the shorter distance the cursor and the target has, the shorter movement time and the lower error rate are measured in the task of selecting a static target.

Cursor Techniques. The Area cursor [9] and the Bubble cursor [5] are fundamental ideas of using unique cursors to facilitate the target selection task. The Area cursor is a technique to enhance the static target selection with a cursor by attaching the activation area around it. [5,9,11] Hasan et al. [7] used the circular area cursor to evaluate it in the moving target selection task. The Bubble cursor is an improved version of the Area cursor. [5,12] Its shape changes dynamically to engulf the nearest target. By this feature, users can distinguish the target which is currently selectable. Ninja cursors [10] places multiple cursors in a display so that the average distance between the targets and the cursors becomes shorter than using a single cursor.

2.2 Selection of Moving Targets

Hasan et al. introduced new methods, Comet and Target Ghost, and evaluated the effectiveness of some types of cursors and techniques in the selection of moving targets. [7] They compared the traditional cursor, the Area cursor [9], the Bubble cursor [5], Comet, and the Target Ghost version of them. (8 conditions) Though the Area cursor and the Bubble cursor are invented to select a static target, they are also effective to facilitate the selection of a moving target. Comet is a method for facilitating the selection of a moving target, which attaches another activation area whose shape is like a comet tail to the targets. Target Ghost is also a technique for the selection of a moving target, which add proxy targets to the scene. When triggered, there occur paused targets called proxy targets while the original targets and scene continue moving, and users can select the static proxy targets instead of the original moving targets.

Comet is one of the approaches of the moving target selection by enlarging the selecting area of the targets, and Target Ghost is a kind of the approaches to pause the moving targets. A problem with these approaches is that they alter the visual representation of the scene, either adding a comet tail or ghost proxy. This may not be desirable in some applications because the additional visuals hide critical information on the screen. Inspired by these seminal works, we present a complementary moving target selection technique without changing visual representation.

2.3 Modification of Control-Display Mapping

The Sticky cursor is one of the techniques which modifies the mapping of the physical mouse motion to the virtual cursor motion. This idea has been presented in various publications. For example, Blanch, Guiard, and Beaudouin-Lafon [2] proposed a technique, called semantic pointing, which modifies the motor size to change the control-display (C-D) ratio. This technique can facilitate the static pointing (target selection) task by dynamically adjusting the ratio according to the distance to targets. Lécuyer et al. [13] presented an interaction technique to simulate textures in desktop applications without a haptic interface, by modifying the motion of the cursor on the computer screen. It helps users to successfully conjure a mental image of the topography of the macroscopic textures. Fung et al. [4] introduced, kinematic templates, an end-user tool for defining content-specific motor space manipulations in the context of editing 2D visual compositions.

3 Proposed Method

3.1 Problem Formulation

Figure 2a shows three basic steps to select a static object. (1) users move the cursor, (2) it reaches the object, and (3) users click to select the object.

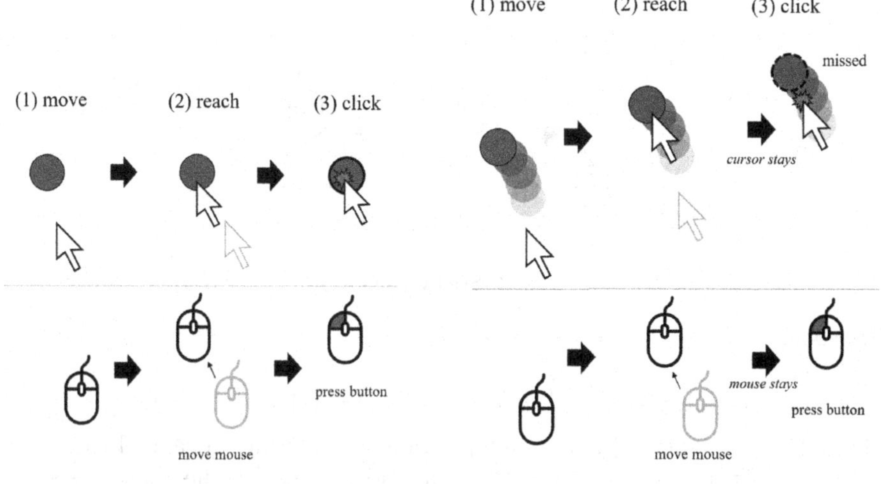

(a) Steps of selecting a static object. (b) Problem of selecting a moving object.

Fig. 2. Difference between selecting a static and a moving object.

However, selecting a moving object is different from a static object that the object is always moving between these three steps. Figure 2b shows the problem of selecting a moving object via a traditional cursor. The object can escape the mouse cursor after the cursor reaches the object before the user presses the mouse button. One can certainly avoid this error by continuously moving the mouse following the moving target until click, or click as soon as possible before the escape, but it is difficult to do so in practice.

3.2 Sticky Cursor

We proposed, *Sticky Cursor*, a technique that allows a cursor to stick to a moving target (i.e. moving together with the target without physically move the mouse) before selecting it. Figure 3 shows the "sticky" feature for moving object selection.

Below shows the algorithms of the traditional (standard) cursor and the proposed cursor.

Traditional.

$$c(t_{i+1}) = c(t_i) + \{m(t_{i+1}) - m(t_i)\}$$

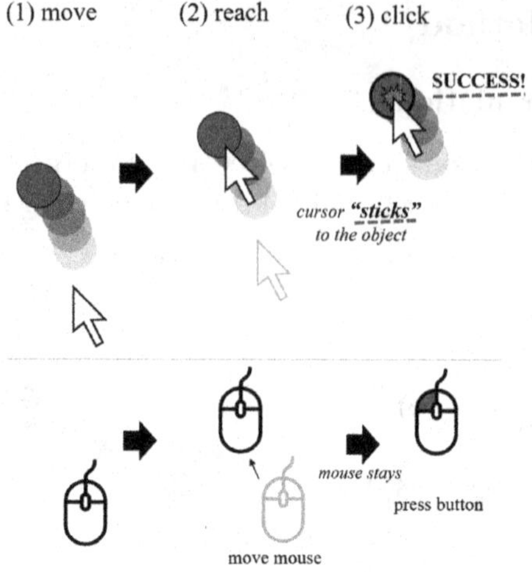

Fig. 3. Sticky Cursor.

Proposed.

$$c(t_{i+1}) = c(t_i) + \{m(t_{i+1}) - m(t_i)\} + \{o(t_{i+1}) - o(t_i)\}$$

where $c(t), m(t)$, and $o(t)$ represent a position of cursor, mouse, and object under the cursor at time t, respectively. With the "sticky" feature the relative position of the cursor to the target does not change as long as the user intentionally move the cursor away from the object. From a different point of view, the motion of the mouse causes the relative motion of the cursor to the target.

4 Evaluation

We ran a user study to compare the proposed "sticky" cursor to a traditional "non-sticky" cursor (i.e., a cursor does not stick to the moving object) in a moving target selection task. The experiment prototype was developed as a WebGL application with Unity 2D, and the user study was conducted via a Web browser. The interface design of the Sticky cursor experiment was mainly referred to the experimental design in the work by Huang, Tian, Li, and Fan [8]. The values of the parameters, the speed and the size of the targets, were determined through a number of pilot studies.

4.1 Participants

Sixteen participants took part in the user study. Eleven participants conducted it online, and five participants did it onsite. Fourteen were male and two were female. They ranged in ages from 19–73. (19–29 years old: 11, 30–39 years old: 3, above 60 years old: 2) And thirteen were right-handed, one was left-handed, and two were ambidextrous. Twelve of them were used to using a computer and a mouse, while four were beginners. Participants were paid an Amazon Gift card $5 for volunteering.

4.2 Goal and Hypothesis

In the experiment, we compared the performance of the traditional cursor and the sticky cursor in a 2D moving target selection task. The participants were asked to select a target object (red) moving from end to end of the experimental field, avoiding dummy objects (gray) moving in the same manner. Based on the "sticky" feature, we hypothesized the following:

H1: the "sticky" feature will save the process of readjusting the coordinate of the cursor according to the target motion, and it will result in shorter selection time.

H2: the "sticky" feature will prevent the target object from passing through the cursor which is placed at its previous position, and thus it will reduce the total number of error clicks.

H3: on the other hand, since the sticky cursor also sticks to the dummy objects, the number of the dummy object clicks will increase.

H4: in using the sticky cursor, it takes a bit of time to check if the cursor is now sticking to the target object correctly, and therefore the Sticky cursor will be more effective on the reduction of the total error clicks for those who spends more time to complete the task.

4.3 Apparatus

We ran the experiment mostly online. A mouse (not a trackpad), a regular Windows PC, the display whose resolution can be changed into 1920 × 1080, and a web browser (Chrome, Edge, Firefox, Opera) are the required setups of the online experiment. We tested each listed Web browser in advance to check if it was able to run the experiment with it correctly. We instructed the online participants to fix the display resolution to 1920 × 1080 before the experiment and to conduct it in a full-screen mode. However, since it was difficult to fix the size of the online participants' display, the display size was varied for each online participant for this time. In order to compare the sticky cursor with a cursor that participants use in daily life, we did not fix the DPI (Dots Per Inch) of the mouse.

4.4 Task in the Experiment

The experiment consists of 3 times of the practice, 20 times of the moving target selection task and a questionnaire. The task is to move the cursor to a moving Target object (red circle in Fig. 4) and click it, using the traditional cursor or the sticky cursor. We instructed the participants to select it as fast and as correctly as they could.

When each task starts, a target object and 10 dummy objects (grey circle in Fig. 4) appear at an boundary of the field. The target object is always one in each task, and it moves straight from end to end in the experimental field. But at the same time, the dummy objects also move in the same manner. When the cursor is placed on a target or dummy object, the icon of the cursor changes into a hand. (Fig. 4b) If the user successfully clicks the goal target, it is a success.

If the user wrongly clicks a dummy object or background, then it is an error. An error is not the end of a task and the user can continue the task until either the participant successfully clicks the target object, or the target object go outside of the field (failure). A single task always results in either success or failure with varying number of errors.

The target object and a dummy object might overlap below the cursor. (Fig. 4c) In such cases, we gave priority to the dummy object in this experiment. The cursor sticks to the dummy object, and clicking on the overlap is considered as an error.

Participants worked on 3 tasks as practice and worked on 40 tasks in the main task, 20 with the sticky cursor and 20 with the traditional cursor. Half of the participants worked on 20 tasks with the sticky cursor first and then switched to the traditional cursor. The other half worked in the opposite order.

The layout, namely the initial coordinates and the direction of the targets, of the 20 tasks are fixed, and the order of the set is randomized at the beginning of the 20 tasks. After the 40 tasks of the experiment, participants were required to answer a questionnaire.

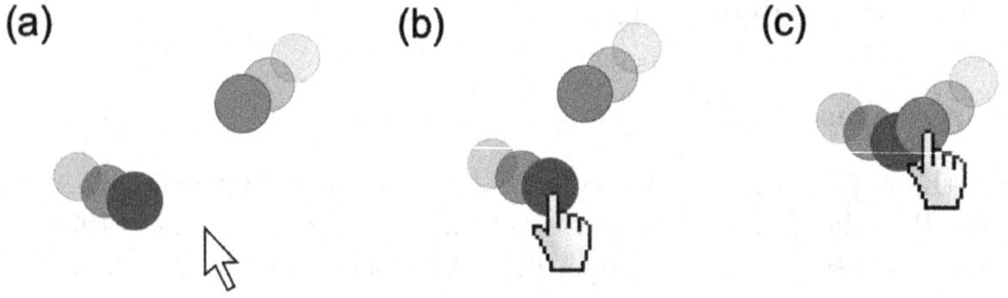

Fig. 4. User task in the experiment. (Color figure online)

4.5 Measurement

During the tasks, we recorded the completion time from the occurrence of the target object to the end of the task, the number of successful clicks of the target object, the number of failures that they miss the target object, and the number of error clicks. Two kinds of error clicks, clicks of dummy objects and clicks of the empty place of the field, were counted separately. Missing the target object is considered to be more fatal than error clicks.

4.6 Interface Design

The interface design was inspired by Huang et al.'s work [8], and we made some adjustments to assess the usefulness of the Sticky cursor. Our interface design of the experiment, see Fig. 5.

The size of the application field (white) was developed to be 1440 × 1080 resolution in a full-screen mode. A counter of the current result of the trials is placed in the top-left of the field, and participants can check it during the task. And the activation area of the cursor is the top-left single point of the icon.

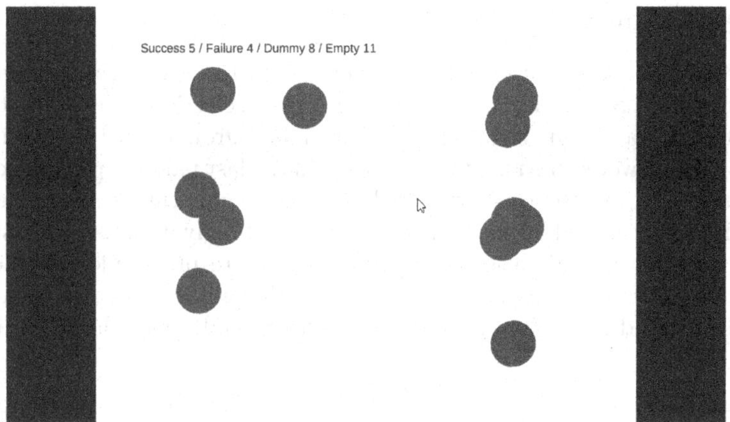

Fig. 5. Interface design of the Sticky cursor experiment.

We made four major modifications from the design of Huang et al.'s work. First is the background color. We used the white background for visibility. Second is the disabling of the bounce of the target. In the previous work, the targets bounce on the ends of the field, but this feature is likely to be unnatural in many cases. Thinking of applications that includes the moving target selection, such as the air traffic control systems or the video surveillance systems, it is a rare case that the moving virtual object bounces in the display, unless the real object that the virtual one is representing does bounce. Thus we did not introduce this feature, and regarded the Target object's passing across the end of the field as the lost of the target, which is a fatal error. Third is the removal of the randomness of the target occurrence. The initial coordinate and the moving direction of the targets are random in the previous work, but this might cause the dispersion of the condition of the tasks and the result might become unstable. Hence we made the set of conditions, on which the task might not be too difficult, and ran the experiment in a random order of the set. Fourth is the counter during the task ongoing. This is meant to enable the participants to check the progress.

4.7 Speed and Size of the Targets

In the task of moving target selection, there are a number of factors that influences the result. Above all, we thought the speed and the size of the targets were considerably important elements. Thus, we ran a pilot study to decide the suitable value of these parameters. In the pilot study and the user study, we configured the same speed and size between the target object and the dummy objects. Referring to the previous works [7,8] and conducting some tests, we made two choices for each, the speed of 360 or 480 pixels/sec and the width or the diameter of the target circle of 90 or 120 pixels. The pilot study showed the most stable (less variance) result with the condition of the speed at 360 pixels/sec and the width of 120 pixels. Therefore, we determined the speed at 360 pixels/sec and the width of 120 pixels and conducted the user study on this condition.

4.8 Questionnaire

After the experiment, the participants were asked to fill a questionnaire about their subjective ratings about the moving object selection tasks. Questions in the first part was about some pieces of their background. In the second part, participants answered the result of the tasks. In the last part we questioned about their subjective preference of the sticky cursor, comparing to the traditional cursor. It was measured on a Likert scale from 1 (strongly disagree) to 5 (strongly agree) how they thought the sticky cursor was more preferable, whether they thought it was easier to use, and whether they thought it was easier to get used to. We also asked its advantage and disadvantage, and its applicable situations.

5 Results

We compared the result data of the traditional cursor and the Sticky cursor, using t-test and Poisson test. ($\alpha = 0.05$ in both tests) We assumed that the number of success, failure, dummy, and empty follow a Poisson distribution, and that the completion time follow normal distribution. In the following subsections, we investigated on the failure rate, the number of clicks on dummy objects per trial, the number of clicks on empty place per trial, the completion time per trial, the total number of error clicks ($dummy + empty$).

5.1 The Number of Failure

Each condition, the traditional cursor and the sticky cursor, had the data of 16 participants. The graph in Fig. 6a shows the averages of the Failure rate (the number of Failure divided by the number of trials) of two conditions. The error bars in the graph indicated the standard errors. Also, the graph of Fig. 7(b) is the histogram of the result data. The means of the numbers of Failure were 4.38 [%] (Traditional), 2.19 [%] (Sticky), and the standard errors were 1.76 point (Traditional), 0.761 point (Sticky).

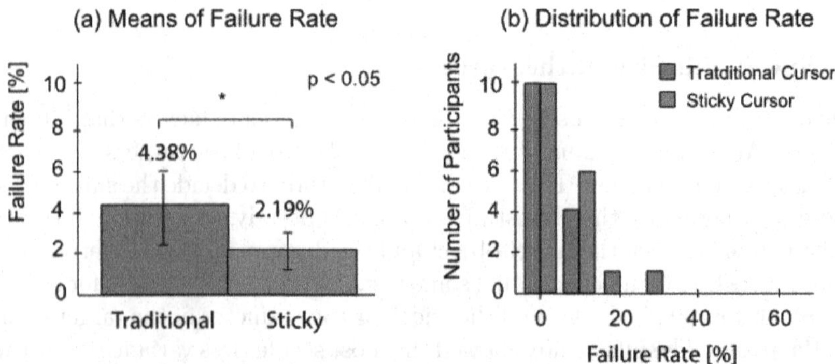

Fig. 6. Results of the failure rate. (a) Means of the failure rate and (b) Histogram of the failure rate.

We run a Poisson test on the data (we computed Poisson distribution from the traditional condition, and computed probability of obtaining the result of the sticky condition). The result was $p = 0.03 < 0.05$, which indicated the failure rate of the sticky condition is significantly lower than that of traditional condition.

5.2 The Number of Error Clicks

Figure 7 shows the number of clicks on dummy objects or on Empty places per trial. The number of the data was 16 in each condition. The means of the number of Dummy were 0.0625 (traditional), 0.0844 (sticky), and the standard errors were 0.0219 (traditional), 0.0289 (sticky). And the means of the number of Empty were 0.319 (traditional), 0.156 (Sticky), and the standard errors were 0.0700 (traditional), 0.0242 (sticky).

We run a Poisson test on the number of dummy clicks. The result was $p = 0.0900 > 0.05$, which shows that the difference was not significant between those two conditions. As for empty, the result of a Poisson test was $p = 1.31107 < 0.05$. This indicates that the difference in the number of empty clicks is significant.

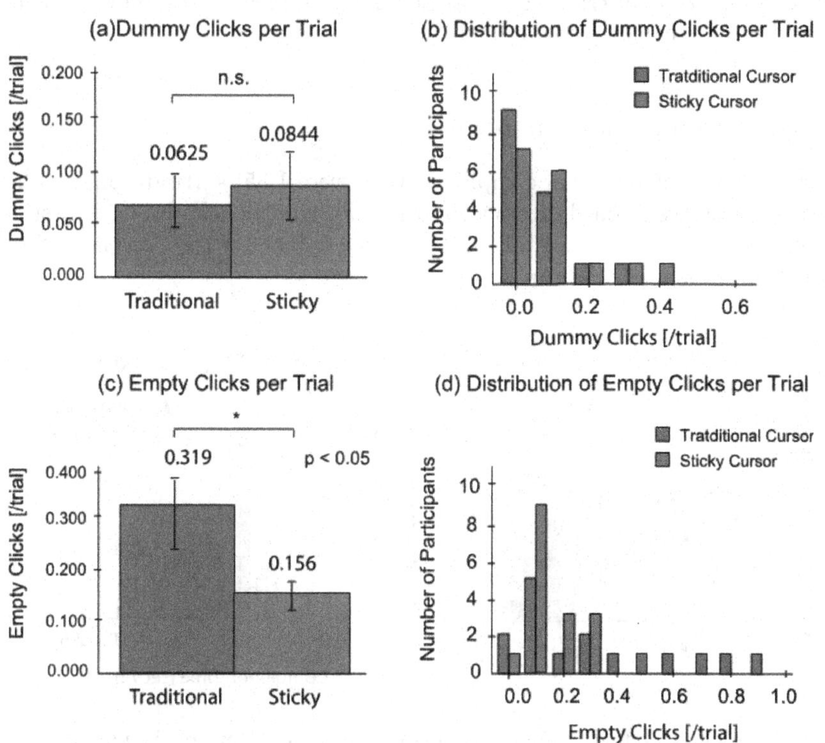

Fig. 7. Results of the error clicks. (a) Means of the number of clicks on dummy objects, (b) Histogram of the number of Dummy, (c) Means of the number of clicks on Empty place, and (d) Histogram of the number of Empty.

In addition, we examined the total error clicks (*dummy* + *empty*). Figure 8 shows the means were 0.381 (traditional), 0.240 (sticky), and the standard errors were 0.0843 (traditional), and 0.0449 (sticky). The result of a Poisson test was $p = 2.31105 < 0.05$. This indicates that the difference in the number of total error clicks is significant.

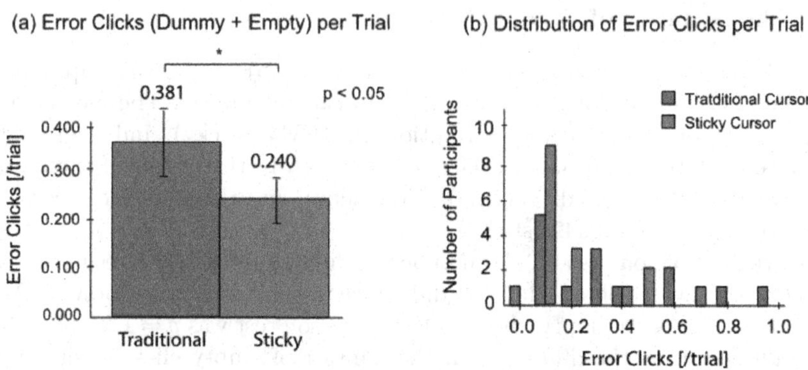

Fig. 8. Results of total error clicks. (a) Means of the number of total clicks and (b) Histogram of the number of total error clicks.

5.3 Task Completion Time

Figure 9 shows the means of completion time were 1.35 [s] (traditional), 1.23 [s] (sticky), and the standard errors were 0.112 [s] (traditional), 0.0755 [s] (sticky). We conducted Welch's t-test. The result was $p = 0.388 > 0.05$, so the difference was not statistically significant.

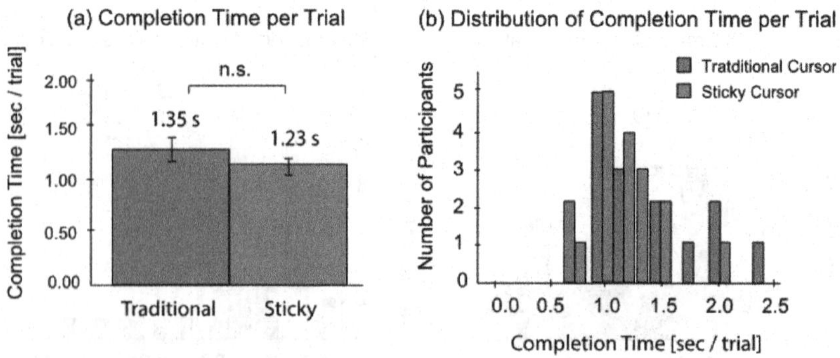

Fig. 9. Results of the task completion time per trial. (a) Means of the number of total clicks and (b) Histogram of the number of total error clicks.

5.4 Questionnaire Results

Figure 10 shows the distribution of the subjective ratings was. 8 of 16 participants equally liked the sticky cursor, and 6 participants preferred it to the traditional cursor. And 10 participants answered that the sticky cursor is easy to use to some extent. Also, 10 participants positively evaluated the easiness to get used to the sticky cursor.

About the sticky cursor, participants answered an advantage and disadvantage of the sticky cursor. They raised such advantages as the fact that they could concentrate on clicking after they placed the target once, or that the sticky cursor would be useful especially in the situation that they were not used to used the mouse cursor and that the target they wanted to select was moving quickly not surrounded by other moving targets. And they answered such disadvantages as the fact that they could not feel the difference when targets were slow, and that they did not distinguish which target the cursor was sticking to if the targets were overlapping.

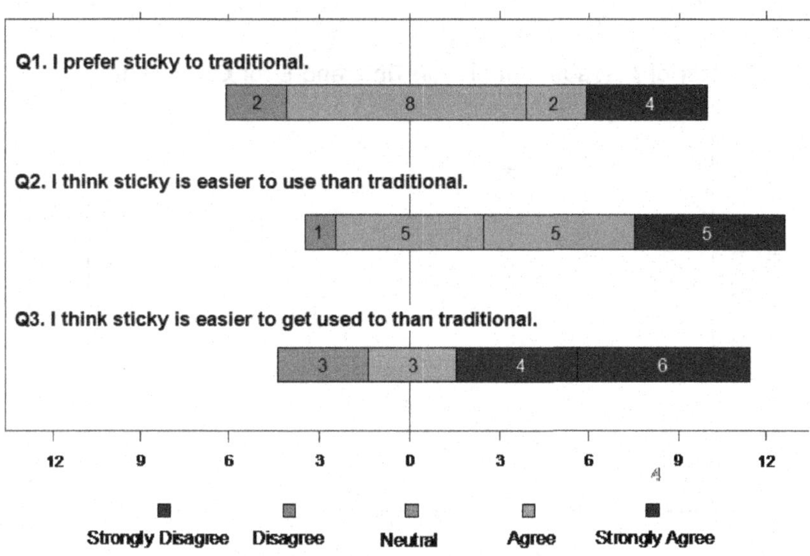

Fig. 10. Questionnaire results.

6 Discussion

The sticky cursor showed lower means of the Failure rate, the number of Empty clicks, the total number of error clicks, and the completion time. On the other hand, the mean of the number of dummy clicks was higher than that of the traditional cursor. The results of the statistical test indicated the difference in the means between the traditional cursor and the sticky cursor, except for the number of dummy clicks and the completion time.

As for hypothesis ***H1***, the result showed a shorter completion time with the sticky cursor, but the difference was not significant. So ***H1*** was neither supported or denied. Yet the result supported the hypothesis ***H2*** with a high possibility (>99.9%). It can be said that the sticky cursor reduces the total number of error clicks. About hypothesis ***H3***, the result showed that the sticky cursor might have some effect on the increase of the number of dummy clicks, but the Poisson test shows that the possibility that it was a co-incidence was $9.00\% > 5\%$. The hypothesis ***H3*** was neither supported or denied. On the other hand, the Poisson test indicated that the number of empty clicks were reduced by the sticky cursor with high possibility (>99.9%). It can safely be said that the sticky cursor have a positive effect on the reduction of the number of clicks on empty place.

Regarding the hypothesis ***H4***, we created a scatter plot of the average completion time and the difference of total error clicks (Sticky – Traditional) of the participants, see Fig. 11. And their correlation coefficient was -0.715. Therefore, it is possible to say that the sticky cursor was more effective for those who took longer time to complete the task, and that this experiment supported the hypothesis ***H4***.

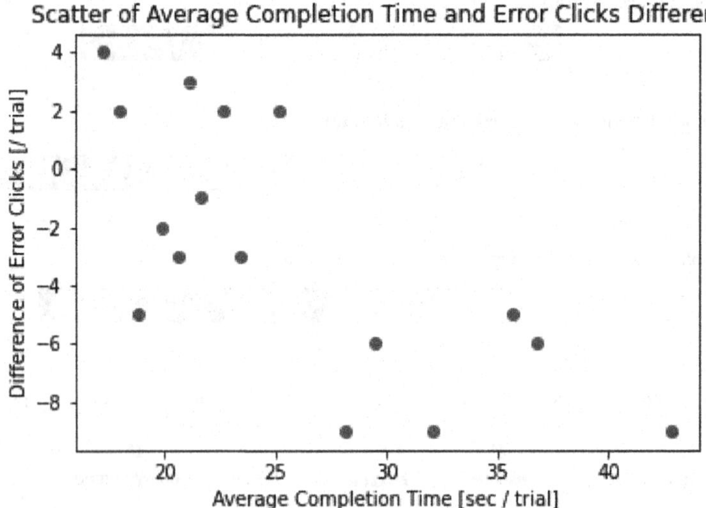

Fig. 11. The scatter plot of the average completion time and the difference of the total number of error clicks. (Sticky – Traditional)

7 Future Directions

7.1 Limitations

There are a few limitations with the proposed technique. First is that the sticky cursor is designed for indirect (relative) pointing devices and cannot be used with direct (absolute) pointing devices such as a pen tablet or a touch display (unless we physically drive these devices). Second is about the overlapping area of the targets. In this experiment, we gave priority to the dummy objects to be stuck to in the overlapping area. But even if the dummy objects were placed in front of the target object, they were sometimes confused at which target they are pointing, and they mistook that they could click the target object. There are a few limitations with the user study as well. This experiment was conducted mainly online, so we might lack the explanation to them. Also, the size of the display could not be fixed for this time. The easy conditions, the number of participants, and the inconsistency of the display were the limitations in this experiment.

7.2 Future Work

We see various future directions of this work.

- Making it possible to switch on and off the sticky function. In this experiment, we implemented the sticky cursor which can stick to targets all the time. However, the cursor which users can select if it should stick to targets may be useful in many situations. It is conceivable to assign a switching function to some mouse button and to conduct the experiment with this button. In addition, to make it visible which target the sicky cursor is sticking to by changing the color of the target or some other method.
- Varying the area of the targets in which the sticky cursor sticks to. In this experiment, such an area was set to the whole shape of the targets. However, the effectiveness or the easiness of the Sticky cursor may be improved by shrinking or expanding such area, though expanding the area may cause some confusion.
- Comparing the sticky cursor with other techniques. The sticky cursor has a feature of the fact that it does not enlarge the activation area of the cursor or the selectable area of the targets. This feature is concerned with the density of the targets. Though the effectiveness of the Sticky cursor is also reduced in the dense situation, it is conceivable that its degree of reduction is smaller than the other techniques, since enlarging the area makes the field denser.

7.3 Applications

We suggest some applications of the sticky cursor technique. First is for the situation of automatically scrolling a web page or an electronic book. The content or sentence which users are now reading is set to be the target, and the cursor sticks to it, so that it can reduce the possibility to miss the content and can facilitate users to follow the automatically flowing sentences. Second is for the seek bars in the video-sharing site. When a video is playing, the current point of the seek bar always moves to right. In most cases, the current point was enlarged to make it easy to select, but this causes the difficulty to click the immediate former or latter time of the current point. By using the sticky cursor, there might be less need to enlarge the current point and the usability could be improved.

Third is for the management of food deliverers. These days, the use of food delivery services was increasing. Food deliverers are moving almost all the time in working, so it might be difficult to select them and grasp the current status with GUIs. Since the icons of them will have some distance in the field, the sticky cursor might be effective to facilitate the management of them.

8 Conclusion

In this study, we introduce, Sticky Cursor, a pointing technique that makes a cursor stick to a moving target (i.e. move together with the target) before selecting it. We ran a user study to compare the proposed "stick" cursor and a traditional (standard) "non-sticky" cursor in a moving object selection task. The results showed that the sticky cursor helped the participants to select (point and click) the moving object more correctly (precisely) than the traditional cursor. In addition, most of the participants preferred the sticky cursor for selecting moving objects and felt the sticky cursor is easy to use and get used to it during the task. We believe this technique can be used in many applications while we discussed possible applications.

Acknowledgement. The experimental reward of this study was paid from the research fund of Igarashi laboratory. I thank to Assistant Professors in the laboratory, Tsukasa Fukusato, Kazutaka Nakashima, and Seung-Tak Noh for advising us from different viewpoints, and Yuta Fukushima and Yuuma Shiota for participating a pilot study of this experiment.

References

1. Bezerianos, A., Dragicevic, P., Balakrishnan, R.: Mnemonic rendering: an image-based approach for exposing hidden changes in dynamic displays. In: UIST 2006: Proceedings of the 19th Annual ACM Symposium on User Interface Software and Technology, pp. 159–168 (2006). https://doi.org/10.1145/1166253.1166279
2. Blanch, R., Guiard, Y., Beaudouin-Lafon, M.: Semantic pointing: improving target acquisition with control-display ratio adaptation. In: Proceedings of the SIGCHI Conference on Human Factors in Computing Systems (CHI 2004), pp. 519–526 (2004). https://doi.org/10.1145/985692.985758
3. Fitts, P.M.: The information capacity of the human motor system in controlling the amplitude of movement. J. Exp. Psychol. **47**, 381–391 (1954)
4. Fung, R., Lank, E., Terry, M., Latulipe, C.: Kinematic templates: end-user tools for content-relative cursor manipulations. In: Proceedings of the 21st Annual ACM Symposium on User Interface Software and Technology, pp. 47–56 (2008). https://doi.org/10.1145/1449715.1449725
5. Grossman, T., Balakrishnan, R.: The bubble cursor: enhancing target acquisition by dynamic resizing of the cursor's activation area. In: Proceedings of the SIGCHI Conference on Human Factors in Computing Systems (CHI 2005), pp. 281–290 (2005). https://doi.org/10.1145/1054972.1055012

6. Grossman, T., Kong, N., Balakrishnan, R.: Modeling pointing at targets of arbitrary shapes. In: Proceedings of the SIGCHI Conference on Human Factors in Computing Systems (CHI 2007), pp. 463–472 (2007). https://doi.org/10.1145/1240624.1240700
7. Hasan, K., Grossman, T., Irani, P.: Comet and target ghost: techniques for selecting moving targets. In: Proceedings of the SIGCHI Conference on Human Factors in Computing Systems (CHI 2011), pp. 839–848 (2011). https://doi.org/10.1145/1978942.1979065
8. Huang, J., Tian, F., Li, N., Fan, X.: Modeling the uncertainty in 2D moving target selection. In: Proceedings of the 32nd Annual ACM Symposium on User Interface Software and Technology (UIST 2019), pp. 1031–1043 (2019). https://doi.org/10.1145/3332165.3347880
9. Kabbash, P., Buxton, W.A.S.: The "prince" technique: Fitts' law and selection using area cursors. In: Proceedings of the SIGCHI Conference on Human Factors in Computing Systems (CHI 1995), pp. 273–279 (1995). https://doi.org/10.1145/223904.223939
10. Kobayashi, M., Igarashi, T.: Ninja cursors: using multiple cursors to assist target acquisition on large screens. In: Proceedings of the SIGCHI Conference on Human Factors in Computing Systems (CHI 2008), pp. 949–958 (2008). https://doi.org/10.1145/1357054.1357201
11. Labrune, O.C.J.B., Pietriga, E.: Dynaspot: speed-dependent area cursor. In: Proceedings of the SIGCHI Conference on Human Factors in Computing Systems (CHI 2009), pp. 1391–1400 (2009). https://doi.org/10.1145/1518701.1518911
12. Laukkanen, J., Isokoski, P., Räihä, K.J.: The cone and the lazy bubble: two efficient alternatives between the point cursor and the bubble cursor. In: Proceedings of the SIGCHI Conference on Human Factors in Computing Systems (CHI 2008), pp. 309–312 (2008). https://doi.org/10.1145/1357054.1357107
13. Lécuyer, A., Burkhardt, J.M., Etienne, L.: Feeling bumps and holes without a haptic interface: the perception of pseudo-haptic textures. In: Proceedings of the SIGCHI Conference on Human Factors in Computing Systems (CHI 2004), pp. 239–246 (2004). https://doi.org/10.1145/985692.985723
14. MacKenzie, I.S.: A note on the information-theoretic basis for Fitts' law. J. Mot. Behav. **21**, 323–330 (1989)
15. MacKenzie, I.S.: Fitts' law as a research and design tool in human-computer interaction. Hum.-Comput. Interact. **7**(1), 91–139 (1992). https://doi.org/10.1207/s15327051hci0701_3
16. MacKenzie, I.S., Buxton, W.: Extending Fitts' law to two-dimensional tasks. In: Proceedings of the SIGCHI Conference on Human Factors in Computing Systems (CHI 1992), pp. 219–226 (1992). https://doi.org/10.1145/142750.142794
17. Wobbrock, J.O., Cutrell, E., Harada, S., MacKenzie, I.S.: An error model for pointing based on Fitts' law. In: Proceedings of the SIGCHI Conference on Human Factors in Computing Systems (CHI 2008), pp. 1613–1622 (2008). https://doi.org/10.1145/1357054.1357306

A Preliminary Study on Eye Contact Framework Toward Improving Gaze Awareness in Video Conferences

Kazuya Izumi(✉), Shieru Suzuki, Ryogo Niwa, Atsushi Shinoda, Ryo Iijima, Ryosuke Hyakuta, and Yoichi Ochiai

Research and Development Center for Digital Nature, University of Tsukuba, Tsukuba, Japan
izumin@digitalnature.slis.tsukuba.ac.jp

Abstract. Gaze information plays an important role as non-verbal information in face-to-face conversations. However, in online videoconferences, users' gaze is perceived as misaligned due to the different positions of the screen and the camera. This problem causes a lack of gaze information, such as gaze awareness. To solve this problem, gaze correction methods in videoconference have been extensively discussed, and these methods allow us to maintain eye contact with other participants even in videoconference. However, people rarely make constant eye contact with the other person in face-to-face conversations. Although a person's gaze generally reflects their intentions, if the system unconditionally corrects gaze, the intention of the user's gaze is incorrectly conveyed. Therefore, we conducted a preliminary study to develop an eye contact framework; a system that corrects the user's gaze only when the system detects that the user is looking at the face of the videoconferencing participant. In this study, participants used this system in a online conference and evaluated it qualitatively. As a result, this prototype was not significant in the evaluation of gaze awareness, but useful feedback was obtained from the questionnaire. We will improve this prototype and aim to develop a framework to facilitate non-verbal communication in online videoconferences.

Keywords: Gesture and Eye-gaze Based Interaction · Eye Contact · Gaze Awareness · Video Conferencing · Video-mediated Communication · Gaze Interaction

1 Introduction

1.1 Background

People have been freed from the constraints of location and can communicate without gathering in one place with the widespread use of remote communication through online videoconferencing systems. However, video conferencing has a serious problem in that it lacks non-verbal feedback, including eye contact, in comparison to face-to-face meetings [10,11,15]. In the lack of such non-verbal information in a conversation, the participants in the conversation try to compensate for the lack of non-verbal information by increasing the amount of talk, which in turn reduces the efficiency of the communication [17]. Many researchers have tried to achieve the same level of non-verbal feedback in videoconferencing as in face-to-face conversations.

M. Kurosu and A. Hashizume (Eds.): HCII 2023, LNCS 14011, pp. 484–498, 2023.
https://doi.org/10.1007/978-3-031-35596-7_31

Among the non-verbal information in face-to-face conversations, gaze, especially eye contact, plays an important role [3]. Eye contact helps to share one's interests and feelings [9, 13], builds trust [14] and helps in lowering social anxiety disorder [18]. However, due to the physical misalignment between the camera and the screen position, the gaze information is lost and the eye contact is not made. In a general video conferencing environment, where the camera is placed above the screen, when the user is looking at the screen, the image from the camera makes the user appear to be looking down [8].

1.2 Research Motivation

To solve the problem of lack of eye contact due to misperceived gaze, research has been conducted on gaze correction mainly based on the information from the user's eye tracking [5, 19, 20]. For example, Vertegall et al. [20] set up cameras side by side and used an eye tracker to maintain eye contact between users by switching the image to the camera closest to the front of the user's gaze in the video. Hsu et al. [5] detected the position of the faces of the video conference participants on the screen and processed the images so that the user's pupil position is directed to the front, on the assumption that the user's eyes are facing the participant's face. Tausif et al. [19] proposed a method that uses an XY plotter to move the camera behind the screen vertically and horizontally in accordance with the user's gaze. In addition, FaceTime from Apple, Inc. has added the ability to direct a user's gaze to the camera on a smartphone in real time using image processing. Nvidia Broadcast from Nvidia, Inc. has also added the ability to direct a user's gaze to the camera on PC in real time. Thus, many approaches have been proposed to improve the lack of eye contact by continuously correcting the gaze in real time, allowing us to always have eye contact with the other participant in an online videoconference.

However, these approaches redirect the user's gaze forward in all situations, so that the conversation partner is always in eye contact with the user. In both face-to-face and videoconferencing, people rarely make eye contact with their interlocutor [2]. During casual conversation, people look at the other person 61 % of the time, and only about half of that time is there mutual eye contact [1]. In addition, Bailenson et al. [2] have pointed out that videoconference participants often feel tired after a meeting because of the constant gaze of the other participant.

In general, the gaze behaviour of participants in a conversation reflects their intentions, such as expressing interest or requesting turn taking [6, 20]. However, unconditional correction of gaze to the front would misrepresent the user's intention by gaze. For example, even if a videoconference participant is looking at a browser in another window, the gaze may be corrected and other participants may think they are being looked at. Therefore, simply by always redirecting the user's gaze to the camera in online videoconferencing, it is not possible to communicate all the eye contact that is possible in face-to-face conversations.

Therefore, this paper examines whether it is possible to appropriately convey both eye contact and other gaze interactions to the other party in an online videoconference by reducing the frequency of gaze correction. Specifically, we implemented and evaluated in a preliminary study eye contact framework; a system that corrects the user's gaze only when the system detects that the user is looking at the face of the videoconferencing participant. With this system, videoconferencing users can only make eye contact when they are looking at each other. We hypothesised that this would allow users to make appropriate eye contact while preventing other gaze behaviours from being inadvertently transmitted to the other party, and specifically evaluated changes in users' qualitative responses.

2 Related Work

We review the role of gaze and eye contact in conversation and approaches to correcting gaze in videoconferencing, and summarise the purpose of this research in the last section.

2.1 Role of Eye Contact in Video Conferences

Eye contact in conversations has many different roles [3]. Eye contact helps to share one's interests and feelings [9, 13], builds trust [14] and helps in lowering social anxiety disorder [18]. It also plays an important role in multi-party communication as turn taking, such as encouraging people to talk [6, 20]. Vertegaal et al. [20] suggested that there are two roles for eye contact: "*Eye contact is used to convey whom one speaks or listens to.*" And "*Eye contact is used to regulate intimacy and arousal in conversations.*". In addition, if participants in a video conferences cannot observe the eye contact of other participants, they will not be able to accurately estimate whether they are being asked or expected to speak, and they will avoid speaking because they will not be able to measure the intimacy of the communication. O'Malley et al. [17] stated that participants in online video conferences speak and gaze at the other participants more than in face-to-face meetings. This suggests that the lack of nonverbal information leads to a lack of confidence in the mutual understanding of the conversation, which is overcompensated for by increasing the level of both verbal and nonverbal information. Thus, the gaze plays an important role as one of the non-verbal information in a conversation, and the lack of gaze information especially eye contact in video conferences, has a significant negative impact on communication and results in less engagement of the conferences.

Lack of eye contact in video conferences is mainly caused by the gap between the participant's gaze on the video conference screen and the participant's gaze on the camera. In order to maintain eye contact with the participants in video conferences, the gap between the user's gaze and the camera's optical axis needs to be kept within 1°C in the horizontal direction and within 5°C in the vertical direction [3]. However, in a setup where the camera is placed at the top of a 24 in. monitor, the parallax from the camera when the user is looking at the center of the screen can be as much as 15°C, resulting in a significant lack of eye contact [8]. Improving the lack of eye contact is a matter of solving this gap in gaze, and various researches has been conducted as discussed in the next section. Maintaining eye contact in video conferencing has been a challenge for many years, and various methods have been tried [4, 5, 7, 8, 16, 19, 20]. There are two main methods of gaze correction: static gaze correction, assuming that the user's gaze and face position are static, and dynamic gaze correction, where the gaze is corrected dynamically based on the user's gaze.

2.2 Static Gaze Correction in Video Conferences

In this section, researches on static gaze correction is introduced. There are two main approaches to correcting eye contact: hardware-based approaches and software-based approaches. The hardware-based approaches achieve eye contact by matching the optical paths of the display and the camera, or by enabling the user to view the video conference image and the camera at the same time [7, 16]. For example, in Clearboard [7], a half-mirror is set up as a screen and a camera captures the image of the user reflected in the half-mirror, thereby matching the gaze of the user looking at the screen with the gaze of the user being captured by the camera. MAJIC [16] uses a projector to project images onto a thin transparent film and installs a camera behind the film to match the optical paths between the camera and the display. On the other hand, software-based approaches manipulate the video sent to the video conferencing system, such as the research that rotates the image from the camera in three dimensions to make the captured user looking at the display face the front [8].

However, since the position of the user's face and the direction of their gaze are not fixed in actual video conferencing, eye contact will not be made in these systems if the user looks slightly away [20]. In current multi-party video conferencing applications, the images of each participant are displayed in a tiled arrangement, and the position of the participants' faces is not fixed. In addition, the participants sometimes look at other application windows, such as referring to documents. Therefore, it is difficult to maintain eye contact with static eye correction.

2.3 Dynamic Gaze Correction in Video Conferences

With the development of computer vision technologies and the detection of the user's gaze with high accuracy and high frame rate, researches have been conducted on tracking the user's gaze and dynamically correcting the gaze. In hardware-based approaches, GAZE-2 [20] responded to changes in the user's gaze by installing multiple cameras and an eye tracker behind a half-mirror and switching the image sent to the video conference system to the camera closest to the user's viewpoint. In addition, Tausif et al. [19] responded to changes in the user's gaze by using an XY plotter to move the camera behind the screen vertically and horizontally according to the position of the user's face and gaze, enabling eye contact to be maintained. In a software-based approach, methods were proposed to redirect the user's face and eyes in the image [4, 5, 21, 22]. For example, Look at Me! [5] corrects the user's eye ball rotation based on the position of the participant's face in the video conference image and generates the image as if the user is facing the front.

2.4 Purpose of This Study

Research on tracking the user's gaze and redirecting the gaze have made it possible to make eye contact at all times, regardless of the user's gaze direction. However, in face-to-face meetings, participants do not always look at each other's faces, and often look elsewhere as well, such as at the documents at hand [16]. Participants spend a significant amount of time during a conversation avoiding eye contact with each other, and if there is a third object, such as a blackboard, participants spend less than half the time looking at each other's faces [2]. Bailenson et al. [2] also found that Zoom Fatigue, a peculiar fatigue of video conference participants, is caused partly by the perception that all participants' faces are projected in front of them and that they are constantly being watched throughout the meeting. It is said that one of the reasons for this is that all participants' faces are projected in front of them, giving the illusion that they are being watched at all times during the meeting. Thus, it is thought that constant support for eye contact would conversely reduce the efficiency of the meeting and cause fatigue.

The goal of this research is to develop a nonverbal communication framework that enables users to communicate nonverbal information, including eye contact, to others in online videoconferencing in a way that they intend. In this paper, we conducted a preliminary study focusing on the eye contact framework. By introducing the framework to all videoconferencing users, eye contact will only occur when they look at each other, and eye contact communication will be realised similarly to face-to-face conversation.

3 System

This section describes the system used to evaluate the eye contact framework. The system consists of a software component and a hardware component. The software component detects whether the user is looking at the participant's face and decides whether to correct the user's gaze. The software component then sends a signal to the hardware component, which corrects the gaze. Figure 2 shows the system usage, Fig. 2 shows an overview of the system and Fig. 3 shows the entire system flow. The implementation of the software and hardware parts will be described in the next sections.

3.1 Software Component for Detection of the User's Gaze

The software component performs the following processes:

1. Detect the user's gaze point and determine whether the user is looking at the participant's face.
2. If the system determined that the user is looking at the participant's face, calculate the target coordinates and rotation angle of the camera for gaze correction from the user's gaze point and gaze vector information.
3. The calculated information of the target coordinates and rotation angle of the camera is sent to the hardware component via serial communication.

The target coordinates are calibrated as described in the next section, and the destination (x, y) is normalised to the range [0, 1]. The hardware component moves the camera based on the target and rotation angle information received from Arduino for gaze correction (Fig. 1).

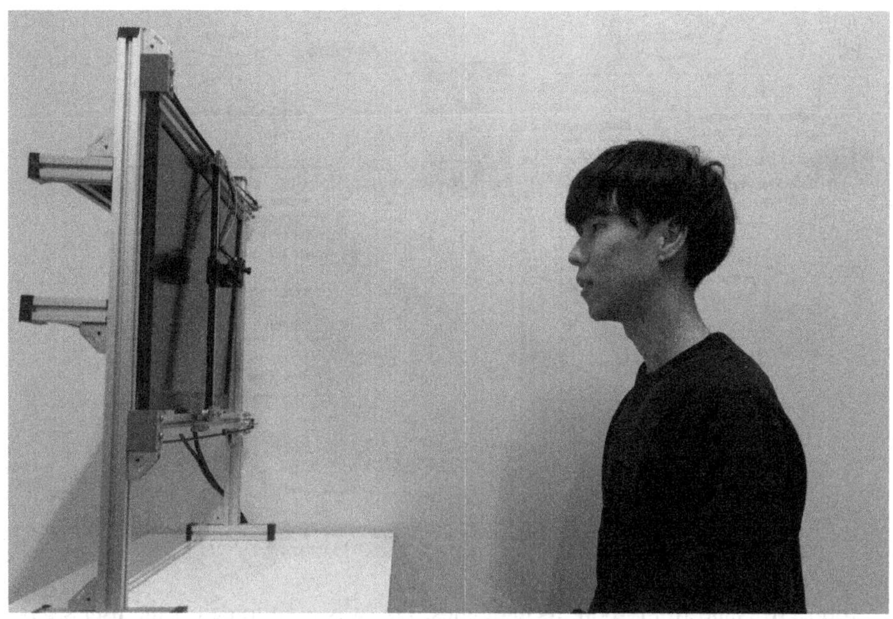

Fig. 1. System usage

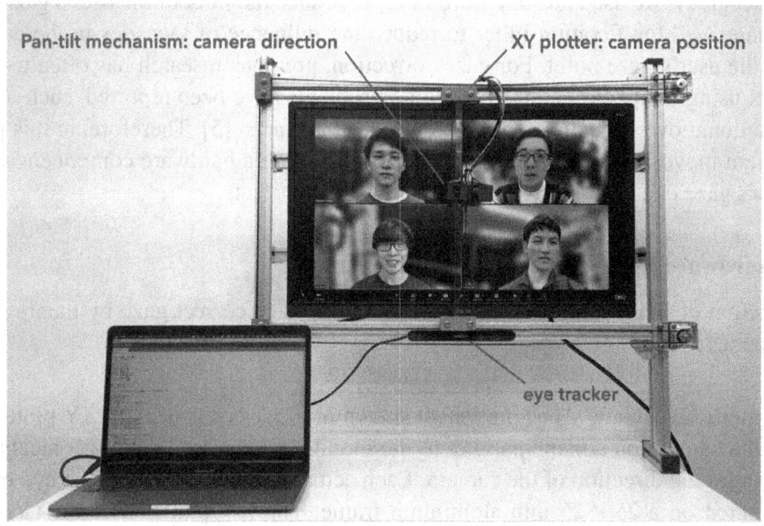

Fig. 2. System overview

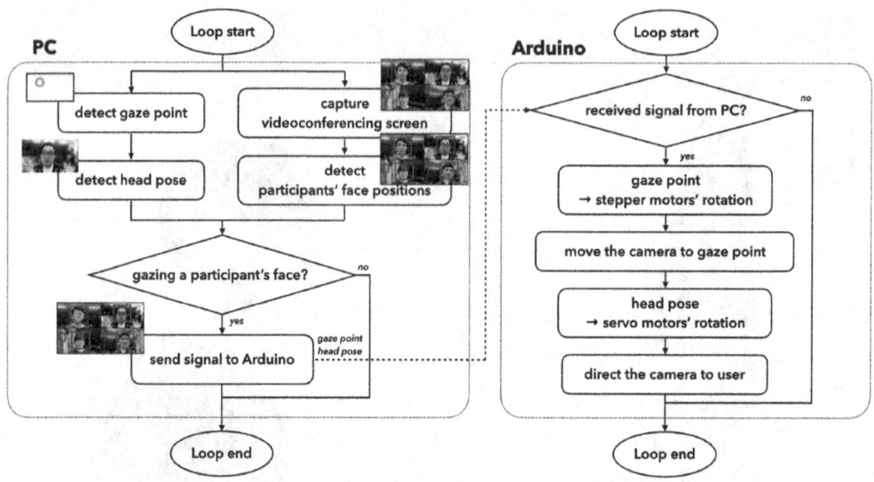

Fig. 3. System flow

Tobii Pro Nano from Tobii Technologies, Inc. was used to detect the user's gaze point and gaze vector, and MediaPipe Face Detection[1] was used to detect the faces of the videoconference participants in the video. To obtain the user's gaze point with higher accuracy, we used the One Euro Filter to reduce the jitter of the user's gaze point coordinates and the Fixation Filter to reduce the influence of saccades in the calculation of the user's gaze point. For gaze correction, previous research has often used the methods using image processing, but some problems have been reported, such as high computational overhead and generation of visual artifacts [5]. Therefore, in this paper, the system moves the camera in front of the monitor in a hardware component so that the user's gaze can be corrected without any visual artifacts.

3.2 Hardware Component for Gaze Correction

This section describes the hardware component used to correct gaze by manipulating the camera.

Component Overview. The component shown in Fig. 2 consists of an XY plotter that moves the camera on a plane parallel to the monitor screen, and a pan-tilt mechanism that changes the direction of the camera. Each actuator, the monitor and the eye tracker are mounted on a 25×25 mm aluminium frame. The XY plotter uses the CoreXY[2] mechanism to reduce the weight of the moving part and increase the speed of camera movement. The mounting adapters for the pulleys of the XY plotter were 3D printed, and the mounting adapters for the monitor and stepper motors were laser cut. Each actuator is connected to an Arduino Uno and is controlled by information received from the software component via serial communication.

[1] https://google.github.io/mediapipe/solutions/face_detection.html.

[2] https://corexy.com/.

Calibration. After assembling this system, the user must first calibrate the system to avoid attempting to move the camera out of range of the monitor screen. First, the user moves the camera to the upper left corner of the monitor's LCD screen. Next, the user operates the XY plotter from a calibration program and moves the camera to the bottom right of the screen. This calibrates the camera's range of movement. In the program, the coordinates of the camera's movement are replaced by the number of rotations of the stepper motor in the XY plotter and stored in the program (Fig. 4). This allows the hardware component to operate the actuator based on the camera position and angle information specified by the software component via serial communication.

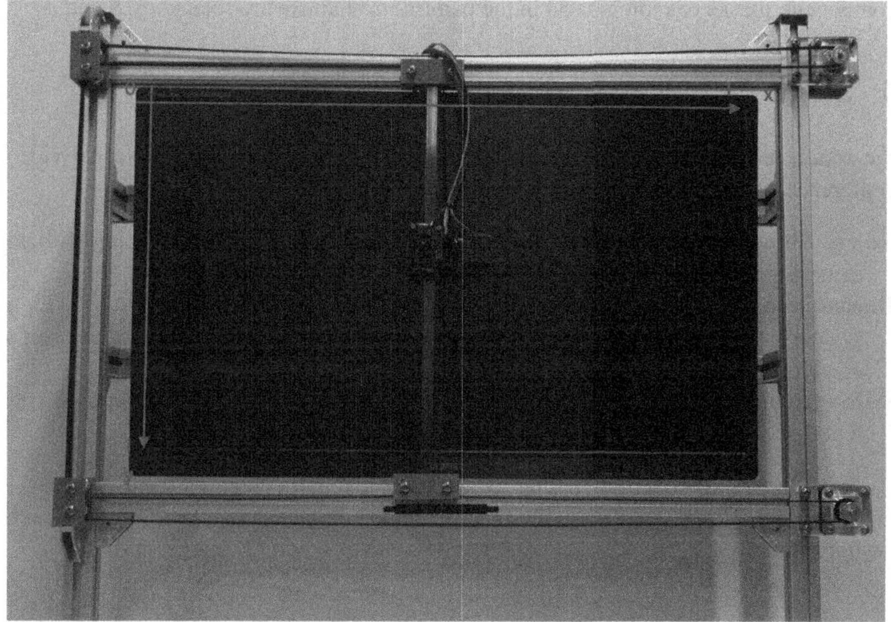

Fig. 4. XY plotter coordinates; normalized from 0 to 1.

Camera Manipulation. The software component calculates the coordinates of the camera's destination on the monitor and converts them into the number of rotations of the stepper motor mounted on the XY plotter, which is then sent to the hardware component. From the calibration, the number of motor rotations required to move the camera from the origin to the end point is defined as $X_{MAX} and Y_{MAX}$. If the camera is to move to coordinate (x, y) $(0 <= x, y <= 1)$, the number of rotations of the stepper motors, stepx and stepy are calculated as follows:

$$step_x = round(x \times X_{MAX}), step_y = round(y \times Y_{MAX}) \tag{1}$$

When the software component sends this information to Arduino via serial communication, Arduino rotates the stepper motor so that the rotation numbers become $step_x$ and $step_y$. The current rotation number is stored in Arduino and the required number of rotation steps $\Delta step_x$ and $\Delta step_y$ are calculated as follows:

$$\Delta step_x = step_x - step_x^{now}, \Delta step_y = step_y - step_y^{now} \tag{2}$$

where $step_x^{now}$, $step_y^{now}$ are the current number of rotation steps. If $\Delta step_x, \Delta step_y$ are positive and negative respectively, the stepper motor is rotated forward and backward. If the rotation angles θ and ϕ $(-60 <= \theta, \phi <= 60)$ are sent from software component, the servo motors used in the pan-tilt mechanism are rotated by θ and ϕ.

4 Study

We conducted user study to evaluate the system in comparison with the usual video conference system, under the following three conditions:

No eye contact correction (No Correction) An ordinary video conferencing without camera manipulation or image processing.

Unconditional eye contact correction (Unconditional) Video conferencing with a system using camera manipulation that keeps correcting gaze regardless of the user's attention.

With eye contact framework (Proposed) Video conferencing with our proposed system that corrects the gaze depending on the user's attention.

From these experimental conditions, we evaluated and compared the user engagement, the user's impression about their conversation opponent and user's fatigue of each design system.

Participants and Study Design

A total of 12 (5 males, 7 females; age range: 19–51, *M*= 25.9, *SD*= 10.9) participants took part in the study. Participants were divided into groups of four, and each group participated in the study one at a time. Each participant participated in a video conference in a well sound obstructed space. The video conference was done a total of three times changing the experimental conditions, no correlation, correlation and design and answered a questionnaire asking about their experience after each video conference. At the end of all three meetings, the participants evaluated the best and worst experience from the three system designs and the reasons for the answer. In order to take a counterbalance, the order of the system designs was switched between groups.

This study was conducted face-to-face with close consideration to COVID-19. Zoom from Zoom Video Communications, Inc. was used for video conferencing application. Noise reduction software was used during the video conference to prevent the implemented equipment noize interfering with the audio of the video conference.

4.1 Procedure

First, the study overview and procedure was explained, participants agreed to the consent form. After the participants moved to different rooms, they were asked to participate in the video conference system with a microphone and video camera turned on. In conducting this system study, a virtual background which is a function in video conference application was used to prevent the participants from getting distracted by the transition of the background caused by camera movement.

After a five minute ice-break session, video conference was done three times with each system condition. The following process was done in each condition.

System Explanation and Calibration. After explaining the system used in the next video conference, eye tracker calibration with Tobii Pro Eye Tracker Manager was done in five minutes. Participants were required to position their face as the calibration system guidance and the system calibrated five gazing points on the screen. Finally checked if the eye tracing for each participant has no significant error.

Speach. Each participant gave a 30 s speech with the theme prepared for the participants to get familiar with the used system and to avoid the novelty effect caused by the system.

Discussion. Discussion requires mutual conversation which gives opportunities for frequent speaker and attention change. Therefore, eye contact holds an important role to follow the context of the conversation and lead to poor conversation experience without it. In addition, speakers judge the audience's interests with eye contact which makes the speaker unconfident without it. From the reasons above, we conducted a seven minute discussion to evaluate if eye contact was successfully taken and context was easy to follow from eye contact.

Questionnaire. Questionnaires were prepared on experimental conditions of thes session and conservation experience, the user experience of the system, TPI [12], and fatigue after the meeting. There was a five minute break before repeating this procedure for the next design system. After all the study was over, participants completed a questionnaire to rank the meeting conditions and their overall opinions about the study. Each condition took half an hour, and the entire study took two hours.

4.2 Result and Discussion

Figure 5 shows the qualitative results. Questionnaires are the following: "*How frequently eye contact did you have with the participants?*", "*How often were you aware of the camera during the videoconference?*", "*Did the camera movement interfere with your discussion?*", "*Did the participants look directly at you or listen to you?*", "*Did you get a feel for the intention of participants?*" and "*Did you understand why the participants were looking at you?*"

We validated that the data is normally distributed through the Shapiro-Wilk test and satisfies the assumptions of an analysis of variance (ANOVA). As a result, the Proposed condition was not significant ($p > 0.05$) in terms of TPI and gaze awareness. However, Figure X shows that the Unconditional condition tended to be more aware of the camera than the others, and the camera tended to interfere with the discussion. This result shows that the Unconditional condition tends to be less useful in videoconferencing. Possible reasons for this include the camera's movement interfering with the videoconferencing screen, sound problems, and the delay between detecting eye movement and actually correcting the camera.

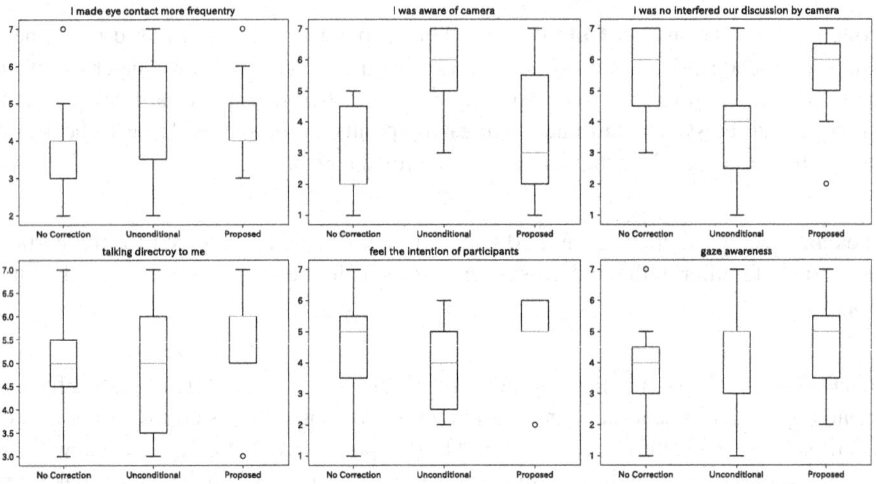

Fig. 5. Qualitative results regarding TPI and gaze awareness between No Correction condition, Unconditional condition and Proposed condition.

In addition, the paritipants evaluated the best and worst experiences from the three conditions. From the results, 58 % of the participants answered that the proposed system was the best experience in 3 conditions, with the reasons given as "*the system conveyed the eye movement of participants well*" and "*eye contact occurred appropriately with the other participants.*"

Insight. The results showed that the proposed system was not advantageous for videoconferencing, but tended to improve gaze awareness compared to other corrections. The feedback we received was: "*I was disturbed by the camera moving too much*" and "*Our discussion was disturbed by the moving camera during the videoconference*". The reason why the study did not show significant results is that these defects, such as the camera movement noise of the hardware component, were uncomfortable for the participants. By improving these defects, the proposed system could be useful in videoconferencing systems. This is suggested by the fact that many participants answered that the proposed system was relatively the best experience among the three conditions.

5 Limitation and Future Work

The results of the user study showed that the proposed system has the potential to reduce the risk of unintentional transmission of the user's gaze to the other participants in a videoconference. However, there are some limitations to the proposed system and the experiment.

Visibility of the Videoconferencing Screen. In this paper, an XY plotter is used to move the camera position, but the questionnaire results show that the screen was difficult to see due to the XY plotter. Therefore, in the future it may be possible to make the XY plotter less conspicuous by changing to a camera manipulation system that uses a thin wire instead of a belt as part of the XY plotter. Alternatively, a compact camera running on the monitor could greatly improve the user's screen visibility.

Cost of Installing the System. In order to use the system, users need to purchase and assemble the parts themselves, which is a significant barrier to using the system. In addition, the eye tracker device used in this study is expensive, but there is a possibility that OSS such as WebGazer.js could be used as a substitute. In this study, we used an eye tracker device because we needed to detect the gaze point with relatively high accuracy in order to detect the participants' facial area, but we will also consider systems that can use commercially available webcams and such OSS to reduce installation costs.

Comparison of Gaze Correction Methods. There are two methods of gaze correction: one is to manipulate the position of the camera, as in the proposed method, and the other is to use image processing. The advantage of the image processing method is that the latency to correct gaze is very low. However, image processing causes visual artefacts, and the model size increases to correct such artefacts, which increases the computational load. In contrast, the proposed method, which manipulates the camera position, does not cause visual artifacts and can correct the user's gaze with a small computational load, but the problem is that the manipulation noise and latency are significant. In the future, we would like to verify video conferencing views that take this into account in combination with other eye interaction methods. For example, we will explore combining the two correction methods, such as using image processing to primarily correct gaze, and using an XY plotter to physically change the camera position to correct when visual artifacts are expected to occur.

Lack of Quantitative Evaluation. In this paper, we have evaluated the system in terms of the interlocutor's impression, but we have not been able to discuss how much eye contact was made using the system and how much mutual eye contact was actually made by using the system. In the future, we will have to carry out these quantitative evaluations as well as updating the system.

6 Conclusion

This paper verifies the prototype of a system that allows users to make eye contact without losing the context of their non-verbal communication. Using the proposed system, videoconferencing users can make eye contact only when looking at each other. Previous work has addressed the issue of how to complement eye contact in videoconferencing, which is one of the most important non-verbal information in face-to-face conversations. However, the problem with these researches is that they have always corrected the gaze without considering the user's intention, resulting in always eye contact.

The preliminary study in this paper showed that gaze awareness during videoconferencing tended to be slightly improved by using this system, and the questionnaire results suggested the usefulness of the eye contact framework. In addition, some improvements to the system were found, such as the disruption of the meeting by the camera's manipulation noise. By making the above improvements and conducting the verification again, this system should be more efficient in videoconferencing.

In the future, we will analyse more information about gaze in conversation, such as what people are looking at, what they are looking at, and what they want to pay attention to, and aim to construct an eye contact framework that enables eye contact communication in videoconferencing as in face-to-face meetings.

Acknowledgement. This work was funded by JST CREST Grant Number JPMJCR19F2, Japan. We are grateful to Associate Prof. Hiromi Morita for lending us the Tobii Pro Nano for our study.

References

1. Argyle, M., Cook, M.: Gaze and mutual gaze (1976)
2. Bailenson, J.N.: Nonverbal overload: a theoretical argument for the causes of zoom fatigue. Technol. Mind Behav. **2**(1) (2021). https://doi.org/10.1037/tmb0000030
3. Chen, M.: Leveraging the asymmetric sensitivity of eye contact for videoconference. In: Proceedings of the SIGCHI Conference on Human Factors in Computing Systems, pp. 49–56. CHI 2002, Association for Computing Machinery, New York, NY, USA, April 2002. https://doi.org/10.1145/503376.503386
4. Ganin, Y., Kononenko, D., Sungatullina, D., Lempitsky, V.: DeepWarp: photorealistic image resynthesis for gaze manipulation. In: Leibe, B., Matas, J., Sebe, N., Welling, M. (eds.) ECCV 2016. LNCS, vol. 9906, pp. 311–326. Springer, Cham (2016). https://doi.org/10.1007/978-3-319-46475-6_20
5. Hsu, C.F., Wang, Y.S., Lei, C.L., Chen, K.T.: Look at me! correcting eye gaze in live video communication. ACM Trans. Multimedia Comput. Commun. Appl. **15**(2), 1–21 (2019). https://doi.org/10.1145/3311784
6. Iitsuka, R., Kawaguchi, I., Shizuki, B., Takahashi, S.: Multi-party video conferencing system with gaze cues representation for turn-taking. In: Hernández-Leo, D., Hishiyama, R., Zurita, G., Weyers, B., Nolte, A., Ogata, H. (eds.) CollabTech 2021. LNCS, vol. 12856, pp. 101–108. Springer, Cham (2021). https://doi.org/10.1007/978-3-030-85071-5_8

7. Ishii, H., Kobayashi, M.: ClearBoard: a seamless medium for shared drawing and conversation with eye contact. In: Proceedings of the SIGCHI Conference on Human Factors in Computing Systems, CHI 1992, pp. 525–532. Association for Computing Machinery, New York, NY, USA, June 1992. https://doi.org/10.1145/142750.142977
8. Jaklič, A., Solina, F., Šajn, L.: User interface for a better eye contact in videoconferencing. Displays **46**, 25–36 (2017). https://doi.org/10.1016/j.displa.2016.12.002
9. Kim, S., Billinghurst, M., Lee, G., Norman, M., Huang, W., He, J.: Sharing emotion by displaying a partner near the gaze point in a telepresence system. In: 2019 23rd International Conference in Information Visualization - Part II, pp. 86–91. ieeexplore.ieee.org, July 2019. https://doi.org/10.1109/IV-2.2019.00026
10. van der Kleij, R., Maarten Schraagen, J., Werkhoven, P., De Dreu, C.K.W.: How conversations change over time in face-to-face and video-mediated communication. Small Group Res. **40**(4), 355–381 (2009). https://doi.org/10.1177/1046496409333724
11. Lee, P.S.N., Leung, L., Lo, V., Xiong, C., Wu, T.: Internet communication versus face-to-face interaction in quality of life. Soc. Indic. Res. **100**(3), 375–389 (2011). https://doi.org/10.1007/s11205-010-9618-3
12. Lombard, M., Ditton, T.B., Weinstein, L.: Measuring presence: the temple presence inventory. https://academic.csuohio.edu/kneuendorf/frames/LombardDittonWeinstein09.pdf, https://academic.csuohio.edu/kneuendorf/frames/LombardDittonWeinstein09.pdf. Accessed 4 Mar 2022
13. Majaranta, P., Räihä, K.J.: Twenty years of eye typing: systems and design issues. In: Proceedings of the 2002 Symposium on Eye Tracking Research & Applications, ETRA 2002, pp. 15–22. Association for Computing Machinery, New York, NY, USA, March 2002. https://doi.org/10.1145/507072.507076
14. Nguyen, D.T., Canny, J.: Multiview: improving trust in group video conferencing through spatial faithfulness. In: Proceedings of the SIGCHI Conference on Human Factors in Computing Systems, pp. 1465–1474. CHI 2007, Association for Computing Machinery, New York, NY, USA, April 2007. https://doi.org/10.1145/1240624.1240846
15. Nguyen, D.T., Canny, J.: More than face-to-face: empathy effects of video framing. In: Proceedings of the SIGCHI Conference on Human Factors in Computing Systems, CHI 2009, pp. 423–432. Association for Computing Machinery, New York, NY, USA, April 2009. https://doi.org/10.1145/1518701.1518770
16. Okada, K.I., Maeda, F., Ichikawaa, Y., Matsushita, Y.: Multiparty videoconferencing at virtual social distance: MAJIC design. In: Proceedings of the 1994 ACM Conference on Computer Supported Cooperative Work, CSCW 1994, pp. 385–393. Association for Computing Machinery, New York, NY, USA, October 1994. https://doi.org/10.1145/192844.193054
17. O'Malley, C., Langton, S., Anderson, A., Doherty-Sneddon, G., Bruce, V.: Comparison of face-to-face and video-mediated interaction. Interact. Comput. **8**(2), 177–192 (1996). https://doi.org/10.1016/0953-5438(96)01027-2
18. Stephenson, G.M., Rutter, D.R.: Eye-contact, distance and affiliation: a re-evaluation. Br. J. Psychol. **61**(3), 385–393 (1970). https://doi.org/10.1111/j.2044-8295.1970.tb01257.x
19. Tausif, M.T., Weaver, R.J., Lee, S.W.: Towards enabling eye contact and perspective control in video conference. In: Adjunct Publication of the 33rd Annual ACM Symposium on User Interface Software and Technology, UIST 2020 Adjunct, pp. 96–98, Association for Computing Machinery, New York, NY, USA, October 2020. https://doi.org/10.1145/3379350.3416197
20. Vertegaal, R., Weevers, I., Sohn, C., Cheung, C.: GAZE-2: conveying eye contact in group video conferencing using eye-controlled camera direction. In: Proceedings of the SIGCHI Conference on Human Factors in Computing Systems, CHI 2003, pp. 521–528. Association for Computing Machinery, New York, NY, USA, April 2003. https://doi.org/10.1145/642611.642702

21. Wood, E., Baltrušaitis, T., Morency, L.P., Robinson, P., Bulling, A.: GazeDirector: fully articulated eye gaze redirection in video. Comput. Graph. Forum **37**(2), 217–225 (2018). https://doi.org/10.1111/cgf.13355
22. Xia, W., Yang, Y., Xue, J.H., Feng, W.: Controllable continuous gaze redirection. In: Proceedings of the 28th ACM International Conference on Multimedia, pp. 1782–1790. Association for Computing Machinery, New York, NY, USA, October 2020. https://doi.org/10.1145/3394171.3413868

Intentional Microgesture Recognition for Extended Human-Computer Interaction

Chirag Kandoi, Changsoo Jung, Sheikh Mannan, Hannah VanderHoeven, Quincy Meisman, Nikhil Krishnaswamy, and Nathaniel Blanchard(✉)

Colorado State University, Fort Collins 80523, USA
{Nikhil.Krishnaswamy,Nathaniel.Blanchard}@colostate.edu

Abstract. As extended reality becomes more ubiquitous, people will more frequently interact with computer systems using gestures instead of peripheral devices. However, previous works have shown that using traditional gestures (pointing, swiping, etc.) in mid-air causes fatigue, rendering them largely unsuitable or long-term use. Some of the same researchers have promoted "microgestures"—smaller gestures requiring less gross motion—as a solution, but to date there is no dataset of intentional microgestures available to train computer vision algorithms for use in downstream interactions with computer systems such as agents deployed on XR headsets. As a step toward addressing this challenge, we present a novel video dataset of microgestures, classification results from a variety of ML models showcasing the feasibility (and difficulty) of detecting these fine-grained movements, present a demonstration of a novel keyframe detection method as a way to increase recognition accuracy, and discuss the challenges in developing robust recognition of microgestures for human-computer interaction.

Keywords: Human-computer interaction · Gesture recognition · Microgestures

1 Introduction

Gesture recognition is a current focus of extensive ongoing research and development in HCI and computer vision. As extended reality technology becomes increasingly prevalent, it is anticipated that people will increasingly use gestures as a means to interact with computer systems, rather than traditional peripheral devices. Previous research has shown that the use of hand gestures, such as pointing and swiping, in mid-air can result in fatigue ("gorilla arm") [7], making them unsuitable for extended use. In order to address this issue, Way *et al.* [26] have proposed the use of smaller hand motions, known as "microgestures," which

C. Jung and S. Mannan—These authors contributed equally to this work.

M. Kurosu and A. Hashizume (Eds.): HCII 2023, LNCS 14011, pp. 499–518, 2023.
https://doi.org/10.1007/978-3-031-35596-7_32

require less movement. These microgestures are intended to mitigate the issue of fatigue and are adaptable to multiple situations such as human-object interaction and driving a car [4,6,17–19]. In addition, microgestures are suitable replacements for general gestures if there are physical space constraints while interacting with XR systems. Beginning with simple microgestures for communicating between human and computer, the study of microgestures has potential to facilitate delivery of complex information using microgesture sequences. Despite the potential benefits of utilizing microgestures for human-computer interaction, there exists no dataset of intentional[1] microgestures for the purpose of training computer vision algorithms for downstream interactions with computer systems, such as agents deployed on XR headsets. In order to address this challenge, this paper introduces a novel video dataset of microgestures and investigates the performance of various machine learning models in classifying these gestures. Additionally, we discuss challenges and considerations in developing robust recognition of microgestures for human-computer interaction.

Our research aims to better understand the challenges posed to recognition algorithms by microgestures, which are characterized by their subtle and fast nature. These properties make the task of gesture classification difficult, creating a challenge for those working in the field of vision-based gesture recognition for use in HCI. In response to this challenge, we created the "Microgesture" dataset, a novel dataset that combines both real and synthetic microgestures, providing a valuable resource for gesture classification. The Microgesture dataset is the largest dataset of its kind, containing both real and synthetically-rendered videos for the task of hand gesture recognition. The dataset includes 3,234 RGB-D videos captured in real-world scenarios from 10 different people, as well as 3,920 RGB videos generated synthetically. In addition, we developed a taxonomy of 49 semantically-distinct gestures with the goal of eventually improving human-computer interaction inputs. We anticipate that the Microgestures dataset will serve as a benchmark for future research efforts, providing a valuable resource for the academic and wider research community.

Our specific contributions include:

- A novel video dataset consisting of real and synthetically-generated microgestures.
- Classification results from a variety of computer vision models over this dataset.
- A demonstration of a novel, computationally-efficient technique to increase baseline accuracy through intelligent keyframe selection.

[1] On occasion, research in the computer vision community has used "microgesture" to refer to unconscious movements that indicate emotional state (e.g., [2]). We use "microgesture" in the HCI sense, referring to some *intentional* movement intended to convey information to a system.

2 Related Work

In this section, we summarize some of the earlier, relevant work in modeling and recognizing gestures, including key datasets and algorithms, and describe how our methods differ from previously-existing methods.

2.1 Datasets

There are a number of publicly-available datasets in the field of vision-based gesture recognition, including ChaLearn ISO/ConGD [25], Jester [15], EgoGesture [29] IPN Hand [1], nvGesture [16], and HaGRID [8]. It is important to keep in mind that these datasets lack synthetic data.

The Jester dataset [15] is the largest dataset containing 148,092 videos that were collected from 1,300 different human subjects, covering 27 distinct actions, totaling over 5 million frames. The authors propose that larger datasets are necessary to recognize complex and subtle gesture features. We have the same motivation for our dataset and create both synthetic and real data to give a wider sample to recognition algorithms. The Jester authors also note the elimination of the requirement for any external or wearable devices in their study, which we also adopted in our research.

The IPN hand dataset [1] is a continuous gesture dataset which contains 4,000 gesture instances with more than thirty different representative scenarios at 640 $\times$ 480 pixels at 30 frames per second. The IPN dataset has been enhanced by incorporating more features of real data to effectively train large deep learning networks. Building on this concept, we generated synthetic data using HDR (High Dynamic Range) images to add further diversity to the dataset.

EgoGesture [29] presents a dataset primarily focused on a first-person perspective, with over 24,000 gesture samples from 50 subjects, including 83 static and dynamic gesture classes. The authors propose that hand gestures are intuitive and natural for communicating with computers, and a first-person perspective in XR technology offers a unique human-centered viewpoint. We believe such approaches have the potential to revolutionize human-computer interactions through the integration of microgestures.

The HaGRID dataset [8] aims to improve hand gesture recognition systems for various industries through device-human interaction. The dataset consists of 552,992 Full HD RGB images including 18 hand gestures and a "no gesture" class, with at least 34,730 unique scenes. While HaGRID focused on static hand gestures, our study emphasized the examination of dynamic hand gestures.

The iMiGUE dataset [13] for emotional AI research focuses on nonverbal microgestures, with 32 gesture categories, 2 emotions, and 18,499 samples from 72 subjects, obtained from online video interviews. iMiGUE assesses a model's ability to identify emotions by considering microgestures as an integrated whole, not just isolated prototypes in a sequence. This holistic approach matches our method for recognizing hand microgestures (Sect. 4).

The nvGesture dataset [16] contains 25 gesture classes (1,532 samples) of dynamic gestures from 20 subjects. The authors introduced nvGesture to address the challenge of detecting and classifying hand gestures in real-world human-computer interaction systems.

Finally, Wolf et al. [27] proposed a taxonomy for categorizing microgestures based on usability and scenarios, which provides a useful framework for design and evaluation. This taxonomy is used in our research to design microgestures.

2.2 Algorithms

The Jester dataset [15] has been used to show the capabilities of gestures in human-computer interaction and their potential applications in a wide range of industries, such as automotive, gaming, home automation, and consumer electronics. In constructing their networks [15], the authors employed a methodology using spatio-temporal filters as it effectively represented spatio-temporal data in previous approaches, e.g., [20]. Their model was trained using a stochastic gradient descent (SGD) algorithm, with a learning rate of 0.001, for a total of 100 epochs, and with no data augmentation being employed during the training process. The final model achieved a top-level accuracy of 93.81%.

The IPN dataset [1] was designed to effectively detect and categorize the input stream; to accomplish this, they employed two hierarchical model structures, incorporating multimodal (RGB+depth) 3D CNN models with HarD-Net (Harmonic Dense Networks) to achieve state-of-the-art results. The video sequences were segmented into isolated gestures using manually annotated beginning and ending frames. For the real data used in our study, we used the same methodology and manually annotated the beginning and ending frames.

In their study, the EgoGesture authors [29] adopted a multimodal approach, utilizing both hand-crafted and deep-learned features to address two key tasks: classifying gestures in separated data and identifying gestures in continuous data. The authors demonstrated a high level of performance, achieving an 89.7% classification accuracy for segmented ego gestures in RGB-D data and a 0.718 Jaccard index using the LSTM-C3D-LL6s8 method for spotting and recognition in continuous data. For our research, we have chosen to focus on segmented data, where we have extracted frames from both synthetic and real datasets.

The HaGRID authors [8] used SSDLite with MobileNetV3 for hand detection, with ResNeXt-101 as the best for gesture classification and ResNet-152 for leading hand classification.

The iMiGUE authors [13] present a Seq2Seq-based unsupervised encoder-decoder model for microgesture recognition without labeled data. TSM [12], a supervised 2DCNN RGB modality, was used with a top 1 accuracy of 61.10% and top 5 accuracy of 91.24%.

The nvGesture dataset [16] was collected in both real and simulated environments using a head-mounted camera in both RGB and depth modalities. The proposed method, which combines color, depth, and optical flow, achieved 98.2% accuracy.

In this study, we investigate the classification of microgestures, a challenging task due to the fast and subtle nature of microgesture hand movements. Our proposed Microgesture dataset, to the best of our knowledge, is the first and most extensive dataset of its kind for microgesture classification.

3 Microgesture Dataset

Figure 1 presents a visual overview of the different components of the Microgesture dataset: real and synthetic images against different backgrounds and in different orientations.

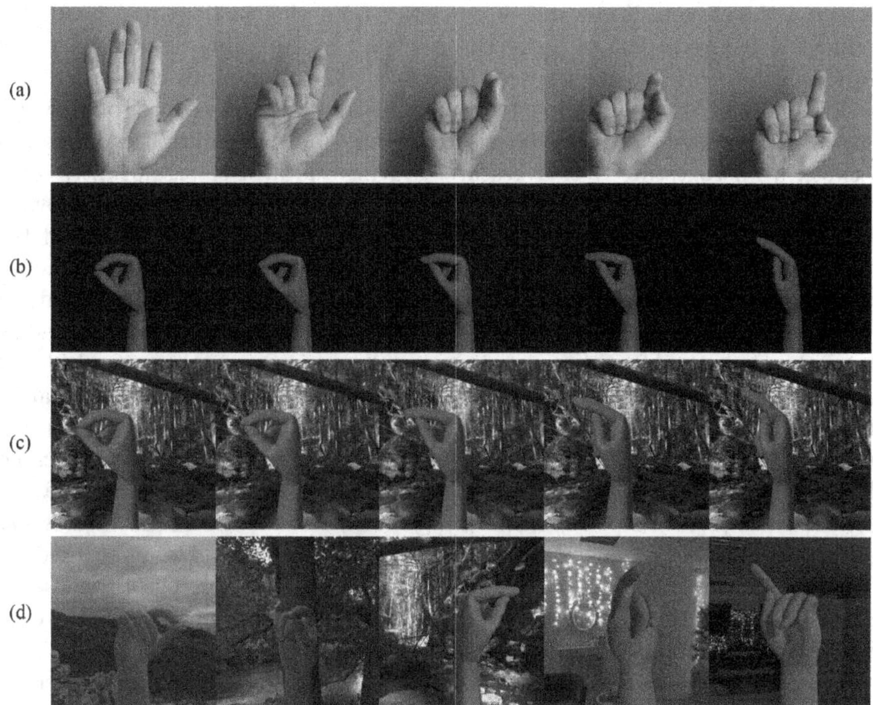

Fig. 1. The dataset includes the following specific types of data: (A) Sequences of cropped real-world images capturing the gesture from beginning to end; (B) Sequences of synthetic images depicting the same gesture against a black background; (C) Sequence of synthetic images against a HDRI (High Dynamic Range Image) scene; and (D) Sequence of synthetic images featuring various HDRI backgrounds, including nature, night, urban, indoor, and outdoor settings, as well as different angles around the Z-axis.

3.1 Data Collection

We followed the gesture semantics proposed by Kendon [9] and elaborated by Lascarides and Stone [11], among others, and capture the pre-stroke, stroke (semantic head), and post-stroke of each gesture in the microgesture dataset.

Data collection consisted of two segments: recording participants making the 49 microgestures for the real dataset, and creating and rendering animations of the 49 microgestures for the synthetic dataset.

To record participants, we used the Microsoft Kinect Azure camera to record both RGB and depth (Fig. 2) at a resolution of 1,920 × 1,080 for 30 frames per second. Three Kinects were syncronized and positioned with a backdrop of a green screen approximately 30–40 cm away from the participant's hand. Each Kinect was angled at the central point where participants made the microgestures — this was done to maximize the amount of data being captured. Every Kinect was between 30 cm and 40 cm away from the participants' hand. We included a 10 s recording of a checkerboard at the beginning of each recording session in the event anyone wanted to perform their own depth calibrations.

Prior to recording, participants were informed of the procedure to follow for making the microgestures. Emphasis was placed on explaining the differences between a microgesture over a gesture. Moving the arm or significantly moving the wrist would not qualify as a microgesture. For instruction on how to make each microgesture, participants were shown the synthetic data and the researcher performing the microgesture. Participants were allowed to practice making each microgesture as the recording proceeded. When they were ready to perform they would enter the starting position which was an open palm facing the center camera. After the participant made a microgesture, we marked if it was made correctly. The use of an "incorrect label" to remove gesture frames that are performed incorrectly ensures that the final dataset only contains gestures that are performed correctly. The frequency of incorrect gestures indicated the difficulty performing that gesture caused participants. Overall the data collection, *Index finger swipe right*, *Index finger swipe down*, and *Index finger swipe left* had 21, 15, and 15 mistakes respectively. Each participant was recorded for about 45 min which allowed for 1–4 rounds of making each microgesture. Participants were randomly assigned to start with their left or right hand and would switch between rounds.

To create the synthetic data, a 3D model of a hand was created using Blender 3D software. All 49 gesture animations were then played on the rigged hand, and the videos were generated with 2,000 × 2,000 resolution and 30 frames per second. The background was created using a black image and five High Dynamic Range Image (HDRI) scenes that were randomly provided to the software as a background of hand gestures. These five HDRI scenes were broken down into five categories: night, urban, indoor, and outdoor, and each category has four images for that scenario. The angle of the hand in each video was randomly chosen around the Z-axis (in the coordinate system used, the Z-axis is up-down).

Fig. 2. This image represents the three Microsoft Kinect cameras with a green screen setup for real data collection. (Color figure online)

3.2 Data Statistics

For the real dataset we had 10 participants (60% were male and 40% were female). We collected a total of 66 videos containing 49 gestures each. This resulted in 66 instances of each microgesture and 3,234 total instances. From this total, we excluded gestures that were incorrectly made by participants, leaving us with 3,054 instances from which 184,107 frames were extracted.

For the synthetic dataset, 80 videos of each microgesture were created, all evenly split between the left and right hands. The background for both the left and right hands were split such that both had 20 videos with the black

Table 1. Comparison of existing gesture datasets, including ours.

Datasets	Samples	Labels	Subjects	Scenes	Task
ChaLearn ISO/ConGD [25]	47,9339	249	21	1	classification, detection
IPN Hand	4218	13	50	28	classification
Jester Dataset	148,092	27	1376	N/A	classification
EgoGesture	24,161	83	50	6	classification, detection
nvGesture	1532	25	20	1	classification, detection
HaGRID	552,992	19	34,730	34,730	classification
iMiGUE	18,499	32	72	N/A	classification
Microgesture (Ours)	301,707	49	10	21	classification

background and 20 videos with the HDRI background. 3,920 total videos were created from which 117,600 frames were extracted.

The number of frames per gesture in real data varies between 60 and 81 frames due to the different participant speeds when making the gestures, while in the synthetic data each of the 30-frame gestures is captured at a consistent speed. The data statistics of our dataset are represented in Table 1 — we also compare our gestures with other gesture datasets that are currently accessible online.

3.3 Dataset Characteristics

We designed all 49 gestures in this dataset to be easy, fast, and low-effort (and hence low-fatigue over the long term), since these are essential qualities for micro-gestures to have when considering HCI applications. We classified the gestures into 17 distinct groups by features of the gesture. We called this gesture categorization a two-level hierarchy. Level 1 of the hierarchy consists of the gesture groups and level 2 includes the individual gesture types. Table 2 describes the taxonomy of all 49 gesture classes.

Table 2. Comprehensive table of all 49 gestures. The second column lists the 17 groups of gestures, while the third column lists all 49 gestures. The second and third columns are named as level 1 and level 2 gestures, respectively, in the two-level gesture hierarchy.

	Level 1	Level 2
1	Single tap index	Tap on distal phalanx of index finger w/ thumb
2		Tap on middle phalanx of index finger w/ thumb
3		Tap on proximal phalanx of index finger w/ thumb
4	Single tap middle	Tap on distal phalanx of middle finger w/ thumb
5		Tap on middle phalanx of middle finger w/ thumb
6		Tap on proximal phalanx of middle finger w/ thumb
7	Single tap ring	Tap on distal phalanx of ring finger w/ thumb
8		Tap on middle phalanx of ring finger w/ thumb
9		Tap on proximal phalanx of ring finger w/ thumb
10	Single tap last	Tap on distal phalanx of last finger w/ thumb
11		Tap on middle phalanx of last finger w/ thumb
12		Tap on proximal phalanx of last finger w/ thumb
13	Double tap index	2x tap on distal phalanx of index finger w/ thumb
14		2x tap on middle phalanx of index finger w/ thumb
15		2x tap on proximal phalanx of index finger w/ thumb
16	Double tap middle	2x tap on distal phalanx of middle finger w/ thumb
17		2x tap on middle phalanx of middle finger w/ thumb
18		2x tap on proximal phalanx of middle finger w/ thumb

(continued)

Table 2. (*continued*)

	Level 1	Level 2
19	Double tap ring	2x tap on distal phalanx of ring finger w/ thumb
20		2x tap on middle phalanx of ring finger w/ thumb
21		2x tap on proximal phalanx of ring finger w/ thumb
22	Double tap last	2x tap on distal phalanx of last finger w/ thumb
23		2x tap on middle phalanx of last finger w/ thumb
24		2x tap on proximal phalanx of last finger w/ thumb
25	Tap once	Index finger single tap
26	Tap twice	Index finger double tap
27	Move	Index finger swipe up
28		Index finger swipe down
29		Index finger swipe right
30		Index finger swipe left
31		Select with index finger
32	Numbers	One
33		Two
34		Three
35		Four
36		Five
37	Rotate (In air)	Rotate index finger anti-clockwise
38		Rotate index finger clockwise
39	Rotate (Rub)	Rub thumb on index finger anti-clockwise
40		Rub thumb on index finger clockwise
41	Slide	Slide thumb backward on index finger
42		Slide thumb forward on index finger
43	Open/close	Hand open
44		Hand close
45	Zoom	Zoom out using palm
46		Zoom out with index finger and thumb
47		Zoom in using palm
48		Zoom in with index finger and thumb
49	Snap	Snap

4 Model Training and Evaluation

To train models on the real dataset, using standard machine learning practice, we considered two different ways of dividing the data into training, validation, and test segments (splits): a split where all data from individual participants were grouped together (a "participant-wise" split), and a split where they were not (hereafter, a "traditional" or "gesture-wise" split). For traditional gesture-based distribution, 80%, 10%, and 10% of gestures were allocated to the train, validation, and test sets, respectively. Since the allocation was done by level 2 gestures, the dataset contained an equal portion of level 1 gestures for the train, validation, and test sets. The dataset of the traditional split was used for fine-tuning various methods including SOTA models (see Table 3). With the participant-wise data split, our goal was to show where and using which models the trained visual features would applicable to general cases where the individual person has never been seen before by the model. We assigned gestures belonging to a male and female participant to the validation and test sets respectively, and the gestures of the remaining participants were allocated to the training set. The training on the participant-wise split was done for level 1 gestures only (see Table 4).

4.1 Random Classification

We first established a random chance classification baseline. For each video in the test set, we assigned the predicted class randomly, and computed classification accuracy and other metrics for these random predictions. We then averaged these metrics across 10,000 iterations of randomly guessing to minimize any noise from the random labeling.

4.2 Landmark-Based Model

Our second baseline approach uses 3D joint positions extracted from the videos rather than raw visual features. Videos were preprocessed to extract landmarks on the hands using MediaPipe [14]. MediaPipe is a two-stage pipeline that tracks hands using 21 landmark points made up of X, Y, and Z coordinates. MediaPipe processes each frame into an array of landmarks normalized relative to the image dimensions. Figure 3 shows extracted landmarks superimposed on a video frame. MediaPipe performs well for detecting hands on a frame by frame basis, and has been used in many projects to aid in static single frame gesture classification, however, not much work has been done to classify gestures that span multiple frames, like exist in this dataset, and no works have explored microgestures.

We established a model baseline using this landmark-based approach by selecting 10 frames starting at the 20th frame for every video in the dataset. Extracted landmarks from the collected frames were then fed into a neural network classifier (details in Sect. 4.4).

4.3 Computer Vision Models

We evaluated various computer vision models to determine the feasibility of detecting microgestures with a computer vision method. Models were evaluated on a both level 1 and level 2 of our gesture taxonomy. Following general practice in gesture recognition, we focused on action recognition and gesture recognition models which we fine-tuned for our dataset. The action recognition models we evaluated were VideoMAE [22], Multiscale Vision Transformers (MViT) [3], 3D ResNet [5], and C3D [23]. Note that we used pretrained weights for VideoMAE and 3D ResNet whereas MViT and C3D were initialized with random weights

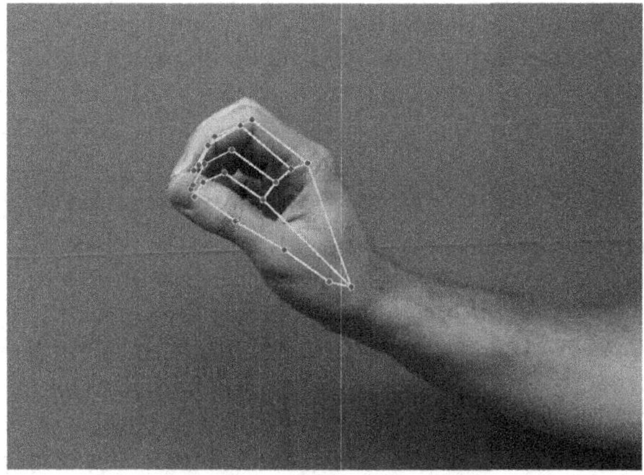

Fig. 3. Extracted landmarks superimposed on video still.

(see 4.4). The gesture recognition models, based on Köpüklü et al. [10] used a ResNeXt [28] architecture. These models were pretrained on two different datasets: EgoGesture [29] and nvGesture [16], following the training details of each respective work.

4.4 Training Details

We trained all models on the gesture-wise and participant-wise splits of our dataset. To train the action recognition models, we used 1,000 epochs to fine-tune/train VideoMAE, MViT (base), 3D ResNet, and C3D with a batch size of 8 for VideoMAE and 16 for the others. For all these models, we used an SGD optimizer with a learning rate of $1e^{-4}$. The input images were resized to $I \in R^{3\times224\times224}$, except for when fine-tuning the gesture recognition models, where the input size was $I \in R^{3\times112\times112}$ [16, 29]. These models were checkpointed every 5 epochs and the best-performing checkpoints were used for evaluation.

In addition, 480 epochs were used to fine tune the state of the art gesture recognition models (batch size of 16 and a learning rate of $1e^{-4}$ were used). 480 epochs was chosen to make a direct comparison to the best-performing checkpoint of VideoMAE.

For the landmark-based model, we used a 2-layer feed-forward neural network with 20 and 10 units, respectively, all with ReLU activation, followed by a final softmax classification layer. The model was trained for 100 epochs with an Adam optimizer, a learning rate of 0.001, sparse categorical cross-entropy loss, and a batch size of 16.

5 Results

Our results present precision, recall, macroaveraged F1, and top-k classification accuracy for multiple models, including the landmarks-based classifier. We also contextualize the results by presenting the "random chance" baseline (Sect. 4.1). Metrics were calculated using the Scikit-learn package, which first calculates macroaveraged F1 over each class and then averages the F1 scores for all classes.[2]

5.1 Results on Gesture-wise Split

Table 3 compares all classification results. Ultimately, VideoMAE exhibited the best performance over both vision and landmark-based models. The top-k accuracy of vision models indicate that the visual features of microgestures are learnable with neural networks, indicating the potential to utilize microgestures in HCI applications that use such models. Interestingly, the models that were pretrained on EgoGesture and nvGesture exhibited similar performance to 3D ResNet, which is based on action recognition, indicating that pre-training on gesture may not provide particular benefits. For gesture-wise classification at the more fine-grained level (level 2 in our taxonomy), C3D barely performed better than random classification and the landmark-based model was on par with or slightly worse than random, showing that classification at this level of granularity is difficult enough to likely require a custom deep learning model fine-tuned on the dataset.

5.2 Results on Participant-wise Split

As shown in Table 4, the performance of most models on the participant-wise split was lower than on the level 1 gesture-wise split. The exception is 3D ResNet, which showed comparable performance. In addition, MViT and C3D models showed a little performance gap from the random chance model, indicating these models are poor fits for microgesture classification. Generally, the drop in accuracy when training and evaluating on different participants is expected — such evaluations approximate how well a trained model could be expected to generalize to an unseen participant.

6 Discussion

Figures 4 and 5 show confusion matrices for all four action recognition models trained on the gesture-wise level 1 and level 2 classes, respectively. Classifiers generally performed similarly across both levels — for example, C3D (top-left) made the most mistakes on both levels while VideoMAE (bottom-right) performed best. Although both C3D and VideoMAE show similar results on the UCF101 dataset (90.4% and 91.3%, respectively), VideoMAE substantially outperforms C3D on our real dataset for both levels, indicating there are specific design decisions that successful microgesture models will need to address [21–23].

[2] As a result, classes with lower than average sample support and lower than average F1 may cause overall macroaveraged F1 for a model to fall below both average precision and recall.

Table 3. Reported metrics: precision, recall, F1, and top-k accuracy for all evaluated model architectures. The level column indicated higher (1–17 classes) or lower (2–49 classes) levels of abstraction for the defined classes.

Level	Model	Precision	Recall	F1	Top-1	Top-3	Top-5
1	Random	9.70	9.03	9.27	10.92	–	–
	Landmarks	14.85	14.86	11.59	19.37	54.93	72.54
	VideoMAE	74.38	73.67	72.72	75.74	94.49	97.79
	MViT[1]	52.67	52.41	51.60	52.86	83.57	92.50
	3D ResNet	63.68	58.81	60.36	61.79	92.50	98.21
	C3D[1]	31.77	32.27	31.70	35.71	69.29	83.21
	Köpüklü et al. [10][2]	54.57	53.99	53.03	54.93	85.92	92.61
	Köpüklü et al. [10][3]	57.75	56.38	56.03	59.15	88.03	92.96
2	Random	6.91	6.33	6.27	6.34	–	–
	Landmarks	3.79	7.21	3.63	7.40	20.78	33.45
	VideoMAE	67.58	64.90	64.79	65.07	90.44	96.32
	MViT*	41.27	39.39	38.16	39.29	67.50	77.14
	3D ResNet	44.88	43.03	41.35	43.57	78.93	91.43
	C3D*	8.73	9.86	8.87	9.64	25.00	41.07
	Köpüklü et al. [10][2]	44.78	41.02	40.45	41.20	73.24	82.04
	Köpüklü et al. [10][3]	55.18	48.67	48.19	48.59	72.89	82.04

Table 4. Metrics for the 17 level 1 classes (participant-wise train-test split)

Model	Precision	Recall	F1	Top-1	Top-3	Top-5
Random	14.84	17.48	15.11	14.18	–	–
VideoMAE	25.05	25.87	20.25	30.15	66.18	81.61
MViT[1]	5.35	11.16	6.69	15.44	29.41	44.12
3D ResNet	63.24	55.14	56.27	57.35	89.71	95.59
C3D[1]	12.37	18.18	13.05	18.38	43.38	57.35
Köpüklü et al. [10][2]	30.03	32.03	27.67	34.04	68.09	78.01
Köpüklü et al. [10][3]	26.42	34.97	26.09	31.21	61.70	74.47

[1]Trained from scratch.
[2]Pretrained on EgoGesture.
[3]PreTrained on nvGesture.

Figure 6 shows confusion matrices plots for all four action recognition models trained on the participant-wise split. We can see that all models had similar and better performance for the *single tap middle* and *number* gesture classes, with 3D ResNet (bottom-left) making the fewest mistakes. In addition, 3D ResNet was robust to *Double tap index*, *Double tap middle*, *double tap ring*, and *double tap last*.

6.1 Misclassfications

Comparing the best-performing models, VideoMAE and 3D ResNet, for both data splits, we can see what common microgestures are difficult for neural net-

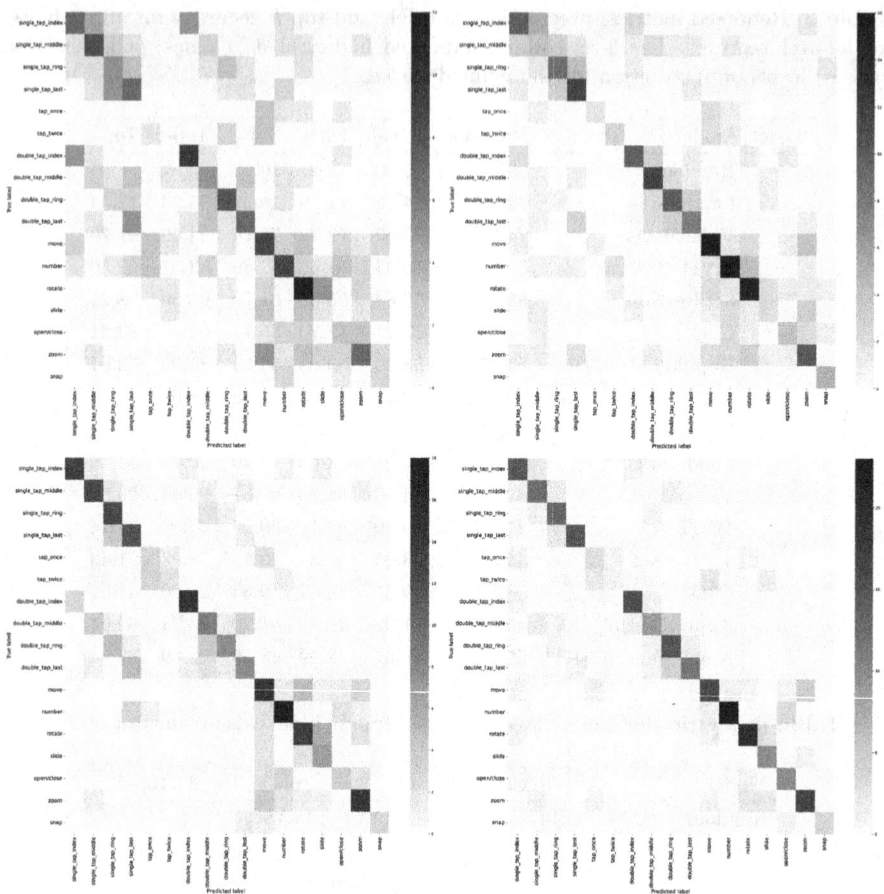

Fig. 4. Confusion matrices for level 1 gesture classes for the traditional split. From top left: C3D, MViT, 3D ResNet and VideoMAE.

work models to distinguish. For the level 1 gesture-wise split, both models have trouble identifying the *tap twice* and *tap once* classes. Looking at the fine-grained microgestures from level 2, VideoMAE is unable to predict the *slide thumb forward on index finger* (ID 42 — see Table 2) microgestures, and 3D ResNet is unable to predict the similar *slide thumb backward on index finger* (ID 41) microgesture, perhaps indicating that these subtle distinctions, even down to the finger level, are difficult for recognition models in general.

Looking at the confusion matrices from the participant-wise split (Fig. 6) we can also see that 3D ResNet and VideoMAE have difficulty in identifying the *tap twice* and *slide* gesture classes.

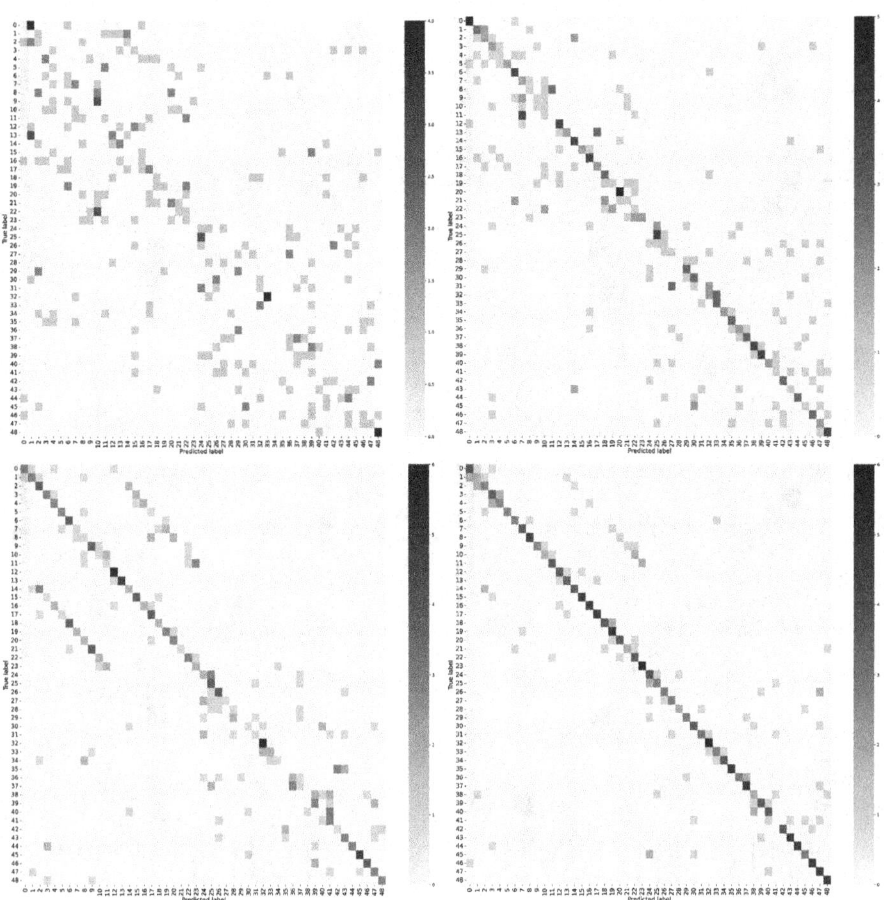

Fig. 5. Confusion matrices for level 2 gesture classes for the traditional split. From top left: C3D, MViT, 3D ResNet and VideoMAE.

6.2 Key Frame Selection for Landmarks

Recognizing more complex gestures is substantially easier if precise key frames are identified prior to recognition, since this preemptively filters excess noise. Since the landmarks-based approach performed poorly yet is fast to train, but also used a constant frame selection across all videos, we wanted to investigate if smarter selection of frames could improve this model's performance. We developed a key frame annotation solution that locates key frames using a three stage pipeline. First, a simple binary classifier recognizes the general static shape of a gesture of interest (a "hold"). Next frames in a gesture video are grouped by relative changes in motion to create "segments." Finally, we identify segments with some percentage of frames in "hold" using another binary classifier. Using this data, we can identify the start and end of the key frames, along with the start

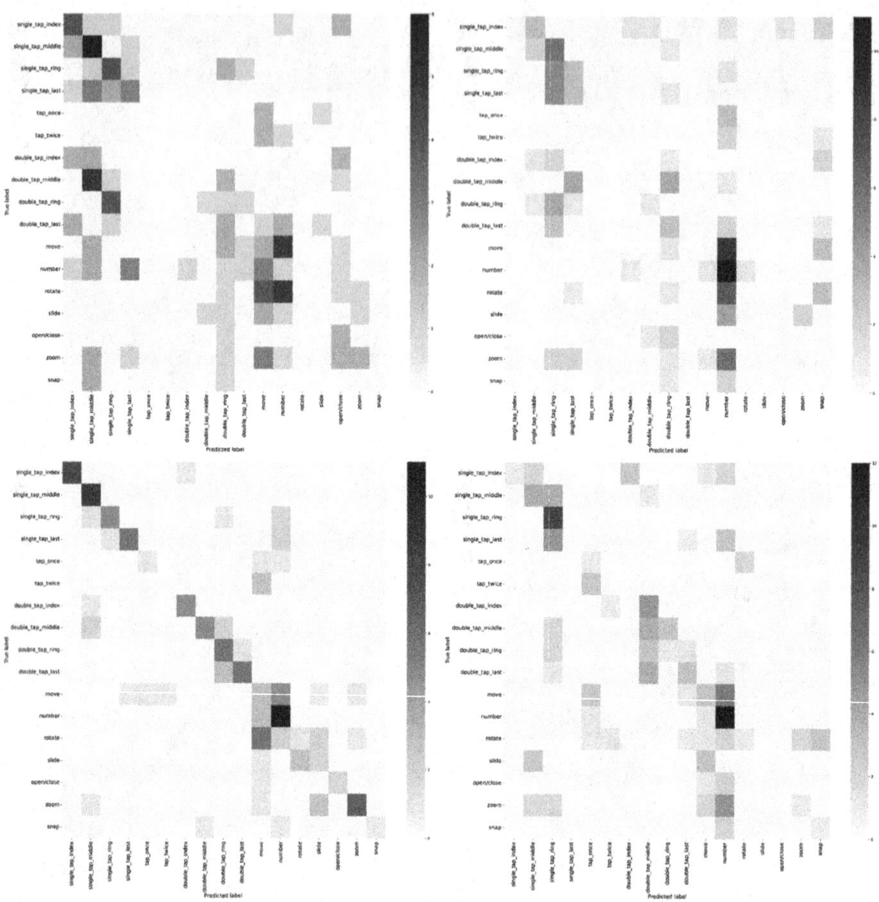

Fig. 6. Confusion matrices for level 1 gesture classes for the participant-wise split. From top left: C3D, MViT, 3D ResNet and VideoMAE.

and end of the "peak" segment, which contain the most still frames in "hold" and could be considered the peak of the key frames [24]. We hypothesized that we could improve the overall performance of the landmark-based classifier over multiple frames using these annotated values to select dynamic features on a per-gesture basis.

To test this procedure, an additional experiment was run on a subset of the Microgesture data. The gestures included in the subset were *snap*, *two*, *index finger swipe right*, *hand close*, and *zoom in with palm*. We trained a feedforward neutral network on the subset to retrieve key frames using the same hyperparameters defined in Sect. 4.4, using a leave-one-out split for each of the 10 participants. Tables 5 and 6 show the average performance and standard deviation of classification using the dynamic key frame selection compared to the static method, run on the same 5 gestures [24]. The increase in performance using the dynamic method shows promise as a solution to improve the overall performance of the landmark based model if trained using the dynamic key frames across the entire dataset. This makes sense, since the microgesture movements are quite small and the key frame identification eliminates excess noise.

Table 5. Average reported metrics: precision, recall, F1, and top-k accuracy. 10 frames were gathered for both methods. Static collection started at frame 20 of each video. Dynamic started at the unique key frame location for each individual video.

Method	Precision	Recall	F1	Top-1	Top-3
Static	35.28	39.16	33.86	41.48	83.49
Dynamic	66.35	66.48	62.78	69.10	89.10

Table 6. Standard deviation of reported metrics: precision, recall, F1, and top-k accuracy.

Method	Precision	Recall	F1	Top-1	Top-3
Static	23.99	20.36	21.97	21.16	9.78
Dynamic	22.80	19.00	22.00	18.28	9.86

7 Future Work

Here, we presented a novel microgesture dataset to serve as a benchmark and to encourage research into the use of microgestures interactive systems. However, the current dataset has only minimal egocentric data (Sect. 3.1) and thus limits the ability to adopt microgestures in XR contexts — microgestures are particularly important for XR contexts where the user could conceivably interact with the system throughout the day.

From an HCI perspective, future work should evaluate how effective our set of microgestures are from both a fatigue estimation perspective and from a usability perspective. In parallel, computer vision research should focus on identifying which gesture types are most easily recognized by trained systems. In this work, we showcase the feasibility of detecting various microgestures, but future work can likely surpass these baselines since we did not explore custom models.

Our novel technique for intelligent key frame selection increases both performance and training efficiency — where training modern computer vision models as we used can each take between 1–5 days, the classifier portions of the key frame selection pipeline can be trained in a matter of minutes, and the entire procedure approaches the accuracy of some of the top-performing vision models.

This technique is discussed in more detail in [24], but was evaluated only on a subset of the dataset. A larger evaluation is the subject of future work.

8 Conclusion

Microgestures represent a naturalistic and low-effort strategy for human-computer interaction. However, prior to this work, microgesture datasets were limited at best, especially from the perspective of what would be needed to study them from an AI application perspective. Our novel microgesture dataset includes video recordings of a hierarchy of microgesture types from a multitude of participants. Further, it contains synthetic videos of gestures being performed which can be augmented with various backgrounds or variations to improve the robustness of the trained model.

Our experimental results, which compared random chance, landmark-based, and computer vision models, show how well micoregestures can be recognized by a computer vision system. While these results showcase the feasibility of detecting microgestures, they also highlight the difficulties that need to be overcome for an interactive system to capitalize on microgestures. We offer some solutions to bolster this performance, such as our novel technique for intelligent key frame selection that provides a substantial increase in recognition performance on the landmark data. While this is just the start of the work that needs to be accomplished to integrate microgestures into HCI applications, we believe it provides a solid foundation on which the HCI and AI research communities can build.

Acknowledgement. This work was partially supported by the National Science Foundation under awards CNS 2016714 and DRL 1559731 to Colorado State University. The views expressed are those of the authors and do not reflect the official policy or position of the U.S. Government. All errors and mistakes are, of course, the responsibilities of the authors.

References

1. Benitez-Garcia, G., Olivares-Mercado, J., Sanchez-Perez, G., Yanai, K.: Ipn hand: a video dataset and benchmark for real-time continuous hand gesture recognition. In: 2020 25th International Conference on Pattern recognition (ICPR), pp. 4340–4347. IEEE (2021)
2. Chen, H., Liu, X., Li, X., Shi, H., Zhao, G.: Analyze spontaneous gestures for emotional stress state recognition: a micro-gesture dataset and analysis with deep learning. In: 2019 14th IEEE International Conference on Automatic Face & Gesture Recognition (FG 2019), pp. 1–8. IEEE (2019)
3. Fan, H., Xiong, B., Mangalam, K., Li, Y., Yan, Z., Malik, J., Feichtenhofer, C.: Multiscale vision transformers. In: Proceedings of the IEEE/CVF International Conference on Computer Vision, pp. 6824–6835 (2021)
4. Freeman, E., Griffiths, G., Brewster, S.A.: Rhythmic micro-gestures: discreet interaction on-the-go. In: Proceedings of the 19th ACM International Conference on Multimodal Interaction, pp. 115–119 (2017)

5. Hara, K., Kataoka, H., Satoh, Y.: Can spatiotemporal 3d CNNs retrace the history of 2d CNNs and imagenet? In: Proceedings of the IEEE conference on Computer Vision and Pattern Recognition, pp. 6546–6555 (2018)
6. Häuslschmid, R., Menrad, B., Butz, A.: Freehand vs. micro gestures in the car: driving performance and user experience. In: 2015 IEEE Symposium on 3D User Interfaces (3DUI), pp. 159–160. IEEE (2015)
7. Hincapié-Ramos, J.D., Guo, X., Moghadasian, P., Irani, P.: Consumed endurance: a metric to quantify arm fatigue of mid-air interactions. In: Proceedings of the SIGCHI Conference on Human Factors in Computing Systems, pp. 1063–1072 (2014)
8. Kapitanov, A., Makhlyarchuk, A., Kvanchiani, K.: Hagrid-hand gesture recognition image dataset. arXiv preprint arXiv:2206.08219 (2022)
9. Kendon, A.: Gesture: Visible Action as Utterance. Cambridge University Press, Cambridge (2004)
10. Köpüklü, O., Gunduz, A., Kose, N., Rigoll, G.: Real-time hand gesture detection and classification using convolutional neural networks. In: 2019 14th IEEE International Conference on Automatic Face & Gesture Recognition (FG 2019), pp. 1–8. IEEE (2019)
11. Lascarides, A., Stone, M.: A formal semantic analysis of gesture. J. Semant. **26**(4), 393–449 (2009)
12. Lin, J., Gan, C., Han, S.: Tsm: temporal shift module for efficient video understanding. In: Proceedings of the IEEE/CVF International Conference on Computer Vision, pp. 7083–7093 (2019)
13. Liu, X., Shi, H., Chen, H., Yu, Z., Li, X., Zhao, G.: imigue: an identity-free video dataset for micro-gesture understanding and emotion analysis. In: Proceedings of the IEEE/CVF Conference on Computer Vision and Pattern Recognition, pp. 10631–10642 (2021)
14. Lugaresi, C., et al.: Mediapipe: a framework for perceiving and processing reality. In: Third Workshop on Computer Vision for AR/VR at IEEE Computer Vision and Pattern Recognition (CVPR), vol. 2019 (2019)
15. Materzynska, J., Berger, G., Bax, I., Memisevic, R.: The jester dataset: a large-scale video dataset of human gestures. In: Proceedings of the IEEE/CVF International Conference on Computer Vision Workshops (2019)
16. Molchanov, P., Yang, X., Gupta, S., Kim, K., Tyree, S., Kautz, J.: Online detection and classification of dynamic hand gestures with recurrent 3d convolutional neural network. In: Proceedings of the IEEE Conference on Computer Vision and Pattern Recognition, pp. 4207–4215 (2016)
17. Neßelrath, R., Moniri, M.M., Feld, M.: Combining speech, gaze, and micro-gestures for the multimodal control of in-car functions. In: 2016 12th International Conference on Intelligent Environments (IE), pp. 190–193. IEEE (2016)
18. Sharma, A., et al.: Solofinger: robust microgestures while grasping everyday objects. In: Proceedings of the 2021 CHI Conference on Human Factors in Computing Systems, pp. 1–15 (2021)
19. Sharma, A., Roo, J.S., Steimle, J.: Grasping microgestures: eliciting single-hand microgestures for handheld objects. In: Proceedings of the 2019 CHI Conference on Human Factors in Computing Systems, pp. 1–13 (2019)
20. Song, Y., Demirdjian, D., Davis, R.: Tracking body and hands for gesture recognition: natops aircraft handling signals database. In: 2011 IEEE International Conference on Automatic Face & Gesture Recognition (FG), pp. 500–506. IEEE (2011)
21. Soomro, K., Zamir, A.R., Shah, M.: Ucf101: a dataset of 101 human actions classes from videos in the wild. arXiv preprint arXiv:1212.0402 (2012)

22. Tong, Z., Song, Y., Wang, J., Wang, L.: Videomae: masked autoencoders are data-efficient learners for self-supervised video pre-training. arXiv preprint arXiv:2203.12602 (2022)
23. Tran, D., Bourdev, L., Fergus, R., Torresani, L., Paluri, M.: Learning spatiotemporal features with 3d convolutional networks. In: Proceedings of the IEEE International Conference on Computer Vision, pp. 4489–4497 (2015)
24. VanderHoeven, H., Blanchard, N., Krishnaswamy, N.: Robust motion recognition using gesture phase annotation. In: Digital Human Modeling and Applications in Health, Safety, Ergonomics and Risk Management. Human Body, Motion and Behavior: 14th International Conference, DHM 2023, Held as Part of the 25th HCI International Conference, HCII 2023. Springer (2023)
25. Wan, J., Zhao, Y., Zhou, S., Guyon, I., Escalera, S., Li, S.Z.: Chalearn looking at people RGB-d isolated and continuous datasets for gesture recognition. In: Proceedings of the IEEE Conference on Computer Vision and Pattern Recognition Workshops, pp. 56–64 (2016)
26. Way, D., Paradiso, J.: A usability user study concerning free-hand microgesture and wrist-worn sensors. In: 2014 11th International Conference on Wearable and Implantable Body Sensor Networks, pp. 138–142. IEEE (2014)
27. Wolf, K., Naumann, A., Rohs, M., Müller, J.: A taxonomy of microinteractions: defining microgestures based on ergonomic and scenario-dependent requirements. In: Campos, P., Graham, N., Jorge, J., Nunes, N., Palanque, P., Winckler, M. (eds.) INTERACT 2011. LNCS, vol. 6946, pp. 559–575. Springer, Heidelberg (2011). https://doi.org/10.1007/978-3-642-23774-4_45
28. Xie, S., Girshick, R., Dollár, P., Tu, Z., He, K.: Aggregated residual transformations for deep neural networks. In: Proceedings of the IEEE Conference on Computer Vision and Pattern Recognition, pp. 1492–1500 (2017)
29. Zhang, Y., Cao, C., Cheng, J., Lu, H.: Egogesture: a new dataset and benchmark for egocentric hand gesture recognition. IEEE Trans. Multimedia **20**(5), 1038–1050 (2018)

Improving Hand Gesture Recognition via Infrared Tomography of the Wrist over Multiple Wearing Sessions

HongMin Kim(✉) and Ian Oakley

Ulsan National Institute of Science and Technology, Ulsan, South Korea
khm489@gmail.com

Abstract. Smartwatches now enable a wide range of end user applications. However, despite their increasingly sophisticated capabilities, the bandwidth of the user input that they support remains strongly limited by the small size of their touch screens. Numerous techniques have been proposed to improve this situation by integrating novel sensing systems and input modalities. A prominent approach here has been to detect gestures made by the hand wearing the watch with sensors capable of imaging either the associated distortions to the surface of the wrist, or changes to the wrist's internal structures. While performance of such systems is promising (e.g., gesture accuracy of up to 93.3%), most studies currently examine performance during single studies and sessions. As such they fail to take account of the variability in measurement of wrist shapes and/or structures that might result from minor changes in sensor placement each time a device is donned. To explore the impact of this type of natural variability, we conducted a study using a watch strap prototype implementing infrared tomography to image the surface of the wrist during hand gesture production. While recognition performance during a single session of wearing this device was high (92.1%), it dropped substantially when the device was removed and re-worn between training and testing (to 22.9%). To alleviate this problem, we explore whether calibration processes that seek to maximize the consistency of sensor placements can yield improved performance. A study studies achieves this via IMU-based measurement of sensor placement similarity between sessions and shows greatly improved inter-session performance (up to 86.7%). Based on this result, we suggest that IMU based calibration of sensor placement can improve the real-world performance of gesture input systems based on wrist imaging techniques.

Keywords: Wrist wearable input · Consistency · Infrared tomography

1 Introduction

The market for wrist-sized wearable devices is growing and their form factors are diversifying. As a result, the devices have become more technically advanced and versatile - serving not only as a traditional watch, but also as a device

M. Kurosu and A. Hashizume (Eds.): HCII 2023, LNCS 14011, pp. 519–531, 2023.
https://doi.org/10.1007/978-3-031-35596-7_33

for communicating, managing personal health, and providing entertainment [8]. However, most smartwatches today are not considered standalone devices, but rather paired with a smartphone [2]. There are many possible explanations for this, but a key reason is the poor usability of their input technologies, such as their reliance on small touch screens [14] and the requirement to use both hands for input [5]. Due to the unique wrist-mounted form factor of these wearable devices, we argue there is a need to investigate and improve the performance of input approaches that do not rely on both hands. Systems that enable effective and reliable input using only the hand that is wearing the watch will significantly improve the usability of this class of devices [3].

Many companies and researchers have explored alternative modalities and sensing techniques that enable better interaction on smartwatches. One-handed input techniques, particularly those that recognize the poses or gestures made by the hand wearing the watch, have attracted frequent attention. Sensing techniques to enable these systems include the use of an IMU to measure changes in wrist angle [3], electrical impedance tomography to image the internal structures of the wrist [21], and infrared transmission and reflection to assess changes to its outer shape [13]. While these diverse technical approaches robustly demonstrate the value of the wrist as a source of information about input actions made by the hand, we identify a need to improve the real-world applicability of such systems. Specifically, we note that most existing examples in the research literature report performance results from a single session (involving wearing a device once) [9] or require lengthy dedicated calibration or training processes each time they are worn [4]. Performance over more extended periods, or in situations where users are reluctant to provide training, remains unknown.

In this paper, we explore this issue by combining two modalities - motion sensing and Infrared (IR) tomography - to assess and improve the performance of smartwatch-based gesture classification over multiple wearing sessions. This paper presents the sensing hardware, study design, and results of two evaluations. The sensing system follows a recent implementation of wrist IR tomography for a smartwatch [9], and the studies involve participants reproducing a series of hand gestures cued on a screen. Participants wear and remove the sensing system three times during each experiment to assess performance over multiple sessions. In the first study, participants naturally put on and take off the sensing band. In contrast, in the second study, they are supported in maintaining a similar fit between sessions by viewing interactive data from an IMU. In each study, we investigate how to create models that achieve peak classification performance in terms of accuracy in discriminating each hand pose both within and between different sessions.

The single session results confirm those from a prior IR tomography study [9]: for classifiers trained and tested on data from a single session, we report a high level of hand pose recognition accuracy (91.2%). However, when classifiers were trained on data from one session and tested with data from another, performance dropped precipitously to 22.4%. This result suggests that small changes in sensor placement on the wrist can dramatically impact performance. However, when an IMU-based calibration process designed to minimize sensor placement variability occurred at the start of each session, hand pose recognition accuracy increased to 86.1%. Based on these results, we argue the proposed IMU-based calibration method is a promising approach to improve the consistency of smartwatch hand pose input techniques and, consequently, the usability of wrist-based hand gesture classifiers designed for smartwatches.

2 Related Work

The proliferation of consumer wearable devices has led to a substantial body of research on interaction (especially input) techniques tailored to their unique usage contexts. For example, for wearable wrist devices, researchers have proposed approaches to improve the usability of their touchscreen by optimizing tapping or stroking for text input [15], and by exploring temporal [11] or spatial [6] touch patterns to achieve rapid command execution.

Another approach has been to increase input options by adding touch surfaces to the wristband [12] or edge [5,10] of the watch. These novel touch surfaces can be combined with standard touchscreen input to increase input efficiency, as shown in Ahn et al.'s [1] text input system for smartwatches. In this system, tapping on the side of the device selects different keyboard regions to be displayed on the screen, allowing for larger individual keys. Other researchers have proposed typing on a smartwatch using the motion of the watch, captured by dedicated [17] or built-in [19,20] motion sensors. These studies have shown that combining two or more modalities can improve user interaction. However, all of these approaches require both hands for input.

Researchers have also explored smartwatch input systems that avoid input with the opposite hand using various techniques. Prominent examples include using body motion detection via trackers [3], hand gesture recognition via electrical impedance tomography (EIT) [7,16,18,21], wrist angle tracking via time-of-flight (ToF) IR light modules [13] and hand gesture recognition via IR light reflection and transmission tomography [9]. Both motion-based and tomography-based input approaches are particularly promising because they are single-handed, requiring only the hand wearing the watch. However, unlike two-handed input systems, such as touch screens or surfaces, there is little prior research on multi-sessions scenarios involving a user wearing their device over multiple sessions. This omission represents a problematic data gap that highlights the need for studies that evaluate the performance of same-hand smartwatch gesture recognition systems over different sessions.

3 Hardware and Software Prototyping

As shown in Fig. 1, we constructed a prototype that captures both IR tomography (to detect hand gestures) and wrist orientation (to adjust the device and sensor placements). The prototype is composed of 14 identical 3D printed modules (Sindoh PLA), each containing an IR emitting LED (Osram SFH4557, 860nm)

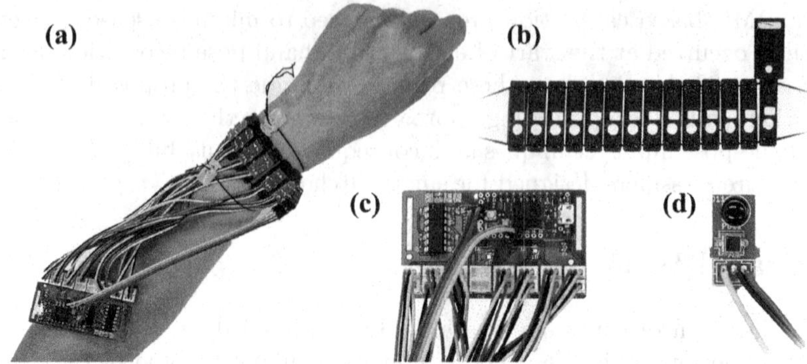

Fig. 1. Hardware prototype used in this work. The image on the left(a) shows the arm wearing the prototype. The prototype is composed of 3D printed pieces (b), a PCB featuring a Teensy 4.0 microcontroller, OP Amps, and other electric components (c), and a set of modular PCBs containing IR-emitting LEDs and receivers (d).

and an IR receiving photodiode (Osram BPW34). Each module is connected to the others with a rubber cord typically used for fastening clothing. An OP Amp (LM324N) with a gain of 1M served as a trans-impedance amplifier to measure the current from the diodes. To switch between different IR emitters and photodiodes, we used two 16-channel analog multiplexer switches (TI CD74HC4067). We set a 10ms warm-up time for the IR emitters, which is in line with the specifications of the LEDs (12ns raise and fall time). The photo-diodes have a raise and fall time of 100ns, but this does not impact our system as they are always active. Each IR LED cycle (on for 10ms and off for 10ms) takes 20ms, meaning one full capture cycle took 280ms (20ms times 14). We placed SparkFun's 9DOF stick (ST LSM9DS1) - to capture motion data - on a 3D printed piece which has additional housing shown in Fig. 1(b). A Teensy 4.0 controlled the IR emitters and captured data from the photodiodes and the IMU. The software for the experiment was written using the Processing development environment and communicated with the Teensy board via USB. Due to its use in closely related prior work [9], we selected an MLP (Multi-Layer Perceptron) classifier in one-vs-rest mode (Scikit-learn) as the basis for assessing performance in our system. We configured this classifier with one hidden layer of 24 neurons and applied the L-BFGS training algorithm ($\alpha = 0.05$).

4 Study1: Proof of Concept and Multi-Session Performance

To explore the impact of multiple sessions on performance with our prototype, we replicated (and extended) a recent study of IR tomography hand pose recognition [9]. We achieved this by using the same set of 12 hand poses (Fig. 2) and data capture procedures (visually cued hand pose production and ten repetitions of each pose) for a single session. However, we also captured data from two

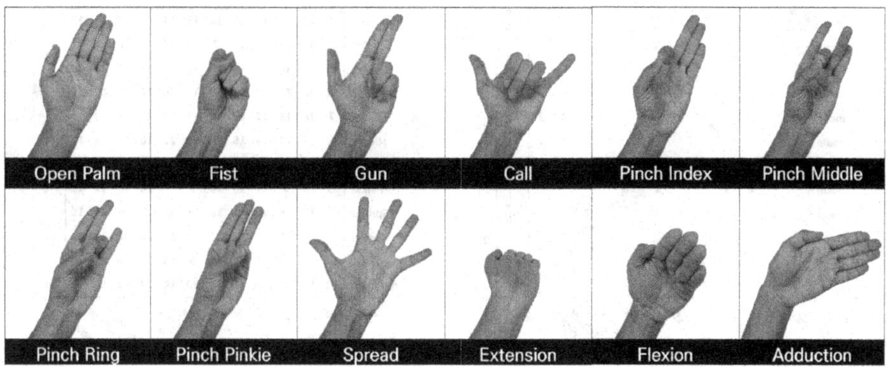

Fig. 2. Hand pose set used in both Study 1 and Study 2, adopted from [9].

further sessions to extend this prior work. Each of these additional sessions mirrored the first, but participants were required to take off and re-wear the sensor before starting each. The goal was to compare hand pose recognition performance between the first (or training) and the subsequent (or testing) sessions. In total, we collected data from 3,600 trials: ten participants by twelve hand poses by ten repetitions by three iterations.

4.1 Participants

A total of 10 participants (mean age = 27.1, σ = 6.64) were recruited through a social networking site for members of a local university. 8 were male and 2 were female, and all were right-handed. We asked about their familiarity with smartphones, smartwatches, and other wearable smart devices using a 5-point Likert scale questionnaire. As a result of this questionnaire, participants reported high familiarity with smartphones ($\mu = 4.7$, $\sigma = 0.48$), moderate familiarity with smartwatches ($\mu = 2.7$, $\sigma = 1.06$), and low familiarity with other wearable smart devices ($\mu = 1.2$, $\sigma = 0.42$). Approximately 10 USD in local currency was paid for participation.

4.2 Procedure

The study was conducted in a dark laboratory environment to avoid variations in the lighting conditions. During the study, participants sat in a non-adjustable chair and placed the arm wearing the prototype on a desk. We asked them to perform these steps:

Instructions: Before the study began, we provided instructions and explained the procedures. Participants then completed an informed consent form. They were told that they could ask questions about the study at any time and that they could take a short break at any time during the study if they felt tired. We

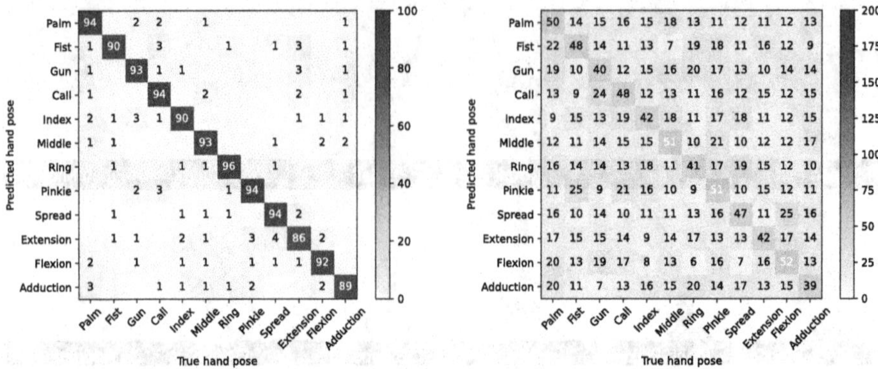

Fig. 3. Confusion Matrix of the results of Study 1. Cross-validated classification of hand poses trained and tested on first session data (left), classification of hand poses in second and third sessions based on training using data from the first session (right). Data are numerical totals (#).

instructed them to minimize their arm movements as much as possible during the study. We also recommended that they rest their arm for at least 3 min between sessions to reduce fatigue.

Task: Participants then wore the prototype on their wrist and placed their arm on the desk. A laptop computer was located on the desk in front of them. It displayed study instructions in the form of pictures of the hand poses they were asked to perform. For each pose, they were asked to imitate the shown hand for a period of five seconds. After the initial adoption of the pose, an experimenter manually started acquisition of the IR tomography data. The combination of hand poses was randomized for each trial, and each participant performed each pose ten times. At the end of the trial, they were asked to lower their arm, rest, and then remove and re-wear the prototype. They repeated this task a total of 3 times.

4.3 Results and Discussion

To evaluate hand pose recognition accuracy in light of prior work, we need to consider two cases: when both the training and testing occur in a single session and when the training uses poses from one session and the testing uses data from subsequent sessions. Results from the first analysis serve as a proof of concept that the system works and support comparisons between our device and data with prior systems and studies deploying similar systems and evaluations. Results from the second evaluation explore the reliability of these results after users take off and re-wear a device. We conducted the first analysis using per-user MLP classifiers and a 10-fold leave-one-out cross-validation process. In each fold of this analysis, classifiers were trained on 90% of the data and tested on the remaining 10% (composed of one gesture of each class). As illustrated in the confusion matrix in Fig. 3 (left), the accuracy of the hand pose classification with this approach was high: 92.1% ($\sigma = 6.01$). In the second analysis, all data from the first session was used to train the system, and all data from the second and third sessions served as the test set. As the confusion matrix illustrated in Fig. 3 (right) shows, the accuracy of hand pose classification in this analysis was low: 22.9% ($\sigma = 7.91$). This result indicates that the simple act of wearing and re-wearing the sensing device on the wrist represents a substantial practical barrier to achieving good hand pose classification performance. As taking off and re-wearing a watch is a daily practice for most users, this issue represents a severe real-world problem impacting the viability of wrist-based hand classification systems.

The results show extreme differences between within-session and between-session performance. A likely explanation is that sensor placement variability each time the device is worn leads to changes in the sensor readings that are sufficient to confound the performance of the classifiers. More consistent measurements may be achievable if the sensors can be mounted in a consistent position on the wrist. In turn, this may improve classifier accuracy over multiple sessions.

5 Study 2: Impact of IMU-Based Sensor Fitting

We designed an IMU-based fitting method to improve the consistency of sensor placements in wrist-worn devices and, in turn, improve the hand pose classification performance they can achieve. To evaluate the performance of this system, we conducted a follow-up study. The study investigated whether our IMU-based fitting method successfully improved hand-pose classification performance.

The study began with participants wearing the smartwatch prototype on their wrist and placing their palm on the table for three seconds to record the IMU data to establish the baseline position of the prototype on the wrist. After recording the baseline IMU data, participants performed hand poses according to a series of on-screen instructions, following the methods described in Study 1. They then removed and re-wore the prototype and were required to adjust its position while reviewing the IMU data. Their task was to ensure the currently sampled IMU data (in terms of roll, pitch, and yaw) closely matched the IMU data recorded at the start of the first session. Finally, they performed the complete set of hand poses once again.

The goal was to compare hand pose recognition performance between the first (or training) session and the second (or testing) sessions in light of the IMU-based sensor placement procedure. In this study, in total, we collected data from 2,400 trials: ten participants by twelve hand poses by ten repetitions by two iterations.

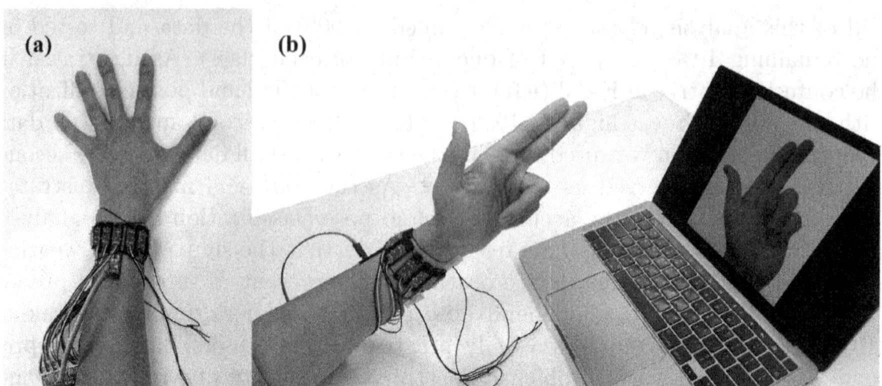

Fig. 4. The pose when collecting IMU baseline data (palm flat on table, (a)) and while reproducing hand pose cued on the screen (elbow resting on table, (b)). The IMU unit is shown in red in the left image. (Color figure online)

5.1 Participants

A total of 10 participants (mean age = 29.6, $\sigma = 7.26$) were recruited through an online forum associated with a local university. 7 were male, 3 female, and nine were right-handed. They indicated their familiarity with smartphones, smartwatches, and other wearable smart devices using a 5-point Likert scale questionnaire. From this questionnaire, they reported high familiarity with smartphones ($\mu = 4.3$, $\sigma = 0.48$), moderate familiarity with smartwatches ($\mu = 2.4$, $\sigma = 0.84$), and low familiarity with other wearable smart devices ($\mu = 1.3$, $\sigma = 0.67$). Participants in this study were compensated with approximately 10 USD in local currency.

5.2 Procedure

The environmental setting of this study was very similar to the first study. We ensured the laboratory environment was dark to prevent signal variations due to changing lighting conditions, prepared a non-adjustable chair for participants to sit in, and had participants place their arms on a desk in front of them. We asked them to perform these steps:

Instructions: Instructions mirrored those in Study 1. Before the study began, we provided and explained the procedures, and participants completed a consent form. They were told they could ask questions about the study at any time and informed that they could take a short break at any point during the study. We instructed them to minimize their arm movements as much as possible during the study. We also recommended that they rest their arm for at least 3 min between the two sessions to reduce fatigue.

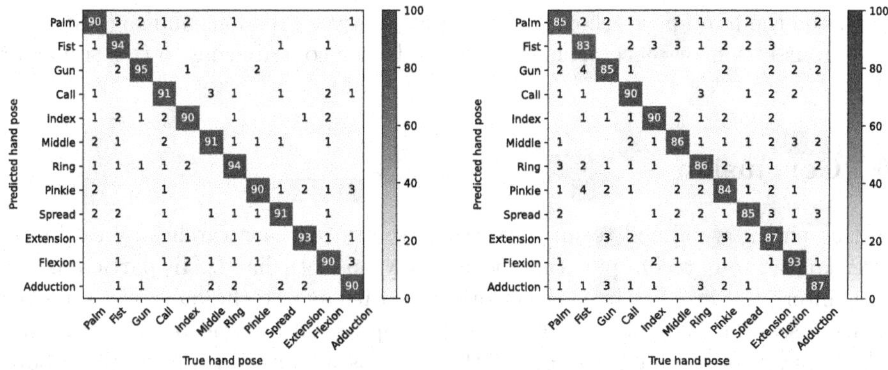

Fig. 5. Confusion Matrix of the results of Study 2. Cross-validated classification of hand poses trained and tested on first session data (left), classification of hand poses in second session based on training using data from the first session (right). Data are numerical totals (#).

Task: First, participants placed the prototype on their wrist and their palm flat on the table (Fig. 4(a)). Following the instructor's guidance, they waited for approximately 3 s while baseline IMU data was collected from the prototype's IMU. They then rested their arm on the table and, as in Study 1, viewed and mimicked (for five seconds each) a series of hand poses shown on a laptop screen. After adopting each pose, an experimenter manually triggered the acquisition of the IR tomography data. The combination of hand poses was randomized for each trial, and each participant performed each pose ten times. At the end of the session, they lowered their arm, rested, and then removed and re-wore the prototype for another session. While donning the device, they again placed their hand palm down on the table. They then adjusted the prototype position so that the IMU readings matched the previously acquired baseline IMU data in terms of roll, pitch and yaw.

5.3 Results and Discussion

In this study, we evaluated the consistency of hand pose recognition accuracy between the two study sessions. We again constructed an MLP classifier using a same-session 10-fold cross validation procedure to characterize within-session performance and used the first session as training data, and the second as testing, to establish performance between sessions.

As illustrated in Fig. 4 (left), the results for the same session showed that the classifier achieved an average accuracy of 91.6% ($\sigma = 5.91$), which is consistent with the data from the first study. However, the accuracy between sessions (with the first session as training and the second as testing) reached a mean accuracy of 86.7%($\sigma = 7.13$) (Fig. 5, right). This represents a substantial improvement (of 63.8%) over the results reported in the first study. This improvement indicates that the IMU-guided sensor placement adjustment procedure positively impacted the hand pose recognition accuracy between sessions and suggests that variations in sensor placement are a major factor contributing to this source of error.

6 Conclusion

In this paper, we aimed to improve the usability of smartwatches by exploring alternative input techniques that do not rely on both hands. In particular, we were interested in investigating performance with such techniques over multiple wearing sessions. We focused on an existing approach to hand pose recognition, which uses the internal structure of the wrist as a source of information about the input actions performed by the hand. We used the combination of IMU and IR tomography to evaluate the performance of smartwatch-based hand pose recognition over multiple wearing sessions.

We conducted two studies. In each, participants reproduced a series of on-screen hand gestures in two or more separate wearing sessions. We examined gesture recognition accuracy for classifiers trained and tested on data from the same session and those trained and tested on different sessions. While within-session performance was high in both studies (92.1% in Study 1 and 91.6% in Study 2), our first study (which did not include any special procedures to improve consistency of sensor placement) showed low performance in terms of between-session classification accuracy (22.9%). To improve this low accuracy, our second study incorporated an IMU-based sensor positioning step to reduce variability in sensor placement. The between-session results of our second study indicate that this was highly successful: we recorded a classification accuracy of 86.7% when training in one session and testing in another in Study 2. This figure represents a substantial improvement over the results from Study 1.

Despite these positive results, there are some limitations to the reported work. Some of these are methodological. In particular, while the value of careful alignment of sensor positions (by tracking IMU data) is apparent in Study 2, our Study 1 protocol did not include measurement of this data. As a result, we lack an assessment of how well the sensor positions were aligned in the first study. This clouds the interpretation of the results. A more robust study protocol would rigorously monitor and control this factor throughout the study. In addition, although we are interested in more realistic use scenarios for one-handed gesture input systems, our studies were conducted during single visits (although the sensors were worn and re-worn several times). Investigating performance over extended periods is a clear next step for this work. Other limitations reflect the cumbersome nature of our solution: participants had to manually adjust the wristband while adopting a specific hand posture and closely tracking the sensor data. This is a tedious process. Future work should explore whether other approaches to dealing with variability in sensor placement, such as training on data from multiple wearing sessions, can provide similar improvements in performance to those observed here.

In conclusion, based on the strong results shown in Study 2, we argue that the IMU-based calibration process is a promising approach to improve the performance of smartwatch hand gesture recognition. In addition, this research highlights the importance of considering the impact of natural variations (e.g., in terms of how devices are worn) on the performance of wearable sensing systems and the potential for sensor calibration during donning to improve their real-world performance.

Acknowledgements. This research was supported by the Basic Science Research Program through the National Research Foundation of Korea (NRF) funded by the Ministry of Science, ICT and Future Planning (2020R1F1A1070699).

References

1. Ahn, S., Heo, S., Lee, G.: Typing on a smartwatch for smart glasses. In: Proceedings of the 2017 ACM International Conference on Interactive Surfaces and Spaces, ISS 2017, pp. 201–209. Association for Computing Machinery, New York, NY, USA (2017). https://doi.org/10.1145/3132272.3134136
2. Chen, X., Chen, W., Liu, K., Chen, C., Li, L.: A comparative study of smartphone and smartwatch apps. In: Proceedings of the 36th Annual ACM Symposium on Applied Computing, SAC 2021, pp. 1484–1493. Association for Computing Machinery, New York, NY, USA (2021). https://doi.org/10.1145/3412841.3442023
3. Gong, J., Yang, X.D., Irani, P.: Wristwhirl: one-handed continuous smartwatch input using wrist gestures. In: Proceedings of the 29th Annual Symposium on User Interface Software and Technology, UIST 2016, pp. 861–872. Association for Computing Machinery, New York, NY, USA (2016). https://doi.org/10.1145/2984511.2984563
4. Huh, J.H., et al.: Wristacoustic: through-wrist acoustic response based authentication for smartwatches. Proc. ACM Interact. Mob. Wearable Ubiquitous Technol. **6**(4) (2023). https://doi.org/10.1145/3569473
5. Kim, H., Kim, M., Oakley, I.: A mobility evaluation of tilt panning and offset sensing smart watch input. In: The 5th ACM Workshop on Wearable Systems and Applications, WearSys 2019, pp. 5–10. Association for Computing Machinery, New York, NY, USA (2019). https://doi.org/10.1145/3325424.3329665
6. Lafreniere, B., Gutwin, C., Cockburn, A., Grossman, T.: Faster command selection on touchscreen watches. In: Proceedings of the 2016 CHI Conference on Human Factors in Computing Systems, CHI 2016, pp. 4663–4674. Association for Computing Machinery, New York, NY, USA (2016). https://doi.org/10.1145/2858036.2858166
7. Li, X., et al.: Dynamic hand gesture recognition using electrical impedance tomography. Sensors **22**(19) (2022). https://doi.org/10.3390/s22197185, https://www.mdpi.com/1424-8220/22/19/7185
8. Lin, H.P., Shih, Y.Y., Pang, A.C., Lou, Y.Y.: A virtual local-hub solution with function module sharing for wearable devices. In: Proceedings of the 19th ACM International Conference on Modeling, Analysis and Simulation of Wireless and Mobile Systems, MSWiM 2016, pp. 278–286. Association for Computing Machinery, New York, NY, USA (2016). https://doi.org/10.1145/2988287.2989150

9. McIntosh, J., Marzo, A., Fraser, M.: Sensir: detecting hand gestures with a wearable bracelet using infrared transmission and reflection. In: Proceedings of the 30th Annual ACM Symposium on User Interface Software and Technology, UIST 2017, pp. 593–597. Association for Computing Machinery, New York, NY, USA (2017). https://doi.org/10.1145/3126594.3126604
10. Oakley, I., Lee, D.: Interaction on the edge: offset sensing for small devices. In: Proceedings of the SIGCHI Conference on Human Factors in Computing Systems, CHI 2014, pp. 169–178. Association for Computing Machinery, New York, NY, USA (2014). https://doi.org/10.1145/2556288.2557138
11. Oakley, I., Lee, D., Islam, M.R., Esteves, A.: Beats: tapping gestures for smart watches. In: Proceedings of the 33rd Annual ACM Conference on Human Factors in Computing Systems, CHI 2015, pp. 1237–1246. Association for Computing Machinery, New York, NY, USA (2015). https://doi.org/10.1145/2702123.2702226
12. Perrault, S.T., Lecolinet, E., Eagan, J., Guiard, Y.: Watchit: simple gestures and eyes-free interaction for wristwatches and bracelets. In: Proceedings of the SIGCHI Conference on Human Factors in Computing Systems, CHI 2013, pp. 1451–1460. Association for Computing Machinery, New York, NY, USA (2013). https://doi.org/10.1145/2470654.2466192
13. Salemi Parizi, F., Kienzle, W., Whitmire, E., Gupta, A., Benko, H.: Rotowrist: continuous infrared wrist angle tracking using a wristband. In: Proceedings of the 27th ACM Symposium on Virtual Reality Software and Technology, VRST 2021, Association for Computing Machinery, New York, NY, USA (2021). https://doi.org/10.1145/3489849.3489886
14. Siek, K.A., Rogers, Y., Connelly, K.H.: Fat finger worries: how older and younger users physically interact with PDAs. In: Costabile, M.F., Paternò, F. (eds.) INTERACT 2005. LNCS, vol. 3585, pp. 267–280. Springer, Heidelberg (2005). https://doi.org/10.1007/11555261_24
15. Turner, C.J., Chaparro, B.S., He, J.: Text input on a smartwatch qwerty keyboard: tap vs. trace. Int. J. Hum.-Comput. Interact. **33**(2), 143–150 (2017). https://doi.org/10.1080/10447318.2016.1223265
16. Wu, Y., Jiang, D., Duan, J., Liu, X., Bayford, R., Demosthenous, A.: Towards a high accuracy wearable hand gesture recognition system using EIT. In: 2018 IEEE International Symposium on Circuits and Systems (ISCAS), pp. 1–4 (2018). https://doi.org/10.1109/ISCAS.2018.8351296
17. Xiao, R., Laput, G., Harrison, C.: Expanding the input expressivity of smartwatches with mechanical pan, twist, tilt and click. In: Proceedings of the SIGCHI Conference on Human Factors in Computing Systems, CHI 2014, pp. 193–196. Association for Computing Machinery, New York, NY, USA (2014). https://doi.org/10.1145/2556288.2557017
18. Xu, X., et al.: Enabling hand gesture customization on wrist-worn devices. In: Proceedings of the 2022 CHI Conference on Human Factors in Computing Systems. CHI 2022, Association for Computing Machinery, New York, NY, USA (2022). https://doi.org/10.1145/3491102.3501904
19. Yeo, H.S., Lee, J., Bianchi, A., Quigley, A.: Watchmi: applications of watch movement input on unmodified smartwatches. In: Proceedings of the 18th International Conference on Human-Computer Interaction with Mobile Devices and Services Adjunct, MobileHCI 2016, pp. 594–598. Association for Computing Machinery, New York, NY, USA (2016). https://doi.org/10.1145/2957265.2961825

20. Zhang, C., Yang, J., Southern, C., Starner, T.E., Abowd, G.D.: Watchout: extending interactions on a smartwatch with inertial sensing. In: Proceedings of the 2016 ACM International Symposium on Wearable Computers, ISWC 2016, pp. 136–143. Association for Computing Machinery, New York, NY, USA (2016). https://doi.org/10.1145/2971763.2971775
21. Zhang, Y., Harrison, C.: Tomo: wearable, low-cost electrical impedance tomography for hand gesture recognition. In: Proceedings of the 28th Annual ACM Symposium on User Interface Software & Technology, UIST 2015, pp. 167–173. Association for Computing Machinery, New York, NY, USA (2015). https://doi.org/10.1145/2807442.2807480

A Comprehensive Evaluation of OpenFace 2.0 Gaze Tracking

Evan Kreiensieck(✉), Yan Ai, and Linghan Zhang

George Mason University, Fairfax VA, 22030, USA
{ekreien,yai,lzhang37}@gmu.edu

Abstract. Gaze tracking is widely used for various human-computer interaction (HCI) applications. One of the exciting pieces of gaze tracking and analysis software is Openface 2.0, an open-source and powerful facial landmark tracking toolkit that enables real-time head pose tracking, eye gaze estimation, and action unit recognition with webcams. However, despite its various advantages, many researchers are concerned about the low accuracy and unstable performance of OpenFace 2.0, mainly gaze tracking. Indeed, the authors of OpenFace describe their gaze tracking as an estimation instead of accurate computation, with certain limitations which are not systematically explored or explained by the authors or previous research. Therefore, this paper aims to evaluate OpenFace 2.0 gaze tracking under various experimental settings. Specifically, the results may provide insightful information about how OpenFace 2.0 gaze-tracking performance may change when conditions such as the distance between users and the camera, lighting, camera position, user head pose, and facial obfuscation vary. The evaluation could especially benefit researchers who intend to use OpenFace 2.0 gaze tracking in less favorable environments and settings.

Keywords: OpenFace 2.0 · Gaze Tracking · HCI

1 Introduction

Eye tracking plays significant roles in HCI and ergonomics research communities, various research fields, and applications related to cybersecurity, psychology, user experience, education, assistive technology, etc [17,30,36,41,47]. For instance, given the uniqueness of individuals' eye gaze patterns [30], researchers analyze eye gazes for biometric-based user authentication [23,53] and deep fake detection [34,37]. Moreover, previous research shows that individuals' eye gaze patterns can effectively reveal their emotional and cognitive status [48]. Abdrabou et al. propose to detect password reuse by analyzing users' gaze patterns and typing behavior [14]. Similarly, some researchers use gaze patterns to classify individuals' emotions [31,43], measure students' comprehension and engagement [40,44], and detect distracted or fatigued drivers [15,45,49]. Furthermore, eye gaze patterns can be informative and applied for assistive technology. For

Supported by George Mason University.

M. Kurosu and A. Hashizume (Eds.): HCII 2023, LNCS 14011, pp. 532–549, 2023.
https://doi.org/10.1007/978-3-031-35596-7_34

instance, D'Mello et al. claim that eye gaze can be applied to reduce bias and detect when just-in-time care is needed [20]. Müller et al. analyze eye gaze patterns to predict users' speaking intentions to mediate conversations between parties [38]. Hsieh et al. find that eye-gaze assistive technology could improve computer activities and technology usability for children with severe motor and communication difficulties [26]. The entertainment industry has adopted eye gaze tracking in virtual reality and augmented reality systems [19,35,39] and gaze-based HCI applications [18,52] to enhance user experiences. Despite different purposes and experimental designs of eye gaze tracking, a critical requirement of eye gaze-based research or applications is the high accuracy of gaze tracking.

Most commercial eye gaze tracking systems rely on sophisticated hardware like infrared lights and infrared cameras, high-speed cameras, specialized eyeglasses and VR headsets, and designated software and complex algorithms to achieve that. For example, a biosensor solution provider, iMotions, supports screen- or wearables-based eye tracking devices and software suites for gaze data analysis [1,2,5,8,10,11]. Although iMotions also enables webcam-based gaze tracking, the developers warn about its performance degradation due to the inferior hardware [4]. Similarly, Tobii offers accurate screen- and wearable-based eye tracking solutions for various research purposes and individual entertainment applications [12]. Given the hardware limitations, Tobii implements webcam-based head pose tracking instead of eye gaze tracking for gaming [13]. These solutions provide users with raw eye gaze data and statistical analysis of eye gaze features regarding gaze fixations and saccades. In comparison, Eye-Tracking takes a further step to enable eye gaze tracking and gaze-based cognitive load calculation [9]. Whereas EyeTech focuses on supporting gaze tracking-based assistive technology, which enables people with complex communication needs (e.g., brain or spinal injuries or cerebral palsy) to communicate with their eye gazes [3]. Despite the high accuracy and powerful software supports, commercial eye gaze tracking solutions are challenging to adopt by academia due to their expensiveness (e.g., Tobii eyeglasses cost over $15,000), complex and rigid setup and calibration procedures [50].

Researchers aim to implement affordable, accurate, and flexible eye gaze tracking solutions with off-the-shelf devices. Existing eye gaze tracking research work can generally be categorized into model-based and appearance-based methods. Model-based methods achieve better performance in controlled in-lab experiments when experimental settings are constrained, and specialized sensors such as thermal or infrared cameras can be used [28,42]. These methods require at least one light source to create glints on the users' cornea. Then they use 2D or 3D regression models to calculate the gaze of point (GoP) based on the users' eye parameters, the glints' coordinates, and camera and screen coordinates [29]. By contrast, appearance-based methods estimate eye gazes from typical camera feeds or pre-recorded videos or images. They rely on pre-trained models to compute the current gaze data [50]. Appearance-based methods have more advantages in unconstrained environments, making them appealing for real-world applications. Therefore, many researchers work on improving the accuracy and feasibility of appearance-based eye gaze tracking. For example, Indolia et al. adopt a convolutional neural network to reduce parameter number and avoid over fitting [27].

Among existing eye gaze tracking solutions, OpenFace 2.0 is especially popular since it is an open-source, powerful facial landmark tracking toolkit that enables head pose tracking, eye gaze estimation, and action unit recognition on images, videos, and real-time webcam recordings [16]. OpenFace 2.0 uses key algorithms like Convolutional Experts Constrained Local Model (CE-CLM) and strategies such as deep model simplification, smart multiple hypotheses, and sparse response maps to achieve accurate, real-time gaze estimation without advanced hardware, such as a GPU. Moreover, OpenFace 2.0 is pre-trained with two of the largest datasets (i.e., IJB-FL [33] and 300VW [46]), which are collected under various environmental settings. OpenFace 2.0 supports different operating systems like Ubuntu and Windows and various programming languages, including Matlab, Python, and C++ [16]. However, OpenFace 2.0, especially its eye gaze tracking, possesses several issues. For instance, OpenFace 2.0 make assumptions about camera parameters based on camera resolution. Such assumptions make it necessary to conduct both camera and user calibration for accurate gaze tracking [6]. Moreover, researchers find that OpenFace 2.0 could only provide proper relative gaze angle estimations instead of exact absolute values [6]. Authors of OpenFace 2.0 verify such a conclusion [7]. Indeed, the authors evaluate OpenFace 2.0 eye gaze tracking with the MPII image dataset [51] and obtain satisfactory results. However, many researchers or HCI applications require gaze tracking based on real-time camera recordings. On the OpenFace 2.0 forum, researchers propose many other concerns regarding the eye gaze tracking of OpenFace 2.0.

Therefore, this paper aims to comprehensively evaluate OpenFace 2.0 eye gaze tracking under different environmental and experimental conditions. Specifically, the evaluation is conducted with different user-camera distances, lighting conditions (e.g., light intensities, light source angles, and light source colors/wavelengths), camera positions relative to the screen, users' head poses, gaze moving speeds, and face obfuscation with glasses or not. We choose such settings based on common use cases of eye gaze tracking for HCI research or applications in recent years. For example, driver eye gaze tracking is an important research topic since the drivers' gaze patterns could reveal critical driving safety information like the drivers' attention, cognitive, and fatigue status. One of the challenges of driver gaze tracking is that the outdoor lighting varies at different times of the day, affecting camera performance and, hence, gaze tracking accuracy. Therefore, it is crucial to understand gaze tracking accuracy with various lighting conditions. Moreover, related work focuses on evaluating and comparing the performance of commercial eye tracking solutions [22,25] or evaluating gaze tracking under controlled environments [50]. We believe this work is the first comprehensive evaluation of OpenFace 2.0 gaze tracking and thus could benefit those who intend to use it for real-time gaze tracking-based HCI research or applications in less favorable experimental settings or even in unconstrained, day to day situations.

2 Method

2.1 Recruitment and Participants

We recruit participants via email from the George Mason community. In total, 11 participants attend this study, whose ages range from 18 to 22 years old. Participants that typically wear glasses are asked to remove them except for the experiment measuring OpenFace 2.0 gaze tracking performance when glasses obstruct the participants' eyes. Given the short distances (equal or less than 1.5 m) between the screen and the participants and the sizes of designed dots for gaze focuses, the participants with low and moderate myopia could still focus their gazes on and move their gazes along the designated dots. Therefore myopic participants would not impact the evaluation of OpenFace 2.0.

2.2 Apparatus

One of the most appealing features of OpenFace 2.0 is that it supports normal web cameras for gaze tracking. Therefore, we use the RGB camera of an Intel RealSense D4351i and a 26-inch monitor for all the experiments. Although it is possible to improve the distance measurements between the user and the camera with the depth camera on the D4351i and enhance the gaze estimation accuracy, we disable such a feature since we focus on evaluating OpenFace 2.0 without extra modifications and improvements. Moreover, we also cover the IR projector on the D4351i so that it does not affect OpenFace 2.0 functioning, especially the lighting experiments. Indeed, we notice obvious degradation of OpenFace 2.0 gaze tracking when the IR projector is on. The D4351i has an effective range of 30 cm to 3 m. The RGB camera has a frame resolution of 1920×1080, a frame rate of 30 fps, and a sensor resolution of 2MP. We choose the 26-inch monitor since it enables us to locate fixation points at different angles of the participants on the monitor. We conduct general experiments in typical office lighting conditions. A laser distance finder was used to confirm the distances from the monitor before the start of each new experiment, as seen in Fig. 1.

2.3 Experimental Design

During experiments, the participants are required to look at the 5 dots that appear and disappear in sequence on the monitor. This dot animation is implemented in our experiment program, which runs in parallel with OpenFace 2.0 program. Specifically, we design the dots as grey circles shrinking in size, with a red dot in the center of each grey circle. The center red dot is a constant 15 pixels in diameter. The grey circle that closes in to the red dot starts as 100 pixels in diameter and shrinks over the course of 5 s. This is done to help participants maintain their focus on each dot for the entire time required. Only one

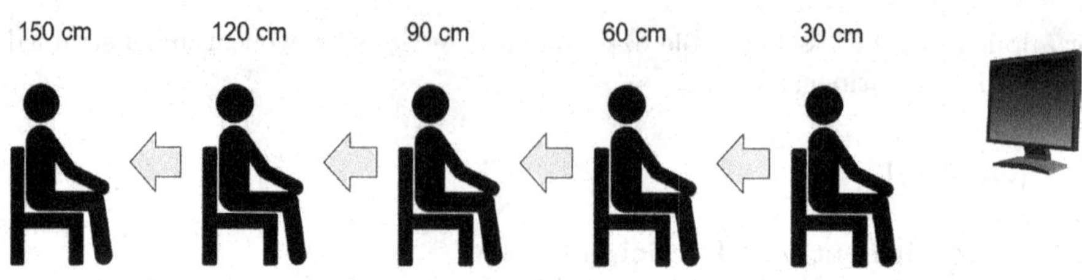

Fig. 1. Distance Experiment Set Up

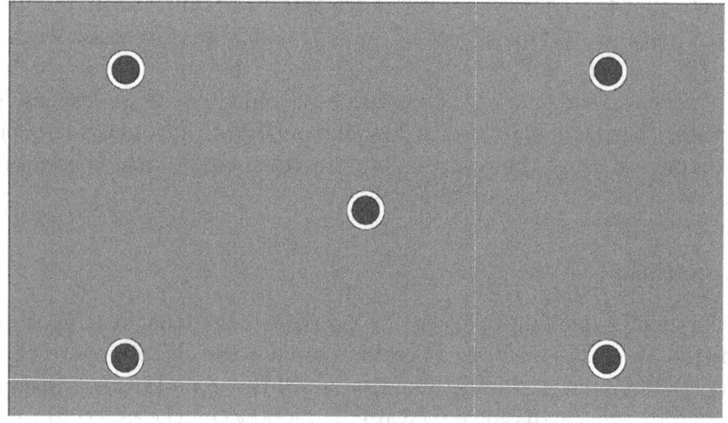

Fig. 2. Image of 5 Dot Pattern

dot is on screen at a time. Figure 2 shows the pattern the dots would create if they were simultaneously on-screen. The first dot appears in the top left corner, then they appear one at a time in a clockwise fashion, ending with the dot in the center. We require participants to fixate their eye gazes on each dot from when it appears until it disappears. In the moving dot experiments, the participants look at a dot moving horizontally across the screen at different speeds. By observing a moving dot, we can evaluate OpenFace 2.0's performance when gaze speed changes.

2.4 Experimental Setup

In the default experimental setup, participants sit 60 cm away from the monitor, facing forward at the camera, which is located at the bottom of the monitor. This default setup is applied to all experiments unless otherwise stated. Before experiments, we adjust the participants' seat heights so that when they look straight ahead, their eye levels are roughly aligned with the center of the monitor. This results in better tracking results and simplifies the calculation of the ground truths. Before experiments, we adjust a single experimental variable and hold all

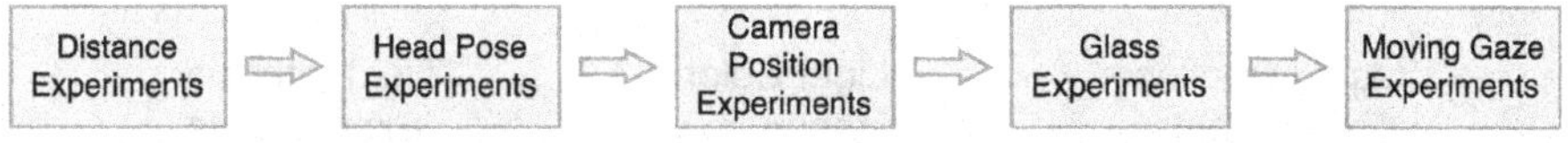

Fig. 3. General Experiment Order

others constant. These variables include the participant's distance to the camera, head pose, facial obfuscation, camera position, the direction of lighting, the color of lighting, and the color/wavelength of lighting.

2.5 Experimental Procedures

We conduct a sequence of experiments as shown in Fig. 3. Specific experimental procedures are elaborated on below. First, we adjust the distance participants sit from the camera. Then distance is held static while head pose is adjusted. The next experiments evaluate camera position, the impact of glasses, and lastly, gaze speed. Each experiment takes between 5 and 10 min, resulting in each participant needing about an hour to complete the entire set of experiments. After each experiment, the researcher positions the participant and any necessary factors needed for the next experiment.

Camera Calibration. Gaze tracking accuracy could be improved by introducing camera and user calibrations. In this work, we only implement camera calibration before experiments. We do not consider user calibration as it requires considerable effort from each user and requires a new calibration whenever the relative coordinates between the user, the camera, and the monitor change. Such requirements are not always feasible in HCI applications. In comparison, camera calibration eliminates the image deformation caused by lens distortion. We conduct one camera calibration at the beginning of all experiments using the same camera. OpenFace 2.0 makes assumptions about camera parameters like focal length and optical center based on the camera resolution. To calibrate the false parameters, we set up a checkerboard pattern in front of the camera and then use OpenCV to produce the true intrinsic camera parameters [24]. Eventually, we pass the measured parameters to OpenFace 2.0.

Distance Experiments. We evaluate the impact of distance between the camera and participants with five distances, i.e., 30, 60, 90, 120, and 150 cm. We choose such distance ranges considering common HCI use cases and the distance limitation of the camera. For example, when using the OpenFace 2.0 eye gaze tracking on laptops, the users usually sit in front of the laptop at distances of around 30 cm. Whereas if we apply OpenFace 2.0 for driver gaze tracking, we usually locate the camera on top of the dashboard. In that case, the distance between the driver and the camera can be over 120 cm. Before each experiment, we confirm the distance with a laser range finder. Specifically, we require participants to hold the range finder at their nose bridges, pointing at the monitor.

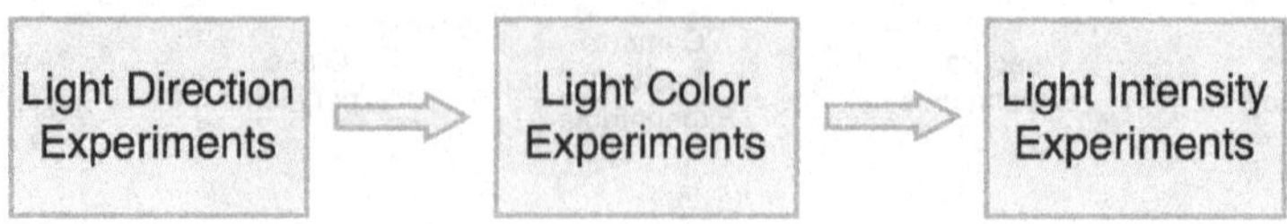

Fig. 4. Lighting Experiments

We help the participants to adjust their distance to the monitor by moving their chairs.

Head Pose Experiments. OpenFace 2.0 locates facial landmarks for eye gaze angle calculation. Therefore, the performance of gaze tracking may vary with different head poses. During these experiments, we require the participants to turn their heads to -40, -20, 20, and 40°C. We mark these angles with tapes on the ground for the participants' reference. Participants were then asked to repeat the 5 dot animation procedures for each angle listed previously. Participants were warned that they might not be able to hold their focus on some dots when sitting at -40 and 40°C to the camera but were asked to do their best within comfort. These angles were chosen to offer various levels of facial obfuscation without turning the participants to the point of not being able to see the dot animation.

Moving Eye Gaze Experiments. In this set of experiments, we change the default experimental design. The participants are required to follow a single dot moving across the screen from left to right at 3 different speeds with their eye gazes. Specifically, the dot takes 12, 8, and 4 s to move across the screen, corresponding to speeds of 4.80, 7.19, and 14.39 cm/s, respectively. We request the participants to repeat each experiment 3 times. We carry out these experiments to address HCI applications, such as reading or driving, where a person may change their gaze angles rapidly. This experiment will help future users to understand OpenFace 2.0's performance under such use cases.

Lighting Experiments. Lighting conditions are critical for camera performance and gaze-tracking solutions. Therefore, we design three sets of experiments to evaluate OpenFace 2.0 gaze tracking under different lighting conditions, including light intensities, light source angles, and light colors/wavelengths. Existing work evaluates gaze tracking systems' performance (but not OpenFace 2.0) in general outdoor environment [50]; there is no comprehensive evaluation of gaze tracking or OpenFace 2.0 in different lighting settings. The order of experiments related to lighting conditions took place in the order outlined in Fig. 4.

First, we shift the angles of light sources. To control the light directions, we turn off the overhead lights in the lab and set up a bar light with diffusing plastic cover (to protect the participants' eyes) at predetermined angles of -90, -45, 45, and 90°C from left to right to the participants. Using these angles, we

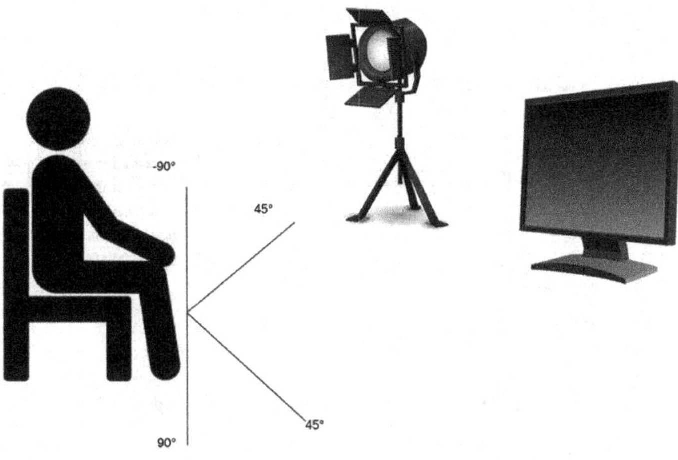

Fig. 5. Set Up for Angled Lighting

could produce deep or shallow shadows across the participants' faces. The bar light was not placed directly in front of the participants (angle = 0) as they cannot conduct the experiments when the light shines directly in their eyes even with the diffusing plastic cover. Next, we change the color of the light source by putting red, green, and blue plastic colored sheets over the bar light. This set of experiments is necessary for OpenFace 2.0 gaze tracking evaluation since researchers may collect gaze data in environments with complex light settings. The bar light was placed to the side of the monitor, so the participants' face was evenly lit without making it impossible for them to see the screen, as seen in Fig. 5. In the light color experiments, we also use an IR emitter to illuminate the participants' faces with infrared light since many gaze-tracking systems use such light sources to make it easier to separate human pupils [32]. Lastly, we adjust the ambient light intensities to simulate light levels at night by turning off the overhead lights, bringing the light level of the participant's faces to 20 lux. We compare that low light level to regular ambient light of an office, which is about 400 lux.

3 Data Analysis

3.1 Data Collection

OpenFace 2.0 outputs a comma-separated value (.csv) file containing basic information (frame index, timestamp, confidence, success, etc.), gaze-related data (gaze angles and eye landmark coordinates), pose data, facial landmark coordinates, etc. We focus on gaze-related data estimation. Therefore, we extract only the timestamps, confidence (reliability of current results), and averaged gaze angle in the x- and y-axes from the .csv file generated by OpenFace 2.0. Moreover, we write a Python program to generate dots at predefined coordinates on

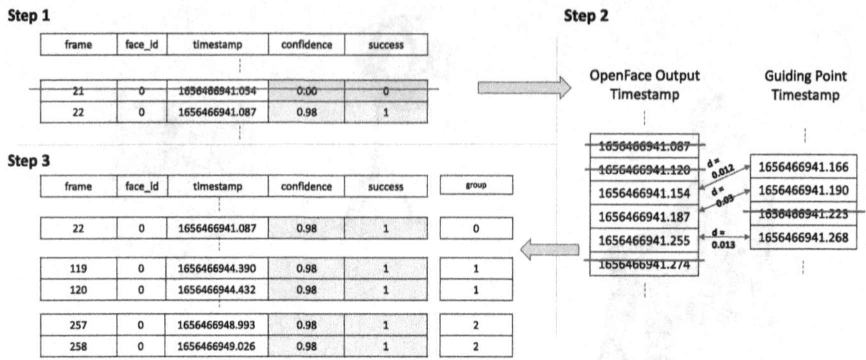

Fig. 6. Steps of Signal Preprocessing

the screen. This program also produces a .json file that contains the real-time 2D coordinates of the leading dot and the associated time stamps. The timestamps of the two files enable us to map the measured gaze angles to the corresponding ground truth.

Additionally, the size of the monitor (in centimeters) and the distance between the participants' nose bridge and the monitor surface are measured and the latter is recorded for each experiment. Before each trial, these values are taken by a range finder with an accuracy of 0.1cm. These data are used to calculate the ground truth of gaze angles. Before the final analysis of the experiment data, we need to perform signal preprocessing and denoising to reduce the errors caused by OpenFace failure frames and outlier data points.

3.2 Signal Preprocessing

The purpose of signal preprocessing is to eliminate invalid data and convert the raw data into a form more convenient for further analysis.

We first remove invalid frames which have confidence values lower than 0.98. During the experiments, we find that sometimes OpenFace 2.0 could fail to capture user's facial features even when the person stays stationary. Usually, this happens in the first few seconds of recording, and then OpenFace 2.0 will work stably. Therefore, we always start the program a few seconds after OpenFace 2.0 runs and discard the first few seconds of OpenFace data. In some rare cases, the recording contains many frames with low confidence values even after the first minute and could corrupt more than 10% of total frames. We discard such recordings and repeat these experiments.

Next, we match the timestamps of the gaze angles generated by OpenFace 2.0 and those of the leading dot on the screen. OpenFace 2.0 runs at different frame rates based on the experimental computers' configurations. On our experimental laptop, the frame rate of OpenFace 2.0 gaze tracking is around 30 fps. During experiments, we run OpenFace 2.0 and the experiment (leading dot) program simultaneously and sample the ground truth (leading dot coordinates) at a frame rate of 30 fps. Nevertheless, OpenFace 2.0's sampling frequency is not always stable. Indeed, it can be lower or higher than 30, and the value fluctuates throughout the process. After we remove invalid data, the OpenFace output is less than 30 frames per second. Based on our previous testing of OpenFace 2.0, when we find two frames from the two files (.csv and .json), whose timestamps have a time difference that is less than 0.02 s, we consider them as a matched pair.

The last step is to classify the output gaze angles into five groups. The number of groups is decided by experimental design. This step is only necessary for the gaze fixation trials. There are three gaze movement experiments where the leading dot moves at constant speeds on the screen. In these cases, we can group the OpenFace output frames with the ground truth points' timestamps. The purpose of this step is to simplify the analysis.

Figure 6 shows exemplary results of each step. In Step 1, the deleted row has a confidence value of 0.0 and a success indicator of 0. Thus, it's discarded. The frames with a success indicator of 1 are highlighted green and kept. In Step 2, we start with the OpenFace output data. If there is no frame from .json file with a time difference smaller than 0.02s, then we delete this frame of OpenFace output. This process is the same for the .json file frames. In Step 3, we group the OpenFace output frames based on the .json file's timestamps of each leading dot and add a group number to each frame. This is the first phase of data preparation.

3.3 Signal Denoising

The second and final phase of data preparation is denoising. Humans make small, fast eye movements even when trying to focus on one target [21]. We consider these frames as outliers and discard them. We do this for experimental data when gaze fixation is required. For moving gaze experiments, the position of gaze points constantly changes. Therefore, the participants only focus their eye gazes on a specific screen coordinate for around 0.02 s (given a fixed frame rate of 30fps of leading dot program) and produce insufficient data for denoising. For the fixed gaze experiment, we use standard deviation as the filtering standard and remove the gaze angles that are too far away from the rest. The second step is to handle the noises in the dataset. Human's uncontrollable eye movements or OpenFace 2.0 errors could introduce such noises.Empirically, we use the moving average method to process the gaze angles with a window of 9 frames.

Figure 7 shows signal denoising results of one of the fixed gaze experiments. In Fig. 7(a), the outliers are identified by the 2-sigma process. First, we compute the mean value of the point's x and y coordinates and the standard deviation within each point group. Then the points that fall outside the 2 sigma range are eliminated. Figure 7(b) contrasts pre-denoising and post-denoising data using moving average. We could observe that after denoising, the measured gaze angles change smoothly with fewer noises.

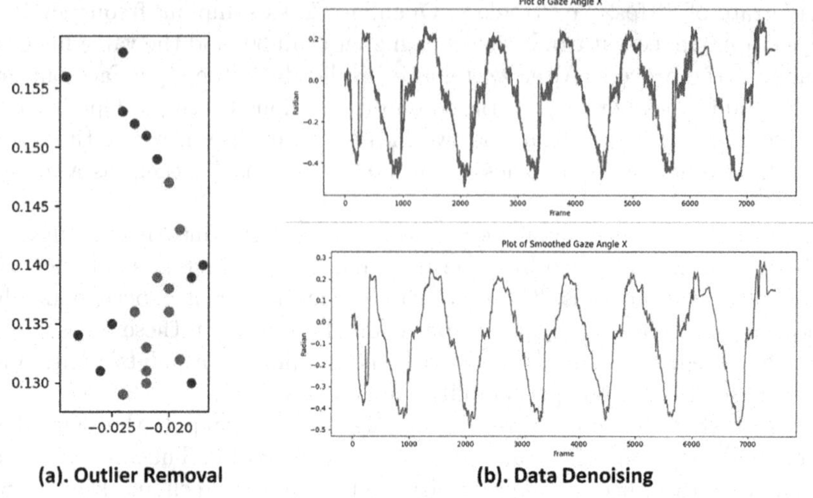

Fig. 7. Signal Denoising

3.4 Ground Truth Calculation

Before the experiments, we help the participants adjust their relative positions to the monitor so that when they look straight forward at the monitor, the average of their left and right eyes' coordinates are aligned with the center of the screen, i.e., their gaze directions should be perpendicular with the screen surface. The world coordinate system's origin is the screen's upper right corner, per the document of OpenFace 2.0. Also, given the monitor specifications and the pixel locations of the gaze leading dots, the leading dots' world coordinates can be obtained. Knowing the coordinates of the center of two eyes and the leading dot, we can easily calculate the ground truths of gaze vectors. Eventually, we decompose this vector into x, y, and z subvectors and compare that with the gaze angles output of OpenFace 2.0, which are given in fraction of the unit vector in the x and y directions. The OpenFace output's gaze angles are compared with the ground truth values to evaluate the accuracy of estimation.

4 Results

4.1 Impact of Distance from Camera

As shown in Fig. 8, at 30 cm from the camera, the average error of OpenFace 2.0 gaze tracking is 19.6°C, the highest of any distance. This could be because when the participants sit close to the monitor and camera, minute eye movements can cause significant gaze angle changes, thus resulting in relatively larger errors. When participants sit 60 and 90 cm away, the average error drops to 10°C, then even farther at 120 cm, to 7.9°C. At 150 cm from the camera, the error increases again to 13.7°C. Although the camera supports up to 3 m, when participants sit further away, the camera uses less pixels to describe the participants' eyes and therefore affects landmark localization of OpenFace 2.0 and gaze tracking. The results show that OpenFace 2.0 functions best when users sit between 60 to 120 cm away from the camera.

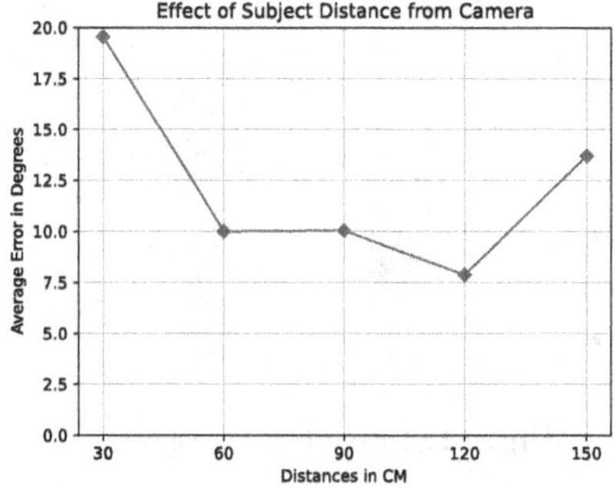

Fig. 8. Impact of Distance from Camera

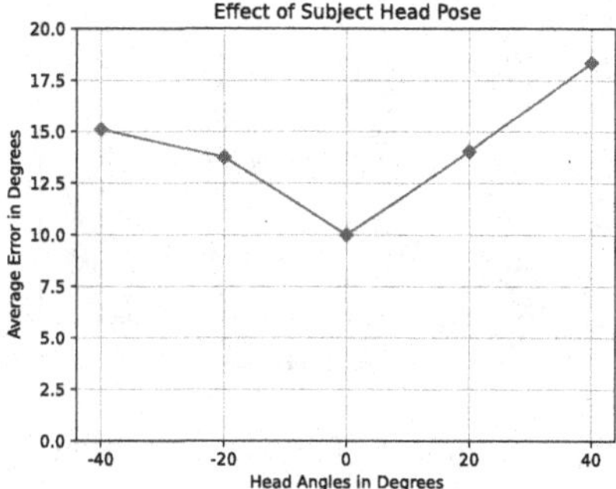

Fig. 9. Impact of Head Pose

4.2 Impact of Head Pose

For the first experiment testing the impact of head pose, participants were seated 60 cm away from the camera and turned 40°C to their left. This setup resulted in an average error of 15°C was measured. The next two parts of the experiment were done with participants turned slightly to their left and right (20°C in both cases). Figure 9 illustrates the gaze tracking results when participants' head poses change. These yielded average errors of 13.8 and 14.1, respectively. Turning to the right at 40°C resulted in an average error of 18.4°C. When turned to steeper angles, either left or right, OpenFace 2.0 results in a higher error. The results suggest that it could be significant to set up the camera at proper locations so that the users' head angles are minimized when using OpenFace 2.0 for gaze tracking.

4.3 Impact of Camera Position

By default, the camera is placed at the bottom of the monitor. In this experiment, to test the impact of camera position on Open Face's accuracy, we move the camera either to the side of the monitor or above it. The results in Fig. 10 show that all positions except for the bottom performed similarly, with average errors of about 13.5°C. When the camera was placed at the bottom of the monitor, the average error was 10°C. These positions were chosen to give an idea of how OpenFace's accuracy changes when the camera is placed in different locations.

Aside from performing best at the bottom of the monitor, other positions did not impact the accuracy significantly. This result is consistent with previous research.

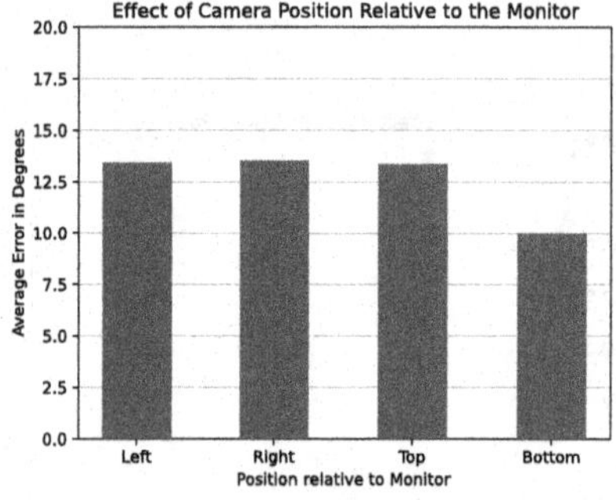

Fig. 10. Impact of Camera Position

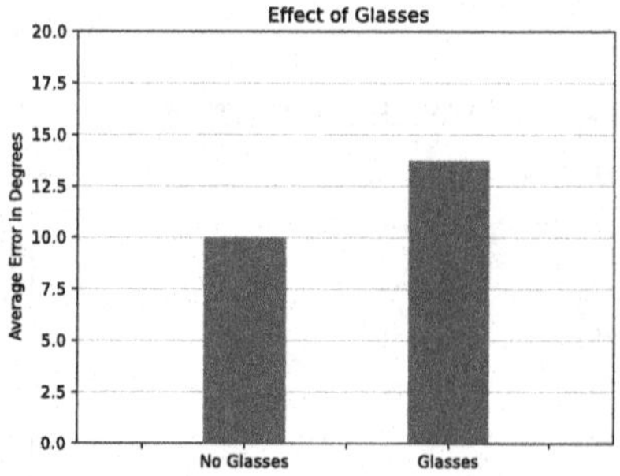

Fig. 11. Impact of Glasses

4.4 Impact of Glasses

Theoretically, when the users wear glasses, eye tracking performance drops since the glasses may affect the cameras' functioning and the landmark recognition of OpenFace 2.0. Our experimental results verify this hypothesis. As we can observe in Fig. 11, the average error when glasses were not worn was 10°C, whereas the average error when glasses were worn was 13.7°C. All other experiments were done without wearing glasses, even if participants typically wore them. This decision was made because participants could still fixate their gaze on the center of the dots for the required time, regardless of whether they typically wore glasses or not.

4.5 Impact of Gaze Speed

As illustrated in Fig. 12, when the users' eye gazes follow the leading dot traveling across the 26-inch monitor in 4 s (4.8 cm/s), 8 s (7.19 cm/s), and 12 s (14.39 cm/s), the gaze angle errors calculated by OpenFace 2.0 are 7.6, 7.7, and 7.5°C. The error is fairly close at every speed, differing only by .2°C. We do not consider higher gaze speeds since, based on participants' feedback, they could hardly fixate their gaze on the moving dot when it moves at 14.39 cm/s. It is possible for participants to change their eye gaze directions at higher speeds when they initiate such movements. Nevertheless, it is hard to obtain the ground truth in such cases.

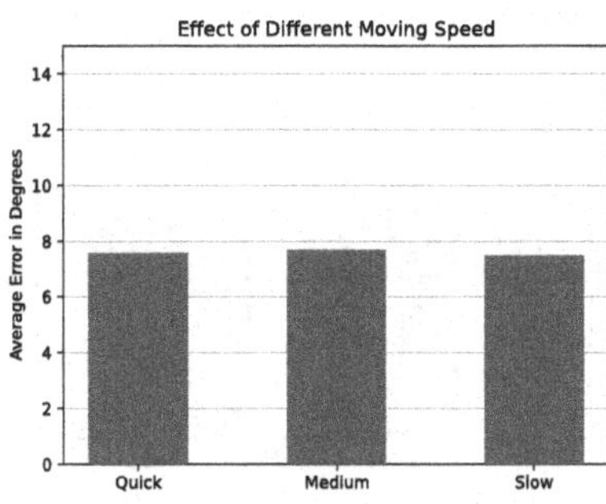

Fig. 12. Impact of Gaze Speed

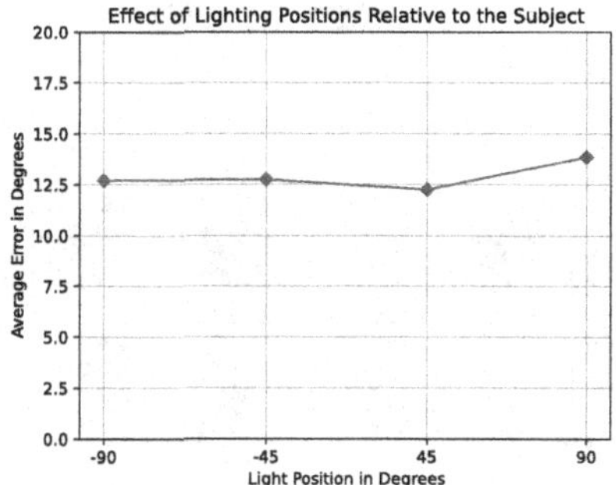

Fig. 13. Impact of Lighting Position

4.6 Impact of Light Position

In Fig. 15, we could notice that the accuracy changed very little when the lighting angle was moved. When the light was directed onto the participant directly from their left, the average error was 12.7°C. At 45°C to their left, the average error is 12.8. When the light is directed from 45°C to the participant's right, the average error drops to 12.3°C. Shining the light directly from the participant's right resulted in an average error of 13.9. These angles were chosen so that different depths of shadow would be cast across participants' faces, limiting the view of the camera and OpenFace 2.0. OpenFace 2.0 performs similarly regardless of which direction the light is coming from. When comparing Fig. 10 and Fig. 15, we could notice that with the same camera position (at the bottom of the screen), when the light is angled, the OpenFace 2.0 gaze tracking performance decreases.

4.7 Impact of Type of Lighting

We use four types of lights in this experiment. Figure 14 shows the impact of light color/wavelength on OpenFace 2.0 eye tracking. Using a red light to illuminate participants' faces resulted in an average accuracy of 11°C. Using the green light provided an average error of 12.4°C. Blue light results in the highest average error of 13.6°C. Lastly, the infrared emitter resulted in an average error of 11.6°C. In each case, the light was placed directly next to the monitor to minimize any shadow, as the impact of the direction of lighting was tested previously.

4.8 Impact of Intensity of Lighting

Turning the overhead light off gave lighting conditions of about 20 lx. In these darker lighting conditions, OpenFace 2.0 achieves an average error of 12.2°C (Fig. 15). Lighting conditions of 400 lx result in an average error of about 10°C. These two levels were chosen to understand how OpenFace 2.0 performs in dark scenarios as opposed to a well-lit office space. We assume extreme high light intensity will largely affect OpenFace 2.0's performance. Nevertheless, participants are not conformable conducting experiments in such situations.

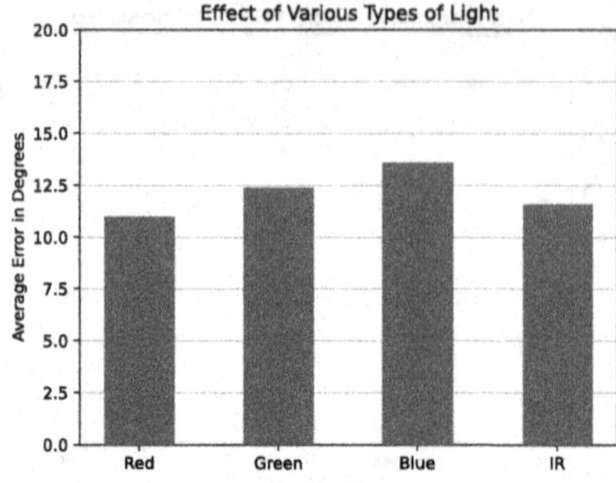

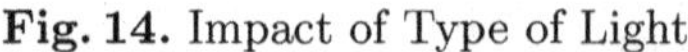

Fig. 14. Impact of Type of Light

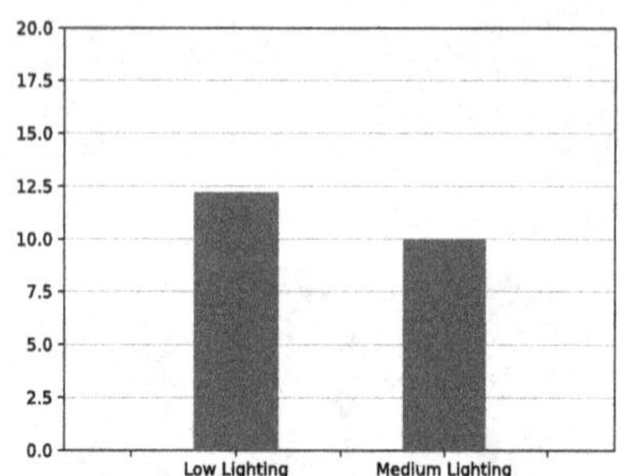

Fig. 15. Impact of Level of Lighting Impact of Lighting Position

5 Conclusion

In this paper, we present a comprehensive evaluation of OpenFace 2.0 gaze tracking under different environmental and experimental settings. We found that OpenFace performed with consistent average error in a variety of conditions that limited the information available to OpenFace in some way. By testing individual conditions in a controlled manner, we find that OpenFace 2.0 gaze tracking performs best in the range of 60–120 centimeters when the user is turned towards a camera placed at the bottom of a monitor, without glasses, and in a well-lit environment. While many of those conditions may seem intuitive, our experiments show that researchers using OpenFace can expect fair results when gaze speed varies, single-color lighting is used, directional lighting is used, or users are turned slightly from the camera.

References

1. Argus science etmobile eye tracking glasses, hardware specifications. https://imotions.com/hardware/argus-science-eye-tracking-glasses/
2. Eye tracking: Screen-based, detect visual attention in controlled environments. https://imotions.com/biosensor/eye-tracking-screen-based/
3. Eyeon, the technology gap felt around the world. https://eyetechds.com/eye-tracking-products/the-eyeon-platform/
4. imotions module: Eye tracking screen based. https://imotions.com/products/imotions-lab/modules/eye-tracking-screen-based/
5. imotions research software, the world's leading human behavior research tool. https://imotions.com/platform/
6. Output quality (gaze direction underestimation, default face measures). https://github.com/TadasBaltrusaitis/OpenFace/issues/969m
7. Output quality (gaze direction underestimation, default face measures 969). https://github.com/TadasBaltrusaitis/OpenFace/issues/969
8. Pupil labs invisible, hardware specifications. https://imotions.com/hardware/pupil-labs-invisible/

9. Remote solution: Eyeworks + fx3. https://www.eyetracking.com/fx3-remote-eye-tracking/
10. Smart eye ai-x, hardware specifications. https://imotions.com/hardware/smart-eye-ai-x/
11. Smart eye aurora, hardware specifications. https://imotions.com/hardware/smart-eye-aurora/
12. Tobii eye tracker 5. https://gaming.tobii.com/product/eye-tracker-5/
13. Tobii horizon. https://gaming.tobii.com/horizon/
14. Abdrabou, Y., et al.: "your eyes tell you have used this password before": identifying password reuse from gaze and keystroke dynamics. In: CHI Conference on Human Factors in Computing Systems, pp. 1–16 (2022)
15. Abouelnaga, Y., Eraqi, H.M., Moustafa, M.N.: Real-time distracted driver posture classification. arXiv preprint arXiv:1706.09498 (2017)
16. Baltrusaitis, T., Zadeh, A., Lim, Y.C., Morency, L.P.: Openface 2.0: facial behavior analysis toolkit. In: 2018 13th IEEE International Conference on Automatic face & Gesture Recognition (FG 2018), pp. 59–66. IEEE (2018)
17. Beddiar, D.R., Nini, B., Sabokrou, M., Hadid, A.: Vision-based human activity recognition: a survey. Multimed. Tools App. **79**(41), 30509–30555 (2020)
18. Bisen, D., Shukla, R., Rajpoot, N., Maurya, P., Uttam, A.K., et al.: Responsive human-computer interaction model based on recognition of facial landmarks using machine learning algorithms. Multimed. Tools App. **81**(13), 18011–18031 (2022)
19. Clay, V., König, P., Koenig, S.: Eye tracking in virtual reality. Journal of eye movement research 12(1) (2019)
20. D'Mello, S.K., Tay, L., Southwell, R.: Psychological measurement in the information age: machine-learned computational models. Curr. Dir. Psychol. Sci. **31**(1), 76–87 (2022)
21. Doshi, A., Trivedi, M.M.: Head and eye gaze dynamics during visual attention shifts in complex environments. J. Vis. **12**(2), 9–9 (2012)
22. Funke, G., Greenlee, E., Carter, M., Dukes, A., Brown, R., Menke, L.: Which eye tracker is right for your research?Performance evaluation of several cost variant eye trackers. In: Proceedings of the Human Factors and Ergonomics Society Annual Meeting, vol. 60, pp. 1240–1244. SAGE Publications Sage CA: Los Angeles, CA (2016)
23. Ghosh, S., Dhall, A., Sharma, G., Gupta, S., Sebe, N.: Speak2label: using domain knowledge for creating a large scale driver gaze zone estimation dataset. In: Proceedings of the IEEE/CVF International Conference on Computer Vision, pp. 2896–2905 (2021)
24. Herrera, D., Kannala, J., Heikkilä, J.: Joint depth and color camera calibration with distortion correction. IEEE Trans. Pattern Anal. Mach. Intell. **34**(10), 2058–2064 (2012)
25. Housholder, A., Reaban, J., Peregrino, A., Votta, G., Mohd, T.K.: Evaluating accuracy of the Tobii eye tracker 5. In: Kim, J.-H., Singh, M., Khan, J., Tiwary, U.S., Sur, M., Singh, D. (eds.) IHCI 2021. LNCS, vol. 13184, pp. 379–390. Springer, Cham (2022). https://doi.org/10.1007/978-3-030-98404-5_36
26. Hsieh, Y.H., Granlund, M., Odom, S.L., Hwang, A.W., Hemmingsson, H.: Increasing participation in computer activities using eye-gaze assistive technology for children with complex needs. Disability and Rehabilitation: Assistive Technology, pp. 1–14 (2022)
27. Indolia, S., Goswami, A.K., Mishra, S.P., Asopa, P.: Conceptual understanding of convolutional neural network-a deep learning approach. Proc. Comput. Sci. **132**, 679–688 (2018)

28. Jiang, J., Zhou, X., Chan, S., Chen, S.: Appearance-based gaze tracking: a brief review. In: Yu, H., Liu, J., Liu, L., Ju, Z., Liu, Y., Zhou, D. (eds.) ICIRA 2019. LNCS (LNAI), vol. 11745, pp. 629–640. Springer, Cham (2019). https://doi.org/10.1007/978-3-030-27529-7_53
29. Kar, A., Corcoran, P.: A review and analysis of eye-gaze estimation systems, algorithms and performance evaluation methods in consumer platforms. IEEE Access **5**, 16495–16519 (2017)
30. Katsini, C., Abdrabou, Y., Raptis, G.E., Khamis, M., Alt, F.: The role of eye gaze in security and privacy applications: Survey and future HCI research directions. In: Proceedings of the 2020 CHI Conference on Human Factors in Computing Systems, pp. 1–21 (2020)
31. Khan, F.: Facial expression recognition using facial landmark detection and feature extraction via neural networks. arXiv preprint arXiv:1812.04510 (2018)
32. Kim, H.C., Cha, J., Lee, W.D.: Eye detection for gaze tracker with near infrared illuminator. In: 2014 IEEE 17th International Conference on Computational Science and Engineering, pp. 458–464. IEEE (2014)
33. Kim, K., Baltrusaitis, T., Zadeh, A., Morency, L.P., Medioni, G.: Holistically constrained local model: Going beyond frontal poses for facial landmark detection. Technical report, University of Southern California, Institute for Robotics and Intelligent ... (2016)
34. Li, M., Liu, B., Hu, Y., Zhang, L., Wang, S.: Deepfake detection using robust spatial and temporal features from facial landmarks. In: 2021 IEEE International Workshop on Biometrics and Forensics (IWBF), pp. 1–6. IEEE (2021)
35. Li, T., Liu, Q., Zhou, X.: Ultra-low power gaze tracking for virtual reality. In: Proceedings of the 15th ACM Conference on Embedded Network Sensor Systems, pp. 1–14 (2017)
36. Lim, J.Z., Mountstephens, J., Teo, J.: Emotion recognition using eye-tracking: taxonomy, review and current challenges. Sensors **20**(8), 2384 (2020)
37. Masood, M., Nawaz, M., Malik, K.M., Javed, A., Irtaza, A., Malik, H.: Deepfakes generation and detection: state-of-the-art, open challenges, countermeasures, and way forward. Appl. Intell. 1–53 (2022)
38. Müller, P., et al.: Multimediate: multi-modal group behaviour analysis for artificial mediation. In: Proceedings of the 29th ACM International Conference on Multimedia, pp. 4878–4882 (2021)
39. Mutasim, A.K., Stuerzlinger, W., Batmaz, A.U.: Gaze tracking for eye-hand coordination training systems in virtual reality. In: Extended Abstracts of the 2020 CHI Conference on Human Factors in Computing Systems, pp. 1–9 (2020)
40. Paidja, A.N.R., Bachtiar, F.A.: Engagement emotion classification through facial landmark using convolutional neural network. In: 2022 2nd International Conference on Information Technology and Education (ICIT&E), pp. 234–239. IEEE (2022)
41. Pantic, M., Pentland, A., Nijholt, A., Huang, T.: Human computing and machine understanding of human behavior: A survey. In: Proceedings of the 8th International Conference on Multimodal Interfaces, pp. 239–248 (2006)
42. Pathirana, P., Senarath, S., Meedeniya, D., Jayarathna, S.: Eye gaze estimation: a survey on deep learning-based approaches. Expert Syst. Appl. **199**, 116894 (2022)
43. Rahdari, F., Rashedi, E., Eftekhari, M.: A multimodal emotion recognition system using facial landmark analysis. Iranian J. Sci. Technol. Trans. Elect. Eng. **43**(1), 171–189 (2019)
44. Sathik, M., Jonathan, S.G.: Effect of facial expressions on student's comprehension recognition in virtual educational environments. Springerplus **2**(1), 1–9 (2013)

45. Seebeck, C.: Real Time Labeling of Driver Behavior in Real World Environments. Ph.D. thesis (2021)
46. Shen, J., Zafeiriou, S., Chrysos, G.G., Kossaifi, J., Tzimiropoulos, G., Pantic, M.: The first facial landmark tracking in-the-wild challenge: Benchmark and results. In: Proceedings of the IEEE International Conference on Computer Vision Workshops, pp. 50–58 (2015)
47. Strohmaier, A.R., MacKay, K.J., Obersteiner, A., Reiss, K.M.: Eye-tracking methodology in mathematics education research: a systematic literature review. Educ. Stud. Math. **104**(2), 147–200 (2020). https://doi.org/10.1007/s10649-020-09948-1
48. Tao, J., Tan, T.: Affective computing: a review. In: Tao, J., Tan, T., Picard, R.W. (eds.) ACII 2005. LNCS, vol. 3784, pp. 981–995. Springer, Heidelberg (2005). https://doi.org/10.1007/11573548_125
49. Zhang, S., Abdel-Aty, M.: Drivers' visual distraction detection using facial landmarks and head pose. Transport. Res. Record. 03611981221087234 (2022)
50. Zhang, X., Sugano, Y., Bulling, A.: Evaluation of appearance-based methods and implications for gaze-based applications. In: Proceedings of the 2019 CHI Conference on Human Factors in Computing Systems, pp. 1–13 (2019)
51. Zhang, X., Sugano, Y., Fritz, M., Bulling, A.: Appearance-based gaze estimation in the wild. In: Proceedings of the IEEE Conference on Computer Vision and Pattern Recognition, pp. 4511–4520 (2015)
52. Zhao, R., Wang, K., Divekar, R., Rouhani, R., Su, H., Ji, Q.: An immersive system with multi-modal human-computer interaction. In: 2018 13th IEEE International Conference on Automatic Face & Gesture Recognition (FG 2018), pp. 517–524. IEEE (2018)
53. Zhou, B., Lohokare, J., Gao, R., Ye, F.: Echoprint: two-factor authentication using acoustics and vision on smartphones. In: Proceedings of the 24th Annual International Conference on Mobile Computing and Networking, pp. 321–336 (2018)

Text Entry on Smartwatches Using Continuous Gesture Recognition and Word Dictionary

Thamer Horbylon Nascimento[1(✉)], Juliana Paula Felix[2], Jhon Lucas Santos Silva[2], and Fabrizzio Soares[2]

[1] Federal Institute Goiano – Campus Iporá, Iporá, GO, Brazil
thamer.nascimento@ifgoiano.edu.br
[2] Instituto de Informática, Universidade Federal de Goiás, Goiânia, GO, Brazil
fabrizzio@inf.ufg.br

Abstract. This work proposes the development of a method for text entry in smartwatches using continuous gesture recognition, *Naïve Bayes* classifier and a word dictionary. We performed an evaluation with experts to validate the proposed method. To perform text entry, a user inserts characters through simple gestures, based on geometric shapes, thus, a character is drawn by a user using a set of proposed gestures. We use *Naïve Bayes* classifier to identify the character that user is entering without the user having to draw it completely. Finally, we use a trie as a dictionary of words to predict words that can be written, considering characters already inserted. We also used the relative probability of word usage in the prediction process. The evaluation with experts showed that it is possible to insert phrases in smartwatches using the proposed method and that the words were inserted correctly.

Keywords: Smartwatch · Text Entry · Continuous Gesture Recognition · Word Dictionary

1 Introduction

Smartwatch is a wearable device that is attached to user's wrist and because it is an emerging technology, its use is constantly growing [10,13]. They allow you to perform various everyday tasks, such as replying to a message or email, as well as using them to control other devices. Therefore, it is important to create fast and efficient interaction methods for these devices.

In our previous work [14], we developed a method that uses continuous gesture recognition and *Naïve Bayes* classifier to insert characters in smartwatches using simple geometric shapes, such as straight lines and curves. Results show that using this method, a character can be inserted using only two interactions. Our work also shows that users were receptive to methods that use continuous gesture recognition on [11,15,17] smartwatches.

Therefore, this work aims to develop a method that allows you to enter text on smartwatches using continuous gesture recognition, *Naïve Bayes* classifier

M. Kurosu and A. Hashizume (Eds.): HCII 2023, LNCS 14011, pp. 550–562, 2023.
https://doi.org/10.1007/978-3-031-35596-7_35

and a word dictionary. For this it is necessary specifically: to recognize gestures, insert characters from performed gestures and finally, predict words that can be inserted with these characters. Thus, we present in this work results of the research for text entry in smartwatches using continuous gesture recognition, Naïve Bayes classifier and word dictionary.

Next sections detail the contents that are relevant to understanding the results. The next section presents the related work, then we will explain the developed prototype and the details of the method. Soon after, we will approach the evaluation with specialists, in sequence, the results and finally, the conclusions.

2 Related Work

Gong et al. [7] presents *WrisText*, a method that performs text input on smartwatches using only one hand, for this, it uses a similar wrist movement and works similarly to a joystick. Cha et al. [4] have developed a text input method called *Virtual Sliding QWERTY (VSQ)*, which uses a virtual *QWERTY* layout keyboard and a "Tap-N-Drag" method to move the keyboard to the desired position. Wong et al. [21] presents "FingerT9" as a method that uses the interaction of the thumb with the fingers to allow the entry of text in smartwatches using a single hand, for this, the layout of the T9 keyboard was mapped to the finger segments and sensors are used to capture which segment the user touched.

Oney et al. [19] presents a method called *Zoomboard*, which allows the user to touch the area of the desired character and a magnification of it is presented to the user to be enlarged again or to allow the user to select it. Darbar et al. [6] developed *ETAO Keyboard*, an application for smartwatches that shows the most frequent characters of the English language on the main screen, in this way, users can enter them with a touch, as well as the main numbers and symbols with a double tap.

Nebeling et al. [18], created *WearWrite*, an application that allows the collaborative writing of articles, in which the user can send or accept notifications directly from their smartwatch. Gordon et al. [8], developed *WatchWriter* which is a keyboard where the user uses the finger to enter text, it supports touch and gesture typing in addition to using statistical decoding. The keyboard proposed by Hong et al. [9], allows the user to swipe left and right by switching between halves of a *QWERTY* keyboard.

In our previous work, we proposed a prototype for a text input method in smartwatches based on geometric shapes. This prototype aims to allow the user to insert a character with up to two interactions using geometric shapes [14]. Results of our work show that users were receptive to methods that use continuous gesture recognition on smartwatches, they also show that it is possible to use it to insert characters using only two interactions [11,14,16,17].

In the light of these applications for text entry, this work presents a method that allows the entry of text with the insertion of words and phrases, an evaluation with specialists is also carried out to validate the proposed method.

3 Prototype

We developed a prototype that allows the user to enter text on smartwatches using simple gestures based on geometric shapes. Characters are inserted by users using a set of gestures composed of straight lines and curves validated in our previous work [14]. This set is composed of vertical line, horizontal line, diagonal lines, circumference and semicircles that can be seen in Fig. 1.

Fig. 1. Shape of gestures developed to compose characters.

To enter a character, the user uses the gestures shown in Fig. 1. After performing the gesture, the first step is to recognize it using the continuous gesture recognition algorithm, then it is passed on to the *Naïve Bayes* classifier to identify which characters can be inserted from the gestures performed, for Finally, a search is carried out in a dictionary of words stored in a trie to identify which words can be inserted from the characters that the gestures represent.

Therefore, we developed a method that allows the user to input text as words and phrases using a set of gestures based on geometric shapes validated in our previous work [14]. For this, we use a continuous gesture recognition algorithm, a *Naïve Bayes* classifier and a trie. Figure 2, presents the structure of the developed method.

The trie is used as a dictionary of words, in this way, each character selected by the user is inserted in the trie. The dictionary is also used to check for available words with the characters returned by the *Naïve Bayes* classifier. This step is performed using the already entered characters (word prefix) and the word dictionary. In this way, only the characters that can be entered are displayed to the user.

The most probable character is selected, as well as the words that can be entered by it. The character will be automatically inserted after 2 s if there is no user interaction, however, the other characters are sorted according to their probability and displayed to the user. At this moment, the user can perform three actions:

- Confirm selection of the most likely character or select an option displayed to him, in this case the character is inserted into the trie;

- Select a word;
- Perform a new gesture, in this case, repeat the process shown in Fig. 2.

In order to validate the proposed method, we developed a prototype for the "Wear Os" system that was installed on the smartwatch *"Fossil Gen 4"* to carry out an evaluation with specialists. The next subsections detail the developed method.

3.1 Continuous Gesture Recognition

We used the continuous gesture recognition algorithm proposed by (Kristensson and Denby) [12] to recognize the gestures performed by the user. This algorithm can recognize a gesture before it is finished with high accuracy.

As it is capable of predicting partial gestures, it is not necessary for the user to complete the gesture for it to be recognized, making it possible to quickly perform the action desired by the user. Because, the continuous gesture recognition algorithm and being able to predict partial gestures, can recognize a gesture before it is finalized, moreover, it is able to predict them with high accuracy. [12].

As we use the continuous gesture recognition algorithm, it is not necessary for the user to finalize the gesture for it to be recognized. In this way, the prototype

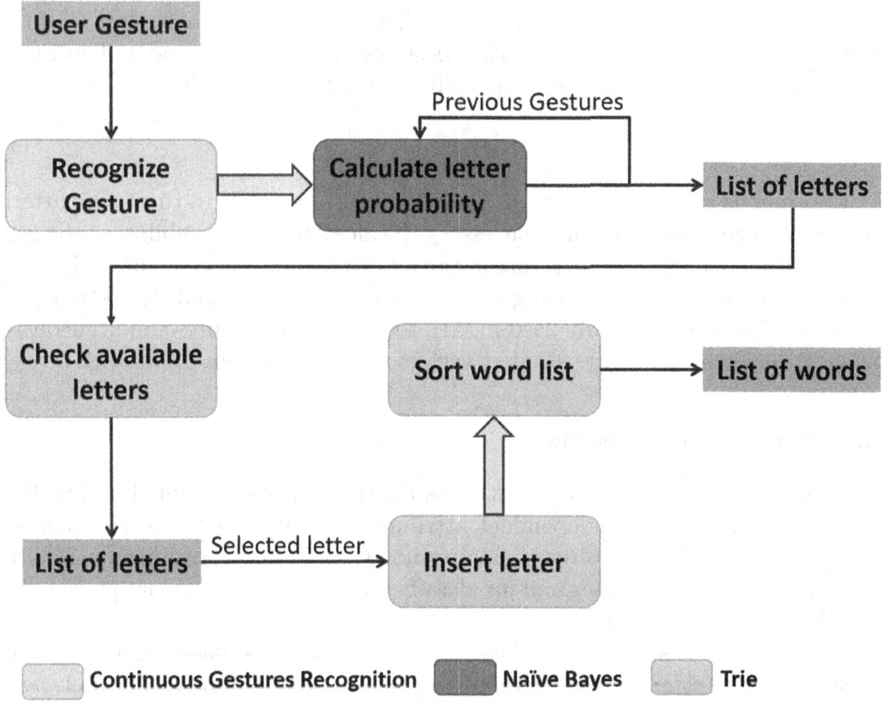

Fig. 2. Structure of the method developed for text entry.

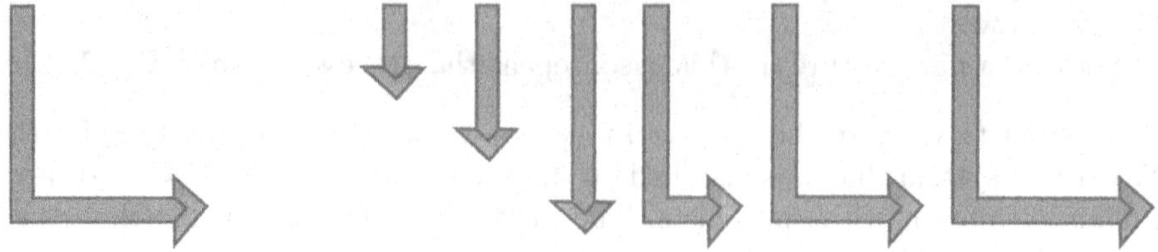

Fig. 3. Full model to the left and segments of the gesture to the right. Adapted from [12].

was designed to recognize a gesture and show the available characters when the user performs a gesture of at least 2 cm.

Algorithm uses a technique that considers a gesture as a template and divides it into several segments. Therefore, the segments describe the partial sections of the model in an increasing way [12]. As illustrated in Fig. 3, the direction of the gesture is represented by an arrow. A complete gesture, i.e. a template, shown on the left with its partial segments on the right.

A model can be considered to be a vector of points ordered in relation to time, that is, a vector of points ordered relative to the way in which the movement should be produced, a gesture is segmented into several parts and in increasing movements.

A model is represented by w is a pair (l, S), where l is the description of the model and S is a set of segments that describe the complete model. The Eq. 1, describes a complete model ordered with respect to time T [12],

$$S = [s_1, s_2, ..., s_n]^T. \tag{1}$$

Continuous gesture recognition algorithm considers each gesture as a pattern to be recognized, therefore, it is necessary to calculate the probability of the gesture in execution being each gesture of the set. To reduce the recognition time, we used a technique for parallelizing gesture recognition with multithreading proposed in [17] and successfully used in [11], to compare n gestures simultaneously, being n the capacity of threads that the smartwatch can run in parallel.

3.2 Naïve Bayes Classifier

Naïve Bayes is a classifier that works with the concept of conditional probability. Considers conditionally independent attributes. Despite this, it is widely used, has good results and requires a small amount of data for training [5,22]. Its operation is based on classes and for classification it uses conditional probability and Bayes' Theorem [5,20].

Whereas the classifier *Naïve Bayes* works with classes, based on the characteristics of each element, the classifier calculates the probability of this element belonging to a certain class of its training set [5]. The calculation of probabilities is performed using Bayes' theorem, represented in the Eq. 2:

$$P(C_k|x) = \frac{P(C_k)p(x|C_k)}{P(x)} \tag{2}$$

We used a *Naïve Bayes* classifier proposed in our previous work to identify the possible characters to be inserted based on the gestures performed by [14] users. Each character was defined as a class, so when defining which class one or more gestures belong to, the classifier will be defining the character.

For each inserted gesture, we calculate the probability of all classes, that is, all characters and, if the user inserts a new gesture, a new calculation is performed. These steps can be viewed in Fig. 4.

3.3 Word Dictionary

In this work we used a dictionary with words from the English language and the relative probability of using the words. However, by changing the dictionary, the method can be used in other languages.

Figure 5, displays an example of the trie structure used to store words used in this work. In this example, all nodes of interest have their edges highlighted. Nodes of interest correspond to the last character of a word. In this way, a word is composed by the character of the node of interest and the characters of all its ancestors.

We can see that all leaf nodes and some internal nodes have highlighted edges. In Fig. 5 the following words are stored: **computer, computers, computing, entry, end, enter, entered, mobile, movie, movies, text, ten** and **test**.

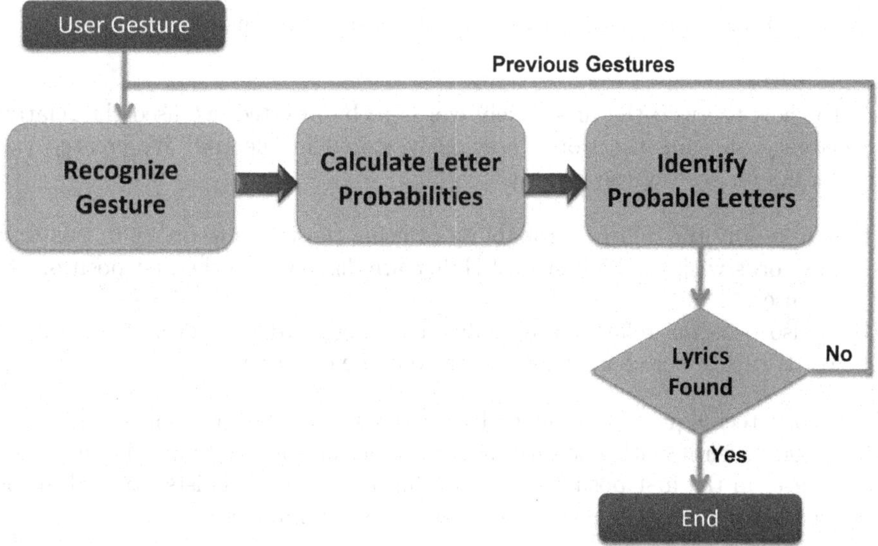

Fig. 4. Steps for character recognition with performed gestures (Adapted from [14]).

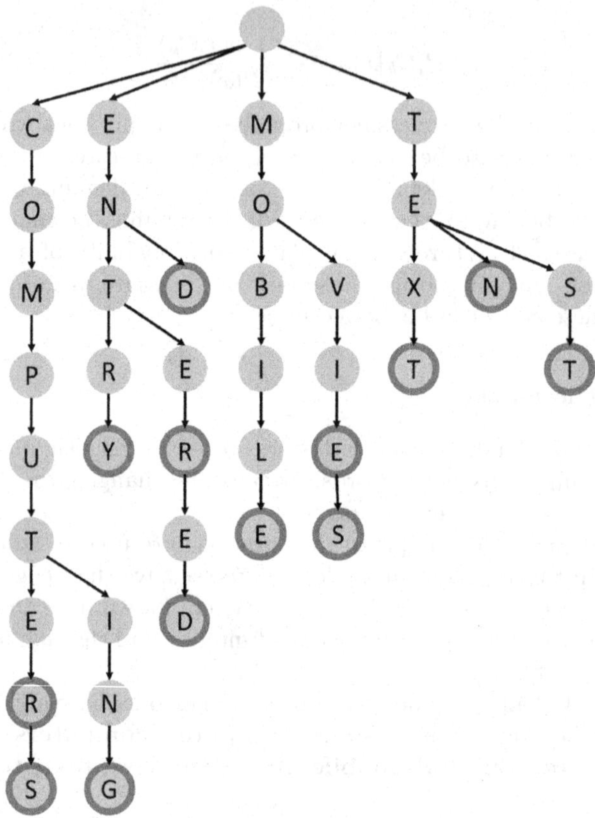

Fig. 5. Illustration of the trie's structure used to store and retrieve words.

To show the user the most likely words to be inserted, we used the relative probability of using the words previously stored in the trie. We created two techniques for sorting the word list:

I. It uses only the relative probability of using the words to order, in this way, the words with the highest probability are displayed in the first positions to the user;
II. It also uses the relative probability of using words, however, it prioritizes words with fewer characters to carry out the ordering.

Second technique was developed with the aim of allowing words with fewer characters, even if, with a lower relative probability of use, to also be displayed to the user in the first positions. The evaluation with specialists exposed in the Sect. 4 section shows the results of these sorting techniques.

4 Expert Evaluation

In order to validate the proposed method, the application was installed on the smartwatch *"Fossil Gen 4"*, with the following specifications: 1.4 in. round screen, 454 × 454 pixels, 4GB RAM memory, Qualcomm's Snapdragon 2100 processor with 1.2 GHz ARM Cortex A7 4-core. The method was tested and evaluated in an exploratory study by volunteer experts, during the experiment, the experts entered text on the device using the gestures shown in Fig. 1. The experts were instructed to insert phrases used in their daily lives.

4.1 System Usability Evaluation

At the end of the experiment, we applied an adaptation of the System Usability Scale (SUS) questionnaire to the experts to verify the usability of the method. In the usability test, we verified the efficiency and effectiveness of the method, as well as the satisfaction of the specialists when using the method. The experts' perception of the developed method was explored in the experience test.

SUS [2] was used because it allows evaluating a wide variety of products and services and is independent of technology. It has 10 questions that are answered using the Likert scale with scores between 1 and 5, with 1 meaning "completely disagree" and 5 corresponding to "completely agree". Table 1, shows the questions of the questionnaire.

Table 1. Usability questionnaire. Adapted from [2]

Q1	I would use this system to perform text entry on smartwatches in my daily life	↑
Q2	I find the system unnecessarily complex.	↓
Q3	I found the system intuitive and easy to use.	↑
Q4	I think I would need the help of a person with technical knowledge to use the system	↓
Q5	I think the various functions of the system are very well integrated..	↑
Q6	I think the system has a lot of inconsistency.	↓
Q7	I imagine people will learn to use this system quickly..	↑
Q8	I found the system very complicated to use.	↓
Q9	I felt confident using the system.	↑
Q10	I needed to learn several things before using the system.	↓

(↑ - Positive Question, ↓ - Negative Question).

SUS questionnaire statements are alternated between positive and negative statements, this is done to avoid biased responses and for the evaluator to read and analyze each question and decide whether to agree or disagree with the question. Thus, to calculate the score of odd answers, one must subtract 1 from 5 from the score assigned by the user $(x - 1)$, where x is the score assigned by the user. For even answers, the score assigned by the user must be subtracted from 5, that is, $(5 - x)$, where x is the score assigned by the user. Therefore, all answers will be scored from 0 to 4, with 4 being the best score. After that, the score of all answers is multiplied by 2.5, making the score of each question stay in the range of 0 to 10 and the sum of the scores in the range of 0 to 100. The author points out that this score is not a percentage , but a general measure of perceived usability. To be considered good usability the score needs to be at least 68 [2,3].

Considering the score obtained in the SUS questionnaire, Bangor et al. [1], defined a scale of descriptive adjectives according to the punctuation of the answers. The Table 2, displays the adjectives of the SUS according to the score of the answers. In the next section we detail the evaluation results.

Table 2. Descriptive Statistics of SUS Scores for Adjective Ratings. Adapted from [1].

Adjective	Mean SUS Score
Worst Imaginable	12.5
Awful	20.3
Poor	35.7
OK	50.9
Good	71.4
Excellent	85.5
Best Imaginable	90.9

5 Results and Discussion

Developed prototype was used in an evaluation with specialists and we applied a usability and experience test. At the end of the test, the experts answered a questionnaire based on the questionnaire adapted from the SUS, shown in Table 1. Average score for each question in the questionnaire is shown in Fig. 6.

In the previous section, we presented a system rating adjective scale that uses the sum of question scores to rate a system proposed by Bangor et al. [1]. The sum of the average score of the questions was 90, which places the developed prototype in the "Excellent' category. However, when analyzing the individual scores of the questions, it is possible to identify favorable points for the developed prototype and also points to improve.

Question 1 obtained a score of 8.5, so, according to the evaluation, there are strong indications that users would use the method developed for text entry on smartwatches in their daily lives. The scores for questions number 2 and number 3 show that the evaluators found the prototype easy to use and without complexity, this can also be seen in the score for question number 4, as the evaluators considered that people with little technical knowledge can use the prototype without the help of an experienced person to help.

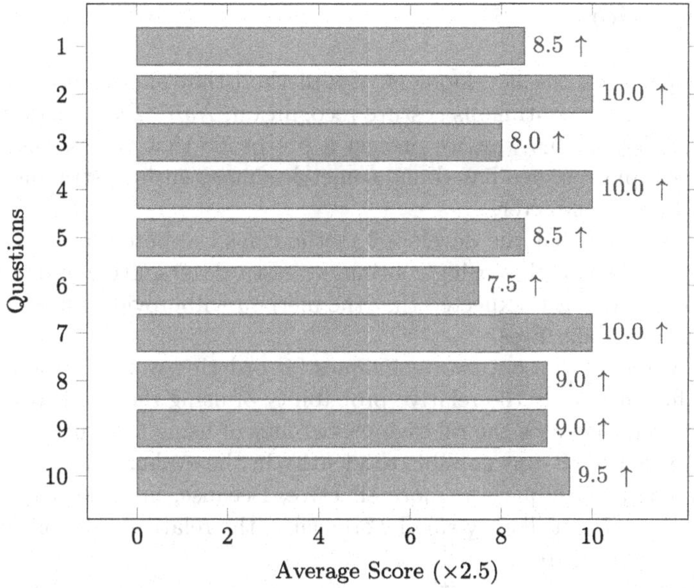

Fig. 6. Normalized Average score for each statement in the questionnaire.

When analyzing the scores of questions number 5 and 6, we can observe that it is possible to improve the consistency of the prototype, but that the functions of the prototype are integrated. With the score of question 7, it is possible to verify that the evaluators considered that people will learn to use the prototype quickly, as well as, they thought that users will learn to use it quickly, as can be seen in the score of question 8. The scores for questions 9 and 10 show that the evaluators felt confident when using the prototype and that they did not need to learn anything new to use it.

We also observed that the words could be inserted correctly easily and quickly, as the method allowed inserting phrases with few interactions. It was also observed that using the continuous gesture recognition algorithm, it was possible to recognize a gesture without the user having to finalize it, thus allowing a quick interaction between the user and the prototype.

Use of the trie as a dictionary of words allowed filtering the available words, in this way, the prototype only shows the user the characters that can be inserted considering the prefix of the word already inserted.

During the experiments, we identified that the sorting technique that uses only the relative probability of using words made it difficult to insert words with smaller numbers of characters. Finally, experts found it easy to perform text entry using the prototype.

6 Conclusions

This work proposes the development of a method that allows entering texts in smartwatches using continuous gesture recognition, *Naïve Bayes* classifier and a word dictionary. In this way, we present a prototype that allows users to enter text using simple gestures based on geometric shapes such as straight lines and curves to draw a character.

Results showed that the developed method has the potential to be used for text entry in smartwatches using continuous gesture recognition and a word dictionary. In this way, it is expected that the method will provide a new experience to users in their daily lives.

In this work, we present two techniques for ordering words in the prediction step. The first uses only the relative probability of using the words to order and the second that also uses the relative probability of using the words, but prioritizes smaller words. It was possible to identify in the evaluation with specialists that the second technique was more effective. Because, in some situations, the first technique did not display small words since the relative probability of using larger words was greater.

Results of the evaluation with specialists showed that the developed method has potential and to be used in the entry of texts in smartwatches. Therefore, we hope this method will provide a good experience for users when entering text on smartwatches.

Next stage of this research will be the development of new word prediction techniques. Soon after, the prototype will be tested on other smartwatches and usability and user experience tests will be carried out.

References

1. Bangor, A., Kortum, P., Miller, J.: Determining what individual SUS scores mean: adding an adjective rating scale. J. Usabil. Stud. **4**(3), 114–123 (2009). ISSN 1931–3357
2. John Brooke. Sus: A 'quick and dirty' usability scale. In: Usability Evaluation in Industry, pp. 189–194. Taylor and Francis, London, First Edn. (1996)
3. Brooke, J.: SUS: a retrospective. J. Usabil. Stud. **8**(2), 29–40 (2013)
4. Cha, J.-M., Choi, E., Lim, J.: Virtual sliding qwerty: a new text entry method for smartwatches using tap-n-drag. Appl. Ergon. **51**, 263–272 (2015). ISSN 0003-6870. https://doi.org/10.1016/j.apergo.2015.05.008. https://www.sciencedirect.com/science/article/pii/S0003687015000915
5. Chen, L., Wang, S.: Automated feature weighting in Naive Bayes for high-dimensional data classification. In Proceedings of the 21st ACM International Conference on Information and Knowledge Management, CIKM 2012, pp. 1243–1252. ACM , New York, NY, USA (2012). https://doi.org/10.1145/2396761.2398426. ISBN 978-1-4503-1156-4
6. Darbar, R., Dash, P., Samanta, D.: Etao keyboard: text input technique on smartwatches. Proc. Comput. Sci. **84**, 137–141 (2016). https://doi.org/10.1016/j.procs.2016.04.078, http://www.sciencedirect.com/science/article/pii/S187705091630093X

7. Gong, J., et al.: Wristext: one-handed text entry on smartwatch using wrist gestures. In Proceedings of the 2018 CHI Conference on Human Factors in Computing Systems, CHI 2018, pp. 1–14, New York, NY, USA (2018). Association for Computing Machinery. ISBN 9781450356206. https://doi.org/10.1145/3173574.3173755
8. Gordon, M., Ouyang, T., Zhai, S., Watchwriter: tap and gesture typing on a smartwatch miniature keyboard with statistical decoding. In: Proceedings of the 2016 CHI Conference on Human Factors in Computing Systems, CHI 2016, pp. 3817–3821, New York, NY, USA (2016). Association for Computing Machinery. ISBN 9781450333627. https://doi.org/10.1145/2858036.2858242
9. Hong, J., Heo, S., Isokoski, P., Lee, G.: Splitboard: a simple split soft keyboard for wristwatch-sized touch screens. In: Proceedings of the 33rd Annual ACM Conference on Human Factors in Computing Systems, CHI 2015, pp. 1233–1236. Association for Computing Machinery, New York, NY, USA (2015). ISBN 9781450331456. https://doi.org/10.1145/2702123.2702273
10. Horbylon Nascimento, T., et al.: Using smartwatches as an interactive movie controller: a case study with the Bandersnatch movie. In:L 2019 IEEE 43rd Annual Computer Software and Applications Conference (COMPSAC), vol. 2, pp. 263–268 (2019). https://doi.org/10.1109/COMPSAC.2019.10217
11. Horbylon Nascimento, T., Soares, F.: Home appliance control using smartwatches with continuous gesture recognition. In: Streitz, N., Konomi, S. (eds.) HCII 2021. LNCS, vol. 12782, pp. 122–134. Springer, Cham (2021). https://doi.org/10.1007/978-3-030-77015-0_9
12. Kristensson, P.O., Denby, L.C.: Continuous recognition and visualization of pen strokes and touch-screen gestures. In: EUROGRAPHICS Symposium on Sketch-Based Interfaces and Modeling (2011)
13. Lutze, R., Waldhör, K.: Personal health assistance for elderly people via smartwatch based motion analysis. In: 2017 IEEE International Conference on Healthcare Informatics (ICHI), pp. 124–133 (2017). https://doi.org/10.1109/ICHI.2017.79
14. Nascimento, T.H., Soares, F.A.A.M.N., Irani, P.P., Oliveira, L.L.G., Soares, A.S.: Method for text entry in smartwatches using continuous gesture recognition. In: 2017 IEEE 41st Annual Computer Software and Applications Conference (COMPSAC), vol. 2, pp. 549–554 (2017). https://doi.org/10.1109/COMPSAC.2017.168
15. Nascimento, T.H., et al.: Method for text input with google cardboard: an approach using smartwatches and continuous gesture recognition. In: 2017 19th Symposium on Virtual and Augmented Reality (SVR), pp. 223–226 (2017). https://doi.org/10.1109/SVR.2017.36
16. Nascimento, T.H., Soares, F.A.A.M.N., Nascimento, H.A.D., Vieira, M.A., Carvalho, T.P., Miranda, W.F.: Netflix control method using smartwatches and continuous gesture recognition. In: 2019 IEEE Canadian Conference of Electrical and Computer Engineering (CCECE), pp. 1–4 (2019)
17. Nascimento, T.H., et al.: Interaction with platform games using smartwatches and continuous gesture recognition: a case study. In: 2018 IEEE 42nd Annual Computer Software and Applications Conference (COMPSAC) (2018)
18. Nebeling, M., et al.: Wearwrite: crowd-assisted writing from smartwatches. In: Proceedings of the 2016 CHI Conference on Human Factors in Computing Systems, CHI 2016, pp. 3834–3846. ACM, New York, NY, USA. (2016). https://doi.org/10.1145/2858036.2858169. http://doi.acm.org/10.1145/2858036.2858169. ISBN 978-1-4503-3362-7

19. Oney, S., Harrison, C., Ogan, A., Wiese, J.: Zoomboard: a diminutive qwerty soft keyboard using iterative zooming for ultra-small devices. In: Proceedings of the SIGCHI Conference on Human Factors in Computing Systems, CHI 2013, pp. 2799–2802. ACM, New York, NY, USA (2013). https://doi.org/10.1145/2470654.2481387. ISBN 978-1-4503-1899-0
20. Taheri, S., Mammadov, M., Bagirov, A.M.: Improving Naive Bayes classifier using conditional probabilities. In: Proceedings of the Ninth Australasian Data Mining Conference, vol. 121, AusDM 2011, pp. 63–68. Australian Computer Society, Inc., Darlinghurst, Australia, Australia (2011). ISBN 978-1-921770-02-9
21. Wong, P.C., Zhu, K., Fu, H.: Fingert9: leveraging thumb-to-finger interaction for same-side-hand text entry on smartwatches. In: Proceedings of the 2018 CHI Conference on Human Factors in Computing Systems, CHI 2018, pp. 1–10. Association for Computing Machinery, New York, NY, USA (2018). ISBN 9781450356206. https://doi.org/10.1145/3173574.3173752
22. Zaidi, N.A., Cerquides, J., Carman, M.J., Webb, G.I.: Alleviating Naive Bayes attribute independence assumption by attribute weighting. J. Mach. Learn. Res. **14**(1), 1947–1988 (2013). ISSN 1532-4435

Analysis and Considerations of the Controllability of EMG-Based Force Input

Hayato Nozaki[1](✉), Yuta Kataoka[1], Christian Arzate Cruz[2], Fumihisa Shibata[3], and Asako Kimura[3]

[1] Graduate School of Information Science and Engineering, Ritsumeikan University, Kusatsu, Shiga, Japan
{nozaki,y-katao}@rm2c.ise.ritsumei.ac.jp

[2] Global Innovation Research Organization, Ritsumeikan University, Ibaraki, Osaka, Japan
arzate@rm2c.ise.ritsumei.ac.jp

[3] College of Information Science and Engineering, Ritsumeikan University, Kusatsu, Shiga, Japan
{fshibata,asa}@rm2c.ise.ritsumei.ac.jp

Abstract. Using electromyography (EMG) measurements for user interfaces (UIs) is widely employed as an interaction method. Some advantages of using EMG-based input are that it does not require a physical controller and can be operated intuitively with small body movements. Existing work has explored different novel interaction methods for UIs using EMG. However, it is still unclear how precisely users can control the force and what kind of control pattern is easier for them to use. Thus, this paper analyzes the effect of EMG-based force input on control accuracy and mental workload. We constructed a pointer-tracking application that inputs force strength from forearm EMG. Tracking accuracy and mental workload were evaluated under the conditions of multiple tracking patterns and hand gestures. The results showed that EMG-based input accuracy was affected by the way in which the force was applied (e.g., strengthened, weakened, or fluctuated). We also found that hand gesture type did not influence accuracy or mental workload.

Keywords: Muscle–computer Interface · Electromyography · Force Input · Performance Evaluation

1 Introduction

Electromyography (EMG) is a technique for measuring the change in muscle potential over time that is produced by skeletal muscles. There have been efforts to improve EMG measurement devices [1, 2]. In addition, multiple applications in various fields use EMG as input (e.g., entertainment, healthcare, and education [3]). In part, the use of EMG devices is popular because they can estimate the posture or specific body movements of users [4, 5]. For example, EMG-based input allows intuitive manipulation by small body movements without a physical controller [6–8].

M. Kurosu and A. Hashizume (Eds.): HCII 2023, LNCS 14011, pp. 563–572, 2023.
https://doi.org/10.1007/978-3-031-35596-7_36

Previous studies have analyzed the controllability of the force estimated from an EMG signal [9, 10]. The studies discussed the validity of input in the UI with EMG compared to physical input methods. However, it is not clear which hand gestures or methods of applying force (e.g., keep strong/weak force) enable a user to control the input force more accurately and with less strain.

Therefore, we investigated how a user can track different applied force patterns (e.g., ascending or descending lines) at different muscle activation levels under the next six hand gestures: fist, grip, pinch, and push on a surface with the index finger, thumb, and palm. The evaluation included qualitative and quantitative measures. To understand the accuracy, we computed how well users perform given force patterns. We also administered a six-question questionnaire to assess the mental workload. This experiment provides the first approximation of the relationship between performance force, accuracy, and mental workload.

Human–computer interaction (HCI) researchers can use these results to design new hand gestures at various performing strengths or with a dynamic force input (which changes over time). This can lead to a wider range of interaction methods for EMG-based applications.

The contributions of this paper are as follows:

- We are the first to analyze the effects of EMG-based force strength input on control accuracy and mental workload.
- We clarify the features that can accurately control EMG-based force strength.
- We clarify that certain hand gestures do not influence input accuracy or mental workload.

2 Related Work

In this section, we provide use cases of the muscle–computer interface and some foundational research for our paper. We then describe the literature that explores EMG-based input accuracy. We also point out that our experimental condition is novel compared to previous studies.

2.1 EMG-Based Devices for User Interfaces

EMG signals enable intuitive UI operation in real-time. Thus, controlling user interfaces through EMG is widely practiced in HCI research. Becker *et al.* demonstrated the gradual adjustment of lamp brightness using EMG-based force strength [6]. Benko *et al.* realized a variety of sketching brush strokes using forearm EMG [11]. These studies utilized EMG amplitude information as the inputted strength.

Furthermore, EMG-based input enables human assistive activity. For example, Rosen *et al.* developed a powered exoskeleton system controlled by forearm EMG, which is naturally controlled by humans [12]. Rakasena *et al.* also proposed an electric wheelchair controlled by forearm EMG [13]. A variety of applications have used forearm EMG as an input method. In contrast, in this study, we analyzed the impact of different EMG-based input approaches on controllability and mental workloads.

2.2 Detecting Gestures with EMG-Based Signals

The state of the human body can be estimated by extracting and learning the features of an EMG signal. The advantage of utilizing EMG is that it requires only simple measurements without large body movements. Much research has estimated human states, for example, gestures and behaviors, from EMG signals using machine learning [9, 14]. In addition, the human body is composed of many muscles; therefore, the muscles of the face, legs, arms, and other body parts have been utilized for estimations [15, 16]. Many studies have estimated body movements from EMG signal features. In this study, we analyzed continuous tracking accuracy measured from EMG potentials.

2.3 Continuous Tracking with EMG-Based Input

The ideal interaction with a UI is that the user intuitively and comfortably controls the target object, as expected. Several studies have investigated the influence of the EMG-based force input of the forearm on tracking accuracy. Yamagami *et al.* performed a cursor-pointing task to analyze the controllability of the target trajectory [17]. The literature reports that EMG-based control showed higher accuracy than a physical controller. Lobo-Prat *et al.* performed a one-dimensional tracking task using EMG-, force-, and joystick-based interfaces [18]. Corbett *et al.* also conducted a similar tracking task to compare EMG and force-based interfaces [19]. Their results revealed that EMG-based operations have comparable or better controllability than other input methods. However, these studies examined accuracy under the conditions of a single gesture or a simple tracking pattern. To the best of our knowledge, this study is the first to consider multiple gestures and the way force is applied to evaluate tracking accuracy as well as mental workload.

3 Experiment

The main objective of this user study was to find the effects of EMG-based force input on control accuracy and mental workload. For that goal, we designed a two-factor repeated measures ANOVA on input accuracy and mental workload. We introduced the independent variables *gesture* and *control patterns*. As dependent variables, we evaluated input accuracy and mental workload scores using NASA-RTLX [20].

3.1 Apparatus

We built an application using Unity (Ver. 2020.3.15) to visualize the exerted EMG (Fig. 1, Fig. 2a). The application runs at 120 frames per second with a display resolution of 1920 $\times$ 1080 pixels. We used the same EMG measurement device as in [21] (Fig. 2c). The amplitude range of the device was –1.25 to + 1.25 mv. The surface EMG signals were amplified 1000 times, and then, A/D conversion was applied to the signals. The measured signal was transmitted to the computer via serial communication at a sampling frequency of 1000 Hz. Two electrodes were attached 20 mm apart on the dominant forearm [22]. The reference potential was set by letting the participants grasp the wrench.

The general frequency range of EMG signals was from 5 to 500 Hz; therefore, we used the same frequency range in the experiment [23]. The signal filters used a high-pass filter to cut low-frequency noise below 5 Hz and a low-pass filter to cut high-frequency noise above 500 Hz. A band-pass filter was also applied to eliminate humming, with a cutoff frequency of 55–65 Hz (Table 1).

An EMG signal contains positive and negative amplitudes; thus, the measured EMG signal was rectified and smoothed. We used the percentage of the root mean square (%RMS), which is a widely used indicator for smoothing EMG [3, 24]. The %RMS represents the myoelectric potential ratio of the measured RMS to the maximum voluntary contraction (MVC). The window size was 300 ms, with an overlap of 299 ms. Each RMS value corresponds to the white pointer in the Unity application.

3.2 Hand Gestures

A variety of hand gestures are used to interact with a user interface [25]. It is important to compare the controllability and mental workload between multiple gestures to design interactions. Thus, we selected six types of static hand gestures that do not move the forearm: fist, grip, pinch, finger push (index finger), finger push (thumb), and palm (Fig. 2b). The advantage of these gestures is that they do not change the hand position compared to dynamic gestures (e.g., swipe, slide, and tap). In this study, we focused on static gestures that can be employed for a variety of UI operations.

The electrodes were affixed to the muscle position corresponding to the hand gesture. Specifically, we attached electrodes to the extensor digitorum muscle for the fist and grip conditions. The flexor carpi radialis muscle corresponded to the finger push conditions (index and thumb). The brachioradialis muscle corresponded to the palm condition. The flexor pollicis longus muscle corresponded to the pinch condition.

3.3 Task

The participant controlled a pointer to keep it within the area of a blue target figure moving from the right side of the screen. The pointer moved up and down, ranging from 0% to 100%, depending on the %RMS. Tracking accuracy was calculated for each of the six hand gestures. The target figure (control pattern), which refers to the method of applying force, was randomly shown from seven patterns (Fig. 3). The types of target figures are divided into the following categories:

- Straight line (L1: low, L2: middle, L3: high)
- Diagonal line (L4: uphill, L5: downhill)
- Curved line (L6: inverted U-curve, L7: U-curve).

The pointer was counted as correctly controlled if it was positioned inside the target diagram. Each diagram had a range of $\pm 5\%$ from the center (Fig. 3). The duration of each diagram was 5 s. The seven types of target figures flowed in random order, with intervals of 5 s. One trial took 70 s ((5-s tracking time + 5-s intervals) $\times$ 7 target figures).

The trial was repeated six times, which is the number of hand gestures. The accuracy of each target diagram was calculated by dividing the duration of the correct position by 5 s.

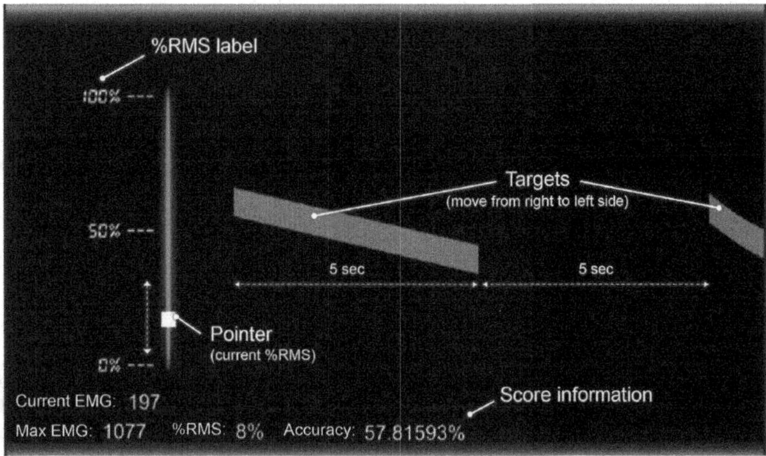

Fig. 1. The application for visualizing the input force used in the experiment. The participant adjusted the force strength so that the pointer stayed inside the blue target figure. The participants' maximum force strength was mapped to 100%.

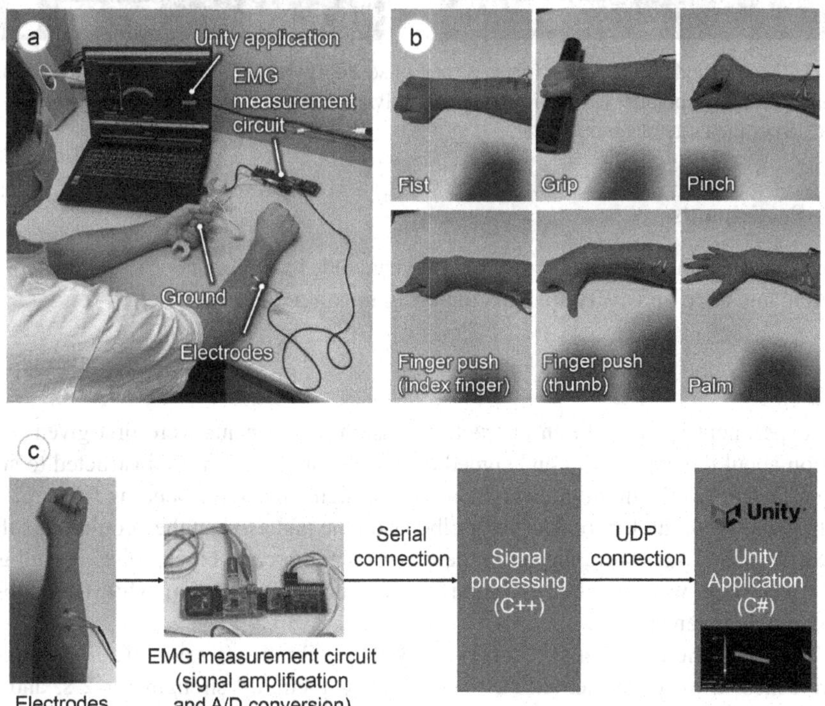

Fig. 2. Experiment setup. a) The participant controlled the strength of the force measured with EMG while viewing the measurement application. b) We set up six types of hand gestures: fist, grip, pinch, finger push (index finger), finger push (thumb), and palm. c) The measured EMG was sent to the application through the measurement device [21] and filter processing.

Table 1. EMG processing parameters.

Sampling frequency	1000 Hz
Window size	300 ms
Overlap window size	299 ms
Indicator	RMS
Filters	High pass: 5 Hz Low pass: 500 Hz Band-pass: 55–65 Hz

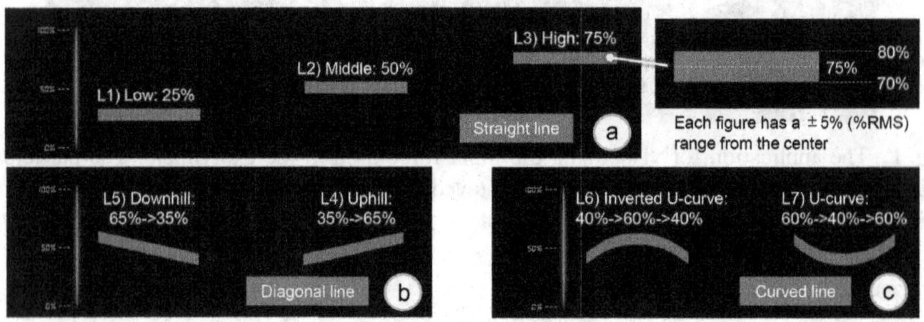

Fig. 3. The methods for applying force. A total of seven figures (L1–7) were presented per hand gesture task. The pointer was counted as correctly positioned if it was located within ± 5% (%RMS) of the target diagram center.

3.4 Participants

Twelve participants (four women, $\overline{X} = 21.2$ years old; 11 right-handed) volunteered. All participants were university students majoring in computer science.

3.5 Procedure

The experiment began with an instruction session. Participants were first given information about the experiment and signed a consent form. They were instructed to sit in a chair in front of the monitor, keep their back straight, and avoid bending forward. The participants were guided to place their elbows on the table so that they could relax their forearms. Floor mats were placed in the experimental area to block noise. For all gestures, electrodes were attached to the participants' dominant forearm, while the opposite arm held the wrench.

The instruction session was followed by the calibration session. The participants were asked to measure their MVC. They exerted their full strength for 2 s, and the average RMS was calculated as the MVC. This measurement was repeated for the six gestures. The measured MVC corresponded to 100% of the range that the pointer could move.

Once the participants concluded their task, we asked them to answer the NASA-RTLX questionnaire [26]. It contained six questions that assessed mental workload on a

20-point scale. The procedure was repeated until all hand gestures were evaluated, with sufficient breaks to avoid muscle fatigue. The order of the conditions was randomized. Finally, we conducted exploratory interviews to better understand the user experience. We collected 504 ratings (12 participants × 7 target figures × 6 gestures) on input accuracy and 72 ratings (12 participants × 6 gestures) on the NASA-RTLX score. The entire procedure took about 50 min.

4 Results and Discussion

The average tracking accuracy in each condition is shown in Fig. 4. The error bars indicate standard errors. The accuracy data were analyzed using a two-way ANOVA with *gesture* and *control pattern* factors. The statistical analysis revealed that the main effect of the *gesture* factor was not significant ($F_{(5,55)} = 1.588$, $p = .178$), and the interaction was not significant ($F_{(30,330)} = 1.079, p = .360$). In contrast, the main effect of the *control pattern* factor was significant ($F_{(6,66)} = 64.558, p < .001$). Furthermore, we employed a post hoc test using Holm multiple comparisons ($\alpha = 0.05$, two-sided test) for the *control pattern* factor and confirmed significant differences (Table 2).

The statistical analysis showed that the smaller the force strength, the higher the accuracy (L1, L2, and L3). The L6 conditions, which required force strength fluctuation, was as accurate as the L2 condition needed to maintain an intermediate force intensity. The L7 condition showed statistically higher accuracy than the L6 condition. Moreover, the task of relaxing the force (L5) showed higher accuracy than strengthening the force (L4). The results showed that the EMG-based force strength and the way in which the force was applied had an impact on tracking accuracy. The participants commented that maintaining a strong force (L3) made it difficult to track the diagram. This comment was reflected in the experimental results. However, the type of static hand gesture showed no statistical differences in tracking accuracy. This suggests that the muscle intensity and the way the force was applied had more influence on tracking accuracy than the posture of the hand.

The average NASA-RTLX scores for the conditions are shown in Fig. 5. A higher score represents a higher mental workload. The error bars indicate standard errors. The mental workload (NASA-RTLX) data were analyzed using a one-way ANOVA. As a result of the analysis, the main effect was not significant ($F_{(5,55)} = 1.912, p = .107$). The statistical analysis showed that mental workload did not differ regardless of the types of hand gestures. Therefore, Fig. 4 and Fig. 5 reveal that input accuracy depends on the method by which force is applied; however, the types of hand gestures did not influence the input accuracy or mental workload scores. Participants stated the following: "I feel fatigued in the first condition compared to the other gesture because nothing is held," and "In the grip condition, the gripped object is large and hard, so it makes me tired controlling it." We could not conclude that the difference in the gestures could not be attributed to the mental workload. However, the comments suggested that the gripping condition of the object may have an impact on the mental workload.

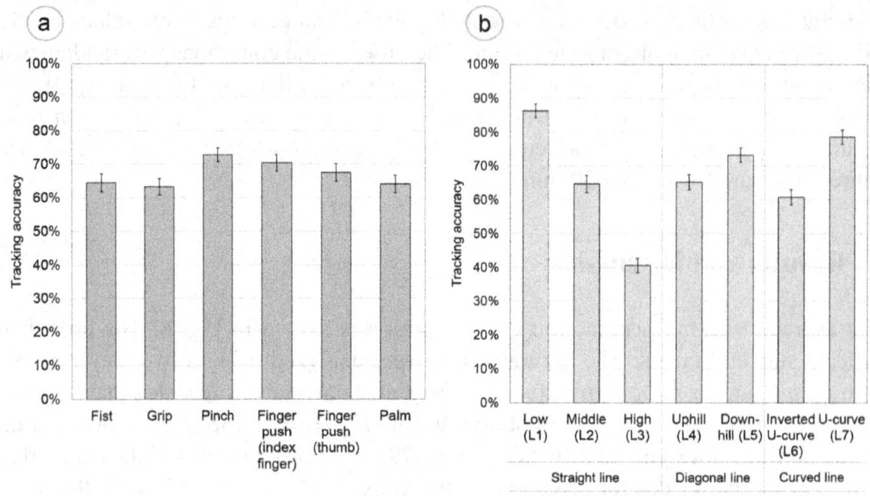

Fig. 4. Results of the experiment on input accuracy. We evaluated the input accuracy for each factor: a) gesture, b) target figure.

Table 2. Significance of the target figure. The highlighted values show significant differences.

	L1	L2	L3	L4	L5	L6
L2	<.001	N/A	N/A	N/A	N/A	N/A
L3	<.001	<.001	N/A	N/A	N/A	N/A
L4	<.001	.806	<.001	N/A	N/A	N/A
L5	<.001	.005	<.001	.009	N/A	N/A
L6	<.001	.217	<.001	.162	<.001	N/A
L7	.002	<.001	<.001	<.001	.120	<.001

5 Conclusion

In this study, we explored the input accuracy and mental workload of EMG-based force strength by measuring multiple hand gestures. We built an application to measure tracking accuracy from force inputs. We defined seven control patterns and evaluated the accuracy and mental workload for six types of hand gestures. Through the experiment, we demonstrated that (1) EMG-based input accuracy was affected by the way force was applied. Specifically, (2) the smaller the force strength, the higher the tracking accuracy, and (3) the task of relaxing the force showed higher accuracy than strengthening the force. We also found that (4) the types of hand gestures did not influence tracking accuracy and (5) the mental workload scores.

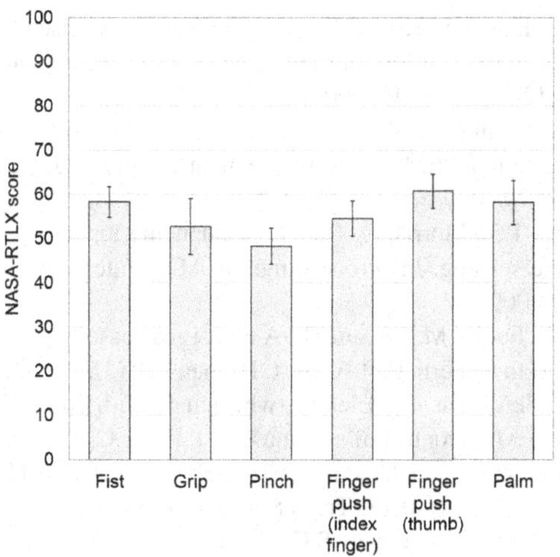

Fig. 5. Results of the experiment for the mental workload for each hand gesture.

The experimental results may provide fundamental knowledge for designing user interfaces that use EMG as a force input. In future work, we plan to conduct a time-series analysis of the EMG data in this experiment. We are also interested in analyzing the controllability of force input with other body parts.

References

1. Beniczky, S., Conradsen, I., Henning, O., Fabricius, M., Wolf, P.: Automated real-time detection of tonic-clonic seizures using a wearable EMG device. J. Neurol. **90**, 428–434 (2018)
2. Benalcázar, M.E., Jaramillo, A.G., Jonathan, A.Z., Páez, A., Andaluz, V.H.: Hand gesture recognition using machine learning and the Myo armband. In: Proceedings of European Signal Processing Conference (EUSIPCO), pp. 1040–1044 (2017)
3. Saponas, T.S., Tan, D.S., Morris, D., Balakrishnan, R., Turner, J., Landay, J.A.: Enabling always-available input with muscle-computer interfaces. In: Proceedings of ACM Symposium on User Interface Software and Technology (UIST), pp. 167–176 (2009)
4. Xia, P., Hu, J., Peng, Y.: EMG-based estimation of limb movement using deep learning with recurrent convolutional neural networks: EMG-based estimation of limb movement. Artif. Organs **42**(5), E67–E77 (2018). https://doi.org/10.1111/aor.13004
5. Zhang, Q., Hosoda, R., Venture, G.: Human joint motion estimation for electromyography (EMG)-based dynamic motion control. In: Proceedings of IEEE Engineering in Medicine and Biology Society (EMBC), pp. 21–24 (2013)
6. Becker, V., Oldrati, P., Barrios, L., Sörös, G.: Touchsense: classifying finger touches and measuring their force with an electromyography armband. In: Proceedings of ACM International Symposium on Wearable Computers (ISWC), pp. 1–8 (2018)
7. Hartmann, B., et al.: Computer keyboard and mouse as a reservoir of pathogens in an intensive care unit. J. Clin. Monitor. Comput. **18**, 7–12 (2004)
8. Greenberg, S., Fitchett, C.: Phidgets: easy development of physical interfaces through physical widgets. In: Proceedings of ACM symposium on User Interface Software and Technology (UIST), pp. 167–176 (2001)

9. Chu, J.U., Moon, I., Lee, Y.J., Kim, S.K., Mun, M.S.: A supervised feature-projection-based real-time EMG pattern recognition for multifunction myoelectric hand control. IEEE/ASME Trans. Mechatron. **12**(3), 282–290 (2007)
10. Ngeo, J.G., Tamei, T., Shibata, T.: Continuous and simultaneous estimation of finger kinematics using inputs from an EMG-to-muscle activation model. J. Neuroeng. Rehabil. **11**(1), 1–14 (2014)
11. Benko, H., Saponas, T.S., Morris, D., Tan, D.: Enhancing input on and above the interactive surface with muscle sensing. In: Proceedings of ACM Interactive Tabletops and Surfaces (ITS), pp. 93–100 (2009)
12. Rosen, J., Brand, M., Fuchs, M., Arcan, M.: A myosignal-based powered exoskeleton system. IEEE Trans. Syst. Man Cybern. Part A: Syst. Humans. **31**(3), 210–222 (2001)
13. Rakasena, E.P.G., Herdiman, L.: Electric wheelchair with forward-reverse control using Electromyography (EMG) control of arm muscle. J. Phys. Conf. Ser. **1450**(1), 1–7 (2020)
14. Raurale, S.A., McAllister, J., del Rincon, J.M.: Real-time embedded EMG signal analysis for wrist-hand pose identification. IEEE Trans Signal Process. **68**, 2713–2723 (2020)
15. Fridlund, J., Schwartz, G.E., Fowler, S.C.: Pattern recognition of self-reported emotional state from multiple-site facial EMG activity during affective imagery. J. Psychophysiol. **21**, 622–637 (1984)
16. Winter, D.A., Yack, H.J.: EMG profiles during normal human walking: stride-to-stride and inter-subject variability. J. Electroencephalogr. Clin. Neurophysiol. 402–411 (1987)
17. Yamagami, M., Steele, K.M., Burden, S.A.: Decoding intent with control theory: comparing muscle versus manual interface performance. In: Proceedings of CHI Conference on Human Factors in Computing Systems (CHI), pp. 1–12 (2020)
18. Lobo-Prat, J., Keemink, A.Q., Stienen, A.H., Schouten, A.C., Veltink, P.H., Koopman, B.F.: Evaluation of EMG, force and joystick as control interfaces for active arm supports. J. Neuroeng. Rehabil. **11**, 1–13 (2014)
19. Corbett, E.A., Perreault, E.J., Kuiken, T.A.: Comparison of electromyography and force as interfaces for prosthetic control. J. Rehabil. Res. Dev. **48**, 629–641 (2011)
20. Hart, S.G., Staveland, L.E.: Development of NASA-TLX (Task Load Index): results of empirical and theoretical research. J. Adv. Psychol. **52**, 139–183 (1988)
21. Ishikawa, K., Akita, J., Toda, M., Kondo, K., Sakurazawa, S., Nakamura, Y.: Robust finger motion classification using frequency characteristics of surface electromyogram signals. In: Proceedings of International Conference on Biomedical Engineering (ICoBE), pp. 362–367 (2012)
22. Jensen, C., Vasseljen, O., Westgaard, R.H.: The influence of electrode position on bipolar surface electromyogram recordings of the upper trapezius muscle. J. Appl. Physiol. Occup. Physiol. **67**, 266–273 (1993)
23. Ozdemir, M.A., Kisa, D.H., Guren, O., Onan, A., Akan, A.: EMG based hand gesture recognition using deep learning. In: Proceedings of Medical Technologies Congress, pp. 1–4 (2020)
24. Saponas, T.S., Tan, D.S., Morris, D., Turner, J., Landay, J.A.: Making muscle-computer interfaces more practical. In: Proceedings of SIGCHI Conference on Human Factors in Computing Systems (CHI), pp. 851–854 (2010)
25. Rautaray, S.S., Agrawal, A.: A novel human computer interface based on hand gesture recognition using computer vision techniques. In: Proceedings of Intelligent Interactive Technologies and Multimedia (IITM), pp. 292–296 (2010)
26. Byers, J.C., Bittner, A., Hill, S.: Traditional and raw Task Load Index (TLX) correlations: are paired comparisons necessary? Advances in Industrial Ergonomics and Safety l, pp. 481–485. Taylor and Francis (1989)

Research on RGB-d-Based Pilot Hand Detection in Complex Cockpit Environment

Cheng Qian, Zhen Wang(✉), and Shan Fu

Department of Automation, Shanghai Jiao Tong University, Shanghai, People's Republic of China

b2wz@sjtu.edu.cn

Abstract. With the rapid development of the aviation industry, human error has replaced mechanical failure as the main cause of aviation accidents, which makes "human factors" increasingly popular. In human factors research, hand detection is very important for analyzing pilot behavior. However, in the complex environment of the cockpit, common hand detection methods have poor accuracy because of light and background. In this paper, we propose a new hand position detection and contour extraction method based on RGB-D information for cockpit scenes. In the pre-processing stage, this method uses depth images of the unobstructed cockpit scene for background modeling and the median filtering method is used to process depth images. After that, the result of subtracting the depth background from the depth image and image segmentation using the threshold are applied to extract the contour of the pilot's arm. Next, we use the region growing algorithm on the depth image to find the location of the top of the pilot's arm, which is the location of the hand, and use it as the seed point for using the region growing algorithm on the RGB image. Finally, the region growing algorithm combining RGB and YCbCr color spaces is used for the extraction of hand contour. The results show that the method proposed in this paper can effectively reduce the influence of lights and background in the cockpit and achieve the goal of hand localization and hand contour extraction in complex scenes.

Keywords: RGB-D information · hand detection · aviation human factors

1 Introduction

With the rapid development of the aviation industry, the number and frequency of civil aviation accidents has been decreasing year by year. However, the statistics show that the percentage of civil aviation flight accidents related to human error is over 70%. Human error has replaced mechanical failure as the main cause of aviation accidents, which makes "human factors" increasingly popular.

Available aviation accident statistics show that, the most direct manifestation of human error is the pilot's behavioral errors. Therefore, it is important to monitor and identify the pilot's operational behavior.

Of all the physical behaviors of the crew in the cockpit, hand actions are the most obvious, meaningful, and valuable to study, and are relatively easy to obtain behavioral

M. Kurosu and A. Hashizume (Eds.): HCII 2023, LNCS 14011, pp. 573–584, 2023.
https://doi.org/10.1007/978-3-031-35596-7_37

information. The study of pilot hand actions can provide theoretical support for optimizing cockpit design, verifying crew minimum airworthiness provisions, ergonomic analysis and evaluation, improving flight quality, and reducing pilot errors and mishandling. Therefore, hand detection is of high research value as an important method for behavioral analysis.

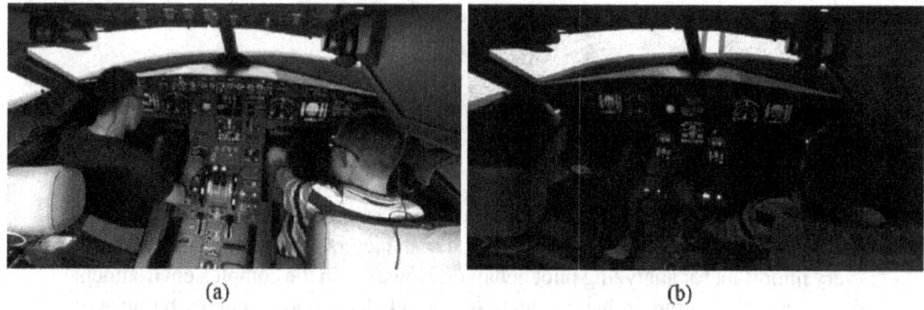

Fig. 1. Complex illumination and background in aircraft cockpit: (a) normal light (b) low light

However, in the complex environment of the cockpit, common hand detection methods have poor accuracy because of the complex illumination and background in aircraft cockpit (see Fig. 1).

Current research on hand detection has different problems, including computational speed, scene adaptation, and detection accuracy. The data glove-based method [1, 2] mainly uses the relevant equipment to locate and track the human hand directly. The disadvantage of this method is that the use of wearable devices may affect the pilot's operations, makes this solution unsuitable for pilot hand detection. For aircraft cockpit environments, image-based hand segmentation methods are more suitable for obtaining more research-worthy operational data. The main method for detecting a human hand from an existing image is generally to extract the ROI of the hand from the background using features that are clearly different between the hand and the background (e.g. skin color [3, 9], edges [4], shape, etc.) and then to accurately obtain the exact shape of the hand in the image by filtering, morphological processing and contour extraction. The main methods commonly used for hand image segmentation are skin color segmentation, motion information segmentation, clustering methods (K-means algorithm [5]), contour-based [6] segmentation and depth-based [7] segmentation methods. Region growth [8] aggregates pixels or sub-regions into larger regions based on growth rules (growth neighborhoods and judgment thresholds) to form region blocks, which are then segmented. The most commonly used skin color segmentation method segments possible skin color regions by a skin color threshold in the color space (RGB, HSV, YCbCr [10]) and then recognizes hand gestures [11, 12]. Although skin color is the most obvious recognition feature [13] of a human hand, skin color recognition is easily disturbed by the actual environment. Wang [14] discusses hand detection and contour extraction methods in complex environments and specific applications. Wen [15] introduces a depth-based method using hand motion analysis to evaluate the performance of the secondary task when driving, and a background subtraction-based 3D spatial hand localization method is used to localize the left and right hands. Zhao [16] proposes a vision-based hand detection method. K-curvature is used to detect the operational key points of the hand, and the center of the hand is determined by combining image area moments and a palm maximum circle fitting algorithm. Keskin and Wang [17, 18] has implemented real-time hand tracking and gesture recognition based on color or depth images using deep learning methods.

In a complex cockpit environment, the accuracy of traditional hand detection methods is poor due to the complex illumination and background in the aircraft cockpit. The current research on hand segmentation mainly focuses on technical solutions, such as skin tone threshold segmentation, pixel clustering The current research on hand segmentation mainly focuses on technical solutions, such as skin tone threshold segmentation, pixel clustering, foreground and background segmentation, and region growing, but each solution has different problems, including computational speed, scene adaptation, and detection accuracy, where the main problem is the interference of environmental factors. Therefore, traditional methods need to be improved to address these problems.

This paper proposes an accurate pilots' hand detection method with high efficiency and (light) adaptive capability. The proposed method implements hand segmentation and contour extraction based on RGB-D information. The effectiveness of the proposed method is verified by data collected in a simulated cockpit scene.

2 Method

This paper introduces a new hand detection method based on RGB-D information for cockpit scenes. The key points of the proposed method are as follows:

1. Dividing the hand detection task in the cockpit into two parts, including the delineation and optimization of the region of interest containing the hand and the detection of the hand coordinates;
2. In addition to the color information commonly used in other hand detection methods, depth information collected by the intel Realsense D455 camera in the cockpit is also used for hand position detection;
3. Using depth images to reduce the effect of light and background on hand detection in the cockpit;
4. Using color information to optimize the raw detection results in depth channel (Fig. 2).

In the pre-processing stage, the proposed method uses depth images of the unobstructed cockpit scene for background modeling and a median filter is used to remove noise and smooth the image.

After that, background subtraction was applied to extract the area of the pilot's arm.

Next, region-growing algorithm is used on the depth image to find the location of the top of the pilot's arm, which is the approximate location of the hand. After finding the location of the hand, a region of interest including the hand is segmented. This region excludes a large number of factors that are not relevant to pilot's hand, such as cockpit background, windows, and other parts of the body. Using depth information for raw hand detection and then using color information for fine hand contour detection is one of the main innovations of this paper.

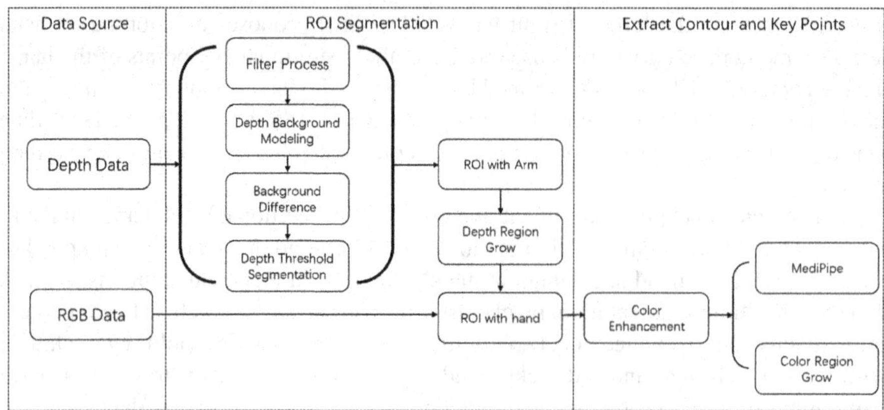

Fig. 2. Specific process of algorithm module

The region of interest is also segmented in the aligned color image by recording the coordinates of this region.

During aircraft flight, the cockpit is always in dark light conditions, which deprives the color image-based hand detection method of most of its data source.

To solve this problem, this paper uses MSRCR (Multi-Scale Retinex with Color Restoration) algorithm for the current region.

Finally, the method proposed in this paper implements hand key point detection (Google's MediaPipe hand detection algorithm) and hand contour extraction in this region.

2.1 Data Acquisition

During the data acquisition phase, the Intel RealSense D455 was used to capture RGB-D information in the cockpit. The Intel RealSense D455 has the advantages of a wide viewing angle, large measurement range, high measurement accuracy, and a wide range of adjustable resolution and sampling rate. Since there are limited locations in the cockpit where the camera can be mounted, the camera can be mounted on the top panel or behind the pilot between the seats to capture and record behavioral data from the back of the pilot's seat in an approximate first-person view.

The acquisition results from the RealSense camera were saved as color and depth images, respectively, with sampling parameters of 848 $\times$ 480 at 30 FPS. The depth images captured by the depth camera can avoid the effect of lighting variations. By using a good depth image, hand detection can be achieved under various lighting conditions.

2.2 ROI Segmentation

Data Pre-processing. In the pre-processing stage, image filtering and enhancement functions are added. Color images and depth images captured by the Intel RealSense D455 depth camera often have defects, especially depth images, such as missing depth (there are more points or areas with a depth value of 0), the interference effect of noise is very large, and the resolution is much smaller than the resolution of color images. It can also be affected by the surface material of the object, and the camera cannot capture the reflected infrared light and thus cannot obtain the depth information of that point. Noise has a large impact on the accuracy of hand detection and must be reduced by filtering the image prior to subsequent detection. The more common filters such as Gaussian filter, median filter, considering the special environment of the cockpit, the median filter is used in this stage. The median filter is a nonlinear filter that takes the median pixel value in the filter kernel as the filtered pixel value of the target point, which is very effective for pretzel noise and can preserve the edge information in the image.

Arm Segmentation. The use of depth images to improve the accuracy of hand detection can be divided into three steps. (see Fig. 3). First, the background of the depth image of the unmanned scene of the cockpit is captured with a depth camera. Second, the depth image of the manned scene is differenced from the depth image of the unmanned scene to obtain the body region. Third, a suitable threshold is set to segment the differential image based on the fact that the pixel value of the device region is close to zero, while the pixel value of the body region is much larger than the pixel value of the device region. Given a suitable threshold, the binarized image of the body region can be roughly segmented by setting the pixel points with values less than this threshold to 0. Using this image as a mask, the region of interest is extracted over the original depth image.

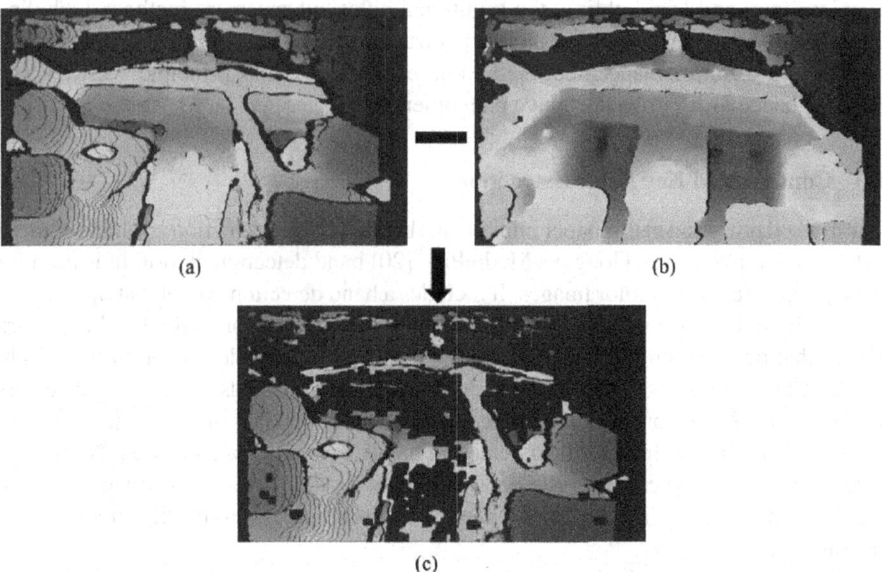

Fig. 3. Arm Segmentation: (a) depth image with pilots (b) depth image without pilots (c) region with body

Depth Region Grow. Region-growing algorithm is used on the depth image to find the location of the top of the pilot's arm, which is the approximate location of the hand. This method makes it possible to determine the approximate position of the pilot's hand in different lighting conditions. After finding the location of the hand, a region of interest including the hand is segmented. This region excludes a large number of factors that are not relevant to pilot's hand, such as cockpit background, windows, and other parts of the body. Using depth information for raw hand detection and then using color information for fine hand contour detection is one of the main innovations of this paper. The advantage of the proposed method is that it simplifies the processing and reduces the amount of data to be processed per image, achieving a reduction in processing time. At the same time, the proposed method allows subsequent image-processing algorithms to focus on local areas containing key information and increases the accuracy of the algorithm.

MSRCR. The region of interest is also segmented in the aligned color image by recording the coordinates of this region. Although a large number of irrelevant factors were excluded, the current color images are still not ideal when used for hand detection. The lighting in the cockpit has a significant impact on the accuracy of hand detection. During aircraft flight, the cockpit is always in dark light conditions, which deprives the color image-based hand detection method of most of its data source. To solve this problem, this paper uses MSRCR [19] (Multi-Scale Retinex with Color Restoration) algorithm for the current region. MSRCR algorithm uses a color recovery factor to adjust the proportional relationship between the 3 color channels in the original image, bringing out information from relatively dark areas and eliminating the defects of image color distortion. The local contrast of the processed image is improved and the brightness is similar to that of the real scene. After comparison, for scenes such as darkness, overexposure, and backlighting, the traditional color enhancement methods including gamma conversion, adaptive threshold equalization for limiting contrast do not perform as well as the color enhancement method based on the Retinex principle. MSRCR can better enhance or improve the above phenomenon.

2.3 Contour and Key Point Extraction

The method proposed in this paper implements hand key point detection and hand contour extraction in this region. Google's MediaPipe [20] hand detection algorithm is used for hand point detection in color images. It includes a hand detection model that operates on the entire image returning hand bounding boxes with orientation and a hand landmark model that operates on the image region defined by the hand detector returning high-fidelity 3D coordinates of the 21 hand points. MediaPipe Hands trains palm detectors instead of hand detectors because estimating the bounding boxes of rigid objects such as palms and fists is much easier than detecting hands with articulated fingers. After hand detection on the whole image, the hand landmark model performs accurate key point localization by regression on 21 3D hand joint coordinates within the detected hand region.

After using the Mediapipe hand detection algorithm for color images, there are a large number of false detections due to the complex environment in the cockpit. The method proposed in this paper can restrict the location of the hand region so that the detection results of the MP algorithm can be filtered to exclude the false detection results and select the hand location with the highest probability.

Compared with the traditional region growth algorithm, the region growth algorithm used in this paper has been improved in terms of growth criterion. The region growing algorithm combining RGB and YCbCr color spaces and using hand position points as seed points is used for the extraction of hand contour. The traditional method has the following characteristics:

1. the region growth is performed with the gray value of pixel points or the value of a certain color space.
2. the absolute value of the value of neighboring pixel points is used as the distance measure.

The region growth algorithm used in this paper improves the growth criterion as follows:

1. By combining information from multiple color spaces for region growth, information from a total of five channels in both YCbCr space and RGB space is used for the calculation, and the weights are adjusted according to the difference in information importance.
2. Using region growth on depth images to narrow the region growth boundary on color images to avoid wasting resources by overgrowth.
3. Relative Euclidean distance is used as the distance metric instead of absolute value. Calculation method is:

$$d_i = \frac{\sqrt{k_1(R_i - \overline{R})^2 + k_2(B_i - \overline{B})^2 + k_3(Y_i - \overline{Y})^2 + k_4(Cb_i - \overline{Cb})^2 + k_5(Cr_i - \overline{Cr})^2}}{\sqrt{k_1 R_i^2 + k_2 B_i^2 + k_3 Y_i^2 + k_4 Cb_i^2 + k_5 Cr_i^2}} \tag{1}$$

where, d_i denotes the improved relative Euclidean distance between the current pixel to be determined and the adjacent generated region. The pixel continues to grow in the region as a growth point if the *di* of the pixel is less than the specified threshold. $\overline{R}, \overline{B}, \overline{Y}, \overline{Cb} and \overline{Cr}$ is the average of *R, B, Y, Cb,* and *Cr* channels in the adjacent generated region. R_i, B_i, Y_i, Cb_i, and Cr_i indicate the values of the *R, B, Y, Cb,* and *Cr* channels of the pixel to be determined. k_i is a constant factor indicating the weight.

3 Result

To evaluate the proposed approach, the proposed hand detection and contour extraction algorithms are applied to flight tasks executed by real pilots in a level D full flight simulator. In the experiment, the behavior of the pilot was recorded by RGB-D camera, and the pilot performed their tasks in various scenarios, including complex scenarios of changing lights and night navigation (lighting failure).

The results of the proposed hand contour extraction method in this paper are shown in Fig. In the extraction results for different hand gestures, it can be seen that the proposed region growing method combining multi-color space and using a new distance metric can achieve better contour extraction results even under dark light conditions.

Compared with the method using a single color space and traditional distance metric, the segmentation accuracy of this method is higher (see Fig. 4).

The results of the proposed detection algorithm combining depth-based hand region segmentation and MP hand detection algorithm are shown in (Fig. 5).

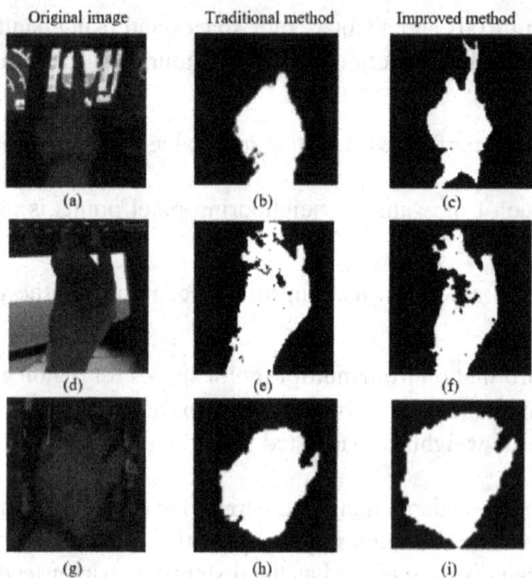

Fig. 4. The result of hand contour extraction

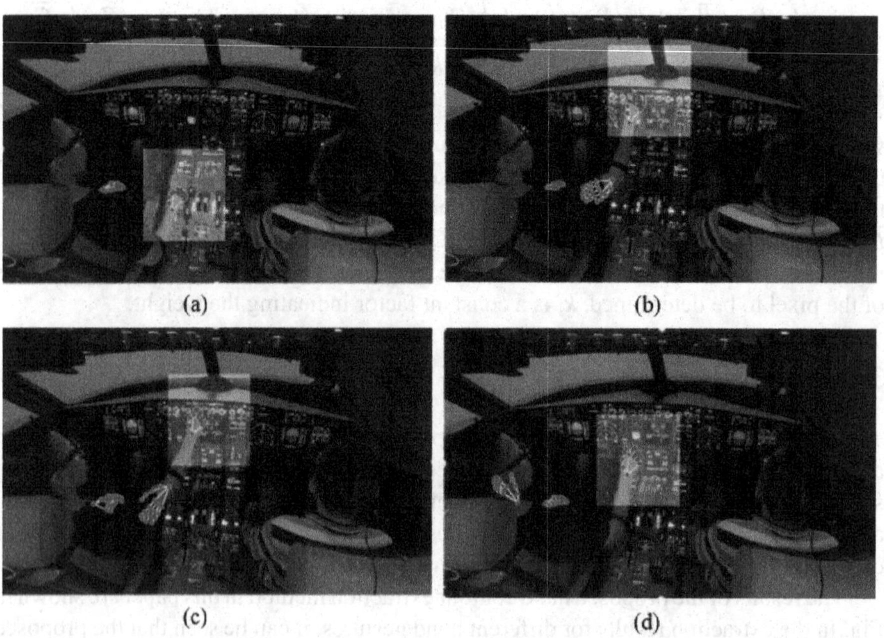

Fig. 5. Detection Results: (a) free (b) Turning knob (c) Turning knob (d) moving

The highlighted square area in the figure represents the valid hand position range. MP hand detection results within this square area are considered reasonable hand detection results, while detection results outside this area are considered erroneous detection results.

A frame is considered to be correctly detected if the hand region is extracted correctly in that frame and the MP algorithm successfully detects the hand key point coordinates in that frame.

The video of the pilot performing the mission with a duration of 27 s is selected as the experimental sample, and the frame rate of the Realsense camera is 30, so the total number of video frames is 900.The counting statistics of the video frames are shown in Table 1.

Table 1. Detection result of 900 frames

	Fail detection	Correct detection
Number of frames	87	813
Proportion in 900	9.7%	90.3%

According to the detection results, the accuracy of the detection method proposed in this paper is 90.3%. Compared with the detection results obtained by applying the MP hand detection algorithm alone without applying the method in this paper, the current detection results filter out the hand positions with the highest probability, which significantly improves the availability of hand coordinate points and provides the basic data for subsequent pilot behavior analysis. The result is satisfactory considering the interference of various factors such as the complex illumination and background in aircraft cockpit. The errors in the detection results are mainly caused by the missing arm part in the depth image after differencing. This will be improved in a subsequent study.

4 Discussion

For hand contour segmentation, the proposed method has higher accuracy than conventional method. The conventional method uses a single color space. The disadvantage of the conventional method is that it may use color channels that are not related to skin tones, which can lead to overgrowth. In addition, a single color space does not provide sufficient information during region growth. The contour extracted by this method is not complete. The proposed method uses multiple color spaces (RGB and YCbCr). It excludes information that is not very useful in the RGB color space (e.g., green). Also, considering that the segmentation target is the hand, the proposed method combines the information in the skin color space (YCbCr). The proposed method reduces the problem of overgrowth and allows the edges of the pilot's hands in the color image to be separated from the background of the device with accurate and complete contour. The conventional method uses a traditional distance metric. Conventional distance metric makes it possible for region growth to miss the skin tone part or grow to the device part by mistake. The proposed distance metrics adds information about the regions that have grown and assigns weights to each color channel. Therefore, the extracted contours of the proposed method are more complete and accurate. In addition, the ROI identified by the proposed method can be used as a boundary for region growth to avoid growing to areas where hand is impossible to be there.

For hand key points detection, the proposed method improves the practicality and accuracy of MP in the complex environment of the cockpit. There are a large number of error cases in the detection results of the mediapipe-only method. These error results are not useful for analyzing the behavior of the pilots. The proposed method determines the ROI with hand by depth images. The depth image has the property of not being affected by light. In addition, Subtraction results of manned and unmanned depth images exclude the influence of the device background. Thus, the ROI with hand excludes the influence of light and background. By using the ROI with hand to filter the MP detection results, the proposed method can select the most accurate result.

However, the determination of the hand position after segmentation of the arm in the depth image is unreliable. The proposed method uses threshold segmentation to extract the body contour, which is strongly influenced by the selection of the threshold. In addition, if the depth camera is moved during the experiment, the background needs to be re-modeled.

5 Conclusion

This paper implements a hand key point detection and hand contour extraction method based on color and depth information. The completed hand detection and contour extraction algorithms are applied to flight tasks executed by real pilots in a level D full flight simulator.

The light in the cockpit is not constant for pilots during flight missions. The method in this paper relies on depth information to determine the hand position even in low light conditions, thus filtering out the correct hand key point coordinate detection results. The method in this paper provides an innovative improvement to the growth criteria of the traditional region growth algorithm. The method in this paper uses multi-channel information from multiple color spaces, while using a new distance metric instead of the traditional distance metric. The method can segment the entire hand contour after color enhancement of the hand region in dark light conditions.

The method in this paper still has some shortcomings, such as the determination of the hand position after segmenting the arm in the depth image is not robust, which causes the algorithm to select the wrong hand key points. To solve this problem, the combination of depth and color information to optimize the hand position determination will be considered in future studies. Second, issues such as classification when detecting multiple hands simultaneously will also be addressed in future studies.

In subsequent studies, the detection and segmentation accuracy of the algorithms proposed in this paper will be further optimized. At the same time, these detection results can be used to determine the pilot's operating status and analyze the pilot's behavior, which is important for the study of human error in aviation human factors.

References

1. Mummadi, C.K., Philips, P.L.F., Deep Verma, K., et al.: Real-time and embedded detection of hand gestures with an IMU-based glove. Informatics MDPI. **5**(2), 28 (2018)
2. DelPreto, J., Hughes, J., D'Aria, M., et al.: A wearable smart glove and its application of pose and gesture detection to sign language classification. IEEE Robot. Autom. Lett. **7**(4), 10589–10596 (2022)
3. Chung, H.Y., Chung, Y.L., Tsai, W.F.: An efficient hand gesture recognition system based on deep CNN. In: 2019 IEEE International Conference on Industrial Technology (ICIT), pp. 853–858. IEEE (2019)
4. Jesna, J., Narayanan, A.S., Bijlani, K.: Automatic hand raise detection by analyzing the edge structures. In: Shetty, N.R., Patnaik, L.M., Prasad, N.H., Nalini, N. (eds.) Emerging Research in Computing, Information, Communication and Applications, pp. 171–180. Springer, Singapore (2018). https://doi.org/10.1007/978-981-10-4741-1_16
5. Celebi, M.E., Kingravi, H.A., Vela, P.A.: A comparative study of efficient initialization methods for the k-means clustering algorithm. Expert Syst. Appl. (2013)
6. Paul, S., Bhattacharyya, A., Mollah, A.F., Basu, S., Nasipuri, M.: Hand segmentation from complex background for gesture recognition. In: Mandal, J.K., Bhattacharya, D. (eds.) Emerging Technology in Modelling and Graphics: Proceedings of IEM Graph 2018, pp. 775–782. Springer Singapore, Singapore (2020). https://doi.org/10.1007/978-981-13-7403-6_68
7. Johnson, D., Damian, D., Tzanetakis, G.: Detecting hand posture in piano playing using depth data. Comput. Music. J. **43**(1), 59–78 (2020)
8. Songhua, W.: Research on image region growing segmentation algorithm. Science and Technology Innovation Guide (2015)
9. Bandini, A., Zariffa, J.: Analysis of the hands in egocentric vision: a survey. IEEE Trans. Pattern Anal. Mach. Intell. (2020)
10. He, Q., Wang, W., Xiao, R.F.: fast hand detection and tracking for human-robot interaction. In: 2022 IEEE 17th Conference on Industrial Electronics and Applications (ICIEA), pp. 1441–1446. IEEE (2022)
11. Shaik, K.B., Ganesan, P., Kalist, V., Sathish, B.S., Jenitha, J.M.M.: Comparative study of skin color detection and segmentation in HSV and YCbCr color space. Proc. Comput. Sci. **57**, 41–48 (2015)
12. Kolkur, S., Kalbande, D., Shimpi, P., Bapat, C., Jatakia, J.: Human skin detection using RGB, HSV and YCbCr color models. arXiv preprint arXiv:1708.02694 (2017)
13. Li, C., Kitani, K.M.: Pixel-level hand detection in ego-centric videos. In: Conference on Computer Vision and Pattern Recognition, pp. 3570–3577. IEEE (2013)
14. Wang, J., Wang, Z., Shan, F., Huang, D.: Research on hand detection in complex scenes based on RGB-D sensor. In: Kurosu, M. (ed.) Human-Computer Interaction. Interaction Techniques and Novel Applications: Thematic Area, pp. 147–158. Springer International Publishing, Cham (2021). https://doi.org/10.1007/978-3-030-78465-2_12
15. Wen, H., Wang, Z., Fu, S.: Secondary task behavioral analysis based on depth image during driving. In: Kurosu, M. (ed.) Human-Computer Interaction. Design and User Experience Case Studies. LNCS, vol. 12764, pp. 473–485. Springer, Cham (2021). https://doi.org/10.1007/978-3-030-78468-3_32
16. Zhao, Y., Wang, Z., Lu, Y., Fu, S.: A visual-based approach for manual operation evaluation. In: Harris, D., Li, W.-C. (eds.) Engineering Psychology and Cognitive Ergonomics. Mental Workload, Human Physiology, and Human Energy. LNCS (LNAI), vol. 12186, pp. 281–292. Springer, Cham (2020). https://doi.org/10.1007/978-3-030-49044-7_23
17. Keskin, C., Kıraç, F., Kara, Y.E., et al.: Real time hand pose estimation using depth sensors. In: Consumer Depth Cameras for Computer Vision: Research Topics and Applications, pp. 119–137 (2013)

18. Wang, J., Mueller, F., Bernard, F., et al.: Rgb2hands: real-time tracking of 3d hand interactions from monocular RGB video. ACM Trans. Graph. (ToG) **39**(6), 1–16 (2020)
19. Wang, J., Lu, K., Xue, J., et al.: Single image dehazing based on the physical model and MSRCR algorithm. IEEE Trans. Circuits Syst. Video Technol. **28**(9), 2190–2199 (2017)
20. Zhang, F., Bazarevsky, V., Vakunov, A., et al.: Mediapipe hands: on-device real-time hand tracking. arXiv preprint arXiv:2006.10214 (2020)

A Self-contained Approach to MEMS MARG Orientation Estimation for Hand Gesture Tracking in Magnetically Distorted Environments

Pontakorn Sonchan(✉), Neeranut Ratchatanantakit, Nonnarit O-larnnithipong, Malek Adjouadi, and Armando Barreto

Department of Electrical and Computer Engineering, Florida International University, Miami, FL, USA
{psonc001,nratc001,nolarnni,adjouadi,barretoa}@fiu.edu

Abstract. There is increasing interest in using low-cost and lightweight Micro Electro-Mechanical System (MEMS) modules containing tri-axial accelerometers, gyroscopes and magnetometers for tracking the motion of segments of the human body. We are specifically interested in using these devices, called "Magnetic, Angular-Rate and Gravity" ("MARG") modules, to develop an instrumented glove, assigning one of these MARG modules to monitor the (absolute) 3-D orientation of each of the proximal and middle phalanges of the fingers of a computer user. This would provide real-time monitoring of the hand gestures of the user, enabling non-vision gesture recognition approaches that do not degrade with line-of-sight disruptions or longer distance from the cameras. However, orientation estimation from low-cost MEMS MARG modules has shown to degrade in areas where the geomagnetic field is distorted by the presence of ferromagnetic objects (which are common in contemporary environments). This paper describes the continued evolution of our algorithm to obtain robust MARG orientation estimates, even in magnetically distorted environments. In particular, the paper describes a new self-contained version of the algorithm, i.e., one requiring no information from external devices, in contrast to the previous versions.

Keywords: MARG module · Orientation Estimation · Magnetic Disturbance

1 Motivation

1.1 Interest in Intuitive Means of Computer Input

The rising pervasiveness of virtual and augmented reality applications in human-computer interaction is currently driving an increasing interest in computer input mechanisms that are more natural and better matched to those environments [12]. There is an active search for methods to track the position and configuration of the user hands and fingers as a way to interact with the computer. Many of the approaches being investigated

M. Kurosu and A. Hashizume (Eds.): HCII 2023, LNCS 14011, pp. 585–602, 2023.
https://doi.org/10.1007/978-3-031-35596-7_38

are based on multi-camera vision systems. However, the introduction of Micro Electro-Mechanical System (MEMS) modules containing tri-axial accelerometers, gyroscopes, and magnetometers, in the past 20 years, seemed to, potentially, open up a completely different approach to hand tracking, with distinctive advantages and challenges.

1.2 Inertial and Magnetic Tracking Approach

The emergence of miniature MEMS accelerometers and gyroscopes in the 1990's and 2000's [3] sparked interest in their use for tracking segments of the human body in ways similar to the application of accelerometers and gyroscopes for navigational purposes, which had already been in practice for decades. This approach would be highly convenient for our goal of tracking of the articulated segments of a computer user's hand through a glove instrumented with several of these sensor modules [1, 8, 9, 13]. Unfortunately, it was discovered that the performance characteristics of the MEMS accelerometers and gyroscopes was much inferior with respect to their navigational counterparts. Soon MEMS magnetometers were added to the ensemble with the intent to improve the orientation estimation performance achievable by the sensor modules. Nonetheless, practice has shown that the same type of algorithms used for navigational tracking cannot be simply mapped to the MEMS MARG modules. New approaches have emerged that seek to use all the information available from the three sensor modalities contained by the MARG module.

We have previously developed the "Gravity Magnetic Vector with Double SLERP" (GMV-D) orientation estimation algorithm for MEMS MARG modules [10, 11, 16–18], where we emphasize the need to selectively increase or decrease the weight given to each of the sources of information in the module, according to the instantaneous operational conditions of the MARG.

In this paper we will first describe the GMV-D orientation estimation algorithm, overall. Then we will describe in detail how the trustworthiness parameters, α and μ, are obtained, with special emphasis on the novel approach taken to obtain values of μ that do not require any information from outside the MARG module for their computation. In the next sections we represent vectors and quaternions through boldface variables. In addition, we invoke a few well-established properties of quaternions as representations of 3-D rotations, which are fully developed in texts focused on the topic of quaternions, such as [2, 4] and [23].

2 The GMV-D MARG Orientation Estimation Algorithm

2.1 Conditional Involvement of Available Information Sources

Many of the previously proposed approaches for MARG orientation estimation seek to use all available forms of information (readings from all three types of sensors), to obtain a final orientation estimate. It seems, however, that the effective emphasis of most of the previous approaches is to "maximize" the involvement of the information sources in the estimation, targeting some theoretical goal in the estimate. For example, the Kalman Filter seeks to provide the linear estimator yielding the smallest variance in the estimate

[22]. However, many of the approaches do not deliberately include provisions to restrain or block the involvement of some forms of available information when those elements of information may not be trustworthy. The lack of such provisions could result in large estimate errors that persist for long intervals, given the fact that the estimate resulting from one iteration is fed back and used as a central factor in the estimation for the next iteration.

This may happen, for example, when the assumptions made for the use of signals such as accelerations and magnetic fields are not actually fulfilled at the moment in which they are used for the estimation. The alternative approach followed in our proposed method (GMV-D) is to assess, in every iteration of the algorithm, if the preconditions are met, and actively suppress the involvement of the corresponding sources of information, when they are not met. That is, GMV-D implements a form of conditional involvement of the available information sources.

2.2 Information Flow in the GMV-D Algorithm

The information flow through one iteration of the GMV-D algorithm is displayed in Fig. 1. At the beginning of each iteration, the latest set of gyroscope readings, $\boldsymbol{w}$, accelerometer readings $\boldsymbol{a}_0$ and magnetometer readings, $\boldsymbol{m}_0$, will be read. The gyroscope readings, $\boldsymbol{w}$, will be first processed by a "De-biasing" stage, in which a linear model of the buffered samples of the gyroscope readings acquired during the most recent quasi-static interval is used to compensate for the possible bias in the gyroscope signals. This yields an "un-biased" set of angular rotation speeds, $\boldsymbol{w}_B$, which will be the ones effectively used for the algorithm. It should be noted that, historically, this kind of bias removal has been shown to be insufficient to eliminate the bias in gyroscope readings completely, and it is because we acknowledge the imperfection of this bias removal that the orientation estimation based on gyroscopic readings has to be corrected using other sources of information, in the GMV-D algorithm.

An initial (quaternion) orientation estimate, $\boldsymbol{q}_G$, is defined by recursive integration of gyroscope measurements. To do this, the un-biased gyroscope readings are converted to a "quaternion rate of change", $\dot{\boldsymbol{q}}$, as indicated in Eq. 1, where $\otimes$ represents quaternion product and $\boldsymbol{q}_0$ is the quaternion representing the orientation before the latest unbiased rotational speeds (cast as a quaternion) $\boldsymbol{w}_B$, are considered. Then, the rate of change is "accumulated" (integrated) into the newest instantaneous gyroscope-based orientation quaternion, $\boldsymbol{q}_G$, through Eq. 2, where Δt is the sampling interval and $\boldsymbol{q}_0^*$ is the quaternion conjugate of $\boldsymbol{q}_0$.

$$\dot{\boldsymbol{q}} = \frac{1}{2}\boldsymbol{q}_0 \otimes \boldsymbol{\omega}_{\boldsymbol{B}} \tag{1}$$

$$\boldsymbol{q}_G = e^{((\Delta t)\dot{\boldsymbol{q}} \otimes \boldsymbol{q}_0^*)} \otimes \boldsymbol{q}_0 \tag{2}$$

If the bias had been *completely* removed from $\boldsymbol{w}_B$, this initial estimation of the orientation of the MARG would already be correct. However, unavoidable offset remnants in the gyroscope signals cause orientation "drift" in this $\boldsymbol{q}_G$ estimate that must be corrected periodically.

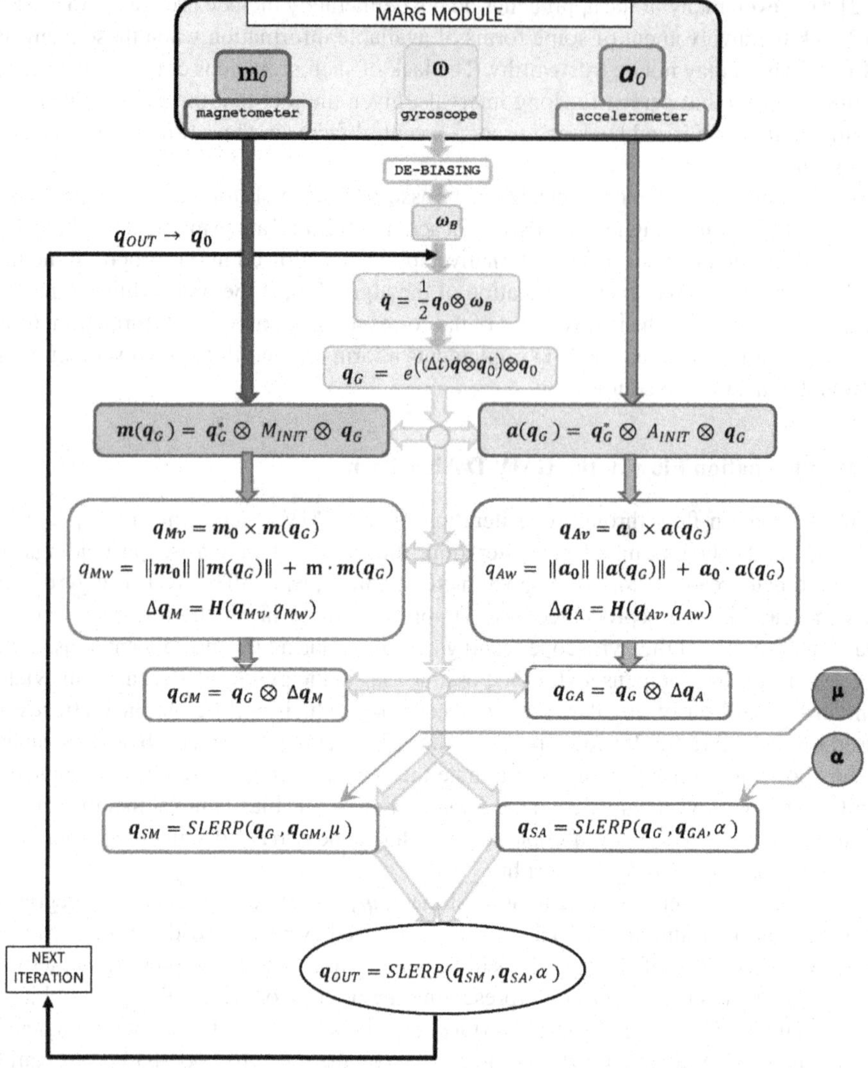

Fig. 1. Information flow during 1 iteration of the GMV-D MARG orientation estimation process. The computations of α and μ are explained in Sect. 3.

The two lateral columns shown in Fig. 1 symbolize the two pipelines of additional information that GMV-D implements to develop and apply quaternion correction components on the basis of magnetometer readings (left column) and accelerometer readings (right column). Both these pipelines have the same type of functionality. Therefore, only the right (accelerometer-based) pipeline will be described in detail at this point, letting the reader apply an analogous explanation to the functionality of the left (magnetometer-based) pipeline.

In GMV-D, both accelerometer-based and magnetometer-based corrections:

1. Are developed on the assumption of the existence of a uniform vector field,
2. Encode the degree to which the assumption is verified in a scalar parameter,
3. Use the parameter to modulate the significance of the corresponding correction.

The scalar trustworthiness parameters are α, for the accelerometer-based correction, and μ for the magnetometer-based correction, and each takes on values only in the closed interval [0, 1]. Their meaning and calculation will be detailed in subsequent sections. Here the basic explanation of GMV-D will assume that they are available in each iteration.

Observing the right pipeline in Fig. 1, we see that its objective is the computation of a quaternion orientation estimate, $\boldsymbol{q}_{\mathrm{GA}}$, which has been "fully" corrected on the basis of accelerometer readings. That is, $\boldsymbol{q}_{\mathrm{GA}}$ is obtained by modifying the initial estimate, $\boldsymbol{q}_{\mathrm{G}}$, by full application of an "acceleration orientation adjustment", $\Delta\boldsymbol{q}_{\mathrm{A}}$, which will tweak the incrementally constructed quaternion to match the orientation informed by the current accelerometer readings. As detailed in [18], the quaternion, $\Delta\boldsymbol{q}_{\mathrm{A}}$, which encodes that additional rotation, can be inferred considering the (vector) cross product of the instantaneous acceleration measured, $\boldsymbol{a}_0$, and the direction of the acceleration vector that would be derived by mapping the initial measurement of the gravitational acceleration, $\mathbf{A}_{\mathrm{INIT}}$, to the current orientation of the body frame of the MARG, $\boldsymbol{a}(\boldsymbol{q}_G)$, which we call the "computed acceleration". $\mathbf{A}_{\mathrm{INIT}}$ is the 3-dimensional vector recorded from the accelerometer readings at startup, when the orientation of the MARG body frame is adopted as the orientation of the fixed inertial frame, with respect to which the orientation of the body frame will be expressed, from that moment on. The mapping of $\mathbf{A}_{\mathrm{INIT}}$ to the current orientation of the MARG body frame is calculated according to this useful property of quaternions [2, 4, 23], with $\boldsymbol{q}_{\mathrm{G}}$ as the quaternion that represents the orientation of the second (body) frame, with respect to the first (inertial) frame.

$$\boldsymbol{a}(\boldsymbol{q}_G) = \boldsymbol{q}_G^* \otimes A_{INIT} \otimes \boldsymbol{q}_G \tag{3}$$

In the absence of gyroscope drift, the "computed acceleration", $\boldsymbol{a}(\boldsymbol{q}_{\mathrm{G}})$, would ideally match the measured instantaneous acceleration (gravity) in direction, so that no "orientation adjustment" (i.e., difference), $\Delta\boldsymbol{q}_{\mathrm{A}}$, would need to be considered. However, in the likely event that persistent residual gyroscope drift might have distorted the basic estimate of the MARG body frame, the vector and scalar parts of the additional orientation change, $\Delta\boldsymbol{q}_{\mathrm{A}}$, that could supplement the mapping of $\mathbf{A}_{\mathrm{INIT}}$ to actually match $\boldsymbol{a}_0$ can be computed as shown in Eqs. 4 (vector part) and 5 (scalar part).

$$\boldsymbol{q}_{Av} = \boldsymbol{a}_0 \times \boldsymbol{a}(\boldsymbol{q}_G) \tag{4}$$

$$q_{Aw} = ||\boldsymbol{a}_0||\ ||\boldsymbol{a}(\boldsymbol{q}_G)|| + \boldsymbol{a}_0 \cdot \boldsymbol{a}(\boldsymbol{q}_G) \tag{5}$$

Then, $\Delta\boldsymbol{q}_{\mathrm{A}}$ is obtained by concatenating both parts into a quaternion, as indicated by the $\boldsymbol{H}$ operator, in Eq. 6:

$$\Delta\boldsymbol{q}_A = \boldsymbol{H}(\boldsymbol{q}_{Av}, q_{Aw}) \tag{6}$$

Once this supplementary rotation quaternion, $\Delta \boldsymbol{q}_{\mathrm{A}}$, is obtained, it is effectively applied to define the quaternion $\boldsymbol{q}_{\mathrm{GA}}$, which encodes the MARG orientation estimate that assumes complete appropriateness of the accelerometer correction and has applied it to the latest available basic orientation estimate $\boldsymbol{q}_{\mathrm{G}}$:

$$q_{GA} = q_G \otimes \Delta q_A \tag{7}$$

It should be noted that a completely analogous reasoning supports the computational steps illustrated on the left column of Fig. 1, to yield $\boldsymbol{q}_{\mathrm{GM}}$, a quaternion encoding the results of modifying the original estimate of MARG orientation, $\boldsymbol{q}_{\mathrm{G}}$, on the basis of applying a magnetometer-based correction in full. Similar to the process described for the right column of Fig. 1, except that referring to the magnetic field, a "computed magnetic vector" is obtained by now mapping the initial magnetic field recorded at startup, $\mathbf{M}_{\mathrm{INIT}}$, to the MARG body frame, using $\boldsymbol{q}_{\mathrm{G}}$. The potential orientation "difference", $\Delta \boldsymbol{q}_{\mathrm{M}}$, between the "computed magnetic vector" and the instantaneous output from the magnetometer is calculated with equations similar to Eqs. 4, 5 and 6, and then applied with an equation similar to Eq. 7. This yields $\boldsymbol{q}_{\mathrm{GM}}$, a quaternion that represents the MARG orientation initially obtained from integration of gyroscopic signals but then fully corrected on the basis of instantaneous magnetometer readings,

At this point in the GMV-D iteration there are 3 prospective estimates for the MARG orientation: $\boldsymbol{q}_{\mathrm{G}}$, which was obtained merely updating the final MARG orientation estimate obtained from the previous iteration, $\boldsymbol{q}_0$, with the gyroscopic measurements from this iteration (in Eqs. 1 and 2); $\boldsymbol{q}_{\mathrm{GA}}$, the estimation in which the basic $\boldsymbol{q}_{\mathrm{G}}$, has been infused with information from the current accelerometer measurements, applying the accelerometer-based correction "fully"; and $\boldsymbol{q}_{\mathrm{GM}}$, the orientation estimate which has been infused with information from the current magnetometer measurements, applying the magnetometer-based correction "fully". It has already been pointed out that, in spite of the "de-biasing" procedure performed on the readings from the gyroscope, even $\boldsymbol{w}_{\mathrm{B}}$ is likely to still contain persistent remnants of bias errors which will develop drift in $\boldsymbol{q}_{\mathrm{G}}$, unless it is corrected. Therefore, the corrections derived from accelerometer or magnetometer readings *should be used, but only to the extent that the preconditions required in each of those corrections are met*. Otherwise, an inadequate accelerometer-based or magnetometer-based correction would actually degrade the correctness of the orientation estimation further (for the current *and future* estimation results).

Figure 1 shows that GMV-D formulates the final orientation estimate as a combination of $\boldsymbol{q}_{\mathrm{G}}$, corrected using information from the accelerometer and $\boldsymbol{q}_{\mathrm{G}}$, corrected using information from the magnetometer, but only after the "strength" of each of these corrections is scaled in proportion to a single scalar trustworthiness parameter which is instantaneously assessed for each of the sources of information: $0 \leq \alpha \leq 1$ for the accelerometer correction and $0 \leq \mu \leq 1$ for the magnetometer correction. The specific meaning and formulation of these 2 parameters will be detailed in the next section, where the new approach for calculating μ without relying on signals that are external to the MARG module will be highlighted.

The scaling of the full-strength corrected orientation estimates, $\boldsymbol{q}_{\mathrm{GA}}$, and $\boldsymbol{q}_{\mathrm{GM}}$ is implemented as quaternion interpolation from $\boldsymbol{q}_{\mathrm{G}}$ to $\boldsymbol{q}_{\mathrm{GA}}$, controlled by α, and from $\boldsymbol{q}_{\mathrm{G}}$ to $\boldsymbol{q}_{\mathrm{GM}}$, controlled by μ, respectively. In both cases the interpolation approach used is the

Spherical Linear Interpolation (SLERP), which is defined as follows for interpolating from a quaternion $\boldsymbol{q}_1$ towards a quaternion $\boldsymbol{q}_2$, under control of the parameter h [21]:

$$\Omega = cos^{-1}(\boldsymbol{q}_1 \cdot \boldsymbol{q}_2) \tag{8}$$

$$SLERP(\boldsymbol{q}_1, \boldsymbol{q}_2, h) = \frac{\boldsymbol{q}_1 \sin((1-h)\Omega) + \boldsymbol{q}_2 \sin(h\Omega)}{\sin(\Omega)} \tag{9}$$

Therefore, the scaled accelerometer-corrected quaternion, $\boldsymbol{q}_{SA}$, and the scaled magnetometer-corrected quaternion, $\boldsymbol{q}_{SM}$, are given by:

$$\boldsymbol{q}_{SA} = SLERP(\boldsymbol{q}_G, \boldsymbol{q}_{GA}, \alpha) \tag{10}$$

$$\boldsymbol{q}_{SM} = SLERP(\boldsymbol{q}_G, \boldsymbol{q}_{GM}, \mu) \tag{11}$$

Figure 1 shows that GMV-D derives its final orientation estimate quaternion through a second tier of SLERP interpolation, from $\boldsymbol{q}_{SM}$ to $\boldsymbol{q}_{SA}$, under control of α.

$$\boldsymbol{q}_{OUT} = SLERP(\boldsymbol{q}_{SM}, \boldsymbol{q}_{SA}, \alpha) \tag{12}$$

3 Formulation of the Trustworthiness Parameters

3.1 Accelerometer Correction Trustworthiness, α

It is known that two "vector observations" are not sufficient to independently define the 3-D orientation of a moving rigid body [7]. However, our approach uses a pair of observations of the gravitational acceleration vector field (assumed constant throughout the operating space of the MARG) to infuse additional information into the MARG body orientation estimation, implementing a *correction* of $\boldsymbol{q}_G$.

Within the context of our proposed application of MARG modules for hand tracking as an input mechanism for human-computer interaction, the local gravitational field is, indeed, uniform. That is, the vector representing the acceleration of gravity all around the prospective working space of the MARG can be considered as oriented perpendicular to the horizontal plane, pointing downwards, with the same magnitude. Unfortunately, the tri-axial accelerometer in the MARG does not exclusively respond to the gravitational acceleration, but, instead, the output of each of its 3 axes (X, Y and Z), will contain projections of the so-called "linear acceleration" superimposed on the components of the gravitational accelerations they sense. This "linear acceleration" refers to the acceleration that the MARG experiences when it is in movement, with a varying speed. Therefore, accelerometer-based corrections imply the presumption of immobility in association with both "vector observations" used for them, which are, in reference to Fig. 1, (an average) of the acceleration measured at startup, $\mathbf{A}_{INIT}$, and the instantaneous acceleration recorded at any GMV-D iteration, $\boldsymbol{a}_0$.

GMV-D requires that the system be initialized while the MARG is static (and in a location where the geomagnetic field is undistorted). Furthermore, it is established that the orientation of the MARG body frame at startup will become the default inertial frame of reference (with respect to which the orientation of the MARG body frame will be characterized in all future iterations). According to that operational requirement, $\mathbf{A}_{INIT}$ should, indeed, be exclusively a reflection of the gravitational acceleration. But, expectedly, there will be some iterations in which the MARG will be in motion and, therefore, its accelerometer axes will report the superposition of gravity components and the corresponding "linear accelerations". It follows that, in iterations when the MARG is far from static, an accelerometer-based correction of the type contemplated in GMV-D should not be applied in full strength, and instead should be significantly restrained. This restraint on the accelerometer-based corrections is accomplished in GMV-D by having a single scalar parameter, $0 \leq \alpha \leq 1$, control the SLERP interpolation from the uncorrected $\boldsymbol{q}_G$ to the "fully corrected" $\boldsymbol{q}_{GA}$, yielding $\boldsymbol{q}_{SA}$, where accelerometer-based corrections which do not fulfill the necessary precondition (i.e., when $\alpha \approx 0$) will be essentially bypassed.

Accordingly, α must parametrize the level of (approximate) immobility of the MARG. In our work, we have used the Yost Labs 3-space USB MARG module, which internally computes a Confidence Factor, from 0 to 1, that can be read by issuing a command to the MARG and indicates "how much the sensor is being moved at the moment. This value will return 1 if the sensor is completely stationary and will return 0 if it is in motion. This command can also return values in between indicating how much motion the sensor is experiencing." [24]. Therefore, we compute α by reading this parameter and simply applying a linear function to precipitate the decrease of α when the MARG departs even slightly from immobility (and re-enforcing the lower bound of 0 and the upper bound of 1, in α). We have confirmed that, for other MARG modules that may not output such a Confidence Factor, one can be derived from the variance of the accelerometer axes and the gyroscope axes [14].

3.2 Original Magnetometer Correction Trustworthiness, μ

In the case of the two "vector observations" made on the geomagnetic field within the operating space of the MARG, the violation of the field uniformity assumption is not due to a sensor ambiguity. In this case the actual magnetic field is, actually, not uniform in some regions of space. A local distortion of the magnetic field may occur because of the presence of an object which produces an additional magnetic field of its own (e. g., permanent magnet). A local magnetic field distortion may even be due to a ferromagnetic object which simply provides a path of lower magnetic permeability to the lines of magnetic flux, causing them to experience detours. Whichever the cause, the magnetic vector in the neighborhood of these magnetic disruptors will likely be different in direction and/or magnitude from the geomagnetic field, which is uniform within the reduced operating volume that we would contemplate for a human-computer interaction application of the MARG module. Unfortunately, contemporary built environments (dwellings, offices, laboratories, etc.) are bound to be constituted in part by structural elements containing these magnetic disrupters. In addition, many types of contemporary furniture pieces (e.g., desks, filing cabinets, etc.) will also contain ferromagnetic components, such that distortions of the geomagnetic field in the operating space of the

MARG, and their associated negative impacts on orientation estimates, cannot be ruled out [15, 19, 20].

On the other hand, within the prospective use of the MARG for human-computer interaction, the assumption may be made that those magnetic disrupters will likely be at constant locations (or moving slowly) within the operating space of the MARG. Accordingly, we previously sought to consider the level of distortion of the geomagnetic field as a function of the spatial location of a point, or rather a small "voxel" (e.g., 2 x 2 x 2 cm.), being considered. This initially seemed an appealing approach when we were developing a system for orientation *and position* tracking of the MARG module, utilizing a 3-infared-camera system (OptiTrack V120 Trio) to read the real-time X, Y, Z position of an infrared reflective marker attached to the MARG module. Having available the X, Y, and Z position of the MARG every time its orientation was estimated allowed us to, under some circumstances, assign a μ value to the "current voxel" and store it in a 3-dimensional map of the μ values within the expected operating space of the MARG (meant to be attached to a glove worn by the computer user, for that previous application). For the sake of caution, the μ value of all the voxels would be initialized to a value of 0, so that the magnetic corrections would be "blocked" in regions of space for which the system did not yet have evidence of an acceptable magnetic trustworthiness (μ close to 1).

During each iteration, GMV-D would first determine if the value of α is above a minimum threshold (exclusively for this purpose), $\alpha > \alpha_{THR}$. Only if that is the case, such that the accelerometer-based correction, $\boldsymbol{q}_{GA}$, can be considered to represent the true MARG orientation, the process of calculating a μ value for the current voxel could proceed. If the current value of α is found to be adequate, the accelerometer-corrected orientation, $\boldsymbol{q}_{GA}$, can be used to map $\boldsymbol{M}_{INIT}$ to the current MARG body frame, yielding a computed magnetic vector $\boldsymbol{m}(\boldsymbol{q}_{GA})$, which should (ideally, in the case in which there is no magnetic distortion at the current location of the MARG), closely approximate the direction determined by the current readings of the 3 magnetometer axes, in vector $\boldsymbol{m}_0$.

In general, the cosine of the 3-dimensional angle between the directions of $\boldsymbol{m}(\boldsymbol{q}_{GA})$ and $\boldsymbol{m}_0$, that is, $\cos(\gamma)$, can be found computing their dot product. That cosine is already a parametrization of the direction disparity of the computed magnetic vector and the actual magnetometer readings, with values from -1 (totally opposite directions) to + 1 (exactly the same direction). Associating that directional disparity to the magnetic distortion in the current location of the MARG, a decrease of $\cos(\gamma)$ from + 1 towards -1 would indicate the presence of a proportionally significant magnetic distortion at the current location of the MARG. The corresponding value of $0 \le \mu \le 1$ is computed by first applying a linear function to $\cos(\gamma)$, in order to more severely penalize any decrease from the ideal value of + 1, and then overwriting any negative results with a value of 0. A more detailed explanation of this initial formulation of μ, with the involvement of the positional information provided by the 3-infrared-camera system, can be found in [18].

3.3 New, Self-contained Magnetometer Correction Trustworthiness, μ_K

While the conceptualization of the magnetic distortion level, and consequently, the μ value as a function of X, Y, Z location is appealing from the physical point of view and could lead to the development of "re-usable" μ maps in cases where the MARG system is utilized repeatedly in the same room without frequent furniture re-assignments, it has a significant affordability drawback. MEMS MARG modules are particularly attractive in many circumstances due to their low cost (less than $20 USD for each wired module, bought in large quantities). But the involvement of a calibrated multi-IR-camera setup immediately raises the prospective overall cost of a combined tracking system. In addition to its higher cost, a system that requires multiple cameras would increase the time and complexity of the corresponding setup process.

Therefore, we have tackled the challenge of defining a new, alternative magnetometer-correction trustworthiness parameter, which we have designated as μ_K, that does not require any type of information from devices that are external to the MARG module under consideration. That is, we have developed a "self-contained" implementation of GMV-D where the new μ_K is used.

The goal in the development of μ_K and its use in GMV-D is to detect when the MARG has entered an area with significant distortion of the geomagnetic field, prior to the computation of the final orientation estimate of MARG orientation, $\boldsymbol{q}_{\mathrm{OUT}}$, for the current iteration. Accordingly, we will consider the human-computer interaction context in which the MARG is being used and leverage the (relatively) low range of speeds in the hand movements of a human computer user, so that we can adopt (tentatively, and just for the purpose of μ_K computation) the $\boldsymbol{q}_{\mathrm{OUT}}$ estimation resulting from the *previous* iteration, which we will designate $\boldsymbol{q}_{\mathrm{OUTprev}}$, as a useful approximation to the MARG orientation in the current iteration.

Under this assumption, we will "map back" the magnetic vector sensed in this iteration, $\boldsymbol{m}_0$, to the inertial reference frame, resulting in the vector $\boldsymbol{m}_{0\mathrm{i}}$:

$$\boldsymbol{m}_{0i} = \boldsymbol{q}_{OUTprev} \otimes \boldsymbol{m}_0 \otimes \boldsymbol{q}^*_{OUTprev} \tag{13}$$

This is necessary, so that the currently detected magnetic field *referenced to the inertial frame* can be properly compared against the initial (undistorted) magnetic vector recorded at startup, $\boldsymbol{M}_{\mathrm{INIT}}$, which is also referenced to the inertial frame. Once both magnetic vector directions are referenced to the same (inertial) frame we develop two intermediate parameters, μ_{KA} and μ_{KM}, which quantify the discrepancies in terms of angles and magnitudes between $\boldsymbol{M}_{\mathrm{INIT}}$ and $\boldsymbol{m}_{\mathrm{oi}}$, respectively.

The angular discrepancy is first assessed as the angle λ between the vectors through their inner product:

$$\lambda = \cos^{-1}\left[\frac{\boldsymbol{M}_{INITit} \cdot \boldsymbol{m}_{0i}}{||\boldsymbol{M}_{INIT}||\,||\boldsymbol{m}_{0i}||}\right] \tag{14}$$

Based on λ, we have formulated μ_{KA} to drop faster as the angle departs its ideal value of 0 (which would indicate no angular discrepancy, likely due to the absence of magnetic distortion). This is implemented through this linear equation:

$$\mu_{KA} = 1 - 1.5\lambda \tag{15}$$

In order to formulate μ_{KM} as a more specific quantification of the magnitude discrepancies between $\boldsymbol{M}_{\mathrm{INIT}}$ and $\boldsymbol{m}_{\mathrm{oi}}$, we defined a "penalty" parameter that grows from 0 only when it takes place simultaneously with considerable misalignment between $\boldsymbol{M}_{\mathrm{INIT}}$ and

$\boldsymbol{m}_{\mathrm{oi}}$, which is more likely attributable to actual magnetic distortion in the magnetic field currently sensed by the MARG:

$$penalty = \left[\frac{||\boldsymbol{m}_{0i}||}{||\boldsymbol{M}_{init}||}\right](\lambda) \tag{16}$$

and

$$\mu_{KM} = 1 - penalty \tag{17}$$

where any negative results for μ_{KM} will be overwritten with a value of 0.

The fusion of μ_{KA} and μ_{KM} takes place in a few steps, starting with the average of, μ_{KA} and μ_{KM} to define an intermediate result μ_1:

$$\mu_1 = [\mu_{KA} + \mu_{KM}]/2 \tag{18}$$

This intermediate parameter μ_1 is channeled through a First-In-First-Out (FIFO) structure, so that the current and immediately previous 5 values are available in any iteration. From these group of μ_1 values the minimum is extracted as μ_2. This is done so that spurious transient increases in the instantaneous value of μ_1 will still not be allowed to apply a strong magnetic correction, reserving that possibility for instances when μ_1 has been consistently high.

Finally, μ_{K} is obtained using μ_2 as a factor, where the other factor is α. This serves as a blocking mechanism that will "disable" large values of μ_2 computed during rapid movements which would be in violation of the initial assumption of slow or moderate motion (I.e., when α is not close to 0, we can better justify the use of $\boldsymbol{q}_{\mathrm{OUTprev}}$ as a valid approximation of the current MARG orientation).

$$\mu_K = (\mu_2)(\alpha) \tag{19}$$

4 Evaluation Protocol

4.1 Setup

We sought to assess the level of resilience that the GMV-D, with the newly formulated μ_{K}, would exhibit in estimating MARG orientation even in regions of space with known significant magnetic distortion. To that end, we designed a sequence of translations and rotations of the MARG that includes manipulations in both a magnetically undistorted area (A) and a magnetically distorted area (B), with the sequence starting and ending at a third position (also undistorted) that acted as "home location" (H). The Yost 3-Space Mini Wireless MARG module we used follows the "left-hand coordinate" convention, by default, and recorded data at sampling intervals of 70 ms. The 3 locations were arranged as a (horizontally) mirrored "L", with location (A) at the intersection of the 2 strokes of the L. The H-to-A stroke was approximately 30 cm. in length and ran North-to-South. The A-to-B stroke was approximately 40 cm. in length and ran East-to-West. The setup was placed away from iron furniture and all the necessary supports were made of wood. To create the magnetic distortion at B, a 0.5 x 3.8 x 37.5 cm steel bar was placed at B, right under a horizontal cardboard that served as a horizontal plane reference where H, A and B were located.

4.2 Manipulation Sequence and Poses

In each testing run, the MARG would be initialized (startup) at H, under magnetically undistorted and static conditions, as required by the algorithm. The module case laid flat with its "thickness" (its -Y axis) parallel to the plumb line ("POSE_1"). Then the following actions would be taken in the first half of the test run (not magnetically distorted):

Translation without rotation, H to A, keeping POSE_1 orientation throughout

+ 90° rotation about the Z body axis, defining POSE_2, and return to POSE_1

+ 90° rotation about the X body axis, defining POSE_3, and return to POSE_1

+ 90° rotation about the Y body axis, defining POSE_4, and return to POSE_1

Combined + 90° in X and - 45° in Y, defining POSE_5, and return to POSE_1

Then the MARG would be translated, without rotation, from A to B (landing in POSE_6, which is the same orientation as POSE_1) and the sequence described above would be replicated exactly, but now in B, i.e., within the magnetically distorted region:

+ 90° rotation about the Z body axis, defining POSE_7, and return to POSE_6

+ 90° rotation about the X body axis, defining POSE_8, and return to POSE_6

+ 90° rotation about the Y body axis, defining POSE_9, and return to POSE_6

Combined + 90° in X and - 45° in Y, defining POSE_10, and return to POSE_6

Finally, the MARG would be translated, without rotation, from B to H.

The resilience of a given orientation estimation algorithm can then be assessed by the similarity of the results obtained for poses 1-trough-5, in the magnetically undistorted region (A), in which most algorithms will provide satisfactory orientation estimates, and the results obtained for poses 6-through-10, in the magnetically distorted environment (B).

In the next section we display the time evolution of the orientation estimation quaternion components obtained from GMV-D, with μ_K, as well as those from benchmark orientation estimations: Kalman Filter [22] (computed within the YOST 3-Space MARG), and the Madgwick [5] and Mahony [6] algorithms, implemented in Matlab, as made available by Sebastian Madgwick at: at https://x-io.co.uk/open-source-imu-

and-ahrs-algorithms/. (Since the Matlab implementations posted by Madgwick are for a sensor that follows the "right-handed" coordinate convention, the sensor data directions needed to be reassigned and "re-sampling" had to be performed to obtain data sequences at an equivalent sampling rate of 256 Hz, which is the condition expected by the implementations provided in the website. Similarly, the output quaternion components needed to be re-organized.)

5 Results and Discussion

This section presents the results obtained from the GMV-D algorithm, using the newly proposed μ_K parameter for two representative sequences of manipulations which followed the schedule described in Subsect. 4.2. For each one of the sequences, we first present the evolution of the novel parameter μ_K and its μ_{KA} and μ_{KM} components, accompanying the evolution of quaternion components from GMV-D and from the on-chip implementation of a Kalman Filter (KF). Then we compare the quaternion evolution from GMV-D with the corresponding results from two other contemporary methods.

5.1 Results from Two Experimental Sequences

Figure 2 displays on its top panel the evolution of the values of the components μ_{KA} and μ_{KM}, the overall novel parameter μ_K and the evolution of the 4 components of the orientation quaternion computed by GMV-D, where the timing of the poses held in the magnetically undistorted region (A) is indicated by blue underlined numbers ($\underline{1}$, $\underline{2}$, $\underline{3}$, $\underline{4}$, $\underline{5}$), and the timing of the poses held in the magnetically distorted region (B) is indicated by red underlined numbers ($\underline{6}$, $\underline{7}$, $\underline{8}$, $\underline{9}$, $\underline{10}$). For comparison, the evolution of the quaternion components calculated by the on-chip Kalman Filter are also shown. It should be noted, in this top panel, that both GMV-D and KF report essentially the same quaternions for the first part of the record (poses $\underline{1}$, $\underline{2}$, $\underline{3}$, $\underline{4}$, $\underline{5}$), which were held in the magnetically undistorted area. However, for the poses held in the magnetically distorted area (poses $\underline{6}$, $\underline{7}$, $\underline{8}$, $\underline{9}$, $\underline{10}$), the results from GMV-D and KF differ considerably. Since the sequence of orientations is the same as for the first part of the record, the GMV-D output seems correct as it closely resembles the patterns generated for the first half. In contrast, the KF output for the second half is markedly different from its output for the first half, indicating that the KF orientation estimator has succumbed to the presence of the magnetic distortion in B. It is also interesting to note that GMV-D is disregarding the prospective magnetometer-based corrections during poses $\underline{6}$, $\underline{7}$, $\underline{8}$, $\underline{9}$, $\underline{10}$, as evidenced by the zero value acquired by μ_K during that interval.

The bottom panel of Fig. 2 serves the purpose of comparing the evolution of components from the GMV-D quaternion (showed, again, with the timing of the poses indicated by underlined numbers), to the evolutions of quaternions generated from the same accelerometer, gyroscope and magnetometer data by the Madgwick and Mahony algorithms. The same comments made above for the output of the Kalman Filter apply to the outputs of these two other algorithms. All in all, these figures confirm that GMV-D has displayed a much higher level of resilience to the distortion of the magnetic field, by appropriately suppressing (μ_K close to 0) the involvement of the magnetometer signals in the correction of the initial orientation derived by integration of the gyroscope signals.

The two panels in Fig. 3 are organized in the same way as for Fig. 2 and simply present the results from a different experimental run, where the timing of the rotations in the same sequence is slightly different. The same general behavior and conclusions derived from Fig. 2 apply to Fig. 3 as well.

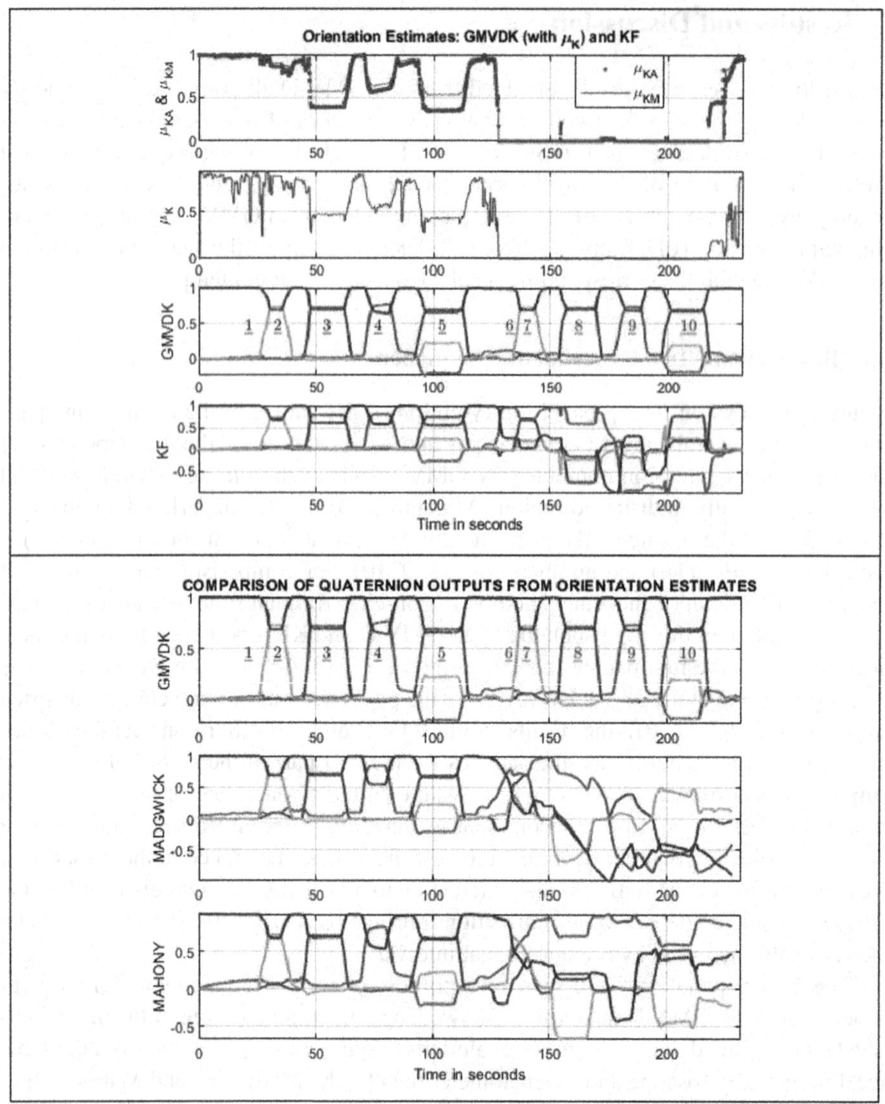

Fig. 2. – **Record 1** [TOP] Time evolution of the μ_K magnetometer trustworthiness parameter and its components μ_{KA} and μ_{KM}, along with the 4 components of the resulting orientation quaternion produced by GMV-D. The blue underlined numbers indicate the timing of the poses held in the magnetically undistorted location. The red underlined numbers indicate the timing of the poses held in the magnetically distorted location. The 4 quaternion components generated by a Kalman Filter are shown for comparison. [BOTTOM] Components of the GMV-D quaternion are compared with those generated by the Madgwick and Mahony algorithms.

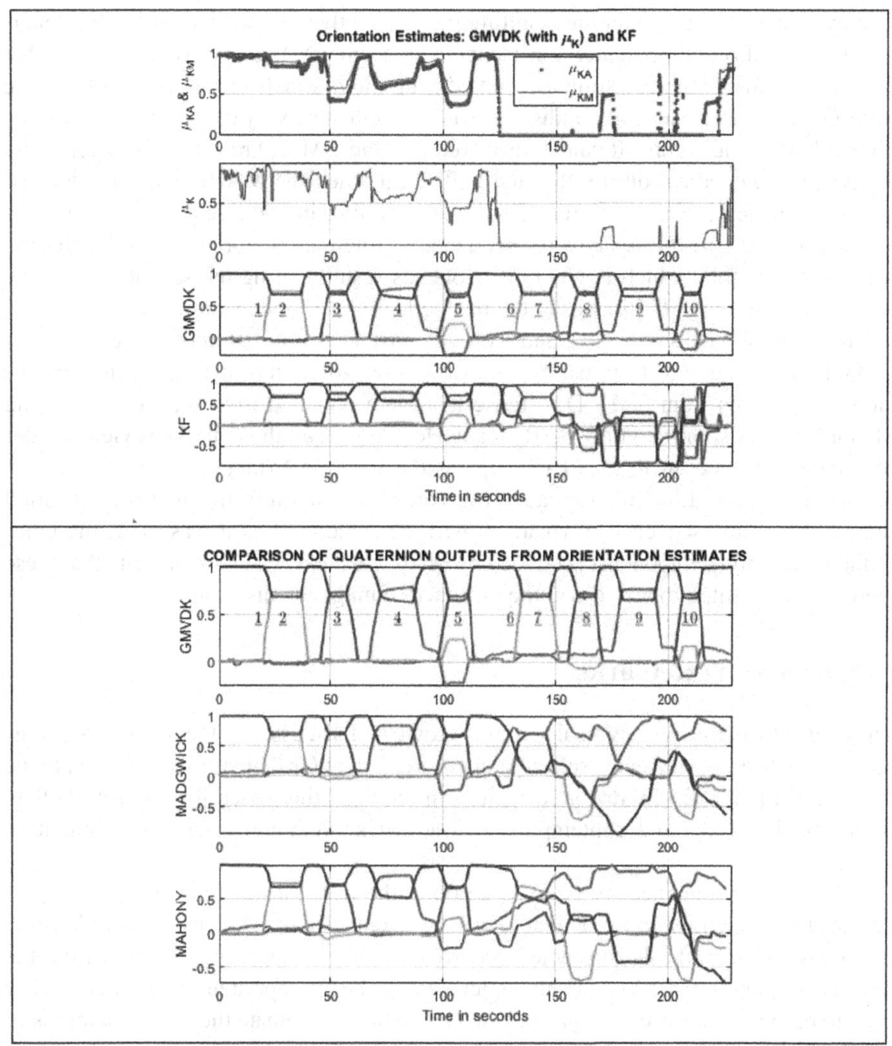

Fig. 3. – **Record 2** [TOP] Time evolution of the μ_K magnetometer trustworthiness parameter and its components μ_{KA} and μ_{KM}, along with the 4 components of the resulting orientation quaternion produced by GMV-D. The blue underlined numbers indicate the timing of the poses held in the magnetically undistorted location. The red underlined numbers indicate the timing of the poses held in the magnetically distorted location. The 4 quaternion components generated by a Kalman Filter are shown for comparison. [BOTTOM] Components of the GMV-D quaternion are compared with those generated by the Madgwick and Mahony algorithms.

5.2 Discussion

The top panel of Figs. 2 and 3 confirm that the newly proposed μ_K parameter effectively drops to 0 during the portion of the recordings in which the MARG was in the neighborhood of the magnetically distorted location, B. Both the μ_{KA} and μ_{KM} components display a sharp decrease and the resulting μ_K is effectively cancelled during that interval. The evolution of the quaternion components from GMV-D and from KF show that both algorithms yield very similar results during the first half of the record (while the MARG was in a magnetically undistorted area) but display very different results for the second half of the record. It can be observed that the GMV-D results closely resemble the results it generated during the first half, even when the MARG was now located in the magnetically distorted area. This is reasonable, since the sequence of rotations performed in B *was the same* as the sequence of rotations performed in A. Therefore, it is the KF method which is yielding erroneous results during the second part of the recording, while the MARG was in the magnetically distorted location (B).

The bottom panels of Figs. 2 and 3 provide further confirmation of the resilience of GMV-D to magnetic distortions, by comparing the evolution of the orientation quaternion components from GMV-D to those that were obtained from the Madgwick and Mahony methods for the same MARG data. Here, again, all three methods yield similar orientation estimates while the MARG operated in location A (magnetically undistorted) but generated very different orientation estimates for location B (magnetically distorted region). Since the sequence of rotations was the same in B as it was in A, the unfamiliar quaternion components produced by Madgwick and Mahoney indicate that these methods had limited robustness to the presence of magnetic distortions.

6 Concluding Remarks

The results from two prototypical test runs shown and discussed in the previous sections seem to confirm that the new "self-contained" version of GMV-D is more resilient to the existence of magnetically distorted regions in the operating space for the MARG than some classical (KF) and contemporary (Madgwick, Mahony) orientation estimation algorithms.

The autonomy gained by GMV-D through the new formulation of μ_K is important at the conceptual and practical levels. Conceptually, it has presented a plausible mechanism to identify the suspected occurrence of local magnetic distortion from the sensors contained in the MARG alone, leveraging the appropriateness of one modality (i.e., iterations with large-enough α), when available, to evaluate the appropriateness of a different modality (i.e., to compute μ_K as a trustworthiness parameter for the magnetometer information). Practically, the "self-contained" character of the new version of GMV-D relieves potential users of this approach pursuing only the determination of orientation from having to include in the setup a typically much more expensive position tracking device. Furthermore, the new GMV-D might be suitable for pairing with a lower-resolution position tracking system when seeking the combined determination of position and orientation. In that respect, the new version of GMV-D may finally allow the utilization of MARG sensors for human-computer applications such as hand-tracking without a strong dependency on particularly expensive high-end vision tracking components.

Acknowledgments. This work was supported by the US National Science Foundation grants CNS-1532061 and CNS-1920182.

References

1. Abyarjoo, F., Barreto, A., Abyarjoo, S., Ortega, F.R., Cofino, J.: Monitoring human wrist rotation in three degrees of freedom. In: 2013 Proceedings of IEEE Southeastcon, pp. 1–5 (2013)
2. Hanson, A.: Visualizing Quaternions. Morgan Kaufmann Series in Interactive 3D Technology.: Morgan Kaufmann. Elsevier Science distributor, Boston, p. 498 (2006)
3. Johnson, R.C.: 3-Axis MEMs gyro chip debuts. EE Times (2009). https://www.eetimes.com/3-axis-mems-gyro-chip-debuts/
4. Kuipers, J.B.: Quaternions and rotation sequences: a primer with applications to orbits, aerospace, and virtual reality, p. 371. Princeton University Press, Princeton, N.J, xxii (1999)
5. Madgwick, S.: An efficient orientation filter for inertial and inertial/magnetic sensor arrays. Report x-io and University of Bristol (UK) **25**, pp. 113-118 (2010)
6. Mahony, R., Hamel, T., Pflimlin, J.-M.: Nonlinear complementary filters on the special orthogonal group. IEEE Trans. Autom. Control **53**(5), 1203–1218 (2008)
7. Markley, F.L., Mortari, D.: Quaternion Attitude Estimation Using Vector Observations. J. Astronaut. Sci. **48**(2–3), 359–380 (2000). https://doi.org/10.1007/BF03546284
8. O-larnnithipong, N.: Hand motion tracking system using inertial measurement units and infrared cameras. In: Electrical and Computer Engineering Department. Florida International University, Miami, Florida, USA (2018)
9. O-larnnithipong, N., Barreto, A.: Gyroscope drift correction algorithm for inertial measurement unit used in hand motion tracking. IEEE SENSORS. **2016**, 1–3 (2016)
10. O-larnnithipong, N., Barreto, A., Tangnimitchok, S., Ratchatanantakit, N.: Orientation correction for a 3D hand motion tracking interface using inertial measurement units. In: Kurosu, M. (ed.) HCI 2018. LNCS, vol. 10903, pp. 321–333. Springer, Cham (2018). https://doi.org/10.1007/978-3-319-91250-9_25
11. O-larnnithipong, N., Barreto, A., Ratchatanantakit, N., Tangnimitchok, S., Ortega, F.R.: Real-time implementation of orientation correction algorithm for 3D hand motion tracking interface. In: Antona, M., Stephanidis, C. (eds.) UAHCI 2018. LNCS, vol. 10907, pp. 228–242. Springer, Cham (2018). https://doi.org/10.1007/978-3-319-92049-8_17
12. Nonnarit, O., Ratchatanantakit, N., Tangnimitchok, S., Ortega, F., Barreto, A.: Hand tracking interface for virtual reality interaction based on MARG sensors. In: 2019 IEEE Conference on Virtual Reality and 3D User Interfaces (VR), pp. 1717–1722 (2019)
13. O-larnnithipong, N., Ratchatanantakit, N., Tangnimitchok, S., Ortega, F.R., Barreto, A., Adjouadi, M.: Statistical analysis of novel and traditional orientation estimates from an IMU-instrumented glove. In: Antona, M., Stephanidis, C. (eds.) Universal Access in Human-Computer Interaction. Multimodality and Assistive Environments. HCII 2019. Lecture Notes in Computer Science(), vol. 11573, pp. 282–299. Springer, Cham (2019). https://doi.org/10.1007/978-3-030-23563-5_23
14. Ratchatanantakit, N.: Digital processing of magnetic, angular-rate, and gravity signals for human-computer interaction. In: Electrical and Computer Engineering Department, Florida International University, Miami, Florida, USA (2021)
15. Ratchatanantakit, N., O-larnnithipong, N., Barreto, A., Tangnimitchok, S.: Consistency study of 3D magnetic vectors in an office environment for IMU-based hand tracking input development. In: Kurosu, M. (ed.) HCII 2019. LNCS, vol. 11567, pp. 377–387. Springer, Cham (2019). https://doi.org/10.1007/978-3-030-22643-5_29
16. Ratchatanantakit, N., Nonnarit, O., Sonchan, P., Adjouadi, M., Barreto, A.: Live demonstration: double SLERP gravity-magnetic vector (GMV-D) orientation correction in a MARG sensor. In; 2021 IEEE Sensors, p. 1 (2021)

17. Ratchatanantakit, N., O-larnnithipong, N., Sonchan, P., Adjouadi, M., Barreto, A.: Statistical evaluation of orientation correction algorithms in a real-time hand tracking application for computer interaction. In: Kurosu, M. (eds.) Human-Computer Interaction. Technological Innovation. HCII 2022. Lecture Notes in Computer Science, vol. 13303, pp. 92–108. Springer, Cham (2022).https://doi.org/10.1007/978-3-031-05409-9_8
18. Ratchatanantakit, N., O-larnnithipong, N., Sonchan, P., Adjouadi, M., Barreto, A.: A sensor fusion approach to MARG module orientation estimation for a real-time hand tracking application. Inf. Fusion **90**, 298–315 (2023)
19. Roetenberg, D., Luinge, H., Veltink, P.: Inertial and magnetic sensing of human movement near ferromagnetic materials. In: Second IEEE and ACM International Symposium on Mixed and Augmented Reality 2003, pp. 268-269. IEEE (2003)
20. Roetenberg, D., Luinge, H.J., Baten, C.T.M., Veltink, P.H.: Compensation of magnetic disturbances improves inertial and magnetic sensing of human body segment orientation. IEEE Trans. Neural Syst. Rehabil. Eng. **13**(3), 395–405 (2005)
21. Shoemake, K.: Animating rotation with quaternion curves. SIGGRAPH Comput. Graph. **19**(3), 245–254 (1985)
22. Simon, D.: Kalman filtering. Embedded systems programming, vol. 14, no.6, pp. 72–79 (2001)
23. Vince, J.: Quaternions for Computer Graphics. Springer, New York, p. xiv, p. 140 (2011)
24. YostLabs 3-Space Sensor Miniature Attitude & Heading Reference System with Pedestrian Tracking User's Manual (2017)

One-Handed Character Input Method Without Screen Cover for Smart Glasses that Does not Require Visual Confirmation of Fingertip Position

Takahiro Yamada, Toshimitsu Tanaka(✉), and Yuji Sagawa

Meijo University, Shiogamaguchi 1-501, Tenpaku-Ku, Nagoya, Japan
223441701@ccmailg.meijo-u.ac.jp

Abstract. We have developed a one-handed character input method that allows you to use a regular smartphone as an input device. Each character is entered in two steps.

Japanese hiragana characters are divided into 10 groups of 5 characters each, and alphanumeric characters are divided into 8 groups. In the first step, you select a group by rotating your thumb around the base of your thumb. Place your thumb on the left half of the touch screen and rotate your thumb clockwise that enables to switch groups in ascending order. You can see the group name on your smart glasses. You can also reveal the group in descending order by moving your thumb counterclockwise from the right half. The displayed group is selected when you remove your thumb from the touch screen.

In the second step, one character in the group is selected by a tap or a flick. This operation is the same as the well-known flick input. However, taps are accepted anywhere in the bottom half of the screen. Flicks and taps are distinguished by the movement on the touch screen, so you can start flicks anywhere on the touch screen. In both steps, the touch position is only roughly specified. Therefore, you do not need to see your finger to operate.

In an experiment targeting beginners, the average input speed of 6 subjects was 18.4 [CPM] when each of them enters about 250 characters, and the total error rate was 3.3%.

Keywords: Character input · One-hand operation · Touch typing · Smart glasses · Mobile

1 Introduction

More recently, head-mounted displays (HMDs) have been used in virtual reality, 3D computer games, the metaverse, and more. Smart glasses, which are see-through type HMDs, allow you to see the virtual image superimposed on the real scenery. In particular, Vuzix Blade and Nreal Air have the same shape as regular glasses, so you can wear them around town without feeling awkward. So you can use smart glasses as a mobile display for your PC or smartphone on the go.

M. Kurosu and A. Hashizume (Eds.): HCII 2023, LNCS 14011, pp. 603–614, 2023.
https://doi.org/10.1007/978-3-031-35596-7_39

Both virtual and real images can be seen through smart glasses, but it is not a good idea to perform input operations on a smartphone and see the results on smart glasses. The distance from the eyes to the virtual screen is set to 2.5–5.0m for normal smart glasses, but the distance between the smartphone held in the hand and the eyes is only 0.5m. So our eyes cannot focus on both distances at the same time. As a result, we are forced to alternately look at our smartphones and virtual screens. This causes eye strain.

Most of the applications on computers and smartphones can be operated using pointing and keyboard input. With pointing, move the cursor displayed on the screen with the mouse or touchpad and click. You don't need to look at your hand for this operation. Smartphones are operated by touching the screen with a finger, but it is possible to replace it with a pointer operation with a mouse. Many smartphones come pre-installed with telephone or QWERTY software keyboards. Telephone keyboards have fewer keys than QWERTY keyboards, but still have about 20 keys. Software keyboards require a visual aid to select a key because you can't find the keys by touching them with your fingers. Therefore, as a character input method to replace the software keyboard, several input methods that do not require looking at the hand have been developed.

The method that we presented at HCII2022 [1] uses a smartphone covered with a plate with holes as an input device. Touch operation is possible only in the holes. Since you can predict the position of your finger by touching the edge of the hole, you can operate without looking at your finger. However, in order to use a smartphone for general purpose, it is necessary to attach and detach the cover every time you enter characters. In addition, estimating the finger position by the tactile sense of the fingertip has a larger error than visual confirmation, so the input error rate is high.

Therefore, we have developed a method without a cover. The input device is a bare smartphone. You can enter characters with simple operations such as tapping, flicking, and turning. The places where these operations are performed are only loosely restricted, for example the top or bottom, or left or right of the touch screen. In addition, you can check the characters that can be selected on the screen. Therefore, you can operate without looking at your hand.

2 Related Researches

Many techniques have been developed for entering text outdoors or on the move.

Speech recognition [2–4] is a popular technique for entering text without using a keyboard. If you speak clearly in a quiet place, the recognition rate is sufficiently high, but misrecognition increases in a noisy city. A significant drawback is that the speaker's voice is heard by others, so the speaker's privacy is not protected. Another drawback is that it takes a lot of time and effort to fix typos with just voice commands. In addition, it cannot be used in places where quietness is required.

Another developed method is to use fingers, hands, or arm gestures to select characters from an on-screen keyboard displayed on a head mounted display [5–7]. These methods require motion capture devices such as game controllers, motion sensors, and depth cameras to detect hand position and arm orientation. Such devices should be carried outdoors. The on-screen keyboard takes up a lot of screen space. The input speed is not fast with the method of pointing characters on the screen keyboard one by one.

A method of typing on a 3D virtual keyboard in mid-air [8, 9] has been developed, but mastering this method requires training.

Gesture-based methods can also be used in mobile environments. However, you should carry a motion detection device such as a data glove [10] or finger ring [11, 12], a video camera for motion capture, or a game controller with an accelerometer. Also, in a crowded place, the method of drawing letters in the air [11] cannot be used because the arm will bump into nearby people. Virtual keyboards that project key patterns on to the back of a hand or arm have been developed [13, 14]. However, you must select a key after visually confirming the position of your fingertip. All of those methods require looking at both a nearby hand and a faraway virtual screen, so eye-focus problems cannot avoid.

Methods have been developed to detect the position of the thumb by attaching touch sensors [15, 16] or micro touch panels [17] to the fingers. With these, one-handed eyes-free character input is possible. These sensors and panels get in the way, come off, or break when users grab things with your hands. However, it is not practical to attach and detach the sensors and panels every time you enter characters.

There are devices on the market that allow you to enter characters just by tapping fingers. Tap Strap 2 [18] is a device with five rings connected by a string. Each ring detects taps of the inserted finger. Fingers in tapping can also be detected by the TapXR [19] worn on the wrist. If you can memorize the finger combinations assigned to letters, you can type them quickly without visual aids, but it takes a lot of practice.

Some methods specify the character from the orientation and rotation of the wrist [20–22]. However, it is difficult to input long sentences by these methods because the wrist gets tired. It also takes a long time to learn, as you have to memorize the wrist movements assigned to each letter.

As a character input method for smart glasses used outdoors, there is a demand for (1) a portable input device, (2) operability with one hand, and (3) no need to visually confirm the finger position. The first condition is essential for carrying the device. A second condition is required to hold a bag, grab a strap, hold an umbrella, or open a door with the other hand. The third is necessary to avoid vision-taxing focusing problems caused by alternately looking at the hand and the virtual screen.

We presented a method satisfying these three conditions at HCII2022 [1]. Its input device is a smartphone covered with a plate as shown in Fig. 1. The black part of the cover is cut out. Enter one character in two steps. In the first step, select one of the groups of 5 characters with a stroke. A stroke begins at one of the four endpoints of the cross-shaped hole and ends at one of the other endpoints. In the second step, select one letter in that group by tapping or flicking within the cross-shaped area. Holes placed in the corners are used to type space, backspace, enter, etc.

You can predict the position of your finger by touching the edge of the hole, so you can operate without looking at your finger. However, the four endpoints of the cross-shaped area and the four circles, which are the touchable positions, are close to each other and have similar outlines, so selection errors are likely to occur. Also, unfortunately, you cannot use your everyday smartphone as an on-demand input device. This is because the cover must be firmly fixed to the touch panel. In order to eliminate the inconvenience of carrying a specific input device additionally, we have developed a method that does not require a screen cover.

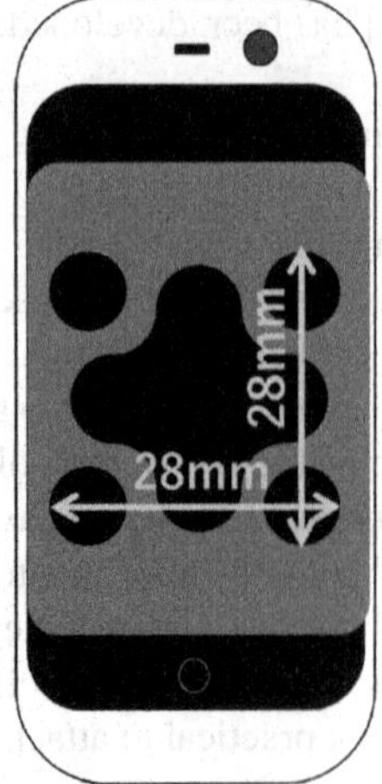

Fig. 1. The input device with a screen cover from the previous method.

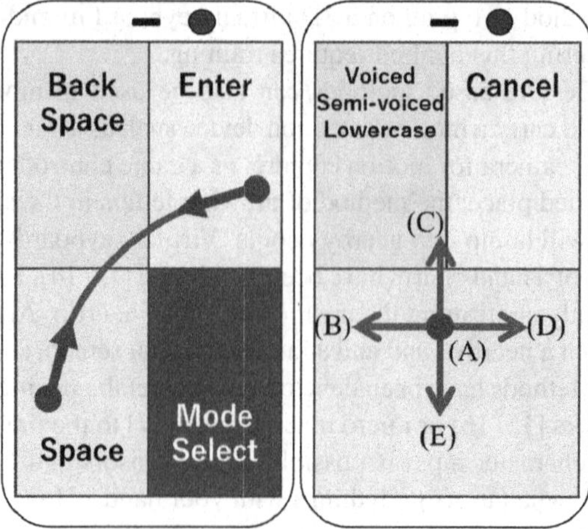

Fig. 2. Function allocation and input operation of the proposed method.

3 Proposed Method

In the proposed method, one character is selected in two steps as in the previous method. So, in the first step, one out of ten letter groups is selected. In the second step, select one character out of the five characters contained in the selected group. However, we have improved the operation to reduce misoperation. Also, the restrictions on the touch position have got less.

At the first step, the touch screen is divided vertically and horizontally into four regions, as shown in Fig. 2(a). Space, backspace, and enter are assigned to the lower-left, upper-left, and upper-right areas, respectively. The bottom right area is difficult to touch because the thumb has to be bent a lot when operating with the right hand. Thus, we assign this area the function for switching alphanumeric mode and Japanese hiragana mode, because this function is used less frequently.

When holding a smartphone with one hand, the place where the tip of the thumb can reach when the base of the thumb is turned is the easiest to touch. The red arc in Fig. 2(a) shows the path of the thumb when turned. So we decided to select a letter group with that thumb rotation. Hiragana characters are divided into 10 groups of 5 characters each, as shown in Fig. 3. Alphanumeric characters are divided into 8 groups. Touch the left side of the screen with your thumb and move it clockwise. There are no position restrictions as long as the touch is to the left of the centerline. When the distance traveled exceeds a certain length, the first group will appear on the screen. "あ" is displayed in hiragana mode, and "a" is displayed in alphanumeric mode.

After that, every time you move your thumb a certain distance, the display switches to the group on the right in Fig. 3. Moving your thumb back to the left also moves the displayed group back. The displayed group can be selected by lifting your finger from the screen. This operation can also be initiated from the right side. In this case, moving

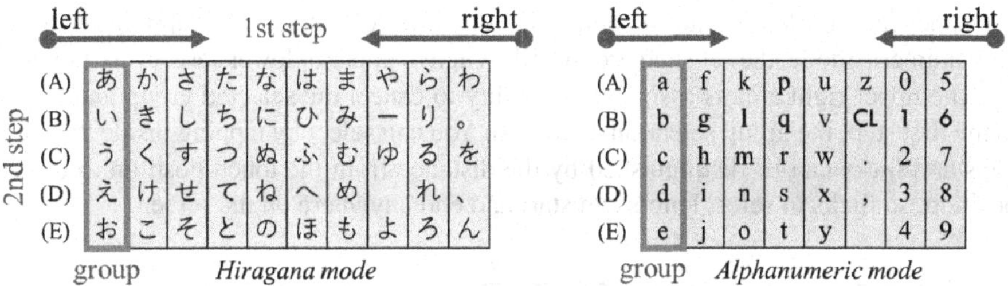

Fig. 3. Character groups and character selection process.

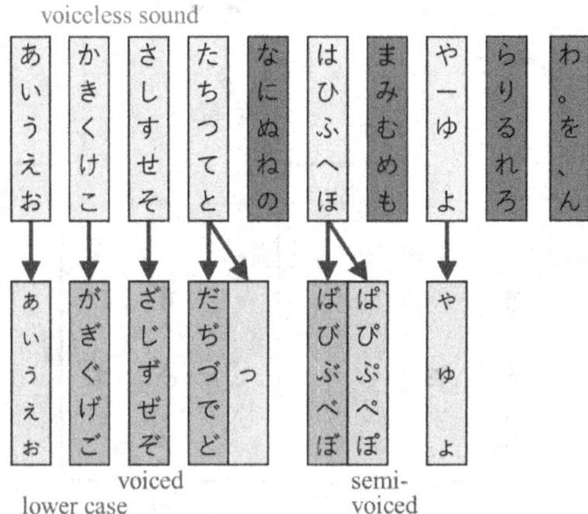

Fig. 4. Some hiragana groups are switched to related voiced, semi-voiced, or lowercase groups by tapping upper left area.

the thumb to the left displays the character groups in reverse order, starting with the last group. This touch interaction occurs in the four tap areas shown above, but group selection and taps can be separated by distance traveled. If the distance from the touch position to the up position is less than a threshold, the system considers the action to be a tap, otherwise it considers it a group select.

Flick keyboard is the most popular text input method, at least on Japanese smartphones. Here, 5 characters are assigned to one key. The user taps or flicks a key to select a single letter. Many people are familiar with this operation, so we decided to select characters in the same way in the second step. Specifically, the first character in a group can be selected by tapping. In the second step, the touch screen is divided into upper and lower parts. The bottom area is used for this tapping. The second through fifth characters of the group can be selected by flicking left, up, right, or down respectively.

The upper part is further divided into left and right as shown in Fig. 2(b). By tapping upper left area, some hiragana groups are switched to related voiced, semi-voiced, or lowercase character groups as shown in Fig. 4. The upper groups in Fig. 4 are the pre-change groups selected in the first step. Groups painted gray are voiceless sound only and cannot be changed. Groups with two variations will change to voiced letters by tapping the upper left area once, and to semi-voiced or lowercase letters by tapping again. In alphanumeric mode, the selected group will switch to upper or lower case, every tapping.

The upper right area is assigned the ability to cancel the selected group and return to the first step, the group selection operation. You can select by tapping inside the area. Taps and flicks can be distinguished by the distance from the touch position to the up position, so flicks to select letters can start and end anywhere on the screen.

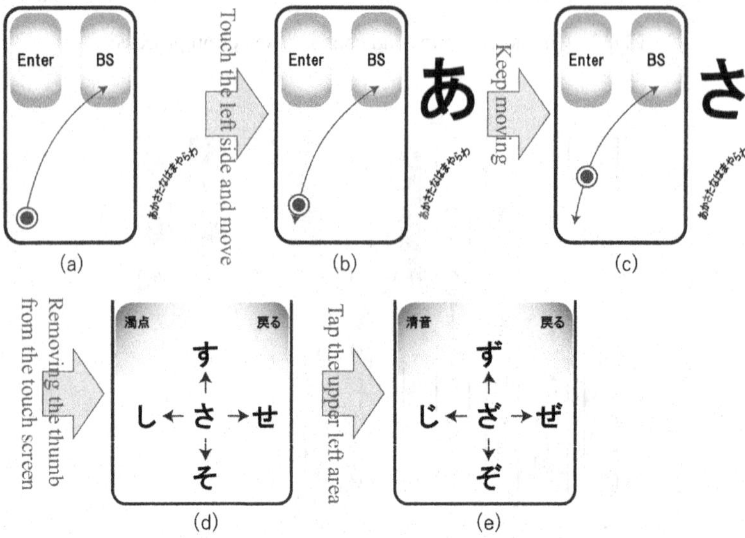

Fig. 5. The display of the input guide changes as the input operation progresses.

A guide image is displayed on smart glasses to assist operations. Figure 5(a) is an image of standby. If you place your thumb on the upper left area and move it to the right, the image switches to Fig. 5(b). The large letters on the right indicate which group is selected when you lift your thumb off the touch screen. Each time you move your thumb a certain distance, the displayed groups change. If you release your thumb while the "さ" group is displayed as shown in Fig. 5(c), the guide image will change to Fig. 5(d) and the five characters included in the group will be displayed. The position of the letter indicates the direction of the flick to select it. For example, the character "し" can be selected with a left flick.

4 Experiments and Results for Beginners

In this chapter, we will evaluate the beginners input speed and error rate.

4.1 Procedure of Beginner Experiment

As an input device, we used Unihertz Jelly Pro JPRO-03, a micro smartphone equipped with Android 7.0. In the experiment, Jelly Pro detects touch gestures, updates input guides, displays task words, and records input operations. A small monitor displays information to subjects instead of smart glasses in this experiment. The number of test subjects is 6. Prior to this experiment, they had never used this input system.

At the beginning of the experiment, the subjects were given a 10-min presentation on the operation procedure for character input, the meaning of the input guide display, the experimental procedure, and precautions. Subjects were then asked to type the characters as accurately as possible. Each subject sat in a chair in a normal posture, grabbed the Jelly Pro by his right hand, and operated the input system with his thumb. In this experiment, subjects put their hands in black bags to hide their thumbs, as shown in Fig. 6.

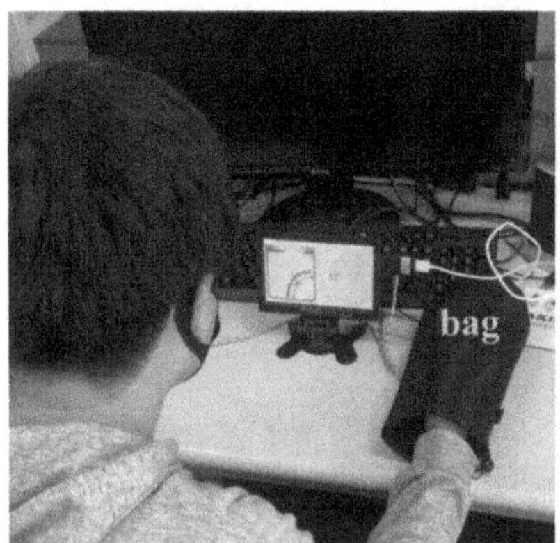

Fig. 6. A subject during an experiment.

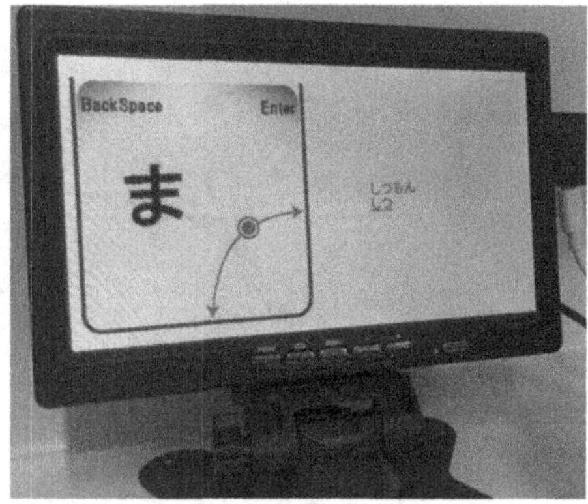

Fig. 7. Monitor display during experiment.

Subjects enter 5 hiragana words in one task. In the experiment, this task is repeated 10 times every between with a 3-min break. Each task starts when a subject's thumb touches the input device. A single task word written in hiragana is displayed on the right side of a small monitor placed in front of the subject. The characters entered by the subject appear just below the task word. On the left side of the monitor, an input guide will appear as shown in Fig. 7. After entering all the characters of the task word, tap the upper right area to input Enter. Then the next word is displayed. Enter is accepted even if some of the characters you input do not match the words in the task. Enter 5 words to complete one task.

The task words were selected from the word list of the Balanced Corpus of Contemporary Written Japanese (BCCWJ) [23] of the National Institute for Japanese Language and Linguistics. From each of the 4, 5, and 6-letter nouns in hiragana notation, 100 words were extracted in order of frequency, excluding numbers and quantifiers. Then words which are same in hiragana notation but different in Kanji notation were merged. Frequency of the merged word is sum of frequency of the original words. Finally, the top 50 words in frequency from each of 4, 5, and 6-letter words were selected. Those 150 words have been combined into one list. In the experiment, 5 words are randomly selected from the list for each task.

4.2 Results of Beginner Experiment

The thin line in Fig. 8 is the input speed of each subject. The thick line indicates the average input speed of the 6 subjects. The input speed of each test subject varied greatly from task to task. The average input speed also fluctuates, but basically increases with the number of tasks. However, after the third task, the speed increase was slow. The average input speed of the first task is about 11 [CPM: characters per minute]. In the 10th task, it reached 18.4 [CPM].

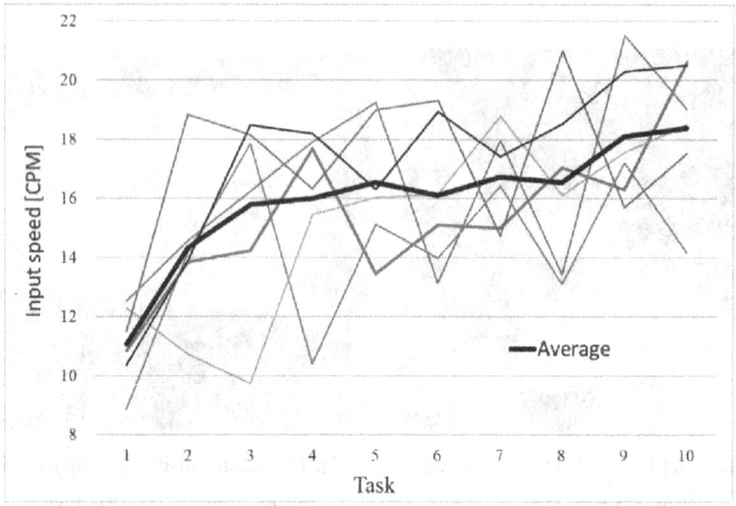

Fig. 8. The input speed of each of the 6 beginners and their average.

Figure 9 shows the total error rate (TER) [24]. Each thin line is a beginner's TER. Graphs vary greatly by subject and task. This is because only about 25 characters are entered for each task, so one error character increases TER by about 4%. The average TER of the 6 beginners, indicated by the bold line, decreased slowly in the second half of the experiment, and reached 3.3% at the tenth task.

Input speed and total error rate were compared with the previous method using screen cover [1]. As shown in Fig. 10, the input speed decreased by about 20% at the 10th task. Since the operation of selecting a character from a group of characters is the same for both methods, this difference in speed is likely due to the difference in group selection operations. In the proposed method, it is necessary to confirm on the guide image which group will be selected when the thumb is released from the touch screen. The former method, on the other hand, does not require confirmation as it selects with different strokes for each group. Therefore, it is thought that the input speed has slowed down for the confirmation time.

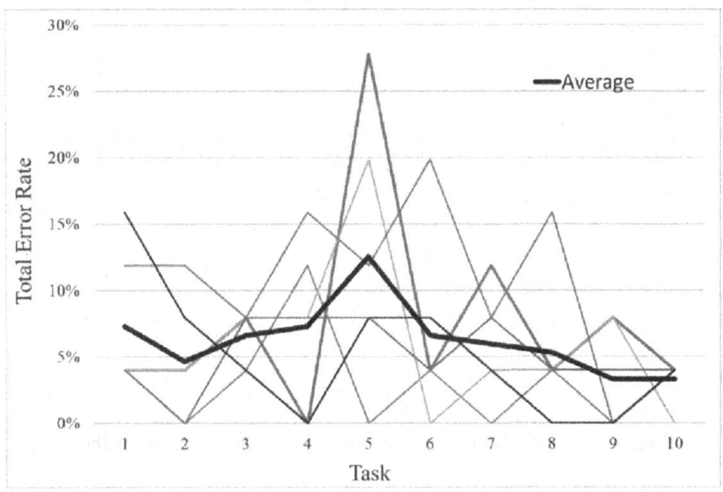

Fig. 9. The total error rate of each of the 6 beginners and their average.

Contrary to prior expectations, the total error rate of the proposed method was slightly reduced over the previous method, as shown in Fig. 11. The proposed method has looser constraints on the touch position than the conventional method. The decrease in TER is thought to be due to a decrease in input errors due to touch position deviation.

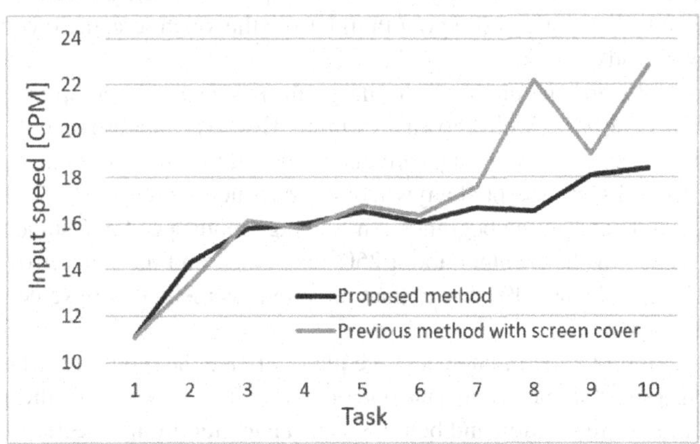

Fig. 10. Comparison of input speed with the previous method.

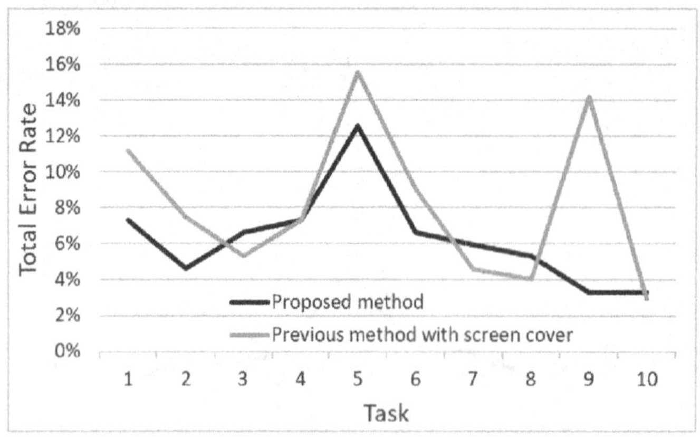

Fig. 11. Comparison of total error rate with the previous method.

5 Conclusion

We have developed a one-handed character input method that allows you to use your regular smartphone as an input device. Each character is entered in two steps. Hiragana is divided into 10 groups of 5 characters each. The first step is to select a group by rotating the thumb around the base of the thumb. Place your thumb on the left half of your smartphone's touch screen and rotate your thumb clockwise to reveal one group on your smart glasses. Continue moving to switch groups in ascending order. The displayed group is selected when you remove your thumb from the touch screen. So you don't have to look at your hands.

In the second step, one character in the group is selected by a tap or a flick. This operation is the same as the well-known flick input. However, taps are accepted anywhere below half the screen. Flicks and taps are distinguished by the movement distance from touch to up, so flicks are accepted anywhere on the touch screen.

In an experiment targeting beginners, the average input speed of 6 subjects was 18.4 [CPM] when each of them enters about 250 characters, and the total error rate (TER) was 3.3%. The speed was 20% slower than the previous method with screen cover. The TER was almost same.

In order to improve the input speed, we plan to make the input procedure one step. When holding a smartphone in one hand and operating it with the thumb, the most natural thumb movements are rotation and bending. The character group selection operation in the proposed method is just that rotation. But, flicking to select a character from the group is up, down, left, and right with respect to the smartphone screen, so you must move your thumb by the combination of the rotation and bending/stretching. So, we replace the selection by taps and flicks to the selection by length of the bended thumb. Rotate your thumb until you see the group you want to select, then flex your thumb in continue. When the character you want to enter is displayed, you lift your thumb off the touch screen and select it. The motion of this operation is one-step and easy to execute. Thus, input speed may be improved.

References

1. Tanaka, T., Ogawa, N., Tsuboi, R., Sagawa, Y.: One-Handed character input method for smart glasses that does not require visual confirmation of fingertip position. In: Kurosu, M. (eds.) Human-Computer Interaction. Technological Innovation. HCII 2022. Lecture Notes in Computer Science, vol. 13303, pp. 165–179. Springer, Cham (2022). https://doi.org/10.1007/978-3-031-05409-9_13
2. Alexa Voice Service Overview (v20160207). https://developer.amazon.com/docs/alexa-voice-service/api-overview.html. Accessed 14 Jan 2023
3. Use Siri on all your Apple devices. https://support.apple.com/en-us/HT204389. Accessed 14 Jan 2023
4. Google Assistant is better than Alexa or Siri. https://www.cnbc.com/2019/06/19/google-assistant-beats-alexa-and-siri-at-recognizing-medications.html. Accessed 14 Jan 2023
5. Grubert, J., et al.: Text entry in immersive head-mounted display-based virtual reality using standard keyboards. In: 25th IEEE Conference on Virtual Reality and 3D User Interfaces, VR 2018 - Proceedings, pp.159–166 (2018)
6. Boletsis, C., Kongsvik, S.: Text input in virtual reality: a preliminary evaluation of the drum-like VR keyboard. Technologies **7**(2), 1–10 (2019)
7. Yu, C., et al.: Tap, dwell or gesture?: Exploring head-based text entry techniques for HMDS. In Proceedings of the 2017 CHI Conference on Human Factors in Computing Systems, pp.4479–4488 (2017)
8. Boletsis, C., Kongsvik, S.: Text input in virtual reality a preliminary evaluation of the drum-like VR keyboard. Technologies **7**(2), 31 (2019). https://doi.org/10.3390/technologies7020031
9. Adhikary, J., Vertanen, K.: Typing on Midair virtual keyboards: exploring visual designs and interaction styles. In: Ardito, C., et al. (eds.) INTERACT 2021. LNCS, vol. 12935, pp. 132–151. Springer, Cham (2021). https://doi.org/10.1007/978-3-030-85610-6_9
10. Fujitsu Develops Glove-Style Wearable Device. http://www.fujitsu.com/global/about/resources/news/press-releases/2014/0218-01.html. Accessed 14 Jan 2023
11. Fujitsu Laboratories Develops Ring-Type Wearable Device Capable of Text Input by Fingertip. https://www.fujitsu.com/global/about/resources/news/press-releases/2015/0113-01.html. Accessed 14 Jan 2023
12. Ring Zero. https://www.techinasia.com/ring-zero-new-start-japanese-wearable, https://www.g-mark.org/award/describe/42290?locale=en. Accessed 14 Jan 2023
13. Haier Asu Smartwatch, https://www.digitaltrends.com/smartwatch-reviews/haier-asu-review/. Accessed 2023/1/14
14. NEC develops ARmKeypad Air, a contact-free virtual keyboard for a user's arm. https://www.nec.com/en/press/201607/global_20160713_01.html. Accessed 14 Jan 2023
15. Wong, P., Zhu, K., Fu, H.: FingerT9: leveraging thumb- to-finger interaction for same-side-hand text entry on smartwatches. In: Proceedings CHI 2018, Paper No.178 (2017)
16. Whitmier, E., et al.: DigiTouch: reconfigurable thumb-to-finger input and text entry on head-mounted Displays. In: Proceedings ACM IMWUT2017, vol.1, no.3, Article 133 (2017)
17. Xu, Z., et al.: TipText: eyes-free text entry on a fingertip keyboard. In: Proceedings of the 32nd ACM Symposium on User Interface Software and Technology, pp.883–899 (2019)
18. Tap Strap 2. https://www.wired.com/review/tap-strap-2/. Accessed 14 Jan 2023
19. TapXR. https://www.forbes.com/sites/charliefink/2021/10/12/tapxr-bracelet-enables-typing-without-a-keyboard/?sh=612e2b662d7f. Accessed 14 Jan 2023
20. Sun, K., et al.: Float: one-handed and touch-free target selection on smartwatches. In: Proceedings CHI2017, pp.692–704 (2017)

21. Gong, J., Yang, X., Irani, P.: WristWhirl: one-handed continuous smartwatch input using wrist gesture. In: Proceedings UIST2016, pp.861–872 (2016)
22. Gong, J., et al.: WrisText: one-handed text entry on smartwatch using wrist gestures. In: Proceedings CHI2018, Paper No.181 (2018)
23. The word list of the Balanced Corpus of Contemporary Written Japanese of the National Institute for Japanese Language and Linguistics. https://ccd.ninjal.ac.jp/bccwj/en/freq-list.html. Accessed 14 Jan 2023
24. Soukoreff, W., MacKenzie, S.: Metrics for text entry research: An evaluation of MSD and KSPC, and a new unified error metric. In: Proceedings of ACM CHI2003, pp.113–120 (2003)

Author Index

M. Kurosu and A. Hashizume (Eds.): HCII 2023, LNCS 14011, pp. 615–617, 2023.
https://doi.org/10.1007/978-3-031-35596-7

Printed in the United States
by Baker & Taylor Publisher Services